D0081251

International Handbook
on
Race and
Race Relations

International Handbook on Race and Race Relations

EDITED BY

Jay A. Sigler

Greenwood Press

NEW YORK • WESTPORT, CONNECTICUT • LONDON

HT
1521
.I485
1987

Library of Congress Cataloging-in-Publication Data

International handbook on race and race relations.

Bibliography: p.
Includes index.
1. Race—Handbooks, manuals, etc.   2. Race
relations—Handbooks, manuals, etc.   I. Sigler, Jay A.
HT1521.I485   1987   305.8   86-33651
ISBN 0-313-24770-6 (lib. bdg. : alk. paper)

Copyright © 1987 by Jay A. Sigler

All rights reserved. No portion of this book may be
reproduced, by any process or technique, without the
express written consent of the publisher.

Library of Congress Catalog Card Number: 86-33651
ISBN: 0-313-24770-6

First published in 1987

Greenwood Press, Inc.
88 Post Road West, Westport, Connecticut 06881

Printed in the United States of America

∞

The paper used in this book complies with the
Permanent Paper Standard issued by the National
Information Standards Organization (Z39.48-1984).

10 9 8 7 6 5 4 3 2 1

JESUIT - KRAUSS - McCORMICK - LIBRARY
1100 EAST 55th STREET
CHICAGO, ILLINOIS 60615

To Janet

CONTENTS

TABLES	ix
PREFACE	xi
INTRODUCTION	xiii
Australia *by Henry Albinski*	1
Brazil *by Anani Dzidzienyo*	23
Canada *by Doug Daniels*	43
Fiji *by Ralph Premdas*	67
France *by Alan B. Anderson*	101
India *by Raj S. Gandhi*	117
Japan *by Yung-Hwan Jo*	129
Malaysia *by C.E.R. Abraham*	155
Netherlands *by Joed H. Elich*	167
New Zealand *by Andrew D. Trlin and Paul Spoonley*	191
Singapore *by John Clammer*	213
South Africa *by Paul Rich*	233
Sudan *by Ann Lesch*	263
Switzerland *by Carol Schmid*	281
Thailand *by Suchitra Punyaratabandhu-Bhakdi and Juree Vichit-Vadakdan*	301

Trinidad *by Stephen D. Glazier*   321

Union of Soviet Socialist Republics *by Samuel P. Oliner*   339

United Kingdom *by Barrie Axford*   369

United States *by Jay A. Sigler*   395

West Germany *by Lutz Holzner*   423

BIBLIOGRAPHICAL NOTE   449

APPENDIX: RACIAL/ETHNIC DIVISIONS   455

INDEX   467

ABOUT THE CONTRIBUTORS   479

TABLES

1 Potential Economically Active (PEA) by Sex and Color, According to Groups and Monthly Income   37

2 Manual and Nonmanual Workers and Their Income According to Color, 1976   38

3 Educational Opportunities, by Race   39

4 Earnings, by Race   40

5 Population of Fiji, by Ethnic Group   68

6 Communal System of Representation in Fiji, 1966   79

7 Composition of the Proposed Parliament   81

8 Composition of the Senate   81

9 Land Distribution in Fiji   87

10 School Enrollment, by Race, 1958 and 1968   91

11 Examination Pass Rate, by Race, 1967   92

12 Civil Service Personnel, by Race, 1974   93

13 Police Force Personnel, by Race, 1974   93

14 Fijian Armed Forces   94

15 Minority Groups in Japan   130

16 Number of Koreans in Japan, 1909–1985, Selected Years   132

17 History of the Legal Status of Koreans in Japan   138

18 Marriage Trends of KJs, 1965–1981, Selected Years   143

19 Major Ethnic Origin Groups in New Zealand, 1981   193

20 Proportion of the Maori Population Living in the
    Cities and Boroughs, 1951–1981, Selected Years   199

21 Maori Pupils as a Percentage of the Total Secondary
    School Population in New Zealand, 1963–1983,
    Selected Years   201

22 Percentage of Non-Maori and Maori Pupils Leaving
    School Without any Certification, 1963–1983,
    Selected Years   201

23 Percentage of School Leavers with University
    Entrance or Higher Qualifications, 1963–1983,
    Selected Years   202

24 Population by Ethnic Groups, 1931–1980, Selected
    Years   216

25 Foreign Nationals in Switzerland, 1860–1983,
    Selected Years   283

26 Foreign Residents in Switzerland in 1983   291

PREFACE

The chapters that appear in this book were selected mostly on the basis of the expertise of the authors, all of whom have done recent and penetrating studies on race relations in important areas of the world. The nations chosen for study present some sort of geographic balance, but other factors also entered into the choice. Nations such as South Africa, the United States, Brazil, and Trinidad were chosen for obvious reasons, whereas Australia and New Zealand were picked because they are developing some progressive policies in the field of race relations. In the United Kingdom and the Netherlands the subject of race relations has just emerged on the public agenda. France, West Germany, Japan, and Switzerland may be viewed as unusual choices in view of their small racial minorities, but the evidence shows that race relations problems are emerging in those nations. It is hoped that the global treatment of the subject presented here will provide a rounded view of race and race relations all over the world.

Each contributor to this volume was given a common format and, to the extent that national conditions allowed, each adhered to that format. The result is a sharply focused treatment of a subject which, for all its importance, has been treated with some timidity in the academic community. I hope that this book will provide a useful source for further work in this subject area.

The contributions presented here are more descriptive than prescriptive, tending to describe, as closely as possible, what has actually been happening in race relations. Perhaps many other social scientists, determined to unearth some clues as to why race consciousness or race attitudes have emerged, would prefer to dwell on issues of causation. But there is a genuine need to describe the conditions in many of the world's societies objectively and factually without becoming overly involved in current controversies or becoming an advocate for particular policies. Every attempt has been made to avoid those traps here. The commentaries are enlightened and as balanced as possible. Nonetheless, the contributors were not asked to conceal their own attitudes or to hide their feelings. Hence, the chapters are informative without being bloodless; they are scholarly without being pedantic or recondite. If they are also controversial in many respects, that, I think, is unavoidable.

Each author has recently been in the nation which he or she has written about, thereby enhancing the reliability of the sources as well as the authenticity of the studies. The contributors have had direct and recent access to the best available information on the nation they describe.

I am aware that I have been a source of difficulty for some authors. While I regret the deadlines and sometimes the dictatorial approach, I believe the end product has been worthwhile. To all the fine experts and scholars who have endured my lash, I extend my profound appreciation. Without exception, the chapters exhibit the highest traditions of scholarship. All the contributors gave generously of their valuable time to an enterprise that took several years to accomplish.

Special thanks are due to my editor, Mim Vasan, who constantly urged me on to greater efforts. My graduate assistant, Nancy Hart, has played an important role in manuscript preparation, as has my wife, Janet Sigler. The Rutgers University library staff has worked diligently on my behalf, especially B. J. Swartz. Sandra Cheesman has lent a hand and so has Anthony Mitchell, who helped me locate some contributors. Despite its complexity, this project has been an exhilarating one, reflecting the best efforts of many hands and many minds. Now that the book is completed, I hope that it will stimulate further work in this very important field.

INTRODUCTION

The concept of "race" is still little understood by experts and laypersons alike. Whether races are "real" or are socially imposed artificial categories has been hotly debated by scholars. In one recent study of American teachers of physical anthropology, doubters and rejecters of the concept of "race" numbered around 50 percent.[1] Periodically, another salvo is fired in this controversy to "prove" that races exist as a physical fact or, on the other hand, that they are social inventions created to serve some social, economic, or political purpose, usually to the disadvantage of the minority group defined as a "race." Indeed, sometimes, especially in colonial settings, a minority differentiates itself from the majority population on racial grounds.

Contributions presented in this book are designed to prove not the existence of races, but rather the prevalence of racial categories in many societies. Each chapter demonstrates that "race," however defined in the context of the particular society, has salience for the lives of members of the society. Race is an important factor not only in South Africa and the United States, but also in supposedly more homogeneous societies like France, West Germany, Switzerland, and Japan. The research summarized here should arouse complacent citizens to the fact of race in their own nation, for race-thinking appears to be a worldwide phenomenon, whatever the anthropologists may eventually conclude.

As has been pointed out by Pierre van den Berghe, "much of the literature on race relations during the last three decades has dealt with the United States and has been written by scholars who lacked comparative experience."[2] American scholars have tended to dominate the writing and thinking about race relations. This does not mean that America has a monopoly on problems of race relations. On the contrary, the United States has devoted more attention to remedies for inequitable race relations than most other nations have. A comparative approach to race relations would reveal that problems of race are much more common in other nations than has been realized.

The essays in this volume are based on the notion that race can and should be examined on an international basis. This may result in findings that race relations in the Netherlands and the United Kingdom, for example, are just emerging as issues on the public agenda. Other contributors report that race patterns are quite different in Europe, Asia, and Africa from those in the Americas. This book sheds light on areas of race relations that have been neglected and overlooked, partly because of academic fashion and partly because of the disrepute of the concept of "race." As some of the authors suggest, "race" is virtually a tabu subject in some societies, partly as a residue of Nazi race theory. This volume presents an opportunity to reconsider the accepted wisdom or to learn anew about the salience of race in many nations.

The leading scholar on comparative race relations, Graham Kinloch, holds that the nature and type of relations between racially distinct groups varies with social structures.[3] He claims that some societies are governed by racial "elites...which subordinate indigenous populations, import other race groups for purposes of economic exploitation, and rationalize their power monopoly on the basis of assumed racial superiority."[4] Such societies are common under colonialism, which, says Kinloch, produces a heavily dogmatic racialist elite. Certainly, many examples of such situations spring to mind, but some of the essays show that race thinking is even occurring in postcolonial settings, as in France, the Netherlands, the United Kingdom, and West Germany. These nations have, in effect, imported their race problems after losing most of their colonies. Kinloch differentiates between colonial-influenced types and noncolonial-developed types (including Western Europe) but has not addressed the situation in sufficient detail.[5] In fact, given the evidence provided in this volume, it is increasingly difficult to draw grand generalizations about the impact of the colonial experience on the development of race relations and race thinking.

The special situation of racial politics in South Africa is given detailed attention by Professor Paul Rich. The peculiar institutions in that society are grounded on a special set of historical developments. Race relations in South Africa were never beneficial for racial minorities, even before the rise of official apartheid. Neither colonialism nor crude Marxism fully accounts for developments there. Yet some important lessons in the management of race relations may be learned from the South African experience. The relative position of white minorities and black majorities in South Africa may be changing even as this book is written, but the attempt to construct a minority rule regime at the foot of black Africa seems to have been an experiment in futility.

Marxist theorists prefer another grand explanation for the concept of race. Many Marxists contend that race is a socially defined category that is purely a product of the development of capitalism.[6] Seen from this perspective, the race issue is a means of exploiting the workers: by creating tensions among workers, workers can be prevented from seeing their true antagonists, the owners of the means of production. According to Marxism, under capitalism the ruling class is racialist, striving for ideological domination over society. If these premises are true, then it would seem to be difficult to improve race relations in a capitalist country in a major way. Reducing racial tensions would seem to be counterproductive. If race is merely an ideological concept within the class struggle, then it is devoid of any genuine meaning and so too is "race relations." Both may be invalid products of well-meaning liberal sociology.[7] The whole literature of race relations obscures the issue of social class and, seen from this perspective, may be designed to do so. Not all Marxists hold the view that race and race relations are irrelevant to deeper forces of social classes under capitalism, but the appearance of race factors is an undeniable fact of social life, whatever the causes and functions of the "ideology of race." The contributors to this volume are not Marxists, but they are prepared to admit that race relations are related to, if not determined by, class position. The long chapter on race and race relations in the Soviet Union shows that even noncapitalist societies employ racial thinking. The chapter on Canada, however, reveals Marxist insights.

In this book, the relevance of race and race relations is also seen from the point of view that subsumes race into ethnicity rather than into social class. The distinction between race and ethnicity is deeply dependent on the particular conditions that prevail in specific societies.[8] In Trinidad, as Stephen Glazier points out, there are thirteen ethnic groups, with five separate white groups, East Indians, West Indians, and several black groups. Yet the most powerful groups are the Creoles and, to a lesser extent, the Chinese. He clearly demonstrates that in Trinidad race has a meaning quite distinct from ethnicity. Creoles enjoy their supremacy mostly because of their light skin color, which makes them superior to dark-skinned Creoles and to all non-Creoles. This essay deserves close attention because Trinidad has been the subject of extensive research by sociologists and anthropologists concerned with the relationships among race, ethnicity, and class. For similar reasons, the chapter on Singapore by John Clammer shows that race is a different, and more salient, factor in that nation than religion, ethnicity, or class. Experts may disagree about the extent of such differences, but in the view of the editor and the authors, race is not a mere subcategory of ethnicity.

Dr. Ann Lesch's article on the Sudan elucidates the distinctions between religious, tribal, and racial factors in that area. In Africa, tribal

identities do not tend to be racial. But, as Dr. Lesch indicates, the amal-
gam of religion, race, ethnicity, and geography may become an increasingly important social and political factor on that continent, even if race
alone is not a controlling factor.

Finally, the universality of race relations problems must be noted. An
example from the recent past provides a vivid illustration. In September
1985, Japanese Prime Minister Yasuhiro Nakasone was forced to apologize for a racial slur he had made in referring to American racial
groups. Nakasone had made a speech in Japan in which he had attributed
Japanese accomplishments to the high levels of intelligence of its citizens.
This situation was compared unfavorably to the situation in the United
States in which educational levels were allegedly held back by "blacks,
Puerto Ricans, and Mexicans." Although Nakasone initially refused to
apologize for these remarks, he ultimately issued a "clarification," stating
his words "were not intended to imply any racial discrimination." The
fact is that Japan has a very small racial minority in its midst, the Koreans,
who remain on the fringes of Japanese society. But discrimination against
that group does exist. Japan, one of the most racially homogeneous
nations in the world, has its own racial problems, even though its Prime
Minister would like to appeal to his nation's sense of racial superiority.
Interestingly, Nakasone felt compelled to fire his own education minister
a few weeks prior to his speech mentioning American races. The reason
given was that, among other things, his minister was openly anti-Korean
in his views of recent historical events.

No nation is entirely free of race relations problems. These articles
show that the subject of race relations retains its high political and social
significance in many nations. No nation is a racial utopia. On the contrary, even Brazil, long held by social scientists to be a successful example
of comfortable race relations, suffers from severe problems of its own.
No nation, it seems, can claim to have solved race relations problems
altogether, but as this book shows some have done far better than others
in coping with those problems.

Few societies will admit to having racial distinctions and policies, because it is more politically acceptable to explain that social differences
are really ethnic, hence less deeply rooted and less based upon bias and
prejudice. Yet, even the most enlightened and progressive nations—
such as the Netherlands, Australia, West Germany, and Switzerland—
appear to have genuine racial social arrangements, whatever official
agencies may choose to call them. Moreover, the Soviet Union is by no
means free of race relations problems, even if the government prefers
to speak of "nationalities." Of course, there may be some disagreement
among scholars as to the proper labeling of particular social systems,
but findings that a given society has racial distinctions should not be

taken to mean that the special racial situation of the Union of South Africa are paralleled in other nations. The social fact of race is quite different from an official policy of racism or apartheid.

It may be concluded that the racial problems of the world are never racial in the biological sense. They may be seen as one aspect of the cultural problem created by the overseas expansion of European civilization. Christopher Columbus, at first charmed by the Indians in the New World, soon decided that the natives of Hispaniola could form a cheap source of slave labor for the Spanish settlers. The Portuguese reached the same conclusion when they explored the African coasts in the fifteenth century. Probably, the concept of racial differences has gradually evolved since that time. Although there has always been a natural human tendency to treat strangers as different and potentially hostile, this tendency is not the same as racial stratification. Until group differences are coupled with biological connotations, the notion of race cannot be said to be operative. The modern sense of the word did not become prevalent until the nineteenth century.[9] The twentieth century gave birth to a conscious ideology of racism and to the liberal sociology that has sometimes been given the name, "race relations."

As a field of academic study, race relations has been associated with the development of American sociology. Beginning in the 1920s, scholars defined the contours of an area of concern in such a way as to emphasize the salience of racial factors in social relationships. To some extent this scholarship was designed to expose the abuses in America against blacks. As such, there was an ameliorative quality to much of the writing. Race relations and the extirpation of racism became entangled, and sometimes confused, especially after World War II. In preparing this book there was no effort to probe into racial ideologies and the theoretical roots of race prejudice. Those subjects have been treated very well elsewhere.

There is a quality of liberal reformism still evident in many textbooks about race relations. To the extent that the research dwells upon contemporary problems, it is hard to distinguish from journalism or benevolent aspirations. There is a very extensive bibliography of race relations literature, but much of it falls into the category of well-intended social description. The essays in this volume aim to provide the detailed historical information, the dynamic and sophisticated culture-free analysis which has been lacking in the comparative literature of race relations.[10] However, when examined in the historical, legal, and political context of particular societies, race relations can be a distinct area of study. Even though issues of race, class, nation, religion, culture, and ethnicity are much intertwined, it is the task of sound scholarship to locate the differences. Whether or not race relations constitute a class of social relations different in kind from the relationships among other social groups is a matter of hot dispute among scholars. The evidence assembled here suggests that it is a distinct and meaningful category of analysis.

Obviously, the recognition that race relations problems exist is a precondition for dealing with those problems. Anti-discrimination and immigration policies are largely determined by the prevalent attitudes toward race and race relations. The formulation of decent public policy in these areas depends upon an accurate understanding of the current state of race relations. It is my hope that a comparative approach will provide a basis for sound policies toward minority groups. The scholarship of comparative race relations needs clarification, too, but carries with it policy implications as societies search for ways to meet the legitimate aspirations of racial minorities. Sound scholarship will identify the social existence of race, while avoiding turning the social fact into an ideology that supports racism.[11]

NOTES

1. See Leonard Lieberman, Larry Reynolds, and Robert Kellum, "Institutional and Socio-Cultural Influences on the Debate over Race," *Catalyst* 15 (1983): 45–63.

2. Pierre L. van den Berghe, *Race and Racism* (New York: John Wiley, 1967), p. 4.

3. Graham Kinloch, *The Dynamics of Race Relations* (New York: McGraw-Hill, 1974).

4. Ibid., p. 225.

5. Graham Kinloch, *The Sociology of Minority Group Relations* (Englewood Cliffs, N.J.: Prentice-Hall, 1979), p. 180.

6. Oliver C. Cox, *Caste, Class and Race* (New York: Doubleday, 1948).

7. Robert Miles, *Racism and Migrant Labour* (London: Routledge & Kegan Paul, 1982).

8. See Pierre L. van den Berghe, *Race and Ethnicity* (New York: Basic Books, 1970), p. 10.

9. Michael Banton, *The Idea of Race* (Boulder, Colo.: Westview Press, 1977), pp. 156–72.

10. Graham C. Kinloch, "Comparative Race and Ethnic Relations," *International Journal of Comparative Sociology* 22 (1981): 257–71, calls for these empirical improvements and for deeper theoretical insights.

11. Van den Berghe supports the view of race presented here, that it is a "social label attributed to groups of people in particular societies at particular times, on the basis of inherited phenotypical characteristics," meaning skin color, stature, hair texture, facial features, and similar characteristics. However, van den Berghe also observes that an ideology that supports racial classifications and their social consequences "is called racism." See Pierre L. van den Berghe, *The Ethnic Phenomenon* (Amsterdam/New York: Elsevier, 1981), p. 29.

International Handbook
on
Race and
Race Relations

AUSTRALIA

Henry Albinski

A RACIAL CONTEXT

Up to the first half of the twentieth century, Australia was one of the world's most homogeneous societies. Its European population was overwhelmingly Anglo-Celtic. Persons of non-European extraction, predominantly Aborigines, accounted for under 2 percent of the total. But by the mid–1980s, Australia had been transformed into one of the world's most diverse, migrant societies. The proportion of the Anglo-Celtic component had dropped to about 70 percent, attributable mostly to white migrants and their offspring whose origins were outside the British Isles. But the nonwhite element in Australia had also risen, both absolutely and proportionately.

At the time of the first European settlement in 1788, Aborigines numbered about 300,000. At the turn of the twentieth century, when the Australian colonies federated, there were only about 67,000. Disease, public neglect, and even a measure of deliberate extermination had shrunk their numbers to the point that their extinction was widely expected. Aboriginal mortality and morbidity rates continue to stand far higher than those for the general population. Aboriginal life expectancy, for instance, is about twenty years shorter. Recent decades, however, have witnessed a marked improvement in Aboriginal conditions and, in turn, a recovery in Aboriginal numbers. The Australian population is currently about 15.5 million; in 1983, there were 160,000 full- and half-blood Aborigines.

A much more striking rise in Australia's nonwhite population has resulted from Asian migration. During the nineteenth century, tens of thousands of people from the Asia/Pacific region, mostly Chinese and Pacific Islanders, entered Australia as indentured or as other types of workers. White opinion toward nonwhites became intense. Most were deported, and a racially exclusionist, "White Australia" policy became entrenched. Between the wars, nonwhite numbers sank to barely over 20,000. Changes in immigration policy, especially from the late 1960s, have made a profound difference. Between 1971 and 1980, a quarter of all migrants to Australia were Asians. In 1983–84, about 40 percent were Asians, numbering over 25,000. Most Asian migrants have entered under normal migration procedures, but since the late 1970s very large numbers have been Indochinese refugees. During 1974–84, about 88,000 Indochinese refugees arrived. On a per capita basis, Australia has accepted more Indochinese refugees than any other nation. The percentage of Asian-born migrants in Australia rose from 1.8 percent in 1976 to 2.6 percent in 1981 to 2.9 percent in 1983, with the percentages of persons of Asian extraction residing in Australia, of course, being higher. Some projections for the turn of the twenty-first century have placed the resident Asian population at up to 10 percent of the total, and there have been speculations that Australia will eventually evolve into a Eurasian society.

Even if these projections prove far off the mark, the fact remains that the Australian racial mix has undergone rapid and considerable change. It has happened in a society that for most of its experience deliberately, even boastfully, defended its racial homogeneity and for the most part regarded nonwhites with pity, contempt, or fear. Australia's recent encounter with race relations is therefore especially instructive. Following an examination of the roots, and then of the nature and range of contemporary policies toward nonwhite groups and toward multiracialism at large, the analysis will consider the incentives and disincentives that have conditioned recent race-related policies. The concentration will be on domestic factors, including the state of popular opinion, but external factors will also be taken into account. We will also be concerned with identifying some of the major, systemic implications that are arising or may arise for an Australia that is increasingly becoming racially heterogeneous.

POLICY ROOTS

Earlier, racially related policies that guided the Australian colonies in the nineteenth century, and then the federal government and the several states after federation in 1901, sprang both from what Australians thought of nonwhites and from how they came to construe their own society and its purpose. Almost from the outset, contacts between Aborigines and convicts and administrative personnel, and later emancipated convicts and free settlers, carved a gulf whose legacy was to shape and inform race relations generally:

It would be difficult to find two cultures of greater contrast than the European and the traditional Aboriginal; the former exploitative and competitive, the latter conservationist and cooperative. Even without the problems posed by differences of language, technology, and external appearances, it is doubtful that a meaningful dialogue could have been established between the two people for their aspirations were diametrically opposed.[1]

Aborigines were regarded not only as primitive, but also as useless or indeed as obstructive. They lacked hierarchical organization and martial skills. White convict labor precluded their utilization even in the most menial employment, and their nomadic, hunter-gathering habits conflicted with stable, ownership-related European versions of land and its use. Their vulnerability to disease and alcohol made them appear an unvigorous people. Under the impact of the European presence, their personal and social denigration cultivated an image of Aborigines as disposable, subordinate objects of comedy, pity, and occasional convenience.

Early Australian society itself was formed from a convict population, operating in a convict environment, and later from free migrants predominantly drawn from a relatively depressed socioeconomic stratum and lacking experience in dealing with racial diversity. What emerged was the dominance of petty bourgeois values; insular, socially and class conformist, and practical minded. There was little room for idealism or for *noblesse oblige* impulses that otherwise might have flowed from a noticeable socioeconomic or educated elite. Aborigines became the lowest rank, a depressed element in Australia's stratification system.

Ironically, it was the depressed and mocked condition of the Aborigines which, with the end of convict transportation by the mid-nineteenth century, caused labor shortages that induced the importation of cheap, indentured labor, especially Chinese. Later in the century, labor shortages prompted the importation of South Sea islanders, or Kanakas, for work on the Queensland sugar plantations. But many Chinese deserted their employers to find their fortune during the gold rushes in Victoria and New South Wales, and others slipped into Australia directly. Two decades later, following the discovery of gold in Queensland, another wave of Chinese entered. Riots erupted on the goldfields in all three colonies. The Chinese came to be regarded as an economic threat and as a social blight. For the sheltered homogeneous Australian community, it was not difficult to transpose intolerance of Aborigines to others. The Chinese were racially and culturally unlike white Australians, and the industry of Asians and islanders made them appear more despicable than the hapless, numerically declining Aborigines.

The alleged degeneracy of Chinese, and by inference other Orientals, raised the stakes of protecting Australia against racial dilution. The putative threat to Australia's social and ultimately economic and political integrity was made more graphic by the country's position as a white and civilized outpost on the edge of a swarming and a so-called covetous Asia. In fact, it has been asserted that "Racism is the most important single component of Australian nationalism."[2] In this context nationalism refers to the development of a sociopolitical ethos, a sense of community, and not just national or patriotic feelings. Indeed, Australia was arguably a community before it became a nation. Political democracy, advanced social programs, and the entrenchment of working-class and rural interests became part of a myth of social purpose. Since Asians were regarded as unassimilable, they were therefore a barrier to development and nation-building: a danger to what was perceived to be a virile, thriving community of free people.

Given these circumstances, the attendant policy outputs were not surprising. An initial laissez-faire approach toward Aborigines was being replaced by forms of "protective" policy by the middle of the nineteenth century. This entailed the gathering of Aborigines into settlements, originally under religious mission auspices and by the late nineteenth century through colonial governments. Although a humanitarian motive was involved, the action also reflected the view that Aborigines were unfit to be absorbed into the general Australian society and that it was charitable to "smooth the dying pillow" as they as a people gradually became extinct. In large part segregated from the bulk of Europeans, who were domiciled in cities and were preoccupied with nation-building, Aborigines became the victims of public ignorance and apathy. The absence of federal organization dispersed jurisdiction among the states, and the absence of federal or state "bill of rights" meant at best minimal stewardship rather than anything like equal rights for Aborigines. The limited financial resources of a small population occupying a giant and often stern island continent left little for Aborigines. Queensland and Western Australia, with heavy Aboriginal concentrations, were among the least prosperous states. To the end of World War II, many Aboriginal children had hardly any education, and many others were prohibited from attending white schools. Until 1926 the vote was prohibited to most Aborigines in New South Wales. Well beyond World War II, full-blooded Aborigines were essentially deprived of the franchise federally, and in Western Australia, Queensland, and the Northern Territory, whose nonstate situation continues to place it under ultimate federal control.

Policy toward Asians was largely reflected in their exclusion. Both before and shortly following federation, most Asians and islanders were deported or left voluntarily. The nonwhites born outside Australia who remained were for the most part denied citizenship rights, though eligibility for social welfare privileges was gradually liberalized. Only a trickle of Asians was admitted after federation, and then under very extenuating circumstances. The instrument chosen, modeled on the Natal system in South Africa, was the dictation test. Without any specification of race, it could be and was used to discourage and block migration by nonwhites; it originally required written competence in any European language and later in any language—at the discretion of the examiner.

CURRENT STATE OF POLICY

Postwar changes in race-related policies, while not sudden or somehow predetermined, have nevertheless produced a corpus of legislation and practices diametrically different from those of previous times. It is useful to notice the range and character of these policy changes, and then to assess the motives and forces behind them, their reception, and finally their systemic implications.

In broad-stroke terms, Australian policy first moved toward a removal of formal discrimination, and then turned toward the provision of various supportive programs to protect and advance disadvantaged individuals or groups. These trends broadly coincided with trends in what the outlines of Australia's sociocultural (not just racial) relations generally should be. The earlier approach, favoring "assimilation" of subcultural and racial groups into the broader stream of the Australian community, was replaced by "integration," under which diverse ethnic and racial heritages could be preserved, even fostered, under an accommodating Australian rubric.

Changes in policy enabled nonwhite aliens to take citizenship, originally after prolonged residence and later on the same basis as others. In 1958, the dictation test as such was removed. By the early 1960s, nonwhites who were "distinguished and highly qualified" could migrate, and by the end of the decade the terminology was changed to "well qualified." By the early 1970s, all discriminatory migration provisions were abolished, including the previous ineligibility of nonwhites to receive assisted passage. Despite some appearances to the contrary, however, the large Asian intake has resulted from coincidental factors rather than from deliberate favoritism.

As of the passage of the Racial Discrimination Act of 1975, Australia has progressively legislated against racial (as well as ethnic, religious, and national origin) discrimination at large, making incitement to racial hatred or promotion of racial superiority an offense. A Human Rights Commission was formed in 1981. Although federal legislation continues to emphasize conciliation rather than coercion, its features have been strengthened over time. Australia has ratified the International Convention on the Elimination of All Forms of Racial Discrimination (ICCPR). It has also adhered to the International Covenant on Civil and Political Rights, and after a time withdrew its original reservations to the ICCPR.

As of 1985, the Australian Labor party government continued to consider a bill of rights, grounded on ICCPR principles.

Should an Australian bill of rights be adopted, it would, in the first instance, almost surely be statutory legislation rather than constitutionally entrenched. This is because considerable practical difficulties are involved in ratifying constitutional amendments. All the same, several Australian states have themselves enacted legislation and established machinery to combat discrimination and other breaches of human rights. The federal government's stated position is that *it* "is the appropriate standard-bearer in human rights matters. Federal measures should (nevertheless) not infringe upon constructive developments which take place in our States and which are consistent with our international obligations." It is also important that, since the mid–1970s, the High Court of Australia has been sympathetic to the idea of extending federal jurisdiction across state boundaries. Inter alia, it has invoked the Australian Commonwealth's exclusive external affairs power in relation to international conventions to which Australia has subscribed. The precedents are to date very limited, but this was the rationale expressed in a 1982 case (*Koowarta v. Bjelke-Petersen*), in which the Court invalidated Queensland efforts to deny purchase of a lease of land by an Aboriginal.

Federal and state approaches toward Aborigines have come to entail policy measures and considerations that would have been nearly unimaginable before World War II. A milestone in the process of new policies was the passage in 1967 of a constitutional amendment authorizing Canberra to make laws on behalf of Aborigines generally, with the effect of superseding state prerogatives. All states save Queensland have agreed to transfer their Aboriginal-related administrative apparatus to the federal government. Aborigines now enjoy the same franchise as do others. Most of the earlier practices that imposed restrictions of right of movement and various forms of social behavior have now been rescinded.

The simple dismantling of overtly discriminatory policies toward Aborigines has, however, become only one facet of a larger and in a sense more delicate and elusive undertaking. With some early signs shortly before World War II, and then with fuller force until the mid–1960s, Australian federal and state government policy assumptions favored assimilation; that is, that Aborigines would be encouraged to assimilate gradually into the wider community. But it was conceded that assimilation was untenable. Most Aborigines live in remote or rural or country town areas. Most lack the educational, economic, and sociopolitical skills needed to enter and to function viably within the wider community. These considerations were compounded by deeply held Aboriginal attachments to traditional practices, to religious sites, and to land. But their attachment to land is special; they feel not that land was or is an economic resource which might "belong" to them, but that *they* belong to the land.

Under the Fraser Liberal-National Country party (later Liberal-National party) government, reserve lands in the federally controlled Northern Territory were turned over to Aborigines on an inalienable basis, and Aborigines could lay claim to Crown land, based on traditional ownership submissions. South Australia has explicitly ceded lands. Other land models have been adopted elsewhere, except that Queensland has legislated lease or "deed of grant in trust" but not freehold practices, and otherwise has maintained restrictions on Aboriginal land claims.

The Hawke Australian Labor party government entered federal office in early 1983 with a commitment to further reforms. It passed National Heritage legislation designed to protect various Aboriginal areas from damage to the environment and to sacred sites. It has transferred lands in the Northern Territory, as at Kakuda and Ayers Rock, for ownership by Aborigines but with leasing for national park use. It was especially concerned that *uniform* legislation be adopted between Canberra and the states, and that Aborigines enjoy a veto over mining on their lands. Legal rulings have prevented the Northern Territory government from frustrating federal government land policy there. Likewise, the High Court has ruled that South Australian legislation is not in conflict with the Racial Discrimination Act simply because it restricts access to specific lands to traditional owners; that is, that Aboriginal land rights are a proper form of affirmative action on behalf of racial or ethnic groups requiring special protection.

By 1985, the Labor government had nevertheless reconsidered its position. Future legislation guidelines would not, for example, foreseeably include an Aboriginal right of veto over mining.[3] The Hawke government adopted the approach that future legislation should actually weaken *existing* land-use veto power. While Aborigines in the Northern Territory do not hold formal ownership over minerals on their lands, standing federal policy has been that mineral exploration is to be carried out with Aboriginal consent and on the basis of negotiation with mining companies. Technically, Canberra can presently invoke a national interest clause to override Aboriginal veto to permit mining activity, but this can be done only with the concurrence of both houses of Parliament and for most purposes is not a viable option.

An important rationale underlying existing federal land law is that affected Aboriginal communities are able to transact royalties and other payments with mining companies. This has been perceived as a means for Aborigines to acquire new housing and other facilities, and to gain a measure of independence from the welfare society to which many dispossessed and impoverished Aborigines had become resigned. This feature of Aboriginal land law is part of a network of structures that have been erected by the federal government to negotiate, lobby, and otherwise represent the Aboriginal community. There are, for instance, Land Councils to assist and protect the interests of Land Trusts, which hold Aboriginal land. The Land Councils negotiate with mining companies but are accountable to traditional Aboriginal groups. A similar rationale animates the Aboriginal Development Commission, which was formed in 1980 to assist Aboriginal individuals and communities to set up and run businesses and to provide housing loans. Government outlays to the commission also enable it to administer a program of grants in aid to Aboriginal housing associations to build, buy, or renovate houses.

The federal government has experimented with mechanisms intended to reduce historical Aboriginal powerlessness and to provide meaningful input channels to the established political system. The major, present-day forum for the sharing and dissemination of views is the National Aboriginal Conference, a thirty-five-member body of nationally elected Aborigines. The Council for Aboriginal Development, a small body attached to the Minister for Aboriginal Affairs, is the principal institutionalized advisory structure. There are other specialized bodies, for instance, in the domains of education and health.

Aborigines have continued to benefit from substantial public outlays that provide medical, educational, training, and other services. Between 1970–71 and 1982–83, federal expenditure on Aboriginal assistance rose tenfold. Special efforts have been made to recruit Aborigines into colleges and universities, and to place them in responsible public positions as their skills and interest might warrant. By end of 1984, there were still only three or four Aboriginal lawyers and no physicians—but two Aborigines had been inducted into the Department of Foreign Affairs, and the highest ranking official in the Department of Aboriginal Affairs was himself an Aboriginal.

The prospective role of nonofficial sectors and of the general citizenry in complementing government efforts at reducing racial discrimination and opening opportunities for minorities has been acknowledged. In 1982, the Australian Ethnic Affairs Council was converted to the Australian Council for Population and Ethnic Affairs. The previous body's brief was to combat racism through public education. The new body's brief was extended to work against prejudice affecting Aborigines. Under both rubrics, the emphasis has been on the public's own awareness and contributions. There is some parallel with the federal government's approach to settling Indochinese refugees. Most Indochinese newcomers are introduced to Australia through government-provided centers where they undergo English language and orientation courses to equip them for housing, education, employment, and settlement within the community. But the community has also been engaged. Some refugees are moved directly into the community, and are provided with private sponsors such as families, groups, and organizations. The migrant center refugees are themselves set loose unattended, but they are bolstered for a time by private, prearranged hosting schemes. Throughout Australia, racial minorities have been incorporated into a network of multicultural efforts. These include culture, electronic media, educational, and other outlets.

According to the federal government and those who subscribe to its assumptions, "Australia is a young and developing nation whose multicultural society is one of its great assets. It will be a major tragedy if racial prejudice, ethnic stereotyping and discrimination are allowed to play a significant role in our developing nationhood."[4]

INSPIRATION FOR POLICY: EXTERNAL FACTORS

Only a generation or two ago, the above assumption would have been startling to the great majority of Australians. Today it enjoys considerable credence. But how far has the conversion gone, and under what inspiration or incentives? Do considerable patches of serious resistance remain, and are there significant disincentives as well as incentives for pursuing strong policies aimed at extirpating overt discrimination, as well as at compensating for historical prejudice, injustice, and disadvantage?

Explicitly or by inference, external considerations have consistently played a major role in bringing about the postwar remodeling of Australia's race-related policies. The effect has been especially pronounced on Australia's admission and handling of Asians. After the war, Australia greatly intensified and diversified its international role. Decolonization in Asia and the Pacific created a host of independent nonwhite states in Australia's neighborhood. For diplomatic, security, and commercial reasons, it became imperative for Australia, as a white and prosperous, Western-oriented, yet underpopulated nation on the edge of Asia, to avoid severe criticism by and isolation from nonwhite and Third World nations generally. In part, Australia wished to avert or deflect various claims on it, and interference in its domestic policies affecting nonwhites. The irony is that, while Australia originally reasoned that it could protect itself from undesirable consequences by excluding Asians, it later concluded that its national interests were served by admitting them. An important incentive dictating generosity toward Indochinese refugees has been the need to relieve refugee pressures on, and otherwise to impress the members of the Association of Southeast Asian Nations (ASEAN) community, with whom Australia feels it must foster a special relationship.

In 1984, the intramural Australian debate over the appropriate scale

of Asian migration intensified. With foreign policy as well as party political considerations in mind, the Labor Foreign Minister complained
that some ranking spokespersons of the federal opposition were guilty
of "straight out political opportunism," and "they don't give a damn
about the awful consequences and costs that could [be raised] for Australia" by damaging its interests in the Asia-Pacific region.[5]

International calculations have likewise constrained Australian approaches toward its Aboriginal population. Getting on with the Third
World has added incentives to its treatment of indigenous blacks, and
Canberra has wished to limit and neutralize Aboriginal protests being
carried into the international and especially nonwhite community: "My
government treats with great seriousness any suggestion that international human rights standards are not being upheld in Australia. We
are especially concerned by any such criticisms when they come from
within the Australian community itself."[6] These remarks were made in
response to an Aboriginal complaint before a United Nations body against
Western Australia's handling of a 1980 land rights dispute, and the
federal government's failure to take direct action. Aborigines have continued to seek international forums for their complaints, especially within
the ambit of the World Council of Indigenous Peoples. The Australian
government has found itself thrust more prominently into presenting
anti-discrimination positions, at times with Aboriginal observers present
at such deliberations.

Over the years, such Aboriginal militants have made contact with European peace movements, have taken an interest in causes sponsored by
Libya and by the Irish Republican Army, and have tried to enlist Australia's Middle Eastern oil suppliers in the Aboriginal cause. Aborigines
lobbied Asian-Pacific and African delegates at the 1981 Commonwealth
Heads of Government meetings in Melbourne, and threatened to disrupt
the 1982 Commonwealth Games in Brisbane unless the state of Queensland yielded on Aboriginal land rights. They assisted the World Council
of Churches investigating team, which laid a racist indictment at Australia's doorstep.

INSPIRATION FOR POLICY: DOMESTIC FACTORS

The domestic factors that have contributed to race-related policy reforms have been cumulatively impressive, though they often came about
fortuitously or may not have been clearly recognized when their influence was being exerted. The substantial cosmopolitanization of postwar
Australian society, induced by more complex external involvements and
attitudes, product and commercial diversification, substantial exposure
to tourists, overseas students and business and professional visitors, educational and cultural strides, and the advent of diverse migrant groups

certainly contributed toward more reflection and openmindedness among general and elite publics alike. Paradoxically, traditional Australian cultural values such as egalitarianism, "far go," and an emphasis on *group* rights may, in selective ways, have weakened resistance to change regarding racially distinctive peoples.

Australian society has also been affected by a pricking of its conscience. Since the late 1960s, there has been a heightened sense of Australian national identification and pride. This has brought the Aboriginal legacy into more prominent and sympathetic focus. Widespread revelations of historical injustices and a widening, personal exposure to Aborigines by urban whites have made the Aboriginal plight more publicly evident than in the past. Even if most Europeans do not fathom Aboriginal society and mores, they in measure can empathize with the nature of the Aboriginal appeal. Because Aborigines are "in the minority and are relatively powerless, their claims must be (and often is) one that will arouse feelings of sympathy or of guilt in the majority—hence the emphasis (by Aborigines) on spirituality, on conservation and on destruction of a people."[7]

A perceptible "conscience" factor has also shaded acceptance of Indochinese refugees. Refugees are by their nature an unfortunate and dispossessed group. Australia's own military involvement in the Vietnam conflict, judging by press opinion as well as often unspoken public thinking, has left a feeling of humanitarian responsibility for the casualties of its aftermath. Family reunion schemes, which apply to refugee as well as to regular migrants, have added a touch of compassion to migrating programs as well as intimating that racially and otherwise unusual migrants are likely to integrate more successfully.

Regular Asian and then Indochinese refugee migrants were more readily acceptable because of the sequence in which postwar migrating programs developed. As noted earlier, Asian migrants were originally admitted on a small and selective basis, and the process was quite unobtrusive. In addition, Australia had already absorbed large numbers of non-Anglo-European migrants before Asians began to arrive. The notion of being confronted with persons of different stock was already in place. A pluralistic society became easier to sustain, respecting Aborigines as well as Asians.

Economic circumstances have also played their part. The initial years of the growing Asian migration were years of general prosperity, offering little cause of popular fears of job and other economic undercutting. Moreover, regular Asian migrants have tended to be persons of reasonable education and of middle-class skills and outlooks, and often with English language competence. This circumstance has placed them above the socioeconomic status of many Eastern and Southern European white migrants, and has helped to dispel historical anxieties about Asians stereotyped as being an unsavory lot who would "live off the smell of an oil rag." Wealthy and entrepreneurial Asians have been keenly sought under Australia's Business Migration Program.

In part because of their English language deficiencies, Indochinese refugees as a group are less economically competent than are regular Asian migrants, and they run high unemployment rates. But they often compete for employment with non-Anglophone "ethnic" migrants rather than with established Australians. There have been more Chinese than ethnic Chinese refugees, and it is the Chinese who bring a strong tradition of work and enterprise. Australian economic conditions worsened in the 1980s. The actual recipient per capita costs associated with settling Indochinese refugees, or with meeting their unemployment charges— or indeed with disproportionate investments made in Aboriginal welfare—are high. The fact remains that these groups represent a very small fraction of the population. As an advanced and prosperous nation, Australia can quite handily absorb the burden imposed on its financial and administrative resources.

Economic and noneconomic factors affecting policy changes tend to blur. We will later stress public perceptions and acceptance of these groups. Our comment here is on several fairly objective measures of racial minority integration. Aborigines have only very recently and in very small numbers begun to enter the professions and otherwise to gain distinction. But the rate of improvement is swift, at least somewhat dispelling feelings that Aborigines are light years removed from mainstream society and are unreconstructable. Aborigines continue to suffer from exceptionally high rates of incarceration for drunkenness, disorderly conduct, and various other offenses. The gradual removal of legal discrimination, combined with the movement toward evenhandedness, has begun to erode a negative reputation. Aborigines are now, with some frequency, being seen in major cities. In a few instances such as the inner Sydney suburb of Redfern, they are very much in evidence. While most of the new Aboriginal city dwellers are poor and not especially well integrated into the wider community, they at least are increasingly viewed as a natural rather than a distant and exotic feature of the Australian scene.

Asians far outnumber Aborigines and have overwhelmingly settled in the large cities. Mostly because of their planned arrival and strong social and economic credentials, regular Asian migrants have integrated well. Indochinese refugees understandably have a more mixed record. There is evidence that some refugees of Chinese extraction have affiliated with secret Chinese criminal societies. Vietnamese refugees as a group are strongly anti-communist, and as a result there have therefore been occasional uproars over the presence in Australia of visiting students or dignitaries from present-day Vietnam. In general, however, both Chinese and ethnic Vietnamese have had low crime rates and have adjusted reasonably well. It should be borne in mind that the great majority of Indochinese refugees have been admitted as part of an *orderly* program and after being subjected to various screening procedures. Some observers have noted that in fact

it is rather more difficult for traditional Asian societies to accommodate new ethnic or religious minorities than it is for Australia where the values associated with ethnic pluralism and religious toleration are the accepted orthodoxies of the political culture as a whole. The common belief that Vietnamese refugees could fit more easily into the countries of South-East Asia is quite wrong-headed.[8]

In the event, while the Vietnamese Chinese tend toward exclusivism, they work hard. Ethnic Vietnamese value work less, but interact more with the general community and tend to take up Australian citizenship shortly after becoming eligible. The Vietnamese are inclined to cluster in big city neighborhoods in such suburbs as Fairfield and Cabramatta in Sydney and Springvale in Melbourne. But those who acquire English competence and a measure of economic well-being often move to other neighborhoods.

On balance, the cause of immigration reform and of supportive policies for Aborigines and other resident nonwhite groups has been undertaken in a manner that has done more good than harm. This was especially clear regarding the dismantling of racially restrictive immigration barriers. The lobbying effort on behalf of this cause was centered on the Immigration Reform Group. Its approach was reasoned and moderate, and undercut much of the conventional wisdom behind standing firm on Asian migration. As with the campaign for the admission of Asians, a substantial pro-Aboriginal reform movement arose, at first mostly among white Australians and much of it expressed through voluntary and church groups. Some of the effort, such as during the "freedom rides" in northern New South Wales in the early 1960s, spotlighted the condition of Aborigines. An early and important result was the dialogue about and subsequent adoption of the 1967 constitutional amendment.

Aborigines themselves have become active in promoting their cause. A few became involved with racial movements such as the Black Power party. But the party never really caught on and expired. Others have looked to the outside for help, and still others have demonstrated for their cause within Australia by such acts as erecting a "Aboriginal embassy" outside Parliament House in Canberra or through public marches and other demonstrations. This has happened most conspicuously in Queensland, where Aboriginal grievances have been particularly noticeable. Actual violence, however, has been virtually absent. Perhaps the most celebrated instance of disturbance occurred at Noonkanbah, in Western Australia, when the Western Australian government launched a paramilitary operation to force a mining company to drill for oil on a site Aborigines had declared sacred. There are a number of Aboriginal militants about. But it is well to remember that the various Aboriginal consultative/advisory groups created by the national government serve a useful input function. In addition, in keeping with their design, they provide such input in an orderly way and help to diffuse potentially more intemperate Aboriginal representations.

Policy reform touching on nonwhites has for the most part been sustained by considerable, major, federal party agreement, at least up to the mid–1980s and possibly including the mid–1980s. As will be seen later in this article, in 1984 a prominent debate arose over whether Australia was accepting too many new Asian migrants. The point to be made here is that, after harsh words and imputations of bad will between the Liberal-National (L-NP) party opposition and the Labor government, both sides modulated their positions. During the 1984 electoral campaign the L-NP did not urge a rewritten, racial balance policy and did not make immigration an electoral issue. On being returned to office, the Australian Labor party (ALP) government changed the migration rules, including reduction of the number of planned Indochinese refugees. The actual 1983–84 refugee figure of 10,000 was scaled down to 8,000 and then to 6,000. More emphasis was to be placed on family reunions, and tighter skills and language competence were to be imposed on regular migrants. De facto, the proportion of white migrants was expected to rise.

Much the same thing happened on the controversial subject of Aboriginal land rights. The L-NP has gone on record that it regrets its previous, generous legislation of land rights in the Northern Territory, and has promised to vest responsibility for land rights in the states themselves. The ALP's intent was to legislate uniform, nationwide land rights, Aboriginal veto power over mining, and other land use. Under pressure from some states including Labor-governed Western Australia, a mining industry that claimed injury to itself and ultimately to the health of the national economy, and with an eye to electoral opinion, it backed down. It even indicated that it would dilute the Aboriginal land use powers in the Northern Territory previously legislated by the L-NP, as well as its intent to check the spread of new Aboriginal land claims. Again, the major parties converged, and a form of grudging consensus was seemingly restored.

Nonwhite members of the Australian electorate remain small, but will increasingly play some part in conditioning federal or state/territorial parties to avoid alienating these constituents. Aborigines have yet to make a meaningful electoral impact, but like whites they now are subject to compulsory enrollment and voting, and in the Northern Territory they represent 25 percent of the population. Parties must already take into account the vote of Asians, who by the mid–1980s represented a more numerous eligible electorate than ethnic Greeks. In the early 1980s, Australian Asians were inclined to support the L-NP. By the 1984 federal election they favored Labor, most likely because they felt that the L-NP had tried to exploit the concerns being voiced about excessive Asian numbers in the country.

PUBLIC ATTITUDES

In 1981, a visiting team from the World Council of Churches asserted that "Racism is entrenched in every aspect of Australian life."[9] Taken at face value, this statement is a powerful indictment and seems to run counter to the various postwar impulses that have been conducive to change, reform, and even public compassion.

Over the years, a variety of vociferous groups with open or implied programs aimed against Asians, Aborigines, or minorities and dissidents have come and gone, and some, such as the League of Rights, have survived over many years. But they have attracted only a tiny public membership and have had very little practical, political effect. A Labor Minister for Immigration lost his seat in the 1974 election in part because of a massive and often virulent campaign against his reformism and support for minority groups. Later efforts to dislodge progressively minded Liberal immigration/ethnic affairs ministers failed badly. Despite a vigorous campaign, an extremist, independent candidate polled only about 1.3 percent of the vote in a 1984 federal by-election.

Direct discrimination on the part of the white community lingers but has clearly declined over the years. Overt, interracial violence is very rare and episodic, usually limited to encounters with Aborigines in country towns and to work site outbursts involving refugees in the large cities. As best as can be determined, informal relations with racial minorities have improved. Ready acceptance of Aborigines in particular, however, has not been achieved. A survey of middle management males conducted during 1978–81 indicated that only 11 percent were prepared to accept and socialize with Aborigines; lesbians ranked just above Aborigines in acceptance, and prostitutes just below.[10] The fact that "Negroes" were more than three times as likely to be fully accepted as Aborigines did, however, suggest that cultural/stylistic as well as racial ingredients structure attitudes. The Human Rights Commission's experience has not uncovered egregious racism, though most complaints received have predictably related to racist statements and materials aimed at Aborigines. Nonsystematic investigations have pointed to noticeable white neighbor acceptance of Indochinese refugees in the Sydney and Melbourne suburbs where they are concentrated.

In summarizing survey data, it is possible to detect trends in public disposition toward public policy themes affecting racial minorities. Some broad conclusions seem applicable whether the object of opinion has been Asian or Aboriginal. First, white Australians are by now much better disposed to support, or at least acquiesce in, policies that are positive toward other races than they were a generation or two ago. Second, further policy measures favoring racial minorities have by now become suspect among many, if not most, white Australians. By the early and mid–1980s, Australians were disapproving of having the volume of migration from Asia increased, and in fact there was a feeling that Asian migration ought to be reduced. Similarly, white Australians were opposed to conceding to Aborigines generous, Australia-wide land rights, especially as such rights might include veto power over development projects.

Another conclusion to be drawn is that the responses of the white community mask subgroup attitudes, which themselves can be instructive. For example, West Australians and Queenslanders have been among the most resistant to granting generous land rights to Aborigines. Those states have an especially high ratio of Aborigines and are the ones where newly found prosperity inordinately depends on resource development. Among those most distressed about a continuing, heavy flow of Asian migrants have been persons in the oldest age groups whose views were shaped during times of more traditional thinking about race; young people, who especially in an environment of high national unemployment are not yet settled and secure in jobs; and semi- and unskilled working-class Anglo-Irish *and* ethnic whites, who feel their jobs threatened by unskilled but ordinarily hard-working Indochinese refugees.

It is also hardly surprising that the preferences of white Australians are sensitive to publicity that may surround racially related issues. In this sense, sharp debate among political and other elites has a flow-on effect on the mass public. Opposition to generous Aboriginal land rights hardened perceptibly under the impact of the mining industry's widely publicized warnings about the economic consequences Australia would suffer because of the federal Labor government's quarrels with other governments (including the ALP-controlled West Australian government), and of the federal opposition's reconsideration of previous L-NP land policy.

The public's attention to Asian migration became sharply focused as of early 1984. The precipitant was the outspoken position of Professor Geoffrey Blainey of the University of Melbourne, one of Australia's most distinguished historians and respected for his sympathy toward racial minorities. In effect, Blainey warned that on both social and economic grounds Australia was moving too fast in attempting to absorb large numbers of Asians: "we could easily create, in our own cities, tensions and troubles that restrict the options open the next generation of Australians as well as souring permanently the quality of our nation's life."[11] Blainey's comments stirred a whirlpool of controversy in which the federal government and opposition parties flayed one another and into which the media, academics, and various interested groups quickly entered. Prior to the Blainey debate, the public had been relatively quiescent about Asian migration. Once the debate had become a kind of national pastime, 58 percent of the public indicated that immigration was an "important personal issue" for them, and the proportion of those wishing to curtail Asian migration rose.[12]

A related observation on white opinion is that not only does public salience ascribed to race-related issues decline when political and media debate is dampened, but also that to most appearances Australians as a national electorate do not rank racially related issues high. By inference they do not structure their vote according to their perceptions of which party best reflects their preferences on these issue areas. During the late 1984 federal electoral campaign, Aboriginal issues held virtually no interest for the electorate. Government handling of migrant problems attracted under 4 percent of respondents, and only 9 percent felt that reduction in Asian migration was among the issues most important to them.[13] In contrast, a clear majority was on record as in principle preferring a slowdown of Asian migration.

SOCIETY, SYSTEM, AND RACE

Neither informal evidence nor empirical data sustain a conclusion that present-day Australian society is overtly racist. There is a very significant economic root that underlies much of the resistance to such policies as generous Aboriginal land rights or a heavy flow of Asian and especially Indochinese refugee migration. Of course, it can be argued that such views may be misplaced or exaggerated; that many Australians are simply wrong in their assessment; and that the de facto scapegoating that results carries its own systemic implications. Japanese as such apparently suffer little, if any, antipathy among Australians. It is useful to bear in mind that hardly any Japanese migrate to Australia. Not only do they not compete for jobs, but also their image is that of investors and merchants, of people who have contributed to Australia's postwar economic growth and prosperity; of sophisticated people in business suits or of well-mannered tourists. It may also be helpful to glance at recent outcries that visiting Asian students have been filling college and university places to the extent that Australian students have been squeezed out. The great majority of overseas students are in fact Asians, and they tend to concentrate on vocationally directed programs of study such as business and engineering. There are also the areas where, in the midst of a job-minded educational climate among students, Australians have also sought admission in uncommon numbers. While low Social Economic Status (SES), working-class Australians react against Indochinese refugees who are construed as job threats, the perceived displacement of Australians by visiting Asian students for scarce yet career-significant university courses has been a particular concern of the middle and upper middle classes. In the 1984 federal election campaign alluded to earlier, the electorate overwhelmingly listed economic issues, notably unemployment, as most salient.

Australia's traditions and political culture must also be placed in perspective. We have mentioned the forces that have worked toward modification, in favor of change in race-related outlooks and policies. Still, despite its increasing heterogeneity as a society, an Australia encumbered by a historical conditioning that chooses commonality, even conformity, rather than diversity within its ranks has not yet been able to make the final and successful leap: "While Australians may generally agree on the desirability of a degree of cultural pluralism in Australia, it is less clear that a similar consensus exists on the shape of a multiracial Australia."[14]

Prejudice and suspicion in the Australian context is particularly understandable because of the exceptional, historically firm racial character of the country and of the numerous cultural and economic props that upheld exclusivism and defensiveness. Present-day race relations and attitudes, moreover, are much more complex than can be denominated simply as white/nonwhite. We have already hinted at aspects of this phenomenon. Hence, despite fears about Asian migration that were voiced during the Blainey debate, Australians preferred Asians to Aborigines as neighbors, but continued to feel a sense of collective responsibility for helping depressed Aborigines.[15] Although most Australians perceive Aborigines as actually or potentially less "threatening" than Asian migrants, they continue to see Aborigines, *apart* from the racial factor, as a downtrodden yet culturally and stylistically unappealing group. We are reminded of the small clue found in the 1978–81 middle management survey, in which Negroes were found to be more than three times as acceptable as were Aborigines. Continuing the argument about the complexity in Australian race relations, it should be emphasized that some of the most outspoken opposition to Indochinese refugees has emanated from white ethnic migrants, who have not been exposed to the traditional Australian political culture. A number of ethnic migrants have expressed fear of competition and even of contamination from disease from Vietnamese migrants. For some ethnic whites the refugees have become a convenient group, available for denigration and at times the object of outright racism. In some cases relations between Indochinese refugee migrants of Chinese and ethnic origin have become couched in suspicion and cultural disdain. Some articulate Aborigines have made it quite plain that "While the Aboriginal people are in poor health, ill-housed and uneducated, we can't afford a novelty cause like the Indo-Chinese one."[16]

Postwar public policies aimed at removing racial barriers and fostering Aboriginal well-being have tended to move somewhat ahead of opinion. In the 1970s and very early 1980s, opinion was inclined to accept the changes that were taking place. Events such as the vigorous debate set off by Blainey, and perhaps the sharp relief of the Aboriginal land rights controversy, appear at least temporarily to have fractured what might have seemed like a consensus on immigration and racially related policies. Some of the interplay took on abusive, *ad hominem*, and racist overtones, and the public evinced keen interest. One inference to be drawn is that the earlier, so-called consensus was shallow; that Australian society has not yet come to comfortable or even working terms with what it is or ought to be as a society in light of profound population changes, rising Aboriginal militancy and claims, and a host of externally and domestically generated influences over the past thirty or forty years. It may in fact be salutary that with fundamental, racially related questions being brought before it in high relief, the Australian public and its leadership will over time evolve a more firmly anchored and confident, yet prudently assessed, sense of national and societal priorities. This would not necessarily mean the retraction of sympathetic and generous approaches toward nonwhites, but it could mean changes in degree and inflection. For instance, it is not illegitimate for a major mining company to have raised, and for the public and politicians to weigh, the notion that, if federal policies applicable in the Northern Territory were to be extended across Australia, potentially one-third of the nation's land could be under inalienable tenure and the control of Aborigines, who could set the terms of mining and other economic development. "It implies no disrespect or no lack of recognition of Aboriginal aspirations to question whether, in the interests of the nation as a whole that situation is desirable."[17] Nor is it improper for Australia to ventilate and to weigh the various arguments as to whether the sum of its interests dictates particular levels, composition, and societal integration of migrants.

Almost certainly, however, further debate will reveal that the momentous strides of the last few decades toward policies and attitudes of acceptance, fairness, and commitment of effort and resources aimed at racial minorities will not be reversed. Even if Australia does not become multiracial in genuine fact, idiom, or spirit, it will very likely continue to accommodate. While such a vision may not be inspiring, complex conditions and Australian pragmatism will probably not yield a much different result.

NOTES

1. M.J.E. King-Boyes, *Patterns of Aboriginal Culture: Then and Now* (Sydney: McGraw-Hill, 1977), p. 99.

2. Humphrey McQueen, *A New Britannia. An Argument Concerning the Social Origins of Australian Radicalism and Nationalism* (Ringwood, Vic.: Penguin, 1970), p. 42.

3. Senator Gareth Evans, Minister for Resources and Energy, address to the U.N. Commission on Human Rights, Geneva, February 6, 1985; in *Australian Foreign Affairs Review* 56 (February 1985): 85.

4. W. G. Wojak, Chairman, Federation of Ethnic Committees' Councils of Australia, in "Foreword" to Frances Milne and Peter Shergold, *The Great Immigration Debate*, 2d ed. (Sydney: Federation of Ethnic Committees' Councils of Australia, 1984), p. viii.

5. William Hayden, Minister for Foreign Affairs, statement in Bangkok of August 3, 1984; in *Age* (Melbourne), August 4, 1984.

6. Remarks by Lloyd D. Thomson, Australian Ambassador to the Office of the United Nations at Geneva, before the U.N. Subcommittee on Prevention of Discrimination and Protection of Minorities, September 3, 1980; in Australian Information Service, Embassy of Australia, Washington, *Media Release*, September 1980, p. 1.

7. Kenneth Maddoc, *Your Land Is Our Land: Aboriginal Land Rights* (Ringwood, Vic.: Penguin, 1983), p. 182.

8. Robert Manne, "The Blainey View—The Politics of Asian Immigration to Australia 1975–1984," *Dyason House Papers* 11 (September 1984): 13.

9. Elizabeth Adler et al., *Justice for Aboriginal Australians: Report of the World Council of Churches Team Visit to the Aborigines June 15 to July 3, 1981* (Sydney: Australian Council of Churches, 1981), p. 9.

10. *Bulletin*, March 10, 1981.

11. Geoffrey Blainey, *All for Australia* (North Ryde, NSW: Methuen Haynes, 1984), p. 163.

12. McNair Anderson Poll, *Sydney Morning Herald*, May 7, 1984.

13. Morgan Gallup Polls, October 23 and November 5, 1984.

14. Nancy Viviani, *The Long Journey: Vietnamese Migration and Settlement in Australia* (Melbourne: Melbourne University Press, 1984), p. 158.

15. SSC and B Lintas survey, in *Australian*, June 18, 1984.

16. Charles Perkins (then Deputy Secretary, Department of Aboriginal Affairs, later Secretary), interview with Robert Drewe in *Bulletin*, August 15, 1981.

17. MIM Holdings submission, in *Australian*, October 18, 1983.

BIBLIOGRAPHY

Albinski, Henry S. "Majority-Minority Relations in Australia." *Humboldt Journal of Social Relations* 10 (Fall/Winter 1982–83): 83–115.

Blainey, Geoffrey. *All for Australia*. North Ryde, NSW: Methuen Haynes, 1984.

Cousins, David, and John Nieuwenhuysen. *Aboriginals and the Mining Industry:*

Case Studies of the Australian Experience. Sydney: Allen and Unwin/Committee for Economic Development of Australia, 1984.

Grassby, Al. *The Tyranny of Prejudice*. Blackburn, Vic.: Australasian Educa Press, 1984.

Gurr, Ted Robert. "Outcomes of Public Protest Among Australia's Aborigines." *American Behavioral Scientist* 26 (January/February 1983): 353–73.

Hanks, Peter, and Bryan Keon-Cohen. *Aborigines and the Law*. Sydney: Allen and Unwin, 1984.

Maddock, Kenneth. *Your Land Is Our Land: Aboriginal Land Rights*. Ringwood, Vic.: Penguin, 1983.

Manne, Robert. "The Blainey View—The Politics of Asian Immigration to Australia 1975–1984." *Dyason House Papers* 11 (September 1984): 12–20.

Milne, Frances, and Peter Shergold, eds. *The Great Immigration Debate*. 2d ed. Sydney: Federation of Ethnic Committees' Councils of Australia, 1984.

Palfreeman, A. C. *The Administration of the White Australia Policy*. Melbourne: Melbourne University Press, 1967.

Price, A. Grenfell. *White Settlers and Native Peoples*. Westport, Conn.: Greenwood Press, 1972.

Rivett, Kenneth. *Australia and the Non-White Migrant*. Melbourne: Melbourne University Press, 1975.

Rowley, C. D. *A Matter of Justice*. Canberra: Australian National University Press, 1978.

Stanbury, Peter, ed. *The Moving Frontier: Aspects of Aboriginal-European Interactions in Australia*. Sydney: Reed, 1977.

Stevens, F. S., ed. *Racism: The Australian Experience. A Study of Race Prejudice in Australia*. Vol. 1, *Prejudice and Xenophobia*. 2d ed. Sydney: ANZ Book Co., 1974; Vol. 2, *Black Versus White*. New York: Taplinger, 1972.

Viviani, Nancy. *The Long Journey. Vietnamese Migration and Settlement in Australia*. Melbourne: Melbourne University Press, 1984.

Willard, Mary. *History of the White Australia Policy to 1920*. London: Frank Cass, 1967. (Corrected edition.)

Yarwood, A. T. *Asian Migration to Australia. The Background to Exclusion 1896–1923*. Melbourne: Melbourne University Press, 1967.

———, and M. J. Knowling. *Race Relations in Australia: A History*. North Ryde, NSW: Methuen Haynes, 1982.

BRAZIL

Anani Dzidzienyo

A RACIAL CONTEXT

In the last fifteen years, an increasing number of studies and analyses have appeared, dislodging Brazil from its hitherto privileged and somewhat impregnable position as a racial haven. It is not the case that Brazil has suddenly been transformed into a run-of-the-mill variant of global race relations, or even that the recent work undertaken by both Brazilian and foreign students in the field has dramatically altered the perceptions of those who have formerly defended Brazil's exceptionality to the conflictual race relations patterns elsewhere in the world. What is incontrovertible is the import of analyses based on a more critical examination of the literature in the social sciences and the humanities and on data from census and national household research.

By 1987, therefore, it could no longer be argued that it was impossible to determine the racial composition of the Brazilian population because of the scarcity of hard data or the irrelevance of the question premised on the notion of the indivisibility of the Brazilian people. Population statistics now provide more reliable data. Many recent writers have redressed the earlier lyrical picture most often associated with the works of Gilberto Freyre.

The available evidence suggests, in the words of Valle da Silva, that it is increasingly costly not to be white in Brazil, whether in schools or marketplace, or whether in urban or rural areas.[1] Ninety-eight years after the abolition of slavery (1888) in Brazil, blacks continue to be disproportionately represented in the nation's lowest socioeconomic levels. Both the available data and the perennial denunciations of Afro-Brazilian politicians provide a powerful indictment of the grossly disadvantaged position of Afro-Brazilians within the polity.

The economic crisis has wrought a heavy toll on the Brazilian people as a whole since the late 1960s. Nonetheless, it would not be accurate to point to the recent economic deterioration as the sole reason for Brazil's racial inequity, just as an equally single line of unbroken misery through-out the ninety-eight years of abolition appears to be unduly pessimistic. Be that as it may, we do not have enough examples either of successful individual mobility for Afro-Brazilians to justify unlimited faith in this traditional route to improvement for Afro-Brazilians, or of better in-terpersonal relations resulting from Brazil's historically unfettered race relations. No amount of smoother interpersonal relations, lack of out-ward physical violence, or expression of pride in the Afro-Brazilian religious and cultural heritage and practices has proven to be a sufficient counterpoint to the overall disadvantaged status of Afro-Brazilians as a group. Although slavery, manumission, and abolition are not the whole explanation of the Afro-Brazilian predicament, they provide major clues for present-day societal attitudes toward Afro-Brazilians.

INDIANS IN BRAZIL

The special situation of Indians in Brazil deserves some attention here. Less than 1 percent of the Brazilian population can be considered Indian. Official sources are unreliable, giving estimates ranging from 45,000 to 1.2 million, depending on the source or the political purposes to be served by the estimate. There are about 160 distinct tribes in Brazil today, most of which have about 1,400 members, but some have a mere handful. In most cases these tribes were formally politically autonomous, rather like separate nation-states. Whenever tribes sought contacts with Brazilian national society, they asked to meet the chief of the society, the President of Brazil. Consequently, it is inaccurate to speak about the Indians of Brazil as a single entity. They have never been united, and only recently have they begun to cooperate among themselves as a pro-tection against the inroads of the larger Brazilian society.

Much of the tension between Indian tribes and the Brazilian state centers on the issue of land policy. In 1500, when the Portuguese arrived, 100 percent of the territory of what is now Brazil was claimed by one or another Indian tribe. Today, Indians control less than 5 percent of the land. There are just over 160 remaining islands of Indian land, and all of these are threatened by the policies of national development which the federal government has consistently pursued. Land and its demar-cation from further invasion has become the central issue for all Indian tribes.

Government initiatives have been directed at "integrating" the Indian into Brazilian society. This apparently means eliminating the very cat-egory of "Indian" in order to reduce the claims of inheritance which might otherwise impede economic and industrial development in various regions, especially in Amazonia and Mata Grosso. "Emancipation" for Indians has been the national catchphrase. In application, the term means removal of protections for Indian lands and culture, in spite of Brazil's Constitution which seems to give such protections to Indians. Invasion of Indian lands by non-Indian settlers continues at a rapid pace, while efforts to designate homeland areas for Indian tribes have been generally unsuccessful.

The government Indian agency (FUNAI, the National Foundation for Indians) has been in operation since 1967, replacing a less active agency. FUNAI is part of the Ministry of the Interior and is subordinate to the minister of that department. Rather than sponsor more acts that would protect Indian interests, most presidents of the Indian agency have decided to promote "integration" instead. In fact, FUNAI has been at odds with anthropologists who have usually sided with Indian groups against integrationist policies.

In 1983, an Extraordinary Ministry for Land Affairs was formed and was given final authority on all land issues, thereby overriding FUNAI policies. The problem of protecting Indian land rights may be treated with much less seriousness than national development issues. While not all Indian land will be lost to bulldozers, the risk of further losses of such lands is very high.

The very question of Indian identity is at issue. Outright Indian repression was once a government policy, but now the favored approach is toward "integration." The vision of Brazil as ethnically homogenous has served Brazilian policymakers well. This approach conceals the differences in color which still affect Brazilian life, but in the process the Indians can be virtually defined out of existence rather than being exterminated. Battles with Indian tribes still take place from time to time, with the tribes usually losing. Meanwhile, the failure of various Indian groups to unite politically makes the emancipation or integration of Indians a popular and successful approach to national development. In a society devoted to national homogeneity, racial attitudes toward Indians are never openly discussed but the implication that Indian tribes are not worthy of protection is hard to avoid.[2]

HISTORICAL BACKGROUND

The system of slavery in Brazil, some have argued, was a relatively gentle institution, with good masters who established an intimate relationship with their slaves within the patriarchal household. But in the dissenting view of one of Brazil's foremost historians, José Honório Rodrigues, slavery was a virtual concentration camp; the inmates demonstrated their opinion of its living conditions through frequent revolts, flight, and the creation of alternate communities, none of which reflect a climate of pacific cooperation between masters and slaves.

Even before Brazil attained independence from Portugal in 1822, parts of Brazil were rocked by major slave rebellions, the most notable being the 1835 revolt of African Muslims in Salvador da Bahia, that most African of Brazilian cities. This revolt resulted in massive repression not only of the suspects or Muslims, but also all blacks in an unleashing of racism.

Robert Conrad has commented on how difficult it was for dark people in slave-holding Brazil to attain freedom and on how precarious it was to maintain once achieved. There was no certainty that freedom would become a permanent condition: "This reality of oppression and disrespect for the rights of blacks and mulattoes contrasts sharply, in fact with the well-known but exaggerated Brazilian reputation for benevolence and generosity."[3]

In nineteenth-century Brazil, black life and activities were strictly policed. The gatherings of blacks, whether free or slaves, their religious and recreational activities, their music, their work—all were subject to police control, and the consequences of that control have persisted into the twentieth century. Indeed, it was not until January 1976 that *candomblés*, the Afro-Brazilian religious temples, were permitted to operate in Bahia without a police license. This latter-day legitimizing of a long-standing Afro-Brazilian institution indicates the dynamic nature of the interplay between Afro-Brazilian society and the larger society. After centuries of repression, the religion, music, and other cultural institutions of Afro-Brazilians are now openly recognized as important components of Brazilian society and the national culture. It remains to be seen, however, how a specifically cultural recognition will translate into material improvement of the Afro-Brazilians' political, economic, and social conditions.

The issue of Brazil's national image and its implications, as discussed by Vianna Moog, is most illuminating. When asked to cite the "highest," most edifying aspect of their civilization, Brazilians unhesitatingly point to their nation's almost complete absence of insoluble racial problems.[4]

There are many, however, who do not believe that this image is realistic. Both Brazilian and non-Brazilian students of Brazilian society have examined this issue in an attempt to bridge the gap between image and reality. Florestan Fernandes' landmark study, *The Negro in Brazilian Society* (1969), focuses on the postabolition "integration" of blacks into a growing economy which also absorbed large numbers of European immigrants.[5] Fernandes attempts to establish that the problems resulting from Brazil's archaic socioeconomic structures with their roots in slavery can be superseded by the modernizing process. Carlos Hasenbalg's 1985 study of racial discrimination challenges this position.[6] Hasenbalg demonstrates that, far from being superseded, the structures of discrimination and inequality are undergoing a modernizing process that rebounds to the prejudice and increasing victimization of Afro-Brazilians. Thomas E. Skidmore has shown that the whitening ideology, which was largely predicated on the need to de-blacken the population, is not the best evidence of liberality or commitment to racial equality.[7] Octavio Ianni has continued to explore the race and class dimension of the society to show the spuriousness of attempting to separate the two where Afro-Brazilians are concerned.[8] Clovis Moura's focus on the transformation of blacks from good slaves to bad citizens, and on the pitfalls and contradictions inherent in the very model of individual mobility as a solution to the problems of Afro-Brazilians, represents one of the most consistently insightful and rigorous Afro-Brazilian contributions to this process of reevaluation.[9]

In any discussion of contemporary Brazilian culture, it is imperative to recognize the pioneering role of two individuals: Sergio Buarque de Holand and Gilberto Freyre. Buarque has profiled the Brazilian's essential commitment to cordiality,[10] and Gilberto Freyre, now eighty-six years old, wrote the groundbreaking study *The Masters and the Slaves* (1965), probably the single greatest influence in creating Brazil's image with regard to race relations both at home and abroad.[11] While Freyre's work provided a strong counter to the Aryan, Eurocentric view of Brazilian society by stressing the African contribution, he would later become the butt of critics, including younger Brazilian intellectuals such as Carlos Guilherme Mota who criticize the unduly conservative framework of his contributions.[12]

In a category all by himself is Abdias do Nascimento, who has combined political activity with academic debate while constantly denying that he is concerned only with the academic resolution of the Afro-Brazilian problem. For Nascimento, the issue is both an intellectual and a practical one involving the political empowerment of Afro-Brazilians. He believes that Brazil's image as a tolerant, racially democratic society remains both "hollow and needs to be combatted unceasingly."[13] Precisely because he has been engaged in this combat for more than half a century (which in itself is a testimony to his courage, endurance, and persistence), he has remained a controversial figure among Afro-Brazilians and other Brazilians. In his mind, changes in political position, party affiliation, and strategy are all subsumed under the nonnegotiable position of the primacy of the Afro-Brazilian struggle. He would compare Brazilian race relations to those of South Africa and states that the proverbial camel, hump and all, will more likely pass through the eye of the needle than Afro-Brazilians, generally speaking, will improve their lot. Obviously, his view clashes with the national self-image.

John Rex describes a wide range of situations that can be labeled examples of racial discrimination: group scapegoating, stereotyping, unfair access to opportunities in the economic and political system, the forcing of a minority to assimilate into a dominant culture or face segregation. None of the preceding mechanisms, as Rex sees it, needs involve the forcible manipulation or unleashing of violence.[14]

As far as the victims are concerned, discrimination may consist in doing nothing to help narrow the gap between blacks and the beneficiaries of the status quo; it might reside in not interfering in discriminatory acts practiced by others; or it might involve an unawareness of the existence of discrimination or the failure to designate a discriminatory situation as such.

In the Brazilian case, Nascimento pointedly challenges such a causal relationship, arguing that blacks and whites have lived closely together for hundreds of years without any perceptible increase in the chances of blacks becoming any less victimized by what he sees as a Kafkaesque race-relations pattern.[15] But therein precisely resides a fundamental problem: national myths whose continued existence becomes a serious impediment to the protest viability of victimized groups. As Mota has observed: "The tepid waters of Brazilian national character, from an ideology of cordiality to 'racial democracy,' are currents which bolster the ideological elaboration of the system which emerged after the revolution of 1930."[16]

Fernandes regards ideologies and utopias as sacred rituals and mystifications that serve the needs of the powerful. Racial democracy was created as an ideology because of the need to compel individuals and groups to comply to desired social rituals.[17] Who is black in Brazil, and who are the Afro-Brazilians? There are no simple and straightforward answers to these questions.

DEFINITIONS OF BLACKNESS

We define black as (1) all those who are visibly and incontrovertibly black in appearance; (2) those whose outward appearance would enable them to choose categories other than black if they so desired, though residual blackness is perceptible; and (3) those who do not initially appear to be black but who themselves acknowledge a black component in their makeup. Well-known examples of the third category are Clovis Moura, Eduardo de Oliveira, and Alceu Collares. In terms of our definitions, those who would fit in category (2) and (3) but who would choose to emphasize their otherness are excluded. Also excluded from consideration are those who are recognizably black but who choose to underplay or negate their blackness. With regard to black sociopolitical activities, and bearing the above definitions in mind, an individual such as the football genius, Pelé, who is undeniably black but who does not identify with black issues, is also inconsequential to our analysis.

According to our defintion, Afro-Brazilian and Afro-American (North American), or the more cumbersome Afro-Anglo-American, share more characteristics than not, hence, invalidating Carl Degler's differentiation between Brazil and the United States.[18] The point is not that mulattoism has not and does not exist, but that its validity as an "escape hatch" clearly demonstrates its intrinsic limitation.

Nor do we accept the rationalization of Mauricio Solaun and Sidney Kronus because their own explanation conceals a paradox: the relative acceptance of miscegenation by whites and infusion of blacks through all levels of the class structure and the relative tolerance of Latin America in racial matters (infused racial system) does not mean that blacks are tolerated. The low level of racial strife in Brazil both singly and collectively negates the undesirability of Negroid racial features.[19] It is of very little comfort to know that the criterion of exclusion from elite membership on racial grounds is a better indicator of discrimination than the concentration of blacks in the lower classes in Latin America.[20] The slave heritage and historical class phenomenon, argue Solaun and Kronus, and not deliberate racial discrimination, account for the situation. This compels us to ask whether that heritage will terminate at some point.

Another problem is the relative lack of black testimony or support in articulating the general Latin American view. Neither miscegenation nor whitening has resulted in the total disappearance of blacks from Latin America. This should have some sobering effect on the conceptualization of the black presence there. In Latin America, unlike the United States, the polity is viewed as having racial differences that have political implications in terms of power that is exercised and the access to it; black deprivation is generally accepted in spite of official attempts to equalize opportunities between blacks and whites; and, finally, the legitimacy of black organizations within the Latin-American polity is questionable. These differences are more meaningful for purposes of comparing race relations in the two Americas than purely legal or aesthetic considerations. As I. M. Lewis points out, there is some illogicality in assuming that the rejection of prejudice in a society proves its absence. The reverse may in fact be the case.[21]

Brazil's sterling reputation in the area of race relations was inexorably bolstered by comparison with other systems, particularly that of the United States. It was a comparison fraught with possibilities for both satisfaction and frustration. On the one hand, the comparison focused on the contrast between legal, social, and cultural forms of racial exclusion and discrimination—which reached their apogee in the United States—and Brazil's more tolerant and more flexible patterns. On the other hand, little attention was paid to finding actual black witnesses to

Brazil's purportedly more elastic notion and practice of race relations. A careful examination of the Brazilian situation would have revealed that, affirmations of nonracism and segregation notwithstanding, the visibly black affirmers or public articulators of nonracism were conspicuous by their absence. Neither national nor foreign observers appear to have noticed this evidence.

From its very inception, racism was endemic to the Portuguese colony of Brazil (1500–1822) in terms of the dominant society's interactions with blacks. The question of whether or not racism proceeded from or caused slavery aside, once slavery was in place the authorities were faced with maintaining a visibly different part of the colonial and postcolonial population under control. This control extended to every aspect of their lives—habitation, clothing, physical mobility, education, worship, marriage, acceptability as a litigant, and recreation. Legal provisions recognizing exceptionality notwithstanding, a historical tradition of assuming black social disability until competence could be proven can be seen as an intrinsic part of Brazilian society and race relations.

We have little evidence of either continuing improvement or deterioration in the quality of race relations and racism in Brazil from the colonial period to the present. If the index of open physical violence as a measure of conflictual race relations patterns favored Brazil in the past, the present appears to be more problematic. The coexistence of strong individual nonracism and strong institutional racism, bolstered by a distinction between prejudice (disposition) and discrimination (behavior), makes it ludicrous to legally declare "prejudice" a misdemeanor. It is also apparent that U.S. race relations patterns have been altered by sociopolitical pressures exerted by Afro-Americans. As a result, blacks have been absorbed into structures of power and prestige, although only lighter complexioned individuals seem to be visible in the national political economy, with a few notable exceptions. Herein also lies the very conundrum of Brazilian race relations.

In the absence of legal impediments that have explicitly barred blacks in Brazil from public office, education, business, the military, the diplomatic service, and the arts, the lack of the black presence in these areas becomes even more intriguing. If, in fact, what has been operational is an economic or social class prejudice that can be surmounted by acquiring the necessary socioeconomic and educational tools, which are theoretically open to all, how is one to explain the disproportionate representation of blacks at the lowest socioeconomic level? Is there an unbroken line from the past to the present which militates against the future? Or are the blacks' bleak prospects today merely a function of the deteriorating economic conditions that have ravaged the lives of all Brazilians?

The difficulty inherent in providing satisfactory and convincing answers to these questions is intrinsic to the historical and contemporary conceptualization of the problem. Slavery was the point around which everything revolved; multiracialism as a feature of slave society did not indicate nonracism.

The abolition of slavery would highlight what had been a latent problem. Abolition released racism, which had been latent and obscured by the slave system. Following abolition, all persons of color were free but were presumed freedmen, thereby equating those who acquired status through freebirth with those who had just been liberated: All were anonymous peasants whose only mention in the town newspaper was always in connection with their appearance before the police. They were described as "thieves, drunks, whores, disturbers of the peace."[22]

CONTEMPORARY CONDITIONS FOR BLACKS

Brazilians have constantly eschewed open racist behavior, while at the same time acknowledging the existence of discrimination based on social class. The positing of individual and group coexistence against its variant, based on exclusive racial considerations, contains an inherent advantage: it justifies the dominant society and its particular interpretation of the development of Brazilian social history and race relations patterns. Individual successes verify the openness of Brazilian society, according to the dominant view. To impute the successful working of the system exclusively to the deviousness of the dominant sectors of the society, however, runs the risk of ignoring or underestimating the extent of diffusion and legitimization in those very sectors objectively victimized by the system.[23]

Since unmistakably black individuals could not achieve the desired goal of physical whitening, the alternative was to postulate "social whitening," attainable through individual economic, education, and professional efforts. But social whitening was built on the same racist foundation that elevated whiteness and devalued blackness, with the added disadvantage of maximizing the chances of a sociopolitical fragmentation of the collective nonwhite group within the society. Those individuals seeking social and economic mobility were forced to avoid public stances as well as group action. As Hasenbalg has observed:

Social whitening corresponds to the popular notion that "money whitens" because it activates the mechanism of partial status compensation. Colored persons successful in education and economic terms are perceived and treated as lighter rather than as people who are of the same complexion but lower status. The adoption of white norms and values by upwardly mobile non-whites implies that the black group of origin is transformed into a negative point of reference.[24]

RACE AND CLASS AND THE AFRO-BRAZILIAN PREDICAMENT

The uses and limitations of (black) racial solidarity have concerned black spokespersons in both Brazil and the United States. Central to this question is the perceived sharing of certain characteristics. The extent to which such commonalities override any religious, class, or political differences is offset by the example of those individual blacks who could be perceived to have attained a measure of success in areas where the great majority of the group remains in a depressed state of existence. While that depressed majority might derive some comfort and inspiration from the example of individual achievers, can those achievers correctly be perceived as bona fide members of the group if they have made a point of disassociating themselves from the group?

Although these concerns are common to both Brazil and the United States, the two countries have adopted different modalities toward their resolution largely because of differences in the socioeconomic racial politics of each country.

In Brazil, the overriding emphasis on individual mobility, coupled with the illegitimacy of converted group effort, has resulted in fragmented efforts at racial politics. The odd black who succeeds in getting a foothold in the elite structure, albeit at the lowest level or in such areas as sports, would not ordinarily be expected to become the spokesperson for the race because such public articulation would immediately be perceived as too political at best or as an exercise in confrontational politics at worst.

The Brazilian popular expression, "Money whitens," perhaps says it best both as an inspiration to blacks and as a guarantee to the larger society that no massive whitening of blacks would occur as a result of the sudden acquisition of wealth. Thus, both whites and blacks are pacified, bringing about a "social peace"—though for different reasons. And because of both the terminological and empirical fragmentation of the "black group," it is possible to slide along the racial continuum, away from blackness.

The political and organizational consequences of this situation were not lost on some blacks, or perhaps more accurately in this context, "people of color." If this lack of solidarity was to be combatted, the ruinous distinction between blacks and mulattoes would have to disappear. Hence, the need arose to emphasize blacks and mulattoes. As a tactic, this move to blur the terminological distinction faced considerable odds given the general inclination toward dissociation from the black end of the racial spectrum, a position reinforced by general societal values and norms.

But then what about those rare individuals who make an undisguised vocation of proclaiming blackness, thus going against the very grain of a fundamental and powerful societal etiquette? Abdias do Nascimento, perhaps the most vocal and persistent Afro-Brazilian dissenter alive today, argues that the fate of a whole race far outweighs any niceties and etiquette which have actually reinforced the oppression of black people. This radical view has set Nascimento apart from all other Brazilian political activists who have tried to change Brazil's race relations, rescuing the debate from the dark oblivion to which all issues considered subversive of the social order are consigned, and concurrently opening up possibilities for improving what is he considers Brazil's dismal record vis-à-vis Afro-Brazilians.

THE AFONSO ARINOS LAW AND BRAZILIAN RACE RELATIONS

More than any other piece of legislation bearing on Brazilian race relations, the legislation named after Afonso Arinos de Mello Franco—popularly referred to as the Afonso Arinos Law but properly known as Law No. 1390 (1951)—has been the subject of unending debate since its passage. For both defenders and critics of Brazilian race relations, it has come to symbolize what should be in the matter of the law and race relations. Discussion of the congressional proceedings culminating in the passage of this law might help elucidate its capabilities and limitations.

The law was enacted during Arinos' "elected" presidency of 1951–54 as distinct from the period of authoritarian and semiauthoritarian rule spanning 1930–45. Arinos introduced the legislation because of his deep conviction that racial or color prejudice constituted a shocking and disrespectful violation of human rights, discrediting Arthur, comte de Gobineau's superiority/inferiority of the race hypothesis. Since Brazil is a largely mestizo country and a country of immigrants, it is not surprising that many sociological and anthropological studies have been devoted to the subject. Arinos urged the legislative branch to ensure the proper application of scientific findings in governmental policy in order to operationalize Brazil's constitutional guarantees and international agreements. Otherwise, they stood in danger of becoming mere declarations out of tune with ordinary law.

Arinos argued that the federal constitution was clear on the subject: it guaranteed equality to all Brazilians before the law,[25] prohibited the dissemination of propaganda manifesting racial or color prejudice,[26] and declared that public offices were open to all Brazilians.[27] Nevertheless, he noted that it was commonly known that certain civilian careers, such as the diplomatic corps, were closed to Negroes; that the Navy and Air Force created unjustifiable difficulties for Negroes who wanted to enter the officer corps; and that other restrictions existed in various sectors of administration:

There will be no laws capable of destroying them, there has never been any law which could uproot such profound sentiments and change the mentality of a people, but this does not prevent us, through adequate legal measure, from eliminating some of the public manifestations of this prejudice.[28]

In subsequent years, the so-called Afonso Arinos Law became the object of both praise and condemnation. Some stated that its very existence was emblematic of Brazil's commitment to anti-racism, while others underscored its lack of bite and hence its general ineffectiveness in dealing with the problems of racial discrimination against black Brazilians. To his credit, Arinos has recognized how difficult the law is to implement when the burden of proof remains almost exclusively with victims of discrimination. For their part, blacks, given the realities of Brazilian society, are unlikely to go marching into police stations to lodge complaints as a first step in a potentially costly legal battle, the outcome of which is unpredictable. Successful test cases under the provisions of the law are conspicuously lacking.

Afro-Brazilian groups and individuals, their political and ideological differences notwithstanding, agree that the Afonso Arinos Law is ineffective. It has become a rallying point for those who criticize the Brazilian way of dealing with the racial issue—citing a law that has shown itself to be totally ineffective in the face of even flagrant acts of discrimination against Afro-Brazilians. But the law has still not been amended. Editorial comments are written; extensive press coverage is given to episodic acts of discrimination in which calls are made for the "Afonso Arinos Law to take its full course"; and high public officials express interest in specific incidents. But these incidents quietly slip into predictable oblivion until another such occurrence.

Any observer of Brazilian race relations who has actually read the proceedings in Congress which culminated in the passage of the law might very well wonder whether or not both its defenders and detractors have not overburdened this piece of legislation with powers it cannot exert, intentions not originally imputed to it, and confusions that should not have arisen. Ultimately, a distinction has to be drawn between prejudice and discrimination. The Afonso Arinos law appears to be much more concerned with prejudice than with discrimination. If a fault can be pointed to, it is not exclusively of Afonso Arinos de Mello Franco's creation.

Florestan Fernandes argued that the emergence of an independent or alternative black position on Brazilian race relations necessitated that black activists take an anti-white stance, not because of racism but as a tactical measure. It was one way of smashing the paternalistic and debilitating framework that had prejudiced independent black sociopolitical and economic activity in Brazil. Its other tactical advantage was that it served as a means of self-identity. It is precisely in this process that traditional and radical sectors collided. At once, black movements could be seen as both reactionary and potentially destructive of the actual or potential united front of the oppressed against the conservative forces on the one hand, and as victims of leftists and subversive radical propaganda, thereby constituting a threat to the Brazilian polity on the other hand. To attain a genuine racial democracy, or in the words of Fernandes, "racial democracy of a revolutionary kind," it was necessary to clarify the confusion between multiracialism and nonracism on the one hand, and the equation of the absence of U.S.-style Jim Crowism with the absence of institutional racism on the other hand.[29]

SUMMARY AND CONCLUSIONS

The problem of racial solidarity has occupied black spokespersons in both Brazil and the United States. Central to this issue are the questons of (1) how much all blacks, depending, naturally, on the definition of blackness, shared commonalities, over and above religious, class, and political differences, and (2) what to do about individual blacks who attained identifiable success in situations where the great majority of their group continued to be a depressed state. While some comfort and inspiration might be derived from the success of these individuals, could they continue to be so perceived if they, in fact, made a point of dissociating themselves from the group? Although these concerns are common to both Brazil and the United States, the two countries have adopted different approaches to resolution.

In Brazil, the overriding emphasis on individual mobility has resulted in fragmented efforts at united politics. A successful individual does not ordinarily assume a group racial identity. The odd black who succeeds in getting a foothold in the elite structures, albeit at the lowest level in areas such as sports, is not ordinarily expected to wear the mantle of race spokesperson. Quite the contrary, such a person characteristically avoids such protest.

Stanley Hoffman (1981) has delineated two possible lines of response for a nation facing political change: (1) fundamentalist and (2) constructive. In the fundamentalist response, an attempt is made to find remedies, not in the spirit that led to past successes, but in the mythified recipes that worked before, in the rituals of national celebration, in the rationalizations that attribute troubles or temporary decline to internal dissolvent forces or evil men and ascribe recovery to rediscovery of traditional ways. In contrast, a constructive response aims at mobilizing all reserves for innovation, at using all that remains healthy and hopeful in order to master the challenge imaginatively.

The first approach may make people feel temporarily better, because it not only provides an explanation for discomfort and disorientation but assures that what will work now is familiar. However, it rests on denial, it denies that there is something radically new to be faced and that something equally new may have to be invented.[30]

The changes within Brazil's society, economy, and politics, and the Afro-Brazilians' increasing insistence on their right to pose questions about race relations that diverge from the views of the dominant society underscore the relevance of Hoffman's words in discussing Brazilian race relations.

The statistics presented in Tables 1–4 below provide evidence of the divergence of life-styles of different racial groups in Brazil. Race differences obviously account for some differences in opportunities. Those unfamiliar with Brazilian life need to be aware of the salience of race in Brazil, and should see that blackness is an important factor in the distribution of social goods and opportunities.

NOTES

1. Nelson da Valle Silva, "Updating the Cost of Not Being White in Brazil," in Pierre-Michel Fontaine, ed., *Race, Class, and Power in Brazil* (Los Angeles: Center for Afro-American Studies, 1985).

2. See Greg Urban, "Developments in the Situation of Brazilian Tribal Populations from 1976 to 1982," *Latin American Research Review* 20 (1985): 7–25.

3. Robert Edgar Conrad, *Children of God's Fire: A Documentary of Black Slavery in Brazil* (Princeton, N.J.: Princeton University Press, 1983), p. 317.

4. Clodomir Vianna Moog, *Bandeirantes and Pioneers*, L. L. Barrett, trans. (New York: G. Braziller, 1964).

5. Florestan Fernandes, *The Negro in Brazilian Society* (New York: Columbia University Press, 1969).

6. Carlos Hasenbalg, *Race Relations in Modern Brazil* (Albuquerque: University of New Mexico Press, 1985), based on his doctoral dissertation of 1978, completed at the University of California at Berkeley.

7. Thomas E. Skidmore, "Race and Class in Brazil: Historical Perspectives," in Pierre-Michel Fontaine, ed., *Race, Class, and Power in Brazil* (Los Angeles: Center for Afro-American Studies, 1985).

8. Octavio Ianni, "Research on Race Relations in Brazil," in Magnus Morner, ed., *Race and Class in Latin America* (New York: Columbia University Press, 1969).

9. Clovis Moura, *Os Quilombos e a Rebēlio Negra*, 2d ed. (Sao Paulo: Brasiliense, 1981).

10. Sergio Buarque de Holand, *Ráizes do Brasil*, 10th ed. (Rio de Janeiro: J. Olympio, 1976).

11. Gilberto Freyre, *The Masters and the Slaves* (New York: Alfred A. Knopf, 1965).

12. Carlos Guilherme Mota, "A Democracia, Racial e Outros Mitos," *Isto É* (January 10, 1977): 36–39.

Table 1
**Potential Economically Active (PEA) by Sex and Color, According
to Groups and Monthly Income**

PEA	TOTAL	White	Black	Yellow	Mixed	No/decl.
Total (thousands)	39728 (100%)	22489 (100%)	3702 (100%)	1022 (100%)	12309 (100%)	207 (100%)
To ½ M.S.	11,5%	7,5%	20%	13,5%	16%	12,3%
½ to 1 M.S.	22,5%	18,3%	32,5%	19%	27,2%	34,6%
1 to 2 M.S.	25,2%	25,7%	24,8%	19,8%	24,9%	29,5%
2 to 3 M.S.	9,5%	11%	6%	7,9%	8,1%	8,8%
3 to 5 M.S.	8,2%	10,6%	3,9%	10,7%	5%	4,2%
Over 5 M.S.	9,8%	14,3%	2%	11,9%	3,9%	3,1%
w/o income	13%	12,3%	10,5%	16,8%	14,6%	7,1%
Men (thousands)	28184 (100%)	15880 (100%)	2579 (100%)	756 (100%)	8815 (100%)	153 (100%)
To ½ M.S.	6,7%	4,1%	10,9%	10,2%	9,8%	5,3%
½ to 1 M.S.	22,0%	16,9%	34,8%	19,8%	27,4%	35,1%
1 to 2 M.S.	27,2%	26,3%	29,8%	21,8%	28,5%	34,3%
2 to 3 M.S.	11,1%	12,5%	7,6%	8,6%	10,0%	11,7%
3 to 5 M.S.	9,7%	12,5%	4,9%	11%	6,3%	5,3%
Over 5 M.S.	12,1%	17,7%	2,4%	14,5%	4,9%	3,4%
w/o income	10,8%	9,7%	9,3%	13,7%	12,9%	4,6%
Women (thousands)	11545 (100%)	6608 (100%)	1122 (100%)	266 (100%)	3495 (100%)	54 (100%)
To ½ M.S.	23,1%	15,5%	40,8%	22,9%	31,7%	32,3%
½ to 1 M.S.	23,6%	21,5%	27,4%	16,6%	26,7%	33,3%
1 to 2 M.S.	20,3%	24,1%	13,3%	14,2%	15,9%	16,1%
2 to 3 M.S.	5,7%	7,5%	2,5%	6,1%	3,3%	0,4%
3 to 5 M.S.	4,5%	6,3%	1,5%	9,8%	1,8%	1,2%
Over 5 M.S.	4,1%	6,2%	1%	4,6%	1,3%	2,1%
w/o income	18,3%	18,6%	13,2%	25,4%	19,1%	14,3%

M.S. = Minimum Salary, an official minimum standard.

Source: IBASE, *Dados da Realidade Brasileira*, p. 53.

Table 2
Manual and Nonmanual Workers and Their Income According to Color, 1976

WORKERS	TOTAL	WHITE	BLACK	MIXED
Total	100%	56,6%	9 5%	30,8%
Nonmanual	100%	77°₀	2,6%	17,9%
Urban manual	100%	55,4°₀	10,5%	30,9°₀
Rural manual	100%	48,3°.	11,6°₀	35,9%
INCOME				
Total	100°₀	71,7°/₀	5,2%	19,8%
Of Nonmanual workers	100°/₀	85,4°₀	1,3%	10,2%
Of urban manual	100°₀	65,8°₀	7°₀	24%
Of rural manual	100°₀	57°₀	9,3%	29,9%

13. Abdias do Nascimento, *Racial Democracy in Brazil: Myth or Reality* (Ibadan, Nigeria: Sketch Publishing, 1977).

14. John Rex, *Race Relations in Sociological Theory* (London: Widenfeld & Nicholson, 1970), p. 130.

15. Nascimento, *Racial Democracy in Brazil*, pp. 7–8.

16. Mota, "A Democracia," pp. 36–37.

17. Florestan Fernandes, *The Negro in Brazilian Society*, J. D. Skiles, trans. (New York: Columbia University Press, 1969), p. 264.

18. Carl Degler, *Neither Black nor White: Slavery and Race Relations in Brazil and the United States* (New York: Macmillan, 1971).

19. Mauricio Solaun and Sidney Kronus, *Discrimination Without Violence: Miscegenation and Racial Conflict in Latin America* (New York: John Wiley, 1973), p. 4.

20. Ibid., p. vi.

21. See I. M. Lewis, *Race and Color in Islam* (New York: Harper & Row, 1971), p. 103.

22. Warren Dean, *Rio Claro: A Brazilian Plantation System, 1820–1920* (Stanford, Calif.: Stanford University Press, 1976), p. 153.

23. See Hasenbalg, *Race Relations in Modern Brazil*.

24. Ibid., p. 5.

25. Art. 31.

26. Art. 141.

27. Art. 184.

28. *Diário*, November 17, 1950, p. 8159.

29. Florestan Fernandes, "The Negro in Brazilian Society: Twenty-five Years Later," in Maxine L. Margolis and William G. Carter, eds., *Brazil: Anthropological Perspectives* (New York: Columbia University Press, 1979), p. 283.

Table 3
Educational Opportunities, by Race

Colors In School	White	Black	Brown	Yellow
No Schooling and Less Than 1 Year of Schooling	11,297,322	3,023,724	13,323,074	42,521
1-3 Years	13,940,845	2,085,650	9,840,036	79,145
4-8 Years	22,564,715	2,034,203	9,328,874	276,682
9 Years Or More	9,071,438	304,531	2,122,057	273,593
No Years Of Study Undetermined And No Declaration (Response)	936		112	
TOTAL	56,875,256	7,448,108	34,614,153	671,941

Source: *Veja*, "Race and Poverty," November 11, 1983, p. 91.

30. Stanley Hoffman, "The New Orthodoxy," *The New York Times Review of Books* 28 (1981): 23–24.

BIBLIOGRAPHY

Brookshaw, David. "Black Writer in Brazil." *Index on Censorship* 6, no. 4 (July/August 1977): 37–44.

Burns, E. Bradford. *A History of Brazil*, 2d ed. New York: Columbia University Press, 1980.

Conrad, Robert Edgar. *Children of God's Fire: A Documentary History of Black Slavery in Brazil*. Princeton, N.J.: Princeton University Press, 1983.

Table 4
Earnings, by Race

Earnings on Ethnic Basis	White	Black	Brown	Yellow
Up to 1 minimum salary ($100)	7,712,951	1,980,245	7,710,350	33,023
More than 1-2 minimum salaries	6,931,477	941,344	3,781,677	55,366
More than 2-5 minimum salaries	6,339,195	466,911	2,206,600	118,733
More than 5				
No earnings	2,824,398	294,646	1,879,307	41,863
No declaration	108,637	9,894	60,723	1,603
TOTAL	27,512,423	3,770,473	16,231,672	376,406

Source: *Veja*, "Race and Poverty," November 11, 1983, p. 91.

Damata, Gasparino. "Eles Tem Direito a Um Lugar no. Sol." *Revista do Globo*, March 24, 1956.

Dean, Waren. *Rio Claro: A Brazilian Plantation System, 1820–1920*. Stanford, Calif.: Stanford University Press, 1976.

Degler, Carl. *Neither Black nor White: Slavery and Race Relations in Brazil and the United States*. New York: Macmillan, 1971.

De Oliveira, Lucia Elena Garcia, Rosa Maria Porcaro, Araugjo Costa, and Tereza Christina. *O lug do Negro na Forca de Trabalho*. Rio de Janeiro: Fundacao Instituto Brasileiro de Georgrafia e Estatistica, 1985.

Dzidzienyo, Anani. "The 'Afonso Arinos Law' and Brazilian Race Relations: A Return to the Source." Unpublished, Brown University, April 1986.

———. *The Position of Blacks in Brazilian Society*. London: Minority Rights Groups, 1971, 1979.

Fernandes, Florestan, "The Negro in Brazilian Society: Twenty-five Years Later." In Maxine L. Margolis and William E. Carter, eds. *Brazil: Anthropological*

Perspectives (Essays in Honor of Charles Wagley). New York: Columbia University Press., 1979.

———. *The Negro in Brazilian Society*. Jacqueline D. Skiles, trans. New York: Columbia University Press, 1969.

Fontaine, Pierre-Michel. *Race, Class, and Power in Brazil*, Los Angeles: Center for Afro-American Studies, UCLA, 1985.

———. "Research in the Political Economy of Afro-Latin America." *Latin American Research Review* (1980).

Freyre, Gilberto. "The Afro-Brazilian Experiment." *UNESCO Courier*, 1977: 1–12.

———. *The Masters and the Slaves: A Study in the Development of Brazilian Civilization*. New York: Alfred A. Knopf, 1965.

Gonzalez, Lelia. "The Black Woman's Place in Brazilian Society." Unpublished paper, 1985 and beyond. A National Conference sponsored by the African American Women's Political Caucus and Morgan State University, Baltimore, Md., August 9–10, 1984.

Hartman, C., and Charles Husband. *Race as News*. New York: UNESCO Press, 1974.

Hasenbalg, Carlos A. "Brazilian Racial Democracy: Reality or Myth?" *Humboldt Journal of Social Studies* 10, No. 1 (Fall/Winter 1982–83).

———. *Race Relations in Modern Brazil*. Albuquerque: Latin American Institute, University of New Mexico, 1985.

Ianni, Octavio. "Research on Race Relations in Brazil." In Magnus Morner, ed. *Race and Class in Latin America*. New York: Columbia University Press, 1969.

Instituto Brasileiro de Analises Sociaia e Economicas (IBASE). "O Negro no Mercado de Trabalho" (Versao Preliminar). Rio de Janeiro, November 1985.

Karasch, Mary. "From Porterage to Proprietorship: African Occupations in Rio de Janeiro, 1808–1850." In Stanley L. Engerman and Eugen D. Genovese, eds. *Race and Slavery in the Western Hemisphere*. Princeton, N.J.: Princeton University Press, 1975.

Mitchell, Michael. "Racial Consciousness and the Political Attitudes and Behavior of Blacks in Sao Paulo." Ph.D. diss., Indiana University, 1977.

Mota, Carlos Guilherme. "A Democracia Racial e Outros Mitos." *Isto É* (January 10, 1977): 36–39.

Nascimento, Abdias do. "Racial Democracy in Brazil: Myth or Reality?" Ibadan, Nigeria: Sketch Publishing, 1977.

———. *Mixture or Massacre: The Genocide of a Black People*. Rio de Janeiro: Afrodiaspora, 1979.

Raphael, Alison. "Samba and Social Control: Popular Culture and Racial Democracy in Rio de Janeiro." Ph.D. diss., Columbia University, 1981.

Reis, Joao Jose. "Slave Rebellion in Brazil: The African Moslem Uprising in Bahia, 1835." Ph.D. diss., University of Minnesota, 1983.

Sanders, Thomas. "Brazilian Population in 1982: Growth, Migration, Race, Religion." UFSI Reports, Universities Field Staff International, Inc., No. 42, 1982.

————. "Economic and Social Characteristics of the Brazilian Population." UFSI Reports, Universities Field Staff International, Inc., No. 43, 1982.

Skidmore, Thomas E. *Black into White: Race and Nationality in Brazilian Thought.* London: Oxford University Press, 1974.

Solaun, Mauricio, and Sidney Kronus. *Discrimination Without Violence: Miscegenation and Racial Conflict in Latin America.* New York: John Wiley, 1973.

Stam, Robert. "Slow Fade to Afro: The Black Presence in Brazilian Cinema." *Film Quarterly* 36, No. 2 (Winter 1983): 36–45.

Toplin, Brent. "Exploding the Myths: Racial Polarization in the Developing Giant." *Blackworld* (November 1972): 15–22.

CANADA

Doug Daniels

This chapter summarizes the many waves of labor migration and internal conflicts that built the mixture of nationalities that now make up the Canadian nation-state. Its theoretical focus owes much to theorists like Samir Amin in political economy and Eric Wolf in anthropology who have studied the growth of the world as a system, particularly from the period of European mercantile expansion in the 1500s onward. This will necessitate a criticism of many of the commonplaces of mainstream social science and government policy such as "visibility theory"—the notion that somehow the more exotic looking nationalities are the most oppressed, or the notion that British colonialism in Canada was much more benign than French or American variants. The article also emphasizes the explicitly political expressions of race and nationality, since these are the most accessible statements of need, consciousness, and conflict available to us.

A RACIAL CONTEXT

Canada's history of relations between nationalities and races can be summarized as follows: After the 1759 defeat of a presumably less developed form of French colonialism in New France, the pioneers of British colonialism rose to economic ascendancy in the rapid building of the nation of Canada. By virtue of their pioneer status, an Anglo-Saxon economic elite remains at the top of the "vertical mosaic" of Canada's classes, nationalities, and races (Porter, 1965). Since the Peace of Paris in 1763, and the Confederation in 1867, the Canadian democracy has sought to widen its social base to include all subsequent immigrant nationalities into all levels of the class structure. Successive waves of immigrants are seen as "starting at the bottom" and working their way to the highest levels over the course of generations. This dominant model makes allowances for "bottlenecks" in the march of upward mobility caused by economic crises during which immigrant populations have been subject to temporary phases of radical politics. Each return to economic expansion, however, has meant a normalization of the process of upward mobility, political assimilation, economic democracy, and cultural tolerance (pluralism or multiculturalism). Variants of this dominant view have been presented by some critical liberal and Marxist scholars who portray a somewhat rougher road to the "embourgeoisement" and passivity of once radical working classes after they have established themselves.

The dominant scholarly view also makes many fine (and often hard) distinctions among racism, nationalism, religious bigotry, ethnocentrism, "nativism" (the chauvinism of those born in Canada versus those who arrived later), and attempts to build a science of minority relations around these distinctions, the most popular of which is the visibility of the oppressed. Once again, this dominant liberal model has a parallel among Canadian radical scholars who have attempted to decide which groups in Canada can be considered "nations"—the Quebecois, the Indians and Metis, the so-called third force of non-Anglo, non-French Euro-Canadians, and so forth.[1] Although some of these definitional disputes relate to practical political strategies for achieving a national territory (an independent Quebec, autonomous regions for native peoples), others remain bound to the strict limitations of traditional legalities of the Canadian Constitution and official state ideology, as reflected in such mainstream textbook titles as *Two Nations, Many Cultures: Ethnic Groups in Canada* (Elliot, 1983).

This article presents an alternative to this dominant view. It follows through the implications of the perception that Canada is fundamentally an economic colony and neo-colony—first of Britain, then of the United States (Teeple, 1972; Panitch, 1977). It also attempts to demonstrate that Canada's economic, political, and cultural-national life has much more in common with Third World neo-colonies than the proponents of the dominant "vertical mosaic" model would ever suspect.

In this alternative view, Canada's development is seen first as a series of chronic crises of stagnation which have been resolved by importing new labor forces to produce new staple products for export, supplanting both the dominance of the old export staple and the people who processed this staple. Each change of staple has necessitated the abandonment and often the repression of one group of producers, followed by the importation and control of another. These changeovers of staple production have been accompanied by racial-national confrontations. The most militant of these confrontations have been not between subject groups but between the Anglo-Canadian state and "obsolete" labor forces of the various nationalities administered by the Anglo-Canadian ruling classes. A number of historic examples are pursued in the following pages.

Second, despite the model of economic assimilation and upward mobility, the Anglo-Canadian ruling class has remained as impenetrable to later or "lesser" Canadian nationalities as has the economic elite of many more transparently colonial societies (Clement, 1975 and 1983). With the concentration of wealth in late monopoly capitalism, it is extremely unlikely that this Anglo-Canadian ruling class will become less impermeable. Although other nationalities have achieved entry to the middle classes in the professions and some small to medium-sized businesses, they have not made it to the "haute bourgeoisie." Even the most numerous and recently most militant non-Anglo nationality, the Quebecois, have only made it to the level of "state elite" (Olsen, 1980) rather than becoming owners of large blocks of capital. They have achieved entry to this state elite primarily through the vehicles of the Liberal party and the Parti Quebecois and the use of nationalization and creation of "Crown corporations" and other state agencies run by political appointees. The tiny exceptions to this rule from the Franco-Canadian and Jewish Canadian nationality remain just that—tiny exceptions in an overwhelmingly Anglo-Canadian capitalist class.

The attempt by Canadian governments and resource industries to foster a "Red Capitalism" among Canadian native peoples has similarly created a state-funded political elite. Some of these leaders have managed to transmute their political influence into some material wealth, but this has been and will almost certainly remain at a very small scale (O'Malley, 1980).

Third, the alternative view is suspicious, not only of the myth of economic democracy, but also of the unqualified claims to a Canadian history of political democracy. Each extension of democratic rights beyond the Anglo-Canadian kin-based elite of the nineteenth century (the "Family Compact," with its political arm in Quebec called the "Château Clique") has been won only after prolonged sruggle, often with arms. Thus, the franchise was extended to the largely Irish and Scots working classes below the English rulers of Upper Canada by the Mackenzie-Papineau rebellions of 1837–38. The demand for franchise and regional government by the Scots Halfbreeds and French Metis of the Northwest Territories was escalated to the "Riel Rebellions" of 1871 and 1885. In line with Paul Sweezy's argument that ruling classes grant their subject classes the vote only when the subject classes are sufficiently coopted to use the vote in ways that are no threat to ruling class hegemony (Sweezy, 1984), Chinese immigrants were not granted the vote until after the 1930s Depression and Canada's Indians only in the late 1950s, well after their semiautonomous subsistence economies were so vitiated that there was no realistic hope of a renewed life outside of the welfare state that followed World War II. In the twentieth century, the recurrent use of mass deportations, mass internment, and other forms of political harassment of the people seen as "dangerous foreigners" (Avery, 1979) makes us regard continual repression and surveillance of immigrant populations as the *norm*. The 1960s–70s, a period of liberal humanism and state-encouraged multiculturalism, represents an exceptional interlude that may well return to the bleak "normality" as the current economic crisis deepens. A number of historic examples of "normal repression" against the nondominant nationalities are presented later in this chapter.

Fourth, despite a thread of right-wing nationalism and nativist jingoism in many immigrant groups (especially East European emigrés in the Soviet epoch), the preponderant expression of immigrant politics has been radical democratic in the nineteenth century and populist and socialist (including Marxist socialism) in the twentieth century. This dominant aspect of Canadian radical politics was interrupted in the postwar period by a combination of prosperity and intense repression known as McCarthyism (which itself followed deportations of "foreign" radicals in the Great Depression). Once again, as the global economic crisis returns, we are seeing many signs of the return to this "normal radicalism" among the Third World immigrants and native peoples of Canada who arrived too late to take part in economic upward mobility and assimilation. Their arrival postdated the economic downturn of the Vietnam War, the OPEC crisis, and probably the "long wave" of economic contradiction that many see in the present world economy (Frank, 1982).

This period also witnessed a rekindling of progressive currents among now "established" immigrants in the form of the Canadian version of liberation theology now sweeping the mainstream churches. This movement evolved from a previous phase of populist/socialist "social gospel" Christianity which helped build the populist/social democratic coalitions of the 1920s and 1930s and which elected self-described socialist provincial governments on the prairies. The point that many have overlooked in their study of "Agrarian socialism" (Lipset, 1950) is that British Fabianism may have had its ideological impact on the largely Anglo-Canadian leadership of Canadian social democracy, but that the first social democratic government was elected in 1944 in the only province where the majority of the population was from neither of the "founding races" (British, French). Rather, the background was overwhelmingly Central and Northern European and native peoples, who brought with them many currents of radicalism from a Europe that was in an age of democratic revolution from 1848 to 1917, a period that nicely overlaps the greatest period of Canadian immigration. Although a moderate social democracy was the main expression of progressive politics among the

Anglo-Saxon working class, left-wing politics among the East Europeans, Finnish, Jewish, and other nationalities consistently gravitated to more radical forms seeking basic transformation of Canadian society. These included the Industrial Workers of the World (Scott, 1975), the Farmers Unity League, the Communist party of Canada, and other formations (see Abella, 1973; Dahlie and Fernando, 1981).

Fifth, most cases of repression can be explained better in terms of political economy than in racial or "visibility" terms. Even such famous "proofs" of the visibility theory, such as the bad treatment of Chinese contract labor and business (compared to European immigrants) or Japanese internees in World War II (compared to German), must take into account the following factors of political economy.

The Chinese arrived in the mid-nineteenth century when the tiny British outpost on Vancouver Island was in a very fragile state without clear British sovereignty and was under pressure from Japanese, Russian, and American claims to the area. Its sovereignty was not secure until well after confederation (1867), the second Riel Rebellion (1885), and the completion of the transcontinental Canadian Pacific Railway and the accompanying trade protectionism of the "National Policy." The British mercantile class felt very threatened by both Chinese and Japanese merchants (including labor contractors) who stood some chance of supplanting Lord Douglas' little flock as the main entrepreneurs in the area (see Chan, 1983, and Knight and Koizumi, 1976). Or are we to assume that the entrepreneurial skills and ability to amass capital—which Chinese and Japanese have demonstrated so successfully in Southeast Asia—were somehow inoperable in Canada? It is here that we must seek the explanation to the unique bans and exorbitant fees leveled against Oriental immigration, rather than in skin color.

With regard to the seizure of Japanese fishing boats and other property in World War II and their mass internment, whereas Germans were subjected to relatively mild repression and only selective internment in the same period, the following explanation may be given. Most German immigrants were fairly well absorbed as farmers and laborers in a stable (though stagnant) prairie economy, whereas the crisis in the West Coast fisheries was severely exacerbated in the 1930s Depression. The uneasy balance between Indian, Japanese, and Euro-Canadian fishermen was temporarily "resolved" by the attack on that nationality group which was weakened by their supposed link to an enemy imperialist power—Japan.[2] It should also be pointed out that progressive Japanese and Euro-Canadian fishermen's unions fought the tripartite racial divisions throughout this period, while the fisheries industry profited from the expropriations (see Knight and Koizumi, 1976 for a Japanese unionist's account; see also North, 1974, and Sunahara, 1981).

Finally on the question of internment of people because of their supposed "visibility," one must note the remarkably little-known internment of Ukrainians and other Euro-Canadians whose homelands were part of the Austro-Hungarian Empire in 1914–18. With the powers of the War Measures Act (which was also used against the rising of Quebec nationalism in October 1970, with full military occupation in peacetime), between 7,000 and 8,000 Central Europeans were interned as "enemy aliens" and many more were prosecuted for anti-conscription propaganda. Once again, as in the Japanese internment, many actual pro-imperialist activists like the pro-Kaiser Bishop Budka were freed, while hundreds of socialist and pacifist Ukrainians, Poles, and other "Austrians" were deported or remained interned to the end of the war (Potrobenko, 1977, pp. 103ff). This bitter chapter in Canadian history—which preceded further anti-Slavic persecution in the 1920s and followed the 1919 Winnipeg General Strike—is perhaps so little known because it does not fit the more comforting liberal model of racial visibility that has been used to "explain" Japanese internment. Only in the wake of successful demands from the Japanese victims of internment for an official apology and financial compensation by the Canadian government has the decades-old grievance of the Ukrainians and other East Europeans seen the light of day.[3]

The Anglo-Saxon nationality, has been the major base of support for both small and large "c" conservatism as supporters of the Conservative party, and Social Credit. It has also been the recruiting base for "nativist" movements against immigrants, including those generated in response to the Winnipeg General Strike of 1919, the Ku Klux Klan on the prairies in the 1920s, and the "new right" racist groups that have attached themselves to the current Conservative party. French Canadians and the "Third Force" nationalities have favored the Liberal party as their means of "liberal" defense and expression, dating from the Riel Rebellion and the Klan. Social democratic and socialist parties have enlisted support on the class and nationality basis discussed above.

All this is not to say that Canadians of British descent are marked by some sign of Cain or that they are incapable of producing progressive leaders (J. S. Wordsworth, T. C. Douglas) and even martyrs (Norman Bethune in the Spanish Civil War and revolutionary China). However, the preponderant political expression of Anglo-Canadians for conservatism and reaction must be laid down to the role selected for them as representative owners for British and American capital (see Myers, 1972). They were dominant in land, timber, and mineral distribution and have become dominant in management and in the better-paying jobs in industry.

The French Metis, on the other hand, were forced to flee, fought again in 1885, lost, and reemerged as a political force only in the mid-twentieth century (see Dobbin, 1981).

As perhaps an ultimate irony, even the Communist party of Canada (CPC) experienced a prolonged line struggle between the Anglo-Saxon leadership and the Finnish and Slavic nationalities that made up the great bulk of the membership. This took the form of rank-and-file resistance to comintern policies, ostensibly of "bolshevization," but in content also included an endorsement of Stalin's abusive policies toward the peasantry for surplus extraction for industrialization, as well as the loss of autonomy of non-Russian nationalities in the USSR. This conflict culminated in a major purge of 1,000 members in the early 1930s, an event which many historians point to as the great downturn for the CPC (see D. Avery, "Ethnic Loyalties and the Proletarian Revolution: A Case Study of Communist Political Activity in Winnipeg, 1923–36," in Dahlie and Fernando, 1981). Future scholars may well note how the Anglo leadership insisted on the policies of Stalin, while former serfs from Finland and Eastern Europe advocated more benign policies toward peasants and nondominant nationalities (policies later known as "Maoism").

Is it more useful to look at Anglo-Canadians as the "first among equals," first merely because they were first on the scene as "Canadians" in the long series of colonial events, and first among equals in a steadily opening and widening democracy of wealth and power? Or is it more useful to examine Anglo-Canadians as a somewhat softer version of the white dominant group in South Africa, which also has never really opened up its doors to either successive or "native" groups and has permitted mixed and subordinate races only to the lower middle-class level? This proposition—preposterous as it may appear at first—should be taken as seriously as Amin's proposition that South Africa itself is not a backward country, but rather is a foreshadowing of the most advanced form of capitalism where immigrant and migratory labor forces of "inferior" nationalities are regulated in *1984* fashion by a privileged ruling/ supervisor nationality (Amin, "The Future of South Africa" in Amin, 1980a). That this is not a "science fiction" model is evidenced by the massive and increasing role of migratory labor in Europe and other parts of the First World (see "The New Nomads: Immigration and Changes in the International Division of Labour," Dixon et al., 1982a).

That the demographic ratios of superior to inferior workers may be different should not dull us to the nature and probable evolution of relations between the nationalities in Canada. We should consider the increase in the ratio of temporary seasonal laborers compared to landed immigrants (Caribbean workers for the Ontario tobacco and fruit harvests; Mexicans in British Columbia and Alberta for temporary agricultural and resort labor; temporary European workers in northern resource industries) and ask whether Canada's leaders may indeed be gravitating to something resembling the South African model rather than the democratic commonwealth of property and toil that has been Canada's self-perception for many decades.

Perhaps Canadian liberalism, too, can be peeled back like layers of an onion, from the most vulnerable nationalities, until only the upper levels of the Euro-Canadian core enjoy the benefits of liberal democracy. If Canada moves to a variation of the South African model, the ethnic and class antecedents and prerequistites certainly exist in its history and present social structure, its "vertical mosaic." Of course, should the world economy experience a major rejuvenation paralleling that which followed World War II, and should monopoly capitalism somehow open itself for upward mobility of the type unknown since the nineteenth century, then the critical model presented here would become little more than the product of an overactive imagination. On the other hand, if the trends that have been perceived are valid, the model will serve as a guide to much of the real world of politics at the turn of the twenty-first century when increased class polarization will take the empirical form of increased distance between the nationalities and "races."

There is yet another major argument against the dominant "visibility theory." The sharpest and most overt acts of racial/national/religious oppression in Canada have developed in ways that have nothing whatsoever to do with "color." In addition, the most serious conflicts have not been sectarian squabbles between dominated nationalities but rather have been directed by the state, with its social base in the Anglo-Saxon elite, against a series of national and religious formations. Aside from the victims of interimperialist rivalry mentioned above, these social groups have in some fashion impeded the indefinite expansion of capitalism in Canada. Among these groups are precapitalist kinship-based communal peoples (the native peoples of Canada); the Metis and other radical democrats under Riel who sought to build a commonwealth of labor on the farmlands and Indian hunting land of the prairies; religiously based and ethnically identified utopian communities (the pacifist Doukhobors and the Hutterites); and immigrant political formations who fought for a noncapitalist social order in Canada (Ukrainians, Finns, et al., as well as the many Jews active on the left and the many anti-fascist Jews who were denied access to Canada during the years of the holocaust; see Abella, 1979).

Each of these groups has been the subject of military or paramilitary surveillance and repression by the state. This repression has ranged from all-out war against the Indians and Metis, including genocide of the Beothuk Indians of Newfoundland,[4] to cultural repression (the seizure of Indian children for rapid assimilation in residential schools). It has also included legal and economic harassment (the Doukhobor and Hutterite colonies) and the use of intensive surveillance and agent provocateurs against the native "Red Power" movement in the 1960s (see

Brown, 1973). These confrontations, along with the repression of single unemployed young males in the 1930s in the labor camps (largely on a nonracial basis, although part of a long history of abuse of bachelor workers, immigrant or otherwise)[5] are the most extreme in Canadian history and they constitute the outstanding crises of race/national relations in Canada. All of them can be explained, however, without the rise of "race" or "visibility" except in the narrowest empirical sense. Let us examine these examples using the methodology of political economy rather than the idea of "race." (For a discussion of race, visibility, and policies of multiculturalism of "visible" traits, see note 6.)

The main thesis here is that the nodes of greatest conflict in Canadian race/nationality relations are at the frontier of capitalist expansion, not in some trivialized dispute over items of dress, diet, or dance—nor even religion per se or color. These crises often occur at the critical juncture when capitalist developers have decided to move from one form of staple production to another, such as the transition from the fur trade to the wheat economy on the prairies—a transition that required the military defeat and displacement (or containment on reserves) of Metis and Indians.

Communal peoples, whether kinship based or religiously based, have regularly fought tenaciously to hang on to a world where prestige is not based on possession but on wisdom and leadership, where social relations are highly egalitarian and cooperative, and where each individual can play a respected, productive role in society. Native peoples have fought to protect this communal mode in the past, and they now defend it even in its distorted and "vestigial" forms in northern Canada today. In spite of the remarkable power of the capitalist "universal market" to dissolve everything by the universal solvent of the cash nexus (Braverman, 1974), Canada's native peoples and communally oriented religious communities have struggled against a system where law, kin, sex, love, and nature are subject to the laws of the market, and nothing is produced simply for "use" alone.

Amin sees this autonomous and varied "patterning of use values" as the real definition of culture. This is the theoretical way of stating what native peoples and others recognize intuitively while they express their demands in the language and forums of the dominant capitalist society— its courts and parliaments—as aboriginal land and economic claims, claims to nationhood, the corresponding right to "Indian government," and parallel demands from other groups. In an attempt to retain some flexibility of their besieged social systems, the native groups have struggled desperately to maintain a land base on which they can have a diversified "cushion," of noncapitalist ways of making a living. Meanwhile, the international crisis of capitalism treats their nationalities to 80 to 90 percent unemployment rates in a countrywide environment of 10 to 12 percent official unemployment. Despite distortions of the welfare state, alcoholism, and the depredations of police and welfare workers who take away so many adult males and "neglected" children, the kinship-based native communal formation tries desperately to survive on the reserves and in nonofficial rural communities.[7]

Quite simply, when the native mixture of "jobs" is successful, it provides for a very free and varied life that would be the envy of many factory-bound and office-chained workers and professionals. Similarly, the remnants of the kin-based communal social order are indeed the kernel of the community and "identity" so desperately sought by the participant-victims of North American consumerism.

Many writers, including those who write for the financial press, have commented on the tenacity and intransigence of the native groups that are most auspiciously located geographically and socially to repel the assault of the multinationals. Despite the commercialization of the aboriginal rights struggle by the multimillion-dollar land claims industry, the ideals of a homeland that is more than a marketplace have struck a chord in the native people that goes far deeper than immediate economic demands for a better way of living. The chord has resonated with astonishing breadth among a wide variety of groups who are resisting the universal market—from "fringe" groups of ecology and life-style that are caricatured so demeaningly by the mainstream press, to respectable church groups like the Anglican Synod of Canada and even the Pope himself on his recent tour of the Northwest Territories.

The movement as a whole has been saddled by some of the less cogent ideas from 1960s radicalism, including every variety of religious mysticism, and by such ideas as that one cannot be a "true Indian" and also hold a job and own a motorized toboggan. Many activists from the 1960s who went "back to the land" also found their way into the native movement as community organizers, consultants, administrators, and researchers. Many courageous and "radical" young white people moved into the north as teachers, nurses, and social workers in the late 1960s when the Canadian state and its provincial governments were attempting to "decolonize the north" to give native communities some self-rule— for example, the election of their own school boards and municipal councils. In the past two decades the less mature people and the more foolish ideas have disappeared, leaving native people at the center of a widening and strengthening network of people and movements that can no longer be written off as marginal cranks. They are developing an increasingly clear vision of an alternative society that will avoid the pitfalls of previous experiments in social change.

Now that every continent has been brought into the universal market, capitalism has been forced to seek out its few remaining frontiers, and each new frontier has stirred a hornet's nest of resistance, resulting

ultimately in wider alliances of opponents. Thus, the expansion of multinationals into major oil and uranium development was a direct result
of falling profitability in manufacturing centers. This new thrust necessarily put capitalism into conflict with the few remaining enclaves of
human geography that it had not yet absorbed fully (including women
engaged in domestic labor).[8] The vast mineral-rich northlands of Canada
inhabited successfully by Indians, Metis, and Innuit is the key area of
the 1980s. The point here is that every expansion of capitalism in British
North America has met with resistance, which has often expressed itself
not only in national forms, but also in ideologies that are in varying
degrees explicitly anti-capitalist (Dahlie and Fernando, 1981). Hence,
when the Royal Canadian Mounted Police labeled the native movement
of Canada the "greatest single threat to national security" in the 1960s
(Brown and Brown, 1973), they were following a well-trodden path in
Canadian history.

Indeed, the historical bridge between the radical democracy of Riel[9]
and the decolonizing upsurge of the 1960s is provided by the great Metis
leaders Malcolm Norris and Jim Brady, the founders of the Metis Society
of Saskatchewan (for an excellent biography, see Dobbin, 1981). These
ideological Marxists were active in the populist-social democratic movement and (after 1944) the provincial government of Saskatchewan. Both
died in 1967 resisting the government funding they justifiably feared
would subvert the movement of their people. The historical record will
show that the predominant ideological current of Metis and other oppressed nationalities in Canada has been radical democratic, often anti-
capitalist, and, in the mid-twentieth century, a socialist version of radical
democracy. While it is not the only current, it is the major expression
of those who have been injured by the ebbs and flows of the world
capitalist system.

A history of Canadian race relations can therefore be written without
any recourse to visibility, for the "visibility" of the oppressed had little
or nothing to do with their oppression. This article opened with an
analysis of the native peoples' continuing political and social evolution
as an expression of resistance to the spread of European imperialism in
order to lay the groundwork for the political economic thesis that is
counterposed here to the "common sense" of visibility theory. The remaining segment of this article will present a succinct statement of this
counterthesis, bring the history of other nationalities up to date, and
conclude with an analysis of contemporary debates and the balance of
forces of various ideologies, movements, and scenarios for the future.

The political economy thesis offered here is as follows: Canadian race/
nationality relations can be understood only in the wider context of the
many mechanisms Canadian and international capital has used to attract
and control the flow of labor into Canada. These mechanisms include

the importation of many kinds of single males; several alternative and sometimes overlapping mechanisms for the reproduction of labor power, such as miscegenation (the Metis), the importation of spouses when convenient (New France), the banning of spouses and the provision of prostitutes in their place (Chinese contract labor); and a long series of legal proscriptions and pogroms against Chinese who mingled with "white" women or attempted to hire them as workers in laundries, restaurants, or other Chinese businesses. The mechanisms of deportation and internment have also been used. The Anglo-Saxon ruling class which imported wave after wave of immigrant labor reserved for itself and even for its working class the position of managers and foremen of the nation. At the level of the managerial/professional/bureaucratic class, the Anglo-Saxon hegemony remains strong, and, even at the level of the skilled workers unionized in high-wage, capital-intensive industries, there is a disproportionate representation of Anglos.

Such an analysis, borrowed from similar analyses of Third World countries, may sound rather odd to scholars used to studying Canada in isolation from other dependent countries. Nonetheless, this perspective will provide more fruitful new insights into Canada's national "vertical mosaic" (see Porter, 1965, Clement, 1975, and many writers since). This Anglo-Saxon colonial ruling class has acted much like others in their task of accumulating wealth for the dominant country (first Britain, now the United States) and has regulated each wave of immigrant labor while mediating the struggle between the laborers' demand for a decent living and the dominant country's demand for greater return on investment.

The nationalities sent to different ecotomes on the prairies were like so many species of cattle who adapted to different habitats (Potrobenko, 1977). Even today the human geography of the prairies looks like a jumbled batch of bits of Iceland, the Ukraine, and Norway. The 1920s witnessed other crises and overt repression against the last holdouts of communal noncapitalist religious communities and native societies. This period saw the prolonged repression of the pacifist communal Doukhobors in the Verigin area of central eastern Saskatchewan. These "practical utopians" from Russia who had suffered so greatly in Europe and were the proteges of Count Leo Tolstoy were constantly harassed by the state over forced military conscription, tax laws, and land entitlement laws. Forced to break up their lands into individual holdings "in fee simple," the groupings finally dispersed over the prairies and into British Columbia, where the communards took to fierce sectarian battles which have scarcely cooled even today. Their severe persecution had little to do with their "visibility," since they looked much like other Slavs on the prairies, and everything to do with their communal mode of living. Similar repression was mounted against the Hutterite movement, another Christian communist movement deriving from the Hugenot and Anabaptist streams of Reformation in Europe.

Other communal formations that fell to police-church-business repression were more directly "racial," that is, the Sundance lodges, ceremonies and networks of the Plains Indians centered around the Sundance (an adaptation of the Midewiwin of the woodland Ojibwa). All forms of shamianism, the remnants of the ghost dance, and the peyote cults (all of which reemerged in the 1960s once the actual economy of communalism was broken) were repressed. At the same time, sharp pressures were exerted to divide Indian reserve lands into individual plots, to elect chiefs in "white" fashion rather than by traditional consensus or heredity, and to otherwise induce the native peoples to participate in the prevailing economic and social life of the capitalist society. These pressures met with remarkable resistance. The Eurocentric observer sees a people who refuse to do well at business. The more astute observer sees a group of people who have never countenanced wide gaps of income and status, who had had socially rewarding roles for every member of their society whether as hunter, weaver, medicine person, warrior, horticulturist, or whatever. Truly, the communal past, though not idyllic, exists as a living memory for those who have known it.

Similarly vigorous efforts were made to smash the potlatch of the Kwakiutl and other west coast Indians. Despite the ravages of European diseases, exacerbated by their enslavement and years of warfare, these peoples had a highly autonomous and abundant economic life outside of Canadian capitalism. Their repression began when they stood in the path to vast forest, mineral, and fishery wealth. Their festivals were banned (the potlatch was the pivotal actuarial service for births, deaths, marriages, inheritances, egalitarian redistribution, and economic "insurance" for bad times, and so on), paraphernalia were seized, lodges destroyed, the carving of totems forbidden, and the Indian children kidnapped and sent to boarding schools. This willful destruction of a kinship-based mode of production proceeded even though Indian labor was the only labor cheap enough to make forestry and fishing profitable at a period of very low technological development in the resource industries (Knight, 1978).

The apparently "irrational" resistance to capitalism by the Kwakiutl of the 1920s and the Dene of the 1980s must be related not only to the economic but also to the immensely "human" social advantages their culture offered. Indeed, only by making the sheer economic survival of the Doukhobors, Cree, and Kwakiutl so nearly impossible did the forces of the dominant economy achieve their aim, at least in part. The Kwakiutl were given back their masks and totems in the late 1970s, well after most of them had been Christianized and been absorbed into the market economy. The Cree of the prairies were given back their Cree language classes and cultural institutes after the language was well into decline and the reserves had long proven incapable of sustaining their populations. This pattern will probably repeat itself in the Northwest Territories but with a more liberal veneer. Dene "culture" and political forms will be tolerated in the 1960s liberal fashion, at the same time that the traditional economic base is destroyed by pipelines, the decline of fur and caribou, and the exponential population growth (Daniels, 1981a). Here, too, Indians and Metis and Innuit are more and more coming to resemble the Third World peasantry whose ingenious methods of living off the land are being undermined by the expansion of monopoly and mechanization of the *latifundia*. Such "peasants" have long surrounded Rio de Janeiro and Johannesburg, and in Canada the native equivalents are finding their way to Kenora, Thunder Bay, Churchill, Regina, and other cities that promise little and deliver little.

In summary, then, the main waves of repression in Canadian history have been directed at race and/or nationality groups that have been precapitalist or anti-capitalist, living in either kinship-based or religiously based communal settings. Other recipients of racial-political repression have been nationalities with a strong history of left radicalism. Many of these people were from Eastern Europe and the Mediterranean and were deported in the 1920s and 1930s to fascist and right-wing royalist regimes in Southern and Central Europe where they were imprisoned or executed (Brown and Brown, 1973). Some of the repressed in Canada, though not political, were banned all the same because the Anglo-Saxon state and ruling class sought to bring in a new body of labor.

Conversely, races or nationalities that have migrated to Canada in good economic times and in full acceptance of normal goals of self-advancement have had little trouble, despite their unusual appearance or customs. Much has been made of the antipathy shown to middle-class East Indians from the Uganda diaspora, most of whom were not "anti-capitalist." The arrival of large numbers of East Indian architects, doctors, and other professionals in the 1960s and 1970s stirred intense reaction among professionals in Canada because the new immigrants threatened to grossly overfulfill the annual quotas of professionals that the market allowed. Hence, many of the stories about the Brahmins' suppose cupidity, untrustworthiness, and arrogance were based on bitter intraclass competitiveness. This is reminiscent of fascist anti-Semitism or anti-Chinese hysteria in Southeast Asia, both of which substituted a vulnerable, slightly privileged group as scapegoat for the errors of the real bearers of power.

In the same vein, the Vietnamese and Hoa (ethnic Chinese from Vietnam) refugees who have arrived in Canada in recent years are industrious and willing to abide by the rules and goals of the market, but they have encountered a severe downturn in the market and increased competition at the small business and professional level. They now find themselves victims of far-right racism which among their "sins" even blames them for failing to fight sufficiently well against the Viet Cong!

The long wave of expansion in Canadian and world capitalism began its downturn in about 1967 and suffered an even sharper decline after the 1973 OPEC crisis. The Canadian immigrants who made it "under the wire" so to speak—the Italians, the Portuguese, and the Greeks of the late 1950s and 1960s—were able to take part in some of the upward mobility that has become the official model for Canadian minorities. Those who arrived later, including the off-reserve Indians who migrated to the cities in the late 1960s and Third World newcomers from the Caribbean, the Philippines, and Latin America, came in a period of steady contraction. Following the surfeit of professionals from the Uganda diaspora and the reasonably abundant supply of skilled workers from Canadian sources (after years of importation from Western Europe), the Canadian immigration authorities have increasingly set very limited goals in their search for temporary labor, domestic laborers, servants, nurses' aides, and the like. These economic roles are given to the darker peoples of the Third World, including the Indians, Metis, and Innuit as part of the Third World, or even the "Fourth" World as some call themselves (see Manuel and Poslums, 1974). These unfortunate migrants have had to endure the choice of these very limited economic niches or long stretches of unemployment and desperation. Again, it becomes clear that "visibility" has little to do with the "causes" of their plight.

Lest my colleagues accuse me of reducing everything to the procrustean bed of economic determinism, let me point out that my intention is anything but economism. I do not see a Rooseveltian New Deal on the immediate horizon, nor do I foresee a miraculous cyclical cure to the current economic crisis. Economic crises do not automatically make people jump one way or the other. Indeed, situations of scarcity that "ought" to produce more competition, racism, and tension between the nationalities often produce more cooperation and reduce national-racial isolation. Such cases as the successful growth of the labor movement in the 1930s which crossed national/racial lines contradict economistic interpretations. Rather, we may expect continued refinement and strengthening of political tendencies, tendencies that have built many kinds of progressive movements, trade unions, political parties, and even churches. They have been the result of the necessary joining together of varied racial, national, religious, and regional groupings. Such an alliance is well on its way to developing, chastened by the errors of uncritical emulation of foreign models and also disentangling itself from the less durable ideas of 1960s radicalism. In the long run, this alliance will have the greatest historical agenda. In the shorter term, however, a rather different set of national-racial groupings is ascendant. These are the many national variants of right-wing nationalism that "pair" with the left variant in nearly every ethnic group, rich or poor, dominator or dominated.

For each attempt to create an "Indian government" that would be egalitarian and integrated into a general economic development that would help all Canadians, there are those in the native movement and the multinationals who would gladly set up enclaves resembling the South African Bantustans like the Ciskei or Swaziland, offering cheap labor pools, pleasure resorts, and preserves of small native elites. Indeed, if certain features in the decay of liberalism continue, remarkably negative possibilities will arise for the whole body politic of Canada. For example, some leaders of native organizations are using a particularly backward form of nationalism to roll back many legal, moral, physical, and economic gains of the "popular classes." By virtue of "aboriginal rights" and the federal status of Indian reserves, some native leaders have managed to circumvent human rights legislation that forbids personal or religious discrimination on their reserves, to block the unionization of Indian and Metis workers on and off reserve, to abjure tenure for teachers in reserve schools, to avoid certain standards of occupational health such as in the uranium industry, and even to skirt certain ecological practices.

In other words, Canada's native communities and movements are undergoing a classical situation of neo-colonialism. As in neo-colonial Africa, a wide range of ideologies and practices exist among the native leaderships—from the consensus politics of the Dene to a highly formalized recreation of Westminster parliamentarism among the Federation of Saskatchewan Indian Nations. As in Africa, too, the leaders use their positions to enjoy life-styles that range from exemplary altruism to egregious venality. The struggle for popular mobilization is only now beginning between those leaders and intellectuals who are seeking to fulfill the early glowing promises of the "independence" struggle, versus those who are content with the new accommodation to transnational capital.

For those who seek to ally themselves with other dispossessed nationalities, some established leaders argue in favor of extreme isolationist nationalism (see Dobbin, 1981), whereas others like Russell Means of the American Indian Movement seek to destroy "everything European," including Marxism and Christianity.

CONCLUSION

Of course no one can predict a quick and simple outcome to the struggle between these unfolding tendencies. Far-right ideologies with their thinly disguised racial arguments are gaining in prominence. Lord

Peter Bauer, for example, asked for an end to restraints to those cultural "groups" capable of making money by those who were not (Block and Shaw, 1985). Neo-fascist groups like Citizens for Foreign Aid Reform are spreading alarm about "sociobiology and immigration" and are also disseminating other racist shibboleths. Teacher James Keegstra and publicist Ernst Zundel were recently charged and convicted by Canadian courts for publicly advocating hatred against an identifiable group by producing an expanded version of an anti-Semitic encyclopedia. Their trials have given much publicity to ideas that were long disappearing, and the legal prosecutions may well be seen as signs of weakness in Canadian liberalism. As the argument goes, the trials would not have been necessary had liberalism continued to win "cultural hegemony" over racism by education, art, satire, and means other than legal repression. In spite of the international reputation of Canadian liberalism, race problems of significance are evident.

NOTES

1. Throughout this chapter, this term is used to refer to Indians, Metis, and Innuit. The context should explain references to other Canadians born in Canada. See Leeson et al., 1984, a study of the politics of nationality in the struggle for Canada's constitution.

2. There were indeed Japanese in Canada who favored the imperialism of their fatherland. However, these were the same Japanese Canadians who acted in concert with the Japanese embassy and Canadian authorities to undercut Japanese progressive fishermen's leaders by having them deported, censored, and otherwise harassed.

3. There is also a move to pardon Louis Riel, the Metis leader hanged in November 1885 for treason. Each of these claims seems to have a sort of "two-line struggle" between those who seek a cash settlement for individuals versus those who seek a collective award for the whole nationality. In the 1985 Japanese claim, some young businessmen were pursuing an individualized cash settlement, while the older generation appeared to favor a museum about Japanese history in Canada (including, of course, the internment) and the establishment of a fund or institute to educate people against intolerance and racism ("Time for Fresh Start, Japanese Canadians Say," *Toronto Star*, April 18, 1985, p. A3). The Ukrainian grievance has not yet advanced to this level of tactical demands, if indeed it ever will. Parallel divisions are surfacing in native peoples' claims for "aboriginal rights" (see Daniels, 1981a).

4. My colleague Dennis Bartels, of Memorial University, Newfoundland, has made the Beothuk annihilation issue one of his research specialties. Contrary to interpretations that this *annihilation* was the result of intertribal warfare between Beothuk and Micmac, or an all-out war of whites against Indians, he believes that a major part of the annihilation can be traced to a few zealous families of British settlers. Contrary to claims by such writers as Price (1981), it should be

obvious that British colonialism was as capable of murder, enslavement, and use of machine guns as any other imperial power.

5. The importation of bachelor workers into Canada deserves a major study on its own, as does woman's role, in the long evolution of the Canadian labor force. (For a study of woman's role in the fur trade and the creation of the Metis and capitalist market relations, see Bourgeault, 1983.) Imported bachelor workers have been pivotal to the development of Canada because of the low social costs of their maintenance.

6. Marvin Harris (1971) and others demonstrate that the race concept has no scientific validity on the biological level. The social concept of race is so variable as to be completely unreliable. In Canada in my own work (Daniels, 1981), perceptions of "whiteness" are very much influenced by the level of development of the nation of origin of those under scrutiny, their political stability and pro-Western geopolitical alliance. For example, in a study of several hundred Canadian students, I found that a large percentage considered Spaniards, Italians, and Greeks to be nonwhite; about 100 percent considered Iranians to be nonwhite (survey taken after the fall of the Shah) despite their light skins, while almost 100 percent simultaneously believed Israelis to be white and Arabs nonwhite. Despite their vaunted European connections, Argentinians did not make it as "whites," and Cubans rated about even with Iranians—very *non*white. The same phenomenon of political-economic bias applies in Canada's history of race perception. For example, Potrobenko (1977) argues convincingly that Ukrainian Canadians were not considered truly "white" until they achieved prosperity after World War II. Their previous roles had been of desperately poor farm immigrants from the turn of the century through to the poverty and political agitation of the 1930s Depression and drought. Before World War II, the Slavic standard of living was often not markedly different from that of Amerindian peoples— including the necessity of hunting, trapping, and gathering wild fruits and mushrooms as an absolutely necessary supplement for survival in marginal or drought-devastated farmland.

The race concept in Canadian history has only recently been used in a Pan-European (or "NATO") sense—many decades after Kipling's declarations about the "White Man's burden." Virtually until World War II, the primary popular application of "race" was in practice for national groupings—for example, the Irish "race" (applied to the canalbuilders), the British "race," the German "race," and so on. Even in the 1960s with the emergence of the struggle for Quebecois self-determination, parliamentarians and the press still referred to the British and the French as the two founding "races" of Canada. In the constitutional struggle of the 1970s and 1980s, this was revised to "two founding *nations*," but both formulations excluded Indians and Innuit, regardless of whether they are considered races or (as they themselves claim, see Asch, 1984) nations in treaty with the Crown of England and nations that antedate the European presence in Canada. The Metis regard themselves as the first authentic Canadians, the novel creation of Euro-Indian synthesis in British North America, and their claim to unique and founding nation status is based in part on this self-perception.

Characterizations of racehood and nationhood have been and remain very political in Canada and everywhere else. This mercurial nature is recognized spontaneously in the popular culture, even if not in the theory of our mainstream scholars or the constitutional experts who, for decades, steadfastly refused any recognition of aboriginal titles for native peoples during the patriation of the Canadian Constitution from Britain in the late 1970s (Lesson et al., 1984; Asch, 1984). Unfortunately, the unreliable nature of race characterization has become embedded in Canadian scholarship and politics through the concept of "visible minorities"—those who suffer a higher degree of oppression in Canadian society because of their skin color or other somatic attributes, or because of novel or exotic costume, hair style, or paraphernalia. At first glance, this labeling seems to be a fairly accurate "taxonomy" since the prime victims of racial and national chauvinism in the 1980s are immigrants from Third World countries like India, Jamaica, and Vietnam, as well as "internal immigrants" via the urbanization of displaced native peoples from the Indian reserves and rural areas to Canada's cities. Unfortunately, it is but a short step to the assumption that the physical differences or exotic appearance actually cause oppressive and xenophobic reactions.

Those many scholars, civil servants, and cabinet-level policymakers who espouse visibility theory as their day-to-day "common sense" would feign sophistication and perhaps claim that that is not what they mean. Yet the visibility theory is not just some esoteric question of epistemology or semantics. Rather, it is the core concept of an ideological overview that steadfastly refuses to examine seriously the workings of political economy in Canadian race/nationality relations. Furthermore, the visibility theory has become the pragmatic working theory of the main political, cultural, and intellectual institutions of the Canadian state. The policy-creating institutions include the Department of Manpower and Immigration which, in its 1974 Green Paper on immigration, advised a curtailment of further immigration of people of exotic culture and appearance on the grounds that the "Canadian public" could not withstand further stress on its social fabric. The Secretary of State funds and supervises a vast array of cultural festivals, international exchanges, ethnic pressure groups, native economic and educational development projects, and ethnically oriented selection of individuals to government boards and commissions. In short, the Secretary of State is the arbiter of Canada's official policy of "multiculturalism."

The ideology of "visibility" has permeated the cultural and political bodies of the various ethnic pressure groups of the country. Over the past two decades, millions of dollars have been spent on maintaining some of the visible differences of dress, diet, dialect, and dance via the mechanism of cultural festivals, language programs, grants to minority newspapers, and so forth, all funded by the state. The obsession with these differences has led the Canadian court system to intervene in cases where an East Indian turban or Rastafarian dreadlocks create problems between employers and members of the "visible minority."

Such cultural endeavors and legal problems are the daily grist of the provincial Human Rights Commissions, next to employment and residential tenancy issues. Scholars, too, vex themselves with the polarities of visible cultural traits around which the Canadian experience allegedly revolves, polarities that can be found in every mainstream minorities textbook: "melting pot versus mosaic," and so forth.

Finally, many of the Third World and native pressure groups have arranged themselves into separate caucuses that openly embrace the "visible minority" appellation, and willy-nilly the "theory" that fits the appellation. While all this goes on in the name of a "common sense," more serious problems are festering in the real world of Canadian political economy. There is the overwhelming reality that behind the careful cultivation and preservation of the visible 4d's of multiculturalism—dress, diet, dialect, and dance—all the peoples of Canada are relentlessly proceeding to the capitalist mode of production.

7. In this sense, Canadian native peoples are similar to the vast majority of humanity—the two-thirds who live in Asia, Africa, and Latin America—many of whom derive their livelihood mainly from subsistence activities that are only partially "capitalist" at the same time as they may have to work for wages or piece-work in capitalist industries. For example, the women of the Philippines who work in the free trade zones making silicone chips for computers (Sivan-andan, 1980) derive the bulk of their livelihood from their extended family who ekes out a living on peasant plots. The woman's cash earnings go to buying medicines, small luxuries, like a radio, and basic necessities that are not available from peasant production.

There is much academic debate in world systems theory about whether this peasant/herder/trapper labor is pre- or noncapitalist or a separate mode of production. As Amin (1980) and Dixon, Jonas, and McGaughan (1982) point out, however, without question such "domestic economies" of "natural produce" act as subsidies to the capitalist system as a whole and allow cheap labor rates that would be impossible in countries where workers require substantial wages to survive in a thoroughly cash economy.

The fishing/trapping/wage/welfare formula is rarely sufficient even to meet the costs of the reproduction of labor power, for the native death rate is three times the national average, with deaths by violence four to five times higher and suicides among young Indian males six to fourteen times the national average. This mortality derives not from outright starvation, but from malnutrition of body and the destruction of dignity:

There is, first of all, the fact that the colonized person, who is in respect like the men in underdeveloped countries or the disinherited in all parts of the world, perceives life not as a flowering as a development of an essential productiveness, but as a permanent struggle against an omnipresent death. This ever-menacing death is experienced as endemic famine, unemployment, a high death rate, an inferiority complex, and the absence of any hope for the future (Fanon, 1959, p. 128).

8. Women's domestic labor is rendered redundant by convenience products, disposable cheap clothing, and so forth, at the same time as her labor is demanded in the marketplace as nurse, waitress, seamstress in the textile plant, or silicone chip assembler. It is not a coincidence that the native movement has found spontaneous allies in the women's movement. As part of the native struggle, Indian women have demanded to regain their legal status as Indians if they have lost it by marrying white men. This has not been a clearcut feminist issue. Mineral- and oil-rich reserves have opposed such a move since it would "dilute" the reserve wealth, while poorer reserves have sought to widen Indian status to

illegitimate children, children "enfranchised" by their parents before they have reached the age of consent, and so on.

There is an uneasy relationship between white middle-class feminists and the movement of Third World women in Canada. Besieged Indian communities which are desperately trying to hold the nuclear family together, can scarcely be expected to join the American feminist demand for smashing the nuclear family. The "snatching" of Indian babies by white social workers, even if feminist, and separation of Indian women from their husbands in the "transition houses" for battered wives (even if run by "feminists"), are scarcely progressive alternatives. To put it another way, both "social chauvinism" and "social imperialism" can be seen in certain attitudes of some Euro-Canadian feminists, and it remains to be seen whether they will show more confidence in the abilities of Canada's Third World women to lead their own struggles. This problem surfaced dramatically as rifts within the Canadian women's delegation to the International Women's Conference in Nairobi, July 1985. The problem is also the subject of a teleplay on child apprehension by the Canadian Metis writer Maria Campbell. See also Kenyatta, 1983; Davis, 1983; Dixon, 1983.

9. Riel and other literate Metis leaders were fully aware of ideological currents and movements in other parts of the world. This ideological cosmopolitanism has already been partially documented by Woodcock (1975) and is turning up in the virtual explosion by researchers (Bourgeault, 1983, McLean, 1985) and others. In the French archives, for example, Bourgeault has unearthed an 1886 pamphlet which French socialists directed to Riel, using Riel's name as "nom de plume." Entitled "Socialisme et Colonies," it urges the Metis to ally with French interests against British imperialism. These "socialists" urge Riel to embrace the French Empire rather than the British since the French Empire is more progressive, being republican, having separated church and state, being more rationalist, and having revolutionary origins. Nicer examples of socialists justifying imperialism would not come along until the collapse of the Second International in 1914.

BIBLIOGRAPHY

Abella, A. *Nationalism, Communism and Canadian Labour*. Toronto: University of Toronto Press, 1973.

————, and H. Troper. "The Line Must Be Drawn Somewhere: Canada and Jewish Refugees, 1933–39." *Canadian Historical Review* 60, no. 2 (1979): 300–20.

Amin, S. *Class and Nation, Historically and in the Current Crisis*. New York: Monthly Review Press, 1980a.

————. *Three Essays on World Capitalism*. Madras: Nalanda House (also P.B. 2855 Station D, Ottawa, Canada), 1980b.

————. *The Future of Maoism*. New York: Monthly Review Press, 1984.

Asch, M. *Home and Native Land: Aboriginal Rights and the Canadian Constitution*. Toronto: Methuen, 1984.

Avery, D. *Dangerous Foreigners*. Toronto: McClelland and Stewart, 1979.

Baum, G., and D. Cameron. *Ethics and Economics: Canada's Catholic Bishops and the Economic Crisis*. Toronto: James Lorimer, 1984.

Berger, T. *Report of the Mackenzie Valley Pipeline Inquiry.* Toronto: James Lorimer, 1977.

————. *Fragile Freedoms: Human Rights and Dissent in Canada.* Toronto: Clarke, Irwin & Co., 1982.

Block, W., and D. Shaw. *Theology, Third World Development and Economic Justice.* Vancouver: Fraser Institute, 1985.

Bourgeault, Ron. "Metis History: Class Structure of the Fur Trade." *New Breed Journal* 13, No. 8 (September 1982): 20–22.

————. "Indians, the Metis and the Fur Trade: Class, Sexism, Racism in the Transition from 'Communism' to Capitalism." *Studies in Political Economy* (Ottawa), No. 12 (Fall 1983): 45–80.

Braverman, H. *Labour and Monopoly Capital: The Degradation of Labour in the Twentieth Century.* New York: Monthly Review Press, 1974.

Broad, D. "Unequal Development: The Political Economy of Guatemala." M.A. thesis, University of Regina, Regina, Saskatchewan, May 1981.

Brown, Lorne, and Caroline Brown. *The Unauthorized History of the R.C.M.P.* Toronto: James Lorimer, 1973.

Chan, A. *Gold Mountain: The Chinese in the New World.* Vancouver: New Star Press, 1983.

Clement, W. *The Canadian Corporate Elite.* Toronto: McClelland & Stewart, 1975.

————. *Class, Power and Property: Essays on Canadian Society.* Toronto: Methuen, 1983.

Connelly, P. *Last Hired, First Fired.* Toronto: Women's Press, 1978.

Cox, O. C. *Caste, Class and Race.* New York: Monthly Review Press, 1959.

Dahlie, J., and T. Fernando. *Ethnicity, Power and Politics in Canada.* Toronto: Methuen, 1981.

Daniels, D. "The White Race Is Shrinking: Perceptions of Race in Canada and Some Speculations on the Political Economy of Race Classification." *Ethnic and Racial Studies* 4, No. 3 (July 1981a): 353–56.

————. "The High Cost of Avoiding Political Economy." *Canadian Journal of Native Studies* 1, No. 1 (1981b): 209–16.

————. "Dene Government: Middle Class Dream or Working Reality?" Dene Nation Documents, Yellowknife, N.W.T., 1981c.

Davis, A. *Women, Race and Class.* New York: Random House, 1983.

Dixon, M. *The Future of Women.* San Francisco: Synthesis Publications, 1983.

————, S. Jonas, and E. McGaughan, eds. *The New Nomads: Immigration and Changes in the International Division of Labour. Contemporary Marxism,* No. 5, Synthesis Publications, 1982.

————, T. Platt, R. Bush, and J. Kress. *World Capitalist Crisis and the Rise of the Right.* San Francisco: Synthesis Publications, 1982.

Dobbin, M. *The One-and-a-Half Men, The Story of Jim Brady and Malcolm Norris, Metis Patriots of the Twentieth Century.* Vancouver: New Star Books, 1981.

Elliot, Jean. *Two Nations, Many Cultures: Ethnic Groups in Canada.* Toronto: Prentice-Hall, 1983.

Fanon, F. *Studies in Dying Colonialism.* New York: Grove Press, 1959.

Frank, A. G. "Crisis of Ideology and Ideology of Crisis." *Dynamics of Global Crisis.* New York: Monthly Review Press, 1982.

Frideres, J. *Native People in Canada: Contemporary Conflicts*. Scarborough: Prentice-Hall, 1983.

Gordon, D. *Theories of Poverty and Underemployment*. Toronto: Lexington Books, 1972.

Gray, J. *Red Lights on the Prairies*. Toronto: Macmillan of Canada, 1971.

Haiven, J. *Faith, Hope, No Charity: An Inside Look at the Born Again Movement in Canada and the United States*. Vancouver: New Star Books, 1984.

Harris, M. *Culture, Man and Nature*. New York: Thomas Y. Crowell Co., 1971.

Hawthorne, H., ed. *A Survey of Contemporary Indians of Canada*. 2 vols. Ottawa: Indian Affairs Branch, Queen's Printer, 1966.

Hughes, D., and E. Kallen. *The Anatomy of Racism: Canadian Dimensions*. Montreal: Harvest House, 1973.

Kallen, E. *Ethnicity and Human Rights in Canada*. Toronto: Gage Publishing Co., 1982.

Kenyatta, M. "In Defense of the Black Family." *Monthly Review* 35 (March 1983): 38–45.

Knight, R. *A Very Ordinary Life* (A German-Canadian Study). Vancouver: New Star Books, 1974.

————. *Indians at Work: An Informal History of Native Labour in British Columbia*. Vancouver: New Star Books, 1978.

Knight, R., and I. Koizumi. *A Man of Our Times*. Vancouver: New Star Press, 1976.

Leeson, H., et al. *Canada . . . Notwithstanding*. Toronto: Carswell/Methuen, 1984.

Li, P. "Immigration Laws and Family Patterns: Some Demographic Changes Among Chinese Families in Canada 1885–1971." *Canadian Ethnic Studies* 12 (1980): 58–73.

Lipset, S. *Agrarian Socialism*. New York: Doubleday, 1965.

McLean, D. *1885: Metis Rebellion or Government Conspiracy*. Regina: Dumont Institute, 1985.

Manuel, G., and M. Poslums. *The Fourth World: An Indian Reality*, Don Mills, Ontario: Collier Macmillan, 1974.

Marger, M. *Race and Ethnic Relations, American and Global Perspectives*. Belmont, Calif.: Wadsworth Publishing Co., 1985.

Myers, G. *History of Canadian Wealth*. Toronto: James Lewis and Samuel, 1972.

North, G. *A Ripple, A Wave: The Story of Union Organizing in the B.C. Fishing Industry*. Vancouver: Fisherman Publishing Society, 1974.

Olsen, D. *The State Elite*. Toronto: McClelland and Stewart, 1980.

O'Malley, M. "Red Capitalism: Self Sufficiency for Native Peoples." *Canadian Business* 53, No. 4 (April 1980): 37ff.

Panitch, Leo, ed. *The Canadian State*. Toronto: University of Toronto Press, 1977.

Piper, J. *A Red Paper on the Commercial Fishing Industry in Saskatchewan*. Office of John Richards, MLA for Saskatoon University, April 1974.

Porter, John. *The Vertical Mosaic*. Toronto: University of Toronto Press, 1965.

Potrobenko, H. *No Streets of Gold: A Social History of Ukrainians in Alberta*. Vancouver: New Star Books, 1977.

Price, J. "Historical Theory and the Applied Anthropology of U.S. and Canadian Indians." *Human Organizations* 41, No. 2 (1982): 45–53.

Scott, J. *Plunderbund and Proletariat*. Vancouver: New Star Books, 1975.

Sivanandan, A. "Imperialism in the Silicon Age." *Monthly Review* 32 (July–August) 1980: 24–42.

Sunahara. *The Politics of Racism.* Toronto: James Lorimer, 1981.

Sweezy, P. "Capitalism and Democracy." *Monthly Review* 32, No. 2 (June 1980): 27–32.

Teeple, G., ed. *Capitalism and the National Question in Canada.* Toronto: University of Toronto Press, 1972.

Watkins, M., ed. *Dene Nation: The Colony Within.* Toronto: University of Toronto Press, 1977.

Weaver, S. *Making Canadian Indian Policy: The Hidden Agenda, 1968–70.* Toronto: University of Toronto Press, 1981.

Wolf, Eric. *Europe and the People Without History.* Berkeley: University of California Press, 1984.

Woodcock, G. *Gabriel Dumont: The Metis Chief and His Lost World.* Edmonton: Hurtig, 1975.

Wright, J. *Slava Bohu: The Story of the Doukhobors.* New York: Farrar, 1940.

Further bibliographic materials may be found by consulting the following:

Clement, W., and D. Drache. *A Practical Guide to Canadian Political Economy.* Toronto: James Lorimer, 1978.

Also see the indexing and abstracts of the Canadian Periodical Index or the International Bibliography of Social and Cultural Anthropology. Relevant journals include *Culture*, the official journal of the Canadian Ethnology Society; the *Canadian Review of Sociology and Anthropology; Studies in Political Economy; Canadian Journal of Native Education*; and *Canadian Journal of Political Science.* Excellent coverage of aboriginal rights and refugee issues is provided in the *United Church Observer* and *Project North*.

FIJI

Ralph Premdas

Communal politics in Fiji is fraught with tension, with racial animosity pervading the system. Open expressions of mutual contempt by members of the communal sections in daily intercourse, though subtle and restrained, periodically spill over into public discourse. Practically no one in Fiji's multi-ethnic social setting is free from the corrosive ravages of racial stereotyping that attends cross-cultural interaction. Paradoxically, everyone is aware that the atmosphere of malaise is harmful for intercommunity cooperation. But those same persons who openly condemn the prejudices displayed in routine intercommunal exchanges proceed in the privacy of their own homes and communities to participate in its enactment. Hypocritical professions of concern for one's cross-communal compatriot are as endemic in the system as racism itself. It is a deadly game of serious self-deception.

More than once in recent years, collective racial violence has spilled over into the public arena, threatening to envelop the entire fragile system in conflagration. The year 1968 is particularly remembered in this regard; the electoral competition brought racial feelings to unprecedented intensity. The fear that all restraints will one day be removed in a racial confrontation haunts political leaders. Politics in Fiji has a built-in potential for recurrent instability, stimulated in part by its ethnically plural social structure (Table 5).[1]

The two dominant population groups in Fiji are the indigenous Fijians and the Indians (India); together, they constitute over 94 percent of the total population. These two groups live side by side but in hostility. They do not share basic cultural institutions, and neither is economically independent. They have different economic resources and productive facilities, rendering economic exchange necessary. Until October 1970 when Great Britain granted Fiji independence, these two cultural groups

Table 5
Population of Fiji, by Ethnic Group

Group Population	Number	Percent of Total
Fijian	263,694	43.41
Indian	277,248	50.85
European	3,477	0.64
Part-European	9,673	1.77
Chinese and Part-Chinese	4,263	0.78
Other Pacific Islanders	13,850	2.55
	572,205	100.00

were kept together in outward harmony by the colonial government which served as "umpire." Since independence, they have continually engaged in deeply divisive disputes that directly or indirectly involve racial matters. In all these respects, Fiji conforms uncannily to the plural society model postulated by J. S. Furnivall.[2]

Unlike homogeneous and heterogeneous societies which are fundamentally integrated, plural societies lack an underlying consensus of basic values and are perennially exposed to strife stimulated by ethnonationalism.[3] Political moderation is a scarce commodity in Fiji. Even where it exists by compromise and special arrangements worked out by intercommunal political elites, the social equilibrium can easily be disrupted by ambitious politicians who manipulate stereotypical interethnic fears for support. Called "outbidders" in the jargon of plural society analysts, they disrupt the fragile political order, serving their own interests to the detriment of their unsuspecting followers.[4] Recent events in Fiji illustrate the fearsome power of outbidders. On October 9, 1975, Sakiasi Butadroka, a member of the Fiji House of Representatives, introduced a motion calling for the expulsion from Fiji of all persons of Indian origin, that is, about half the country's population. Ethnic Fijian sympathy for the motion was widespread.[5] Indians feel insecure in Fiji despite constitutional guarantees giving them full citizenship; as a result, large numbers have migrated to other countries. The prejudices of Fijians and Indians represent two sides of a coin; each is frustrated by the other's presence. The current trends in politics and economic life pointing to greater divisions and disparities between the Indians and Fijians bode ill for future communal harmony.

This chapter focuses on Fijian–Indian relations; only where the other elements in Fiji's ethnic mosaic are salient forces are they discussed in appropriate detail. Race and race relations are examined here within the wider ambit of ethnicity. While Fijians and Indians may be differentiated phenotypically, their social identities have evolved through the interplay of cultural and historical forces. Each group today has a consciousness of itself as a separate entity, each endowed with a unique identity. Because putative racial phenotypical features are interwoven in the assertion of ethnic consciousness, the terms "race" and "ethnicity" are used interchangeably. Fijians, Indians, Europeans, Chinese, and others are treated as discrete ethnic and racial groups. Institutional roles are associated with each group, and rigid social stereotypes make it difficult to merge the ethnic components into a unified identity. In the following pages, "Fijian" refers to indigenous persons who have descended from the original inhabitants of Fiji; "Indians" refers to descendants of persons who came to Fiji from India.

A RACIAL CONTEXT

The Making of a Plural Society in Fiji: The Ethnic Groups

Fiji is an archepelago of some 844 islands that lie almost in dead center of the South Pacific. Two islands, Viti Levu and Vanua Levu, account for approximately 87 percent of the total land area of 7,055 square miles. Viti Levu (4,010 square miles), the largest of the two islands, is nearly twice as large as Vanua Levu (2,137 square miles) and dominates life in Fiji generally. It contains 73 percent of the total population and the country's most productive economic facilities, including its sugarfields, factories, hotels, and commercial houses as well as the capital city, Suva. Indians constitute about 55 percent of the population on the two islands, and Fijians only 38 percent. The surrounding islands, some 100 of which are permanently inhabited, are populated predominantly by indigenous Fijians who subsist mainly on traditional agriculture, fishing, and copra harvesting.

Fiji was colonized on October 10, 1874, when Chief Cakobau ceded Fiji to Great Britain. The Deed of Cession bound Britain to protect the Fijians from European commercial interests and to preserve the Fijian way of life. To halt the steady decline of Fijian customs, Sir Arthur Gordon, the first British governor of Fiji, initiated three policies that laid the cornerstone of communalism. First, all land that was not yet alienated to Europeans, consisting of nearly 90 percent of the country, was to remain under Fijian ownership. Although temporarily breached by legislative fiat between 1905 and 1911 when free land transactions were once again permitted, this policy curtailed economic development of the islands because growth depended on the availability of Fijian land for commercial exploitation. Land, then, became an issue. The second policy was the importation of labor to substitute for Fijians. Protection of the Fijian way of life required not only that their land which was an integral part of the traditional culture be kept from alienation, but also that the people be free from the labor impositions of European plantations. If this policy was to be pursued, however, then Fiji as a financially self-supporting colony needed an alternative source of labor for the plantations. The colonial government depended heavily for its revenues on the profits of plantations.

Plantations cannot survive without cheap and abundant labor.[6] Denied this source from among the indigenous population, Governor Gordon recommended the importation of Indian coolies from India as had been done successfully in British Guiana, Mauritius, and Trinidad. From 1979 when the labor indentureship was inaugurated, to 1916, when it was terminated, about 60,537 Indians were introduced into Fiji.[7] About one-half returned to India, the rest remaining under a scheme that allowed them to become legal residents "with privileges no whit inferior to those of any other class of Her Majesty's subjects resident in the colonies."[8] The Indian population grew steadily, finally outstripping the Fijians by 1945. From the policy of labor immigration, then, a new community was engrafted onto Fiji.

The third policy was the establishment of a separate Native Fijian administration through which the British governed the Fijians indirectly; the Fijian hierarchical political structure was recognized, and Fijian chiefs continued to govern their own people. While this policy substantially preserved the traditional Fijian culture by virtually establishing a state within a state, it so protected the Fijians that they would be almost wholly unprepared to compete effectively with the Europeans and Indians once their circle of interaction had expanded beyond the village. The result was the institutionalization of Fijian economic inferiority.

By the mid–1980s, about 40 percent of all Fijians still subsisted mainly in villages. The typical Fijian worker in the monetized modern sector tends to maintain intimate material connections with his or her village. The Fijian community continues to own about 83 percent of the land, which is held communally by over 7,000 patrilineal groups. Fijians who no longer rely on their villages for their income are employed by the government as policemen, army officers, teachers, nurses, medical officers, office workers, and so on. The government services have given rise to a well-to-do Fijian middle class. Many regard the government bureaucracy as their preeminent domain, much as many Indians regard the commercial and sugar sectors as their preserve.[9] Fijian penetration of the business sector has been generally unsuccessful, even when special programs have been established to initiate them into the commercial world. Fijian culture, being communal, noncompetitive, and nonprofit-oriented, has been blamed for the poor performance.[10] To date, Fijians own very few businesses, which are almost totally in Indian, European, and Chinese hands, and consequently contribute less than 10 percent of the national tax. Because of the tight competition they face in other sectors, Fijians have found it necessary to protect the ownership of their land. Land is their main resource base from which they can bargain politically with other groups in Fijian society.

Most Indian immigrants to Fiji came as indentured laborers. They came from many parts of India, from different language and religious groups, and overwhelmingly, without their families. The Indians who remained in Fiji leased or bought land on which they planted their own cane; by the end of World War II, they owned practically the entire sugar-growing business. Today, some 80 percent of cane farmers are Indians. However, most of the lands are leased from Fijians, transforming what would normally be a powerful political base into a tinder box of communal conflict. Sugar is the most significant crop in the economy, providing more than half of Fiji's foreign reserves.[11]

Only about 3 to 6 percent of the Indians came to Fiji as free settlers, mainly Gujaratis, and by 1936 numbered about 2,500.[12] They established businesses, but were later joined by other Indians who left the sugarfields to start small stores and tradeshops. In contemporary Fiji, most small and intermediate-size commercial operations are in Indian hands. Soon the government bureaucracy was challenged, and Europeans who held highly skilled jobs were localized. In the professions, the Indians' incursion into traditional European areas also became significant.[13] At all levels the Indians posed an economic threat to the two other major groups of Fiji. To the Fijians, the Indians were a land threat, and to the Europeans, the Indians challenged their prestige as the group with a monopoly over expert skills in government and the professions. As will be discussed later, the Indians also confronted Europeans in the political arena.

Many Indians and Fijians have moved to urban areas such as Suva and Lautoka. As in the rural areas where Indians and Fijians live apart (Fijians live in small, concentrated, nucleated villages, whereas Indian family units are dispersed on sprawling leased land), in the towns such as Suva similar ethnic residential self-selectivity occurs, thereby making city wards predominantly Fijian or Indian.[14] Census reports reveal that in four-fifths of the enumerated areas on the two main islands, 70 percent of the people are either predominantly Indian or Fijian.[15] Cultural features also separate the two major communities. While English is the cross-communal language, Indians speak Hindustani among themselves and Fijians their indigenous language. The radio stations carry separate programs in Hindustani and Fijian, and, until recently, the educational institutions were segregated. Finally, most voluntary social and economic organizations such as sports clubs and trade unions are predominantly uni-ethnic. Intermarriage between Fijians and Indians is practically nonexistent.

Europeans, although numerically insignificant, have dominated the direction of the colony. First, the traders and planters stamped a capitalist economy onto Fiji. Second, missionaries converted the Fijians to Christianity. Finally, the Europeans, who at first served as instigators of Fijian intertribal conflict, won political domination of Fijian society through the Deed of Cession in 1874.[16] The political imprint was a form of government which at independence in 1970 was a variant of the Westminster parliamentary model. The overall social impact has been the de facto establishment of English ways as the measure of excellence. The *lingua franca* is English. A strong racial dimension has been added to the emerging class system. A color-class continuum was ingrained in the consciousness of practically all citizens, so that things white were deemed superior to things black. Mixed-race and light-skinned persons, for example, who stand in an intermediate position in the color-class continuum tend to hold middle-level skilled occupations and to enjoy middle-class life-styles. Privileges and rewards are skewed in favor of those who are English or who have acquired English cultural traits. Consequently, Europeans are overrepresented as managers, supervisors, professionals, and skilled workers generally.[17] Constituting less than 1 percent of the population, they command high status and income twenty to fifty times over their proportional share. Today, most nongovernment European workers are employed in high executive positions in foreign multinational corporations. Big business remains in the hands of Europeans and European-owned companies.[18]

The remaining population categories are the Chinese, mixed races, and other Pacific Islanders. The Chinese are mainly small businessmen and skilled professional workers. They, like the various mixed races of light pigmentation, enjoy a middle-class socioeconomic well-being and are among the most urbanized of Fiji's population. The other Pacific Islanders are mainly the Rotumans who belong to the adjacent island, Rotuma, which is part of Fiji's territory, and to Solomon Islanders and other nearby island groups which were originally recruited to serve on European plantations. These Pacific Islanders identify politically with indigenous Fijian interests.

Racial Conflict and Social Stereotypes

Racial conflict is endemic in plural societies. Objective conditions generally provide supportive bases for stereotypical images held of each community. However, these stereotypes are crude shorthand summations of diverse traits and simplify and distort reality. While they serve as a defense mechanism against another group, they lend themselves quite easily to manipulation by demagogues who make scapegoats out of a group's own difficulties. These basic characteristics of stereotypes provide some insights into the structure of Fijian–Indian relations.[19] Fijians generally regard Indians as frugal, profit-oriented, unscrupulous, and aggressive. This image derives substantially from Indian commercial activities, even though only a small minority of Indians own or manage businesses. Most Indians are sugar and rice farmers, many of whom are in debt.

The Fijians' economic relationship to the Indians is played out mainly in three areas. First, the Fijian's *mataqali* (Fijian word for clan, as defined by common ownership of land) group leases land to Indians for which rent is paid; the Fijian-controlled Native Land Trust Board negotiates the rental price on behalf of a *mataqali* so that room for rental irregularity is minimal. Second, the Fijian may work seasonally as a laborer on the land which his *mataqali* leases to the Indian. Third, and most significantly, the Fijians may use part of their wages to buy food, clothes, and other articles from Indian stores. More than likely, this type of interaction at the marketplace, where private self-interests predominate, is the source of the image of the Indian as profit-oriented and unscrupulous. In defense, some Indians point out that the Gujaratis who came as free settlers are predominantly Indian businessmen; the typical Indian who is a descendant of indentured laborers is honest and hardworking. Overall, the behavior ascribed to Indians has led to Fijian fears that they will eventually be overrun by an "alien" group in their own native country. Many Fijians believe that Indians are contemptuous of Fijian culture and that alleged Indian disrespect is rooted in cultural arrogance and even feelings of racial superiority.

The Fijian is stereotyped by the Indians as lazy, unambitious, inferior, and manipulable. Indian achievements in cash cropping (sugar), commerce, and the professions stand in stark contrast to similar Fijian achievements. Production for subsistence and not for profit is the critical feature of Fijian traditional economy. Fijians have not sought to accumulate savings for investment. Most Indians view the Fijians as manipulable partly because the Fijians hold the European in awe. The Indians believe that the Europeans have manipulated the Fijians against Indian interests. Indians consider this ironic since it was the Europeans who originally posed a threat to Fijian land and culture. Consequently, Indians see better race relations ahead if the European presence is significantly diluted or totally eliminated.

Ethnic Cleavages: Coinciding and Conflicting Features

Despite the fact that stereotypical categories paint Fiji's communities into rigid ethnic compartments, objective evidence points to important internal divisions within each communal segment as well as cross-sectional overlaps that have significant bearing on race relations. In Fiji, cleavages between the two dominant groups are erected around six major criteria: (1) race, (2) language, (3) religion, (4) culture, (5) occupation, and (6) residence.

Race, language, religion, and culture are primordial differentiators between the two groups, while occupation and residential patterns are secondarily acquired traits. Racial and phenotypical differences serve as the first signals in identifying relationships of ethnic affinity; it is easy at first sight to tell an Indian from a Fijian. Color is not necessarily part of the physical differentiators; many Fijians and Indians share the same pigmentation. Religion is a major divider, with practically all Fijians adhering to Christianity and the Indians overwhelmingly to Hinduism or Islam. Language is also a pervasive separator, for when in their own company Fijians and Indians speak their own tongue. Cultural practices such as rituals and observances around religion, diet, marriage, and family matters literally separate the two groups into worlds apart. Hence, racial, linguistic, religious, and cultural cleavages fall one on top of the other in a pattern of coinciding reinforcements separating Indians and Fijians. To be sure, there are areas of sharing, such as in education and attire, but culture in Fiji encapsulates the essential differences between the two groups. After over a century of sharing the same country and colonial master, cultural convergence has been minimal.

The secondary cleavages—occupation and residential patterns—were acquired from colonial adaptation. Most Indians are rural dwellers who cultivate sugarcane and live in individual homesteads. Most Fijians are also rural residents, but they live in nucleated villages and plant food crops primarily. In towns where Fijians and Indians meet, they live in predominantly Indian or Fijian residential neighborhoods and hold jobs in occupations predominantly staffed by Fijian and Indian personnel.[20] But even here, the occupational and residential structures are not cast in exclusive compartments. Especially in the civil service, Indians and Fijians work side by side. This happens less so in stores and factories. A policy of deliberate cross-communal hiring has created a mixture of Indian and Fijian workers. Urbanization and migration patterns point to increasing Indian–Fijian interaction and residential mixing, but not much of this penetrates the separated cultural systems.

A number of cross-cutting cleavages, a few of which were mentioned above, has moderated the effects of the ethnic compartments in Fiji society. In the same areas of primordial segmentation, important instances of cross-cutting experiences coexist. Specifically, in the language area most Fijians and Indians speak English, which is the language of communication between the two groups. In addition, a number of Fijians speak Hindi and Indians speak Fijian, although this cross-linguistic competence is not very extensive. In the cultural sphere, all Fiji citizens share common educational facilities and teachers in primary, secondary, and tertiary institutions. Separate language schools have only recently been abolished. In the areas of residence and occupation, especially in towns, many cross-crossing experiences are enacted daily. In sports, Indians and Fijians play cricket and soccer together. Fijians and Indians are members in many clubs and associations, especially in Suva which contains nearly a fifth of the country's population. Alexander Mamak has traced in empirical detail the numerous areas where Indians and Fijians share common membership such as unions, clubs, and neighborhood groups, recreational, and professional bodies.[21] Trade unions are still preponderantly uni-ethnic in Fiji, including the two unions representing Fiji teachers. And most associations remain primarily but not exclusively subscribed by one ethnic group.

While major cleavages divide ethnic groups into cultural compartments, each segment is not monolithically unified.[22] Internal divisions within the Fijian and Indian communities have become apparent in the last decade. Within the Indian group, there are Muslims and Hindus, with the Muslims constituting about 15 percent of the Indian population. A further division exists between North and South Indians as well as separate subidentities such as Punjabis and Gujaratis. The politics of this internal differentiation has seen the support of certain Indian subgroups in whole or in part for the Fijian-dominated Alliance party. Traditional Hindu-Muslim antipathy has had political reverberations in Fiji's Indian politics, with many Muslims joining the Fijian Alliance or becoming closet sympathizers. Many Gujarati businessmen are also covert supporters of the Alliance. Within the Fijian section, internal regional and linguistic divisions compounded by coinciding economic disparities split Fijian political solidarity.

These divisions have influenced the formation of the Fijian Nationalistic party and the Western United Front. With only one vote in the House of Assembly, the Fijian Nationalist party voted with the Indian Federation party in a vote of no confidence to oust the Fijian Alliance from office after the March 1977 elections. The Fijian-dominated Western United Front is a coalition partner of the Indian Federation party. The Indians in the Alliance and the Fijians in the Federation party, however, are a very slender and shifting minority and do not constitute a sufficiently powerful force to modify Fiji's deeply bifurcated society. The numbers are too marginal to radically restructure the watershed that separates the races. An overview of Fiji's ethnic cleavages examining its major dimensions—coinciding, cross-cutting, and internal divisions—shows that the common forces are not powerful or pervasive enough to mold a national Fiji hybrid man or woman.

POLICIES, PRACTICES, AND THE PROBLEM OF BALANCE

Ethnic identity in Fiji originated in the colonial order and influenced the claims to niches of power and privilege. In a circular dynamic of reinforcement, the struggle stimulated-intensified competition and ethnic antagonism, justifying further assertions for a system of distribution sensitive to ethnic fears. Specifically, in this section we will examine the perennial problems of political representation, land, and the allocation of employment opportunities in the private and public sectors. To understand how ethnic claims to privileges and power are legitimated, it is crucial to look at the concept of balance.

Not a written constitutional law, the idea of balance has been embedded in Fiji's multiracial politics by practice whereby sectoral preeminence is distributed as follows: (1) the Fijians control the government, in particular the prime minister's office, and also own 83 percent of all the land; (2) the Indians dominate the sugar industry and intermediate-size businesses; and (3) the Europeans own the very large businesses, such as banks, hotels, and factories. This distributive sectoral "balance" is not a rigid formula for the sharing of power in all its details. One ethnic group may penetrate and participate in another group's domain. For instance, the government uses subsidies to encourage the entry of Fijians into businesses, while the prime minister, a Fijian, deliberately appoints several Indians to his cabinet. Fijians lease their land to Indians and others. This limited "mix" has moderated the sharp edges and virtual monopoly rights of the "balancing" concept. At various times in recent Fiji history, the balance was in danger of being upset, leading to efforts to rectify the disequilibrium. For example, in 1981 when Indian population growth threatened to overwhelm the demographic balance, the government initiated two effective policies informally to offset it: (1) a vigorous birth control and family planning program more oriented to the Indian than the Fijian population, and (2) a policy enabling Indians to emigrate from Fiji taking their property with them.

"Balance" assumes asymmetrical areas of dominance and sustains equality by requiring reciprocity. Such exchanges, however, are not imposed by sentiments of love for another community but are informed by self-interest. Each group needs the resources of the other group to survive and maintain its standard of living. Each group is its brother's keeper in a mundane, practical, self-interested sense. It is no more in the interest of the Fijians to deny Indians access to land than for Indians not to pay taxes to the Fijian-dominated government. "Balance" has been an evolving act constantly needing nurture by intercommunal consultation and cooperation. It is not a rigid or written agreement but a dynamic concept that requires revisions and adaptations to be made in contemplation of changes in society. However, "balance" can only be a short-term solution for intercommunal conflict, and its sustenance revolves around amicable relations among intersectional elites.

In the face of rapid social change, "balance" may not easily apply to the new areas of activities. Cross-communal coalitions could emerge to challenge the balancing concept, or technological breakthroughs could bestow overwhelming benefits to one ethnic group leaving others behind. In the following section, we will see how the "balancing" concept has evolved and note the difficulties it confronts in the absence of an explicit formula for its application. In discussing "balance" in relation to representation, land, and employment, Indians and Fijians will enunciate their own ideas of balance to assert dominance and to prevent encroachment on their claimed territory. In effect, "balance" is repeatedly invoked to justify an ethnic claim; its meaning, however, is so manipulated that it serves to legitimate self-interest.

HISTORICAL BACKGROUND

Fijians regard the Deed of Cession as their Magna Carta. Embodied in it is the idea of Fijian "paramountcy," a concept of unspecified definition. Initially, paramountcy was interpreted as endowing superior rights to the preservation of Fijian culture, especially in relation to the claims of European planters to Fijian land and labor. While the British governed, "paramount" rights were conceived as consistent with Fijian political subjection to European rule. When the Indians came to Fiji and eventually demanded equal representation with Europeans in public decision making, the assertion of Fijian "paramount" rights emerged as a counterclaim to the threat of Indian dominance.

At the outset of British colonial rule in 1874, no concession was made for direct popular participation in collective decision making. When an element of popular representation was first introduced in Fiji in 1904, the colonial council included six elected Europeans, two nominated Fijians, and ten European official members. In effect, the two nominated Fijians represented an indigenous population of 92,000, while six elected Europeans represented a white population of 2,440. The 22,000 Indians were completely without representation.[23] The exclusion of the Indian sector, however, was only temporary. By 1916 when a new council was introduced, Indians were allocated only nominated representatives after agitating for the franchise.[24] The impetus for Indian representation came from recently arrived Indian immigrants, mainly Gujaratis, who emulated the nationalist struggle of the Indian Congress in India for equal rights. As British subjects, they demanded equal representation with the white sector of the population.

The European settlers reacted against Indian demands, arguing that their superior representation was justified on the basis of "their large stake in . . . developing the economy of the islands."[25] Up to this point, the Indians were highly regarded by the Europeans, especially for their labor. Intersectional conflict was primarily between the Europeans who wanted land and labor, and the Fijians who wanted to preserve their way of life. The arrival of Indians forged an informal alliance between Indian labor and European capital against the Fijians. But with the intensification of Indian protests for equal representation, the old Indian–European intersectional alignment altered, and a new era of European–Fijian collaboration was inaugurated. The Indian immigrant became a common enemy.

Indian demand for electoral equality was couched in terms of "common roll" (one man, one vote) as distinct from the "communal roll" (sectional representation). Because the Fijians were governed under a separate native administration, the Indian demand for a common roll challenged European control of the colonial council and was interpreted as an attempt to introduce Indian political domination of Fiji. The equation of the demand for a common roll with the alleged desire of Indians to politically dominate the entire society has since become a pervasive theme in the communal politics of Fiji. When the Indian population surpassed that of the Fijian in 1946 and became a clear majority in the entire population by 1966, the menace of Indian hegemony became as ominous as it was allegedly real. The growing Indian economic and educational ascendancy compounded the problem and seemed to provide the foundations for effective takeover.

To the Fijians, Indian domination contravened the Deed of Cession which accorded them paramountcy above all other sectional interests. Fijian "paramount right" then was only seen as threatened by Indians and their demand for common roll. Accordingly, Fijians shared the European view that common roll would cause a fundamental alteration in the distribution of political power and privileges in Fiji. Indians viewed the alternative to "common roll" as the continuation of communal representation and the institutionalization of inequality. In 1929, when the enlarged third colonial council was established, Indians were given three seats, but "almost immediately after taking their seats, they demanded the introduction of a common roll."[26] As a result, the "European members strongly attacked the Indian demand for a common roll on the grounds that it would contribute to a 'definite and absolute breach of faith and honor to the colored race (the Fijians) which the British government was supposed to protect and care for.' "[27] The voting was thirty-three to three against the common roll. The Indian members resigned their seats. When again, in 1933, a new council was composed under the old communal formula, Indian members once more demanded common roll and again resigned from the Council. Over the following years, common roll "in the minds of European and Fijian members [had] be-

Table 6
Communal System of Representation in Fiji, 1966

| COMMUNAL GROUP | REPRESENTATION | |
	POPULATION	SEATS
Fiji-Indians	272,040 (50.8%)	12 (33.45%)
Fijian and Pacific Islanders	244,364 (45.7%)	12 (38.9%)
European, Chinese, & Mixed Races	18,822 (3.5%)	10 (27.8%)

come synonymous with an attempt at political domination by Indians, and each proposal had been voted down."[28]

No significant alteration in the mode of representation was made until 1966. Earlier, in 1963, universal adult suffrage was introduced. It was in 1963 also that Fijians were first allowed to elect directly their representatives from among the Fijian people. Previously, Fijians were nominated to the council. In 1966, a new legislative council in which elected representatives constituted a majority was inaugurated, and a ministerial member system under which elected members were given cabinet supervisory responsibilities came into effect. The "wind of change" inspired by the post-World War II anti-colonial movements in Africa and Asia had reached the Fiji Islands. The wheels of political change were turning rapidly, making their most significant impact in the transfer of the government to local leaders. A full-blown party system came into existence by 1966 consisting of two major parties, the National Federation party (NFP), supported predominantly by Indians, and the Alliance party supported mainly by Fijians, Europeans, Chinese, and others. What did not change under the new political order of 1966 was the communal system of representation, as Table 6 shows.

The table depicts the inequities of the communal system. The European, Chinese, and mixed races group, for example, had only 3.5 percent of the total population in 1966 but had been allocated 27.8 percent of all elected seats. For the first time, however, the European section obtained fewer seats than were assigned to Fijians or Indians. Nevertheless, Fijians and Indians remained underrepresented. After 1966, the struggle to correct these inequities and the debate over the relative merits of the common versus the communal system of representation was carried on mainly by the two political parties representing communal interests. Essentially, as self-government approached, the contest for power shifted from the Indian versus European-cum-Fijian configuration to a bipolar Indian versus Fijian confrontation. The British presence would remain salient until independence, but, increasingly, the definition of political and constitutional relations would devolve to Indian and Fijian party leaders in preparation for independence. How the newly emergent local leaders reconciled Indian claims for common roll against the "paramount" right of the minority Fijians had to be ironed out, like the issues over land and employment opportunities by the political process of bargaining and compromise.

Although the Fijians initially resisted independence, fearing Indian designs to dominate Fiji, they gradually came to accept it as inevitable. The results of the 1966 elections in particular heartened the Fijians since they gave the Fijian-dominated Alliance party an overwhelming victory against the predominantly Indian National Federation party (NFP). The Alliance party, which represented the non-Indian voter, was actually a "federal" party. It consisted of three groups: (1) the Fijian Association representing the Fijian people; (2) the General Electors Association representing Europeans, Chinese, and mixed races; and (3) the Indian Alliance, representing a very tiny splinter Indian group. The Alliance was led by Ratu Sir Kamasese Mara, a prominent Fijian chief. The NFP, on the other hand, was a "unitary" organization; it grew out of the Indian trade union movement that agitated for better working conditions in the sugar industry. The leader of the NFP was A. D. Patel, who died in 1969, and was succeeded by Siddiq Koya, a Fijian-born Muslim Indian. Independence meant that the country required a new constitution, which, in turn, implied that the outstanding issues that separated Fijians and Indians had to be reconciled. Between August 1969 and March 1970, the representatives of the NFP and Alliance met to work out a constitutional solution for Fiji. While the negotiations process cannot be discussed here, we will isolate the areas of agreement and disagreement that bear on race relations.[29]

On the system of representation, the Alliance accepted the common roll as a long-term objective and acceded to the NFP demands that (1) a royal commission be established between the first and second elections after independence to reexamine the entire issue of common versus communal roll, and (2) common roll elections be held for the municipalities of Suva and Lautoka. In the meantime, a system of communal and cross-communal voting would continue. The lower House in the proposed bicameral Parliament was to be composed as shown in Table 7.[30]

Parity of representation was accorded the Fijian and Indian communities, while the European, part-European, and Chinese sectors referred to as "General Electors," although constituting only 3.5 percent of the population, continued to be overrepresented with 15.4 percent

Table 7
Composition of the Proposed Parliament

GROUP AS % OF POPULATION	COMMUNAL ROLE	NATIONAL ROLE	TOTAL
Fiji-Indians (50.8%)	12	10	22 (42.3%)
Fijians & Pacific Islanders (45.7%)	12	10	22 (42.3%)
Europeans, Chinese, & Mixed Races	3	5	8 (15.4%)
	27	25	52

Table 8
Composition of the Senate

Fijian Great Council of Chief's nominees	8
Prime Minister's nominees	7
Opposition leader's nominees	6
Council of Rotuma's nominees	1
	22

of the seats. With regard to paramount rights for Fijians, the NFP conceded that additional "weight" should be allocated to Fijian interests. The device through which this was to be implemented was a second chamber, a Senate, in the National Parliament. It was agreed that the Senate should be composed as shown in Table 8. The power of the Senate resided not only in the representation of superior numbers of Fijians, but also in the amending procedure that entrenched Fijian interests by requiring the consent of the Fiji Great Council of Chiefs on matters related to Fijian land and custom. This it did by requiring a two-thirds majority in each chamber for alternating the Constitution. Here, it must be noted that the Fijian Great Council of Chiefs had eight out of twenty-two seats, that is, more than a third of the seats capable of blocking any constitutional change without their consent. Summing up the impact of these special provisions conceded to Fijian paramount rights, one observer noted that "none of the continuing imbalances in Fiji's parliamentary representation can be rectified without the concurrence of the traditional Fijian leadership."[31]

Representation in the independence constitution was not permanently solved; the delegates from the Fijian and Indian sections deferred resolving the claims of "common roll" versus "communal roll" until after independence had been attained. In 1975, the Royal Commission was appointed. If its recommendations were accepted by the Fijian-dominated government, given the persistence of intransigent racial voting behavior, the Indian communal party would probably have wrested power away from the incumbents.[32] This would have upset the balance in the distribution of spheres of influence, in particular Fijian political control. The recommendations of the Royal Commission were therefore rejected outright by the ruling regime. But with the rejection, a shadow of illegitimacy descended on the government. To Indians, the Fijian prime minister had broken his word for fear of losing power. To Fijians, it was the right thing to do to maintain balance in the system. What was more clear, however, pertained to the future of race relations. The old problem of reconciling the common roll with the communal roll was once again on the political agenda. In the future general elections that were held, the problem of representation and other issues bedeviling the relations between Fijians and Indians would be ventilated openly.

ELECTIONS AND RACE RELATIONS

In multi-ethnic states, elections tend to aggravate racial tensions. The results can adversely affect a defeated group's identity and vital interests. Political campaigns are not conducted over limited issues within the broader context of a shared nationhood; victory is seen as conquest and defeat as rout. A perceived zero-sum calculus of conflict confers special intensity in the stakes of electoral competition. Fear of ethnic domination is often a pervasive underlying theme. For these reasons, election campaigns in these fragmented states expose underlying intersectional sensitivities and air pent-up prejudices.

These harmful effects generally describe the repercussions of elections in Fiji since 1966. Here we will briefly examine the Fiji elections of 1966, 1972, 1977, and 1982 to illustrate the impact of campaigns on race relations. But first the electoral system must be described in more detail. The Fiji constituencies are divided into two types: communal and electoral. Voters are categorized as (1) Fijians; (2) Indians; and (3) General Electors (Europeans, Chinese, part-Europeans, and other Pacific Islanders). Each of the three groups is assigned a fixed number of communal and national seats. Communal seats are for everyone. Hence, during elections, a voter is assigned four choices, one for his or her communal seat and three votes for each of the national seats. The complicated electoral system is simplified by the fact that the two major parties, the Alliance and the NFP, organize voters to cast ballots mainly around two partisan choices.

During the 1966 elections, race in relation to representation was the most prominent issue. The Indian-dominated NFP campaigned by attacking the inequities of the communal component in the electoral system; "speakers" (NFP) denounced the Constitution for perpetuating racial divisions in politics and retarding the growth of national consciousness. They rejected the Alliance argument that the communal voting system was justified to protect Fijians and Europeans. But it was the disproportionate allocation of political privileges to racial groups that they most condemned.[33] Indians felt like second-class citizens and argued that "if they did not oppose the constitution, they might find themselves dominated by Fijians and Europeans when British rule ended."[34] Fijian Alliance candidates also expressed racial fears during the campaign: "The spokesmen insisted that common roll elections would result in Indian political hegemony and the loss of land. Attention was often drawn to the fact that Indians had surpassed Fijians in numbers, education, and wealth."[35] Hence, Fijians, Indians, and Europeans alike shared the common perception that the stakes in the elections were coterminous with the preservation of their autonomy and in the event of electoral loss could lead to racial discrimination and repression.

The Alliance won the 1966 election, but in protest against their underrepresentation in the legislature because of the communal seats, all Indian parliamentarians resigned. In 1968, by-elections were scheduled for the vacated seats. It was in these memorable elections that racial animosity reached an unprecedented peak. The NFP campaigned again demanding common roll. Fijians reacted with ire, fearing Indian domination implicit in their demands. Indian and Fijian confrontations reached a crescendo when Indian candidates won all their vacated seats and the Alliance obtained none. In the immediate postelection period, Indian demonstrators celebrating victory confronted Fijian demonstrators protesting the outcome. Physical clashes occurred sporadically, and tensions between ethnic groups grew to alarming heights when leaders appealed to their communal followers for restraint. Memories, however, were embittered and sustained a trajectory of continued racial malaise.

If the 1968 by-elections adversely affected interethnic amity, the 1972 elections were comparatively peaceful. Several factors facilitated this state of affairs, including the reconciliation of differences between the Fijian and Indian delegates at the independence constitutional conference. A "balance" was struck, with Indians conceding ownership of most land to

Fijians and Fijians acceding to undisputed Indian citizenship in Fiji. A major factor that aided the harmonious aura was fear of courting the acrimony that attended the 1968 elections. As Prime Minister Ratu Mara reminisced: "those were the days when we sailed close to the rocks... we came so near to the edge of the abyss that we could see with unmistaken clearness the dangers that lay there if we did not change course."[36] The results of the 1972 elections gave the Alliance party a resounding victory. In the fifty-two-member legislature, it won thirty-three seats as against nineteen for the NFP. The Alliance victory has been attributed to the fact that, in the atmosphere of cross-communal amity, some 25 percent of the Indian electorate was persuaded to vote Alliance by its promise to promote multiracial policies and protect Indian interests in a Fijian-run regime.[37]

For five years after the London constitutional conference in 1970, Fijian Prime Minister Ratu Mara and Indian Opposition Leader Sid Koya, consulted each other and cooperated in running the government. But communal peace in multi-ethnic societies is a fragile affair. Moderate leaders who attempt to maintain racial harmony by making concessions and compromises are always threatened by "outbidders" who seek to assert chauvinistic claims to the entire national pie. In 1975, both Mara and Koya faced "outbidders" who alleged a conspiracy between communal elites. Mara was challenged by Sakiasi Butadroka who claimed that the Alliance party presided over a government that was inimical to indigenous Fijian interests. Koya confronted a challenge that he had "sold out" Indian interests. Toward the end of 1975 and early 1976, the pressure against Mara and Koya drove them apart.[38]

Butadroka was a former Alliance party member of Parliament and an Assistant Minister for Cooperatives. Because of his open and insistent demand that the government tilt its expenditures in favor of Fijians, he was expelled from the Alliance. Frequently, this demand was accompanied by inflammatory verbal attacks against Indians, such as his infamous comment that "blood will flow."[39] Butadroka formed the Fijian Nationalist party in 1974 with the motto "Fiji for Fijians." His demands struck against the foundations of the 1970 independence Constitution which he charged had preserved the domination of "foreign" interests and races in Fiji. The Nationalists called for an all-Fijian Parliament; multiracialism was condemned. Such institutions as the Native Land Trust Board (NLTB) and the Senate, which were designed specifically to protect Fijian land and customs, were described as "superficial."[40] Like the Fijian prime minister, the Indian opposition leader faced a virulent attack that would ultimately depose him. The criticisms against Koya came from a dissident party faction that charged that he had failed to guarantee Indian access to land at the London constitutional conference.

The March–April 1977 elections were momentous in Fiji's history: the Alliance lost the elections, obtaining only twenty-four out of fifty-two seats in the House of Representatives. The National Federation party won twenty-six seats, while the remaining two seats went to Sakiasi Butadroka and an independent Fijian communal candidate. The diversion of votes from the Alliance to the Nationalists led directly to Federation victory in at least six seats. The Nationalists justified their vote-splitting role among Fijians in terms of providing proof that Fijian rights were neither paramount nor protected.

The March–April elections traumatized the Fijian population, for in the concept "balance" they had felt that the Indian victory violated the Fijian domain. If the victory had been allowed to stand, Indians would have had control over most of the economy, as well as the polity, radically upsetting the distribution of spheres of influence among the Fijians, Indians, and Europeans. Because the Indian-based NFP obtained just half (twenty-six) of the fifty-two seats in the legislature, and, most importantly, because they could not agree on a leader to succeed Ratu Mara, the Fijian governor general invited Mara to form the next government. In the first meeting of the House, the minority Alliance government was toppled in a vote of no confidence, requiring new elections in September of the same year. If the March–April elections must be viewed as a dramatic upset of the "balance," then the September elections should be seen as an attempt to restore it.[41]

The September 1977 elections gave the Alliance an overwhelming victory. It obtained thirty-six seats, the NFP fifteen seats, and an Independent one seat. The Alliance's victory was accountable in part to the self-decimating factional infighting that attended the split of the NFP into two competing camps and in part to the reduced strength of the Nationalists from 25 percent of the Fijian communal votes in March–April to 17 percent in September. During the election campaign, the Alliance government had jailed several of the Nationalists including Butadroka on a variety of charges. The Alliance victory was not in any way traceable to Indian votes in September. In politics that became increasingly racially polarized, the Indian vote for the Alliance fell from 25 percent in 1972 to 16 percent in March–April 1977 and to 14.5 percent in September 1977. Fijian votes for the NFP fell from 2.4 percent in 1972 to 0.1 percent in September 1977. Finally, the Alliance victory was obtained in part because of programmatic alterations from a moderate multiracial party to one that promised more attention to Fijians in response to Butadroka's criticisms. The closer the Alliance moved towards accommodating Fijians, the less attractive it became to Indians. The Alliance's concessions to the Fijian community notwithstanding, Butadroka's support fell only from 20,189 (25 percent) Fijians in March–April to 16,000 (17 percent) in September. Butadroka remained popular among many Fijians, even though the Nationalists did not win a parliamentary seat.

General elections were again held in 1982, and they brought back memories of the racially tense days of 1968. Fijian Prime Minister Mara and the new Indian Opposition Leader Jairam Reddy had exchanged charges over the land issue, culminating in the collapse of communications between them. One observer commented that "the 1982 elections has bequeathed a legacy of bitterness, distrust, and ethnic hostility unprecedented in the history of post-independence Fiji. It is certain . . . that race relations have suffered a severe setback."[42] In the elections, four parties contested: the Alliance, the NFP, the Nationalists, and the Western United Front (WUF).

In the results, the Alliance barely obtained twenty-eight seats and the NFP-WUF twenty-four seats. In popular terms, out of 1,000,300 preferences cast, the Alliance won by only 2,000. The Fijian community was enraged that the NFP had once more come so close in upsetting the "balance" and depriving them of their political claims to paramount rule. It seems that a special dynamic of intense racial tensions is activated when the Indian NFP comes too close to victory, as happened in 1968, March–April 1977, and 1982. With the Indian electoral performance came Fijian assault on all the fundamental areas of constitutional agreement—Indian citizenship, land, and representation. The Great Council of Chiefs, the penultimate leadership body among Fijians, resolved that two-thirds of all seats of Parliament should be reserved exclusively for Fijians. Furthermore, it demanded that in the future the positions of prime minister and governor general be held by Fijians. These measures would guarantee Fijian paramountcy in all foreseeable elections. One Council member called for the deportation of all Indian leaders who challenged Fijian political supremacy. In various parts of Fiji where postelection passions ran high, Indians were threatened with eviction from Fijian land because they voted for the NFP.[43] Another member of the Great Council of Chiefs stated that "blood will flow" if Indians persisted in their quest for political power.

Clearly, elections in Fiji exacerbate and embitter race relations between Fijians and Indians. Fijian insistence on paramountcy is matched by Indian obstinacy in challenging it electorally. The two groups do not share the same perception of "balance" and "paramountcy." The collision of courses destroys cross-communal amity. Butadroka's Nationalists and other outbidders have succeeded in driving communal elites away from the politics of intersectional accommodation.[44]

PUBLIC POLICY AND LAW

The land issue is perhaps the most significant triggering point of Fijian–Indian racial conflict. Fijians own most of the country's land under

Table 9
Land Distribution in Fiji

	ESTIMATED ACRES	% OF TOTAL
Fijian communal land	3,714,990	82.16
Rotuman communal land	11,000	.24
Freehold	368,000	8.15
Crown Lands combined	377,420	9.45

a system of traditional communal tenure that prohibits private individual alienation to non-Fijians. They equate ownership of land with their heritage and identity. In a modern cash economy dominated by Europeans and Indians, land constitutes the Fijians' most powerful pillar of political bargaining. Being mainly farmers, Indians view land as the indispensable means for their survival. Since they own very little of it, however, they require predictable access to land use since alternative avenues of employment are practically nonexistent. The struggle, then, between Fijian owners and Indian lessees is cast in terms of vital needs generating unusual emotional intensity around the issue. There is also a public interest in land. If political stability and economic viability dictate that the Fijian–Indian conflict over land be contained, then this compels the state to strike a balance on one hand between making land available to the tillers (Indians) and on the other assuring Fijians that their land will not be used by others to build an economic base against Fijian interests. Public policy must tread the narrowest of sensitive options, for communal passions become easily inflamed over land. The idea of "balance" seemed to have guided the British administrators: "It is the government's task to frame its land policy so as to preserve a balance between the interests of the two communities."[45]

Fiji has about 4,505,000 acres of land. At the time of Cession, the Europeans had claimed about 1 million acres, but a land commission subsequently recognized only 415,000 acres as legal.[46] Nevertheless, these tracts represent the best agricultural land in Fiji. Since 1874, apart from a brief period between 1905 and 1911 when an additional 100,000 acres of Fijian land were alienated, land policy has remained very tight. Essentially, the government intervened to terminate all private sales in an effort to preserve the Fijian way of life.[47] Land ownership in Fiji is distributed as shown in Table 9.

The freezing of the tenure pattern has bequeathed a legacy of wide disparities in land ownership among the races. Fijians constituting about 45 percent of the population have retained ownership over 83.8 percent; less than 10 percent of this is cultivable. Europeans constituting about 4 percent of the population own in freehold 5.5 percent of prime commercial land. Indians forming about 50 percent of the population own 1.7 percent. The overwhelming majority of Indians are tenants and subtenants who depend on Fijians for leased land. About 62 percent of the leases issued by Fijians are held by Indians. Indians utilize the land mainly for sugar farming; about 80 percent of the sugar farmers are Indians who continue to demand more land on ninety-nine-year leases. Interestingly, up to World War I, Europeans were the most insistent on the release of more land for commercial development, causing antagonistic relations with Fijians. Thereafter, with the termination of the Indian indentureship system and the adoption of Fiji as their home, the pressure for more land came from Indians. As a result, Fijians and Indians were set on a collision course that continues to the present.

Fijian fear of losing their land as well as their desire to retain land unencumbered by long leases for future use led to the enactment of the controversial land reserves policy in 1940. Called the Native Land Trust Ordinance, the legislation established the Native Land Trust Board (NLTB) to administer the leasing of Fijian land and to terminate leases where necessary so as to create "reserves" for future Fijian use. The architect of this legislation, Ratu Sir Lala Sukuna, viewed the reserves policy as the embodiment of Fijian vital interests.

Indians did not share Ratu Sukuna's views of the NLTB, especially the land reserves policy. The selection of land for reserves has yet to be completed. For over three and a half decades, year after year, land leased to Indian families who had no other alternative source of income was taken out of cultivation and placed in reserves policy. First, many farms that went into reserves were not cultivated; they soon reverted to bush.[48] The Indian family who suddenly became landless was forced into an oversupplied pool of farm laborers available for hire. Second, because the length of leases under the new NLTB regulations was erratic with no guarantee of renewal, the insecurity of tenure provided little incentive for the Indian farmer to develop and care for the land. Third, the more land placed in reserve, the more the country lost revenues from taxes, fewer people were employed, and more persons moved into already overcrowded urban areas in search of jobs.[49]

Fijians defend the land reserves policy, saying that the availability of land may provide the incentive for them to cultivate the soil commercially. Because of long leases, many Fijians in a single lifetime may not have the opportunity to use their land. Furthermore, they argue that the overwhelming majority of leases are renewed so that the commotion and criticisms over nonrenewal are exaggerated and unfair.[50] Indians are not happy, especially with the first of these rebuttals, because Fijians already have more than an adequate supply of land, much of which is not cultivated. Consequently, the reserves policy is seen as an expression of jealousy of the Indians' growing prosperity and fear that, in the long run, Indian economic power may be translated into political power.

Caught between the Indians' expansive needs for long-term secure leases and the Fijians' demands for more reserves, the British colonial administrators oversaw the passage of the Agricultural Landlord and Tenants Ordinance (ALTO), which required the NLTB to offer tenants an initial lease for ten years and two similar ten-year periods if the Fijians did not need the land. The legislation was a balancing compromise that temporarily stabilized Indian–Fijian relations over land. Fijian interests in land were safeguarded in the 1970 independence Constitution which validated all Fijian land claims to 83 percent of the country's land and entrenched Fijian land rights by requiring two-thirds of the Fijian Council of Chiefs in the Senate to alter the land-related aspects of the Constitution. Indian access to land was further strengthened in 1976 when an amendment to ALTO (1966) gave leases for an initial twenty-year period instead of ten years, followed by a twenty-year extension.

While the new landlord-tenant legislation contained conflict over the land issue, both parties were still unhappy with the solution, and they continued to exchange racially acrimonious charges that embittered their relations. When Butadroka and the Nationalists appeared on the political scene, they further complicated the situation by insisting on a vigorous land reserves policy. The hardening of relations between the Fijian prime minister and the Indian opposition also spilled over into the land problem. While the Fijian-led government has enacted policies to allay Indian fears about land, it has permitted certain practices to overshadow its intent. The Native Land Trust Board which administers Fijian land and the ALTO (1976) legislation does not contain an Indian representative; in addition, its administrative staff, numbering close to 200, is almost completely made up of Fijians. Furthermore, when the government assumed control over the Colonial Sugar Refinery facilities, the vast amount of freehold Crown land acquired thereby was slated to be turned into Fijian properties. Indians protested by arguing that the land-hungry tenants should be the first served.

As long as Fiji remains an agricultural country and land ownership and sugar cultivation are in the hands of the two separate and hostile ethnic elements, the land issue will continue to be a fundamental feature of race relations. The intensity of sentiments derives from the fact that "land is seen as a scarce resource and competition for it is regarded in ethnic terms. The symbolic significance makes it more than just an ordinary issue."[51]

EMPLOYMENT: PUBLIC BUREAUCRACY AND THE PRIVATE SECTOR

Employment, especially in the public sector, has emerged as a vicious arena in which competitive claims for ethnic shares have attained a special intensity. While the two areas, representation and land, were bound by colonial precedent and yielded to formal compromises, jobs from the modern commercial sector and from the public bureaucracy—both of which expanded significantly in the post-World War II period—were left wide open for competition by the ethnic communities. In the absence of a formula, each group staked its own claims guided by its own interests. In the toss-up, attempts were made to extrapolate the principle of balance in various self-serving guises to this fluid and changing category.

The civil service, the professions, and private business represent the modern monetary sectors in Fiji. It was from jobs in these activities that stable and high incomes were earned and access to modern urban-type services were acquired. The quest for these positions by Fijians and Indians, acculturated to European ways and trained in skills, conferred dignity and status not only to the individual incumbents of these positions but also to the respective communities. Hence, they carried as much symbolic gratification as monetary rewards. Employment opportunities in the modern nonagricultural public and private sectors were limited, however. It would be in this crucible of scarcity for a very highly prized value that government policy would play a crucial part in determining the distribution of benefits.

The public service, including the education service, has become the largest single source of employment in Fiji. Until independence, the highest posts were occupied by European personnel. To gain access, the nonwhite population needed European education and training. English language schools, however, were not set up until 1916: "Prior to 1916, the government took little interest in Fijian and Indian education. In those days, the two state-aided public schools were restricted to children of European descent."[52] Under the Education Ordinances of 1916, the colonial regime initiated policies to assist the development of schools for Fijians and Indians. These schools were segregated into exclusive Fijian, Indian, and European institutions. The separate facilities were not equal, European schools were better equipped and staffed, while "the facilities and opportunities provided for education of children of other races... contrasted greatly."[53] To attain a reasonably high standard, Indian and Fijian schools depended on their own communities for supplementary resources. Because of their lack of land and insecure leases, Indians spent a great deal of money on upgrading their schools. To them, education was the only alternative to land scarcity; it held the promise of employment in the emerging modern public and private sectors. Indian expenditures in education were reflected after World War II in their

Table 10
School Enrollment, by Race, 1958 and 1968

	Fijians	Indians	Europeans	Others
Primary Schools				
1958	31,251	29,779	2,867	5,385
1968	45,404	58,581	2,945	3,982
Secondary Schools				
1958	642	1,751	324	862
1968	3,356	7,268	511	860

Source: *Annual Statistical Abstract, Fiji* (Suva: Government Printery, 1969), Tables 2.4 and 2.5.

steady incremental displacement of many Europeans in positions that required skills. The Fijians' educational achievement was retarded by comparison. A government inquiry assigned the reasons as "the geographical scatter of the Fijians, the isolation of the rural teacher from much intellectual stimulus, the shortage of Fijian primary school teachers, rural poverty, social distractions and other less tangible and psychological factors."[54] Fijian education grew, however, even if at a slower rate than the Indian, and many Fijians would qualify to compete with Indians for positions, especially in the government bureaucracy.

By independence in 1970, large numbers of Indians and Fijians were attending elementary schools, but Indians predominated (Table 10). Fijian students suffered a greater rate of attrition as they moved to high grades in school; this was bound to reflect adversely on their effort to obtain postsecondary qualifications essential for high-paying and senior echelon ranks. Table 11 demonstrates the disparate results in examinations between Fijian and Indian students, suggesting the inferior emphasis Fijians have placed on education and the poor facilities of their schools.

Given the trend in Indian education, it was almost inevitable, then, that most university positions would go to Indians. In 1968, out of 643 graduates with university degrees, 464 were Indians, 77 Fijians, 63 Chinese, and 31 others.[55] Indian employment in the professions underlined an emergent preponderance especially after many European expatriates left after independence.

Table 11
Examination Pass Rate, by Race, 1967 (in percent)

Item	Fijians	Indians	Others
Secondary School Entrance Examination	39.7	61.9	67.9
Cambridge School Certification Examination	44.8	65.4	67.2
New Zealand University Entrance Examination	25.0	30.0	44.7

Sources: *Annual Statistical Abstract, Fiji* (Suva: Government Printery, 1969), Tables 2.13, 2.16, and 2.17; Raj K. Vasili, *Politics in Biracial Societies* (New Delhi: Vikas, 1984), p. 195.

As the state undertook an increasing number of development projects and more services were extended to citizens, the public bureaucracy expanded. In a scheme where merit determined appointments, the public service was swamped by educated Indian personnel. But the concept of balance entered into the picture. After independence, a Fijian-dominated government offset Indian dominance in the private sector by higher Fijian employment in the public bureaucracy. According to R. S. Milne:

The actual number of Fijians in the civil service exceeds the number of Indians although there are fewer Fijians in the population. The educational qualifications of Indians applying to enter the civil service have been higher and their performance in the service's internal examinations have been superior. The current level of Fijian recruitment, therefore, is based not primarily on qualifications but rather on a policy of "racial balance" which in practice results in recruiting slightly more Fijians.[56]

In Tables 12 and 13, it can be seen that Fijians outnumber Indians in the civil service and police force by a small margin. In the armed forces, the Fijians' lopsided representation has evoked vehement protests against the government, which has been charged with obliquely guaranteeing Fijian paramountcy by the threat of an ethnic army (Table 14). In the Ministry of Fijian Affairs and Rural Development, during 1975 there were fifty-one Fijians, four Indians, and one other; and in the Ministry of Fijian Affairs, there were thirty-five Fijians only.[57] In the 1980s, the

Table 12
Civil Service Personnel, by Race, 1974

Fijians	5,414
Europeans	440
Indians	4,716
Others	490

Table 13
Police Force Personnel, by Race, 1974

Fijians	628
Europeans	5
Indians	448
Others	55

Source: Raj K. Vasili, *Politics in Biracial Societies* (New Delhi: Vikas, 1984), p. 195.

Fijian dominance in the public service had become very lopsided especially at the senior echelon levels. This situation has compelled the Indian opposition leader to accuse the government of

implementing a policy designed to ensure that all strategic levels of government are staffed by local personnel, which in effect means that the Fijians are placed in positions of command in order to deliberately create an alienated out group, namely, the Indians. There is little multiracialism at work. This is reflected in all aspects of governmental work and activities, from its composition, its development strategies, appointments to boards, promotions in the Civil Service, its Crown lands policy, everywhere.[58]

For Fijians, however, public service employment is the primary access route to middle-class well-being and status. Their excess numbers are balanced by the Indian domination of the private sector. Fijians constitute only 2 percent of the entrepreneurs in the country. Europeans

Table 14
Fijian Armed Forces

	Fijians	Indians	Others	Total
Regular Force	372	5	19	396
Territoral Force	502	29	32	563
Naval Squadron	59	2	10	71
	933	36	61	1,030

Source: Raj K. Vasili, *Politics in Biracial Societies* (New Delhi: Vikas, 1984), p. 194.

control the largest businesses, while Indians predominate in middle-sized enterprises. Fijian underrepresentation in business is being remedied by a government policy of affirmative action in its Business Organization and Management Unit (BOMAS) which trains Fijians in business practices and extends interest-free loans from the government's Development Bank. Other programs of official "positive discrimination" have been pursued to promote Fijians in business.[59]

The Alliance government has acted in one other major area to aid Fijians. Foreign aid for capital projects has been directed mostly to Fijian regions or to activities benefiting mainly Fijians. Examples include the pine wood industry and its predominantly Fijian-staffed Fiji Pine Commission, the tuna fisheries project, and the sugarcane seaquaqua scheme. To offset this imbalance, the Fiji government has rigorously sought large quotas at high prices for the Indian-dominated sugar industry mainly from the European Common Market. Hence, balance in the ethnic distribution of benefits is not necessarily built in the same activity or institution, but is orchestrated by linking different sectors together.

RECENT DEVELOPMENTS

More than once in recent years, collective violence has threatened to spill over into the public arena. The fear that one day all restraints will be removed in a racial confrontation is very real. Solutions to avert such a catastrophe have been suggested. In 1980, the country's prime minister, who is the leader of one of the two major communal sections, made a major proposal calling for a government of national unity to avert a national disaster.[60] A condition described as "crisis prone" by the prime minister points to the general instability that characterizes a government that fails "to weld into a nation peoples with strong ethnic allegiances."[61] When Jai Ram Reddy of the NFP replied to Mara's proposals, he agreed with the views that condemned the effects of communal politics.[62] He noted that "economic development cannot take place when the two communities which complement each other in the production of goods and services do not work in harmony. We must know that one community cannot prosper when another stands to perish."[63] Both Reddy and Mara predicted that, if current trends continued, conflict and confrontation would eventually lead to communal violence. They shared a solid foundation of consensus that communal politics was divisive, wasteful, destructive, and unwanted.

The prime minister proposed "a government of national unity" which, institutionally, "will be reflected in a Cabinet which draws upon the best talents in the country having in mind, simultaneously adequate representation of the various ethnic groups in Fiji." By working together in a cooperative cabinet arrangement, Indian and Fijian leaders would impart a salutary example to the entire population as a model of good intercommunal behavior. On the question of ethnic proportional representation in the cabinet, Mara proposed that the Indian–Fijian ratio be guided by two factors: (1) relative ethnic population size in the country, and (2) percentage control by the various parties in Parliament and of the majority party as a result of the previous general election (the September 1977 elections). In the House of Representatives at that time, the Alliance had thirty-six members and the Federation party fifteen. Whatever the final numbers of Indians and Fijians would have been under this formula, its anticipated consequences were "to ensure adequate participation by all communities in the decision-making process," thereby nullifying a "sense of alienation in any one or more ethnic groups through apparent or real exclusion." Reddy agreed that the solution to Fiji's communal politics resided in some form of joint government, but whether the form was "consocialism," "coalition," or "government of national unity," it had to be subordinate to the salient issue of honor or what he called "any arrangement that is honourable." The opposition leader said that a joint government could only be forged on the basis that permitted the NFP relatively equal leverage and representation with the Alliance. He called for discussions between the two parties to explore the subject further.[64]

The timing of the Mara proposal coincided with the fact that the Alliance was at its most powerful parliamentary level in its history, while the NFP, plagued by dissension, was at its weakest. If Mara was negotiating from a position of strength, Reddy was dealing from weakness.

In the end, the vital interests of the Alliance, namely, the retention of power and the protection of Fijian interests, would be promoted, but those of its partner, the NFP, would still be locked up in ambiguity.

The leader of the opposition was put in a quandary. His party, weak both in parliamentary numbers and internal cohesion, was challenged to what seemed to be a higher purpose of preserving communal peace in Fiji. Not surprisingly, genuine fears were felt that a powerful Alliance would absorb the Federation party, eliminating the party's identity in a government of national unity. The timing of the Alliance proposals was inopportune for the NFP. Indeed, time was essential to Reddy's strategy in responding to Mara's proposals, so that he could (1) sort out his party's internal difficulties and (2) increase his party's parliamentary strength. The fulfillment of these conditions would give him the leverage to negotiate with the Alliance.

The opposition leader delved critically into various aspects of the Mara proposal. But he also decided to raise some substantive issues that would require urgent attention if a joint government should be agreed on. He pointed to the Alliance government policies that had allegedly sown the seeds of racial discord in the country. He criticized the Alliance policy of reverting Crown land to native reserves, drew attention to the alleged discriminatory hiring practices of the government in favor of Fijians, and commented on the lack of consultation with the opposition on sensitive issues. "Can you sow the seeds of strife and sue for peace? Is this how we build national unity?" Reddy asked. Ratu Mara's response to the opposition leader's comments amounted to a withdrawal of his proposal. Mara blamed his action on the attitude of the Federation party and the opposition leader.

Several factors further complicated the treatment accorded the unification proposals. First, it was a publicly disclosed design; it was not adequately discussed in private by the two major communal leaders before it was tossed into the inevitable turmoil of communally bound public discourse. Second, the proposals became the arena in which a contest for political upmanship transpired at two national conventions. Reddy had to show that he was capable of standing up to the Alliance, while Mara, in response, had to show that he could put down the NFP. The main casualty was the proposals. Finally, the timing of the unification proposals was unsuitable, particularly to the opposition leader, who would have lost his leadership of the NFP had he chosen to negotiate from a position of weakness. In Mara's unification proposal, the NFP would undoubtedly have had to settle for a very subordinate partnership role. Both the Alliance and the NFP had vital internal needs to protect; no serious negotiation was likely to overlook these. Consequently, the proposal fell victim to political exchanges informed by internal communal interests.

CONCLUSION

Ethnic and race relations in Fiji have been marked by tensions that periodically skirt open physical violence. Fijians and Indians are phenotypically different; their cultural institutions are also separate. Politics has stimulated an acute consciousness of each as endowed with a unique identity and with special interests. In a modern society of material scarcity, competition for resources between the major ethnic groups has strained race relations. An ambiguous concept of balance is often invoked to divide the spoils of the system, but, in reality, struggle for policy favors is conducted for whatever part of the pie can be acquired. Periods of cross-communal amity between sectional elites have been torpedoed by outbidders whose demands have driven Fiji close to the brink of racial conflagration. Party politics, structured around ethnic preference, has cast Fiji's ethnic and racial conflict into an intransigent bipolar mold. In May, 1987, a military coup engineered by Lieutenant Colonel Sitreni Rabuka suspended Fijian democracy and gave full power to native Fijians.

NOTES

1. *Fiji Information* (Suva: Government Printery, 1972), p. 1.

2. J. S. Furnivall, *Colonial Policy and Practice* (London: Cambridge University Press, 1948), pp. 304–12.

3. M. G. Smith, "Institutional and Political Conditions of Pluralism," in Leo Kuper and M. G. Smith, eds., *Pluralism in Africa* (Berkeley: University of California Press, 1965), pp. 26–63.

4. See Alvin Rabushka and Kenneth A. Shepsle, *Politics in Plural Societies: A Theory of Democratic Instability* (Ohio: Charles E. Merrill Co., 1972), p. 82.

5. See Ralph R. Premdas, "Constitutional Challenge: Nationalist Politics in Fiji," *Pacific Perspective* 9, No. 2 (October 1980): 30–44.

6. For an excellent treatment of this relationship, see Eric Williams, *Capitalism and Slavery* (London: Andre Deutsch, 1964), pp. 3–30.

7. See Ahmed Ali, "The Indians of Fiji," *Economic and Political Weekly* 8, No. 36 (September 8, 1973): 1655.

8. These words, known as the "Salisbury Dispatch," are often quoted by Indians to assert their rights in Fiji.

9. For a brief description of the results of qualifying examinations which are used as a basis for civil service jobs, see *Report of the Public Service Commission, 1967*, p. 5.

10. See R. F. Watters, *Koro: Economic Development and Social Change in Fiji* (Oxford: Clarendon Press, 1969), pp. 1–48.

11. E. K. Fisk, *The Political Economy of Independent Fiji* (Canberra: Australian National University Press, 1970), pp. 16–17.

12. Ali, "The Indians of Fiji," p. 1956.

13. *Census Report*, 1966.

14. A. C. Walsh, "Fiji's Changing Population: Implications for Race Relations," *Unispac* 8, No. 1 (1970): 1–2.

15. Ibid.

16. See R. A. Derrick, *The Fiji Islands* (Suva: Government Printery, 1966).

17. *Census Report*, 1966.

18. For an exposition of Australian control of big Fiji business, see Amelia Rokotunivuna et al., *Fiji: A Developing Australian Colony* (Melbourne: International Development Action, 1974).

19. See Premdas, "Constitutional Challenge."

20. See Walsh, "Fiji's Changing Population."

21. A. Mamak, *Color, Culture, and Conflict: A Study of Pluralism in Fiji* (New York: Pergamon Press, 1978).

22. See Ahmed Ali, *Plantation to Politics: A Study of Fiji Indians* (Suva: Fiji Times, 1980).

23. Ahmed Ali, "Fiji: The Arrival of the Communal Franchise," *Journal of Pacific Studies* 1, No. 1 (1975): 30.

24. Norman Meller and James Anthony, *Fiji Goes to the Polls* (Honolulu: East-West Center Press, 1967), pp. 11–12.

25. Ibid., p. 12.

26. Ibid., p. 14.

27. Ibid., p. 28.

28. Ibid., p. 15.

29. R. K. Vasili, "Communalism and Constitution-Making in Fiji," *Pacific Affairs* (Spring 1972): 24.

30. Report of the *Fiji Constitutional Conference 1970*, Council Paper No. 5 of 1970 (Suva: Government Printery, 1970), p. 13.

31. P. H. Grocott, "Fiji: The Politics of Communalism," in P. H. Grocott, ed., *Readings in Pacific Politics: Supplement* (Waigani: University Printery, 1976), p. 51.

32. Brig Lal, "Fiji: Politics Since Independence" (Honolulu: Department of History, University of Hawaii, 1984), pp. 8–9.

33. Robert Norton, *Race and Politics in Fiji* (Queensland: University of Queensland Press, 1978), p. 103.

34. Ibid.

35. Ibid., p. 105.

36. Cited in R. S. Milne, "The Pacific Way—Consociational Politics in Fiji," *Pacific Affairs* (September 1975): 413–30.

37. See Mamak, *Color, Culture, and Conflict*, p. 165.

38. See "Party Leaders Fall Out," *Pacific Islands Monthly* (December 1975): 11–12.

39. Premdas, "Constitutional Challenge."

40. Ibid.

41. Ralph R. Premdas, *Communal Politics in Fiji* (Waigani: University of Papua, New Guinea, 1978), Ch. 3; see also Ralph R. Premdas, "Elections in Fiji: Restoration of the Balance in September 1977," *Journal of Pacific History* 14, No. 1 (1980): 189–201.

42. Brij Lal, "The 1982 Fiji National Election and Its Aftermath," *USP Sociological Society Newsletter*, No. 5 (July 1983): 16.

43. Ibid., p. 8.

44. For a critical role played by elites in cross-communal accommodation, see A. Liphart, *Democracy in Plural Societies* (New Haven, Conn.: Yale University Press, 1977), pp. 25–35. For a more detailed discussion of accommodation and elites in Fiji, see Ralph R. Premdas, "Fiji: Communal Conflict and Political Balance in the South Pacific," *Caribbean Affairs* 4, No. 1 (1978): 22–49.

45. D. T. Lloyd, *Land Policy in Fiji*, Occasional Paper No. 4 (Cambridge: Department of Land Economy, University of Cambridge, 1982), p. 241.

46. Jay Narayan, *The Political Economy of Fiji* (Suva: South Pacific Review Press, 1984), p. 23.

47. Ibid.

48. "Cane Farmers: Fiji's Unrewarded Peasants," *Unispac* 7, No. 5 (1969): 1–2.

49. Ashok Desai, "Employment and Its Remedies: A Case Study of Fiji," *Economic Bulletin for Asia and the Far East* 24, Nos. 2/3 (September–December 1974): 23–35.

50. See "NLTB Facts and Figures," *VANUA* (NLTB Journal), (Suva, 1977), p. 1.

51. R. S. Milne, *Politics in Ethnically Bipolar States* (Vancouver: University of British Columbia Press, 1982), p. 65.

52. Mamak, *Color, Culture, and Conflict, Political Economy of Fiji*, pp. 86–87.

53. Narayan, p. 73.

54. Lal, "Fiji: Politics Since Independence," p. 18.

55. Ahmed Ali, *From Plantation to Politics*, p. 143.

56. Ray K. Vasili, *Politics in Biracial Societies* (New Delhi: Vikas, 1984), p. 194.

57. Ali, *From Plantation to Politics*, p. 188.

58. See Ralph R. Premdas, "Towards a Government of National Unity," *Pacific Perspective* 10, No. 2 (1980): 10.

59. Milne, *Politics in Ethnically Bipolar States*, p. 144.

60. "Ratu Mara Speaks on Government of National Unity," *The Fiji Times*, September 2, 1980.

61. Ibid.

62. "Address to the 16th Annual Convention of the NFP" (mimeo), October 1980.

63. Ibid.

64. The quotations are from Reddy's, "Address to the Sixteenth Annual Convention of the NFP" (mimeo), October 1980, pp. 1–2.

BIBLIOGRAPHY

Ali, Ahmed. "Fiji: The Arrival of the Communal Franchise." *Journal of Pacific Studies*, no. 1 (1975): 30–35.

Fisk, E. K. *The Political Economy of Independent Fiji*. Canberra: Australian National University Press, 1970.

Mamak, A. *Color, Culture, and Conflict: A Study of Pluralism in Fiji*. New York: Pergamon Press, 1978.

Narayan, Jay. *The Political Economy of Fiji*. Suva: South Pacific Review Press, 1984.

Premdas, Ralph R. *Communal Politics in Fiji*. Waigani: University of Papua, 1978.

Watters, R. F. *Koro: Economic Development and Social Change in Fiji*. Oxford: Clarendon Press, 1969.

FRANCE

Alan B. Anderson

A RACIAL CONTEXT

France has a remarkably heterogeneous population. Heavy and persistent immigration has played a major role in creating this racial and ethnic diversity; yet indigenous ethnolinguistic minorities collectively comprise between one-third and one-half of the total French population. These native minorities are concentrated around the periphery of France: Bretons to the west, Basques, Catalans, and the Occitanian peoples (Gascons, Languedociens, Provençal) to the south, Corsicans on the island of Corsica, German-speaking Alsatians and Lorringians to the east, and Flemings to the north. Within their home regions those minorities have been struggling, with varying degrees of success, to develop ethnonationalistic movements aimed at achieving regional autonomy.

To these historic ethnic populations may be added the enormous racial and ethnic complexity introduced by immigrants into urban areas. Francophone immigrants have long come into France to work from neighboring Belgium and Luxemburg. They were joined during the nineteenth and early twentieth centuries by political refugees primarily from Central and Eastern Europe: Russians, Poles, Ukrainians, Jews. With the expansion of the French Empire into the Third World, colonial immigrants began and continue to arrive from French colonies and overseas territories: the Caribbean and French Guyana, Reunion in the Indian Ocean, the French South Pacific territories. Many more migrants have come from one-time French colonies which today form part of "la francophonie" (the French-speaking world): Haiti, Lebanon, Indochina, Mauritius and the Seychelles, Madagascar, and many countries in North, West, and Central Africa. Most recently, since the 1960s, hundreds of thousands of labor migrants have entered France, chiefly North Africans

(Algerians, Tunisians, and Moroccans), Turks, and Arabs, and from the Mediterranean countries of Southern Europe (Italy, Portugal, and Spain).

While France still, in fact increasingly, makes a political ideology of the nation-state, implying that France is the homogenous country of one dominant French race, sociological reality is far removed from this view. France is the most heterogeneous country in Europe west of the USSR. It is preeminently a country of racial and ethnic minorities.

IMMIGRATION TRENDS AND POLICIES

A century ago an estimated 2 million foreigners were living in France (half of them Belgians, a quarter Italians). Immigration increased substantially during the 1930s with industrial expansion. But it was not until fairly recently in French history that immigration, particularly from Southern Europe, the Middle East, and North Africa, has soared in virtually all of the industrialized countries of continental Western and Northern Europe. During the late 1960s, there were only some 2 million foreign workers and family members in France. By the early 1980s, this number had more than doubled to about 4.5 million, or approximately 8 percent of the total population of France and 11 percent of the labor force. The total number of foreign workers in Europe was estimated to be 11 million in 1974 (but as many as 15 million, if allowance was made for illegal and unrecorded immigrants), and officially 14.6 million by 1983, or 7.6 percent of the total population of the continent. So almost a quarter of these foreign workers were resident in France alone.

French immigration rates are difficult to analyze, given the complexity of the French immigration system. Migrants from French colonies and territories and migrants possessing French passports can enter France at will, and so are not officially counted as immigrants. Foreign workers entering from other Common Market countries can usually enter France quite easily, especially if they have previously arranged work contracts. Algerians have a special preferential status dating back to the terms of settlement of the protracted Algerian War, when Algeria became independent from France but reserved the right of free entry into France; similar allowances tend to be made for migrants from other former French colonies such as Morocco and Tunisia. Other immigrants have seasonal contracts. Family members may enter as dependents; however, youth grow up to become members of the workforce themselves, while census data consider the half million children born in France to immigrant parents simply to be French. In a recent report on immigrant youth, demographers J. Marange and A. Lebon predicted that within fifteen years more than half of those aged under twenty-five would be of foreign origin.

In recent years there has been considerable fluctuation in immigration within each category. For example, data from the ONI (Office National d'Immigration) reveal that the number of "controlled" permanent workers (*travailleurs permanents controlés par l'ONI*) fell from 20.9 percent of the total immigration flow in 1974 (259, 703) to only 5.3 percent in 1980 (179, 824); the number of workers entering from Common Market countries was quite stable: 4.2 percent compared to 4.4 percent; the proportion of seasonal workers increased from 50.7 percent to 67.0 percent; and the proportion admitted as family members remained consistent: 24.4 percent compared to 23.4 percent. These data exclude, of course, colonial migrants, refugees, and special status migrants. A 1976 study showed that 42.5 percent of immigrants originated outside Europe, 41.8 percent from non-Common Market countries within Europe, and 15.7 percent from Common Market countries.

Again, the principal source countries have changed considerably since the immediate post-World War II years:

	1946	1954	1962	1968	1975	1980	1984
			(populations in thousands)				
African	54	230	429	572	1193		
- North African						1400	
- Algerian					711		805
- Moroccan					260		493
- Tunisian					140		213
- Black African						70	
- Senegalese							35
Turks					51	92	135
Mediterranean					1719		
- Italian	451	508	629	572	463	483	
- Portuguese	22	20	50	296	759	866	
- Spanish	302	289	442	607	497	450	
East European							
- Polish	424	269	177	132	94	70	
- Yugoslavian					70	70	

In 1975, it was estimated that about half of the foreigners in France were of Mediterranean (Italian, Portuguese, or Spanish) ethnic·origin, while a third were of North African origin. But during the past decade the Mediterranean proportion has dropped, while the North African has climbed. Of course, the actual ethnic populations must be far larger than these immigration data would suggest. There is a great deal of confusion of data over foreign workers per se, whether their family members are added (including those born in France), foreign residents in general, and total ethnic populations (many of whom could be French citizens, or colonial migrants, hence not counted in immigration data). Nonetheless, sociologists and demographers now estimate that the Paris urban region (accounting for roughly one-fifth of the total population of France) houses a disproportion of most immigrant ethnic groups: almost all of the Mauritians, at least two-thirds of the North Africans, Turks, and Yugoslavs, half of the Cambodians and Togolais, a quarter of the Portuguese, Vietnamese, and so on.

How have immigration policies been changing most recently? Doubtless the most controversial measures have been the efforts of government as well as industry to persuade or induce a substantial proportion of foreign workers to leave. France began to deemphasize immigration, at least for certain sources, long before such a policy became the trademark of the Mitterrand regime. For example, as early as 1973 the immigration level from African countries was frozen. Actually, an explicit policy of encouraging return migration had been implemented by the Valéry Giscard d'Estaing government at a time when foreign workers were pouring into France. The new policy proved largely ineffective; not only did relatively few foreign workers accept inducements to leave, but also those who did could easily turn around and return again, particularly shorter distance migrants such as Spaniards or Italians. In 1977, a policy of paying each immigrant a "repatriation bonus" of 10,000 francs was inaugurated. (The amount was possibly augmented to as much as 75,000 francs paid by large industrial companies—Peugeot offered 16,500 francs, Cit-Alcatel up to 44,000 francs.) By 1980, however, only 41,000 had accepted. In mid–1979, a policy of involuntary expulsion was also refined to include criminals as well as illegal immigrants resident in France for more than three months without permission. In addition, the government announced a policy of reducing labor immigration by 3 to 5 percent a year, in combination with a reduction in the total number of immigrants who could enter. By the end of 1980, another 20,000 had accepted voluntary return migration; most were blacks and North Africans, though many were Portuguese. The government optimistically projected that a million would leave by 1985, but only a small fraction actually did.

With 11 percent of the total labor force (and doubtless a higher proportion of foreign labor) unemployed, perhaps even the several tens of thousands who did leave would have left anyway. The police were now given special powers to arrest and expel immigrants; this legislation, advocated enthusiastically by Mitterrand, was aimed at the over 400,000 illegal immigrants in the country. It was estimated in 1980 that over

200,000 illegals (and would-be immigrants turned back at the international borders) were sent home, largely to Africa. The plan to reduce the immigrant population by a quarter million a year has largely failed, in spite of the new stringent policies, serious economic recession, and concomitant racial tensions. Yet the government now claims that at least these combined efforts have kept the total population of foreign workers at a static level since 1980.

The very complexity of French laws affecting immigrants, legal efforts to expel immigrants who have run afoul of these laws, the development of a computerized data bank on immigrant workers, the worsening economic situation, and the rapid increase in racism could together hasten an exodus. When the original *aide de retour* (repatriation bonus) policy was first proposed by the Giscard d'Estaing government, the Socialists under Mitterrand called the idea "immoral and racist." By 1983, these same Socialists were proposing to pay returnees double the original amount; within another year a payment of 100,000 francs per worker was being suggested (consisting of the 20,000 francs from the government, as well as several months of unemployment insurance, and a variable grant from the employer, for example, Renault pays 60,000 francs and offers cheap cars, or Citroën pays 25,000 francs). But most of the foreign workers in France elect to remain for any number of reasons: because unemployment rates are far higher in the poor countries from which they came (e.g., 30 percent in Algeria), or because their militancy acquired in leftist labor unions in France would not go well with police in "home" countries, or because their families have been raised or born in France, where they enjoy higher standards of education and living. Nor are "home" countries particularly anxious to receive hordes of return migrants. With high unemployment, Yugoslavia gladly sends a million workers—20 percent of its possible labor force—to employment abroad; Spain exports 2 million workers, Portugal about 1.5 million, and Turkey over 1 million.

IMMIGRANT INTEGRATION: THE USE AND ABUSE OF IMMIGRANTS

It is instructive to review the manner in which the first postwar labor immigrants were recruited by French industry, particularly automobile manufacturers. Citroën, for example, sent recruiting teams to backcountry mountain regions of Morocco to find able-bodied men who could be employed as cheap labor on assembly lines in France. Soon they were joined by their families—an estimated 70 percent sent for their relatives. They stayed for several years or indefinitely in France, only to learn how they were being exploited in the labor force. At first they were prohibited or advised not to join unions, and they were increasingly blamed for unemployment and for taking jobs away from bona fide Frenchmen.

The ready availability of cheap imported personnel was a principal factor in postwar economic recovery throughout Western and Northern Europe. The underemployment of foreign workers could serve to keep wage levels in general down, while permitting the upward mobility of existing French labor into better jobs. Faced with low birth rates and chronic labor shortages, these industrial countries rapidly became increasingly dependent on cheap foreign labor to work in large industries, menial tasks, and services. Through the importation of vast numbers of usually unskilled, illiterate laborers, industrial Europe created a new lumpenproletariat, essential to capitalist industrial expansion yet outcasts from mainstream society. For their part, the existing population, raised on the mythical ideology of the homogeneous nation-state, was not likely to accept the hordes of newcomers except in the capacity of filling the least desirable jobs—the underpaid assembly line workers, sweatshop employees, garbage collectors, and streetsweepers. As the cheapest labor, the new immigrants were not guaranteed a minimum wage. They were often hired by middlemen who chopped off a large portion of even these meager salaries as a commission. Not infrequently, these *agences d'emploi* received the company paycheck, then paid only a portion of it to the worker, who therefore didn't work directly for the company, with the result that the worker might receive only a third to half of the actual company salary. Not only were workers often not paid directly, thereby bypassing minimum wage legislation, but also they worked in the most hazardous conditions: the estimated accident rate for foreign laborers in the late 1970s was about 20 percent per year.

Two-thirds of African workers are employed in the automobile industry; three-quarters of the Paris urban region work in industrial firms employing over a hundred wage-earners each. Renault employs 17,000 foreign workers (17 percent of the company workforce). It comes as no surprise, then, to discover that the greatest labor unrest among foreign workers has been in the automotive industry. While the foreign workers became progressively politicized from a leftist perspective, the largest union in France—the communist CGT (Confédération Générale de Travailleurs)—almost completely ignored their problems and demands. In general, the unions have been more concerned about ensuring that cheap foreign labor doesn't undercut French labor or take jobs away from French labor. Foreign workers have been threatened with expulsion when they launch their own strikes. Still, these strikes have become more effective. The automotive companies had a deficit of 4 million francs in 1982, a year when strikes cost the industry 50,000 cars in lost production. Much of this loss was due to foreign workers' demands for job security, better pay, hardship bonuses, and retraining programs.

It has become a very popular tenet of French racism that foreign workers are primarily responsible for high unemployment. These workers find themselves in double jeopardy—the brunt of racism from fellow French workers and the first to be victimized by layoffs. Although there may be competition for the lowest paying jobs, there is no correlation between unemployment rates and immigrant populations. According to sociologist Jacqueline Costa-Lascoux, "The attempt to substitute a national labour force for immigrant labor has largely been a failure."[1] Even in times of economic crisis and unemployment, there are certain jobs that nationals will simply not take. Fewer than three foreign workers in ten could be replaced by French workers, according to a recent government report. Yet unemployment is estimated to be one-quarter higher among immigrants in France than among the native French. A significant proportion of the over 1.5 million jobless in France are foreigners; according to the Ministère de Travail, the unemployment rate among immigrants nears 30 percent. This is not to suggest, however, that immigrants are the cause of unemployment.

The immigrant minorities of Europe are the orphans of colonialism's dead empires, living on society's fringe in urban ghettoes spawned by loneliness, illiteracy, and poverty. A UNESCO report in 1976 pointed out that young migrant workers in Europe are overwhelmed by a sense of failure, and violence is likely to erupt unless something is done to effectively integrate them. The report suggested that everything contrives to place the young immigrant in a situation bearing the marks of a dependent subculture, triply branded with the characteristics of foreignness, youth, and lack of skills. The people of the host society see these immigrants only as an exploitable commodity to be channeled into cheap, menial work requiring the least technical skill.

The marginalization of the new immigrants means that they are underemployed or unemployed. It also means that they are poorly housed, not eligible for social benefits regarded as fundamental to the rest of society, stereotyped, ostracized, and treated with scorn. Education, when available, is too often second rate, and progress is hindered by language difficulties. The loneliness of single male immigrants, or of married ones who have left their wives and families at home, is endemic; loneliness can breed the desperation leading in turn to excessive spending, alcohol and drug abuse, and prostitution.

Housing usually reflects acute self-deprivation or overcrowding. During the early 1970s, the French government completed its policy of bulldozing the notorious *bidonvilles* (shantytowns). Data from the government of Prime Minister Jacques Chirac indicate that in 1973–74, the population resident in *bidonvilles* was reduced from 38,000 to 22,000. But these shantytowns were replaced by *foyers* and *barraques* in the inner city and certain outer city areas heavily settled by immigrant ethnic groups. Here one finds four to ten people in a single bedroom. In the worst quarters meals are eaten in common rooms lacking chairs or tables.

The poorest housing conditions are found among the most disadvantaged immigrants: the illegal *immigrés clandestins*.

Drug abuse, prostitution, and crime, particularly juvenile delinquency, have become a serious problem in the immigrant ghettoes—all of which serves to reinforce the low opinion the French people increasingly have of *les étrangers* (foreigners). These problems seem to be most prevalent among the restless *beurs*, the young North Africans raised in France. An estimated 70 percent of the immigrant workforce in France has been there longer than a decade, thus breeding this new generation of French-born children caught between two worlds and thoroughly disillusioned with both. On the positive side, the French government, municipalities, and social workers have all been giving priority to job training and education for these youth. Housing conditions and local decision-making powers have been improving slowly in some areas. But there is still—in fact, increasingly—a negative side: rampant racism in the community, in the workplace, in the economy, in policing, and in the political arena.

RISING RACISM

Racism, directed particularly against nonwhite immigrants as well as Jews, has been on the rise during recent years in France. Incidences of overt racist violence and harassment have become commonplace as the French white population has become aware that immigrants now represent one in ten people in France and are claimed to be taking jobs away from Frenchmen, raising the crime rate while lowering the standard of living. In France, a country that has long taken pride in *liberté, fraternité, eqalité*, sociological surveys and electoral politics are revealing majorities with racist attitudes. Moreover, institutional racism seems to have increased. Police randomly stop nonwhites in the street to check identity papers. They stage dawn raids on crowded apartments occupied by immigrants. They have been repeatedly implicated in beatings and shootings of nonwhite immigrants. Both the police and the government have become overanxious in their crackdown on supposed illegal immigrants, resulting in numerous deportations. These stringent measures have done nothing to discourage racism; rather, they have further aroused public disdain for all immigrants, illegal or legal.

North Africans seem to be receiving the brunt of overt racist attacks. To cite some recent random examples: The knifing of an ethnic French bus driver in Marseilles in 1974 by a deranged Algerian touched off an orgy of racial violence, resulting in eleven deaths. In February 1980, an Algerian teenager was "accidentally" shot to death by a policeman in an apartment block in Nanterre—a working-class suburb of Paris heavily settled by nonwhite immigrants. The official report indicated that the policeman stumbled in the dark. A couple of months previously a similar incident occurred in Strasbourg, when a policeman shot a young Algerian at point-blank range. In 1980, young North Africans clashed violently with French residents at a festival in St. Chamas; the car from which gunshots were fired at young and unarmed North Africans was driven by the mayor's assistant. In October 1982, a French sniper opened fire on youths and children in Nanterre, killing a nineteen-year-old Algerian student as he walked out of a mosque. In November, the president of a local rights group in Troyes was wounded by motorcyclists armed with razors. In December, a North African was thrown out of a train by three drunken Foreign Legionnaires near Bordeaux; his head exploded on a telephone pole. And at St. Cyprien Plage, a Frenchman refused to allow an Algerian to enter a nightclub; the furious Algerian shot the doorman and was then in turn beaten to death.

Hardly a week passes in France without racial violence being reported, and the victims, more often than not, are North African or Arabs. Radio-Beur claimed in 1983 that during the past couple of years at least forty racist murders had occurred in France. The almost two-thirds of a million young people of North African descent who have grown up in France, many of them born in France as French citizens, are a rejected generation reviled by white French nationals. In turn, these youths have decided that they will not be humiliated and exploited like their immigrant parents, typecast as poor, delinquent, and uneducated. Disillusioned with French society, they are caught between two cultures and rejected by both.

Black Africans have also been the recipients of racial animosity, although black French citizens and Haitians who have migrated from the Caribbean have long been accepted as part of the French scene. In one recent incident a Senegalese immigrant sleeping on a canal bank in an industrial town north of Paris drowned when he was rolled into the frigid water by a gang of white youths.

Doubtless the spate of terrorist bombings attributed to Middle Eastern factions in Paris during the early 1980s, and continuing today, has not helped to reduce highly negative public opinion about Arabs. At least some anti-Semitic attacks have also been attributed to these factions, notably the Palestine Liberation Organization (PLO). Yet there is ample evidence that the traditional scapegoats for racism in France, the Jews, have been revived as victims of pervasive anti-Semitism. In March 1979, a Jewish restaurant was bombed, and thirty-three students were injured. In October 1980, a synagogue was bombed; four people were killed and nineteen wounded. On August 9, 1982, Jo Goldenberg's, a well-known restaurant on Rue des Rosiers, in the heart of the old Paris ghetto, was attacked with grenades and machine guns; six died and twenty-two were wounded. The next day a bomb exploded outside a formerly Jewish-owned bank (now nationalized). During the past several years, Jewish synagogues, schools, homes, restaurants, and even graveyards have been attacked or vandalized. These could be isolated incidents of anti-Semitism by Middle Eastern factions, as some scholars have suggested; however, they add up to the worst wave of anti-Semitism for decades.

France has had a long history of anti-Semitism, culminating in the Dreyfus Affair of 1894–99 and in the passivity of Frenchmen when some 30,000 Parisian Jews were deported for extermination during World War II. Since then, anti-Semitism seems to have declined; so it is difficult to determine the popular basis for these recent incidents. With more than half (380,000) of France's 700,000 Jews concentrated in the Paris urban region, there would appear to be more popular and official acceptance of this large ethnoreligious minority than there is of newer immigrants, particularly nonwhites. Following the synagogue bombing in October 1980, President Giscard d'Estaing ordered all French schools to give "a lesson for pupils on the pluralist, tolerant and fraternal character of French society." He commented that these criminal acts against Jews painfully echoed past events: persecutions, deportations, and systematic measures. He referred to French Jews as "French among other French": a title not so readily bestowed on nonwhite immigrants or their children.

THE NEW POLITICS OF RACISM

Racism has emerged prominently in the political arena in France. Political parties ranging from far right to far left came to the realization in the national election of 1986 that at least a quarter of all French voters could be won with a racist anti-immigrant platform. The question of the purity of the French race, mythical as it is, has nonetheless become a key political issue, one to which even moderate centrist parties have felt obligated to conform. Local mayors and elected officials are caught between the dilemma of sincerely wanting to improve living and working conditions of immigrants while facing an electorate increasingly hostile to what they consider to be a foreign invasion.

Campaign slogans have played a significant role in rapidly increasing xenophobia and ethnocentrism. In the poor town of Dreux, just outside Paris, where a quarter of the population consists of foreign workers and their families, neo-Gaullists campaigned with the National Front under the slogan "two million unemployed equals two million immigrants. France for the French!" Similarly, the former centrist mayor of Toulon put up posters claiming "Toulon for the Toulonnais!" and pledged to keep the port city from becoming "the dustbin of Europe." Faced with losing his mayoralty to rightists campaigning on a racist platform, the mayor of Marseilles promised as interior minister to further cut back on immigration.

The Socialists under François Mitterrand lost the election after five years as the government, due largely to their comparatively moderate stand on immigration, although this government did attempt to reduce foreign labor immigration and adopted a policy encouraging return migration. The real demise of the Socialist government lay in the rapid spread of racism through traditionally left-voting working classes. Ethnic French workers increasingly had come to resent being a minority in many factories. The industries hardest hit by economic recession and layoffs are precisely those with a high proportion of foreign labor: automotive, construction, mining, and steel. Ethnic French assembly-line workers laid off when foreign workers are kept on the job (probably because they are cheaper labor) strongly resent what they consider reverse discrimination. Add to this the virtual inundation of many working-class residential communities by foreign or nonwhite immigrants, and ample grist is provided for racist political platforms.

Jacques Chirac, mayor of Paris and leader of the neo-Gaullist RPR (Rassemblement pour la République) formed a strong opposition alliance with the UDF (Union pour la Démocratie Française), a loose federation of conservative factions led by former President Valéry Giscard d'Estaing, to successfully defeat the Socialists in March 1986. The most prevalent fomenters of racism are not the main political parties or coalitions, but smaller fringe parties. The most important of these is the FN (Front National), led by Jean-Marie le Pen. He campaigned on a platform to "free France" from nonwhite workers whom (he claims) take jobs away from the native French. An extreme rightist party, the Front National is no newcomer to French politics; however, it never captured more than 2 to 3 percent of the vote. Now it doubled or tripled its strength, winning 7 to 8 percent, and—most significantly—exercised a profound influence as a third force in the 1986 election. Virulently anti-immigrant, Le Pen and the Front National were instrumental in removing the Socialists from government and in pressuring the RPR/UDF to adopt a platform calling for an end to automatic citizenship for children born in France to immigrant parents, for new visa regulations, and for increased identity checks by police in the streets. Complementing the Front National are a host of minor parties and factions which have been even more racist: SAC (Service d'Action Civique), Action Directe, PFN (Parti des Forces Nouvelles), FANE (Fédération de l'Action National Européan), a small neo-Nazi faction that has been replaced by FNE (Fédération des Nationalistes Européans), among many others. These are countered by an anti-racist organization called "SOS Racisme," which has held some impressive demonstrations.

Political scientists and sociologists are not sure where all of this will lead. France is in a state of great political, social, and economic change. What does seem clear is that racism has been increasing; it has become pervasive in French society; and it has permeated contemporary French politics.

NOTE

1. Jacqueline Costa-Lascoux and C. W. de Wenden-Didier, *Les travailleurs immigrés clandestins en France. Études migrations* (Rome, 1981), p. 7.

BIBLIOGRAPHY

Books

Ath-Messaoud, Malek, and Alain Gilette. *L'Immigration Algérienne en France*. Paris: Editions Entente, 1976.

Bastide, Roger, Françoise Morin, and François Raveau. *Les Haitiens en France*. Paris: Mouton, 1974.

Berger, John, and Jean Mohr. *A Seventh Man*. London: Writers & Readers Publishing Cooperative, 1975.

Castles, Stephen, and Godula Kosack. *Immigrant Workers and Class Structure in Western Europe*. New York: Oxford University Press, 1985.

Centre Information Etudes Migrations Méditerranées (CIEMM). *Des Jeunes Algériens en France*. Paris: CIEMM, 1981.

Gordon, David C. *The French Language and National Identity*. Paris: Mouton, 1978.

Gras, Christian, and Georges Livet. *Régions et régionalisme en France*. Paris: Presses Universitaires de France, 1977.

Haymann, Emmanuel. *Paris Judaica*. Paris: Editions Denoël, 1979.

Herfurth, Matthias, and Huberta Hogeweg-De Haart, eds. *Social Integration of Migrant Workers and Other Ethnic Minorities: A Documentation of Current Research*. Paris: Pergamon Press, 1982.

Kramer, Jane. *Unsettling Europe*. New York: Vintage Books, 1981.

Kubat, Daniel. *The Politics of Migration Policies*. New York: Center for Migration Studies, 1979.

Lefort, François. *Du Bidonville à l'expulsion*. Paris: CLEMM, 1980.

Mayo, Patricia Elton. *The Roots of Identity*. Plymouth: Clarke, Doble & Brendon, 1974.

Minces, Juliette. *Les travailleurs étrangers en France*. Paris: Editions du Sevil, 1973.

Parti Socialiste. *La France au Pluriel*. Paris: Editions Entente, 1981.

Petrella, Riccardo. *La Renaissance des cultures régionales en Europe*. Paris: Editions Entente, 1978.

Thomas, Eric-Jean. *Immigrant Workers in Europe: Their Legal Status*. Paris: UNESCO, 1982.

Reports

Adil, Jazouli. *La Nouvelle Génération de l'Immigration Maghrebine*. Paris: CIEMM, Ca. 1980.

Bastide, Henri. *Les enfants d'immigrés et l'enseignement français*. Paris: Institut National d'Etudes Démographiques (INED), 1982.

Bekkal, Khadidja. *Des êtres en négatif: Les jeunes de familles. Algériennes en France*. Vols. 1 & 2. Paris: CIEMM, 1981.

Borel, Jean. *La condition émigrée: Un combat pour l'homme*. Paris: CIEMM, October 1979.

Caillaux, François. *Mythe ou réalité? Notes sur les rétours aujourd'hui en Algérie*. Paris: CIEMM, 1978.

Centre de documentation sciences humaines. *Migrations internationales: Guide des sources documentaires en France*. Paris: CDSH, 1981.

CIEMM. *Immigration: Economie et démographie*. Paris: CIEMM, ca. 1979.

————. *Les cahiers faim—développement: Migrants, force de travail ou partenaires?* Paris: CIEMM, October 1980.

————. *Le gouvernement socialiste et la politique de l'immigration*. Paris: CIEMM, 1981.

————. *Fécondité et mortalité des étrangers en France*. Paris: CIEMM, July/August 1981.

————. *L'Italie; pays d'immigration*. Paris: CIEMM, September-October 1981.

————. *La nouvelle politique migratoire en France*. Paris: CIEMM, November-December 1981.

————. *Déviance et délinquance des jeunes d'origine étrangers*. Paris: CIEMM, January-February 1982.

Costa-Lascoux, J., and C. W. de Wenden-Didier. *Les travailleurs immigrés clandestins en France. Etudes migrations*. Rome: 1981.

Diaz, Manuel. *Retour au Portugal*. Paris: CIEMM, 1979.

Girard, Alain, and Jean Stoetzel. *Français et immigrés: L'attitude Française, l'adaptation des Italiens et des Polonais*. Paris: INED, 1953.

Groupe Oecumenique. *La population Algérienne en France: un communauté en suspens*. Paris: 1980.

INED. *Français et immigrés: nouveaux documents sur l'adaptation des Algériens, Italiens, et Polonais*. Paris: INED, 1954.

————. *Les immigrés du Maghreb: Etudes sur l'adaptation en milieu urbain*. Paris: INED, 1977.

————. *L'argent des immigrés*. Paris: INED, 1981.

Institut National de la Statistique et des Etudes Economique (INSEE). *Recensement général de la Population de 1975: Nationalité*.

Lafay, Nicole, and Daniel Richer. *L'immigration en France en 1979*. Paris: OCDE, 1980.

Levy, Michel Louis. *Les étrangers en France. Population et Sociétés*. Paris: INED, July-August 1980.

Mangin, Stanislas. *Travailleurs-immigrés: Le bilan*. Paris: CIEM, 1982.

Marange, James, and André Lebon. *L'insertion des jeunes d'origine étrangère dans la société française*. Paris: Ministère du Travail, May 1982.

Office National d'Immigration (ONI). *Statistiques de l'immigration*. Paris: 1980.

Perotti, A. *L'immigration en France: Elements pour une analyse*. Paris: CIEMM, 1980.

Pourcher, Guy. *Le Peuplement de Paris*. Paris: INED, 1964.

Power, Jonathan. *Western Europe's Migrant Workers*. London and Paris: Minority Rights Group, Report No. 28, 1978.

SOS Refoulement. *Le Chomage des immigrés*. Paris: 1981.
————. *Les jeunes étrangers en France*. Paris: June 1981.
Sécrétariat d'Etat aux Immigrés, ONI. *La nouvelle politique de l'immigration*. 1981.
Tapinos, Georges. *L'immigration étrangère en France*. Paris: INED, 1975.

Newspaper and Magazine Articles (by date)

Goshko, John. "North Europe Turns Hostile to Invading Migrants." *Toronto Star*, October 19, 1974.
"Migrant Workers Face Failure." Reuter, May 25, 1976.
"Ghetto Blacks Lingering Reminder of Colonialism." Associated Press (AP), June 29, 1977.
"French to Oust Illegal Aliens." Reuter, July 18, 1979.
"France May Limit Foreign Workers." Canadian Press (CP), February 27, 1980.
"Jobs Go Back to French." *Economist and Vancouver Sun*, August 12, 1980.
"French Leader Takes Step to Fight Anti-Semitism." AP, October 9, 1980.
McDonald, Marci. "The Workers on the Right." *Macleans*, October 13, 1980.
"Storm over Neo-Nazi Terror." *Newsweek*, October 20, 1980.
"France Pays Immigrants to Leave to Help Job Situation." Reuter, December 11, 1980.
"Young Africans Battle Prejudice of French Society." *Le Monde* and Reuter, January 7, 1981.
Ulbrich, Jeffrey. "Terror Tightens Its Grip on Paris." AP, July 24, 1982.
Swain, Jon. "Secret Army Linked to France's Underworld." *Toronto Star*, August 1, 1982.
"Six Slain as Gunmen Blast Jewish Restaurant in Paris." Reuter, August 9, 1982.
"Paris Gunmen Came to Kill Jews." *Toronto Star*, August 10, 1982.
"Bomb Rocks Paris One Day After Cafe Massacre." AP, August 11, 1982.
Marrus, Michael. "The Plight of French Jews." *Toronto Star*, August 14, 1982.
"Wave of Terror Spreads." *Globe and Mail*, August 14, 1982.
Utting, Gerald. "Bloody Wave Engulfs Paris." *Toronto Star*, August 15, 1982.
"Mitterrand Declares War on Terrorism." UPI-Reuter, August 18, 1982.
Weinberg, Henry, and Michael Marrus. "Paris Bomb Blast: Debating the Causes." *Toronto Star*, August 21, 1982.
McDonald, Marci. "Peace Approaches—and the Terror Spreads." *Macleans*, August 23, 1982.
Greeley, Andrew M. "French Hatred of Jews Is Old." *Winnipeg Sun*, September 3, 1982.
Dyer, Gwynne. "Integration of Immigrants into European Countries." *Saskatoon Star Phoenix*, September 17, 1982.
"Europe in Economic Sickbed." AP, September 29, 1982.
"Unions Boycott Appeal for Anti-Semitism Meetings." AP, October 10, 1980.
Boggio, Philippe. "France Becoming the Target of Middle East Terrorism." *Le Monde/Manchester Guardian*, November 7, 1982.
McDonald, Marci. "The Guest-worker Crisis." *Macleans*, April 11, 1983.
"Scholars Say Jews in France Gaining Increased Acceptance." Reuter, April 20, 1983.

Kaiser, Colin. "Ugly Waves of Racial Hatred Sweep Across Face of France." *Toronto Star*, December 18, 1983.

"Rising Racism on the Continent: Immigrants Face Economic Hardship and Increasing Prejudice." *Time*, February 6, 1984.

Tillier, Alan. "Paying Off Immigrants in France." *Toronto Star*, April 8, 1984.

Drainie, Bronwyn. "Hatred, Racism and Modern France." *Globe and Mail*, October 19, 1985.

Logeart, Agatha. "Marriage for Sale." *La Monde/Manchester Guardian*, November 24, 1985.

Fraser, John. "Racism is Cracking Europe's Veneer of Tolerance." *Globe and Mail*, March 5, 1986.

Laver, Ross. "Challenge from the Right," and Janssen, Brigid, "France's Growing Racism." *Macleans*, March 17, 1986.

INDIA

Raj S. Gandhi

Since India is a multicultural, multicaste, multilinguistic and multireligious society, the clarification of the terms "race" and "race relations" in India may be extremely difficult. However much one may like to avoid the problem altogether or dismiss the problem as irrelevant, still one must explain the group tensions that have existed in India for centuries.

A RACIAL CONTEXT

We cannot understand the reality of "race" and "race relations" in India without at once coming to grips with caste as one of the most fundamental categories of social differentiation and division in India. Social scientists, though aware that caste and race cannot be confused, do not preclude that the members of the upper castes may exhibit race-like behavioral characteristics in their interactions with the low and the very low castes, and conversely, that in South Africa and Southern United States, Negro-white relations may reflect many castelike characteristics. Here, one should not confuse similarity with identity. However, an immediate question of importance within the Indian context is to find out how caste came to be identified with race. It might also be asked whether in the earlier period of the formation of caste, there was any correlation between the two and how race affects the patterns of interactions in contemporary India. For this purpose, we will briefly examine the racial theory of the origin of caste.

HISTORICAL BACKGROUND: CASTE-RACE CONNECTION

It is not merely a matter of historical accident that a racial factor was a major contributor to the origin of caste in India. Nonetheless, some social scientists strongly disagree that caste and race in Indian context had anything to do with each other at any time, instead maintaining that caste is a culturally unique phenomenon specific to Hindu culture alone.[1] But such a reaction does not serve any pragmatic purpose as it negates any theoretical and empirical comparability of the phenomena exhibiting similar characteristics.[2]

The ghost of caste has haunted the collective memories of the Hindus for 3,000 years, and, though it is an important aspect of their collective conscience, only the linguistic usages of this very ancient people provide any significant insight into the origin of the phenomenon. The Indian language, especially the ancient Sanskrit, has no equivalent of the term "caste." The Portuguese used the term in the sixteenth century, calling the exclusive group of the Hindus *castus*. The Latin root *castus* means "pure," and the Portuguese derivation of *castus* describes "pure blood groups," the term they applied to describe "the Hindu caste groups." Even today, when one asks Hindus which caste they belong to, they may often take it to mean *varna* or *jati*. Both are Sanskrit words. *Varna* means "color," which suggests a person's possible skin color, and when applied to groups, a *varna* scheme suggests the hypothetical racial classification used by the people themselves. Similarly, one meaning of *jati* is race, and it refers to a racial group within which a person is born. It is similar to the membership acquired through *jus sanguinus*. Thus, both terms in their broadest meanings refer to the exclusive racial groups of people in which they acquire their membership by virtue of their birth. Such groups may be further interpreted to mean people who have similar physical attributes. Laypersons further stereotyped them to stand for the groups with common sociocultural characteristics.

The early connection between caste and race is rooted in Indian written (scriptural) history, which may be said to have started with the invasion by the Indo-Europeans (also referred to as Indo-Aryans) around the second millennium B.C. The people who called themselves Aryans (a Sanskrit word, meaning the civilized as opposed to Anaryans, the uncivilized, referring to the original inhabitants of India) are described as the fair-skinned Caucasians, who, when they entered India (probably from the Northwest), came into conflict with the dark-skinned aboriginals. The late professor G. S. Ghurye, basing his arguments on the *varna* system which emerged out of racial contact and conflict, alludes to two contrasting and clashing *varnas* in the sacred Vedic literature as the Aryas and the Dasas (Aryas meaning the masters and the Dasas, the slaves).[3] They betray not only racial indications in the form of their fair and dark skin colors, respectively, but also their superior and inferior socioeconomic statuses based on ownership of mode of production and the political conditions of the time. The tall, fair-skinned masters were the conquerors, and the dark aboriginals (probably exhibiting proto-Australoid physical characteristics) were the conquered serfs.

It is in the Rig-Vedic literature (1,000 B.C.) that we find references to racial distinction, as well as to the Dasas (the serfs or the slaves), the subjugated indigenous inhabitants, as "dark and ill-favored, bull-lipped, snub-nosed, worshippers of the Phallus, and hostile of speech."[4] The greater stress on the purity of blood, the hardening of social divisions as the Aryans settled among the darker aboriginal Dasas, and the intermarriage of the women of the Dasas with the privileged Aryan men led to the formation of the hierarchical four divisions (referred to as the *varnas*) by about 600 B.C.: the priests (the Brahmins); the warrior-rulers (the Kshatriyas-Rajanyas); the peasant-traders (the Vaishyas); and the slave-serfs (the Shudras). How different skin color could be finely graded is only a matter of speculation, but the divisions may be an outcome of interbreeding, the division of labor, the ownership of means of production, and the emergence of a propertyless class at the bottom of the rank-order drawn from the darker aboriginals, and still below them a slowly rising category of the pariahs, the later-day untouchables.[5]

Origin of the Untouchables

The outcastes served the Aryans in menial and dirty tasks, and were regarded as quite outside their social order. They were also referred to as the Chandalas (the carriers and the cremators of corpses), the leatherworkers, and the basket-makers. They were forced to reside outside the villages of the Aryans. They were given special quarters, and they were to be dressed in discarded garments, eat food from broken vessels, and wear only iron ornaments.[6] Although the idea of untouchability was first given expression in connection with the Shudras and the sacrifices performed by the Brahmins, Ghurye also hypothesizes that the untouchables were a degraded group of aborigines. The Brahminic literature of the post-Vedic period reports a great consolidation of the Brahmin group. The idea that an impure person would impart pollution by his or her touch and even by near approach to the members of the exclusive "racial" groups finds clear expression in the law texts of this period, generally with reference to the low of the lowest.[7]

In the Hindu myth of the Primeval Man, the Brahmins are reported to have issued from the mouth of God while the Shudras from the feet of the Lord.[8] In the *Bhagvad Gita* itself, the Lord sanctifies the system, attributing the low birth to material nature and work performed by the person.[9] The top and the bottom of the rank-order are more or less fixed; the relationship between the two exhibits almost the same characteristics as between Negroes and whites. The permanent condition of servitude is attached to the Shudras and the untouchables; they should neither take to education nor accumulate wealth, nor should they come into contact with the Brahmins as the Brahmins would be defiled by their touch. Capital punishment awaits the Shudra if he violates the Brahmin female, but the Brahmin may escape with mild negative sanction should he have sexual intercourse with the Shudra female.[10]

RECENT DEVELOPMENTS: FROM RACE TO CASTE

Herbert Risely, an outstanding spokesman of the racial theory of caste, based his hypothesis on the caste-*varna*-racial endogamy of the conquered group and the sexual exploitation of the subjugated by means of hypergamy. Hypergamy leads to the unintended consequences of producing halfbreeds, much as happened with respect to the mulattoes of the Southern United States, the Anglo-Indians of India, and the Burghers of Ceylon. The ultimate result is a very complicated caste system in which differences in language, worship, food, and occupation are exaggerated to further enforce endogamy.[11] N. K. Dutt,[12] John C. Nesfield,[13] and G. S. Ghurye[14] accept modified versions of Risely's theory. But since Risely was convinced of a strong relationship between caste and race, he attempted to correlate shape of nose, skin color, and racial types of the Indian population and grouped the Indians into Aryan, Dravidian, Aryo-Dravidian, and Monglo-Dravidian. Curiously, these appear to be the linguistic or regional categories, defeating the purpose of a physcial anthropologist.[15] B. S. Guha's attempt to identify six principal racial elements in the Indian population (Negrito, Proto-Australoid, Mediterranean, Western Brachycephal, Palae-Mongoloid, and Nordic) is perhaps more successful.[16] Andre Beteille believes that the Proto-Australoid and Palae-Mongoloid have some correspondence with social divisions in India, the Proto-Australoid being well represented in the aboriginal population of Central and Southern India and the Palae-Mongoloid in Assam and Himalayan foothills.[17]

Color Consciousness

How does the anthropological classification of Indian races correspond with different castes, and to what degree do the differences enter into patterns of interaction? The first question has been answered by Beteille as follows:

If we take skin colour as our criterion, two sets of differences appear to be of particular importance: these are regional and caste-wise differences. The inhabitants of the Northern states, particularly Punjab, Jammu and Kashmir, Rajasthan and parts of Uttar Pradesh are on the whole fairer than those of the

Southern states. Indeed, many North Indians have a vague prejudice against South Indians on account of their dark skin colour.[18]

Similarly, people from the topmost castes are generally fairer than the untouchables. Take, for example, the Nagar Brahmins of Gujarat, the Chitpavan Brahmins of Maharashtra, the Kashmiri Brahmins, and the Saraswat Brahmins of Mangalore. They are generally light-skinned. The untouchables or the pariahs of Madras are usually dark-skinned. But there are many exceptions to this generality in which the untouchables may be fairer than the Brahmins and the Brahmins may be darker than the untouchables. Furthermore, "regional and caste-wise differences often cut across each other. People from the lower castes in North India tend to be on the whole darker than those from some of the highest castes in the South."[19]

With regard to the second question, though the correlations between caste and race do not appear to be significant, they do create certain stereotypes and prejudices, at times recalling the collective memories of the past of Indians. These stereotypes reflect the high social values attached to such physical traits as light skin, tall stature, and finely shaped (sharp) nose. One only has to scan through the matrimonial advertisements in Indian newspapers to prove the explicit preference for such physical features. The Indians' color consciousness is reflected not only in Indian folklore, proverbs, mythologies, and advertisements, but also in social action. For example, the families of dark-skinned girls have to pay a considerable amount of dowry for marriage. The dowry problem creates considerable tension and conflict both within and outside their families. But nowhere in India does one find an organized "racial" conflict based on sharp physical differences and racial antagonisms as one finds between the Negroes and the whites in South Africa. Nor have such differences become the basis of political action.

Varna, Caste, Jati, and "Race"

If we take into account the centuries of Indian history, the intermixture of the Hindus with non-Hindus, hypergamy, sexual exploitation, and the flexibility of the caste system in adjusting to the changing situation without destroying itself, one is struck by the persistence of the memories of "racial" divisions and color consciousness, which made inequality and hierarchy the basic principles of social order.[20] Granted that the "racial" divisions in the strict sense of the term are not descriptively relevant in understanding the Indian situation, how do we understand varna, caste, and jati as hierarchically ordered social divisions? Moreover, in what sense does the behavior of the upper castes exhibit racelike characteristics toward what the Indian government now identifies as the "scheduled castes" (the category that includes untouchables)?

In its ideal typical form, castes or *jatis* form a hierarchy. They are endogamous, and they practice traditional occupations. They do not dine together. The upper castes may enjoy some extra privileges, but the lower castes suffer from disabilities as they practice "despised" or "polluting" occupations. In its extreme form this differentiation is manifested in the practice of untouchability; hence, social and ritual distance is maintained from the untouchables. They are segregated and discriminated against. Although some deviations from the ideal depiction of caste are permitted, there is no disagreement on the degraded position of untouchables.

More recently, M. N. Srinivas has maintained that *varna* and *jati* are two models of the caste system operating in India, *varna* being a Vedic classification and *jati* a local system.[21] But, according to Srinivas, all *jatis* are interdependent. It is not that he is unaware of the exploitation of untouchables, but highlighting the interdependence of all castes (*jatis*) precludes the possibility of analyzing discriminatory racelike practices against the *varna*. Although the *jati* may be a local variant of the system, the fitting of *jatis* into the four *varnas* is the Indians' centuries-old indigenous device for highlighting the social position of the Shudras and excluding the untouchables from the scheme.

The classification of the Shudras into a new category of "the scheduled castes," also referred to as "the deprived classes" or "the backward classes," is a relatively recent phenomenon, having emerged mainly as a result of governmental policy and legal enactments for the removal of certain disabilities.[22] However, the extreme disabilities imposed on untouchables is akin to racelike prejudice and discrimination. Witness the following: the untouchables could be served neither by clean Brahmins nor by barbers nor by tailors; neither could they use public conveniences such as wells nor schools, nor could they enter Hindu temples, nor serve caste Hindus, nor come in close contact with them for the fear of possible pollution.[23] Although the government of India has adopted an active policy of improving the lot of untouchables, its commitment is more on paper than in practice. All educated Indians overtly agree that the racelike prejudice against untouchables ought to be removed, but their covert behavior betrays their true feelings. The covert behavior relates to the attitude of discrimination against untouchables.

Caste-Race Comparisons

Indeed, taking the term "caste" analytically rather than descriptively, Kingsley Davis finds strong parallels between the social position of untouchables and the Negroes in the United States:

In the South as everyone knows, Negroes and whites constitute two castes set apart. Nearly all the features of Indian caste are perceptible in the relations of these two groups. Outstanding among these is the ideology of pollution. In both India and America this magical concept serves to justify the caste structure. It is somehow contaminating to sit beside a Negro, to touch his hand, or to drink from the same cup.... Toilet, eating, hotel, and nearly all other public facilities must be separate for the two groups. The fundamental rule is that Negroes and whites shall never associate in any relation of intimacy that implies equality. Consequently, most of the restrictions imposed on the untouchables in India can be roughly matched with reference to the Negroes in the southern part of the United States.[24]

The controversy concerning parallels between caste and race has preoccupied many sociologists, including Oliver C. Cox, whose views are opposite to those of Davis. Cox maintains that the Indian caste system is a coherent social system based on the principle of inequality, while the American "color bar" contradicts the equalitarian system within which it occurs and of which it is a kind of disease.[25] G. D. Berreman's opinion that Cox has a very distorted, unrealistic view of Indian caste, as derived from the ideal functioning of the caste system rather than the firsthand experience, coincides with Davis's insistence on comparability between caste in India and the United States.[26] This controversy has made many scholars take sides. Gunnar Myrdal has maintained that "not race but racial beliefs are fundamental to the rigid barrier."[27] He emphasizes the parallels between the race situation and the caste system.

The symposium on caste and race sponsored by the 1966 Ciba Foundation compares the Indian caste system with racial stratification, feudalism and slavery in Europe and America, and pariah castes in Japan.[28] Although no clear conclusion emerges from such comparisons, one is tempted to quote Louis Dumont,

the proclamation of equality has burst asunder a mode of distinction centered upon the social, but in which physical, cultural and social characteristics were indiscriminately mixed. To reaffirm inequality, the underlying dualism demanded that physical characteristics be brought to the fore. While in India heredity is an attribute of status, the racist attributes status to "race."[29]

PUBLIC POLICY AND LAWS: PREJUDICE CONTINUES

This brings us to the social, cultural, economic, and political consequences of the Indian caste system, especially the treatment of untouchables (now subsumed under "the scheduled castes") against whom the race-like prejudice is exhibited by the upper castes. The economic exploitation of untouchable laborers, in both the villages and cities of India, has been widespread. The high-caste Hindu landlords try to make village outcastes work for nothing, or they pay them the lowest possible wages. In cities where exchange or contractual relations have developed, the wages may be on a par with those of other castes, but untouchables, if engaged in manual work, are given the lowest possible work. Add to this violence and terror against them and outcastes may refuse to work only at the cost of their lives.

The Indian Constitution (1950) lists the fundamental rights of a citizen. One right covered by Article 17 states that untouchability is abolished, its practice in any form to be forbidden, and that the enforcement of any disability arising out of untouchability will be an offense punishable in accordance with the law. In 1955, the Indian Parliament passed the Untouchability Offences Act. The act outlaws the enforcement of disabilities "on the ground of untouchability" in regard to, *inter alia*, entrance and worship at temples, access to shops and restaurants, practice of occupations and trades, use of water resources, places of public resort and accommodation, public conveyances, hospitals, educational institutions, construction and occupation of residential premises, holding of religious ceremonies and processions, and use of jewelry and finery. The imposition of disabilities was declared to be a crime punishable by a fine up to Rs. 500 (U.S. $70), or imprisonment up to six months.

But the passing of law is one thing and its practice another. In 1961, throughout India, some 65 million violations of this act were reported, and in 1971 80 million. The failure of the law is indicated by the fact that there have been only 700 convictions. Far more disturbing is the fact that the police themselves sometimes carry out unauthorized raids on the hamlets of untouchables and use violence. In view of the news of tensions, terror, violence, and conflict reported from all parts of India between 1971 and 1981, the rate of change in the racist belief and the practice of untouchability could be said to be extremely slow.

SUMMARY AND CONCLUSIONS

Despite the differences between caste and race, the racial context of caste is apparent. There are many parallels between caste and race, especially when one looks at the social-psychological or behavioral-attitudinal similarities. The behavior and the attitudes of the high castes toward the low caste untouchables betray racelike prejudice. The theory of the racial origin of caste lends further support to our hypothesis. The indigenous device of articulating *varna* and *jati* used by Indians indirectly demonstrates that the untouchables are excluded from mainstream Indian society. The color consciousness of Indians symbolically signifies the past history of racial conflict between physically different groups. Although the anthropological racial classification has no direct relevance to the Indians' social or political action, the governmental policy of abolishing untouchability by the enactment of laws has failed in practice. This failure suggests that the prejudice has deeper historical and ideological roots.

R. A. Schermerhorn's[30] recent attempt to subsume "the scheduled castes" under "ethnic minorities" does not enhance our understanding of the social situation in India as the term "ethnic minority" is also used to designate other communal groups such as the Sikhs and the Muslims in India.[31] Both groups have been making newspaper headlines lately, and both are numerical minorities when compared with the caste Hindus. Although the Muslims constitute more than 10 percent of the total Indian population, the Sikhs hardly total 2 percent. But the Hindu-Muslim conflict which surfaced in violence and bloodshed in Gujarat and Kashmir during 1985 and 1986 has deeper roots in Indian society. The hostility is more the result of religious differences, though the Muslims at times overtly assert the feelings of belonging to a different "race." Similarly, the violence of the Sikhs can be attributed neither to anti-caste nor to anti-Brahmin feelings. It is mistakenly attributed to the militancy of the "Sikh race." It is politically motivated, and, unlike the politics of the Muslims, the Sikh movement has an historically passing interest.

Violence has always been a part of Indian society, despite its public preaching of nonviolence. The mosaic of multiple castes, races, languages, and religions gives one the impression of tolerance and coexistence; hence, the political leaders and the intellectual elites alike enthusiastically advocate the ideology of integration.[32] But hidden beneath the cloak of coexistence is the problem of conflict and separation which asserts itself in the name of caste or race.

NOTES

1. Oliver Cromwell Cox, *Caste, Class and Race in India* (New York: Doubleday, 1948), p. 423.

2. Kingsley Davis, "Intermarriage in Caste Society," *American Anthropologist* 43 (1947): 386–87.

3. G. S. Ghurye, *Caste and Race in India* (Bombay: Popular Prakashan, 1969), p. 176.

4. A. L. Basham, *The Wonder That Was India* (New York: Grove Press, 1969), p. 32.

5. Ibid., p. 35.

6. Ibid., p. 145.

7. Ibid., p. 92.

8. Pandharinath H. Prabhu, *Hindu Social Organization* (Bombay: Popular Prakashan, 1961), p. 286.

9. A. C. Bhaktivedanta, *Bhagvad-Gita as It Is* (New York: Collier Books, 1972), p. 35.

10. Ghurye, *Caste and Race*, p. 79.

11. Herbert Risely, *The People of India* (London: Thacker, Spink & Co., 1915), p. 277.

12. N. K. Dutt, *Origin and Growth of Caste in India* (London: Kegan Paul, Trench, Trubner, 1931), p. 5.

13. John C. Nesfield, *Notes and Queries on Anthropology* (London: Routledge & Kegan Paul, 1951).

14. Ghurye, *Caste and Race*, p. 163.

15. Andre Beteille, *Castes: Old and New* (New York: Asia Publishing House, 1969), p. 38.

16. B. S. Guha, *Racial Elements in the Indian Population*, Oxford Pamphlets on Indian Affairs, No. 22 (Bombay: 1944).

17. Beteille, *Castes*, p. 38.

18. Ibid., p. 40.

19. Ibid.

20. Louis Dumont, *Homo Hierarchicus* (Chicago: University of Chicago Press, 1974), p. 21.

21. M. N. Srinivas, "Some Reflections on the Nature of Caste Hierarchy," *Contributions to Indian Sociology, New Series* 18, No. 2 (1984): 153–54.

22. Andre Beteille, "The Future of the Backward Classes: The Competing Demands of Status and Power," in Philip Mason, ed., *India and Ceylon: Unity and Diversity* (London: Oxford University Press, 1967), p. 85.

23. Kingsley Davis, *Human Society* (New York: Macmillan, 1966), p. 380.

24. Ibid., pp. 385–86.

25. Cox, *Caste, Class and Race*, pp. 427–35.

26. Gerald D. Berreman, "Correspondence: Caste, Racism and 'Stratification'," in Louis Dumont and D. Pocock, eds., *Contributions to Indian Sociology* (The Hague: Mouton & Co., 1962), No. 6, p. 123.

27. G. Myrdal, "Chairman's Introduction" in Anthony de Reuck and Julie Knight, eds., *Caste and Race: Comparative Approaches* (London: J & A Churchill Ltd., 1968), p. 2.

28. Ibid.

29. Louis Dumont, "Caste, Racism and 'Stratification'," in Louis Dumont and D. Pocock, eds., *Contributions to Indian Sociology*, No. 5 (The Hague: Mouton & Co., 1961), p. 40.

30. R. A. Schermerhorn, *Ethnic Plurality in India* (Tucson: University of Arizona Press, 1978), pp. 13–17.

31. Ibid., p. 34.

32. I. P. Desai, "Should 'Caste' Be the Basis for Recognizing Backwardness?" *Economic and Political Weekly* 19, No. 28 (1984): 1106.

BIBLIOGRAPHY

Basham, A. L. *The Wonder That Was India*. New York: Grove Press, 1969.

Berreman, Gerald D. "Correspondence: Caste, Racism and 'Stratification'." In *Contributions to Indian Sociology*, edited by Louis Dumont and David Pocock. The Hague: Mouton & Co., 1962, No. 6, pp. 122–25.

Beteille, Andre. "The Future of the Backward Classes: The Competing Demands of Status and Power." In *India and Ceylon: Unity and Diversity*, edited by Philip Mason. London: Oxford University Press, 1967, pp. 83–120.

———. *Castes: Old and New: Essays in Social Structure and Social Stratification*. New York: Asia Publishing House, 1969.

Bhaktivedanta, A. C. *Bhagvad-Gita as It Is*. New York: Collier Books, 1972.

Cox, Oliver C. *Caste, Class and Race in India: A Study in Dynamics*. New York: Doubleday, 1948.

Davis, Kingsley. "Intermarriage in Caste Society." *American Anthropologist* 43 (1947): 386–87.

———. *Human Society*. New York: Macmillan, 1966.

Desai, I. P. "Should 'Caste' Be the Basis for Recognizing Backwardness?" *Economic and Political Weekly* 19, No. 28 (1984): 1106–16.

Dumont, Louis. "Caste, Racism and 'Stratification': Reflections of a Social Anthropologist." In *Contributions to Indian Sociology*, edited by Louis Dumont and David Pocock. The Hague: Mouton & Co., 1961, No. 5, 22–43.

———. *Homo Hierarchicus: The Caste System and Its Implications*. Chicago: University of Chicago Press, 1974.

Dutt, N. K. *Origin and Growth of Caste in India*. London: Kegan Paul, Trench, Trubner, 1931.

Ghurye, G. S. *Caste and Race in India*. Bombay: Popular Prakashan, 1969.

Guha, B. S. *Racial Elements in the Indian Population*. Oxford Pamphlets on Indian Affairs, No. 22. Bombay: 1944.

Myrdal, Gunnar. "Chairman's Introduction." In *Caste and Race in Comparative Approaches*, edited by Anthony de Reuck and Julie Knight. London: J & A. Churchill Ltd., 1968, pp. 1–4.

Nesfield, John C. *Notes and Queries on Anthropology*. London: Routledge & Kegal Paul, 1951.

Prabhu, Pandharinath H. *Hindu Social Organization*. Bombay: Popular Prakashan, 1961.

Reuck, Anthony de, et al. *Caste and Race: Comparative Approaches*. London: J & A Churchill Ltd., 1968.

Risely, Herbert. *The People of India*. London: Thacker, Spink & Co., 1915.

Schermerhorn, R. A. *Ethnic Plurality in India*. Tucson: University of Arizona Press, 1978.

Srinivas, M. N. "Some Reflections on the Nature of Caste Hierarchy." *Contributions to Indian Sociology, New Series* 18, No. 2 (1984): 151–67.

JAPAN

Yung-Hwan Jo

A RACIAL CONTEXT

Korean residents form a large minority in Japan. If the term "race" is a biological and physical concept, while the term "ethnicity" denotes cultural and social characteristics, those Koreans should be called an ethnic minority. As in the case of the Jews in Nazi Germany, however, ethnicity can be treated as "racial" where it is consciously deemed to be so.[1] Children born of Japanese married to Koreans are called "mixed blood children," as are those born of a Japanese and a Caucasian, or of a Japanese and a black.

Though observable differences between Koreans and Japanese are due to differences in cultural heritage, many Japanese think that most of the Koreans are physically distinguishable from them, at least more so than in the case of former outcasts called Burakumin. Anthropologically, Koreans and Japanese have a considerable overlap of ancestral stock. But in the common Japanese perception, Koreans are different: they have greater facial height than the Japanese, are somewhat taller and sturdier, and have no facial and body hair as is noticeable in many Japanese. This is partly because the Japanese race is somewhat admixed with peoples of Malayo-Polynesian background. This does not apply to Koreans.[2] Not unlike Jews, many Japanese adhere to the myth of Japanese uniqueness as a "race," sustained from the beginning of humankind as ordained by Shinto scriptures.

Koreans in Japan can be classified as both a racial and an ethnic minority. If they are viewed merely as an ethnic minority, Koreans are outnumbered by indigenous Burakumin and once-conquered Okinawans, and are not the largest ethnic minority as is often asserted in the literature dealing with Japanese minorities.[3] (See Table 15.) When em-

Table 15
Minority Groups in Japan*

Name (Identity)	Size
Burakumin (indigenous)	2,600,000
Okinawans (conquered)	1,000,000
Ainu (aboriginal)	25,000
Koreans (aliens) +(illegal and unregistered)	642,727[b] – 692,700[c] +30,000 – 50,000[d] or 40,000 – 50,000[e]
Others[f] (survivors of atomic bomb, naturalized foreigners, and interracial offsprings)	500,000

[a]The total represents about 4 percent of the population of Japan, which was estimated to be 118,600,000 in 1982.

[b]Japanese Ministry of Justice estimate, December 1984.

[c]Republic of Korea Ministry of Foreign Affairs estimate, June 1985.

[d]Government census estimate.

[e]Japanese Ministry of Justice estimate, cited in *Mintoren* 32 (1981), p. 7.

[f]Cited from *Japanese Minorities*, MRG Report no. 3 (London: 1983), p. 3.

barrassed by the mistreatment of the Korean minority in Japan, Japanese officials or academicians often claim that the Koreans are a "foreign" nationality in Japan, implying that, as in many countries, foreigners cannot expect to enjoy the same privileges as Japanese citizens. Technically, such a view is a basis for legal defense, but it is not sufficient grounds for a discriminatory Japanese public policy toward the Korean minority.

DETERIORATION IN HISTORICAL RELATIONS

The very existence of the Korean ethnic group in Japan is the direct outgrowth of the Japanese colonization policy toward Korea. Historical relations between the two interacting peoples have influenced their perceptions of each other and subsequent mutual interactions to a large degree.

The interaction of Koreans and Japanese dates back to the period when concepts of "Koreans" and "Japanese" did not exist. In the early fourth century, the Japanese population was significantly affected by an influx of people from the Korean peninsula. By the end of the seventh century, more than one-third of the Japanese nobility claimed Chinese or Korean descent.[4] Those from China and Korea taught the majority of Japanese the rich Indian and Chinese cultural traditions.

Japanese pirates who ravaged some Korean coastal towns from the thirteenth century onward were followed by Toyotomi Hideyoshi, who plundered Korea for seven years from 1592 to 1598. The military campaign left large areas of Korean civilization in ruins and imbued Koreans with an early memory of Japanese brutality.

In 1905, after winning the war against Russia, Japan forced Korea to sign the Korean–Japan Security Treaty which facilitated Japanese annexation of Korea in 1910. The peninsula remained under military rule for a decade while Japanese businessmen and usurers purchased Korean farming lands cheaply. Lands and forests owned by the previous Korean (Lee) dynasty and its government were confiscated.

To make a living, many displaced farmers migrated to Japan or, in some cases, to Hawaii, Manchuria, and Siberia. During the 1920s, the so-called rice-increasing program increased the financial burden of those farmers who were still on their land; many of them escaped their financial problems by immigrating to Japan.

These farmers were joined by laborers who were enticed to Japan to operate machines in the wake of two waves of industrialization, one after World War I and another following the Japanese intrusion into Manchuria and China proper from 1931 to 1938.

Between these two periods of labor influx, a great earthquake hit the Kanto area on September 1, 1923, when Japan was in the midst of an economic depression. Right-wing fanatics started rumors that Koreans were setting fires. Several thousand Koreans were stabbed to death during the week after the earthquake, which further hardened mutual dislike between the two historical brothers.

The 1939–45 period can be characterized as a stage of forcible movement of Koreans to Japan, which a Japanese author called "a modern version of the old slave trade."[5] Laborers were forced to come to Japan to work in mines and factories to produce war materials and construct airfields, and so on. About 1.1 million Koreans were brought to Japan, including about 110,000 who were drafted for direct military service.[6]

The influx of farmers and laborers to Japan increased the size of the Korean minority to 2.4 million by the end of World War II. Immediately after the war, rapid repatriation reduced the Korean population to a little over 500,000 by 1950. (See Table 16.) Most returned to South Korea, their place of origin. The status of Japan's Koreans shifted from "citizens" to "foreigners" with the San Francisco Peace Treaty of 1952. It was also affected by the political division of Korea into two halves.

Table 16
Number of Koreans in Japan, 1909–1985, Selected Years

Year	Number
1909	790
1919	28,272
1920	40,755
1925	133,710
1930	419,009
1938	799,865
1940	1,241,315
1945	2,400,000
1950	544,903
1959	607,533
1974	643,096
1978	659,026
1980	663,183
1985	692,700-642,727 [a]

[a]See Table 15.

Sources: Association of Fighting for Acquisition of Human Rights for Koreans in Japan, *Koreans in Japan* (Ethnic Minority Problem), October 1979: Kitakyushu, *Japan*, p. 4; Homusho Tokei of Korean Alien Residents since 1952, cited in Kwangkyu Lee, *Jaeil Hankukin* [Koreans in Japan] (Seoul: Ilchokak, 1983), p. 81.

Prior to 1945, the Japanese government made some unsustained efforts to improve the working and living conditions of Koreans with its assimilation policy. However, most Koreans resented the policy because it imposed Japanese as the official language in all schools and forced all Koreans to adopt Japanese names. When Japan surrendered in 1945, it lost its chief motive for the policy. To the Japanese, Koreans seemed to swagger about as if they were "nationals of victorious nations"; this inflamed their racial hatred. In the books of Japanese right-wing extremists, Koreans were marked as victims on that day of "freedom" when the Occupation Army left Japan.[7]

Soon after the war, an exclusion policy was introduced which forced Koreans out of the commercial associations. This was followed by a policy of deportation and repatriation of undesirable Koreans as a means of reducing the Japanese "headache" and burden.[8] In 1959, the Japanese government was pressured from within to enter an agreement with North Korea in 1959 that resulted in the repatriation of more than 100,000 of

Japan's Koreans by 1984, and the number of Koreans in Japan was further reduced.[9]

JAPANESE EXCLUSIVENESS AND RACISM

Today, many Japanese parents employ private investigators to inquire into the ancestral roots of prospective sons- or daughters-in-law to avoid marital alliance with anyone of Korean or Burakumin descent.[10] Such overt "racism" or "ethnocentrism" can be traced back to Japanese racist tendencies, as well as to the deteriorating historical developments noted above.

Since the eighth century, there has been no major infusion of new blood into Japan, and the Japanese have developed a picture of themselves as a racially distinct and "pure" group. The theme of uniqueness and homogeneousness often appears in Japanese literature. This was probably aided by the efforts of prewar leaders to mobilize "irrational attachments" to Japan's national polity (*kokutai*), and reinforced partly by the earliest Japanese chronicles and a long seclusion when there were few contacts with foreigners and few records of miscegenation. The Japanese concept of their uniqueness is a "deeply racist concept," according to Professor Edwin Reischauer, an eminent student of Japanese history.[11]

Two recent examples might be cited from a classic publication on the subject written by Changsoo Lee and George DeVos.[12] The popular view that the Japanese are racially unique was strengthened by a best selling book by a Japanese otolaryngologist who demonstrated that the appreciation of insect sounds tends to be the peculiar province of the Japanese. This book, *The Brain of the Japanese People* (1978), emphasized race in a study that dealt with the "Japanese" pattern of linguistic sensitivity.[13] The Koreans, who are native speakers of Japanese, would have shown the same pattern but were ignored. To the author of this book, being Japanese is purely a matter of race and nothing else. Another book written by an international businessman and essayist, *Facial Physiognomy of the Japanese* (1976), epitomizes the myths of Japanese homogeneity which are naively embedded in many Japanese commentaries on their ethnicity.[14]

Herman Kahn once suggested that in some ways Japan is "the most racist nation in the world."[15] The Japanese do not normally notice that they discriminate against Koreans or Chinese because the discrimination is so thorough that the issue does not usually arise. The Japanese could not imagine having a general of Korean parentage while the Chinese could easily do so.

Reischauer argues that the Japanese racial attitude is "not so much a matter of superiority, that is, of equality, but a difference in kind."[16] It might appear to be so to some Caucasians in Japan, where marriage with American whites is preferred to marriage with Koreans. During the war, however, marriage with other Asians was preferred.

Many Asians, especially Koreans, who have experienced the Japanese sense of racial superiority would argue that a major source of Japanese contempt for the Korean "race" has its roots in the "race colonialism" of the Meiji era. As Japan began its policy of colonial expansion to Taiwan and Korea, the peoples in those colonies were pictured by Tokyo as being lazy, inferior, and incapable of self-rule, and were being assimilated as a favor to them. Having defeated China and Russia, Meiji Japan was intoxicated by the discovery of new sources of power, which seemed to provide it with a new meaning of Japanese race against other races by testifying to the superiority of the Japanese. The superiority myth and racial colonialism made the Koreans themselves, in many cases, have a low impression of themselves and their culture.[17]

While Japan has become a leading industrial democracy of the world since the war, the problem of discrimination against its Korean minority is still pervasive. Although some ameliorative steps have been taken in the last decade, more than the degraded minorities like to recognize, the Japanese sense of racial difference, a sort of racist caste type of thinking, remains embedded in Japanese society. For example, when a Japanese mother disciplines her baby, she will often say something like "Korean babies urinate; not Japanese babies," or "Korean babies have runny noses; not Japanese babies."[18]

According to a survey conducted by two Japanese anthropologists regarding Japanese views of thirteen races and ethnic groups, Koreans ranked lowest next to blacks and mixed children of blacks and Japanese.[19] Their preferences were in the order of Europeans, Americans, Russians, and other Asians. However, Japanese support of Koreans' naturalization was greater than that of other Asians such as Filipinos, Indonesians, and Indians. Although Japanese racial discrimination against Koreans has the same emotional and attitudinal basis as the racism against Jews in Nazi Germany and blacks in the United States, as noted earlier, they hardly recognize their own racial discrimination.

THE IMPROVING LEGAL STATUS OF KOREANS

In the Japanese legal system, there is no specific concept of "citizen" (*shimin*) or "citizen's rights" (*shimin ken*) as such; the term "Japanese national" (*Nihon kokumin*) is used instead. It follows that the basic human rights that should be guaranteed to any human being are guaranteed exclusively to the Japanese. In 1965 when the Japan-Korea treaty was drawn up, Ikegami Tsutomi, an official of the Justice Ministry, said in reference to Japanese legal treatment of foreigners: "We are free to boil and eat them or fry and eat them."[20]

He must have had Koreans in mind since 82 percent of Japan's alien residents are, in fact, Koreans. (Eighty-five percent of these are second- and third-generation Koreans born in Japan.)[21] The 1965 treaty included "The Agreement on Permanent Resident Rights," which applies to (1) those who have been residing in Japan continuously since August 15, 1945; (2) those who were born in Japan since that date; and (3) children born after January 16, 1971, of parents who had received permanent residence status under the preceding categories. As the Japanese government was reluctant to promise permanent residency to successive generations of Koreans, it agreed to hold consultations, if requested by Seoul, after 1990.

The South Korean negotiators for the 1965 treaty placed less importance on the legal question of Koreans in Japan because they were preoccupied with securing financial concessions from Japan for the urgent task of rebuilding Korea's deteriorating economy.[22] Thus, the treaty has some shortcomings. Those who fail to acquire acceptance of nationality by the South Korean government are not eligible for permanent residence in Japan.[23] Therefore, those who pledge loyalty to the North Korean government are excluded and have become legally "stateless" temporary residents since Pyongyang has no diplomatic relations with Tokyo. In addition, any Koreans of permanent residence who commit acts of insurrection or political acts prejudicial to the interests of Japan, and those who are sentenced to prison for more than seven years (three years in narcotics cases), are subject to deportation.

The Japanese Nationality law, based on the principle of *jus sanguinis*, has provisions for naturalization for which all Korean residents in Japan are technically eligible. Naturalization means entitlement to the same rights and privileges as a native-born "pure" Japanese. The number of naturalized persons is increasing (estimated to be 140,000 at the end of 1985) but remains small in proportion to the total Korean population in Japan.[24] Their reluctance, if not lack of urgency, in pursuing naturalization is because (1) the majority of Japanese people would still not accept them socially, while they could not effectively fight discrimination as Japanese citizens: (2) they are pressured to use Japanese names, which is tantamount to losing their cultural identity; and (3) to identify with the Japanese who despise Koreans appears to be capitulation to negative Japanese attitudes toward the Koreans.

The pressures that naturalization places on Koreans can be great. In one case, a young naturalized Korean committed suicide because he felt torn between his Korean national origin and his assimilation into a hostile Japanese society, and because hiding his ethnic identity from his girl-friend resulted in a guilt complex.[25]

Thus, the majority of the Korean minority remains in Japan as aliens, legally barred from government franchise, several types of welfare benefits, and employment in government and government-licensed professions. This separates them from other minorities in Japan. However, progress is being made. In 1979, Japan ratified the International Covenants on Economic, Social, and Cultural Rights, and on Civil and Political Rights, and, in 1982, on Refugees. All of these laws have enhanced the cause of human rights in Japan. The passage of these agreements was much to the credit of Japan's political leaders and to international pressure. As part of this process, in June 1979 a memo was sent to President Jimmy Carter warning that his statement that "Japan too should accept its share of Vietnamese refugees" could be offensive to Japanese sensibility. Japanese Foreign Minister Sunao Sonoda, in urging ratification of the refugee treaty in 1982, indicated his embarrassment at the lack of legal protection for aliens in Japan. The Diet hearing and passage of the treaty have helped remove a few legal barriers in receiving social welfare benefits.

The situation of the "outsiders" such as Burakumin and Koreans may not be in full conformity with the nondiscrimination clauses in these covenants. But by a new law public offices are not permitted to inquire into the origins of job applicants. The strategic efficacy of Korean demands has been increased and has resulted in the elimination of nationality clauses in laws pertaining to public housing, allocation of state allowances for children, admission to the National Pension Fund, and loans from the National Treasury of Investment for private housing.[26]

The covenants also prohibit the denial of the right of minorities to enjoy their own cultures, speak their own language, and use their own native names.[27] Hereafter, the ethnic education of Koreans might also be permitted, if not encouraged. Such a step will decrease social pressure on Koreans to renounce their heritage by denying their Korean name, although the result of customs and image patterns cannot be easily changed. Improvements in education and employment for Koreans must be a part of effective amelioration policies.

The right to participate in political activities as aliens is limited in all countries, not just Japan. What is peculiar to the Koreans in Japan is that they enjoyed the right to vote from 1928 to 1945 (although the Japanese did not formally disenfranchise them until 1952). (See Table 17.)Some of the Koreans continued to claim these rights after 1945, especially for veterans compensation and the like. Like other aliens, Koreans are entitled to take part in political activities, but this may lead the government to refuse to renew their residence permit.

UNDEREDUCATION, UNDEREMPLOYMENT, AND ANOMIE

Koreans in Japan (so-called KJs) who pass over naturalization seem to insist on maintaining some self-esteem in being a Japanese "resident" of Korean ethnic origin. But they recognize that too rigid identity as Koreans is inconvenient for life in Japan. Hence, the overwhelming majority of their children attend Japanese schools rather than ethnic schools, which are discouraged by the Japanese government. Ethnic educators, especially those in schools sponsored by North Koreans, wonder why Japanese society tries to "Japanize" the children of Koreans but at the same time discriminates against them in employment. Japanese officials respond by stating that the graduates of "ethnic schools" would face greater discrimination in adapting economically, if not socially, to life in Japan.

As a compromise, many public school systems in areas like Osaka, where more than 20 percent of the enrollees are Korean, have made concerted efforts to offer ethnic studies programs for interested KJ students. But the program suffers from a shortage of qualified teachers. For example, according to one study, many of the teachers in the area did not know the historical background of how Koreans were brought to Japan.[28]

But to many parents of KJ children, barriers to ethnic education are by far secondary to the barriers to admission to Japanese high schools and universities. Fourteen out of thirty-five high schools in Aichi Prefecture either refuse KJs or use stiff entrance criteria against them. The excuses for such discriminatory policy against the KJs include: (1) they tend to make trouble at school; (2) when that occurs, it tends to invite intervention by the KJ organization; (3) their schools offer no ethnic education; and (4) it is too much of a headache for teachers to find places for KJ graduates in companies and at universities.[29]

Unlike Korean-Americans, the Korean minority in Japan is still functionally illiterate and impoverished in many cases. Their children seem to do relatively poorly in school, though they have better educational opportunities than their parents. In this sense they are comparable to American blacks. The unemployment rate among Koreans is much higher than that of American blacks (partly owing to the alien status) in a country with a lower overall rate of employment than the U.S. rate. Among KJs, 26.2 percent of the population is gainfully employed, compared with 49 percent of the Japanese.[30] The Korean youth in Japan tend to develop a negative self-image, as they have witnessed failures around themselves and face an uncertain future.

According to a 1971 survey among one hundred major Japanese firms, 41.5 percent of them said that nationality would be an issue for employment at their firms. In a 1984 survey among 700 firms, one-third of them had employed KJs.[31] In a 1985 survey of 141 firms, 67 percent indicated no discrimination of nationality for employment, and 26 percent of them had hired KJs. Nearly half of them showed willingness to employ KJs in the future, while a slightly lower number hinted ambivalence.[32] The employment situation for KJs has been steadily improving.

Table 17
History of the Legal Status of Koreans in Japan

Year	Events/Law	Effects
1910	Japan's Annexation of Korea	Koreans considered Japanese nationals
1925	General Election Law	All male Koreans enfranchised
1938	Campaign with pressure	Korean names changed to Japanese
1945	Defeat of Japan and occupation by SCAP (a)	Korea liberated, 1 million Koreans repatriated to S. Korea
1945	Chongnyon	Organized in October
1946	Mindan	Organized in October
1947	SCAP Laws	KJs treated like foreigners
1948	Two separate rival governments in Korea	ROK (b) in the South, DPRK (c) in the North
1950	Korean War	Intense conflict between Chongnyon and Mindan

Year	Event	Effect on Koreans
1952	Japan's independence and joining of United Nations	KJs disenfranchised and declared to be complete aliens
1965	Japan-ROK normalization	Treaty Agreement on "Permanent" Resident Aliens (most Mindan members) (d)
1979– 1982	Ratification of Japan's human rights convenants	Liberalizing effects on Koreans of welfare and other benefits
1982– 1986	Stateless and unregistered aliens	Allowed to apply for "special" resident alien (e) status (mostly Chongnyon members)
1991	Renegotiation by ROK of status of KJs	"Special" acts for KJs better than "permanent" resident status

[a]Supreme Command of Allied Powers under General Douglas MacArthur.

[b]Republic of Korea (South Korea).

[c]Democratic People's Republic of Korea (North Korea).

[d]Deportable for more than seven years of imprisonment.

[e]Deportable for more than one year of imprisonment.

Nevertheless, the Korean minority has a greater percentage on welfare rolls and a higher crime rate than other minorities in Japan. The higher crime rate can best be explained by Emile Durkheim's concept of "anomie," as discussed by Robert K. Merton, that is, criminal careers are "actually very often an alternative pattern of achievement for the socially marginal."[33] Indeed, some Koreans have found acceptance in the Japanese underground gangs (Yakuza). According to Lee and DeVos, those degenerate Koreans are more likely to disregard family ties and are more given to the exercise of physical force, thereby contributing to the Japanese perception that Koreans tend to be aggressive and insubordinate.[34]

DISCRIMINATION AND THE KJ RESPONSE

Discrimination against other races and ethnic groups is more or less a universal phenomenon, but few situations are comparable to the treatment of KJs in Japan. The degree of discrimination and its most determinative ingredients are not easily measurable. Racism, and the continuing colonial mentality and policies, are important ingredients, and they in turn are influenced by historical hostility and the national psychological benefits of a scapegoat.[35] The economic necessity of maintaining a cheap working (KJ) class was a factor in the past if less so today; this familiar theme is often heard about Chicanos in the United States.

The difficulties KJs have in finding secure jobs stem from racial discrimination but are aggravated by insufficient skills. Their alien status is used as an excuse for refusing KJs as sojourners. It is estimated that out of about 10,000 eligible KJ youngsters who look for jobs annually, only about 1,000 secure jobs at Japanese firms. The better job prospects for KJs are in working for KJ-managed companies or schools; such interests hire about half of each year's group of entrants into the job market.[36] The remainder ends up self-employed in the restaurant business or in housework. A small number struggle for careers in sports or entertainment fields and succeed as well as blacks in America. An interesting example is the extremely popular movie star Matsuzaka Keiko, whom many Japanese regard as the "most beautiful woman in Japan." But Japanese remain blissfully ignorant of her Korean roots.[37] About 53 percent of the gainfully employed KJs are engaged as craftsmen, production process workers, and laborers, compared to less than 12 percent for Chinese national minorities and about 30 percent for all residents in Japan.[38] The Korean and Chinese minorities have different percentages because the two groups came to Japan for different reasons. Koreans immigrated to Japan primarily as functional "wetbacks," whereas the Chinese came as merchants and traders. In addition, the Chinese encountered less discrimination than the Koreans.

The insecurity in both finding and holding a job is also reflected in the figures for job changes for KJs in a country that has a reputation for lifetime employment. Seventy-five percent of the KJs had changed jobs during their careers; the average worker had worked in 3.8 different positions.[39]

Social stereotypes and unfavorable credit ratings often become barriers to commercial loans. Of the Kanagawa respondents of a 1985 survey, 66 percent of the KJs had met with discrimination in seeking loans or had not approached Japanese banks at all because of the experiences of other KJs. Hence, the self-employed tended largely to rely on loans from financial institutions owned by KJs.[40]

One indicator of the KJ's sense of alienation and discrimination is the number of trusted Japanese friends KJs have. According to the above-mentioned survey, when asked how many trusted Japanese friends they had, 54.7 percent of the KJs interviewed answered "none at all" or "one or two." Only 38.5 percent of the Chinese answered this way.

To avoid various forms of discrimination on the job and at school, KJs often hide the fact of their Korean ancestry by using a Japanese name to help them "pass." Ninety-one percent of the Koreans and 17 percent of the Chinese have a Japanese name in addition to their own. They use different names on different occasions, suffering the emotional conflict this causes as part of daily life in Japanese society.[41]

An overwhelming majority of the KJs and other foreigners have given a negative response to the controversial fingerprinting requirement of the Alien Registration Law. All aliens aged sixteen years or residing in Japan must renew their registration every five years by impressing the print of the left index finger in three documents. Before 1981, the fingerprinting age was fourteen, and the interval was three years. As many as 285,727 KJs were booked on charges of violating alien registration law during the twenty-year period 1947–66.[42] In response to frequent demonstrations and protests staged against the law by KJs, Japanese authorities openly admit that the law is aimed at KJs and claim that it is necessary for public security.[43] The implication is that KJs are disposed to criminality and that a sizable segment of the KJ community is loyal to North Korea. But second- and third-generation Koreans born in Japan complain that Japan is the only country that requires permanent residents to be fingerprinted like criminals and to be punished for failure to carry an alien registration card or to carry a reentry permit to return home after a trip abroad. The permanent residents object to being treated worse than the aliens who reside in Japan temporarily.

There are also legacies of discrimination from World War II. After the war, the Japanese in Sakhalin were repatriated, but not the 44,000 Koreans who were forcibly brought to this former Japanese territory that is now occupied by the Soviet Union.[44] Seoul has pressured the

Japanese government to negotiate with the Soviet Union for their repatriation. For those and other KJs who have been ignored thus far, such as atomic bomb survivors (there were approximately 40,000 Koreans in Hiroshima when the bomb was dropped), disabled veterans, and Hansen's disease and mental patients, Tokyo has begun to show some concern.

Japanese policy toward the KJs has been to reduce their numbers through repatriation to the two Koreas, and to compel the remaining KJs to become assimilated and naturalized. Both the Japanese and many outsiders believe that the second option is the best ethnic strategy to avoid discrimination. This policy demands that the KJs abandon their ethnic, cultural, and linguistic characteristics and become merged with the majority. Some might argue that this is cultural genocide as described in the Convention on Genocide.

ASSIMILATION AND HOW FAR?

For concerned Japanese in and outside the government, an ideal solution for the KJs would be for them to assimilate and become totally invisible as an ethnic group. The feeling is that a different "race" permanently residing in Japan as a minority could create serious social problems in the future as has happened in the United States and elsewhere. They believe in the inevitability of the KJs' assimilation and naturalization.[45] Practically all KJs will inevitably be acculturated, but some of them might wish to retain their Korean names. In this sense, KJs may not be willing to assimilate fully. Even if they do, they might not be completely accepted into the mainstream of Japanese society. In fact, some would argue that total assimilation into the uniform model of Japanese society is not only unfeasible, but may also be undesirable for the future sake of Japanese society itself.

The concept of assimilation has always been repugnant to most KJs, especially those associated with North Korea. But to most Japanese firms, acculturation (assimilating with the Japanese mind) is a necessary, if not sufficient, condition for employment of KJs. Since 1982, the KJs' resistance to the Japanese policy of assimilation has been inarticulate.

Since the Japanese Diet ratified the Convention Relating to the Status of Refugees which requires equal treatment of refugees, the government has amended the National Pension Law, the Child Allowance Law, and other welfare legislation where eligibility had been restricted to Japanese. As this move opened the way for KJs to receive old age pensions and other benefits, KJs became more receptive to the notion of assimilation.[46]

An indicator of increasing assimilation is the number of KJs who marry Japanese as compared to those who marry Koreans. As Table 18 indicates, the mixed marriages have been increasing at the rate of 2 percent

Table 18
Marriage Trends of KJs, 1965–1981, Selected Years (percentages)ᵃ

Year	Inter-Korean Marriages	Mixed Marriages with Japanese
1965	64.7	34.6
1970	56.3	42.4
1975	49.9	48.9
1979	44.8	54.3
1981	42	58

ᵃThe number of marriages per year ranges from 5,693 to 7,041. In recent years, the average has been near 7,000.

Source: Kosei taishin tokei chosabu jinko totai tokei; Gendai Korea, June 1983.

annually, so that by 1985 the percentage might have been as high as 65 percent as compared to the inter-Korean percentage of 35 percent, if the trend continues.

NATURALIZATION AND POLITICAL PARTICIPATION

Naturalization is the KJs' legal response to legal and administrative form of discrimination. From 1952 to 1980, 102,554 KJs became naturalized.[47] (About the same number of KJs were repatriated to North Korea between 1960 and 1985.) Having sensed the reluctance of KJs to naturalize for the reasons noted above, Hidenori Sakanaka, a Japanese bureaucrat writing in a 1976 official monthly publication, encouraged the government to attempt to create a social environment conducive for the KJs to naturalize by widening doors for KJs in education and employment, including civil service, and by urging Japanese firms to cooperate. This article won high praise from his colleagues.[48]

Seiwakai

Seiwakai, an organization consisting of naturalized KJs, was established in 1971. Since most KJs would like to "pass" as Japanese, they would be reluctant to join an organization that would identify their Korean roots. Only 3,000 out of the presumably 50,000 naturalized families have joined the club. A number of those joined it to mediate the marriages of their children to other members. Some of them leave the organization after their children marry other naturalized KJs.[49] The Seiwakai has not become as politically potent as the Japanese American Citizens League in the United States.

In the prewar period, KJs had the right to political participation. From 1931 to 1942, some 240 KJs ran for public office as Japanese citizens, for offices ranging from the Diet to the village council; 43 of these were elected.[50] After the postwar disenfranchisement, only one naturalized KJ ran; he was elected as a city councilman in the city of Yamato.[51]

The KJ rate of tax payment is estimated to be higher than that of the Japanese, and yet they receive fewer benefits from the government.[52] There is a rising demand for KJs to have the right to political participation as well as social welfare benefits equal to those of Japanese nationals. Political participation is advocated, especially in local politics, as a means of avoiding discrimination in local policies and of receiving equal benefits.[53] But civic rights are not likely to be given away to nonnaturalized KJs in the near future, however unique their status might be. It should be added, however, that the KJs close to Pyongyang would oppose demanding such civic rights.

Mindan versus Chongnyon Strategies

The division between the two Korean communities based on allegiance to either North or South Korea remains strong. Hence, their strategies toward the Japanese ethnic policies often differ, except on such issues as opposition to deportation.

The pro-North Korea organization is the Chongnyon (General Federation of Koreans in Japan) with a membership of nearly 270,000. The pro-South Korea organization is the Mindan (Korean Resident Association in Japan) and claims the allegiance of approximately 400,000.[54] A small number claims no affiliation. Hence, the Korean minority should be viewed as more than an issue of Japan's domestic policy; the policies of the two Koreas toward their kinspeople in Japan as well as Japan's ethnic policies often shape the strategic efficacy and outcomes of the KJs' demands and responses.

Chongnyon has a highly bureaucratic, centralized structure that is sponsored by and modeled on North Korean lines. Its members tend to have a stronger ethnic identity. In contrast, Mindan is a loose federation and has remained relatively weak. Chongnyon has preferred repatriation of KJs to North Korea over assimilation and naturalization of KJs, whereas Mindan is more amenable to assimilation, hoping that through acquiescence they may escape discrimination and persecution. Chongnyon prefers politicization of KJs to the promotion of the well-being and social service of KJs, while the Mindan's preferences were the opposite until 1973. After the Kim Dae Jung kidnapping incident in 1973, a pro-Kim group split off from Mindan calling itself Hanmintong (National Congress for the Restoration of Democracy in South Korea and Promotion of Unification). In politics this organization has become closer to Chongnyon than to Mindan.

Chongnyon emphasizes the KJs' withdrawal from Japanese society and allegiance to North Korea. It is attempting to preserve Korean ethnicity, culture, and language through the establishment of its own educational system from kindergarten to university. These ethnic schools are called Kakushu Gakko (various schools) and are accredited by respective prefectural governors. Unfortunately, only 60 of the approximately 900 Japanese institutes of higher learning allow graduates to apply.[55] According to 1981 statistics released by the South Korean Ministry of Education, nearly 80 percent of KJ children (96,378) attend Japanese schools, while 19 percent attend the Chongnyon ethnic schools. Only 1 percent attend the Mindan ethnic schools. The ratio of the Chongnyon to Mindan schools is 95 to 5, but in recent years the Chongnyon has been losing its students to Japanese schools.[56] In addition, a greater number of the Mindan members' children take ethnic courses offered at certain Japanese schools.

In 1950, 92.6 percent of the KJs were supportive of North Korea, and throughout the 1950s 80 percent of the KJs were Chongnyon members. When they were able to repatriate 88,611 of the KJs to North Korea between December 1959 and November 1967, Pyongyang hailed each "unprecedented" shipment from capitalist Japan to socialist North Korea as evidence of the superiority of Korean socialism over Japanese or Korean capitalism.[57] After 1967, the number of Chongnyon members dwindled as the exodus of KJs from Chongnyon to Mindan began. The number of Chongnyon members has been decreasing from over 92 percent in 1950, to nearly 70 percent in 1960, 46 percent in 1970, and 20 percent in 1980.[58] Although these figures may be exaggerated, the steadily shrinking size of Chongnyon has been widely acknowledged. The major reasons behind this shift are as follows: (1) the 1965 treaty of normalization between Seoul and Tokyo favored Mindan members in terms of obtaining permanent resident status and other welfare benefits; (2) Seoul allowed past and present Chongnyon members to visit their families and relatives in South Korea who found that country far better than they had anticipated (77 percent of the KJs' first generation originally came from the southern half of Korea); and (3) North Korean politics and economics have so deteriorated that KJs regard the living standards in the North as too low for those used to Japanese life even at its lowest level.

For these reasons, Chongnyon and Mindan remain competitive and antagonistic toward each other even as North and South Korea are. This reduces the likelihood of integrating their ethnic demands to overcome the various discriminating policies. Both sides waste their resources to mend fences with Seoul or Pyongyang. This divisiveness allows the Tokyo government to exploit their hostility and keep the KJ problem under control.

THE PRESENT SITUATION AND FUTURE ISSUES

The occupational distribution of the KJ population showed some changes from 1974 to 1984. The number of unskilled and skilled laborers and sales personnel decreased by 12 percent, while the number of white-collar workers such as managers, professionals, and those in the service trades increased 8.5 percent. The entertainment field showed a conspicuous increase of 2,588 in 1984. The percentage of KJs gainfully employed increased by 1.2 percent to 27.4 percent in 1984 but still remained low in comparison to the Japanese, of whom 49 percent were gainfully employed, according to 1980 census data. Eighty-five percent of the KJs are of the second and third generation, and they will shape the future of the KJ community.[59] For most of them the divisions between Chongnyon and Mindan, the sojourn mentality, and the preoccupation with homeland politics are less relevant to their current and future lives.

There is some evidence, however, that the third-generation KJs tend to show more interest in restoring their racial and ethnic identity than the second, even though they speak less Korean. The third generation more strongly resists naturalization and mixed marriages as well.[60] (A similar trend occurred with third-generation Japanese-Americans regarding their identity.)

The declining size of Chongnyon has been paralleled by a declining amount of financial assistance from Pyongyang for its ethnic schools over the past ten years. Aid was gradually reduced from 3.9 billion yen in 1974 to 990 million yen in 1985. Since the annual budget is 1.3 to 1.5 billion yen, Chongnyon's ethnic schools have had an annual budget deficit of 500 to 800 million yen in recent years.[61] Owing to the shortage of foreign currency in North Korea, a large portion of the financial assistance given to Chongnyon schools are funds recirculated from the contributions made by the Chongnyon organizations. Their organizational and financial future is bleak indeed, and their ethnic strategies will be compromised by these trends.

As a result of continuing external pressure and consequent measures such as the two International Covenants on Economic, Social, and Cultural Rights and on Civil and Political Rights ratified in 1979 as well as Japan's acceptance in 1982 of the Refugees Convention, important progress has been made in extending social security and human rights systems to resident aliens, largely KJs. Hence, the situation in 1985 has improved markedly since 1980.

KJs are still largely excluded from medical insurance and old age pensions owing to eligibility conditions. For example, fewer than 19 percent of the Kanagawa respondents have joined a pension plan, even when both the workplace pensions (16 percent) and the national scheme pensions (3 percent) are combined. This low enrollment reflects the fact that when the National Pensions Law was amended in 1982 to extend it to alien residents, no interim relief measures were taken for the group thirty-five years and older who were unable to fulfill the requirement of twenty-five years' subscription to qualify for the pension.[62] Okinawans, however, were exempted from the twenty-five year requirement.

Two court cases have been credited with sparking a vigorous civil rights movement, which is now enjoying the support of a growing number of Japanese. Both Chongnyon and Mindan were challenged by emerging, independent civil rights groups to shift their focus from homeland politics toward the plight of KJs. The first case was Chong Sok Pak's court victory in 1974 against Hitachi, the giant electronic firm, for discrimination. His successful application was rejected because he concealed his Korean identity. In the second case, Kyongduk Kim passed his judicial examination and applied to the government's Judicial Research and Training Institute in 1976. His application was rejected because he failed to declare his intent to naturalize. He then petitioned the Supreme Court, and the Japanese Lawyers' Association as well as the Japanese press supported him. To everyone's surprise including his own, in 1977 the Supreme Court rendered a landmark decision upholding his petition. This set a precedent that the citizenship requirement can be waived when the Supreme Court deems it appropriate to do so.[63]

Daniel Sneider has called Kim a "trailblazer in the struggle for civil rights" and compares him to Rosa Parks, a heroine in the black American civil rights movement.[64] Kim has become a leader in the current civil rights movement whose foremost target is the alien registration law as symbolized by its requirement of fingerprinting.

In spite of some improvements, many elusive issues still face the Korean community in Japan. The recently achieved equal status in access to social welfare benefits has not diminished the importance of demands for equal opportunities in higher education and employment. In addition, institutional reforms are necessary but insufficient conditions for reforming the racial consciousness of the older Japanese. Like black Americans, KJs are enjoying an improved living standard, a situation which some Japanese writers regard as equivalent to reducing a source of discrimination. Yet the Korean community remains deprived and poor relative to the Japanese majority, much as the blacks in America.

It has been assumed that KJs use Japanese names in order to avoid discrimination and Korean names as a means of fighting discrimination. This assumption has not been altered, although KJs have shown a slight increase in their willingness to use their own Korean names, partly as a result of a small amelioration of the problems facing them. Such improvement could eventually reduce the symbolic importance of using Japanese or Korean names.

Naturalization with any kind of Korean identity is viewed by KJs not as an escape from discrimination, but as a way to shift the burden of discrimination from the alien group to a minority group. But too many Japanese would rather see naturalization as a part of the process by which KJs amalgamate into the melting pot of the Japanese majority and become "invisible." The question that remains concerns whether Japanese opinion leaders are willing to refrain from pressuring KJs to assimilate and naturalize until the Japanese people show a willingness to accept them into their society. Such pressure might increase or decrease in 1991 when Seoul and Tokyo meet again to discuss KJ issues.

SUMMARY AND CONCLUSIONS

In conclusion, from the vantage point of today, it can be generalized that the Japanese-KJ relationship is becoming comparable to the white-Chicano relationship in the United States. It is better, however, than white-black relationships of the United States. There is also a discernible positive tendency among young Japanese not to share the prejudices of their parents against Koreans or "Chosenjin." The older generation sometimes uses this term with derogatory intonation, to show contempt for the Koreans, much as the word "nigger" is used as a pejorative term for American blacks.

TOWARD IMPROVED RACE POLICIES AND RELATIONS

The Korean communities in Japan together constitute no more than 0.7 percent of the Japanese population. KJs, together with Burakumin, Okinawan, Ainu, and others who hold some form of minority status, are equivalent to 4 percent of the population. In terms of number and self-esteem, KJs are not sufficiently strong to overcome such a covertly oppressive social environment. It is obvious that the concerned young KJs must form coalitions with their counterparts from other minorities and from the Japanese majority. The Korean communities have increasingly been supported in their struggle for greater equality by various sympathetic elements of the society and even by some human rights groups abroad. A KJ group, the Association of Fighting for Acquisition of Human Rights for Koreans in Japan, has managed to present its complaints before the United Nations Commission and Subcommission on Human Rights meeting. Such international recognition has strengthened their case in Japan.

Other political strategies that might be attempted by the KJs are: (1)

utilize certain "issues" to integrate centripetal forces among the conflicting community organizations while publicizing the discriminatory environment and soliciting support throughout the world; (2) increase
associations in schools between minority and majority children and teach
children all the historical facts of Japanese-Korean relations, which might
bring about a change in the parents' attitudes and even create an environment in which KJ children can freely use their own names; (3)
adopt a *jus soli* bias for awarding citizenship to all those born in Japan,
thereby granting second- and third-generation KJs automatic citizenship; (4) if the previous suggestion is too revolutionary, as an intermediate step adopt a special law for KJs through consultation of all concerned,
so that KJs may be treated better than aliens residing temporarily in
Japan. For example, the reentry permit requirement for KJs traveling
abroad might be dropped. The special law should allow KJs to participate
in local government elections and to compete for local government staff
hiring and qualification tests. Finally, (5) KJs should demand affirmative
action policies in the form of employment quotas for deprived minorities
as practiced in the United States.[65]

If Japanese public policy is to reduce the incidence of discrimination against KJs and improve their race relations, the historical and
psychological causes must first be understood by a significant portion
of Japanese society while implementing the strategies listed above. The
Japanese must begin to comprehend that their racial beliefs that their
genetic heritage and historical development are unique has caused
undesirable consequences and animosity. The concerned and young
Japanese, if not the old, must be socialized to the factual view that
their cultural heritage is too interwoven with that of Korea to sustain
the illusion of separate origin. If KJs are to function as new, bona fide
members of Japanese society and citizens of the Japanese state in future generations, their cultural heritage must be accorded respect and
they must be given the right to be of Korean origin.[66] The equation
of citizenship and ancestry may no longer be tenable in modern states,
including Japan.

Outwardly, the so-called problem of the Korean minority is more than
an issue of Japan's domestic policy, since the treatment and behavior of
the KJs reflect the political and ideological complexities of the relations
among Japan, South Korea, and North Korea. But fundamentally, as
this article demonstrates, the Korean problem is a Japanese problem
that is related to a continuing myth of racial superiority, just as the black
problem is a problem of an American identity. How willing the Japanese
are to accept Koreans in their midst without demanding conformity to
the myth of a single-nation society is "the litmus test of an internationalization of Japan."[67] Hence, as one author has argued, the Korean cause
is really "for the sake of Japanese society itself."[68]

NOTES

Thanks are due to Glen Atkin for editing and typing the manuscript, and to Yasuaki Onuma, Katsumi Sato, and Byongyoon Park for interviews in 1982.

1. Duane Lockard, "Race Policy," in F. I. Greenstein and N. W. Polsby, eds., *Handbook of Political Sciences*, Vol. 6 (Reading, Mass.: Addison-Wesley, 1975), p. 245.

2. Interview with Professor Kwangkyu Lee, an anthropologist at Seoul National University, December 1985; C. Lee and G. DeVos, *Koreans in Japan: Ethnic Conflict and Accommodation* (Berkeley: University of California Press, 1981), pp. 5–8.

3. See Yong Mok Kim, "Korean Minority in Japan and Their Dilemma of Cultural Identity," in T. S. Kang, ed., *Nationalism and the Crisis of Ethnic Minorities in Asia* (Westport, Conn.: Greenwood Press, 1979).

4. According to an early Japanese peerage as stated in George A. DeVos et al., *Japan's Minorities: Burakumin, Koreans, Ainu, and Okinawans* (London: Minority Rights Group No. 3, 1983), p. 9.

5. Shiota Shobei, "A 'Ravaged' People: The Koreans in World War II," *The Japanese Interpreter* 7 (Winter 1971): 49.

6. The data compiled in the Japanese Ministry of Welfare are cited in Wooseng Kim, "The Korean Minority in Japan: Their Social and Legal Status, Past and Present" (M.A. thesis, 1971), p. 6; *Koreans in Japan* (Kitakyushu, Japan: Association of Fighting for Acquisition of Human Rights for Koreans in Japan, 1979), p. 4.

7. David Conde, "The Korean Minority in Japan," *Far Eastern Survey* (February 1947): 45.

8. Chun Chon, *Chochonnyon Yonku* [The Study of Chosoren], Vol. 2 (Seoul: Korea University Press, 1972), p. 346.

9. *The Pyongyang Times*, December 19, 1984.

10. Michael Banton, *Racial and Ethnic Competition* (Cambridge, England: Cambridge University Press, 1983), p. 4.

11. See Edwin Reischauer, *The Japanese* (Cambridge, Mass.: Harvard University Press, 1977), p. 411.

12. See Changsoo Lee and George DeVos, *Koreans in Japan*, pp. 300–302.

13. Tadanobu Tsunoda, *Nihonjin no No: No no Hataraki to tosei no bunka* [The Brain of the Japanese People: The Function of the Brain and East/West Culture], (Tokyo: Taishuken Shoten, 1978).

14. Sakamoto Uichiro, *Kanso to Nihonjin: Anata no senzo wa nanizoku ka* [Facial Physiognomy of Japanese: What Race Were Your Ancestors?] (Tokyo: Saimaru Shuppon Kai, 1976).

15. See Herman Kahn, *The Emerging Japanese Superstition* (Englewood Cliffs, N.J.: Prentice-Hall, 1970), p. 73.

16. Reischauer, *The Japanese*, p. 411.

17. *International Documentation #65 (Marginalization of Peoples*, 1974), pp. 14–15.

18. Kwang Kyu Lee, *Jaeil Hankukin* [Koreans in Japan] (Seoul: Ilchokak, 1983), p. 269.

19. Hiroshi Wagatsuma and T. Yoneyama, *Henken no Koso* [Structure of Prejudice], (Tokyo: NHK, 1967), pp. 119–89.

20. *International Documentation*, p. 16.

21. *Tongil Ilbo*, June 22, 1985.

22. Yung-Hwan Jo, "Japanese-Korean Relations and Asian Diplomacy," *ORBIS* (Summer 1967), pp. 310–42.

23. Lee and DeVos, *Koreans in Japan*, pp. 147–49.

24. *Tongil Ilbo*, January 1, 1986.

25. Cited from Masaaki Yamamura in Young Mok Kim, "Korean Minority in Japan," p. 59.

26. "Protection Against Discrimination in Japan," *The Review*, No. 23 (1979), p. 14.

27. Ibid.

28. *International Document*, p. 18.

29. *Sabets Hakusho* [White Paper on Discrimination], Vol. 2 (Tokyo: Mindan, 1978), p. 70.

30. *1985 Statistics of the Japanese Ministry of Justice Cited in Tongil Ilbo*, January 8, 1986.

31. *The Tong-il Ilbo*, June 28, 1985.

32. Cited in *Human Report* (Japanese), 1985, No. 5, pp. 36–55.

33. See Robert K. Merton, *Social Theory and Social Structure* (Glencoe, Ill.: Free Press, 1957).

34. Ibid., pp. 368–69.

35. Richard C. Kagan, "World Order Studies Project: Curriculum Package." Unpublished paper, no date, pp. 17–22.

36. *Sabetsu Hyakusho*, Vol. 1, p. 17.

37. Cited by Herman Pevner in *The Korean Herald*, October 19, 1984.

38. *The Kanagawa* 32, No. 2 (June–July 1985): 2; *Minority Rights Group, Report No. 3*, p. 10.

39. *The Kanagawa*, p. 3.

40. Ibid.

41. Ibid., pp. 3–4.

42. Kwang Kyu Lee, *Jaeil Hankukia*, p. 225.

43. A Japanese official of the Ministry of Justice cited in *Tong-il Ilbo*, June 22, 1985.

44. Out of this number, 7,000 remain "stateless" and probably wish to be repatriated to South Korea where they came from. The remainder were either naturalized Soviet citizens or remained in the Soviet island as North Koreans, cited in *Kyopo Chongchaek Jaeryo* 21 (1985): 116.

45. *Chosa Keppo*, July 1985.

46. "Katsumi Sato," Jainichi Kankoku, Chosenjin no————," *Gendai Korea*, June 1985, pp. 61–64.

47. Yongdal Kim, *Zainichi Chosenjin no kika* [Naturalization of Koreans in Japan] (Kobe: Kyodo Shuppan, 1980), p. 13.

48. *New Kan Keppo*, cited in Kwang Kyu Lee, *Jaeil Hankukia*, p. 314.

49. Kwang Kyu Lee, *Jaeil Hankukia*, pp. 315–17.

50. Journal, Association of Fighting for Acquisition of Human Rights, Vol. 2 (October 1979): 8.

51. Kwang Kyu Lee, *Jaeil Hankukia*, p. 14.

52. *Sabetsu Hyakusho*, Vol. 2 (1978), p. 41.

53. Cited in *Hoe we tong-po* (Summer 1983): 74–75.

54. *Homusho Statistics*, issued in September 1982.

55. Ministry of Education (ROK), *Hae we paken kyowon upmu jae ryo* [Materials on Teachers Dispatched Abroad], 1982, p. 26.

56. Cited in Kim Kyong-Hae et al., *Jaeil Chosen u Minjok Kyoyuk* [Ethnic Education of Koreans in Japan] (Kobe: Kobe Gakksei Seinen Center, 1982), p. 69.

57. Wangse Lee, "Jaeil Chochongnyon ui sungchang Kwachung Kwa Haltong Shiltoe," *Tongil Ronjib* 4, No. 2 (1984): 85.

58. Kwang Kyu Lee, *Jaeil Hankukia*, p. 117.

59. See the 1985 edition of *Zairyu Kaikokujin Tokei* [Materials on Aliens in Japan], (Tokyo: Government Printing Center, 1986).

60. See the survey recently conducted by *Tong-il Ilbo* in its January 18, 1986, issue. Even if the figure is exaggerated, it tells an interesting trend of the third-generation KJs.

61. *Tong-il Ilbo*, January 8, 1986.

62. *The Kanagawa*, p. 3.

63. Kwang Kyu Lee, *Jaeil Hankukia*, p. 378.

64. See Daniel Sneider, "Prejudice in Japan," *The Christian Science Monitor*, November 21, 1985.

65. See *Minority Rights Group Report*, No. 3 (1983): *The Kanagawa*, p. 3; Yung-Hwan Jo, ed., *Political Participation of Asian Americans* (Chicago: University of Illinois [Pacific American Mental Health Research Center] PAAMHRC, 1980).

66. Lee and DeVos, *Koreans in Japan*, p. 381.

67. Sneider, "Prejudice in Japan," p. 6.

68. Ibid.

BIBLIOGRAPHY

Books

Lee, Changsoo, and George DeVos. *Koreans in Japan: Ethnic Conflict and Accommodation*. Berkeley: University of California Press, 1981.

Lee, Kwang Kyu. *Jaeil Hankukin* [Koreans in Japan]. Seoul, Korea: Ilchokak, 1983.

Mitchell, Richard H. *The Korean Minority in Japan*. Berkeley: University of California Press, 1967.

Sabetsu Hakusho [White Paper on Discrimination]. 6 vols., compiled by Mindan, Tokyo, 1977–82.

Wagatsuma, Hiroshi, and Toshinao Yoneyama. *Henken no Koso* [Structure of Prejudice]. Tokyo: NHK, 1967.

Wagner, Edward W. *The Korean Minority in Japan: 1904–1950*. New York: Institute of Pacific Relations, 1951.

Pamphlets, Monographs, and Dissertations

Association of Fighting for the Acquisition of the Human Rights of Koreans in Japan. *Koreans in Japan (Ethnic Minority Problem)*, 2 vols., 1979.

Chosoren Students Survey Committee. *Nihon no Daigaku ni narabu Zainichi Cho-senjin gakusei no ankeito chosa* [A Survey of Korean Students in Japan Attending Japanese Universities]. Tokyo: Chosoren, 1980.

DeVos, George, et al. *Japan's Minorities: Burakumin, Koreans, Ainu and Okinawans*. London: Minority Rights Group, No. 3, 1983.

Jo, Moon Hwan. "The Problems of the Korean Minority in Japan: Goal Conflict and Assimilation." Ph.D. diss., New York University, 1974.

Kang, T. S., ed. *Nationalism and the Crisis of Ethnic Minorities in Asia*. Westport, Conn.: Greenwood Press, 1979.

Marginalization of Peoples, 1DOC No. 65. New York: 1974.

Zainichi Chosenjin Kyoiku-undo to jitsen no hatten wo megashite [*Toward Promotion of Movement and Practice of Educating Koreans in Japan*]. Compiled by Zainichi Chosenjin Kyoiku-Kenkyu zenkoku kyogikai junbi-kai, Osaka: 1982.

Periodicals Dealing with Koreans in Japan

Chosen Kenkyu [Korean Study], later changed to *Gendai Korea* [Modern Korea]. Monthly since 1962, Tokyo.

Hae we dongpo [Overseas Koreans]. Quarterly since 1981, Seoul. Monographs since 1971, Seoul.

Sansenri [3000 ri i.e. Korea]. Quarterly since 1975, Tokyo.

Newspapers

Tong-il Ilbo (Toitsu Nippo) Tokyo.

MALAYSIA

C.E.R. Abraham

This chapter is based on the premise that the dynamic of ethnic and racial interaction in Malaysia is best understood within the class structure of the society. In other words, identities of ethnicity and race as groupings of individuals sharing similar physical characteristics and a common culture are not problematic per se. Racial groups as defined by their color, and ethnic groups as defined by their culture become problematic only when they interact in circumstances of competition for scarce goods and services and when these differences become meaningful in explaining the basis for differences in class positions. There is in fact nothing new in this perspective. Max Weber calls this pattern of social behavior monopolization.

A group of persons monopolizes the distribution of certain material or ideal goods, ideals, rights and duties and makes rules about who shall be qualified to share in them. *For Weber the sociological significance of race was that it is a monopoly-forming factor.*[1]

The theoretical perspective of social structural analysis adopted in this study views the identity and perception of ethnicity and race within the class structure of society. That is, the structure of the society can be seen as being "created by the intersection of the vertical classification of ethnic [and racial] groups with the horizontal stratification of social class."[2]

This article maintains that the macrosociological approach is the best strategy for analyzing the dynamic of ethnic and racial interaction. Accordingly, the phenomena of British imperialism and colonialism in Malaya are seen as crucial for any understanding of the evolution of the country's present-day ethnic and race relations problems. This is not a matter of assigning blame to the colonial masters or "whipping a dead horse." This article proposes to show that imperialism and colonialism created the basis for major social structural problems associated with ethnic and race identities and indeed set the stage for the carryover of the same structural problems into the postindependence society of Malaysia today.

A RACIAL CONTEXT

Although it will be necessary to deal with the concepts of ethnicity and race as mutually exclusive for purposes of definition, it is more meaningful to deal with these concepts within the social structure of the society, that is, incorporating a social class dimension in a Weberian sense.[3] Because of cultural differences, the ethnic category is obviously more applicable in Malaysia than race when used in a biological sense. This is because, although the Malays' racial stock may be traced to Polynesian, Chinese, Mongoloid, Indian, and Dravidian strands, this classification has little real meaning in terms of perceptions of biological differences per se, except possibly in terms of skin color. Broadly speaking, the Malays may be distinguished on the basis of skin color: light brown, yellow, and dark brown or even black. But it is important to realize that race is more easily identified than ethnicity and that perceptions of racial differences are reinforced by ethnic differences.

At what point can the perception of ethnic difference manifest itself in racial difference? At the macro-level the shift in the basis of identity has been traced to colonial policy, notably the situation that existed during the Great Depression. Aware that the Chinese had become the most economically powerful group in the world second only to the British themselves, the government implemented so-called pro-Malay policies aimed at containing Chinese economic expansion. The Chinese community as a whole was depicted as a threat to the Malays, not only economically but also politically.[4]

Thus, although ethnicity denotes cultural cleavages between groups, social structural factors have contributed to the manifestation of these differences as being more meaningful in racial terms. Clearly, when ethnicity and race overlap with social class differences, the differences in racial identity are made more meaningful simply because race is more easily perceived than ethnicity. H. Hoetink has aptly described this situation:

A racial problem only presents itself in those societies where certain members are perceived by themselves and consequently or previously by the rest of society as somatically different. This perception of somatic difference, *together with the awareness of its entailing social consequences* gives the aggregate of these members grouplike qualities.[5]

A somewhat similar situation can arise when an interaction between ethnicity and social class occurs. Hence, group formations in Malaysia may be determined by the interaction of the vertical stratification of ethnicity with the horizontal stratification of social class. This conceptualization has been called "ethclass."[6]

Conceptually, therefore, the terms "ethnic" and "race," used in the context of interaction within a society's class structure can be used interchangeably. In practice, however, because interaction takes place in a situation of competition and because racial stereotypes and popular myths are articulated to serve colonial interests, social tensions and potential conflict situations are more easily manifested in racial consciousness.[7]

THE COLONIAL SITUATION

The British colonial government successfully imposed modern economic and political structures onto the precolonial feudal structure of Malay society. As a consequence, new political and economic institutions were created and the mass immigration of Chinese and Indians into Malaysia took place, creating what has been termed the "plural society."[8] From this macrosocial structure, which produced a startling juxtaposition in the network of interactions between specific ethnic and racial groups, the ethnic and racial problem may be traced.

Ideology and stereotypes also perpetuated and manipulated racial diversity in Malaysia by popularizing negative stereotypes among and between the nonwhites and attitudes of racial superiority among the whites. The role of ideology has its roots in the British world-view during the period when colonial expansion into the Malay states took place. The ideological basis for British imperialism and the justification for the imposition of colonial rule rested on the inefficiency, and indeed the incapacity, of the Malay race to exploit the country's economic resources. Herein lay the fundamental rationalization for imperialism: Because the Malays did not have the capacity to exploit their natural resources, they had no right to keep out the British who were of a more "advanced" civilization. Nor did they have the right to exclude other immigrant groups who had more developed capacities and who were willing to do the dirty work to exploit the area's economic potential.

The greatest degree of inequality in Malaysia is to be found among groups suffering various types of deprivation; therefore, racial and ethnic identity is of crucial theoretical significance for race relations where a government consistently employs racial categories as the basis for allocating rewards.

The colonial situation was responsible for the creation of new social groups in Malaysia. This development is seen in the tin and rubber industries which would lay the economic foundations of modern Malaysia. A new mode of production was developed for these industries and created new institutional structures involving Western capital investment on the one hand and the introduction of an immigrant labor force on the other. The indigenous Malay population was excluded from this modern sector of the economy and other Asians were imported as labor, as a result of which the different ethnic groups were compartmentalized into different economic activities: Malays as peasants and smallholders in the villages, Indians as rubber tappers in the rubber plantations, and Chinese as tin miners and industrial and service workers in the urbanized areas. Consequently, members of one community were not able to interact with members of other communities, and the cultural differences between them were accentuated. Differentiations between them became identified in terms of inherent physical and mental capacities and capabilities to perform "superior" and "inferior" economic functions. Moreover, the ability of a small minority of Chinese immigrants to achieve success as businessmen (and to a lesser extent a few Indians to achieve professional status) reinforced the perception among the Malays that they were being subordinated by the alien immigrant "races." The ensuing mistrust that characterized the relationship between the different groups blurred the perception that they were jointly subordinated to the common colonial masters. Hence, racial perceptions in colonial Malaya differed from those in certain other colonies where a "racially" nonwhite indigenous population shared a common perception of their subordination to their white-skinned colonial masters.

By dealing with ethnic groups as distinct groups and by implementing policies aimed at containment or pacification as distinct groups rather than as an integral part of society, the colonial government approached the ethnic question as an ad hoc administrative exercise rather than as one that needed a political solution. This approach strengthened intraethnic consciousness in organizing economic activities and social services such as education. Since education was privately funded, it was based on the same structure as that of the home country. Finally, by implementing specific policies which were ostensibly intended to "protect" certain groups, ethnic consciousness was heightened, giving rise to racial perceptions. Thus, political action to demand scarce goods and services from the government became based on racial identity and racial consciousness, and led to increasing polarization between groups. Because colonial ideology and economic policies discriminated on the basis of racial affinity, ethnic groups began to identify along racial lines.

The tin and rubber industries were, of course, very important for industrialization in Britain and the United States. Because of these export-oriented industries, Malaya's economy shifted from one of subsistence agriculture to raw material export, thereby making the country more dependent on the international market.

The effective operation of the tin and rubber industries necessitated firm control of the political structure and the introduction of appropriate institutions to facilitate and manage foreign capital investment. These factors helped create a new class structure in the modern economic sector and transformed the precolonial social structure of indigenous Malay society. As a consequence, the feudal class structure of the indigenous society was reinforced through indirect rule, whereas in the tin and rubber industries there initially emerged a basic two-class structure in the Marxian sense: those who owned the means of production and those who sold their labor for wages. With the growth and development of these industries, certain other classes came into existence. At the same time, certain features were peculiar to the social structure of the three different ethnic groups whereby peasants and coolies related differently to their respective class of property owners or employers. The significance of these differences may be seen within the concepts of class, ethnicity, and race. Basic to an understanding of these differences is that they were linked to the political and economic structure as well as to the ideology of the colonial situation.

Colonial policy was steeped in the belief in the superiority of British institutions, and indeed in the British race. The doctrine behind this ideology was that of the "civilizing mission," which, though not new to Europeans, began to be seriously advocated in the nineteenth century. Whereas previously physical differences among peoples were recognized, only during the latter part of the nineteenth century did these differences begin to be seen in terms of theories purporting to explain the inequalities of races. According to Philip Mason, during this period "Britain was soberly and seriously imperialist on the conscious level, smugly aware of Kipling's idea of 'the white man's burden.' " On the vital question of the impact of race relations, he states, "By the end of the [nineteenth] century racism has come into the realm of popular writing and the talk of the streets; *it has invaded Government policy*."[9]

Some scholars have tried to explain ethnic and racial identity and consciousness in Malaysia in terms of communalism, nationalism, and, above all, cultural pluralism. These explanations, notably those associated with cultural pluralism, have taken cultural and ethnic differences as givens and have thereby obscured and distorted the role of class factors. By neglecting to specify the conditions under which class differences can be perceived as coinciding with ethnic differences, cultural pluralists have implied that cultural factors alone can sufficiently explain Malaysia's racial relations. But as emphasized in this study, class factors are crucial in explaining interracial relationships within the colonial situation.

By conducting its dealings through the elite segment of each ethnic group, the colonial administration effectively controlled the state without an extensive military presence. By recognizing and rewarding members of the elite group, a consciousness of class among the upper and lower segments of each ethnic group was created. This upper class consciousness fostered closer cooperation and cohesiveness, not only along intraethnic lines but also in terms of interethnic class consciousness in order to maintain the status quo.

Because ethnic groups were structured vertically within what has been called the "paternalistic model," the peasants and coolies looked to their own leaders within the elite groups to enhance their respective interests.[10] This pattern was a direct consequence of the social structure of colonialism. The peasants and coolies had no other recourse but to seek redress for their grievances through leaders recognized by the government. One result was a paradoxical situation for both Chinese coolies and Indian laborers: despite their awareness of exploitation by contractors and factory owners, ethnic consciousness remained cohesive and strong, thereby inhibiting class consciousness. Of course, government policies discouraging trade unions had a similar effect.

By playing up issues along ethnic lines, the administration managed to prevent the development of working-class consciousness and kept the upper class segments of ethnic groups from becoming involved in nationalist movements.

POLARIZATION OF GROUP FORMATIONS ALONG RACIAL LINES

Although group formations within the Chinese and Indian communities were characterized by a lack of class consciousness, this phenomenon was due to different patterns of internal relationships. Among the Chinese, class consciousness was inhibited by the existence of possibilities for upward mobility within the structure of Chinese industry, as well as by increased ethnic consciousness arising therefrom. Among the Indians, class consciousness was inhibited by caste and ethnic differentiation within a rigid social stratification system which precluded upward mobility. These differences in group formations, though they reflect the ethnic and cultural differences of the groups involved, were caused primarily by the structure of capitalist industry and by the colonial situation within which economic development took place. This same argument also explains the so-called backwardness and lack of economic incentive among the indigenous Malays when compared to the immigrant groups. To put it differently, "Colonial relations in themselves present many common problems that are little if at all affected by the particular nationality or race of those concerned."[11]

As long as growth continued and profits and wealth from its two major industries flowed out of the country, colonial policy was one of laissez faire, and developments in all other related areas, including labor, could be allowed to take their course. This relationship between economic

growth and the maintenance of the political status quo was the foundation of the colonial policy of "pacification" of the Malay ruling class
and the ideological basis for the immigration of alien labor. The colonial
system of government and the resultant social structure were "harmonious," with the different groups well contained within their distinct
ethnic entities and preferring a colonial paternalistic government to administer the country. The colonial administration was nominally effected
on behalf of the Malays, but in reality it was far more in support of
vested interests.[12] In the colonial situation, therefore, the system of communal representation emphasized class interests within ethnic demar-
cations. The colonial government dealt individually with the
representatives of each ethnic group, while there was little relationship
between either the different representatives or members of the different
groups themselves. Moreover, the "harmonious" social structure was due
largely to the absence of social contact, created by the overlapping of
economic and social factors along the lines of an ethnic division of labor:

The creed of "laissez-faire" enabled the British to adopt an attitude of separate
obligation to almost any group which felt itself to be different, *providing its interests
did not conflict too strongly with the basic purposes for which power was secured in the
first instance.*[13]

The basic question that emerges is as follows: what happened to the
harmonious colonial social structure when external factors created a
situation of economic depression and the different ethnic groups were
forced into competing for scarce resources? The problems that needed
solution clearly had economic and social rather than ethnic origins. With
the overlapping of socioeconomic status with ethnicity, economic and
social upheavals were often inextricably intertwined with ethnicity.
Therefore, the class problem in a largely ethnically homogeneous society
would tend to take the form of an ethnic or racial problem in an ethnically
heterogeneous society.[14] There would also be an intraethnic problem
because the respective ethnic entities were held together by traditional
or kinship relationships within specific employment settings, and the
situation of massive unemployment tended to disrupt or dislocate the
stability of such relationships.

The significance of such breakdown effects for political stability was
enhanced by the fact that traditional or kinship relationships no longer
mitigated against class consciousness. For the first time, therefore, the
economic depression created a conflict of interests within and between
the respective ethnic groups in the country. Accordingly, a need arose
for balance in meeting the different demands not only of ethnic groups
but, more importantly, between capital and labor as well. This role obviously fell to the colonial government, and because the government

itself had to protect European and British economic interests, government intervention brought ethnic consciousness between groups into sharper focus. Moreover, because colonial policy during the 1930s Depression emphasized racial identity, ethnic consciousness was manifested in race consciousness. The kind of demands that had to be balanced between European interests and capital on the one hand, and Chinese, Indian, Malay, and labor interests on the other, suggests the kind of conflicting demands involved.

Once encouraged by depression conditions to intervene in the sacrosanct spheres of tin and rubber, the Malayan administrators displayed a growing tendency to hold the balance between capitalistic and native economic enterprise, to arbitrate labour disputes, to implement a programme of social services and to deal with citizenship problems.[15]

The intervention of the colonial government during the Depression must be evaluated against the changing political situation, primarily among the Malays, but also among the immigrant communities, especially the Chinese. Since the essence of government intervention was to balance the economic interests of the respective groups involved, groups that wielded the least political power and that posed the greatest economic threat to European and British interests would stand to lose most. By the same token, the converse also holds, particularly where, as in this case, the Malays had special treaty obligations with the British and, accordingly, rightfully expected special protection. For its part, the colonial government had every reason to give serious attention to Malay demands because the legitimacy of the government itself depended on Malay acquiescence to colonial rule. At the same time, the possibility cannot be ruled out that "giving in" to Malay demands was being used as a rationale for discriminatory policies directed against other groups, which were seen as threatening European and British interests.

CONCLUSION

This study demonstrates that the pattern of race relations in Malaysia is best understood as the product of political, economic, and other social structural variables and, in particular, as a reactive response of the indigenous and immigrant groups, respectively, to the colonial situation. The analysis of the social class structure is especially fruitful in this respect because colonial relations inhibited the development of social class relations, which then manifested themselves in intraethnic and interrace relationships. Because "under colonial domination democratic institutions could scarcely have evolved in the context of economic underdevelopment, inequality and exploitation,"[16] there was hardly any common tendency for contract market-oriented relations to replace traditional status relations. As a result, the indigenous and immigrant groups had to create their own institutions and social organizations to take advantage of such economic opportunities as were available to them.

It was in this pattern of response to these opportunities that the perceptions and conception of race as an independent variable are to be traced. Because of the political constraints imposed on the indigenous population by indirect rule and because they were primarily confined to the subsistence sector of the economy, they were unable to develop socioeconomic institutions to meet the demands of the capitalist market situation in the modern economic sector. Moreover, because they were supposedly protected by treaty obligations by the colonial government with whom they shared token political and administrative power, their inability to participate in the modern sector was attributed to their "backwardness" by the immigrant groups. To this extent, the stereotypes and ideology of the "lazy native" and his inherent inferiority to compete economically with the immigrant groups as a race, which were propagated by the colonial government in the first place, came to be believed by the immigrant groups and, indeed, by the indigenous group itself. On the other hand, the Chinese, having been left entirely to themselves to survive, responded in ways that particularly emphasized their "Chineseness." Operating as immigrants in the context of the colonial situation, they developed norms and values that stressed ethnic solidarity as a means of achieving economic survival and mobility. It is not difficult for this response pattern to be seen as peculiarly "Chinese" and hence to be attributed as a characteristic of the Chinese race as a whole. Race consciousness between the Chinese and indigenous population was further reinforced (1) because of the small family-type economic business units which precluded the employment of outsiders, and (2) because the socioeconomic distance between the two groups was seen as being particularly marked. Finally, the Indians, being unable to assert themselves either politically or economically, and accordingly not a threat to the indigenous population, were not perceived in the context of a race relations situation. For their part, the Indians responded by separating themselves from the other groups and living an isolated existence.

NOTES

1. Ernst Moritz Manasse, *Max Weber on Race, Social Research* 14 (June 1947): 191–221 (italics added).

2. Milton M. Gordon, *Assimilation in American Life* (New York: Oxford University Press, 1964), p. 51.

3. Manasse, *Max Weber*, pp. 191–221.

4. C. E. R. Abraham, "Race Relations in West Malaysia with Special Refer-

ence to Modern Political and Economic Development." PhD. diss., Oxford University, 1967. This article is based on this thesis.

5. H. Hoetink, "Pluralism and Assimilation in the Caribbean," paper delivered at American Sociological Association Meeting, San Francisco, 1969 (emphasis added).

6. Gordon, *Assimilation*, especially pp. 51–52.

7. Collin E.R. Abraham, "Racial and Ethnic Manipulation in Colonial Malaya," *Ethnic and Racial Studies* 6, No. 1 (January 1983): 18–32.

8. According to the 1921 census, the immigrant population exceeded the indigenous population in that year.

9. Philip Mason, *Prospero's Magic: Some Thoughts on Class and Race* (London: 1962), pp. 15–16 (italics added).

10. Pierre L. van den Berghe, *Race and Racism, A Comparative Perspective* (New York: John Wiley & Sons, 1967), p. 27.

11. John Furnivall, *Colonial Policy and Practice, A Comparative Study of Burma and Netherlands India* (Cambridge: Cambridge University Press, 1948), p. 2.

12. Virginia Thompson, Rupert Emerson, and Lennox A. Mills, eds., *Government and Nationalism in Southeast Asia* (New York: Institute of Pacific Relations, 1942), p. 129.

13. T. H. Silcock, *The Commonwealth Economy in Southeast Asia* (Durham, N.C.: Duke University Press, 1959), p. 77 (italics added).

14. Cynthia Enloe, "Multi-Ethnic Politics', The Case of Malaysia," Ph.D. diss., University of California, 1972, p. 270.

15. Virginia Thompson, *Post-Mortem on Malaya* (New York: Macmillan, 1943), p. 5.

16. D. J. Blake, "Compilation Chronicle or History?" A Review of Charles Gamba, *The Origins of Trade Unions in Malaya*, offprint from the *Malayan Economic Review* 8, No. 3 (October 1963): 401–3.

BIBLIOGRAPHY

Barraclough, Simon. "Co-optation and Elite Accommodation in Malaysian Politics." *Contemporary Southeast Asia* 6 (March 1985): 308–18.

Clammer, John R. *Straits Chinese Society*. Singapore: Singapore University Press, 1981.

Hua, Wu Yin. *Class and Communalism in Malaysia*. New York: Biblio Distribution Centre, 1983.

Klitgaard, Robert, and Ruth Katz. "Overcoming Ethnic Inequalities: Lessons from Malaysia." *Journal of Policy Analysis and Management* 2 (Spring 1983): 33–49.

Howell, Signe. *Society and Cosmos: Chewong of Peninsular Malaysia*. London: Oxford University Press, 1984.

Milne, R. S., and Diane Mauzy. *Malaysia Profile*. Boulder, Colo.: Westview Press, 1986.

Naidu, Ratna. *The Communal Edge to Plural Societies: India and Malaysia*. Atlantic Highlands, N.J.: Humanities Press, 1978.

Siaw, Lawrence K. *Chinese Society in Rural Malaysia*. London: Oxford University Press, 1983.

Visaria, Pravin. *The Incidence of Poverty and the Characteristics of the Poor in Peninsular Malaysia.* Washington, D.C.: World Bank, 1981.
Young, Kevin, et al. *Malaysia: Growth and Equity in a Multiracial Society.* Baltimore, Md.: Johns Hopkins University Press, 1980.

NETHERLANDS

Joed H. Elich

Neither the Dutch government nor university researchers realized that the Netherlands had become an immigration country until the late 1970s. In the early post-World War II period, a policy of immigration to Canada, Australia, and New Zealand predominated, which meant that the Dutch were stimulated to leave the country. Initially, they left in significant numbers (up to 50,000 in 1952) but later the number of emigrants dropped to such a low level that the term "emigration country" was no longer justified. In the 1960s, the Netherlands started to recruit migrants from Turkey, Italy, Morocco, and other Mediterranean countries. These workers were considered guest workers, which meant that they were temporary laborers who were supposed to return to their home countries in due course. But many of them stayed for good. Therefore, both the emigration country idea and the temporary migrant workers idea came under attack. Postwar recovery was quicker in the Netherlands than expected and emigration dropped, whereas the booming economy forced many companies to attract foreign workers who did not appear anxious to return home.

Current discussions on race relations have concentrated on the persistent presence of the migrant workers. Another development is also of relevance to this issue: namely, decolonization in both the West and East Indies, which created a stream of people from Indonesia and Surinam.

A RACIAL CONTEXT

The use of the word "race" in Dutch (*ras*) is different from Anglo-Saxon usage. The word is not commonly used either in daily life or in scientific publications. Over the centuries the Dutch have come into contact with people from all over the world, but they have not talked about them in terms of "race." Today few people employ the word "race" in their vocabulary both because of the stigmatization connected with the word and because of the sensitive memories of World War II. Even when people use the word to differentiate between people, they do so in a very concealed way. Mostly, they will mention the country of origin ("they are from Surinam") or stress the differences in attitudes, customs and behavior. Michael Banton argues that "race" is a second-order abstraction.[1] Physical appearances per se, he notes, are no basis for making distinctions; rather, it is the meaning that is being given to those appearances that is important.[2] Many other authors renounce the concept of race, especially in the Netherlands, in preference to the term "ethnicity." This does not mean, however, that physical appearances have become irrelevant for people.

In Dutch, the concept of racism has been as unfamiliar as race. Only recently has the term "racism" entered scientific discussions, probably under the influence of international writings on the issue. According to Frank Bovenkerk, one of the pioneer researchers into Dutch race relations: "Racism is a comprehensive set of ideas about the inferiority of another race. In its crude form it hardly exists any more."[3] This remark is characteristic of the attitude among Dutch scientists, although recently a conflict has developed concerning the range of "racism." Some, like Bovenkerk, want to restrict the term to "race," which means that racism hardly occurs in present-day Netherlands, whereas others want to broaden the meaning of racism to the concept of ethnicity. Banton would agree with the first suggestion and Robert Miles with the second.[4] Apparently, Miles' definition of racism is gaining increasing support among Dutch academics:

we use racism to refer to those negative beliefs held by one group which identify and set apart another attributing significance to some biological or other "inherent" characteristics which it is said to possess, and which deterministically associate that characteristic with some other [negatively evaluated] feature[s] or action[s].[5]

The discussion as to whether or not the concept of racism should be broadened cannot be solved here. It is remarkable that so little has been written on race and racism in the Netherlands where racism has undeniably existed for a long time.

It is not a mere coincidence that Leon Poliakov's standard volume on European racism, *The Aryan Myth*, does not say one word about the situation in the Netherlands. French, German, and English writers have often mentioned the high level of tolerance in the Netherlands toward people of another culture or origin. Even as late as 1969, when the number of immigrants in the Netherlands was starting to grow rapidly, Christopher Bagley concluded that there was much more tolerance in the Netherlands than in Great Britain.[6] The Dutch themselves have always assented and repeated this putative tradition of tolerance. In the Netherlands racism has been unknown, has been denied and unacknowledged over the years, while racism has been pointed at and condemned in other countries like the United States and especially South Africa. The Netherlands' strong rejection of racism in South Africa is sometimes related to the closeness of the history and culture of the two countries. In addition, the Dutch experienced the immediate consequences of racism in World War II when the Nazis captured and killed thousands of Dutch Jews and gypsies.

In an essay entitled "Race: Myth and Reality," the Dutch anthropologist André Köbben described race relations between blacks and whites in general. His article, written in 1964, devotes very few words to the Netherlands: "Needless to say that ancient racial prejudices still exist or even increase in countries where the number of negroes increases like in Britain or the Netherlands."[7] That was all to be said two decades ago, and it is very hard to find the term "race" or descriptions of Dutch race relations in literature. With regard to that alone, we have to broaden the concept of race to ethnicity in order to get an idea of the nature of relations between different groups of foreigners in the Netherlands. The term "ethnicity" has become generally accepted in Dutch social science: some research centers concentrate on ethnic minorities, the Dutch government has launched an ethnic minorities policy, and ethnicity has become a major variable in social science, along with sex, age, and marital status.

A short note on registration in the Netherlands is necessary.[8] As part of the Napoleonic legacy, the Netherlands has a municipal population register like the ones in France and Germany. All residents are required to report to the local authorities any changes in address, marital status, and the like. Nationality and place and country of birth are also registered, whereas race or ethnicity is not. People of foreign ethnic origin are traced by means of nationality and country of birth. This is not always a sound measure inasmuch as many white Dutch were born in Indonesia and some Turks and Moroccans have become naturalized. Considerations of privacy are the basis of this situation, and for the same reasons there has not been a census in the Netherlands since 1971. The population registers, however, give ample information.

Banton maintains that ethnicity is inclusive, whereas race is exclusive. One could also say the following: ethnicity is used by a group mainly to define itself, and race is used by the dominant majority mainly to describe a minority. By using this distinction, Banton is referring to ethnic revival movements, but those have not emerged in the Netherlands since its immigration history is very young. In the Dutch case, therefore, ethnicity seems exclusive rather than inclusive, and the term has probably been introduced by researchers, having read American literature, and government officials. Ethnic groups have been very reluctant to adopt the term "ethnic" for themselves, and only after they discovered the usefulness of it as an instrument to improve their conditions have they resorted to it. The absence of the term "race" in Dutch may have influenced this development. It is noteworthy that ethnic groups prefer to call themselves black race or colored people nowadays. The racial characteristic has become inclusive.

The terminology of race relations in daily speech is highly confusing and constantly changing. "Racism" has become a stigmatizing term to describe any nonsolidary action toward ethnic minorities. One author coined the term "humdrum racism" for pushing blacks in buses and at cashiers' desks as well as ignoring questions from them.[9] In scientific research we must be cautious not to adopt merely fashionable language.

As a term, ethnicity is more important than race in the Netherlands. In order to be able to write a history of Dutch race and ethnic relations, we have to implement wide definitions of the terms. This leaves unanswered the question as to which role physical characteristics play in relations between indigenous and foreign people. The answer to that question is given in the next section.

RACISM BEFORE 1940

Going back in time to find occurrences of racism and statements about the phenomenon is not easy without a firm grasp of the term. One has to look for implicit wordings in which the superiority of one group toward another is expressed in terms of physical, cultural, or behavioral characteristics. Hence, the following overview of several centuries of Dutch racism is limited. The Netherlands have come into contact with many different cultures within their boundaries over the past centuries. Amsterdam has been a cosmopolitan city for a long time and a refuge for British nobility, Spanish and Portuguese Jews, and German, Belgian, and Austrian war refugees.

Between 1540 and 1787, some 50,000 to 70,000 Huguenots fled from France to the then Dutch Republic.[10] Under the reign of Louis XIV, these French Calvinists were coerced to convert to Catholicism. They would have been killed otherwise, and many left the country for Britain and the Netherlands. As what is still called one of the largest efforts of tolerance in Dutch history, the Huguenots were given asylum in the Republic. At that time the House of Orange, the ancestors of the Dutch

Royal family, was conciliatory toward Calvinism; moreover, French was the language of the upper class.

Although physically not different from most Dutch, the Huguenots were described as "excited and vivid with an ardour that could both amaze and irritate the Dutch. Also they were extraordinary energetic and industrious."[11] It is not unlikely that prejudice and discrimination occurred on the basis of difference in language and attitudes between the Dutch and the Huguenots, but the similarities in working zeal and what Max Weber called the "Calvinistic ethos" will have contributed to the integration of the Huguenots. At the end of the eighteenth century, they were hardly recognizable as a group, and today their descendants can only be identified by their surnames such as Boissevain and Huet. In the seventeenth to nineteenth centuries, a considerable migration took place from other European countries to the Netherlands.[12]

A large demand for workers in land reclamation programs attracted thousands of seasonal laborers each year. The reclamation of land from the sea started as early as the seventeenth century in the North Holland polders. The economic expansion and the cultural prosperity in this Dutch Golden Age (Rembrandt, Hals, Vermeer) attracted many workers from abroad. Apart from workers in land reclamation, peat-digging in the east of the country, the arts in the large cities, and commerce throughout the country drew many foreigners. Hardly any mention is made of discrimination against them, and their mostly temporary stay may have been partly responsible for this tolerant attitude. Conditions were similar to present-day situations, with large proportions of for-eigners in the cities (in Amsterdam at one time in the seventeenth century even 80 percent). Yet they do not seem to have provoked outbursts of racism and discrimination.

Conclusions can only carefully be drawn, however, since data on that period are scarce and "racism" and "tolerance" are ambiguous concepts. Tolerance does not always mean acceptance, but very often merely the allowance of people to live their lives as long as they do not bother the indigenous people. Avoiding bothering other people is much easier in a country with a few million inhabitants than in a country with more than 14 million people and one of the highest population densities in the world. Many historians have mentioned the smallmindedness of the Dutch which seems contrary to tolerance.[13] In fact, the two are not incompatible since differences between groups of people have always been noticed in the Netherlands, but acceptance of those differences is not common and most people will avoid different-looking and different-acting people in whatever respect.

The tradition of tolerance was never questioned until about 1970. Only recently has the history of race relations been regarded differently.

Old studies on migrants who came to the Netherlands at the beginning of this century are being reexamined, and the literature and documents are being read from a different perspective to determine the amount of tolerance in the Netherlands at that time.

Looking at history through today's eyes is always precarious; what is called racism today was not necessarily considered the same thing a century ago. Reexamining those old studies, we find it remarkable that the characteristics of non-Dutch migrants were related to their physical appearance as a matter of course. Maybe even more remarkable is that ideas of superiority were not drawn as conclusions and that only implicit expectations with regard to assimilation can be extracted from those texts.

A nice example is F. Van Heek's 1936 study of the Chinese in the Netherlands. At the turn of the century, several hundred Chinese came to the Netherlands for the same reasons they went to many other countries at that time: population pressure, the Tai-Ping riots, 1851–64, and the 1875 famine. Many of these Chinese signed on ships, but with the decline of coal-burning shipping, they were soon unemployed. In 1927, some 3,000 Chinese sailed on ships under the Dutch flag, most of them as firemen. Once unemployed, they had hardly any alternative but to stay ashore in the Netherlands. Their skills were limited, but some managed to earn a moderate living by selling "peanut-cookies" and, more in general, as merchants. In 1933, about 2,000 Chinese were living in the Netherlands and, although this number may seem small, they were probably the largest group with different looks at that time. Their visibility and their deplorable economic situation attracted the attention of Dutch officials.

In what can be considered the first case study of an ethnic group in the Netherlands, Van Heek wrote an account of the problems of these Chinese.[14] He related certain of the problems to their physical build. They were supposed to be able to do the dirty work: to scoop coal in small rooms with hot furnaces on ships as they were used to heat. Apart from negative characteristics, like shyness in establishing contacts with Dutch people, Van Heek mentioned profitable characteristics: the Chinese were handy, innovative, clean, and "from the houses they lived in one could not tell they were Chinese." This kind of ascription and mention of national character was not unusual in the 1930s. "Nature" as an explanation for certain problems was much more common at that time than it is now. After Nazism came to full growth, the concepts of nature and innate characteristics became less and less acceptable in Dutch social science, which is especially obvious in immediate postwar studies. Even today nature explanations are almost a taboo in Dutch social science. The prewar and war period 1933–45 will be covered in the next section, but in general one can state that analyses based on eugenics were not misused on a large scale by social scientists in the Netherlands. According to a recent study, there were few examples of mentioning the distinctiveness of non-Dutch groups.[15] In one instance, somebody mentioned the Indonesian natives' limited capacity of recollection. Still, the 1930s also showed a rise of national socialism in most Western European countries, including the Netherlands.

NATIONAL SOCIALISM: 1933–1945

In the Netherlands the National-Socialist party (NSB) was founded in December 1931. At its height in 1935, the party had 55,000 members and gathered 7.9 percent of the votes in the national elections. There have been many studies on the party and its fascist ideology, the people they attracted, the quarrels between leaders, and the like.[16] Nevertheless, questions of race have hardly ever been researched, and all attention seems to have gone to the attitude toward Jews and the Aryan glorification. The electoral success in 1935 is sometimes explained as the result of a protest against the then established politicians. After that, national socialist support declined, and in 1939 a coalition of Catholics and Socialists came into office.

The National-Socialist party attempted to become the main political group in the Netherlands after the Germans invaded the country in May 1940. Anton Mussert, the NSB leader, dreamed of becoming the leader of the Netherlands, a dream that was never fulfilled. The NSB collaborated with the Germans but was unable to occupy all important jobs in national and local governments. They assisted the Germans mainly in tracing Jews and bringing them to concentration camps. Strangely enough, we know nothing about the NSB attitudes toward other racial and ethnic groups. The NSB leader Mussert had argued against any discrimination toward Indonesian-Dutch. Other groups, although very small in number, did not apparently suffer more severely from the wartime policies than others. An exception were the gypsies, of whom some 250 died in concentration camps.

The main operations were directed against the Jews, and more than 100,000 Dutch Jews died in concentration camps. Much emphasis has always been laid on the resistance of the Dutch during the war. Although it is difficult to tell how many people were involved in resistance movements, their number was probably larger than the number of those in league with the enemy. The Catholic Church was openly against fascism, as was the government-in-exile in Britain, and most of the government officials seem to have been opposed to German fascism.

Racist ideas did exist, and not all scientists kept silent on them. In *Races of Mankind*, S. Steinmetz and his son R. Steinmetz described the theories of race. Whereas the father, a much respected sociologist, denied any relation between physical appearances and intellectual qualities and especially between jewishness and innate inferiority, the son was less convinced. He died before the war, however, and was never able to impose his ideas.[17]

Immediately after the war, a purification of all important positions was carried out, and many ex-NSB members were punished in one way or the other. According to some observers, many notable fascists escaped and were able to continue to spread their ideas. However, this did not happen on a large scale in the Netherlands, and only occasionally have war criminals come into the open. Conclusions must as always be stated with caution since the available data are limited and the history of the role of race in World War II in the Netherlands still remains to be written.

POSTWAR PERIOD: 1945–1970

After World War II, the term "race" was avoided whenever possible. Connotations with the holocaust were painful, and forty years after, the Dutch are still very sensitive to use of the term. On the other hand, fascism and racism have never disappeared completely and already in 1953 ex-National Socialists from the NSB movement founded the National European Social Movement (NESB). They were clever enough not to mention the inferiority of nonwhites or Jews, but their political motives were clear: the disintegration of democracy and the glorification of the Pan-Teuton heritage. Soon thereafter, the Dutch High Court dissolved the NESB, considering it a continuation of the fascist and racist NSB. In the 1960s and 1970s, as is shown later in this article, members of this NESB founded new organizations under other names with seemingly nonracist goals.

For the Netherlands in 1945 the German occupation may have been over, but not all warfare had come to an end: at this time, the colony of the Dutch East Indies which had been under Dutch rule since 1601 tried to free itself from colonial rule. An independence war in 1949 ended in a victory of the Indonesians, approved by the United Nations. The effects of the loss of what became the Republic of Indonesia have been little researched in the Netherlands, but it is certain that this "colonial hangover" made many Dutch bitter, especially right-wing politicians and their adherents. One result of the defeat of the Dutch and the independence of Indonesia was the migration of a group called the Indonesian-Dutch—people with mixed blood who were no longer well liked by the Indonesians and who were given the opportunity to leave the country.

"L'histoire se répète," one could say when Hans van Amersfoort states: "Of all immigrations to the Netherlands that of the Indonesian-Dutch is without doubt, the most spectacular."[18] The migration of the

Huguenots is described in similar words above, and it should be acknowledged that the number of Indonesian-Dutch that had come to the Netherlands was larger than the number of Huguenots in the seventeenth century: between 1945 and 1958, some 250,000 Indonesian-Dutch were repatriated. In addition, their settlement was remarkably easy. We have to take into account, however, that the total Dutch population had increased since the seventeenth century and that a large proportion of those 250,000 returned or went on to other countries like the United States (especially California) and Australia.

The Indonesian-Dutch are people of mixed Dutch and Indonesian origin, who, according to the rules in former Dutch East Indies, were Dutch in a legal sense.[19] Their repatriation to the Netherlands was effected in stages: some came from concentration camps immediately after the war, some after the independence of Indonesia, still others years after independence, and a final group which came to the Netherlands consisted of people who wanted to be Indonesian at first but were not accepted in Indonesia or were forced to leave after the nationalization of Dutch property.

The relatively easy adaptation of the Indonesian-Dutch to Dutch society, their rapid economic and cultural integration, is not easy to clarify. The Indonesian-Dutch have unmistakenly different looks, but this fact did not seem to matter to most Dutch as long as the repatriates did not bother them. This type of tolerance is mentioned earlier. The Indonesian-Dutch did not have to bother the Dutch because they had had education in the Dutch style, were able to speak Dutch very well, found jobs easily because of favorable economic conditions, and were willing to be retrained. In addition, a general feeling of guilt toward the repatriates because the Dutch were not able to keep the colony of the Dutch-East Indies and the generally praiseworthy characteristics of the Indonesian-Dutch (obedience, quiet) may have contributed to their acceptance in the Netherlands. This might also explain why no hatred against the Indonesian-Dutch erupted in the 1950s, when a severe housing shortage existed and many Dutch were encouraged to emigrate because of overpopulation. Most Indonesian-Dutch found their way through Dutch society after initial stays in boarding houses. They have shown a preference for The Hague, the government seat which still has an Indonesian touch.

Some people have taken a new look at the repatriation period and claim that acceptance was not as general as has been suggested. They contend that Indonesian-Dutch were discriminated against because of their skin color and that many prejudices supposedly existed. There have been few studies in this field, and these recent allegations may be the results of a present biased view of history.[20]

A group that resented the loss of Indonesia very much was the political

Farmers Partij (Boeren Partij), a party that has often been connected with fascist and racist propaganda. As a party of anomic, disoriented farmers who rebelled against the established government, it gained strength in the 1960s and won three seats (out of 150) in Parliament in 1962. The Farmers party was the party of the person in the street, the "oppressed," and it attracted people other than farmers as well, including extreme right-wing nationalists. Even though it held negative opinions on minorities and represented strong nationalism and right-wing extremism, the Farmers party, according to Ad Nooij, cannot be called fascist.[21] Relative deprivation, a structural marginalization, and an ambivalent attitude toward democracy did not result in racist actions by Farmers party members. The party lost most of its support in the 1970s and died, when its founder, Farmer Koekoek, disappeared from Parliament in 1981.

From the early 1960s on, the expanding Dutch economy created a shortage on the labor market. As a result, thousands of foreign workers were brought into the country, initially on a private basis but later on the basis of bilateral treaties between the Netherlands, Italy, Spain, Morocco, Turkey, and other Mediterranean countries. Workers from these countries became indispensable to do the "dirty work." They stayed longer than expected and were allowed to bring their families. Their presence seemed to be tolerated by the indigenous population, in the sense described before. The guest workers, as they were called, were considered a necessary but temporary part of Dutch society. These workers were set apart from mainstream society, and their problems were kept isolated from the general Dutch community for a long time. To speak in terms of race and race relations concerning these foreigners would be highly inappropriate.[22]

The number of postwar refugees from Eastern Europe, from Hungary after 1956, from Czechoslovakia after 1968, and from Chile, Vietnam, Turkey, Ethiopia, and recently Sri Lanka has always been limited. These groups have been spread out over the Netherlands and hardly ever caused any discussion or trouble. In one exception, the shooting of a Dutch youngster by a Vietnamese boat refugee resulted in the removal of several Vietnamese families from that particular town.

AFTER 1970: RECENT DEVELOPMENTS AND POLICIES

A distinct change in ethnic relations in the Netherlands occurred around 1970. The percentage of foreigners increased from 1.4 percent in 1968 to 5 percent in 1985, representing the largest increase in any European country in such a short period of time. Furthermore, most of these migrants came from non-Western European cultures.

The Dutch Bureau of Statistics (CBS) uses nationality as an indication of ethnicity. Many ethnics in the Netherlands, however, have the Dutch nationality, particularly migrants from the former colonies of Indonesia and Surinam and the present colony of the Netherlands Antilles. Still, nationality is considered a useful characteristic since naturalization rates are low. Owing to public opposition the Netherlands has not conducted a census since 1971 and we therefore have to rely on municipal data.

After World War II, a global process of decolonialization also affected the Dutch colonies in the Caribbean: the Netherlands Antilles and Surinam. In 1954, the Surinamese became Dutch citizens, which gave rise to an immigration flow of mostly the elite. They went to the Netherlands for study or better jobs.[23] After 1970, a chain migration relating to this early stream started, but the absolute numbers were never higher than a few thousand Surinamese (with Dutch passports) a year. The year 1975 marked the independence of the Surinam Republic, and an enormous increase in the number of migrants was the result. Under a special treaty, the Surinamese were given the choice of going to the Netherlands or staying in Surinam and becoming Surinamese citizens. In 1975 alone, 36,537 Surinamese left their country. Today about one-third of the Surinamese population has migrated to the Netherlands, leaving Surinam in severe economic and demographic straits.

The Dutch government, overwhelmed by the stream of Surinamese, was faced with a shortage in housing, employment, and other facilities. The 1973 oil crisis had its effect on the Dutch economy, and soon a negative image of the Surinamese emerged: people who expected life to be better in the Netherlands than in Surinam and who migrated to benefit from Dutch social security facilities, since there were no jobs for them. Their Dutch citizenship entitled them to those facilities. As a coincidence, a new high-rise suburb near Amsterdam had just been completed in 1975, and many Surinamese ended up in massive apartment buildings which had been planned for the well-to-do. The social problems associated with this type of construction and the unsuitability of the apartments for larger Surinamese families caused indigenous people to move out or stay away from the suburb. The "Bijlmermeer" as it is called, is still synonymous for Surinam ghetto among the Dutch, in spite of costly programs to change the demographic structure of the population and even the alteration of street names. Officially, the Bijlmermeer suburb is now called Amsterdam-Southeast. Van Amersfoort has pointed out the diversity of the Surinamese group, both socioeconomically and racially. There are three main subgroups—Creoles, Hindustanis, and Javanese—each with its own religion and culture.

The Surinamese were the most visible immigrant group after the war: most of them are black as opposed to the light-colored Indonesian-Dutch. Their ability to speak Dutch, their familiarity with Dutch culture as a result of almost three centuries of colonial rule (1667–1954) and the relatively good education of several of them gave them the opportunity to defend themselves and fight for their rights.[24] At the same time, the indigenous Dutch population criticized the aforementioned use of social benefits and made fun of the Surinamese accent.

People from the Netherlands Antilles have not come to the Netherlands in large numbers. The country is still a Dutch colony, although one island, Aruba, got a "status aparte" in 1986 and will become independent in the 1990s. It is difficult to predict whether this change will precipitate a heavy migration from the Antilles to the Netherlands, but since the total population is small, the absolute number of migrants will never be high.[25]

South Moluccans are probably the most well-known Dutch ethnic minority. Their terrorist actions in the 1970s, and especially the two train hijackings in 1975 and 1977, drew worldwide attention. Of course, the small number of terrorists among the Moluccans does not represent the entire community of about 35,000 in the Netherlands.

After the failure of the South Moluccan Republic, established on April 25, 1950, and disrupted by the Indonesian Army on November 3 of the same year, some 4,000 inhabitants of the island of Ambon, soldiers with their spouses and children, came to the Netherlands.[26] Their migration was meant to be temporary until a solution could be found for their problems in Indonesia, but a solution was never found. Easily recognizable by their skin color, although some people cannot tell the difference between a Surinamer and a Moluccan, they were housed together in temporary camps and so did not get the opportunity to settle and integrate within Dutch society. Moreover, their ambition to establish a South Moluccan Republic in the Indonesian archipelago was kept alive. The U.S.'s haphazard support of these ambitions was not necessary to overthrow Sukarno, the anti-Moluccan leader of Indonesia, in 1965. The Suharto regime that followed was not better, and the South Moluccan leader Soumokil was killed in 1966. In the meantime, a government-in-exile had been established in the Netherlands.

Partly owing to these frustrations and the nonacceptance by the Dutch, as well as the political indifference of the Dutch government on the issue of the South Moluccan Republic, many young South Moluccans drifted away. The 1970s terrorist actions are often explained on the basis of this background, compounded by high unemployment among South Moluccan youngsters: four out of ten were unemployed.

The South Moluccans lost a great deal of sympathy in the Netherlands after the train hijackings and other incidents at the Indonesian Embassy. During the hijackings in northeast Netherlands, a total of 388 persons were taken as hostages and four of them died, while a dozen hijackers were killed. Alex Schmid and others conclude that Dutch society has become more closed as a result of the terrorist actions.[27] A long time after the train hijackings, travelers on trains were frightened upon seeing a person who looked like a Moluccan, and some even went as far as to sound the alarm. (The person feared often turned out to be a Surinamer.) The terrorism has probably had an impact on Dutch attitudes toward people who are "different" in general beyond the mere color of their skin.

In 1979, the Dutch government officially admitted that the Netherlands had become an immigration country.[28] Moluccans, Indonesian-Dutch, and Surinamese were likely to stay for their lifetime and so would their children. A majority of the guest workers would not return to their mother countries in spite of their claims to the contrary. Return rates are low, and special programs with premiums for those who go back voluntarily have not been successful.[29]

The government's recognition of the permanence of the migrants' stay required that it develop an immigration policy. Whereas assimilation had been considered the usual process in which migrants adapted to the new country, evidence that this had not happened, resistance against the assimilationist ideology, and the presence of many different migrant groups resulted in a so-called pluralist policy. The development in policy is very similar to that of other countries, and the present pluralist policy in the Netherlands is comparable to similar policies in Canada, Sweden, and Australia and other multicultural societies.[30] Ethnic groups are encouraged to retain their cultural identity and at the same time are given the opportunity to settle in Dutch society. The Dutch pluralist policy does not differentiate between ethnic groups, although more emphasis is placed on programs for the largest groups, that is, the Turks and Moroccans. Several special programs have been developed in the fields of education, housing, and employment. Broadcasts in foreign languages on radio and television have been started only recently. The most important change is that, starting in 1986, foreigners who have been in the Netherlands more than five years will be entitled to vote and enroll in municipal elections.

The term "race" is not used in the pluralist policy whatsoever. Instead, the term "ethnic minority" is utilized, which describes a rather awkward selection of groups, owing to political considerations: Moluccans, Surinamese, Antillians, refugees, Chinese, gypsies, and people from Mediterranean countries. Included are people with and without Dutch nationality, and excluded are Indonesian-Dutch, Jews, and small groups of Asians and Africans. Groups that have entered the Netherlands recently are also excluded. Policies concerning these groups are haphazard, as the approximately 3,000 Tamils who sought entry in vain from Sri Lanka experienced in 1985.

Another tendency should be noted here: nonethnic groups that consider themselves minorities in Dutch society have started to request special attention and special programs, much as the handicapped, homosexuals, and people with minimum incomes have obtained.

Research reveals that many people do not know how many foreigners live in the Netherlands. The actual total in 1985 was 5 to 6 percent. Yet more than half the population believes that more than 10 to 15 percent of those living in the Netherlands are foreigners.[31] People cannot tell the difference between a Muslim Surinamer and an Indonesian, or between a Turk and a Moroccan. Differences in physical appearance are often generalized in terms as black, brown, or colored, as well as in terms of clothing, especially women's clothing. A distinction between "them" and "us" seems more important for many people, and such distinctions are based on many different characteristics: attitudes, speech, class, occupation, number of children, and so on. The term "ethnicity" disguises these concrete characteristics.

Whatever term is used, non-Dutch citizens are set apart in the Netherlands of the 1980s. As shown in the previous section, ethnicity has never disappeared entirely from the political scene, but after the 1930s, national socialists and racists were not vocal in electoral politics. This also changed in the 1970s.

On September 8, 1982, the extremely right-wing political party Centrumpartij (CP) gained 68,386 votes (0.8 percent) in the national elections. Since there is no electoral threshold in the Netherlands, this meant one seat in Parliament and a lot of tumult.[32] It was not the first time a party with obvious anti-migrant ideas had taken part in an election, but it was the first time such a party got enough support for representation in Parliament.

Some people began to talk about a racist electorate and emphasized the importance of race for many voters. Other claimed that the CP-votes were largely the result of general feelings of discomfort with national politics, and they mentioned the history of the Farmers party as a protest party. Those who stated that the CP adherents were xenophobic seemed to have been vindicated after the municipal elections in Almere (near Amsterdam) where the CP gained more than 9 percent of the votes and three seats in the local council. In addition, extreme right-wing parties became more powerful in France (Le Pen), Britain (National Front), and Germany (National Democrat party of Germany—NDP).

These developments caused a lot of turmoil among other political parties, and many letters to the editor appeared in newspapers and weeklies. In 1984, internal troubles and personal quarrels produced rifts within the Centrumpartij. The CP-member of Parliament was expelled from the party. In several municipalities, CP members resigned from the councils, and in public opinion polls support for the CP seems to be down to less than 0.5 percent, which is not enough for one seat.

Does this latest development mean that the Dutch are not as racist as was thought immediately after the Centrumpartij success in 1982? The situation is far more intricate, and research in this field has been limited up to now. Still, we can distinguish several important developments.

First, the permanence of migrants in the Netherlands, which became clear in the 1970s, has made people more aware of the presence of migrants in society. Immigration and pluralist policies have been widely discussed, and any measure or incident concerning migrants has been reported in the press. It is nevertheless difficult to get an idea of the full range of those measures and incidents. As far as incidents are concerned, the awareness of discrimination and racism in the Netherlands seems to be growing and insults, fights, and attacks make headlines in newspapers. To date, two foreigners have been killed on racist grounds. The killing of a young Antillian by a Dutchman of the same age evoked a large demonstration against racism, with the lord mayor of Amsterdam heading the crowd, while a monument was erected for the victim. This makes clear that racist violence is rather uncommon in the Netherlands, compared to that in other countries.

The extent to which these occurrences are exceptional in comparison with earlier times is not known inasmuch as actions against minorities have been poorly documented. Bovenkerk and others are among the few who have tested situations in which two people applied for a job, a white first and a black consequently. It appeared that blacks were refused jobs significantly more often, solely on the ground of their skin color.[33] Thereafter, several researchers have traced discrimination on racial grounds in government policies, and recruitment and dismissal by companies as well as in daily life. Paternalism in school books, irrelevant mention of ethnicity in newspaper articles and overrepresentation of news items of criminal offenses by members of ethnic minorities have been revealed.[34] Humdrum racism has been described extensively, and a survey of racist organizations has been conducted.[35]

Attention to race and ethnic relations has increased in the Netherlands, as has sensitivity to the issue. Even mentioning race may give rise to a lot of trouble. For example, a professor in criminology, Wouter Buikhuisen, wanted to study the relationship between the biological characteristics of human beings and their criminal inclinations. He was not granted any funds because of resistance from fellow researchers and the media against this kind of project.

The Dutch attitude to race and ethnicity might have become hypersensitive over the last few years. The following discussion illustrates this point. An expression in Dutch similar to "black as ink" is "black as soot." In a Dutch folk song about Saint Nicholas, his servant Black Peter is depicted as such, and several authors have recently translated this ancient tradition, celebrated yearly on December 5, in terms of racism. According to those authors, the link between the blackness of Peter and his subordination to the white Saint Nicholas is a clear example of Dutch racism. The song "Peter, black as soot" is therefore transferring racist content from parents to children generation after generation. It is said that Surinamese and other black people mind this custom and therefore Black Peter should be abandoned in the celebration of Saint Nicholas.

Bovenkerk has defended the custom, proving that Black Peter has nothing to do with a different race. He has traced the origin of Black Peter to chimney sweeps in the nineteenth century. They were "black as soot" and came, as Peter supposedly still does in the song, down the chimney.[36] Apart from the question as to whether this proves the non-racist background of the custom, the mere questioning of it and the anger about it characterize the present climate in the Netherlands with regard to race.

MEASURES AGAINST RACISM AND DISCRIMINATION

The Netherlands' increased awareness of racism, the publicity given racist actions, the growing number of studies in this field, and the alert-ness of minorities themselves have resulted in several measures against racism and discrimination. Those measures, both legal and in the domain of guidance, education, and social control, have been started only very recently. Again, this late awakening of consciousness in both government and private organizations can be attributed to the late acknowledgment of the Netherlands as an immigration country and the nonusage of the variable "race" in research.

Ethnic groups themselves have not been very powerful in requesting measures and laws. Some even argue that it has been mostly white bro-kers and intermediate persons who have introduced proposals to change laws. Although a high degree of integration is necessary to know one's way through bureaucracy and established structures in the Netherlands, some members of ethnic minorities have acquired those skills very well. There is another reason why measures have been taken to protect and help ethnic minorities: a sense of justice among politicians and, nega-tively, the fear that Dutch politics would be discredited if nothing were done against racism.

More and more changes of laws and new regulations have come into effect. A report was published in 1983 presenting an overview of all laws that (may) discriminate against non-Dutch citizens. A voluminous book of 500 pages resulted.[37] The media are very alert to distinctions between Dutch and non-Dutch citizens, as a result of which the indigenous Dutch have started to complain about the overattention given to ethnic mi-norities and the neglect of low-income Dutch people. A concise overview of the laws and measures follows.[38]

The first article of the new Dutch Constitution (sanctioned February

1, 1983) reads: "All those in the Netherlands will be treated equally in equal cases. Discrimination on the basis of religion, persuasion, political inclination, race, sex or whichever ground is not permitted" (Article 1.1). The Netherlands government ratified the United Nations treaty on the elimination of all forms of racism in 1966. Since then, pressure groups have pointed out the consequences of such a ratification. No law was sanctioned until 1976. The new constitution is an extra means to oppose discrimination. As has been true in other countries, however, implementation of anti-discrimination laws is difficult. Some people assert that these laws are mere façades. Moreover, those who are likely to discriminate or act racially are unlikely to acknowledge the authority of laws.[39] Nevertheless, by 1986 a dozen laws were operative in the Netherlands. Court cases and condemnations on the basis of these laws have increased during the last few years. The main laws are:

Penal Code

Article ninety: "Discrimination is understood as any form of distinction or any exclusion, limitation, or preference with the purpose to or has the effect of interfering with the acknowledgment, the enjoyment or the pursuit of human rights, and the fundamental freedoms in the domains of politics, economics, culture or any other area of public life."

Articles 137c, d, and e forbid insults in public on the basis of race, religion, or faith, incitement to hatred, or discrimination.

Article four-hundred-twenty-nine forbids partakement in or support of any activity geared to discrimination.

Articles four-hundred-twenty-nine: "Whoever makes a distinction between persons on the basis of race while conducting a business or pursuing a trade, will be taken into custody for a month at most or will be fined up to ƒ 10,000 (US $3,000)."

Civil Code

Article 15 concerns forbidden corporate bodies among those racist parties. This article has not been used to forbid organizations like the Centrumpartij, mainly because of an ongoing discussion as to whether prohibition will produce the desired effects.[40]

There are also articles against discrimination in relation to hotel catering and drinking laws in the International Treaty on Civil and Political Rights, the European Treaty on the Protection of Human Rights and Fundamental Freedoms, in the social laws concerning unemployment and old age benefits, and in a new law on Dutch citizenship. The citizenship law has been modified, making it easier for foreigners to become Dutch citizens. (They can gain citizenship after only three years of living in the Netherlands.)

Upholding these laws and treaties in practice is difficult, and ethnic people are not very prone to use their legal rights. One has to take into account that the Dutch legal system is based on the Code Napoleon and is different from Common Law in Anglo-Saxon countries. It is not common in Dutch law to sue a person, and to produce evidence against a person is rather complicated. This may explain why so few people have actually used these laws against racism and discrimination. In 1981–82, ten court cases were filed under the penal code, and, although that figure was up to 55 in 1982–83, it is still low.

The Supreme Court in the Netherlands has ruled that race as it appears in the U.N. declarations is to be interpreted very broadly. In practice, race is used as an equivalent to ethnicity, and Jews, for instance, are subsumed under race. On the one hand, this rule is in accordance with Dutch tradition in which ethnicity is the most important variable. On the other hand, this usage of the term "race" in official and legal statements is a break with tradition as "race" has generally been avoided.

Ethnicity in the Netherlands is seen as a social problem, not as a substantial political problem, since political opinions on ethnic issues do not vary largely. The government's inattention to ethnic problems seems mostly a matter of complacency; structural changes are not made, not in the least because of fear of protest by the white majority. This situation is crucial in discussions of affirmative action, which is another potential legal measure to improve the circumstances of ethnic groups. While there is consensus about the necessity of caring for the ethnic minorities, affirmative action is meeting a lot of resistance, both because of the attitude of the white majority and because of the idea that legal measures have only limited power to change the situation.[41]

RACE, CLASS, OR RELIGION

Ethnicity in the Netherlands became important in the 1970s, although still less than 6 percent of the Dutch population was foreign born. To call the Netherlands a multi-ethnic country and to impose a multicultural policy might therefore be somewhat premature. Those terms might have more ideological than practical meaning in the Netherlands in the 1980s. Until now, relations between groups have been discussed entirely in terms of race and ethnicity. Dutch history, however, has been marked by other criteria, and the present question is whether these old variables like religion and class are still prevalent or whether they indeed have been wiped out by race and ethnicity.

Traditionally, religion has been the most important criterion for cross-cutting cleavages in Dutch society. Political and other groups have been established around religion, and the relative strength and peacefulness in spite of those divisions are remarkable. Most social institutions used to be split according to religion. One's sports club, school, paper, radio and TV broadcasting corporation, trade union, women's club, and political party—all have been organized along denominational lines. This situation has been called pillarization, which means that there is relatively great isolation between religious groups (Protestants, Catholics, nondenominational, Jews) and only a few contacts at the top of those pillars.[42] This situation protected the Netherlands from violent religious clashes in the 1917–70 period.

Today these traditional divisions and the resulting pluralism have largely disappeared, and religion is no longer an important criterion. The religious parties in Parliament have lost their majority, falling from 53 percent of the votes in 1963 to only 28 percent in current opinion polls. Nondenominational parties have gained support in line with the well-known labor-liberal division. The opening up of the pillarization system has been attributed to secularization, the mass media, and the influx of migrants who brought with them their own religions (mainly Islamic and Hindu). Those groups have started their own pillars with their own religious-based organizations. This situation has added to the pluralism, most strikingly on radio and television, where many small (religious) groups have their own programs.

In general, religion is not as important in politics and daily life as it used to be. Few are judged by their religion, as was the case twenty years ago when Catholic and Protestant school children did not mix, intermarriage was forbidden, and people from the south of the Netherlands, being mostly Catholic, separated themselves from people of the north, being mostly Protestant.

Most ethnic minorities, as is inherent to the term, belong to the lower socioeconomic strata of Dutch society. Exceptions are the Indonesian-Dutch who generally are middle class. Moreover, distinctions between different ethnic groups exist. Surinamese are higher on the stratification ladder than Turks and Moroccans, which is contrary to the British situation where South and East European migrants generally have better positions than black migrants. Race and class do not totally coincide in the Netherlands, and the two are growing more apart from each other.

Robert Miles and Annie Phizacklea, two British social scientists who are widely read in the Netherlands, have argued that class is much more important than race in Western societies.[43] According to them, the proletarianization of immigrants started with their arrival in the North and West European countries. Race is a mere social construction and not a biological fact. It does not help to clarify relations between people, neither for whites nor for blacks. Miles emphasizes the differentiation among blacks, and the Dutch researcher Bovenkerk agrees with him: part of the black mass belongs to the "legion of the unemployed," others to the working class, and still others to the petty bourgeoisie of ethnic entrepreneurs.

This situation is true for the Netherlands, and it is even more so when distinctions between different ethnic groups are taken into account. Certain groups are better off than others, and their stage of migration, that is, the time they have been in the Netherlands, plays a role in the status and economic positions they have acquired. A solid mass of minorities is a myth.

Nevertheless, one must be cautious in stating that class is a more important variable than race. This might be the case in a statistical and theoretical sense. Some people will often not admit that they are in the same socioeconomic class as certain members of an ethnic group.[44] As Miles and others argue, laborers and ethnic groups do not necessarily join in one fight against the bourgeoisie. A recent Dutch study on attitudes among trade union members toward ethnic minorities makes this clear.[45] It would go beyond the scope of this article to explain the importance of class in Dutch society. Research on class divisions within ethnic groups is still limited, and we can hardly conclude anything from that material yet.

CONCLUSION

If we are to conclude that the exclusion of and discrimination against ethnic minorities in the Netherlands has not been a common phenomenon, that race did not play an important role until the 1970s and thereafter mostly an ideological role, that ethnicity in a very broad sense is more common, and that other cross-cutting cleavages like religion and class have also played an important role in Dutch intergroup relations, we are still left with one question. Even if the Netherlands is a reasonable nonracist country, even if tolerance toward ethnic groups exists, though in the sense of "not to be bothered," even if the government tries to avoid discriminatory measures and is made conscious about that constantly, even if in many instances blacks and whites work together, aren't the Dutch ethnocentric and won't they resist allowing others to interfere with the Dutch way of life?

Ethnocentrism and racism are not the same. Banton argues that ethnocentrism is a modern version of racism because the inherent superiority and inferiority of people are proclaimed in terms of ethnicity.[46] It may be incorrect to use the term "ethnocentric" here, for it is not practical. One may be considered ethnocentric when one judges the behavior of a member of another (ethnic) group according to one's own cultural norms. This is almost always a negative judgment, although there may also be positive aspects in the other's behavior. An ethnocentric person is able to tolerate the member of the other group, hoping or expecting that the other person will change his or her behavior and attitudes in due course.

Ethnocentrism in this sense is very common in the Netherlands. People may be prejudiced toward ethnic minorities but at the same time do not think these people should have to leave the country.[47] The reasoning behind this rationale is simple: ethnic minorities have different attitudes and habits, but those can be changed. Foreigners who have adapted to the Dutch style of life, if there is one, are highly acclaimed.

The prejudices concerning ethnic minorities are widespread and add to the idea that they "are indeed different": ethnic minorities smell, they breed too many children, they don't have respect for animals, and they are criminal. Information contradicting these prejudices does not tend to change people's opinions.[48]

Ethnic minorities and other groups are judged on the basis of difference in the Netherlands: the differences can be very small, like occupational status or the way somebody cooks food or decorates his house. Skin color is very often not the basic reason for rejection. Many Dutch people value differences in life-style, and this type of ethnocentrism or defining of in- and out-groups is very strong in Dutch society. "The in-group is best," and therefore others have to be convinced of it.[49] Paternalistic help to members of the out-group, be it ethnic minorities, is common, and there exists an unremitting zeal to help the out-group learn "the best life-style." Very few ethnic organizations can do without a "white" Dutch person, whose mission is to help the ethnics. Köbben has written a history of these persons who do not belong to the minority group but who play the role of solicitor for the group.[50]

A high level of tolerance, together with a structural ethnocentrism, may explain race and ethnic relations in the Netherlands today. On the one hand, there is relative harmony and little violence; on the other hand, there is much talk about ethnic minorities and their different cultures. The necessity of adaptation or retaining cultural identity is a public debate: every Dutch citizen feels that the issue is touching his or her "in-group" life-style. It might be a mere coincidence that the "out-group" of the 1970s and 1980s has a different skin color. The next decade will bring other out-groups.

NOTES

1. Michael Banton, *Racial and Ethnic Competition* (Cambridge: Cambridge University Press, 1983), pp. 32–59.

2. Ibid., p. 77.

3. Frank Bovenkerk, ed., *Omdat Zij Anders Zijn* (Meppel: Boom, 1978), p. 29.

4. Robert Miles and Annie Phizacklea, eds., *Racism and Political Action in Britain* (London: Routledge & Kegan Paul, 1979).

5. Annie Phizacklea and Robert Miles, *Labour and Racism* (London: Routledge & Kegan Paul, 1980), p. 22.

6. Christopher Bagley, *The Dutch Plural Society* (London: Oxford University Press, 1973).

7. André Köbben, *Van Primitieven tot Medeburgers* (Assen: Van Gorcum, 1964), p. 219.

8. Han Entzinger, "The Non-Usage of 'Race' in the Netherlands," *New Community* 8, Nos. 1–2 (1980): 26–30.

9. Philomena Essed, *Alledaags Racisme* (Amsterdam: SARA, 1984).

10. Cees Cruson, *Huguenot Refugees in 17th Century Amsterdam* (Rotterdam: Erasmus University, 1984).

11. I. Schöffer, *De Hugenoten in Nederland* (Delft: 1964).

12. Jan Lucassen, *Naar de Kusten van de Noordzee* (Gouda: s.n., 1984).

13. Johan Goudsblom, *Dutch Society* (New York: Random House, 1967), pp. 31–33.

14. F. van Heek, *Chineesche Immigranten in Nederland* (Amsterdam: Emmering, 1936).

15. Frank Bovenkerk et al., *Toen en Thans* (Baarn: Ambo, 1978), pp. 208–36.

16. Lou de Jong, *Het Koninkrijk der Nederlanden in de Tweede Wereldoorlog*, Vol. 5a (The Hague: Government Publishing Office, 1974).

17. S. R. Steinmetz et al., *De Rassen der Menschheid* (Amsterdam: 1938).

18. Hans van Amersfoort, *Immigration and the Formation of Minority Groups* (Cambridge: Cambridge University Press, 1982), p. 81.

19. Banton, *Racial and Ethnic Composition*, pp. 29–30, is not correct in stating that Dutch-Indonesians are counted as white since such a classification is never made. See also note 8.

20. Annemarie Cottaar and Wim Willems, *Indische Nederlanders, een Onderzoek naar Beeldvorming* (Den Haag: Moesson, 1984).

21. Ad Nooij, *De Boerenpartij: Desoriëntatie en Radicalisme onder Boeren* (Meppel: Boom, 1969).

22. Rinus Penninx, "Research and Policy with Regard to Ethnic Minorities in the Netherlands," *International Migration* 22, No. 4 (1984): 345–66.

23. Amersfoort, *Immigration*, pp. 136ff.

24. T. J. Reubsaet et al., *Surinaamse Migranten in Nederland* (Nijmegen: Instituut voor Toegepaste Sociologie, 1983).

25. Willem Koot and Anco Ringeling, *De Antillianen* (Muiderberg: Coutinho, 1984). Incidentally, these authors state that Antillians are not light-colored, but black.

26. Alex Schmid et al., *Zuidmoluks Terrorisme, de Media en de Publieke Opinie* (Amsterdam: Intermediair, 1982), pp. 21–69.

27. Ibid., p. 63.

28. The publication of a report by the Netherlands Scientific Council for Government Policy (Penninx, "Research and Policy") can be considered the official landmark of this assent. In 1983, a Minorities Report followed, laying out the policy proposals toward ethnic minorities (*De Minderhedennota*, The Hague: Government Publishing Office, 1983).

29. Flip Muus et al., *Retourmigratie van Mediterranen, Surinamers en Antillianen uit Nederland* (The Hague: Ministry of Social Affairs, 1983).

30. Hubert Campfens, *The Integration of Ethno-cultural Minorities* (The Hague: Ministry of Culture, 1979) and Tomas Hammar, ed., *European Immigration Policy*

(Cambridge: Cambridge University Press, 1984). See also Jean Martin, *The Ethnic Dimension* (Sydney: George Allen & Unwin, 1981).

31. Unpublished Public Opinion Poll carried out by the Netherlands Inter-University Demographic Institute, Voorburg, 1985.

32. Jaap van Donselaar and Carlo van Praag, *Stemmen op de Centrumpartij* (Leiden: State University, 1983).

33. Frank Bovenkerk, ed., *Omdat Zij Anders Zijn* (Meppel: Boom, 1978), pp. 31–58.

34. Teun van Dijk, *Minderheden in de Media* (Amsterdam: SUA, 1983).

35. *De Rechterkant van Nederland* (Amsterdam: SUA, 1983).

36. Frank Bovenkerk and Loes Ruland, "De Schoorsteenvegers," *Intermediair* 20, No. 51 (December 1984): 23–39.

37. H. Beune and A. Hessels, *Minderheid—Minder Recht?* (The Hague: Government Publishing Office, 1983).

38. See also Natan Lerner, *The UN Convention on the Elimination of All Forms of Racial Discrimination* (Alphen aan den Rijn: Sijthoff, 1980).

39. Joed Elich and Benjo Maso, *Discriminatie, Vooroordeel en Racisme in Nederland* (The Hague: Ministry of the Interior, 1984).

40. *Congres Recht en Raciale Verhoudingen, Congresbundel* (Utrecht: s.n., 1983).

41. Elich and Maso, *Discriminatie*, p. 119.

42. Arend Lijphart, *Verzuiling, Pacificatie en Kentering in de Nederlandse Politiek* (Amsterdam: De Bussy, 1982).

43. Annie Phizacklea and Robert Miles, *Labour and Racism* (London: Routledge & Kegan Paul, 1980).

44. This section has not taken into account the difference between class and standing ("estate") as brilliantly described by Max Weber in his essay "Klasse, Stand und Partei." This difference, however, is mostly restricted to European situations where there is a difference in life-style between nobility and burghers.

45. Ruud de Jongh, Marion van der Laan, and Jan Rath, *FNV'ers aan het Woord over Buitenlandse Werknemers* (Leiden: State University, 1985).

46. Michael Banton, "The Concept of Racism," in S. Zubaida, ed., *Race and Racialism* (London: Tavistock, 1970), pp. 28ff.

47. Elich and Maso, *Discriminatie*, p. 41.

48. Rinus Penninx, "De Mythe van Verkleurend Nederland," *Intermediair* 20, No. 11 (March 1984): 1–9.

49. Frank Bovenkerk et al., *Vreemd Volk, Gemengde Gevoelens* (Meppel: Boom, 1985).

50. André Köbben, *De Zaakwaarnemer* (Deventer: Van Loghum Slaterus, 1983).

BIBLIOGRAPHY

Amersfoort, H. van. *Immigration and the Formation of Minority Groups: The Dutch Experience 1945–1975*. Cambridge: Cambridge University Press, 1982.

Berg-Eldering, L. van den, et al. *Multicultural Education: A Challenge for Teachers*. Dordrecht: Floris, 1983.

Beyer, G. "The Benelux Countries: Belgium, the Netherlands and Luxemburg." *The Politics of Migration Policies*, edited by D. Kubat. New York: Center for Migration Studies, 1979.

Bovenkerk, F., et al. "Comparative Aspects of Research on Discrimination Against Non-White Citizens in Great-Britain, France and the Netherlands." *Problems in International Comparative Research*, edited by J. Berting et al. Oxford: Pergamon Press, 1979.

Campfens, H. *The Integration of Ethno-cultural Minorities: A Pluralistic Approach.* The Netherlands and Canada, a Comparative Analysis of Policy and Programme. The Hague: Ministry of Culture, 1979.

Ellemers, J. E. "Race Relations in the Netherlands and Their Policy Implications: A Review Article." *Sociologica Neerlandica* 11, No. 2 (1975): 181–87.

Entzinger, H. B. "The Non-Usage of 'Race' in the Netherlands." *New Community* 8, No. 1–2 (1980): 26–30.

Hofstede, B. P. *Thwarted Exodus: Postwar Overseas Migration from the Netherlands.* The Hague: Martinus Nijhoff, 1964.

Houte, H. van, and W. Milgert. *Foreigners in Our Community.* Amsterdam: Keesing, 1971.

Immigrant Ethnic Minorities in the Netherlands. Planning and Development 8 (1981), No. 1. Assen: Van Gorcum.

Netherlands Scientific Council for Government Policy. *Ethnic Minorities.* The Hague: Government Publishing Office, 1979.

————. "The Political Participation of Ethnic Minorities in the Netherlands." *International Migration Review* 17, No. 3 (1983): 445–70.

Rath, J. "The Enfranchisement of Immigrants in Practice: Turkish and Moroccan Islands in the Fairway of Dutch Politics." *Netherlands Journal of Sociology* 19, No. 2 (1983): 151–81.

NEW ZEALAND

Andrew D. Trlin and Paul Spoonley

The study of race relations in New Zealand has been uneven in terms of both the quality of the material produced and its coverage. Relatively few attempts have been made to develop a systematic theoretical framework. In contrast, there have been some excellent studies of various minority groups. This is due to the influence of anthropology which has a long history of research in New Zealand compared with the relatively recent arrivals of sociology and political science.

The presence of an indigenous Polynesian group was an important factor in attracting European-trained anthropologists and collectors. This anthropological tradition is still active, and it is characterized by a concern with the notions of ethnic group and ethnicity. But this emphasis on the cultural uniqueness and adaptations of a particular group has meant that social science research has placed considerably less emphasis on the relations between groups and on the broader questions of the social and economic context. Thus, there are relatively few ethnographic studies of the dominant white group, or on the way in which the issues of racism and ethnicity intersect with economic and political relations. Obviously, these theoretical and empirical inadequacies will be reflected here, compounded by the substantial transformation of New Zealand's race relations in the 1980s.

Before proceeding to the discussion of these issues, there is one epistemological point to be made. Throughout the text the term "race" is used as a socially constructed concept. Patterns of phenotypical variation are invested with social significance, and the task here is to investigate the way in which race is perceived and has meaning in a specific context, New Zealand. (For an elaboration of this point, see R. Miles and P. Spoonley.)[1]

A RACIAL CONTEXT

Throughout this article, the term "Maori" will be used to refer to the original Polynesian inhabitants of New Zealand, the *tangata whenua* (people of the land), while the term "Pakeha" refers to European New Zealanders. Maori is a contrived category to the extent that it derives from early attempts by European settlers to create an inclusive category for the indigenous people of New Zealand. The term is now widely used and accepted, although it necessarily diminishes the important tribal affiliations of the Maori. Pakeha, although an equivalent term, is not universally accepted. Many Pakeha reject it as having a derogatory meaning, which is incorrect, or as inappropriate because of its Maori derivation. This unease signals the way in which the Maori role and contribution to New Zealand society is contested by Pakehas who cling to British cultural traditions. Finally, the other most important racial category is that of Pacific Islander. Both Pakeha and Maori group together quite ethnically separate Polynesians from various Pacific Islands who have migrated to New Zealand, but they are regarded as explicitly different from the indigenous Polynesian, the Maori.

The vast majority of European migrants to New Zealand have been British. New Zealand was colonized by Pakehas in the mid-nineteenth century after a treaty in 1840 that was supposedly intended to protect Maori interests. This treaty, the Treaty of Waitangi, forms an important part of the mythology of Pakehas who see New Zealand's recent history as avoiding the exploitation and oppression that marked European colonization elsewhere in the world. Seemingly unaware of Maori perceptions of the same history and ignoring the open conflict of the late nineteenth century, the Land Wars, Pakehas tend to claim that New Zealand race relations have been something of a model. An important challenge to these attitudes was mounted in the 1970s and 1980s as sociodemographic factors had an impact, and a new form of Maori assertiveness and nationalism politicized race.

Conflict and disease decimated the Maori population in the nineteenth century. From a population base of approximately 250,000 prior to Pakeha settlement, the number of Maoris dropped to 40,000 by 1900. This population tended to be confined to remote rural areas; thus, there was little contact between most Maori and Pakeha. The Pakeha felt that they were witnessing the last stages of a "dying race." But a demographic and cultural renaissance that began in the early decades of the twentieth century has dramatically altered the situation. The full impact was not felt until the late 1960s when Maori migration to urban areas began to nudge issues concerning racism and ethnic identity from the margins of political discourse and public consciousness to center stage. This was underlined by the postwar arrival in New Zealand of large numbers of

Table 19
Major Ethnic Origin Groups in New Zealand, 1981

Group	No.	Percent
European	2,696,568	85.8
Maori	279,081	8.9
Samoan	42.081)	
Cook Island Maori	23,880)	
Niuean	8,079)	
Tongan	6,900)	2.7
Tokelauan	2,274)	
Other Polynesian	699)	
Chinese	18,480	.6
Indian	11,244	.3
Other	54,021	1.7
TOTAL	3,143,307	100.0

Source: New Zealand Census of Population and Dwellings.

Polynesians from various Pacific Islands. By 1981, Polynesians, both Maori and Pacific Islander, were approaching 12 percent of New Zealand's total population and were experiencing a much higher growth rate than the Pakeha population. The postwar generations of Maoris and Pacific Islanders, now urban-born and with a young leadership that was often tertiary-educated, questioned the racism of Pakeha attitudes and behavior. For a list of New Zealand's major ethnic groups, see Table 19.

In New Zealand, race has long been used to legitimate the dominance of the Pakeha, although in a somewhat contradictory way. Despite the propensity of the Pakeha to use race as a means of classifying others and to act on this categorization, there is a widely expressed denial that race is an important consideration in New Zealand or that racial problems exist. This ideological position is undermined by the obvious disadvantages faced by Polynesians and the tendency of Pakehas to identify Polynesian group membership with various negative features. Stereotypes identify Polynesians as being happy, quick-tempered, musical, dirty, uneducated, easygoing, friendly, generous, quiet, and clannish, while Pakehas are described by New Zealanders as being materialistic, self-reliant, arrogant, ambitious, serious, intelligent, progressive, loud, and brash.[2] In a limited survey in 1968, P. H. Curson found that color was a principal feature in identifying the cause of problems in Auckland.[3] He discovered that 43 percent of his respondents believed Pacific Islanders to be mainly responsible for the depressed housing and social conditions of their area, and another 24 percent intimated that they were at least partially responsible. Research on social distance confirms the fact that Pacific Islander groups are held in low esteem by Pakehas.[4] A 1985 survey (the New Zealand Values Study) indicated that 11.9 percent and 18 percent of respondents identified Maoris and Pacific Islanders, respectively, as "undesirable neighbours."[5] Thus, at one level, Pakehas will claim that New Zealand's race relations are relatively harmonious, but in terms of expressed personal attitudes, they will categorize Maoris and Pacific Islanders in racial terms and employ negative stereotypes.

These negative attitudes inevitably mean restricted opportunities for Polynesians as Pakehas in positions of power translate their beliefs into behavior. Gatekeepers, or those who control the allocation and access to resources such as employment, housing, or health, may not be prejudiced themselves, but the nature of dominant attitudes means that they are often forced to act as "reluctant discriminators."[6] For example, the possibility of an adverse reaction from customers, clients, or fellow workers provides an economic reason for being discriminatory. Evidence of such discrimination is provided in the annual reports of the Race Relations Conciliator and the publications of pressure groups such as the Auckland Committee on Racism and Discrimination (ACORD). There is a considerable amount of material on the disadvantages faced by Maoris and Pacific Islanders, although the racist nature of such disadvantages is still disputed by many Pakehas.

The most common response is to claim that "we're all New Zealanders" and racial matters are not or should not be important. The reporting of racial tension and problems is seen by many as creating a situation that has not previously existed. Hence, one favored response is to suggest that some unspecified Marxists are exploiting Maori issues.[7] And 67.4 percent of respondents in a national survey agreed or agreed strongly that "Maoris get a fair go in this country."[8] In this context, it is seen as unreasonable to pursue past injustices or to suggest that majority group practices and institutions disadvantage the Polynesian or other minority groups. It follows that those institutions and practices which recognize the separate needs of the Polynesian are anomalous and at variance with the dominant group's ideological stance. Thus, contrary to specific guarantees in the Treaty of Waitangi, 80.1 percent of New Zealanders polled felt that Maoris "should have the same land rights as other New Zealanders," thereby reaffirming the monocultural expectations of the Pakeha.[9] Similarly, another survey found that 64.1 percent were opposed to the retention of separate Maori parliamentary representation.[10]

But the parameters and direction of such debates have changed in the late 1970s and 1980s. The most important development has been the growth of Maori activist groups who assert *mana Maori motuhake* (Maori sovereignty). An early and influential group was Nga Tamatoa (the young warriors) who were active from 1970. As the decade proceeded, public protests such as the 1975 Land March publicizing Maori land grievances and the occupation of Bastion Point (Auckland) in 1977 provided the impetus for a new wave of Maori activists. The groups included the Waitangi Action Committee, He Taua (avenging party), Maori People's Liberation Movement of Aotearoa, and Black Women.[11] The concern is with Maori self-determination, and the focus is on seeking effective Maori representation in the power structures of New Zealand, on regaining control over Maori land and resources, and on seeing that *Maoritanga* (things Maori) take their rightful place in the institutions and practices of New Zealand. Maori women have played an important role in challenging Pakehas on these points. One of them, Donna Awatere, published three articles in 1982–83 (subsequently published as a book) which constitute the most important and complete statement of Maori sovereignty, a term first popularized in these articles.[12] These groups, along with some Pakeha anti-racist groups, challenge the dominant Pakeha group in two ways.

First, they confront the racism of Pakehas in an assertive and direct manner. The relative absence of debate and concern on these matters in the 1950s and 1960s contrasts sharply with the intensity and power of contemporary debates over racism. And the challenge is not simply presented to conservative groups. In 1981, a tour by South African rugby players to New Zealand produced a major cleavage in the community between supporters and opponents which often resulted in violence as the tour proceeded. Many Maori activists criticized Pakeha liberal and left-wing groups for becoming politically active on apartheid in South Africa while ignoring, or doing relatively little, on matters of domestic racism. This confrontation was an important factor in the appearance of the Awatere articles on Maori sovereignty.

The second issue is one of ethnicity. Maori sovereignty highlights Maori identity and culture and the lack of an equivalent identity for Pakehas. The taunt is that Pakehas cling to the cultural baggage they brought from Britain, and they lack a commitment to a specific New Zealand identity as a result. Because Pakeha culture is unmarked and unacknowledged, many are unable to respond to the challenge and feel intimidated by the Maori confidence in their own identity. There is an alternative response among Pakehas. From the early 1970s, the number of extreme right-wing groups has grown. They first appeared over the issue of sporting contacts with white South Africans, but they have since expanded their political ideologies, campaigns, and membership.[13] They do provide an opposition to Maori and Pakeha activists as they seek to defend British cultural values and practices. And it is the contrary claims and policies of the extreme right and those who seek Maori sovereignty which have influenced conceptions about race in New Zealand in the 1980s.

HISTORICAL BACKGROUND

Historically, two features have a particular bearing on race relations in New Zealand. The first is the penetration of European capitalism into New Zealand and the resulting destruction of Maori economy and society. The second factor is the recruitment of particular groups to meet the demands created by capitalism.

D. Bedggood identifies three stages in the penetration of the capitalist mode of production and the replacement of the lineage mode of production of Maori society.[14] He labels the first period up to 1840 *initial contact*, and this was characterized by the development of links between the capitalist mode of production, based predominantly in Britain, and sectors of the indigenous Maori population. There was little competition between Maori and Pakeha principally because the number of Pakehas was relatively small and there was sufficient land to fill their requirements. P. Adams suggests that the two groups reached an agreement in the 1830s, an agreement that was rapidly discarded in the next stage of contact, the *colonial period*.[15]

This period extends from 1840 until after the Land Wars and represents the major period of destruction of Maori society, or at least those aspects that inhibited or opposed the establishment of the capitalist system. The beginning of the period saw the signing of the Treaty of Waitangi, a treaty that appeared to accord the Maori certain rights and guarantees. The treaty has often been cited as the foundation of "racial harmony" in New Zealand when Maori and Pakeha were joined as one.[16] In reality, the treaty has seldom protected Maori interests. The traditional spiritual and symbolic relationship of the Maori to the land was seen as a barrier to individual ownership and the use of land as a commodity to be bought and sold. From the 1850s, attempts were made to individualize land ownership among the Maori and to make it available to the growing number of Pakeha settlers in contravention of the undertakings of the Treaty of Waitangi. This was accompanied by moves to subjugate other cultural traditions. Legislation such as the 1867 Native Schools Act, for instance, was instrumental in restricting the social viability of the Maori language.

There was limited resistance from the Maori prior to 1855, but the subsequent attack on cultural values produced substantially greater Maori opposition.[17] This resistance threatened the establishment of capitalism in New Zealand, and the state intervened to overcome this obstacle to Pakeha intentions. As a result, there was open conflict between 1885 and 1890 in the Land Wars. Some commentators regard this war as an unfortunate incident that ran counter to the humanitarianism displayed by many Pakehas toward the Maori. In fact, the "humanitarianism" of the missionaries and officials was discarded or modified when obstacles to British authority appeared.

The third stage identified by Bedggood is the *neo-colonial* period which represents the continuing destruction of Maori society and the further establishment of capitalism.[18] In particular, finance capital was diverted to New Zealand, and a local infrastructure was developed. By 1880, the traditional coherence of Maori society had been destroyed, although resistance continued in places such as Parihaka. In the 1890s and the early part of the twentieth century, there was a resurgence of interest in Maoritanga, but by this time the leaders came from those who had been tested in the Pakeha system. As W. P. Reeves has noted, the exhortation from these new leaders, and others, was to discard much of Maoritanga, and Maoris were "prevailed . . . upon from every quarter to do violence to their own identity."[19] In the neo-colonial period, the Maori was seldom a threat to the dominance of capitalism in New Zealand. Elements of the Maori economy remained, but this was because they were either unimportant or of use to the Pakeha. From this period on, overt racism directed at the Maori became unnecessary until after World War II. Other groups became the focus for Pakeha fears and prejudices.

Racism readily appears when there is an economic threat to the welfare of the dominant group.[20] In the last part of the nineteenth century and the early part of the twentieth, this threat was seen as coming from Asian groups, and sometimes from certain European groups (e.g., the Yugoslavs) who migrated to New Zealand.

The first major influx of Asians was led by the Chinese who came to work the South Island goldfields, and almost immediately there was opposition. Parliamentary debates surrounding the 1881 Chinese Immigration Bill, the 1891 Aliens Bill, and the 1899 Asiatic Immigration Restriction Bill, as well as the intent of such legislation, all reflect the racism of the country's politicians and their electorates. Asians were seen as competing unfairly, but they were also held to represent a "threat" to British values and institutions. W. Pember Reeves, a liberal politician who became Prime Minister, referred to Asians as the "yellow barbarians" or "yellow agony," and in 1902, he wrote that racial intermarriage produces a "mongrel and degraded people by no means fitted for self-government."[21] Discriminatory legislation that levied a poll tax on Chinese and that restricted their entry to New Zealand helped placate public racism, and discriminatory laws remained in effect well into the twentieth century.

The Chinese experience illustrates the fact that racism has played an important part in intergroup relations in New Zealand. Other migrant groups faced similar prejudice and discrimination. A. D. Trlin records Pakeha opposition to Yugoslavs on the gumfields (1890–1914) and to their presence as "enemy aliens" during World War I.[22] Another Asian group to face resentment was the Indian community. In South Auckland, for example, many Pakehas refused to lease or sell land to the Indians during the 1920s. They were excluded from membership of the local Growers Association and were not permitted into the local hotel or on the balcony of the theatre. To restrict the entry of Asians to New Zealand, the White New Zealand League was formed in 1926. The league wrote to 200 local bodies seeking support for their aims, and 160 endorsed the principle of a white New Zealand.[23]

This concern over the "threat" posed by Asians produced an act that effectively established a "white New Zealand" immigration policy until the 1970s. Under pressure from the public and groups such as the Returned Serviceman's Association and the trade unions, the Immigration Restriction Amendment Act was passed in 1920. It gave people of British or Irish birth and descent the right of free entry to New Zealand, while all persons of non-British origin had to obtain an entry permit from the Minister of Customs (later the Minister of Labour and Immigration). Pakeha racism was thus codified in legislation.

RECENT DEVELOPMENTS

Since the 1940s, New Zealand has followed the classic pattern of Western capitalist societies by recruiting migrant workers to fill labor shortages in the urban sector. The boom conditions that prevailed after the war saw increased investment in industrial production and produced a demand for labor. The white urban workers were drawn to the more attractive jobs in the growing industrial and service sectors of the economy. This left labor shortages in areas such as the production line and shift jobs. To fill the gaps, New Zealand turned to other sources of labor. One source was the New Zealand hinterland with its large Maori population, and from 1945 when the Maori Social and Economic Advancement Act was passed, the Maori was actively encouraged to migrate to urban areas. The Department of Maori Affairs reports (see 1961 and 1967 as examples) made it quite clear that the department saw little future for the Maori in rural areas. Prior

Table 20
**Proportion of the Maori Population Living in the Cities and
Boroughs, 1951–1981, Selected Years**

	Percent		Percent		Percent		Percent
1951	19.65	1961	33.4	1971	58.5	1981	78.5
1956	24.37	1966	50.5	1976	76.2		

to the war in 1936, only 10 percent of the Maori population lived in a city or borough. Table 20 illustrates the change in the postwar period, with more than three-quarters of the total Maori population now living in cities and boroughs. The other aspect is the concentration in particular cities. In 1945, only one out of every twenty Maoris lived in the Auckland urban area. By 1981, nearly one in four (22.5 percent) of the Maori population lived in Auckland.

The second source of labor was provided by migrants from the Pacific Islands, specifically Western Samoa, the Cook Islands, Tonga, Niue, Fiji, and Tokelau. New Zealand employers still recruited from Europe, principally Britain, but they turned to the Pacific Islands to recruit semiskilled and unskilled labor. The process of recruitment reflected the requirements of a free market economy. The New Zealand government took little interest in the welfare of the migrants, even to the point of ignoring illegal Pacific Island immigrants. The legacy of this pattern of recruitment is reflected in the position of the Polynesian, both Maori and Pacific Islander, in the economic structure and through social and political relations.

Polynesians are concentrated in the less prestigious and low-skill occupational categories. In 1981, the percentage of male workers employed in the category, "Production and Related Workers, Transport Equipment Operators and Labourers" for the total labor force, Maoris, and Pacific Islanders was 43.9, 62.9, and 72.5 percent, respectively. The reverse was true for the category "Professional, Technical, and Related Workers" where Polynesian males were underrepresented. Only 2.3 percent of the Pacific Island male labor force and 2.6 percent of Maoris were in this category, compared to 12.1 percent of the total male labor force.[24] The gap between Polynesian females and the total female labor force in these categories is of the same order. An analysis of the labor force distribution by industry supports the conclusion that there is a significant degree of segregation in employment. The rates of unemployment also differ considerably. In 1981, unemployment rates for males were 3.1, 13.1, and 10.6 percent for non-Polynesians, Maoris, and Pacific Islanders, respectively. For females, the rates were 4.3, 17.5, and 10.9 percent for the same groups. If the rate for the fifteen to nineteen age group is computed, then the difference is even greater. The non-Polynesian rate is 8.8 percent for males and 12.2 percent for females. The same rates for Maoris are 29.9 and 43.4 percent, and for Pacific Islanders, 27.6 and 62.3 percent. Maoris and Pacific Islanders are four times more likely to be unemployed than non-Polynesians, even when sociodemographic factors such as age and educational achievement are compensated for.

One response to the above analysis is to suggest that rural-urban migrants seldom achieve an occupational distribution similar to that of the host society in the first generation. A better comparison is between second- and third-generation descendants of migrants and the host group. In fact, such a comparison shows no lessening in the magnitude of occupational difference. Younger Polynesians (under twenty-five years of age) are as likely to be concentrated in the semiskilled and unskilled sector as previous generations. This is supported by research that shows a reluctance by employers to hire Pacific Islanders for white-collar jobs, even when they had significantly higher qualifications, either in terms of academic qualifications or job experience, than the paired Pakeha applicant.[25] J. Macrae has shown that vertical mobility or movement into better jobs accounts for a greater percentage of Pakeha job moves than is the case for Polynesians. Some 40 percent of Pakeha job terminations are the result of upward mobility compared to 27 percent for Pacific Islanders and 22 percent for Maoris.[26] The same channels of mobility do not exist equally for Pakeha and Polynesian.

Other channels of mobility, notably the education system, do not provide the Polynesian with any greater opportunities. The relatively younger Polynesian population means that they constitute an increasing proportion of the school population (see Table 21), and there is a growing awareness of the special needs and problems of Polynesians.[27] But this concern is not generally translated into academic success by providing the Polynesian with those credentials necessary in contemporary New Zealand. Tables 22 and 23 show that, while the Maori performance has improved in absolute terms, relative to the non-Maori population the gap is still substantial and in the case of higher qualifications still increasing. The education system is helping to reproduce and increase Pakeha dominance, not to reduce it. A similar disparity is reflected in other indices of economic performance and life chances such as income, residential distribution, and health.

The end result in economic terms is that the Polynesian constitutes

Table 21
Maori Pupils as a Percentage of the Total Secondary School
Population in New Zealand, 1963–1983, Selected Years

	1963	1968	1973	1976	1983
Percent Pupils	8.2	8.9	10.1	11.6	13.6

Source: Department of Education, 1964–1984.

Table 22
Percentage of Non-Maori and Maori Pupils Leaving School Without
any Certification,* 1963–1983, Selected Years

	1963	1968	1973	1976	1983
Non-Maori	67.3	47.4	40.3	31.4	27.0
Maori	93.6	79.1	73.5	68.7	61.6
Difference between					
Non-Maori and Maori	26.3	31.7	33.2	37.3	34.6

*This means that the pupil has not passed any of the public academic examinations that are part of the New Zealand education system.

Source: Department of Education, 1964–1984.

part of a reserve army that exists to fill gaps in the labor market during the seasonal high or boom years and can be discarded in the off-season or during a recession. The recession in 1967/68 and the more substantial crises that began in the early 1970s highlighted the vulnerability of the Polynesian position in the New Zealand economy. In a competitive situation, the latent racism within New Zealand, including that of the state, has become much more apparent. The recession reduced the demand for semiskilled and unskilled labor, and the state intervened to restrict the flow of migrants where possible. Previously, there had been little

Table 23
Percentage of School Leavers with University Entrance or Higher Qualifications, 1963–1983, Selected Years

	1963	1968	1973	1976	1983
Non-Maori	15.8	20.5	26.7	29.9	35.9
Maori	1.8	2.6	4.3	4.1	9.2
Difference Between					
Non-Maori and Maori	14.0	17.9	22.4	25.8	26.7

Source: Department of Education, 1964–1984.

consideration of the social consequences of substantial and continued migration to the urban areas, but the recession required the state to weigh the benefits of a continuing immigration flow (Maoris were obviously not subject to the same nationality measures as Pacific Islanders) against the social costs. By the early 1970s, the social costs were held to be too high, and the state intervened to control Pacific Island labor in New Zealand.

A significant part of the campaign involved action against "overstayers." "Overstayers" refers to immigrants who have stayed on in New Zealand after the expiration of a temporary entry permit. The campaign began with the Labour government and reached its peak in 1976 under the subsequent National government in line with their electioneering which portrayed Pacific Islanders as troublesome. In October 1976, the police began to conduct random street checks and houses raids to identify illegal immigrants.[28] Most of the activity occurred in Wellington, Christchurch, and Auckland, and it appears that some 200 street checks were carried out with people who were thought to be Pacific Islanders. A number of mistakes were made, and the police advised Pacific Islanders to carry their passports.

The overstayers campaign was supported by legislative measures. The National government implemented the previous Labour government's scheme to shorten visitors' permits for Tongans from three months to one month, and this was extended to Western Samoans and Fijians in 1976. At the same time, a work permit scheme was introduced for these three groups. The effect of the legislation and the overstayers campaign was to produce a manageable and efficient contract labor system similar to the guest worker schemes operated in Europe.[29] Not unlike the state's stance on the "threat" of Asian migration much earlier in New Zealand's history, the state had responded to a common perception of Pacific Island immigrants as a "problem," although there were also reasonable fears concerning the impact of continued migration in a time of economic retrenchment. But the morality of the moves are put into perspective when it is noted that there are no restrictions on travel between Australia and New Zealand.

PUBLIC POLICIES AND LAWS

Contemporary race relations in New Zealand reflect a complex situation that combines the politics of ethnic nationalism and assertiveness with policies that show an increasing sensitivity on ethnic and racial issues. But alongside these developments, traditional and new forms of racism continue to exist, both in terms of policy and in popular images and behavior. The 1970s and 1980s record a major shift in the politicization of race and ethnicity.

The overstayers campaign was one element that contributed to the changed climate of the 1980s. The socially constructed notion of street violence in the early 1970s clearly identified Polynesians as the problem, and the subsequent moral panic granted state agencies such as the police a degree of legitimacy in targetting Pacific Islanders as troublesome. The Auckland Task Force, for example, was a select group of police officers who operated in groups from late 1973 to ensure law and order on city streets. ACORD (Auckland Committee on Racism and Discrimination) observed the Task Force over a six-week period when 403 people were arrested. The arrests were concentrated in certain parts of the city, with 90.1 percent coming from the Auckland central city area, Newton, Ponsonby, Grey Lynn, Kyber Pass, Newmarket, and Onehunga.[30] More importantly, by the sixth week, 80 percent of the arrests involved Maoris or Pacific Islanders. In comparison with the number of Polynesians arrested by the regular police, this was disproportionately high.

The police role in removing protesters from Bastion Point in 1978 and in trying to preserve order during the Springbok rugby team's tour in 1981, as two examples, attracted further criticism from a number of groups, and polarized the community in a debate over the appropriateness of policing methods. An indication of these community attitudes is provided by a police survey carried out in South Auckland in 1983.[31] Respondents were asked: How do you think the police treat these groups? Europeans were much more likely to respond that Maoris were not treated "hard enough" by the police (21 percent as against 5 percent who felt they were treated "too hard"), while the response was more pronounced concerning the treatment of Pacific Islanders (30 percent as against 4 percent in the two response categories). When Maoris were asked, they were more likely to reply that the police treated them "too hard" (23 percent) as opposed to "not hard enough" (14 percent). And the respective percentages for Pacific Island respondents were 21 percent ("too hard") and 16 percent ("not hard enough"). Thus, more Maoris and Pacific Islanders felt that they were likely to be treated "too hard" than "not hard enough" by the police, an attitude that is *not* shared by Pakehas. But there is also an indication of Maori/Pacific Islander antagonism because both felt that the other should be treated harder by the police. The same survey also showed that Europeans were much more likely to see "racial difference as causing problems between groups" than Maori or Pacific Island respondents (30 percent as against 16 and 18 percent, respectively).[32] Common-sense notions of what causes problems and what should be the appropriate police response differ and tend to reinforce a "problem orientation" toward Polynesians.

But these perceptions and the activities of state agencies such as the police, judiciary, and social welfare services did not go unchallenged. The issue of institutional racism has been an important one in a society where many important functions are state-run (for example, both television channels are state-owned) and where the concept of a welfare state has been an important policy position since the 1890s. A variety of groups such as ACORD (see above) monitored the activities of these agencies, as well as those in the private sector, and organized campaigns to counter institutional racism. They played an important role in beginning the process of sensitizing government departments to the barriers faced by Maoris and Pacific Islanders. The success is reflected in policies recently adopted by the department which oversees management in the state sector, the State Services Commission, and by the major union representing state employees, the Public Service Association. But there is still the question of Polynesian access to power and decision making within these institutions as most are Pakeha-dominated.

One response to these comments would be that Maoris are adequately represented in alternative power structures. In terms of state institutions, their interests are protected by the Department of Maori Affairs, special programs run by the Department of Education, statutory Maori representation in Parliament, and the legislation relating to racial prejudice and discrimination. The Department of Maori Affairs was initially constituted as an agency to deal with Maori land and its powers, and responsibilities have grown. Until recently, however, its role and effectiveness have been marked by a certain ambivalence. The department's advocacy of the Maori case has not always been particularly strong:

New Zealand is fortunate in that it has no real racial problems, but if the Maori is to progress then it must have the understanding and good will of the European population. To obtain this good will the Maori must conduct himself in such a way that he does not bring disrepute upon his race.[33]

Ten years later, the 1967 departmental report confidently expected the pepper-potting of Maori homes throughout Pakeha areas to produce an "increasing rate of intermarriage and integration."[34]

In 1977, a review of departmental policy led to major changes. The new spirit was encapsulated in the *Tu Tangata* (Stand Tall) philosophy of the department's operations. The aim was to decentralize the bureaucracy so that Maori communities throughout New Zealand would be encouraged to develop their own autonomy. Field officers of the department were to service community-controlled programs and to help groups develop their own skills and initiatives. The concept of *Whanau* (family) was given a key role in a number of programs to encourage community and group identity and to avoid relying on welfare and judicial services. A ministerial review committee (1985) saw the role of the department as achieving "equality with the dominant culture in economic, educational, and social terms in a way that preserves cultural integrity, promotes self-independence and uses Maori resources."[35]

The importance of the department lies in the fact that it serves as a barometer of concern. Its recent programs represent an official acknowledgment that there are visible social and economic problems that require a response. But in trying to regenerate a sense of ethnic community and spirit, functions are being transferred to already pressured voluntary community agencies. In addition, in the face of a continuing social and economic disparity between Pakeha and Maori, the effectiveness of the department's programs is limited by the inability to change the basic economic structure of New Zealand society. It is difficult to avoid the conclusion that schemes such as the encouragement of small business ventures are designed to equip the Maori for a more successful adaptation to the Pakeha economic system. Nevertheless, the *Tu Tangata* philosophy has marked an important change in the way a state department relates to its Maori clientele and has given voice, albeit in a limited way, to Maori self-determination.

Another issue is the effectiveness and role of separate Maori representation in Parliament. The four Maori seats were established in 1867 by the Maori Representation Act. Initially, the Maori campaigned vigorously and tried to exert their influence through the seats. But it was quickly discovered that four members were unable to have much influence, and by the 1880s, there was widespread disillusionment.[36] One response was the move for a separate Maori Parliament (*Kotahitanga*).

Maori representation has with few exceptions had little effect on the decision-making process. Prominent Maori politicians did have some impact, but in 1940 and 1957, when the Maori seats held the balance of power in Parliament, there were few gains. Initially, there were four Maori seats and forty general seats. Now, there are still only four Maori seats as against ninety general seats. A central political question is whether to increase the number of Maori seats or to do away with them altogether. In the past, however, the Maori presence has been unable to resolve contentious land issues or even to have the Treaty of Waitangi ratified. Instead, a series of acts have reduced Maori rights over customary land and the amount of land still under Maori ownership. Frustration at the lack of progress led to the resignation of Matiu Rata, a former Minister of Maori Affairs, in 1979. He helped form Mana Motuhake, a political party that stands on a platform of Maori land rights. In subsequent elections it has failed to seriously challenge the Labor party's monopoly on the four Maori seats. Indeed, some of the policies of the Labour government elected in 1984 meet the demands of groups like Mana Motuhake.

A key legislative move by the government is the Treaty of Waitangi Amendment Act (1985). The issue of outstanding land grievances led to the 1975 Land March that went from the north of the North Island to Parliament in Wellington; to the occupation of Bastion Point in 1977; to a number of localized disputes that have been contested legally and by direct action; and to an ongoing protest during annual activities to "celebrate" the signing of the Treaty of Waitangi. The Treaty of Waitangi Act (1975) established the Waitangi Tribunal to ensure that policies and legislation did not contravene the undertakings of the Treaty of Waitangi. In 1983, this tribunal handed down an important decision on an industrial outfall at Motonui in the province of Taranaki. It ruled that the government had an obligation to protect Maori fishing resources and therefore should not let the outfall go ahead as planned. The Prime Minister disputed the finding, but the role of the Waitangi Tribunal in protecting Maori interests according to the Treaty of Waitangi was established. The Treaty of Waitangi Amendment Act allows for cases to be brought retrospectively. That is, land disputes going back to 1840 where the treaty has been contravened and where the claimants can show disadvantage can now be considered by the tribunal. Given the importance of land grievances to Maori concerns, the effectiveness of the tribunal and the legislation under which it operates are critical to future race relations.

Language is also important, and the education system, most notably parts of the state sector and private Maori schools, have responded to the demand that the schools become bilingual and bicultural, if not multicultural. Separate Maori education was established in 1867, but for much of the nineteenth and twentieth centuries, many Maoris were offered a limited education through the alternative system. The first major shifts came in the 1970s with an acknowledgment that *taha Maori* (Maori concerns) ought to be reflected in the school curriculum. This was endorsed in the late 1970s with the establishment of official bilingual schools in the state primary sector. The first was Ruatoki in 1977, and there are now eight. In 1985, the first private primary school was registered. There are no equivalent bilingual schools in the secondary sector, although the private Maori schools and state schools such as Otara's Hillary College offer multicultural education. But the most impressive development has been the establishment of *kohanga reo* (language nests), or preschool centers that encourage *taha Maori* and *te reo Maori* (Maori language). In 1985, there were 410 *kohanga reo* centers, with another 90 to be established by 1986. They serve 6,900 children, a number that grew by 2,075 (55 percent) in fourteen months. The presence in monolingual schools of graduates of the *kohanga reo* presents a major challenge. Certainly, teachers and educationalists appear more sensitive to the issues of ethnicity and racism, but there is also a reaction that explicitly rejects such developments in an attempt to retain the basics of (European) education. These people see *taha Maori* as irrelevant to the needs of a modern, urban society.

Finally, there is the possibility for Polynesians to safeguard their interests through the provisions of the Race Relations Act (1971) and the Human Rights Act (1978). For political purposes, these acts can be cited as evidence that New Zealand is committed to a policy of racial equality. The acts provide a means of redress for those who feel that they have been discriminated against on the grounds of race, ethnic identity, or nationality. Provision is provided for cases to be taken before an Equal Opportunities Tribunal to rule and, if necessary, to impose penalties. The acts have provided some redress in the areas of employment, housing, advertising, and access to public places. But they offer little protection on such occasions as the campaign against overstayers, and the emphasis is one of conciliation and education. For example, the section that deals with racial incitement accounted for 76 percent of the caseload dealt with by the Office of the Race Relations Conciliator in 1984–85, and yet only rarely does prosecution result from such compliants. Between 1971 and 1979, the only prosecution was against members of the National Socialist (Nazi) party. Thus, the tendency is to restrict the use of the full provisions of the acts to extreme types of racism, and for most Polynesians, there are only limited means of responding to racial prejudice and discrimination. (For a fuller discussion of the acts and their operation, see A. D. Trlin.)[37]

SUMMARY AND CONCLUSIONS

The 1970s and 1980s mark a period of substantial change for New Zealand's race relations. The migration of large numbers of Maori to urban centers, especially to Auckland and Wellington, followed by the arrival of Pacific Islanders has greatly increased the proximity of Pakeha and Polynesian. It has also resulted in the proletarianization of the Polynesian migrants.[38] They have become concentrated in certain employment categories and industries, including a disproportionate number of the unemployed, and in certain housing areas. This economic and social position has been highlighted by a recession in the New Zealand economy that began in the 1970s. It has also been endorsed by the activities of the state, and even traditional working-class representative organizations such as the trade unions and the Labour party have been reluctant to respond to the particular concerns of the Polynesians. For these latter groups, the issues of racism and ethnicity have been seen as subordinate or irrelevant to the agendas of class-based organizations. But by the late 1970s, new generations of Maori, urban-born and with very differènt experiences from those of their parents, were beginning to reach political awareness. This new Maori consciousness and the growing evidence of inequity combined to produce an assertiveness and anger that has, if anything, intensified during the 1980s.

Maori sovereignty provided the theme for this political movement, although the label encompasses a variety of ideological and strategic differences. But there are key elements that justify identifying them as a single force. There is a concern with the racist attitudes and behavior of the dominant Pakeha group. These have been challenged, and the negative features of racism are in the process of being negotiated in favor of a more positive relationship which accords status and rights to an ethnic Maori identity. The ethnic nationalism of the 1970s repeats that of earlier Maori movements, especially in the calls to restore land rights and ownership, and the need to provide a more supportive environment for Maori culture. In certain respects, gains have been made with regard to these concerns. Legislation now affirms the guarantees given under the terms of the Treaty of Waitangi in 1840. Maori culture and language are viewed much more positively in the education system. State departments, notably the Department of Maori Affairs but also others, have adopted new policies and structures that are a response to Maori requests. And an increasing involvement with politics and the accumulation of new skills have allowed a Maori leadership to penetrate national political institutions. But these gains have, if anything, been overdue and in many ways have done little to alter the basic institutional structures and practices. And they have been unable to redress the economic disparity between Maori and Pakeha. Many historical grievances remain to be resolved, and the future of *Maoritanga* (Maori culture) as an important part of New Zealand society is certainly not assured. There is also the question of Pacific Island Polynesian concerns. The 1980s reflect a growing politicization among these groups, with another set of expectations of the institutions of New Zealand society. The formation of a new state department for Pacific Islanders acknowledges their growing power, but future directions and debates are still unclear.

For their part, the Pakeha response has varied. Some have a new awareness of their racism and have welcomed the Polynesian challenge as timely. Others have actually affirmed their racism, and the growth in the number of racist and extreme right-wing groups reflects a defense of "British" values and race. Probably a greater number are troubled by events and have little understanding of the issues or sympathy for Maori claims. Pakehas cannot ignore the debates, and racism will continue to play an important role in the political agenda in New Zealand for some time to come. The issues of domestic racism are paralleled by the impact of independence movements in the rest of the South Pacific, many of whom have political or cultural ties with New Zealand's Polynesians, and the ongoing arguments about the relationship between New Zealand and South Africa. Conflict on the second issue began in earnest in 1960 and has divided the community at intervals throughout the 1970s and 1980s, often leading to intense debate and violence. For many, these issues are not divisible from those surrounding Maori sovereignty or racism, and because they have attracted the interest of Pakeha groups and at times mobilized them in protest action, they have served to grant a degree of legitimacy to Maori concerns. The Pakeha response is critical for the future, and while some of the signs are positive, this response is still in the process of being formulated.

NOTES

1. R. Miles and P. Spoonley, "The Political Economy of Labour Migration: An Alternative to the Sociology of 'Race' and 'Ethnic Relations' in New Zealand." *Australian and New Zealand Journal of Sociology* 21, No. 1 (1985): 3–26.

2. T. D. and N. B. Graves, *As Others See Us: New Zealanders' Images of Themselves and of Immigrant Groups* (South Pacific Research Unit: 1974), p. 7.

3. P. H. Curson, "Inter-Ethnic Relations and Assimilation in the Urban Setting: Some Comments on a Socio-Spatial Model of Inner City," *New Zealand Geographer* 31 (1975): 142–59.

4. A. D. Trlin, "Social Distance and Assimilation Orientation: A Survey of Attitudes Towards Immigrants in New Zealand," *Pacific Viewpoint* 12 (1971): 141–62.

5. A. Webster et al., *The Study of New Zealand Values*, Massey University, Heylen, 1985.

6. P. Spoonley, "The Role of Gatekeepers in the Employment of Minority

Groups," in *Proceedings of the Sixth Annual Conference, New Zealand Demographic Society*, 1980, pp. 1–15.

7. *New Zealand Herald*, September 21, 1985.

8. Webster et al., *Study of New Zealand Values*, pp. 30–42.

9. Ibid.

10. S. Levine and P. Spoonley, "New Zealand Attitudes on Apartheid," *Australian and New Zealand Journal of Sociology* 15, No. 3 (1980): 67–68.

11. R. J. Walker, "The Genesis of Maori Activism," *Journal of the Polynesian Society* 93, No. 3 (1984): 267–81.

12. D. Awatere, *Maori Sovereignty*, Broadsheet, 1984.

13. P. Spoonley, "New Zealand First! The Extreme Right and Politics in New Zealand, 1961–1981," *Political Science* 33, No. 2 (1981): 99–127, and "The Politics of Racism: The New Zealand League of Rights," in P. Spoonley et al., eds., *Tauiwi: Racism and Ethnicity in New Zealand* (Wellington, N.Z.: Dunmore Press, 1984).

14. D. Bedggood, "The Destruction of Maori Society. The Articulation of Modes of Production in New Zealand," paper presented at the ANZAAS Conference, University of Auckland, 1979.

15. P. Adams, *Fatal Necessity. British Intervention in New Zealand 1830–1847* (Auckland: Auckland University Press, 1977), p. 35.

16. R. Walker, "The Genesis of Maori Activism," *Journnal of the Polynesian Society* 93, No. 3 (1984): 269.

17. Ibid. and H. Greenland, "Ethnicity as Ideology: The Critique of Pakeha Society," in P. Spoonley et al., eds., *Tauiui*, 22–40.

18. Bedggood, "The Destruction of Maori Society," p. 14.

19. W. P. Reeves, "Rough Ride to Racism. Beyond the Maori Gang Phenomenon," *Dominion* 3 (May 18, 1979): 7.

20. D. Bedggood, *Rich and Poor in New Zealand. A Critique of Class, Politics and Ideology* (London: Allen & Unwin, 1980).

21. W. P. Reeves, *State Experiments in Australia and New Zealand*, Vol. 2 (New York: Macmillan, 1969), p. 353.

22. A. D. Trlin, *Now Respected, Once Despised. Yugoslavs in New Zealand* (Palmerston, N.Z.: Dunmore Press, 1979).

23. K. N. Tiwari, "The Indian Community in New Zealand. A Historical Survey," in K. N. Tiwari, ed., *Indians in New Zealand. Studies in a Sub-Culture* (Wellington, N.Z.: Price Milburn, 1980), pp. 9–11.

24. K. D. Gibson, "Political Economy and International Labour Migration: The Case of Polynesians in New Zealand," *New Zealand Geography* 39, No. 1 (1983): 35–37.

25. Spoonley, "Role of Gatekeepers," p. 15.

26. J. Macrae, "Maoris, Islanders and Europeans. Labour Mobility in New Zealand Industry," in S. Wallman, ed., *Ethnicity at Work* (New York: Macmillan, 1979), p. 168.

27. Department of Education, *He Huarahi. Report of the National Advisory Committee on Maori Education*, 1980.

28. B. K. Macdonald, "Pacific Immigration and the Politicians," *Comment (New Series)* 1, No. 1 (1977): 71–72.

29. Miles and Spoonley, "Political Economy," pp. 12–13.

30. ACORD, *Task Force—A Failure in Law Enforcement. A Disaster in Community Relations*, 1975, p. 3.

31. New Zealand Police, *South Auckland Police Development Plan. Vols I. and II*, 1984, pp. 30–32.

32. Ibid., pp. 33–34.

33. Department of Maori Affairs, *Annual Report* (57), p. 20.

34. Ibid., 1967, p. 14.

35. *Evening Post*, September 11, 1985.

36. A. Ward, "Law and Law Enforcement on the New Zealand Frontier, 1849–1893," *New Zealand Journal of History* 5, No. 2 (1971): 145.

37. A. D. Trlin, "The New Zealand Race Relations Act: Conciliators, Conciliation and Complaints (1972–1981)," *Political Science* 34, No. 2 (1982): 170–93.

38. Miles and Spoonley, "Political Economy of Labour Migration," p. 25.

BIBLIOGRAPHY

ACORD. *Task Force. An Exercise in Oppression*. ACORD, n.d.

———. *Task Force—A Failure in Law Enforcement. A Disaster in Community Relations*. ACORD, 1975.

Adams, P. *Fatal Necessity. British Intervention in New Zealand 1830–1847*. Auckland: Auckland University Press, 1977.

Awatere, D. *Maori Sovereignty*. Broadsheet, 1984.

Bedggood, D. "The Destruction of Maori Society. The Articulation of Modes of Production in New Zealand." Paper presented at the ANZAAS Conference, University of Auckland, 1979.

———. *Rich and Poor in New Zealand. A Critique of Class, Politics and Ideology*. London: Allen & Unwin, 1980.

Curson, P. H. "Inter-Ethnic Relations and Assimilation in the Urban Setting: Some Comments on a Socio-Spatial Model of Inner City." *New Zealand Geographer* 31 (1975): 142–59.

Department of Education. *He Huarahi. Report of the National Advisory Committee on Maori Education*. Department of Education, 1980.

Department of Maori Affairs. *Annual Reports, Appendices to the Journal of the House of Representatives*. Government Printer.

Gibson, K. D. "Political Economy and International Labour Migration: The Case of Polynesians in New Zealand." *New Zealand Geography* 39, No. 1 (1983): 29–42.

Graves, T. D., and N. B. Graves. *As Others See Us: New Zealanders' Images of Themselves and of Immigrant Groups*. South Pacific Research Unit, 1974.

Greenland, H. "Ethnicity as Ideology: The Critique of Pakeha Society." In *Tauiwi. Racism and Ethnicity in New Zealand*, edited by P. Spoonley et al. Wellington, N.Z.: Dunmore Press, 1984.

Levine, S., and P. Spoonley. "New Zealand Attitudes on Apartheid." *Australian and New Zealand Journal of Sociology* 15, No. 3 (1980): 67–68.

Macdonald, B. K. "Pacific Immigration and the Politicians." *Comment (New Series)* 1, No. 1 (1977): 11–14.

Macrae, J. "Maoris, Islanders and Europeans. Labour Mobility in New Zealand

Industry." In *Ethnicity at Work*, edited by S. Wallman. New York: Macmillan, 1979.

Miles, R., and P. Spoonley. "The Political Economy of Labour Migration: An Alternative to the Sociology of 'Race' and 'Ethnic Relations' in New Zealand." *Australian and New Zealand Journal of Sociology* 21, No. 1 (1985): 3–26.

New Zealand Police. *South Auckland Police Development Plan*. Vols. 1 and 2. New Zealand Police, 1984.

Reeves, W. P. *State Experiments in Australia and New Zealand*. Vol. 2. New York: Macmillan, 1979.

———. "Rough Ride to Racism. Beyond the Maori Gang Phenomenon." *Dominion*, May 18, 1979, p. 3.

Spoonley, P. "The Role of Gatekeepers in the Employment of Minority Groups." In Proceedings of the Sixth Annual Conference, New Zealand Demographic Society. New Zealand Demographic Society, 1980.

———. "New Zealand First! The Extreme Right and Politics in New Zealand, 1961–1981." *Political Science* 33, No. 2 (1981): 99–127.

———. "Race Relations." In *New Zealand: Sociological Perspectives*, edited by P. Spoonley et al. Wellington, N.Z.: Dunmore Press, 1982.

———. "The Politics of Racism: The New Zealand League of Rights." In *Tauiwi. Racism and Ethnicity in New Zealand*, edited by P. Spoonley et al. Wellington, N.Z.: Dunmore Press, 1984.

Tiwari, K. N. "The Indian Community in New Zealand. A Historical Survey." In *Indians in New Zealand. Studies in a Sub-Culture*, edited by K. N. Tiwari. Wellington, N.Z.: Price Milburn, 1980.

Trlin, A. D. "Social Distance and Assimilation Orientation: A Survey of Attitudes Towards Immigrants in New Zealand." *Pacific Viewpoint* 12 (1971): 141–62.

———. *Now Respected, Once Despised. Yugoslavs in New Zealand*. Palmerston, N.Z.: Dunmore Press, 1979.

———. "The New Zealand Race Relations Act: Conciliators, Conciliation and Complaints (1972–1981)." *Political Science* 34, No. 2 (1982): 152–60.

Walker, R. J. "The Genesis of Maori Activism." *Journal of the Polynesian Society* 93, No. 3 (1984): 267–81.

Ward, A. "Law and Law Enforcement on the New Zealand Frontier, 1849–1893." *New Zealand Journal of History* 5, No. 2 (1971): 128–49.

Webster, A. C., P. Green, I. Bray, and P. Perry. *The Study of New Zealand Values*. Massey University, Heylen, 1985.

SINGAPORE

John Clammer

A RACIAL CONTEXT

In many quarters it has become unfashionable to refer to the concept of race, both because of the definition problems that have always surrounded the term and because of the sinister political uses to which the notion has been put in recent history. It is intriguing in this respect to find a country in which not only is the concept of race alive and well, but also is used as the main means of social and cultural classification. Such is the case in the Republic of Singapore. Singapore is a remarkable society in a number of other respects, too. Formerly a British colony (as part of what was then Malaya), the tiny 224.5 square mile territory became internally self-governing in 1959 and a totally independent nation in 1965 when its brief two-year absorption into the also recently independent new state of Malaysia came to an abrupt end for political and ethnic reasons. Since then, it has developed from a society largely dependent on the presence of British military bases for its economic survival into the nation with the highest per capita income in Asia (after Japan), one of the highest economic growth rates in the world, one of the highest levels of urbanization, and a history of unusual political stability.

Yet all this has taken place in a society comprised almost entirely of migrants, most of whom came from places of origin geographically and culturally far removed from that of the Malay world of Southeast Asia at the center of which Singapore lies. Today Singapore is one of the most ethnically plural societies in the world, with its population not only divided into the four major categories of Chinese (the great majority), Malays, Indians, and "others" (or persons primarily of Eurasian or European descent), but with each of these four categories further subdivided into numerous subgroups on the basis of language, dialect, place of origin, religion, diet, and often occupation. As a consequence, the social fabric of Singapore is inextricably tied up with race: the street scenes are highly multiracial (a fact compounded by the international nature of Singapore's economy and the high level of tourism); everybody is interested in the race or subethnic classification of everybody else; cultural policy is based on the premise of multiracialism; education, language, and economic opportunities reflect this pluralism.

Two items, which are developed in detail later in this chapter, are of special interest here. The first is that, in the eyes of the government and in folk classifications, there is no doubt that the first principle of this multifaceted pluralism is *race*. Everybody knows what their race is, although as empirical research has shown, most people (including university students) have trouble saying what is meant by their ethnicity. The second is that this primary intuition is constantly reinforced by the fact that people are continually asked to classify themselves by race in such activities as filling in official (or for that matter unofficial) forms. Every citizen and permanent resident of Singapore carries an identity card on which is inscribed his or her race. Once achieved or ascribed, a particular categorization is almost impossible to change.

The reasons for this interesting situation are discussed in the next section, since they are largely historical in origin. But one additional preliminary point needs to be made. Given this fairly extreme pluralism and the common assumption that in such contexts racial strife is almost inevitable, one might suppose Singapore to be one of the most unstable of societies. In fact, the opposite is true: thirty years have now passed since the area's last major case of racial conflict. During the 1969 race riots in neighboring Malaysia, it was greatly feared that the trouble would spill over or reproduce itself in Singapore, but it did not.[1] There are strains, which we will discuss later, but Singapore has enjoyed an enviable record of excellent race relations ever since independence. The location of Singapore—as a primarily Chinese country in the middle of the Malay world (Malaysia to the north, Indonesia to the west and south, Brunei and Borneo to the east, and the Philippines further east again)—would seem to make the situation a very tense one, but in actuality the presence of these neighbors has forced on Singapore the need to maintain good internal social relations between its constituent population groups. In the light of these background factors, we can proceed first to explore the historical dimensions of this multiracialism and then to analyze the more recent developments and contemporary trends.

HISTORICAL BACKGROUND

The history of Singapore is usually said to have begun in 1819 when Sir Stamford Raffles landed on the island and claimed it for the British

East India Company. The background to this event need not detain us here, except to note that Raffles' being there at all must be seen as the result of Anglo-Dutch rivalry in Southeast Asia and especially in the Malay Peninsula and what is now Indonesia. The British were looking for a base as an alternative to Malacca, and Singapore with its highly strategic position for both trade and war and its excellent, sheltered, natural anchorage made it a good choice. It is estimated that when Raffles arrived there were about 150 persons on the island—120 of them Malays and the rest Chinese. The exact figures are uncertain, but they do indicate how far Singapore had declined from its former glories as a center of Malay trade and settlement. The Chinese figures may or may not be accurate, for there is growing evidence that there was a reasonably substantial Chinese colony on the island long before Raffles arrived.[2] Be that as it may, it is clear that the population was very small. Once the British flag was planted, the situation changed rapidly. Almost immediately Chinese from the long-established community in Malacca, 150 miles up the western coast of Malaya, began to arrive to exploit the newly opening opportunities. As the British began the task of developing a town and fortifications, promoting the port and opening up the interior for agriculture, it quickly became apparent that the trickle of (mainly businessmen) Malacca Chinese and local Malays could not provide the labor force necessary for this great transformation, so the doors were opened for immigration, principally from south China. The Chinese were especially favored for their hard work, frugality, and ability to police themselves.

So by the time the first Census of Population was taken in 1871, the population had risen to 97,111, comprising 54,572 Chinese, 26,148 Malays, 11,501 Indians, almost 2,000 Caucasians, and a number of Arabs, Jews, Siamese, and other minorities. Since then, while there have been fluctuations in the proportions of the various ethnic groups, the general pattern has remained unchanged, with a sizable Chinese majority, a substantial Malay minority (who have always constituted the biggest group after the Chinese), a smaller Indian minority, and a small group of people of European or mixed descent, Arabs, Jews, and members of the population of the surrounding countries such as Siam (now Thailand), Vietnam, Ceylon (now Sri Lanka), and Japan.[3] The present figures (as of 1980) are shown in Table 24.

The factors underlying the evolution of these figures are of some interest. Until the 1950s, the primary source of population increase was immigration. Only from 1931 did natural increase become the main source of growth. There are several reasons for this situation: until 1949 (the date of the communist takeover in China), immigration was easy for Chinese; most migrants in the earlier stages of migration were men, who either had wives abroad, died in Singapore, or returned home after

Table 24
Population by Ethnic Groups, 1931–1980, Selected Years

Ethnic Group	1931	1947	1957	1970	1980
	Number				
Total	557,745	938,144	1,445,929	2,074,507	2,413,945
Chinese	418,640	729,473	1,090.569	1,579,866	1,856,237
Malays	65,014	113,473	197,059	311,379	351,508
Indians	52,456	71,927	129,510	145,169	154,632
Others	21,635	22,941	28,764	38,093	51,568
	Percentage				
Total	100.0	100.0	100.0	100.0	100.0
Chinese	75.1	77.8	75.4	76.2	76.9
Malays	11.6	12.1	13.6	15.0	14.6
Indians	9.4	7.7	9.0	7.0	6.4
Others	3.9	2.4	2.0	1.8	2.1

Source: Saw Swee-Hock, *Demographic Trends in Singapore*, Census Monograph No. 1, Department of Statistics, Singapore, 1981.

working in Singapore for some years; and mortality rates were very high until the early decades of this century. In 1933, the Aliens Ordinance restricted the flow of adult male migrants to Singapore and Malaya, but allowed in women and the children of immigrants, thus leading to a gradual normalization of sex ratios.

The origins of Singapore's multiracial society thus lie in colonial policies, particularly the formation of a massive immigrant workforce imposed on an original population that may soon become a minority. (Fiji, Trinidad, and Mauritius are other well-known examples of British policy in this respect.) But the story does not end there. First, the racial mix was unique in Singapore. All other Southeast Asian countries have substantial Chinese minorities: no other, however, has a massive Chinese majority. Second, conditions of colonial life led to segregation of the races into enclaves. This is still remembered in place names in Singapore: Kampong Java (village of the Javanese), Kampong Bugis (village of the Buginese), "Chinatown," and so on. The Chinese settled mostly either in the central city area (where the Chinatown district still is—an area of high-density, very traditional-style Chinese habitation)—or in the interior in vegetable-growing villages or plantations; the Indians in the Serangoon area east of the city center and in the Market Street and High Street districts of the city proper; and the Malays along the coasts, especially the Bedok and Geylang areas to the east and the Pasir Panjang district to the west.[4]

Not only geographical, but also other kinds of distinctions are pertinent. The main ones were (and are): language, religion, and occupation. The four-race model is actually misleading, since each race is actually divided into "subraces," often defined by language. Mandarin, the north Chinese dialect which is the official variety of Chinese in Singapore is the mother tongue of less than 1 percent of the Chinese population. The largest group are speakers of Hokkien, the dialect of the Amoy district of China, followed by speakers of Teochew, Cantonese, Hainanese, Hakka, Shanghainese, and other dialects mostly from south or southwest China, but including one found only in Southeast Asia—the Baba or Peranakan dialect. Similarly, the Indian community is divided along linguistic lines into speakers of Tamil (the majority), other south Indian languages such as Malayalee, north Indian languages such as Hindi and Punjabi, and languages spoken by only a few people in Singapore such as Bengali and Sinhala. The Malay population is more linguistically homogeneous, but even then Javanese, Minangkabau, Bugis, and other dialects or distinct languages are used as well as the *lingua franca*, Malay itself. Thai, Nepali, Japanese, Tagalog, Arabic, and numerous other minority languages as well as English are spoken by the fourth ethnic group—the "others."

The second major differentiating factor is religion. Whereas virtually all Malays were and are Muslims, Chinese were traditionally followers of what is often called Chinese folk religion—a syncretic blend of Taoism, Confucianism, Mahayana Buddhism, ancestor veneration, and spirit-beliefs. Indians, while mostly Hindu, were also Christians, Buddhists (of the Therevada School from Sri Lanka), Muslims (from south India or often from what is now Pakistan), or followers of sectarian religions. Every major and many minor religions can probably be found in Singapore, and adherence to one or another often follows ethnic lines.

A third factor is occupation. Malays tended in the past to be concentrated in fishing and small-scale agriculture. After the coming of the colonial era, many moved into service activities (as drivers, messengers, office attendants) or the colonial police and armed forces. This occu-

pational specialization is still reflected in present-day employment figures. Indians of the merchant class were often to be found in the spice
trade, in textile importing, and in general goods retailing, while their
working-class compatriots entered the estate sector, the railway, or the
Public Works Department (engaged in road building, public-building
works, etc.), specializations that to some extent also carry over to the
present day. The Chinese (other than the Malacca businessmen) tended
toward market gardening, plantation or dock work, high-energy service
activities such as rickshaw pulling, and, after accumulation of capital into
shopkeeping, catering and the provision of specialist services such as
ritual paraphernalia for Chinese funerals and religious observances. Although many elements of this initial specialization still occur (and with
it subethnic specialization, such as Hainanese in the catering trade and
Minangkabau in the selling of Nasi Padang, a favored, highly spiced
cuisine from Sumatra), there has naturally been a broadening of the
economic base of all the racial groups. The implications of this for competition between the races are discussed later in this chapter.

The point to be emphasized here, however, is that these historical
factors are highly relevant to the present situation in multiracial Singapore. The division of the population into the four-race model, the
Chinese majority, the tendency for occupational clustering, and the formation of enclaves all still have their impact, albeit a diminished one.
They have had three major implications. First, Singapore is inherently
multiracial, and political policy since independence has been to accept
this fact and indeed to represent it as a unique and desirable feature of
Singapore. Second, discussions of culture invariably involve questions of
race: is there a Singapore culture, or does Singapore simply comprise
the four cultures of the four main races (although, of course, in a unique
combination)? Cultural policy and the fact of multiracialism are closely
entwined. Third, since colonial times the main vehicle for the manipulation of this pluralism has been education. Continual modifications to
the education system, changes in educational policy, different emphases
on different languages at different times—all are related to the management of the multiracial society. The weight of the past lies more
heavily on Singapore than is at first apparent.

RECENT DEVELOPMENTS

"Recent" in this context really means since independence, for while
"fine tuning" of the multiracial system goes on continually, no major
shifts in public policy have taken place. The small changes are significant
and will be dealt with in the next section. The present section concen-
trates on the working out in practice of the multiracial situation described
earlier. The first independent government of Singapore inherited a pop-

ulation of migrant stock, of great linguistic and religious heterogeneity, and of uncertain loyalty to the new nation. A number of models were available to deal with this problem. A policy of assimilation into the Chinese majority was one possibility but would have been unworkable in practice. First, culturally different minorities are unassimilable into a Chinese community, even if such a solution had been politically acceptable either to the minorities themselves or to the surrounding countries. Second, no one Chinese community existed; rather, there was the amorphous mass described above, with no common language or other unifying principle. The alternative adopted (unlike neighboring Malaysia which is following a gradualist policy of Malayization) was to accept the idea that Singapore was multiracial and probably always will be, and to make this multiracialism the basis of public policy—and indeed enhance this characteristic, which most societies would find rather threatening.

The result has been the enshrining of race as the basis of social classification. Class, caste, religion, or other possible modes of identification do, of course, exist, but the only society-wide, universal, and officially sponsored means of personal, social, and cultural definition is race. This has certain consequences. The first is that a basic principle of social stratification is built into the society from the very start and, once established, is very difficult to eradicate. Whether or not Singapore's multiracial society is moving toward the merging or blurring of racial boundaries will be considered shortly. Second, any system of classification is bound to create ambiguities. For example, Sri Lankans, Nepalis, Pakistanis, and Bangladeshis are all classified as Indians. A further difficulty is that each race has an officially defined mother tongue which is the appropriate one from the list of four official languages—Mandarin, Malay, Tamil, and English. The Indians' mother tongue is thus Tamil, although a Sikh, for example, may define his dialect (on his identity card, for example) as Punjabi. In some cases this creates problems. A Straits Chinese child whose actual home language is a creole language related to Malay will be obliged to study Mandarin in the bilingual school system because it is his mother tongue.

At the microsociological level there are many consequences of this situation for relationships between the races and/or between subethnic categories. An obvious problem is communication. With the spread of English this problem may eventually solve itself, but at present it means that certain languages—Hokkien among the Chinese, Malay between the Malays, Indians, and Chinese—serve as interethnic tongues. One of the attractions of English is that it is a "neutral" language, that is, it is associated as a mother tongue with only a small ethnic minority and so has considerable utility as a means of interracial communication.

Another question, and one of equal importance, is that of interethnic marriage. One of the best indices of spontaneous assimilation is naturally that of marriage. There are no legal disabilities attached to interethnic marriage in Singapore, and yet the rate is low—hovering generally between 3 and 4 percent a year. At first sight at least, there appears to be a paradox here: officially promoted multiracialism has led to very little intimate mixing. But closer analysis reveals two reasons for this low percentage. The first is the multiracial policy itself. By stimulating ethnic awareness, people are made increasingly self-conscious of their race, and so it becomes more difficult to cross out of their race in marriage. The second is that cultural and especially religious barriers come into play. It is normally impossible to marry a Muslim without embracing Islam first, and so marriages between Muslims and non-Muslims are rare, except when conversion of the non-Muslim partner takes place. The Malays have very little objection to interracial marriage as such, provided the partner is Muslim: in other words it is religion, not race, which is the decisive factor. Among Chinese the dynamics work somewhat differently, since there is no one religion to which all Chinese belong. In earlier times marriage between individuals of different dialect groups would have been regarded as an interethnic marriage by the Chinese, but with the spread of Mandarin and English this is no longer the case. Considerations of maintaining the ancestor cult, of how to bring up the children of such marriages, and feelings of racial purity and superiority are now the operative factors. But where Chinese/non-Chinese marriages do occur they are often intrareligious (for example, where both partners are Christians), and the outmarrying partner is usually female. (The female does not carry the family surname and is not responsible for the ancestor cult, since even in a Chinese intraethnic marriage she would adopt the surname and ancestors of her husband.) Incidentally, female children (usually Chinese ones—it is a patrilineal kinship system) are not infrequently adopted by Malay or Indian families as infants, brought up wholly within the adoptive community, and subsequently marry within it, apparently without problems arising.[5]

Important as kinship relationships are to race relations, economic relationships are even more important, since they affect the entire structure of the society and of intergroup relationships in a very fundamental way. For years now Singapore has enjoyed a high rate of economic growth, as a result of which it has enjoyed full employment, rising wages, and a good infrastructure (including government housing provided at prices that are cheap compared with private sector housing). All of these cushion the effects of economic disparities between races. Here we must distinguish between *economic specialization* which is cultural in origin and so is associated with only one racial group (such as the provision of religious services or specific foodstuffs), and *economic stratification* which is generated by structural factors. Economic specialization is natural and relatively unproblematic, but economic stratification involves potentially serious long-term implications. Some figures here are revealing. In 1980 (the last census year), there were only 679 Malay University graduates in Singapore, as opposed to 31,286 Chinese, 3,518 Indians, and 8,519 others. In the same year 71.7 percent of Malays earned less than S$400 per month (approximately US$200), as against 51.8 percent Chinese, 59.8 percent Indians, and 25.6 percent of others. In the category of incomes above S$1,000 per month, only 2 percent of Malays were to be found, as opposed to 10.2 percent of Chinese, 8.6 percent of Indians, and 50 percent of others (which here include expatriate professionals and managers). In Division One (the top scale) of the civil service, in 1980 there were only 181 Malays as opposed to 6,520 Chinese, 698 Indians, and 397 others. Yet in Division Four (the lowest grade), there were 6,281 Malays, 5,765 Chinese, 2,537 Indians, and 795 others. Between 1967 and 1980, the percentage of Division One Malay civil servants marginally declined from 2.4 percent to 2.3 percent, whereas the Chinese percentage rose from 73.5 percent to 84.3 percent. In Division Four, the percentage of Malays rose during the same period from 37.5 percent to 40.9 percent, while that of Chinese declined from 41.9 percent to 37.6 percent.[6]

Education figures and employment figures closely relate to and reinforce each other. Only 0.2 percent of the Malay population are employers, as opposed to 2.4 percent of the Chinese. A total of 4.7 percent of Malays are in the professional and technical category, as opposed to 9 percent Chinese, but 54.2 percent of Malays are in the production sector (i.e., mainly factory production-line work) as opposed to 38.8 percent of Chinese. Many Chinese are self-employed, in small family businesses or other entrepreneurial activities, while Malays tend to be in service occupations, if not in factory work. The Indian community and the others tend to be overrepresented (as a ratio of their distribution in the population as a whole) in the upper occupational categories. Thus, we see an emerging stratification along ethnic rather than class lines, with a resulting rise in dissatisfaction among groups that feel they are being left out of the fruits of economic growth. This feeling is particularly shared by the Malays. Earlier evidence shows that until 1973 economic growth had not led to growing income inequalities between races overall.[7] The problem, however, is that such inequalities as did exist are becoming institutionalized and self-perpetuating.

Another consequence of the employment picture in Singapore is stereotyping—the myth of Chinese energy and Malay laziness in particular—which is used to explain inequalities. There *are* differences in the worldviews of the various racial groups in Singapore, and their coexistence within a single socioeconomic system inevitably creates tensions. Even the view that economic participation differences are to be explained on genetic grounds occasionally rears its ugly head.[8] In summary, while the national ideology of multiracialism and the booming economy have so far acted together to minimize the negative effects of economic inequalities on race relations, the foundation for future problems is being laid, unless policy decisions are devoted to offsetting these imbalances.

Education is the main means of socialization, with the bilingual school system designed both to promote multiracialism and to provide the language skills necessary for survival in the multiracial society. The other agency chiefly responsible for promoting racial mixing is the Housing and Development Board (HDB). This government department provides public housing for approximately 80 percent of the Singapore population in mainly high-rise apartments grouped in "new towns" around the nucleus of the old city. Whereas, as we have seen, ethnic enclaves were common in colonial times, one main social objective of the HDB has been to split up such concentrations and disperse people at random around the new housing estates. This both promotes racial mixing, since a typical housing block will contain members of all or most of the main ethnic groups, and prevents (politically) undesirable concentrations of one race in one place. But despite the physical mixing, it is evident that most people still interact on the basis of networks of their own ethnicity. Even immediate neighbors may have virtually no communication if they do not share the same racial background, but they are likely to have closer links with other families of the same race elsewhere in the same block or in adjacent ones. The policy has not been a great practical success, but it is still pursued in the hope that eventually physical proximity will lead to increasing social and cultural contacts.

The final area that cannot be ignored in any discussion of race relations in Singapore is that of cultural policy. And here considerable ambiguities arise, since no one seems to be exactly clear what the policy is. One version has it that the policy is to bring about a synthesis of the cultures associated with the different races—a "Singapore culture" derived from but also distinct from the source cultures. The other main version is that the idea is to keep and indeed develop the four main source cultures, but to bring them into harmonious relationship with each other. Both of these views tend to see "Singapore culture" as being somewhere in the future—as a yet unrealized goal. A third and somewhat minority view is that Singapore does, of course, have a culture (all functioning societies do) and that the main constituent of this national culture is its multiracialism. The second of these views is the one currently most favored, and it has direct practical consequences for race relations, which are somewhat paradoxical. The paradox is that the promotion of this policy requires that people be made more conscious of their origins, rather than less. Chinese Singaporeans are expected to reflect Chinese culture, Indians, Indian culture, and so on. The predictable result is an intensification of ethnic awareness rather than its diminution. As a result, it is commonly argued that cultural policy works *against* the emergence of a common culture, by promoting what is sometimes called "cultural involution." Culture that does not fit this pattern is regarded as individualistic (and probably Western and "decadent"), but it must not be *too* ethnic, otherwise it is liable to be labeled chauvinistic! The main effect of cultural policy then is to continually reinforce the four-race model. Although this policy does not have immediate or negative effects on day-to-day race relations, it does create one major strain—that of continually "proving" one's racial affiliation by demonstrations of the "appropriate" cultural and linguistic skills.

In summary, recent developments have centered not on legislative means to promote and insure racial harmony, but rather on a range of social policies, especially housing, education, bilingualism, compulsory military service for men, and cultural policies. Although the cumulative effect has been the maintaining of Singapore's excellent record of race relations, one major result has been the institutionalizing of the four racial categories, the expected relationships between them, and the economic niches to be occupied by each of them, rather than in the creative search for alternatives. With the formative period of Singapore now over (i.e., the last twenty-five years of intensive "nation-building"), the social structure and ethnic patterns are beginning to rigidify and to be taken for granted.

PUBLIC POLICY AND LEGAL PROVISIONS

Direct legal provisions for the management of racial relations in Singapore are almost entirely absent in any direct sense. There are no anti-miscegenation laws, for example, or laws regulating access to occupations. There are indirect means, however, and we will consider the leading examples. The first of these is the regulation of associations. In order to be a legal entity, all associations (including clubs, recreational and sporting organizations, and religious, kinship, or cultural societies) have to be registered with the Registrar of Societies, a government monitoring body. The Registrar withholds registration from societies that are not specifically multiracial in intended membership. Existing societies that are necessarily comprised of members of a single race (such as Chinese clan associations) are permitted to continue on that basis, but no new society can now be registered that does not allow for multiracial membership. In practice, many societies, though theoretically multiracial, actually (because of their activities, language medium, or some similar factor) are comprised entirely or almost entirely of individuals of only one race. But the intention of the legal provision in this case is to prevent the formation of groups explicitly intended to be racially exclusive.

A second policy strategy has been through the medium of language policy and educational policy. As mentioned earlier, all education in Singapore is bilingual, normally in the students' mother tongue (i.e., the "appropriate" official language) and English. The mother tongue is intended to be the carrier of culture, whereas English is supposed to serve as the language of commerce and technology and as a nonethnic general means of communication. The reality is more complex inasmuch as the "mother tongues" (according to the official definition) are not in many cases the languages spoken at home, which are likely to be the dialects (rather than Mandarin) in the case of Chinese, and one of the regional languages (rather than Tamil) in the case of non-Tamil Indians. Indeed, Indian students often take Malay as the second language in school. English has therefore emerged as the most important public language, which in turn has led to fears of the erosion of the other languages, especially Mandarin, which is not in any case well rooted.

A number of steps have been taken to deal with this perceived threat to Chinese identity—a "speak Mandarin campaign"; the increasing of the standard for second-language attainment to the elite schools and to the National University; the merging of the two main Chinese-medium daily newspapers into a single (and government-controlled) one; and the insistence that Mandarin and not dialects be spoken on television and radio programs, and in government offices. Language is seen as an essential component of ethnic identity in Singapore and hence is a subject of everlasting debate in relation to cultural and educational policies. The decline in enrollment in Chinese medium schools within the last two years in particular has triggered fears of the gradual disappearance of Chinese culture. The link between this and our earlier discussions of cultural policy and its paradoxes is very evident.

Three other recent developments are also of note. The first is the introduction of religious education into the schools, which is a complete reversal of former, secular, policies. Pupils are taught the religion associated with their own culture—Islam to Malays, Hinduism to Indians, Confucianism to Chinese. Rather than use the policy as a means of promoting racial integration by teaching students about each other's religions, it has become yet another subtle means of reinforcing existing attitudes and ethnic boundaries. The second development is the creation of a Council on Education of Muslim Children (Mendaki in Malay) in order to attempt to raise the level of educational achievement of Malay children to offset the occupational patterns noted earlier, and a recently announced decision (January 1985) to create a statutory board to promote Muslim participation in national development. Government policy has been designed to satisfy the needs of the most important minority— the Malays—in somewhat symbolic ways (such as making land available in each new housing estate for the construction of a mosque), while actually downplaying their participation in other areas (not all Malays are called up for military service, for example), including language. Malay is the national language of Singapore (a legacy of the merger with Malaysia days), but no steps are taken to promote its use, unless one considers half a page in Malay in the main English-medium newspaper such a step. At the same time rather more active steps have been taken to promote Mandarin, while attempting to diminish the significance of monoracial social organizations and associations.

SUMMARY AND CONCLUSIONS

Singapore society's most outstanding sociological feature is its multi-racialism. Race is used as the primary means of social classification both officially (as inscribed on every citizen's identity card) and as a folk device. Social interaction, economic relationships, patterns of friendship and intermarriage, lines of religious cleavage, dress, language, and enter-tainment, and cultural activities—all flow along lines created by the fun-damental racial categorization. Few social scientists today would dispute that "race" is not just a given, but is something created by patterns of social interaction. How questions of phenotype, origin, and so on are interpreted, used, exploited, and so on, is precisely what makes the race question interesting.

In Singapore we see the interaction of two levels of interpretation. The first of these is the official four-race model, taken over from colonial times and enshrined as a fundamental principle of the social structure. In this model, "race" is taken as absolutely unproblematic—as based on physical type and place of origin and as having a particular culture unambiguously associated with each other.[9] The second is the "folk" model. And here there is a particularly interesting fact that the folk version accords very closely with the official one, so no great strains arise between the two. It is an especially Chinese characteristic to put great emphasis on race in this sense, although the idea is much weaker among the other groups in Singapore, which seem to have a cultural rather than racial view of their identity.[10] If this thesis is correct, it would help explain why Chinese-dominated Singapore gives such remarkable prom-inence to the idea of race.

But as we have also noted, this unusual approach to race—its deliberate enhancement—has worked in practical terms. It has meant a booming economy with full employment and rising wages; a feeling of vulnera-bility in the midst of the Malay world; and a highly managed corporate state and a population of almost entirely migrant background, few of whom would want to "rock the boat" by inciting the kind of ethnic discontent that could only damage their affluence.

The four-race model should not give rise to the impression that no interaction takes place between the races—that segregation is complete. This is not true at all. Mixing takes place in housing estates, markets, schools, places of entertainment, recreation spots such as beaches and parks in the popular "hawkers centers" or collections of small stalls selling cooked foods, on public transport, and in places of work. Many friendships, business relationships, and other links are established across racial lines in all of these contexts and more.

A key factor in the creation and maintenance of these relationships is the state. Not only does an organic and highly Durkheimian view of the state prevail in Singapore, but also the agencies of that state move quickly and punitively to squash any manifestations of racially based disorder or conflict. The enhancing of race thus creates a situation in which an ideology has been established (institutionalized multiracialism), which can be manipulated and yet reflects the views of the bulk of the population. Race is thus thought to be natural and something that you "have" as an inevitable consequence of being human. Modernization and urbanization have done little to diminish this deeply rooted sense of racial identity. And, it should be emphasized here, it is race (rather than ethnicity or some alternative sense of identification) which is explicitly recognized and stressed. It follows from this and preceding factors that "situational selection," or switching of identity to suit differing contexts, is not only very difficult (except at a subethnic level, say between Chinese dialect groups or between Malays and Muslim Indians), but also is not desired, especially among the majority Chinese. To a Chinese, modifications in culture, such as loss of a native dialect, would not in any case constitute loss of racial identity. Majority or minority status does not seem to affect this identity either.

All of these factors have broad political implications, one of which is that an assimilation model of race would not be applicable in Singapore, since the different races have such very different world-views and conceptions of what constitutes their own identity. Although cultural borrowing and interaction do occur, separation at the micro-level is still the norm at much beyond a superficial level. (It is interesting to watch people boarding a half-full bus: they will frequently select seats next to persons of their own race if they have a choice.) At the national level, however, there is a high degree of integration, which is reflected in fairly well-shared national goals, participation in a single political system, and shared national symbols, such as the National Day celebrations.

A second implication is the absence of alternatives. At the personal level, it is not possible not to "have" a race—without one, one is unclassifiable, and has no concrete existence. At the national level, three fairly obvious alternatives are not considered. The first of these would be to develop a system not based on race at all. Given the deeply rooted attachment and national commitment to the multiracial model, it does not seem likely that this possibility will ever be seriously discussed. The second would be something along the lines of multiculturalism, that is, the model that a single individual should be bi- or multicultural in the same way that he or she is expected to be bi- or multilingual. Again this possibility has received no public attention; it is thought to be somehow inconceivable.[11] The third alternative would be class. The problem here is that, not only is the government firmly against the idea that class exists in Singapore, but in fact the race model is so strong that incipient class-based movements inevitably collapse along racial lines. Clearly, the government does not want to hear about alternatives or other models (Hawaiian? Brazilian?) since they would tend to upset the equilibrium that everybody is now tacitly committed to preserving. Indeed, it has been suggested that race is a resource for coping with the stresses of modernization by providing a primary identity that cannot be questioned, and as such is desired by individuals in a rapidly changing and potentially alienating social situation. In ethnographic terms, a continual dialectic between the official and folk, or the secondary and primary levels, is always in progress.

What of the future? Signals in this respect are contradictory and hard to interpret, but the operative factors themselves can at least be set out. Singapore has embarked on what is now being called the "Second Industrial Revolution." The first transformed Singapore into an industrial society; the second will move Singapore from labor-intensive and small-scale manufacturing into capital-intensive, high-technology, and internationally linked industries. Many policies, including forcing up wages to make unproductive labor-intensive industries uneconomical or to force technological upgrading on to them, have benefited many in the workforce. But a potential long-term effect will be to give additional advantages to those who already have them (especially in terms of skills and education suitable for exploiting a rapidly developing industrial and commercial environment), and to make it even harder for already disadvantaged groups, especially the Malays, to compete, thus widening economic disparities. On the other hand, the improving infrastructure, rising wage levels, and efforts to stimulate such groups by agencies such as the proposed statutory board for Malays may help alleviate these difficulties. Of all the races in Singapore, the Malays are the most disaffected. "Others" are overrepresented in upper echelon jobs, whereas the Indians, though rather forgotten in national policies, are also overrepresented in good public and private sector occupations. This disaffection is frequently reflected in anti-government voting behavior at elections, although its effects are minimized by the government ensuring that no constituency has a Malay majority. The heavy swing in votes against the People's Action party government in the December 1984 election may be a portent of a new era of greater political participation and pluralism than has hitherto been the case. The integration of the Malays, whose life-style and value system are very different from those of the Chinese, may prove to be the biggest challenge in race relations in the future.[12]

Consequently, the question of whether race-based stratification in Singapore is declining is arguable. With the spread of English, the establishment of a national educational system, mixing in housing estates, occupational mixing, and so on, the historically rigid lines of demarcation have to some extent disappeared. The result has been increasing levels of integration (although the Chinese majority are less accepting on almost all indices of tolerance),[13] but very little assimilation and continuing low levels of interracial marriage. Both class *and* race exist in Singapore, but the question of their precise relationship is too complex to enter into here. Although the four-race model continues to exist, certain structural constraints are present to prevent integration from proceeding very far at the primary group level. Indications are that identification with and loyalty toward Singapore is high, though probably lowest among professionals who have the option to migrate if conditions become more difficult.

One factor must be stressed once again: all discussions of race in Singapore involve politics. Race is highly politicized and highly ideological in Singapore. The government, which has ruled unbrokenly since independence, is committed to the multiracial model, even though it creates many problems (of classification, cultural policy, and so on). The alternatives are not considered—either because the government is already committed to the four-race version, or, because since that version has fared pretty well so far, no one wishes to risk changing the known system. Because of the society's articulation between race and the other subsystems (cultural, linguistic, religious), to many people in Singapore it is quite literally inconceivable that a nonracial alternative is possible. Race is what might be called (again with reference to Durkheim) a "collective representation." It acts as a system of meaning, as a world-view, and as a way of ordering and structuring an otherwise complex and rather messy reality. The unifying force in Singapore is the political culture, which binds all of these diverse elements of a basically migrant society together.[14] Common commitments at one level cushion differences at other levels, and the result is a high level of racial harmony. The government, acting through both politico-legal means—such as the refusal to register new ethnic associations—and through ideological means—such as the promotion of ideas of national identity and "nation-building"—is much in evidence, but grass-roots sociological factors must also be included in the total equation.

The model is not without its tensions: between majority and the minorities, in cultural, linguistic, and educational policies, and in economic stratification. But to date the overriding "system factors" have kept these well under control, not through repression, but through economic growth and ideological persuasion. As Singapore advances into the ranks of the advanced industrial nations, it will be of continuing interest to monitor the relationships between concepts of race, race relations, and socioeconomic development. Of all the issues, however, it is the ideological enshrining of race as the fundamental sociological reality of the society that most catches the eye, leaving aside political questions of whether the alternatives should be given a greater airing. Singapore's solution to the problems of the management of multi-ethnic societies, while it may not be generalizable to other contexts, is of profound interest, both in terms of its conception and, to date, its practical success.

NOTES

1. Leon Comber, *13 May 1969: A Historical Survey of Sino-Malay Relations* (Kuala Lumpur: Heinemann, 1983); Goh Cheng Teik, *The May Thirteenth Incident* (Kuala Lumpur: Oxford University Press, 1971).

2. C. M. Turnbull, *A History of Singapore 1819–1975* (Kuala Lumpur: Oxford University Press, 1977); Lee Loh Ping, *Chinese Society in Nineteenth Century Singapore* (Kuala Lumpur: Oxford University Press, 1978); Carl A. Trocki, *Prince of Pirates: The Temenggongs and the Development of Johor and Singapore 1784–1885* (Singapore: Singapore University Press, 1979).

3. For a detailed study of changing ethnic proportions in the demographic profile of Singapore, see Chiew Seen Kong, "Ethnicity and National Integration: The Evolution of a Multi-Ethnic Society," in Peter S. J. Chen, ed., *Singapore: Development Policies and Trends* (Singapore: Oxford University Press, 1984), pp. 29–64.

4. R.J.W. Neville, "The Areal Distribution of Population in Singapore," *Journal of Tropical Geography* 20(1965): 16–25.

5. Further details can be found in Riaz Hassan, *Interethnic Marriage in Singapore* (Singapore: Institute of Southeast Asian Studies, Occasional Paper No. 21, 1974); Chew Sock Foon and John A. MacDougall, *Forever Plural: The Perception and Practice of Inter-Communal Marriage in Singapore* (Athens, Ohio: Papers in International Studies, Southeast Asian Series No. 45, 1977).

6. For detailed contemporary figures, see David Jenkins and V. G. Kulkarni, "Joining the Mainstream," *Far Eastern Economic Review* June 28, 1984, pp. 26–32.

7. Pang Eng Fong, "Growth, Equity and Race," in Riaz Hassan, ed., *Singapore: Society in Transition* (Kuala Lumpur: Oxford University Press, 1976).

8. Cf. the notorious argument of the now Malaysian Prime Minister—Mahathir bin Mohamad, *The Malay Dilemma* (Singapore: Donald Moore for Asia Pacific Press, 1970). For a locally produced commentary on this debate, see Chan Heng Leng and Chan Chee Khoon, eds., *Designer Genes: I.Q., Ideology and Biology* (Petaling Jaya: INSAN, 1984).

9. A popular view in Singapore which is critically explored in Geoffrey Benjamin, "The Cultural Logic of Singapore's 'Multiracialism,' " in Riaz Hassan, ed., *Singapore: Society in Transition* (Kuala Lumpur: Oxford University Press, 1976).

10. See John Clammer, "Chinese Ethnicity and Political Culture in Singapore," in L. A. Peter Gosling and Linda Y. C. Lim, eds., *The Chinese in Southeast Asia*, Vol. 2 (Singapore: Maruzen Asia, 1983).

11. John Clammer, *Singapore: Ideology, Society and Culture* (Singapore: Chopmen, 1985), pp. 133–37.

12. Ibid., pp. 118–29.

13. Chiew Seen Kong, "Ethnicity and National Integration," in Peter S. J. Chen, ed., *Singapore: Development Policies and Trends* (Singapore: Oxford University Press, 1984).

14. John Clammer, "Symbolism and Legitimacy: 'Urban Anthropology' and the Analysis of Singapore Society," *Jernal Antropologi dan Sociologi* (1985), pp. 10–30.

BIBLIOGRAPHY

Allard, E. "The Social Organization of the Eurasians in the Malay Federation." *Current Anthropology* 5(1964): 422.

Arasaratnam, S. *Indians in Malaysia and Singapore*. Kuala Lumpur: Oxford University Press, 1970.

Azhari, Zahri. "Urbanization and Malay Society in Singapore." *Suara Universiti* 2(1971): 56–59.

Babb, L. A. "Patterns of Hinduism." *Singapore: Society in Transition*, edited by Riaz Hassan. Kuala Lumpur: Oxford University Press, 1976, pp. 189–204.

Bedlington, S. "The Malays of Singapore: Values in Conflict?" *Sedar* 3(1971): 43–55.

———. "The Singapore Malay Community: The Politics of State Integration." Ph.D. diss., Cornell University, Ithaca, N.Y., 1974.

Benjamin, G. "The Cultural Logic of Singapore's 'Multiracialism.' " *Singapore: Society in Transition*, edited by Riaz Hassan. Kuala Lumpur: Oxford University Press, 1976, pp. 115–33.

Blake, M. "Kampong Eurasians in Singapore." *Working Paper* No. 17, Department of Sociology, University of Singapore, 1973.

Buchanan, Iain. *Singapore in Southeast Asia: An Economic and Political Appraisal*. London: G. Bell & Sons, 1972.

Busch, Peter A. *Legitimacy and Ethnicity: A Case Study of Singapore*. Lexington, Mass.: D. C. Heath & Co., 1974.

Chan, H. C., and H. D. Evers. "National Identity and Nation Building in Singapore." *Studies in ASEAN Sociology*, edited by Peter S. J. Chen and H. D. Evers. Singapore: Chopmen, 1978, pp. 117–29.

Chang Chen-tung. "The Changing Socio-Demographic Profile." *Singapore: Society in Transition*, edited by Riaz Hassan. Kuala Lumpur: Oxford University Press, 1976, pp. 271–89.

Chen, Peter S. J. *Singapore: Development Policies and Trends*. Singapore: Oxford University Press, 1984.

Cheng Lim-Keak. *Social Change and the Chinese in Singapore*. Singapore: Singapore University Press, 1985.

Chew Sock Foon, and John A. MacDougall. *Forever Plural: The Perception and*

Practice of Inter-Communal Marriage in Singapore. Athens, Ohio: Ohio University Centre for International Studies, Southeast Asia Series No. 45, 1977.

Chiew Seen Kong. "Relations Between the Principal Ethnic Groups of Malaysia and Singapore." *Southeast Asian Journal of Sociology* 1 (1968): 63–78.

———. "Singapore National Identity." Master's diss., University of Singapore, 1971.

———. "Ethnicity and National Integration: The Evolution of a Multi-Ethnic Society." *Singapore: Development Policies and Trends,* edited by Peter S. J. Chen. Singapore: Oxford University Press, 1984, pp. 29–64.

Clammer, John. *Ethnographic Survey of Singapore.* Singapore: Department of Sociology, University of Singapore, 1977.

———. *The Ambiguity of Identity: Ethnicity Maintenance and Change Among the Straits Chinese Community of Malaysia and Singapore.* Singapore: Institute of Southeast Asia Studies, 1979.

———. *Straits Chinese Society.* Singapore: Singapore University Press, 1980.

———. "Malay Society in Singapore: A Preliminary Analysis." *Southeast Asian Journal of Social Science* 9(1981): 19–32.

———. "The Institutionalizing of Ethnicity: The Culture of Ethnicity in Singapore." *Ethnic and Racial Studies* 5(1982): 127–39.

———. "Chinese Ethnicity and Political Culture in Singapore." *The Chinese in Southeast Asia.* Vol. 2. Edited by L.A.P. Gosling and Linda Y. C. Lim. Singapore: Maruzen Asia, 1983, pp. 266–84.

———. *Singapore: Ideology, Society and Culture.* Singapore: Chopmen, 1985.

Djamour, Judith. *Malay Kinship and Marriage in Singapore.* London: Athlone Press, 1965.

Freedman, Maurice F. *Chinese Family and Marriage in Singapore.* London: HMSO, 1957.

———. "Immigrants and Associations: Chinese in Nineteenth Century Singapore." *Comparative Studies in Society and History* 3(1960): 25–48.

George, T.J.S. *Lee Kuan Yew's Singapore.* London: Andre Deutsch, 1975.

Hassan, Riaz. "The Religious Factor in Inter-Ethnic Marriage in Singapore." *Sedar* 2 (1969–70): 47–51.

———. "Class, Ethnicity and Occupational Structure in Singapore." *Civilizations* 21(1971).

———. *Interethnic Marriage in Singapore: A Study in Interethnic Relations.* Singapore: Institute of Southeast Asian Studies, 1974.

———, ed. *Singapore: Society in Transition.* Kuala Lumpur: Oxford University Press, 1976.

———, and G. Benjamin. "Ethnic Outmarriage and Socio-cultural Organization." *Singapore: Society in Transition,* edited by Riaz Hassan. Kuala Lumpur: Oxford University Press, 1976, pp. 205–20.

Hsieh, Jiann. "The Chinese Community in Singapore: The Internal Structure and Its Basic Constituents." *Studies in ASEAN Sociology,* edited by Peter S. J. Chen and Hans-Dieter Evers. Singapore: Chopmen, 1978, pp. 184–226.

Kassim, Ismail. *Problems of Elite Cohesion: A Perspective from a Minority Community.* Singapore: Singapore University Press, 1974.

Kaye, B.L.B. *Upper Nankin Street, Singapore: A Sociological Study of Chinese House-holds Living in a Densely Populated Area.* Singapore: University of Malaya Press, 1960.

Kuo, Eddie C. Y., and Aline K. Wong, eds. *The Contemporary Family in Singapore.* Singapore: Singapore University Press, 1979.

Kuo, P. A. "Religion, Educational Aspirations and Career Choice Among Chinese Teenagers in Singapore." Ph.D. diss., University of Notre Dame, South Bend, Indiana, 1966.

Lind, Andrew W. *Nanyang Perspective: Chinese Students on Multiracial Singapore.* Honolulu: Hawaii University Press, 1974.

Murray, Douglas. "Multilanguage Education and Bilingualism: The Formation of Social Brokers in Singapore." Ph.D. diss., Stanford University, 1971.

Nam, Tay Y. *Racism, Nationalism and Nation-Building in Malaysia and Singapore.* Delhi: Sadhna Prakashan, 1973.

Pang Eng Fong. "Growth, Equity and Race." *Singapore: Society in Transition,* edited by Riaz Hassan. Kuala Lumpur: Oxford University Press, 1976, pp. 326–38.

Png Poh Seng. "The Straits Chinese in Singapore: A Case of Local Identity and Socio-Cultural Accommodation." *Journal of Southeast Asian History* 10(1969): 95–114.

Sandhu, K. S. "Some Aspects of Indian Settlement in Singapore 1819–1969." *Journal of Southeast Asian History* 10 (1969): 193–201.

Siddique, S., and N. Puru Shotam. *Singapore's Little India.* Singapore: Institute of Southeast Asian Studies, 1982.

Song Ong Siang. *One Hundred Years History of the Chinese in Singapore.* Singapore: Oxford University Press, 1984.

Topley, M. "The Emergence and Social Functions of Chinese Religious Associations in Singapore." *Comparative Studies in Society and History* 3 (1961): 101–39.

Wilson, H. E. *Social Engineering in Singapore.* Singapore: Singapore University Press, 1978.

Wu, David Y. H., ed. *Ethnicity and Interpersonal Interaction: A Cross Cultural Study.* Singapore: Maruzen Asia, 1982.

SOUTH AFRICA

Paul Rich

A RACIAL CONTEXT

The complex mosaic of South African society has long been a source of fascination and interest to students of race, for here there appears to be a veritable microcosm of more general global problems concerning racial conflicts and their resolution. The South African state as such has only existed since the Act of Union in 1910 when the British Parliament bequeathed sovereignty to the former Boer states of the Transvaal and Orange Free State, together with the British colonies of Natal and Cape Colony. There was, however, a deep history of racial and class cleavages in a society that had had many features of frontier expansion and colonial conquest. For some observers, one of the chief features of South Africa has always been the domination of the past over the present. The entrenchment of white minority rule, buttressed by a vehement anti-black racial prejudice, appeared to confirm the survival of older frontier stereotypes formed by the Boer trekkers in their movement into the African interior since the late seventeenth century. More recent analysts, however, have stressed the role of extraneous economic links binding South African society to a capitalist world system and European imperial expansion.[1]

Although it is often easy to discern quite simple historical patterns in the South African past, the forces that have created the contemporary South African dilemma are somewhat more complex, as this chapter seeks to show. Certainly, the long presence of the Boer (now called "Afrikaner") population since the establishment of a freshwater station at the Cape by the Dutch East India Company in 1652 has had a fundamental impact on the society. But by the late eighteenth and early nineteenth century the essentially rural and pastoral Boers had begun to meet other social forces with which they were forced to interact. In the Eastern Cape and later Natal Boer, trekkers and frontiersmen encountered well-organized African societies which they could by no means easily overwhelm in the same manner that they had earlier subjected the San ("Bushman") and Khoi Khoi ("Hottentot") peoples in the Cape. The resulting clash with such peoples as the Zulu, Xhosa, and Basuto led to a long period of protracted warfare which was ended only with the final conquest of the African societies by the end of the nineteenth century. However, despite maintaining a vehement Calvinist religious faith, Boer societies in the nineteenth century would have been unlikely to have achieved the colonial subjection of Africans without the additional intrusion of the British "imperial factor" from the early nineteenth century onward.

The British presence in South Africa stemmed from the annexation of the Dutch Republic of Batavia during the Napoleonic War in 1806, which was later confirmed by the Treaty of Vienna in 1815. The new connection was vital for a number of reasons: it established mercantile links between the Cape and the British imperial metropolis at a time when the British Industrial Revolution was establishing Britain as the dominant industrial nation in the world in the first half of the nineteenth century. From 1820 onward this presence was fortified by the intrusion of an English settler presence in parts of the Eastern Cape and after the 1840s in Natal. The evangelical revival of the early nineteenth century in Britain also ensured a growing missionary presence in South Africa. Bodies such as London Missionary Society (LMS) began to establish mission stations on the colonial frontier as a means of winning over African converts and establishing communities of detribalized ("Kholwa") peasants schooled in more productive methods of agriculture and land maintenance.

HISTORICAL BACKGROUND

By the middle of the nineteenth century, the nascent society of South Africa was characterized by the interaction of Boer, British, and African societies, while in the Cape Colony a mixed race or "Colored" community had been established as a result of white liaisons with San, Khoi Khoi, and African peoples. In addition, from 1860 onward an Indian population began to be established in Natal as a result of the need by white sugar plantation owners for indentured labor and the resistance, before the 1880s, of the Zulu people in that colony to release significant pools of cheap labor to work in the cash economy.[2] From this time onward, South African racial divisions began to crystallize around a fairly rigid color-class gradient, despite the fact that the mid-nineteenth century was the highpoint of Victorian liberalism and the belief in the rights of the individual. The sources for the reproduction of such an ideological ideal in the South African context were generally limited and confined mostly to the Cape Colony where the 1854 Constitution ensured a color-blind franchise in which a small number of educated African voters were able to vote on the basis of an education and property qualification. The Cape's "liberal tradition" rested on the missions, the English-speaking press, and a mercantile community which at this time traded with an African peasantry that had grown up in the Eastern Cape. Trade was conducted especially among the Mfengu ("Fingo") people who had been formed as a consequence of the population dispersal (or *Mfecane*) unleashed by the Zulu expansion under Chaka in Natal in the 1820s.[3] Without tribal chiefs and being accommodative to the tenets of missionary education, the African peasantry in the Eastern Cape appeared to epitomize the Victorian liberal ideal of "civilizing" or "uplifting" the African population. At the same time, the discipline of free labor in a cash economy had been reinforced by freeing Cape Colored labor under Ordinance 50 of 1828 and the abolition of slavery throughout the British Empire in 1834.

The Cape liberal ideal, was increasingly challenged as the century wore on. In the north, a different norm of race relations prevailed in the Boer Republics where, as in the Transvaal Constitution of 1854, there was promulgated the doctrine that there should be no equality between white and black in church or in state. In addition, even though the classical liberal ideal had judged Africans as at least culturally backward, the onset of imperial expansion into Africa by the 1870s and 1880s and the increasing prevalence of Social Darwinist notions of a struggle between races led to a progressive erosion of Cape liberalism. The defeat of the Transkei in 1877 presented the Cape colony with the question of how far it was willing to incorporate large numbers of Africans who had not been schooled through the missions in Western "civilization." The 1833 Cape Native Laws and Customs Commission marked a shift in political thinking away from the classic individualist model toward a more group-oriented approach. This approach recognized African "tribal" law as well as the reality of separate African social norms and customs outside those of the society of the Cape.[4] In Natal, a similar ideological development was occurring as the Secretary of Native Affairs there, Sir Theophilus Shepstone, developed an early version of the doctrine of "indirect rule" by constructing "native administration" on the basis of the authority and legitimacy of the chiefs who became the accomplices of white colonial control.[5]

The period from 1883 to the outbreak of the Anglo-Boer War in 1899 was thus a critical pivot in modern South African history. It was during these years that the doctrines and practices underpinning white power effectively began a process of systematization into what would later, in the twentieth century become known as racial segregation and apartheid. These ideological movements were of crucial importance in the making of South African history. To this point they have frequently been neglected by analysts in favor of an ahistorical interpretation of the structures of white power, or else a more materialistic concern with society's class formation and resulting class conflict. Ideology, however, has always been of single importance in such a society as South Africa where there has not been the overwhelming weight of historical tradition, as in British society, such that ideological premises can be concealed behind a more amorphous "official mind." South Africa, like the United States, has been strongly influenced by political myth, which has often been fabricated by movements seeking to attain power through the mobilization of political opinion. Moreover, the function of this political mythology was historically vital in the literal sense that it breathed life into what were otherwise lifeless social interests at a time when the communication of political propaganda through pamphlets, books, and newspapers was on the increase. The real dynamics of modern South African politics, therefore, are to be located in a crucial period of world history when European imperialism reached a high point of expansion (in the last two decades of the nineteenth century) and became fueled by the advent of industrialization in South Africa through the discovery there of diamonds and gold.

INDUSTRIALIZATION AND SEGREGATION

The growth of diamond mining at Kimberley in the 1870s and later of gold on the Witwatersrand after 1886 had an indelible impact on South African society and race relations. They initiated a rapid process of social and economic change away from the older pastoral and mercantile economy which had been dependent on the export of such products as wool, wine, and ostrich feathers. They also provided a focal point for industrial expansion, which rapidly sucked in large pools of cheap black labor from the surrounding African chiefdoms and tribal reserves. By the end of the century four basic institutions had emerged by which this labor could be controlled in the interests of a smooth flow of migrant labor to service the mining industry: the reserve, the compound, the location, and the servant quarters in white homes.[6] Over the years, the varying importance of these institutions would change, especially as the economic base of the supposedly separate and autonomous reserve would progressively decline with growing population pressure, ecological deterioration, and the erosion of the political legitimacy of the "traditional" chiefly structures that increasingly appeared as the mere agents of white colonial rule. But on these four institutions, it may be argued, rested the more sophisticated ideology of white power and the conception of a "white" South Africa that was so essential for its success. In the years after the Boer War, a restive white population began to be mobilized around segregationist ideological slogans and by the establishment of the South African Union in 1910 around a militant ideology of white settler nationalism.

The system of racial segregation that the newly formed white state began to establish acted in the interests of releasing large pools of cheap black labor power for the burgeoning economy of the towns centered on mining and later secondary industry. The 1913 Natives Land Act was especially important for initiating a process of harmonizing the diverse pattern of white and black landholding in the territories of the Transvaal, Orange Free State, Natal, and the Cape. The South African state effectively embarked on what some observers came to call a policy of possessory segregation in which racial segregation became institutionalized in separate territorial spheres of land ownership.[7] By the end of World War I, this pattern was extended to the towns as well, as urban centers became officially recognized as "white" areas in which Africans were only to reside in order to minister to the labor needs of the resident white population. This was the doctrine enunciated by the 1921 Transvaal Local Government Commission chaired by the high Tory Colonel Stallard. It evolved into legislation with the 1923 Natives (Urban Areas) Act, which denied Africans the right of freehold ownership of property in urban areas and restricted them to specially reserved urban locations, in many cases, these locations were outside the city limits where they could be more easily observed and subject to social control.[8] This urban segregationist system controlled the process of African proletarianization by institutionalizing the pattern of influx control into the urban areas and ensuring that the rural reserve economies continued to act as reservoirs for the labor flow. The workers could be paid artificially cheaply since the wages of single African men did not take account of the subsistence needs of families who were left back in the rural reserve.[9]

The segregationist system was also a product of conscious design in which the diverse interests of the white settler population became to a degree reconciled behind a common ideological umbrella which was seen as shielding "white western civilization" from an advancing black demographic tide.[10] For white farmers, territorial segregation appeared to be the means by which Africans could be kept in the reserve economies as pools of vital farm labor which would otherwise drift uncontrolled into the towns. For white labor, too, territorial segregation was but part of a wider protective system of industrial segregation in which jobs were classified as specifically "white." Thus, although the government passed the Mines and Works Act in 1911 establishing a job color bar on the mines, the Natives Land Act two years later was additionally important as part of a strategy of regulating the flow of African labor to the mines and ensuring the institutional hegemony of white labor, now represented politically through the segregationist South African Labor party. Finally, for mine owners, segregation also represented the culmination of attempts at socially engineering African ethnic communities which would be resistant to too hasty a process of proletarianization and would be subject to the more "traditional" and compliant authority of tribal chiefs.

To this extent, then, South African racial segregation was an important ideological landmark in establishing white supremacy and preventing the breakup of white settler society once the imperial British presence had been removed after Union. White society was rent by increasingly bitter ethnic divisions in the wake of the Anglo-Boer War. Although the first South African government of General Louis Botha and the South African party (SAP) promoted a policy of "forgive and forget" between British and Boers, Afrikaner sectionalism continued to be fomented by nationalist politican brokers, especially after the establishment of the National party under General J.B.M. Hertzog in 1914 and a rebellion by some Boer diehards the following year during World War I. Segregation thus acted, as John Cell has pointed out, as an "interlocking system of economic institutions, social practices and customs, political power, law and ideology, all of which function both as means and ends in one group's efforts to keep another (or others) in their place within a society that is actually becoming unified."[11] It did not completely prevent the breakout of violent social divisions between whites in periods of crisis, such as the bloody Rand Revolt of 1922 when white miners were defeated by the government of General Jan Smuts by troops and planes. But the continuing domination of white South African political discourse by a vocabulary of segregation ensured a certain ideological harmonization that was crucial in laying the basis for the more advanced and sophisticated formulation of apartheid in the 1950s and 1960s.

LIBERAL ACCOMMODATION TO SEGREGATION

A further feature of segregationism's success in South African politics was that it had behind it a degree of intellectual sophistication that was crucial in a young society that had been to a degree cut adrift from the more traditional whig politics of parliamentary government under British imperial rule. With such a restricted parliamentary system confined, for the large part, to white voters, the conventional Victorian path of gradually widening the franchise to ever greater numbers of the electorate appeared effectively foreclosed. One may speculate, however, that if the Cape had been allowed to rule itself without the infusion of more racist northern influences, it might have emulated the Victorian liberal model and ended up with a color-class system along lines similar to Jamaica without formalized racial barriers. But even some Victorian liberal observers such as the traveler and politician James Bryce doubted that South Africa could emulate the model of the ethnically homogeneous societies of Western Europe. In *Impressions of South Africa* (1897) Bryce argued that in two or three generations South African society was likely to be characterized by "Two races ... living on the same ground, in close and economic relations, both those of employment and those of competition, speaking the same language and obeying the same laws, differing, no doubt, in strength of intelligence and will, yet with many members of the weaker race superior as individual men to many members of the stronger."[12] The saliency of Social Darwinism in late Victorian political thought and the belief of "survival of the fittest" among both nations as well as human individuals led to the conclusion that segregating Africans away from white society was beneficient, not only in terms of protecting whites from an ever-present black menace, or *swaart gevaar*, but also in the interests of African societies themselves. In this way, cultural and social traditions could be preserved and the dangers of "miscegenation" and interracial sex and marriage in the denationalizing towns prevented. This indeed was the argument of the liberal writer and novelist Olive Schreiner in the 1890s (though she later changed her views). In 1894 she warned that racial interbreeding and the creation of the "half caste" offended against the basic liberal concern with the right of nationality, for this "half caste" was a "creature without a family, without a nationality, without a stable kind, with which it might feel itself allied, and whose ideals it might accept."[13]

To a considerable degree, therefore, South African segregation was the product of a more general international climate in which ideas of ethnic and racial separation were still deemed intellectually respectable by a liberal intelligentsia in Britain, the United States, and the countries of white colonial settlement. Black races were seen as essentially rural and peasant peoples who were wedded to the norms of country rather than town life, and the existence of specially defined reserves did not connote ipso facto economic exploitation.[14] Thus a number of liberals saw the passage of the Cape of the Glen Grey Act in 1894 by the government of Cecil Rhodes—a law that provided for a measure of local government in African areas of the Eastern Cape—as a milestone in enlightened recognition of the "native question." The Cape liberal lawyer and "friend of the native" Richard Rose-Innes championed the measure as part of a wider policy of "segregation of the races within certain limits and under safeguards, but without compulsion." It still seemed possible, too, for the South African "native question" to be linked to a wider area of land settlement in Southern Africa in which large African areas would be established both north and south of the Zambesi River in the area of Northern and Southern Rhodesia.[15] This indeed was the scope of the investigation of the South African Native Affairs Commission under

Godfrey Lagden which was reported in 1905. Though not specifically advocating territorial segregation, it still assumed that there would be a measure of territorial separation in South Africa along racial lines.[16]

In the wake of the 1913 Natives Land Act whereby only some 9 percent of the total land area of South Africa was demarcated for African occupation, the issue began to assume an increasingly controversial tone politically. Some leading religious figures, such as the Anglican Bishop of Pretoria, lent their moral authority to the idea that the issue could be taken out of white party politics and confined to the realm of specially chosen "native experts," who could deliberate on the subject in an impartial manner.[17] Such ideas gained increasing currency by the end of World War I when there was a wave of black strikes, and the African National Congress (ANC) organized an anti-pass campaign on the Witwatersrand in 1919 and a black mine strike in 1920. The response of the Smuts government was passage of the 1920 Native Affairs Act. This law was widely seen as being in harmony with the emergent colonial doctrines of "indirect rule" through its extension of the Glen Grey idea of local African councils, as well as the establishment of the Native Affairs Commision as a forum for white "native experts." For one of the most articulate of these experts, the Natal educator Charles T. Loram, author of the important book *The Education of the South African Native* (1917), the moment of truth seemed to have arrived. As he wrote to the British High Commissioner, Earl Buxton, in November 1920:

the chief thing is of course to restore the Victorian condition when the natives believed in the European. Today with our democratic and even anarchic conditions we cannot revert to the paternalism of a Grey or a Shepstone.... If General Smuts approves I hope to stump the country in an attempt to awaken a conscience regarding native matters among the Europeans. I have a profound belief in the sense of justice of the white South African.[18]

Thus was born the era of "race relations" in South Africa. An increasingly articulate liberal intelligentsia, allied to the English-speaking universities in Johannesburg, Cape Town, and Durban, now sought to mobilize a white "conscience" on race through the establishment of interracial associations such as the Joint Council movement, begun in 1921, and later the South African Institute of Race Relations, funded in part by the Phelps-Stokes Fund and Carnegie Corporation, in 1929.[19] The white liberals hoped that their activities could (1) generate a more informed discussion on race issues among the white South African public and (2) help forge a more articulate and moderate African political leadership that would avoid the more militant paths of the small South African Communist party (formed in 1921) or the pan-Africanist Garveyites who had been impressed in the early 1920s by the activities of

Marcus Garvey's Universal Negro Improvement Association in the United States.

These ideals, became increasingly qualified by the mounting pressure for a widening of segregation after the election of the Pact Government in 1924 of General James Hertzog's National party in alliance with the Labor party under Colonel Frederic Creswell. A new Department of Labor led to legislation such as the Wage Act of 1925 to help unskilled "poor whites" and the 1926 Color Bar Act to protect skilled and unskilled labor from black competition. The entrenchment of industrial segregation in the mid–1920s marked the growing African disillusionment with both the ideal of a "just" form of territorial segregation and of a fair share in economic advancement in South Africa's advancing industrialization. Thus, although cooperation with the white liberals continued, by the end of the 1920's rising doubts were being expressed by a number of black critics. This was especially so after a Scottish trade unionist, William Ballinger, was brought into South Africa in 1928 to help organize the black International and Commercial Workers Union (ICU) run by the Malawian Clements Kadalie. The exposure of both corruption and bitter divisions in the Union was in part blamed on white liberal meddling. Some critics such as the anonymous "Enquirer," wrote in the black press that the Joint Councils and white liberals were trying to neutralize black political leadership.[20]

The hope for a united African political leadership was continually dashed by personal factionalism and by the absence of a cohesive black middle class. The entrenchment of segregation continually threatened even small African farmers, traders, journalists, and teachers with the ever present threat of proletarianization. The 1921 census, for example, showed that the educated African leadership was tiny, with only 9,756 teachers, ministers, chiefs, and headmen (3 per 1,000) of the population and interpreters and clerks totalling 1,634 (1 per 1,000). "Peasants," on the other hand, totaled 2,382,277 (435 per 1,000), farm laborers 368,122 (126 per 1,000), and mine workers 235,665 (99 per 1,000). In this condition, it was still possible for white missionaries to exercise a good deal of paternal control in the 1920s. The Chamber of Mines newspaper *Umteteli wa Bantu* confidently expected in 1926 that the Joint Councils would become officially recognized by the government as a forum for the ideal of "interracial cooperation."[21]

The following five-year period, 1927–32, may be identified as a crucial watershed in the evolution of South African politics. That period witnessed the beginning of a rapid undermining of the legitimacy of segregationist ideology. Outside South Africa a number of writers and politicians began to attack the tenets of segregationism. In England such figures as Lord Olivier, Norman Leys, Leonard Barnes, and the South African W. M. Macmillan, in a stream of books and articles in the late

1920s and 1930s, warned of its possible extension to the British colonial territories in Africa and of its undermining of basic liberal values of common citizenship.[22] Inside South Africa these warnings appeared to be regularly confirmed as more authoritarian legislation reached the statute books. One of these laws was the 1927 Native Administration Act which bolstered the failing authority of tribal chiefs with strong autocratic powers. In 1932, the Native Service Contract Act supported the powers of white farmers in their control over black farmworkers by extending the period of service on farms to ninety days and gave white agriculturalists virtually feudal powers over their black serfs. Finally, in 1936, the United party government of Generals Smuts and Hertzog agreed on legislation that extended the territorial segregation of the 1913 Natives Land Act by establishing a trust through the Native Trust and Land Act to consolidate the areas of African landholding. The Representation of Natives Act also removed Cape African voters from the common roll and established a Natives Representative Council, together with a limited number of whites, "natives representatives" in the Senate and House of Assembly who were elected by African voters but could not themselves vote in any division of the members of Parliament (MPs) or senators.

After at least three decades when a number of observers had seen a strong resemblance between the South African pattern of segregation and the Jim Crow South, a parting of the way occurred. Liberal opinion in America now began to bend slowly before the pressure of an advancing civil rights movement and to reject the ideas of a segregationist ideology of the South which Gunnar Myrdal in *An American Dilemma* (1944) considered stood in contradiction to the dominant Enlightenment values of the "American Creed."[23] In South Africa, on the other hand, segregationism remained the dominant political ideal in South African political discourse. Even the liberal organizations gathered under the umbrella of the Institute of Race Relations maintained an ambiguous relationship with it. A number of English-speaking liberals were anxious that the "native question" not become an issue of ethnic mobilization in white politics. They therefore sought as far as possible to avoid the Afrikaner nationalists' accusation that they favored maintaining the African franchise in order to gain black votes. This became evident at a National European-Bantu Conference held in Cape Town in February 1929 while the question of legislation on the Cape franchise was still under discussion. C. T. Loram, who had played an important part in the organization of the Joint Councils, urged that the conference not even discuss the subject for fear that it would divide the conference in which representatives of the Dutch Reformed Churches were in attendance.[24] In any event, the conference did discuss the issue, and a number of liberals in the Cape organized around the Cape Native Franchise Association in order to defend the franchise. The second defeat of Smuts' SAP later in the year by the Pact led to the accusation that the liberals had helped Smuts to lose votes in a "Black Manifesto" election. In this election, race was skillfully employed by Pact politicians under Hertzog, who accused Smuts of wanting to swamp white South Africa through his schemes for expanding South African territory to the north.[25]

By the early 1930s, therefore, many liberals became wary of too close an involvement in white party politics and felt their influence could best be exerted through more informal channels. The Joint Councils became increasingly suspect as they either fell in disuse at the local level or were taken over by more militant activists. However, a proposal in 1933 by the Communist party for a program of joint action to fight segregation and police "pickups" of Africans on antiliquor raids, and achieve free compulsory education of African children, was turned down after failure to reach agreement.[26] By this time, the emergence of the Institute of Race Relations directed by its "advisor" J. D. Rheinallt Jones marked a more politically bland approach. Under its president, the philosopher R.F.A. Hoernle, many liberals began to think about some form of political accommodation to segregationism through the idea of racial separation of South African society into separate ethnic communities. By this means, it was hoped, some form of "liberal spirit" could be kept alive in the South African body politic. As Hoernle pointed out in some important lectures in 1939, however (*South African Native Policy and the Liberal Spirit*), this was not an especially practical long-term solution. He gloomily reflected that South Africa seemed to exemplify a more general trend in Europe in which liberal values were being eclipsed under a fascist jackboot.[27]

Despite the further entrenchments of the segregationist doctrine by the South African state in the 1920s and 1930s, the society was not by any means a completely authoritarian police state by the outbreak of World War II in 1939. Still in existence were many of the visible trappings of a liberal democracy for whites, whose electoral power was doubled in 1930 when white women gained the vote. For Coloreds and Indians, too, the full apparatus of segregation had not yet been established. Even so, the Indian population had waged a passive resistance campaign under M. K. Gandhi before 1914 against immigration restrictions, while the 1926 Color Bar Act discriminated against the employment not only of Africans but Coloreds and Indians as well. However, an attempt by the Union government to apply territorial segregation against the Indian population through an Areas Reservation Bill was preempted by its agreeing to meet representatives of the Indian government at a Round Table Conference in Cape Town, December 17, 1926, to January 12, 1927. At that meeting a scheme of assisted emigration was agreed upon, combined with a limitation on the immigration of Indian wives and children and a program of "upliftment" of the Indian population resident in South Africa. Segregation had been averted for the time being.[28]

For the most part, South African domestic politics had been able to evolve more or less unhampered before 1939 by external involvement. However, South African membership as a "white dominion" of the British Commonwealth indicated that where these politics directly affected the interests of another Commonwealth member such as India, it was not yet strong enough to do anything but back down. The onset of war in 1939, began a process by which South African domestic policies became internationalized before an international arena increasingly hostile, in the wake of the Nazi holocaust, to policies based on race. South African relations with Britain did reach a momentary high point of cordiality during the war, as South African Premier General Smuts, who had ousted his rival Hertzog in 1939, forged a close understanding with the government of Winston Churchill. But the old world order was rapidly breaking up and, despite Smuts' assertion before an Institute of Race Relations audience in 1942 that the segregation policy had "fallen on evil days" and that the government welcomed limited black urbanization, its "native policy" appeared increasingly outmoded. Nevertheless, as the war hastened South Africa's secondary industrialization, manufacturers and commercial entrepreneurs showed a growing economic interest in building up a larger domestic market through the establishment of a growing black working class of consumers. Thus, in the early 1940s, a more optimistic attitude concerning South African race relations began to emerge.

An articulate body of opinion was forged through journals such as *The Forum* and *Trek* which looked to increasing South African capital investment in other parts of the African continent as well as an easing of the restrictions of racial segregation. To many economically minded liberals segregation now appeared anachronistic in an era increasingly governed by the logic of both market forces and "rational" managerial decision making.[29] This line of reasoning seemed to be echoed within the appartus of government itself as the establishment of an Industrial Development Corporation under its managing director Dr. H. J. Van Eck led to the managerialist thesis being repeated at the heart of the administration. The language of race implicit in the doctrines of "segregation" and "trusteeship" now appeared to be replaced by blander notions of "industrial development," "training," and "greater productivity" which became the key terms in the early 1940s.[30] A realignment in South African party politics seemed likely, in which a more liberally minded party would emerge to capture the middle ground of politics and isolate the diehard elements on the backveld or platteland who remained an obstacle in the United party and a dominating voice in the National party opposition under Dr. D. F. Malan.[31]

This misperception of South African political processes has been commonplace in the society's history. At a deeper level a more fundamental political reorganization was taking place within the white electorate in response both to domestic political and economic change as well as to rising international hostility and concern. Since the end of World War I, Afrikaner nationalism had been increasingly mobilized as an ideological weapon by a vanguard of militant Afrikaner intellectuals determined to sever South African links with the British Empire-Commonwealth. Through such organizations as the Broederbond (founded in 1918) and the Federasie van Afrikaanse Kulturvereniging (FAK) (founded in 1929), this ideology was instilled into the white Afrikaner electorate in the 1930s and 1940s as it underwent a massive social transformation resulting from the migration from the rural platteland into the cities and establishment as a white working class. The ideological offensive was designed in part to override the possible emergence of a deracialized class consciousness emerging between white Afrikaner workers and their brown and black counterparts. The Afrikaner political elite played on the theme of race as a dividing factor in South African politics. This mobilization in many respects drew on the ideological resonances of segregationism that were already embedded in white South African political culture. It systematized them into a more ethnically specific ideology of Afrikaner political and ideological mission. As Leonard Thompson has recently pointed out, it had the additional attraction of being able to draw on Afrikaner sacred history harkening back to such well-known incidents as the Great Trek, the Battle of Blood River and the Day of the Covenant, and the experience of Boer Women and children being herded into concentration camps during the Anglo-Boer War of 1899–1902. This political mythology proved a valuable mobilizing weapon when such incidents as the centenary of the Great Trek was reenacted in 1938: Afrikaner men grew beards, donned traditional costume, and drove in ox carts in memory of their ancestors.[32]

The linkage of the political ideology to the doctrine of apartheid, or racial apartness, therefore, owed as much to the movements of political consciousness within the self-proclaimed Afrikaner *volk* as to structural factors at the level of the reserve economies. While economic and class determinants were important in the emergence of such a populist movement as the National party in the 1940s, its victory over Smuts' United party in 1948 cannot be mainly attributed to the erosion of the precapitalist mode of production in the African reserves. This argument, which has been cogently made by Harold Wolpe in a famous paper of 1972, fails to account for the historical decline of the reserves much earlier than the 1940s. Indeed, on the basis of pioneering investigations into the reserves in the Eastern Cape such as Herschel and Victoria East by W. M. Macmillan and the Reverend James Henderson in the 1920s, it is clear that many areas had already been reduced to the status of labor reservoirs in the decade after World War I, some two to three decades before the institutionalization of apartheid.[33] The emergence of the apartheid doctrine, therefore, owed far more to autonomous political dynamics than to a simple class offensive as a result of the erosion of the reserves' subsistence base, which had allowed African migrants' wages to be set artifically cheaply.

The history of actual class warfare in South Africa, has been an uneven one, with events like world wars having a considerable impact on the mobilization of African political awareness and strike action. This had been the case after 1918, culminating in the African mine strike of 1920. The same thing happened again after 1945, with the resulting African mine strike of 1946 and the suspension of the Natives Representative Council, which one councillor condemned as a "toy telephone." Apartheid, therefore, should be seen as a more specifically political response by an Afrikaner ethnic leadership concerned not only with becoming the new ruling class running the apparatus of the South African state, but also with establishing more ruthless and effective control over the politically restive African, Colored, and Indian population when, by the late 1940s, white rule in South Africa appeared finite and limited.[34] Before discussing the establishment of this apartheid doctrine, it is first necessary to examine the nature of this black resistance.

BLACK RESISTANCE TO SEGREGATION AND APARTHEID

The ideology of racial segregation has attained some degree of success, despite the apparently lunatic ideal of completely separated ethnic communities in South Africa defined on racial grounds. As Cell has pointed out, segregationism in world terms, along with various Marxist and nationalist ideologies, can be seen, as one of the most successful ideologies in the first half of the twentieth century.[35] One reason for this success lay in its ability to continue a more de facto practice of manipulation of African "tribal" divisions during the nineteenth century into a more systematic practice of divide and rule in the face of an increasing potential for a united African resistance in the twentieth.

It has been a difficult and protracted process for African political leaders in South Africa to build a united and popularly based nationalist movement in opposition to white rule. From the time of Union African society was rent by social, cultural, and economic divisions that continually inhibited this aim, though the African National Congress sought such a goal more or less from its foundation in 1912. The African paper

Tsala ea Becoana (edited by Sol Plaatje) viewed the Congress as "the voice in the wilderness bidding all the dark races of this sub-continent to come together once or twice a year in order to review the past and reject therein all those things which have retarded our progress, the things which poison the springs of our national life and virtue."[36] This essentially Victorian liberal ideal of national growth misunderstood the central political and economic processes occurring in the white South African settler state. For many of the African political elite, schooled in the missions of the late nineteenth century, the ultimate court of appeal still seemed the British government and its essentially whig notions of freedom and justice under the rule of law. The Congress opposed the idea of strike action in 1913 and, though it mobilized action against the Land Act, still had a positive view of segregationist ideals. For some African spokesmen such as J. T. Gumede, it appeared feasible in 1915 to link the idea of submitting African views to the white Parliament in Cape Town with support for the tenets of segregation which "would indeed ensure property and pure citizenship of our natives for, they would have their own government, frame their own laws, have no European to 'play the boss,' and would not be so mixed up as to multiply a people which belong to no pure nationality."[37] From the 1913 Land Act onward, however, the reality was a progressive confinement of African territorial aspirations.

Growing proletarianization and the reservoir function of the reserves thus took some time to permeate the thinking of some African political leaders. In the wake of the post–1918 strikes in which a momentary link had been established with the radical International Socialist League, extension of segregation in the 1920s led to a period of confusion and division which was never satisfactorily resolved before World War II. Many ANC activists still had some hope of maintaining channels of communication with the state, and in 1924 the Congress at Bloemfontein welcomed the opportunities provided by the periodical European Bantu conferences.[38] These channels proved ineffective in reversing government policy, and by the late 1920s legislation boosting the powers of the chiefs under the 1927 Native Administration Act threatened the political influence, such as it was, of the small educated African intelligentsia active in ANC, Joint Council, church, and journalistic circles. J. T. Gumede, the newly elected president of the ANC, spoke in a more militant vein of uniting all South African blacks and forging links with nascent African trade unions through a Congress labor department with its own secretariat.[39] But the splits in the ICU, the Depression of 1929, and a conservative takeover of Congress in the 1930s by a faction of chiefs led by Pixley Seme, the original founder, nullified these hopes. Only in the early 1940s, under Dr. A. P. Xuma, would the ANC begin a further growth in its membership, culminating in a wave of African boycotting of the apparatus of segregation in 1946–47 including the Natives Representative Council (NRC), local Native Administration Boards (established under the 1920 Native Affairs Acts) and a decline in support for liberal interracial organizations like the Joint Councils and the South African Institute of Race Relations (SAIRR).[40]

Black political movements were crucially hampered by the difficulties of mobilizing a nationwide organization. Regional differences tended to hinder the work of perceived "outsiders"which were played upon by the local black press, dependent on white finance, such as *Imvo Zabantsundu* in the Cape and *llange lase Natal* in Natal. Furthermore, the struggle to preserve the African franchise in the Cape led to the formation of a separate organization in the 1930s, the All African Convention, which drew off important talent such as Professor D.D.T. Jabavu, of the African College of Fort Hare in the Eastern Cape. In many respects, an authentically nationalist tradition in African politics had difficulty gaining the upper hand before 1939 because it was continually challenged by both a traditionalist native-chief conservatism and a liberalism geared to "interracial cooperation" with white liberals through the existing parliamentary system.

After 1940, a more general expansion of scale began to occur as a result of wartime industrialization and a new climate of political militancy ushered in by the struggle against the fascist axis. To many South African blacks the signing of the Atlantic Charter by Winston Churchill and President Franklin D. Roosevelt in 1941 guaranteeing political rights and freedoms seemed to apply to them, too, while a new generation of black activists began to emerge with the foundation of the Youth League in the ANC in 1943–44, including such figures as Nelson Mandela, Albert Luthuli, Oliver Tambo, and the nationalist intellectual Anton Lembede. By the war's end, it seemed clear that there was to be no going back to the 1920s and 1930s and that a rejuvenated Congress could become part of a new world order in which doctrines of white supremacy no longer had any part. How this was to occur was by no means obvious, however, to many Congress leaders. Anton Lembede, writing in the paper *llanga* on the need for "winning the confidence of the masses," also warned that the Congress should not be "commuted into a battle ground of European ideologies."[41]

There was a certain naiveté in this approach, for African politics could not be insulated from the rest of African society. Lembede himself discovered this idea when, shortly before his death in 1947, he was offered some £500 from the Afrikaner nationalist *Ossewa Bandwag* who clearly hoped his Africanist aims could be made to coincide with their vision of an ethnicized African politics.[42] African political mobilization was inextricably linked to other political processes in South African society, and, the previous era of "interracial cooperation" was now starting to break up as political divisions polarized. The late 1940s resembled the late 1920s somewhat as political divisions between the conservative chiefly faction and the radical Youth League vanguard widened. On this later occasion, however, the radicals were better organized, the degree of white liberal involvement much reduced, and the course of African nationalism increasingly in tune with the postwar world. Despite his earlier buildup of the ANC organization in the early 1940s, Xuma was accused of siding with the chiefly faction.[43]

In 1949, a new Program of Action indicated that the ANC had moved to a more radical position in the wake of the election of Malan's Nation lists the previous year. The Program outlined a strategy of boycotts, civil disobedience, and strikes and marked a significant change in political tone as the movement sought a more militant posture.[44] It marked the trumph of the "progressives" over the conservative elements in the ANC. The Youth Leaguers were radicalized both by the infusion of more left-wing and Marxist ideals from the communists active in the organization and by the links forged with some movements at the local level.[45] In the Johannesburg suburb of Sophiatown, for example, at the beginning of the school term in 1950 many school children were turned away because of a shortage of school places, and the Youth League began a campaign to organize the children and demonstrate against the lack of accommodation.[46] Thus was a pattern begun among the young at the local level, which a later generation in the mid–1970s was to repeat on a wider and more significant scale.

THE APARTHEID RESPONSE

It is in this increasingly politicized context that the development of the apartheid ideology in the late 1940s should be seen. Some analysts have chosen to focus on it as a specifically Afrikaner ethnic response to the South African pattern of racial politics based on doctrines noted in the ideal of the *Herrenvolk*.[47] Clearly, however, it reflected a deeper crisis in the ideological legitimation of white power after World War II. The 1946 census revealed that whites numbered 2,372,690 and nonwhites totalled 9,045,659, an increase of only a million for whites since Union in 1910 but 4.5 million for the nonwhite population. There were strong demographic reasons for white nationalists to feel they were facing a threat to their identity, enhanced by the rapid rate of urbanization during the war. However, the postwar political crisis represented an important additional dimension in that it upset a whole apparatus of cooption of compliant African political leaders in such bodies as the Natives Representative Council. These underpinned the structure of white power. The deputy Prime Minister Jan H. Hofmeyr wrote with some alarm on the suspension of the NRC to the Prime Minister Jan Smuts in September 1946 that

it means that the hitherto moderate intellectuals of the Professor (Z. K.) Matthews-type are now committed to an extreme line against color discrimination, and have carried the chiefs with them. We can't allow them to be swept into the extremist camp, but I don't see what we can do to satisfy them, which would be tolerated by European public opinion.[48]

The dilemma pinpointed by Hofmeyr reflected the fact that the United party government was trapped between appeasing right-wing white electoral opinion and the increasingly militant black political leadership, which was now more and more distrustful of the whole concept of segregation. The aged leader Smuts was unable to reformulate his policy to meet the crisis before the 1948 election. The new slogan of apartheid appeared to many bewildered whites to offer some hope for the future, while the old segregationist ideal seemed to reflect a white polity with no single political direction. This political "danger" had always haunted white South African politics from before Union, but it had been warded off until World War II as the Afrikaner nationalists continued to accept a degree of political consensus on segregation with their political opponents, arguing only for a further tightening up of measures like Urban Areas legislation restricting the entry of blacks into urban areas. In March 1939, for example, D. F. Malan argued in a speech at Stellenbosch that he differed with Hertzog and the United party only over the issue of establishing a Republic, while segregation was the only policy that could protect the "white race" in South Africa.[49]

This consensus with the white polity broke down during the war years as some Afrikaner nationalist groups such as the Broederbond and the Ossewa Brandwag flirted with fascist ideas of a corporate state. By 1943, Malan, in a motion in the House of Assembly calling for a "new order," sought massive extension in state power over the direction of labor and had a "quota" for white agriculture.[50] The defeat of Nazi Germany in 1945, however, confirmed for mainstream nationalists the need to rely on the existing parliamentary structures to attain power. The National party resorted to the use of apartheid as a slogan quite late: originally formulated by a group of Stellenbosch anthropologists in the early 1940s, the word was extensively used in a commission appointed by Malan on "native policy" in 1947. It was still not included in an Afrikaans dictionary published in 1949. In essence, the term came to mean the establishment of a more positive program of racial segregation compared to the more negative policy of fending off African nationalist demands under the previous United party government. Once the ideological zealot Dr. H. F. Verwoerd, an important Broederbonder, was appointed Minister of

Native Affairs in 1950, this program swung into action, amounting to something little short of a counterrevolution over the following decade and a half.

The Population Registration Act in 1950 began a nationwide process of race classification to accord with the overall apartheid design, while the Mixed Marriages Act outlawed interracial marriages. (Interracial sexual liaisons had been outlawed in the 1927 Immorality Act.) The 1950 Group Areas Act established a nationwide pattern of urban ethnic segregation and extended the previous limitation of Indian landholding in towns and cities under Smuts' 1846 Asiatic Land Tenure and Indian Representation Act. The 1951 Bantu Authorities Act boosted the powers of tribal authorities and abolished the local councils established by the 1920 Native Affairs Act as well as the Natives Representative Council. The apartheid policy sought a massive process of social engineering to redirect African political energies into the reserves and away from the cities, and the 1954 Bantu Education Act sought to impose education in African vernacular languages and to encourage "traditional" African customs and mores. Mission schools were progressively expropriated by the state, leading to an ineffective ANC campaign of boycotting the newly formed state schools. The boycott often proved an ineffective weapon against a resolute state. Aside from organizational weaknesses, the ANC leadership at this stage was ill prepared for mass organization and had few links with the rural peasants and migrant workers.[51]

Dr. Verwoerd sought a massive extension of the original Stallardian doctrine that Africans should only be in urban areas to minister to whites as workers. The 1952 Native Laws Amendment Act limited the rights of Africans in urban areas to those who were born there. The Natives (Abolition of Passes and Coordination of Documents) Act the same year required all Africans, including for the first time women, to carry "reference books" containing photographs as the system of influx control was modernized and updated. The Report of the Tomlinson Commision in 1956, however, pointed out the scale of the task. If a gross income of £120 per annum per farming family was used as the guide to rural living standards, it would still only be possible for 20 percent of those living in the reserves to be adequately provided with land. The report envisioned a development program over the following twenty-five and thirty years that would allow some 10 million people to reside in "Bantu" areas, of which 8 million would be dependent on activities in those areas and the other 2 million on work in the "European" sector. It was calculated that £104,486,000 should be spent on economic development of the reserves in the next ten years, of which £27,4 would be on soil reclamation.

The Tomlinson Report confirmed the direction of the apartheid policy. The government of Johannes Strijdom, who replaced Malan in 1954, welcomed it as substantiating the ideal of "separate development" as opposed to "integration": there was now in South Africa no official recognition of any middle way as in the Smuts years, despite the hopes of some liberal groups that the government might be persuaded to the contrary. The government now had its own intellectual think tank in the form of the South African Bureau of Racial Affairs (SABRA). This agency tried to invent an historical legitimacy for apartheid ideology by seeing it as a logical outcome of the South African past since the original settlement at the Cape in 1652.[52]

The apartheid design proved increasingly effective, however, in overriding black resistance, especially as the 1952 Passive Resistance Campaign mounted by the ANC showed how blind the state was to modes of moral persuasion. The 1950 Suppression of Communism Act had driven the Communist party underground, although various left-wing activists collaborated with the ANC, especially after Chief Albert Luthuli replaced the moderate Dr. Moroka as president in 1952. As a relatively charismatic figure, Luthuli was welcomed as someone who might heal the damaging rift with the Natal Indian community after the 1949 Durban riots in which Zulus had attacked and killed a number of Indians, whose role as traders had induced mistrust and racial hatred. But despite the proclamation of the Freedom Charter at Kliptown proclaiming a democratic program for a new multiracial South African society in 1955, the ANC under Luthuli's leadership got bogged down in a growing number of court cases instigated by the state, as well as charges by a number of former supporters of growing communist control of the organization. Since the 1949 Program of Action, there had been an increasing emphasis on trying to build up a mass movement, and the Passive Resistance Campaign had forged a number of new contacts at the local level.

The movement was still seen as very urban-based, however. In 1954, Secretary General Walter Sisulu, who himself came from Transkei, reported at the Congress' 42nd Annual Conference on the need for incorporating the demands of peasants and farm laborers into the program.[53] But the movement lacked funds and could not establish its own nationwide newspaper, depending on local organs like *Injaniso* in the Cape. Only in 1956 was a working committee established to try and get a Congress paper established.[54] Luthuli appointed a Drought Committee of Congress to help stricken areas in the Transkei and Ciskei in 1956, but no systematic effort was made at this time to reach the peasantry and migrant workers, some of whom started to gravitate toward an Africanist wing critical of the Congress leadership's fraternalization with the white left.[55] The Congress' general populist strategy, such as a campaign for 1 million signatures in the wake of the Freedom Charter, thus did not appeal to all sections of the African population. The fact that the Pan Africanist Congress (PAC) under Robert Sobukwe did split off in 1958–59 was undoubtedly a damaging factor just as the ANC was trying to mobilize popular resistance, such as the three-day Stay-at-Home in 1958. It was on such divisions that the South African state was able to play as it sought to entrench territorial apartheid in the late 1950s through the 1959 Promotion of Bantu Self-Government Act and the promulgation of a separate Transkei Constitution in 1963.

The apartheid ideology in South Africa was thus forged in the context of a growing political struggle that broadly took on a "racial" dimension, though it also had to take account of changing economic determinants as South African secondary industrialization escalated in the 1950s and 1960s. In its original form, it still had many of the trappings of a pastoral vision of African land settlement: Verwoerd's Secretary of Native Affairs in the 1950s, Dr. W. M. Eiselen, had been professor of Volkekunde (ethnology) at the University of Stellenbosch and envisaged the development of both rural villages and small industrial townships for the African population. Dr. Verwoerd, too, warned that apartheid was going to "dislocate social institutions and create new relationships in South Africa."[56] The denial of African proletarianization and permanent urbanization continued to form the basis of apartheid thinking well into the 1960s. Nonetheless, the emergence of an Afrikaner business class and a more pragmatic (*verligte*) view of race relations began slowly to undermine the more dogmatic and *verkrampte* ideal of ethnic separation based on a biblical interpretation of the word of God. But in the wake of the shooting at Sharpeville in March 1960 and the banning of both the ANC and the PAC, apartheid seemed an ever more necessary ideology for the state. It now tried to build up political leadership in the "Bantustans" to rival the exile movements that continued to capture the world's headlines. Between 1960 and 1964, the state apparatus proved surprisingly successful in smashing most radical opposition inside South Africa. The ANC's own underground *Umkhonto we Sizwe* (Spear of the Nation) did not succeed in mobilizing a nationwide resistance movement employing sabotage as a strategy to undermine the white state's power. After the Rivonia trial in 1964, the leader of Umkhonto, Nelson Mandela, was jailed for life along with other leaders such as Walter Sisulu and Govan Mbeki. For over a decade, effective African resistance was quashed, as the white state continued to ram through its apartheid design.

The function of the reserves as labor reservoirs for the white economy grew progressively more complex as the apartheid program began to establish separate ministate apparatuses in the "Homelands" as they came to be called. The Homeland leadership was seen as an alternative source of political appeal to a united African nationalism organized through the ANC or PAC. From 1959 the government channeled funds to the Homelands through the Bantu Investment Corporation, with the aim of building up both an ethnically based African business and political class. Later, the 1967 Physical Planning Act sought to decentralize industrial concerns to "border areas" close to the Homelands in order to draw off ready supplies of black labor. Many white industrialists expressed a reluctance to move out of the main nodal points of economic growth centered on the Pretoria-Witwatersrand-Vereeniging, Western Cape, Port Elizabeth-East London, and Durban-Pinetown complexes. However, the business and commercial class in South Africa, until recently at least, has been generally willing to at least cooperate with the state. This cooperation exemplifies a more general trend observed by the sociologist Herbert Blumer in the 1960s that capitalists generally tend to fit into the prevailing ideological climate of race relations within which they find themselves.[57] "We believe the Government of the day, no less than ourselves, desire the furtherance of the country's economic progress," proclaimed *The Manufacturer* in 1957, "and though we disagree with it in method, we accept that it is sincere in believing its policy to be essential. It is our purpose and our duty to collaborate and cooperate with the Government in such of its policies as directly and indirectly influence industry."[58] With the development of ANC-organized strike action such as the three-day Stay-at-Home the following year, the manufacturing sector found itself echoing the government's concern about the "exploitation" of African workers by "agitators" for political and non-economic purposes."[59]

The Afrikaner-controlled state, therefore, proved remarkably successful in the 1960s in both rebuilding the economy after the flight of overseas capital following Sharpeville in 1960 and extending its appeal to the English in the wake of the narrow victory in a referendum in 1960 on establishing a Republic. South African withdrawal from the Commonwealth enhanced the country's sense of isolation, which undermined what remained of the liberal political tradition inherited from Union. White liberals had organized themselves into a small Liberal party after the United party lost a second time to the Nationalists in 1953. The party never gained a seat in Parliament and remained divided on its relation to the black nationalists, refusing to attend the Congress of the People at Kliptown in 1955 owing to alleged communist influence. The party survived until 1968 when the Prohibition of Political Interference Act made multiracial political parties illegal. The small Progressive party, which split off from the United party in 1959 with Helen Suzman as its lone MP, continued the fight as the government made progressive inroads into civil liberties in the 1960s following the 1963 General Law Amendment Act. This law established detention without trial for up to ninety days with the possibility of rearrest, as Ruth First was to recount in her harrowing prison autobiography *117 Days* (1984).[60]

The liberal organizations in South Africa had a significant reputation internationally. At an international conference on race relations in Hawaii in 1955, the black anthropologist Absolom Vilakazi, then at the Hartford Theological Seminary, wrote that the South African Institute of Race Relations was "by far the most important and effective institution which works for better understanding and harmonious relations amongst the racial groups."[61] In reality, however, the liberal organizations in South Africa at that time faced a crisis not only through their political marginality as the white electorate became increasingly supportive of ever more entrenched racial segregation, but also ideologically in that they had no major political tradition on which to mount a civil rights movement as in the United States. The Natal liberal Edgar Brookes pointed out, for example, that South Africa had no dominant liberal tradition like the "American Creed" identified by Myrdal, to which it could appeal.[62]

For some Institute liberals, therefore, by the late 1950s it was important to reach an accord with the more liberal minded Nationalists around notions of political pluralism by which group as well as individual rights could be fostered. These debates continued through the 1960s. In 1973, the Study Project on Christianity in Apartheid Society (SPRO-CAS) concluded in its political report *South Africa's Political Alternatives* that a form of ethnically based federal system was the answer to the society's political crisis, devolving power away from the white state frightened that any change would destroy Afrikaner ethnic and cultural identity.[63]

For nationalists in the ANC together with more radical liberal and socialist groupings, these ideas perpetuated the category of race in South African society and denied the demands for one person one vote in a single political legislature. The exile of the ANC leadership and the segregation of higher education with the 1959 Extension of University Education Act led to the emergence of a more militant group of black intellectuals from the "bush" universities in the form of the Black Consciousness movement. As successors of the earlier Africanists, this group eschewed any collaboration with white liberals. Their ideas started to have a significant impact in the townships in the wake of the 1976 Soweto revolt of high school children against the teaching of Afrikaans. One of the most prominent Black Consciousness advocates, Steve Biko, was murdered in jail in 1977.

Nevertheless, black politics had to a considerable degree become radicalized down to the local level. This reflected a considerable change from the middle 1950s when the former Youth Leaguer Joe Matthews wrote to Albert Luthuli at the time of the ANC boycott of government schools, "if we think the principles of the Bantu Education Act are pernicious and dangerous we will not hesitate to say our children must be withdrawn. The ANC is directing this advice to the parents NOT to the children who are not in a position to judge what is or is not good for them."[64] By the 1970s, this parental control had largely been lost, and in the last decade the South African townships have seen the appearance of often vicious intergenerational and sectarian conflict as young groups of "comrades" have attacked groups of collaborators, organized boycotts of schools, and, more recently, mobilized strike action extending to the working population. In many contemporary townships, the rule of the "necklace" (a burning tire full of gasoline around the neck of the victim) has come to prevail.

MORE RECENT DEVELOPMENTS

The Portuguese coup in 1974 and the resulting decolonization of Angola and Mozambique reopened a period of political turbulence and unrest in South African politics. This came after a period in which some white politicians had hoped that the tide of African nationalism had been halted at the Limpopo River and a white-dominated "Third Africa" established.[65] In the new political atmosphere, the older discourse of race that had underpinned the conventional apartheid ideology began to be transformed, as the South African state sought to legitimize it more in terms of notions of "ethnicity" and group preservation. Some of the earlier liberal ideas on this matter became partly incorporated in the state's new program of reforming the structures of apartheid as the goal became one of widening the class divisions of the African population and entrenching an urban black working class with rights of freehold land tenure and trade union membership. This was the objective of the 1979 Wiehahn Commission Report. The state has become progressively embroiled in a counterrevolutionary strategy—what it terms "total strategy"—which is concerned with building up a compliant urban African population seeking reformist and not revolutionary change.[66] This task has become progressively more difficult as the country has become more isolated following the attainment of majority rule in Zimbabwe in 1980 under the ZANU-PF government of President Mugabe and the formation of a rival regional grouping the same year in the form of the Southern African Development Coordination Conference (SADCC) consisting of Angola, Botswana, Mozambique, Lesotho, Malawi, Swaziland, Tanzania, Zambia, and Zimbabwe. The struggle against apartheid in the last six to seven years has become progressively internationalized as ANC guerrilla incursions and sabotage attacks have led to South African military responses against neighboring states. Such actions started with an attack by commandos in January 1981 on the suburb of Matola in the Mozambique capital of Maputo, when twelve men were killed.

The government of P. W. Botha has sought to mobilize whites around a growing siege politics, while at the same time making a number of changes in the apartheid system. Petty apartheid, such as segregated swimming pools and park benches, has been slowly eliminated, as have the laws outlawing mixed-race sex or marriage. The pass laws still survive, however, and have been "reformed" by the extension of identity documents to the rest of the population. The prosecutions under the Group Areas have all but ended, and the act itself seems set to be repealed. Politically, the state has changed the parliamentary system after a referendum in 1983 into a tricameral legislature for whites, Coloreds, and Indians, but excluding Africans. The Homelands still remain intact as one of the essential pillars of apartheid. Of the total of ten, four have been proclaimed "independent": Transkei, Ciskei, Venda, and Bophuthaswana. The Kwa Zulu leader, Chief Gatsha Buthelizi, with his organization Inkatha kwaZulu, has so far resisted calls for independence. Instead, he seeks a multiracial solution embracing the whole of Natal, a scheme favored by many in the white opposition Progressive Federal party and some *verligte* Nationalists.

The state has come under growing pressure from the far right-wing Conservative and Herstigte Nasionale (HNP) parties, along with the crypto-fascist Afrikaner Volksbereging which favor a return to more conventional apartheid. With the progress of the sanctions in the West, the Botha government feels it has little to gain by trying to maintain an acceptable international image. Botha himself, however, has now publicly admitted that apartheid is an "outdated" and "colonial" concept. But an attempt by a Commonwealth Eminent Persons Group early in 1986 to establish a dialogue between the Botha administration and the exiled ANC and to free Nelson Mandela from jail met with a sharp rebuff.[67] The state has responded to continuing black unrest with the proclamation of a state of emergency and a clamp-down on the reporting of South African news. The society has retreated further and has failed to meet the basic demands for the abolition of the apartheid system. It thus represents one of the most dangerous flashpoints in the world for racial tension and violence, which some observers have argued is an inherently revolutionary situation.[68] Even if revolution occurs, it will not likely take the form of a simple class struggle against the dominant capitalist system, for the degree to which ethnic categories have been institutionalized in South African society indicates that there will be a complex series of ideological and political interactions between class and ethnic factors. These could vary on a regional basis if the overall authority of the white state structure collapses, leading to a society flying apart into a chaotic pattern of regional alliances and "tribal" rivalries.

The essential key to the society's future lies in building up the African and black educated class as the nucleus of a future administrative apparatus: the contemporary multiracial opposition grouping, the United Democratic Front (formed in 1983), clearly hopes that popular communal mobilization can lead to a nationwide political leadership based on such a class emerging, rather as the ANC had acted in the late 1950s before its banning. The existence of rival Homeland leaderships indicates the difficulty of establishing this objective, while a Black Consciousness grouping exists in the form of the rival Azanian Peoples Organization (Azapo). Therefore, as long as South African society continues to remain isolated from international contact and pressure, the danger of civil war increases. This will not be along simple black-white lines but will intersect along regional, ethnic, and class dimensions as well.[69] Meanwhile, the death rate under the State of Emergency declared on July 21, 1985, continues to rise as the black townships fester in a condition of near civil war with the white state. Over 1,500 blacks have been killed since August 1984, and there seems to be no end to the violence.

NOTES

1. Martin Legassick, Shula Marks and Anthony Atmore, eds. "The Frontier Tradition in South African Historiography," in *Economy and Society in Pre-Industrial South Africa* (London: Longman, 1980), pp. 44–79.

2. Jeff Guy, "The Destruction and Reconstruction of Zulu Society," in *Industrialisation and Social Change in South Africa,* Shula Marks and Richard Rathbone, eds. (London: Longman, 1982), pp. 167–94.

3. Stanley Trapido, "'The Friends of the Native': Merchants, Peasants and the Political and Ideological Structure of Liberalism in the Cape, 1854–1910," in Marks and Atmore, eds., *Economy and Society,* pp. 247–74.

4. Colin Bundy, *The Rise and Fall of the South African Peasantry* (London: Heinemann, 1979), pp. 134–40.

5. David Welsh, *The Roots of Segregation: Native Policy in Colonial Natal, 1845–1910* (Cape Town: Oxford University Press, 1971).

6. Robin Cohen, *End Game in South Africa?* (London: James Currey; Paris: UNESCO, 1986), pp. 8–9.

7. J. Kirk, *The Economic Aspects of Native Segregation in South Africa* (London: P. S. King, 1929), p. 56.

8. Paul Rich, "Ministering to the White Man's Needs: The Development of Urban Segregation in South Africa, 1913–1923," *African Studies* 37, No. 2 (1978): 177–91.

9. Harold Wolpe, "Capitalism and Cheap Labour Power in South Africa: From Segregation to Apartheid," *Economy and Society* 1 (1972): 425–56.

10. Martin Legassick, "British Hegemony and the Origins of Segregation in South Africa, 1901–1914" (London: International Cultural Society, 1973), unpub. ms.

11. John Cell, *The Highest Stage of White Supremacy* (Cambridge: Cambridge University Press, 1982), p. 14.

12. James Bryce, *Impressions of South Africa* (London: Macmillan, 1899), p. 465.

13. Olive Schreiner, "Stray Thoughts on South Africa," *The Fortnightly Review* 60, 355 (July 1896): 17.

14. Paul Rich, "Doctrines of Racial Segregation in Britain, 1900–1944," *New Community* 12, No. 1 (Winter 1984–85): 75–88.

15. R. W. Rose-Innes, *The Glen Grey Act and the Native Question* (Lovedale: Lovedale Press, 1903), p. 33.

16. Cell, *Highest Stage*, pp. 211–15.

17. *The Star,* January 23, 1915.

18. *Bryce Papers,* Bodleian Library, Oxford, C. T. Loram to Earl Buxton, November 18, 1920.

19. Paul B. Rich, *White Power and the Liberal Conscience: Racial Segregation and South African Liberalism, 1921–1960* (Manchester: Manchester University Press, 1984).

20. *Umteteli wa Bantu,* November 3, 1928.

21. *Umteteli wa Bantu,* June 5, 1926.

22. Paul B. Rich, *Race and Empire in British Politics* (Cambridge: Cambridge University Press, 1986), pp. 70–91.

23. Gunnar Myrdal, *An American Dilemma,* Vol. 2 (New York and London: Harper & Bros., 1944), p. 1032.

24. *Report of the National European-Bantu Conference, Cape Town, February 6–9 1929* (Lovedale: Lovedale Press, 1929), p. 33.

25. Rich, *White Power and Liberal Conscience,* p. 38.

26. *Minutes of a Meeting of the Johannesburg Joint Council,* June 11, 1933.

27. Paul S. Rich, "R.F.A. Hoernle, Idealism and the Liberal Response to South African Segregation," unpublished paper presented to History Workshop, Wesleyan University, 1986.

28. Bridglal Pachai, *The South African Indian Question, 1860–1971* (Cape Town: C. Struik, 1971), pp. 117–20.

29. *Trek,* December 5, 1940, July 4 and August 15, 1941; *The Forum,* January 3, 1942; Paul Rich, "Liberalism and Ethnicity in South African Politics," *African Studies,* 35, Nos. 3–4 (1976): 229–51.

30. H. J. Van Eck, "The Law's New Deal For Industry," *The Forum,* December 6, 1941, p. 25.

31. *Trek,* June 1947.

32. Leonard Thompson, *The Political Mythology of Apartheid* (New Haven, Conn., and London: Yale University Press, 1985).

33. Wolpe, "Capitalism and Cheap Labour Power"; Paul Rich, "The Appeals of Tuskegee: James Henderson, Lovedale and the Fortunes of South African Liberalism," *International Journal of African Historical Studies* 20, No. 1 (1987): 1.

34. Heribert Adam and Hermann Giliomee, *Ethnic Power Mobilized* (New Haven, Conn.: Yale University Press, 1979).

35. Cell, *Highest Stage,* p. 18.

36. *Tsala ea Becoana,* October 28, 1911.

37. *Izwi la Kiti,* March 17, 1915.

38. *Umteteli wa Bantu,* January 14, 1924.

39. *Umteteli wa Bantu,* July 9, August 20, 27, 1927.

40. Peter Walshe, *The Rise of African Nationalism in South Africa* (London: C. Hurst, 1970), pp. 268–94.

41. *Ilanga lase Natal,* December 9, 1944.

42. J. Ngubane, *I Shall Not Be Silenced* (unpub. ms., School of Oriental and African Studies, London, n.d.), p. 148.

43. *Ilanga lase Natal,* February 14, 1948.

44. Walshe, *Rise of African Nationalism,* pp. 289–90.

45. *Inkundla Ya Bantu,* January 21, 1950.

46. *S. M. Molema Papers* (microfilm, Institute of Commonwealth Studies, London), L. M. Seepe to Molema, March 6, 1950.

47. L. E. Neame, *The History of Apartheid* (London: Pall Mall Press, 1962), pp. 179–92; Eugene P. Dvorin, *Racial Separation in South Africa* (Chicago: University of Chicago Press, 1952), pp. 56–60; Pierre van den Berghe, *South Africa: A Study in Conflict* (Berkeley and Los Angeles: University of California Press, 1967).

48. J. A. Hofmeyr to J. S. Smuts, September 8, 1946, Jean van der Poel, ed., *Selections from the Smuts Papers* (Cambridge: Cambridge University Press, 1973), p. 82.

49. *Rand Daily Mail,* March 20, 1939; *The Forum,* February 10, 1940.

50. *The Forum,* January 29, 1943.

51. Tom Lodge, *Black Politics in South Africa Since 1945* (London and New York: Longman, 1983), p. 128.

52. N.J.J. Olivier, *Apartheid-Slogan or a Solution?* (Stellenbosch: SABRA, 1954), p. 1.

53. *New Age,* December 1954.

54. *A. Luthuli Papers* (microfilm, School of Oriental and African Studies, London), O. Tambo to A. Luthuli, June 17, 1956.

55. *A. Luthuli Papers,* A. Luthuli to W. Sisulu, March 24, 1956.

56. *Natal Mercury,* September 28, 1948.

57. Herbert Blumer, "Industrialisation and Race Relations," in Guy Hunter, ed., *Industrialisation and Race Relations* (London and New York: Oxford University Press 1965), pp. 220–53.

58. *The Manufacturer,* December 1957.

59. *The Manufacturer,* June 1958.

60. Ruth First, *117 Days* (Harmondsworth: Penguin Books, 1984).

61. Absolom Vilakazi, "Race Relations in South Africa," in Andrew W. Lind, ed., *Relations in World Perspective* (Westport, Conn.: Greenwood Press, 1954), p. 332.

62. Edgar H. Brookes, *South Africa in a Changing World* (Cape Town: Oxford University Press, 1953), p. 108.

63. SPRO-CAS, *South Africa's Political Alternatives* (Johannesburg: Ravan Press, 1973).

64. *A. Luthuli Papers,* J. G. Matthews to A. Luthuli, May 2, 1955.

65. E. Rhoodie, *The Third Africa* (Cape Town: Nasionale Boeklander, 1968).

66. Paul Rich, "Insurgency, Terrorism and the Apartheid System in South Africa," *Political Studies* 32 (1984): 68–85.

67. *Mission to South Africa: The Commonwealth Report* (Harmondsworth: Penguin Books, 1986).

68. Thomas G. Karis, "Revolution in the Making: Black Politics in South Africa," *Foreign Affairs* (Winter 1983/84): 405.

69. John D. Brewer, "Black Protest in South Africa's Crisis: A Comment on Legassick," *African Affairs* 85, No. 339 (April 1986): 283–97; Martin Legassick, "South Africa in Crisis: What Route to Democracy?" *African Affairs,* October 1985.

BIBLIOGRAPHY

Adam, H. *Modernizing Racial Domination: The Dynamics of South African Politics.* University of California Press, 1971.

————. "When the Chips Are Down: Confrontation and Accommodation in South Africa." *Contemporary Crises* 1 (1977): 417–35.

Baker, D. "Race, Power and White Siege Culture." *Social Dynamics,* 1 (1975): 143–57.

Carter, G., T. Karis, and N. Stultz. *South Africa's Transkei: The Politics of Domestic Colonialism.* Evanston, Ill.: Northwestern University Press, 1967.

Clough, M. *Changing Realities in Southern Africa.* Berkeley, Cal.: University of California Press, 1982.

Hampel, R. and B. Krupp. "The Cultural and Political Framework of Prejudice in South Africa and Great Britain." *Journal of Social Psychology,* 103 (1977): 193–202.

Heaven, P.C.L. "Ethnic Polarization in South Africa: Myth or Reality?" *Ethnic and Racial Studies,* 6 (1983): 356–62.

Johnson, R. W. *How Long Will South Africa Survive?* Macmillan, 1977.

Johnstone, F. A. "White Prosperity and White Supremacy in South Africa Today." *African Affairs,* 67 (1970): 124–40.

Lever, H. "Frustration and Prejudice in South Africa." *Journal of Social Psychology,* 100 (1976): 21–33.

————. "Sociology of South Africa." *Annual Review of Sociology* 7 (1981): 249–62.

Louw-Potgieter, J. "Reactions of South African Students to Their Status in Society." *Journal of Social Psychology,* 118 (1982): 87–98.

Luiz, D., and P. Krige. "The Effect of Social Contact Between South African White and Colored Adolescent Girls." *Journal of Social Psychology* 113 (1981): 153–58.

Moodie, D. *The Rise of Afrikanerdom: Power, Apartheid, and the Afrikaner Civil Religion.* Berkeley, Cal.: University of California Press, 1975.

Moodie, M. A. "The Development of National Identity in White South African School-Children." *Journal of Social Psychology* 3 (1980): 169–80.

Morse, S. J. and S. Peele, " 'Coloured Power' or " 'Coloured Bourgeoisie'? Political Attitudes Among South African Coloureds." *Public Opinion Quarterly,* 38 (1974): 317–34.

Price, R. M. "Pretoria's Southern Africa Strategy." *African Affairs,* 83 (1984): 11–32.

————, and C. G. Roseberg. *The Apartheid Regime.* Berkeley, Cal.: University of California Press, 1980.

Stokes, R. "Afrikaner Calvinism and Economic Action." *American Journal of Sociology,* 81 (1975): 62–81.

Welsh, D. "Constitutional Changes in South Africa." *African Affairs,* 83 (1984): 147–62.

SUDAN

Ann Lesch

A RACIAL CONTEXT

The question "Who is a Sudanese?" has been raised ever since independence was achieved in 1956. There is still no agreement on the answer among the diverse groups in the country. Must a person belong to a certain ethnic group or speak a particular language in order to be a first-class citizen? Does one have to subscribe to a certain ideology or faith in order to have full rights? Must all Sudanese speak the same language and hold identical religious beliefs in order to be one people and one nation?

Those groups and political figures who call for an Islamic state in the Sudan and Arabization of all the people believe that the only proper course is to assimilate the non-Arab and non-Muslim peoples into the Muslim Arab aspect of the country. They view the southern third of the Sudan, which is predominantly African and non-Muslim, as a fertile field for religious conversion, and they press for Arabic to be the sole language for administration and instruction. Attempts to force such an ethnic and religious homogenization on the south have led to bitter civil strife that has left deep scars on the country. Efforts by religious parties to press for Islamization have caused profound resentment and contributed to renewed civil war in 1983.

In contrast, government policies that recognize the diversity of the Sudanese people have helped to reduce strife and promote a *modus vivendi* among the various groups. The underlying perspective of that approach is that the Sudan can remain one country only if the multiplicity of its people is recognized and used as the basis for building the country.

The tension between the trend toward instilling homogenization and the trend toward recognizing heterogeneity is fundamental to the Sudan.

What are the components of the Sudanese people that bring about this tension?[1]

The Sudan is the largest country in Africa, covering a million square miles. Its 22 million residents, who live scattered across the wide expanse, differ along lines of ethnicity, language, and religion.

More than fifty ethnic groups can be identified, which subdivide into at least 570 tribes. The principal groups in the north are Arab, Beja, Nuba, Nubian, and Fur. Nearly half the population identifies itself as Arab, but the actual meaning of the term *Arab* remains ambiguous. In the Sudan, the generally accepted definition would include tribes that speak Arabic and claim to have originated in Arabia, even though the genealogy may be fictional. In fact, many indigenous tribes are termed Arab if, over the centuries, they adopted the Arabic language, customs, and Muslim religion.

The Arabs are not homogeneous, since some were originally nomadic and others riverain villagers. Major clashes have occurred between Arab tribes as they contest for territory. Arabs from the Nile Valley have tended to dominate the political and economic life of the country, holding the main government posts in the capital Khartoum, the majority in Parliament, and most of the officers in the armed forces. They also dominate the leading educational institutions, trade unions, and business establishments. As the largest and most centrally located ethnic group, Arabs wield a disproportionate influence over policymaking and over the cultural identity of the country.

Six percent of the population belongs to the Beja tribes, which are concentrated in the east. They live along the Red Sea and in the coastal mountain ranges, and merge into the tribes of Eritrea and Ethiopia to the south. With their own unwritten languages and special customs, they have remained distinct from the Arabs and have clung to their way of life in the remote hills. Nevertheless, the Beja share the Muslim religion with other northern Sudanese and participate in the *sufi* (mystical) religious orders that are prevalent throughout the countryside. The Beja are themselves subdivided into tribes, but they occasionally act as a political bloc vis-à-vis the central government and northern Arab power structure. In the assembly elected in April 1986, for example, the Beja Congress won only one seat, far less than it had held in the past. But several Beja were elected to Parliament through the Democratic Unionist party (DUP), which is dominant is eastern Sudan, and one Beja from the DUP became a Minister.

The Nuba are another geographically localized group, concentrated in the west in the Nuba Mountains of Kordofan. They comprise about 5 percent of the total population. The Nuba tend to be sedentary, living in villages in the hills apart from the Arab cattle-rearing nomads on the savannah. The Nuba have distinct languages and no single religious identification. Some adhere to traditional beliefs, while others have become Muslim or Christian. Like the Beja, they sometimes form a political bloc in an attempt to advance their special interests. Moreover, large numbers of Nuba enlist in the armed forces. On occasion, their leaders have demanded political autonomy along the lines of the south and have even linked up to southern rebel forces, feeling a common identity as non-Arab, African peoples. In the elections of 1986, the Nuba gained 8 out of 158 seats in the assembly, through the Sudan National party led by the Christian preacher Philip Ghabboush. Reverend Ghabboush has formed a bloc in the assembly linking the Nuba and the southern parties.

About 3 percent of the population belongs to the Nubian peoples, who have traditionally lived along the upper reaches of the Nile River, extending into Egypt. The Egyptian and Sudanese Nubian areas formed distinct Christian kingdoms prior to the Muslim conquest of Egypt in the seventh century A.D. Now the Nubians are Muslim, although they retain certain pre-Islamic customs, some of which date back to the Pharaonic era. The Nubians are involved in agriculture, commerce, and political affairs, in which they play a more central role than do the Beja and Nuba. Their cultural interaction is closer with the northern Arab groups, and they retain intense contact with Egypt. Although many Nubians speak their own languages at home, they are relatively well integrated into the political and economic mainstream.

The Fur live in the far west. Although constituting only 2 percent of the population, they, like the Nubians, used to have their own kingdoms. The sultanate of Fur lasted from the fifteenth century until the British occupation in 1898, and the sense of special identity remains strong among the Fur.

Thus, in the north, while the Arab ethnic identity predominates, regional pockets of indigenous groups are present and assert themselves on the political map. Moreover, there are small nonindigenous communities such as migrants from West Africa, who are Muslim but racially African, and from Egypt, particularly Coptic Christian merchants in Khartoum. A few Greek traders and Indian entrepreneurs have also settled in Port Sudan and other towns, but they are marginal politically and socially.

In the southern third of the Sudan, no one ethnic group predominates. The Dinka are the largest group, estimated at 40 percent of the southerners. The Dinka number 10 percent of the Sudanese population as a whole, making them larger than the Beja or Nuba. The Dinka are an important force in Upper Nile and Bahr al-Ghazal provinces, two of the three provinces that constitute the southern region. Other related tribes in those provinces also command weight: the Nuer are nearly 5 percent of the Sudan's population and the Shilluk are 1 percent. Their languages and customs are similar to those of the cattle-trading Dinka, but they compete for influence. The Dinka themselves are divided into numerous groups, which conflict over local territorial and trade issues. Nevertheless, the three Nilotic tribes—Dinka, Nuer, and Shilluk—are sometimes perceived as a powerful demographic and political bloc, particularly in relation to Equatoria, the southernmost province. In Equatoria the population is fragmented into myriad tribes that differ in language, custom, and religion. Moreover, the tribes spill across the borders into the neighboring states of Uganda, Zaire, and Kenya. Overall, the fragmentation in the south is more acute than in the north. Nevertheless, at critical junctures southern political groups and guerrilla movements have united in opposition to pressures from the dominant north. At those moments, local differences are largely set aside in contrast to the distinction between them and the north.

Language is a basic distinguishing mark among the Sudanese people, second only to ethnicity. Only half of the residents speak Arabic as their native tongue. In the north, Arabic is the principal language at home as well as in education, commerce, and government, but in the south a hundred indigenous languages are spoken and English vies with Arabic as the language of the educated residents. Unwritten tribal languages remain important throughout the country, in part because the level of literacy is still low. Only 20 percent of adults are literate, and educational opportunities are limited, especially in rural areas. The tribal languages can be grouped into several clusters. One set is the languages of the Beja tribes in the east, known as northern Cushitic or Hamitic. To the west, some tribes speak Chadic languages, while the Fur of Darfur province and Nuba of the Nuba Mountains have their own languages, unrelated to Chadic. In the south, a wide variety of Nilo-Saharan languages are spoken which tend, as in the north, to overlap with and reinforce tribal divisions.

Religion serves as a third major distinction among the Sudanese people. About 70 percent are Muslim, 23 percent follow traditional beliefs, and 7 percent are Christian. The north is overwhelmingly Muslim, with pockets of Christian tribes in the Nuba Mountains as well as Christian communities in Khartoum, Port Sudan, and a few other towns. The other towns are comprised of partly Christians from abroad, but mostly Sudanese from the south who have settled in the north.

In the south, the majority adhere to traditional beliefs, but as many as 20 percent identify themselves as Christian. The number of Muslims in the south is generally said to be only 5 percent, largely traders and bureaucrats who have moved there temporarily from the north. Some, however, claim that as many as 18 percent of the southerners are now Muslim, largely as a result of conversion.

None of these religious groups is internally homogeneous. The traditional beliefs are rooted in local tribal customs and histories. The majority of Christians are Roman Catholic, but there are also Protestant, Coptic, and Greek Orthodox communities. The Sudan Council of Churches provides an umbrella for their activities. Virtually all Muslims are Sunni but belong to different groups, of which the network of *sufi tariqahs* (brotherhoods) is most pervasive. Such brotherhoods tended to be formed around a local religious preacher, who was revered as particularly devout. In time, these brotherhoods became complex organizations, some of which spread their influence over wide areas that superseded tribal bounds. The khatmiyya order, led by the Mirghani family, is one of the most influential brotherhoods today and provides the underpinning for the Democratic Unionist party. Other local orders are also active but have narrower bases and less political influence.

Overall, the Sudan is a widely diverse country. Languages and religious faiths vary across its expanse, and complex ethnic groups have emerged over many centuries. Nevertheless, one broad divide is most salient politically: the distinction between the largely Arab and Muslim north and the African, largely non-Muslim south. This divide has had major political implications and has embittered the political debate.

HISTORICAL BACKGROUND

Over the centuries, the Sudan never constituted one political unit, and its many peoples lived in relative isolation from each other. The first attempt to establish a centralized administration came with the Turko-Egyptian invasion of 1821. Military garrisons, telephone lines, and tax collection were imposed on the north, but the rulers had far less success dominating the south. The southern tribes resisted their incursions for several reasons.[2] First, they opposed the raids to capture slaves to serve in the Turko-Egyptian Army, a slave trade that decimated many non-Muslim tribes. Second, they opposed government efforts to monopolize the trade in ivory, which was one of their few sources of cash income. Third, the tribes did not want to be controlled by any government. They particularly opposed paying taxes and providing labor for government projects. Finally, there was a clash of cultures and beliefs. The tribes opposed pressure to convert to Islam and to speak and write Arabic, particularly since these influences were not penetrating the south by a natural process but were arriving suddenly through an alien occupying army.

The southern peoples not only resisted the Turko-Egyptian presence but also opposed the Mahdiyya, the Islamic politico-religious movement that emerged in the north in 1881 and ousted the Turko-Egyptian rulers in 1885. Although some southern tribes cooperated with the Mahdi for the limited purpose of expelling the Turkish garrisons, these same tribes opposed the Mahdist troops when they tried to impose centralized administration and tax collection.

Southerners also resisted the Anglo-Egyptian conquest of 1898. British troops entered the south in 1901 but did not subdue tribal uprising until 1920. Once the British consolidated control, they sealed the south off from the north. According to the Closed Districts Order of 1922, no Sudanese who lived outside the south could travel to or live in the south without obtaining a special permit from the British authorities. Moreover, the Permits to Trade Order of 1925 excluded northern tradesmen from traveling in the south. Northern officials were removed, Arab-style dress was banned, and English rather than Arabic was taught in southern schools. The British stated that this policy would end northern pressure on and dominance of the south. It would stop Arab tribes from seizing slaves, cattle, and grain from the south, and end pressure to convert to Islam. But the measures also severed normal contact. In some parts of western Bahr al-Ghazal, for example, the Arabic language, Islam, and Arab customs were already prevalent and were stamped out unnaturally. Over time, the policy exacerbated the inherent differences between the two parts of the Sudan.

British policy would have made sense if the south had been separated from the north and either turned into an independent state or attached to a neighboring African country. Although British officials considered those options, they acceded in 1946 to pressure from northern politicians to keep the south within a united country. Suddenly, after more than twenty years of deliberate isolation, trade and travel restrictions were canceled, mosques were constructed, and northern administrators and teachers were sent south.

Most southern politicians demanded that a federal system be established for the independent country, in which the south would have a separate, elected advisory council. The British and northern Sudanese, however, insisted that a unitary system be established that would centralize administration in Khartoum. Southern concern was so profound that in November 1955, only one month before independence, the southern members of the newly elected Parliament refused to endorse the independence proclamation unless the south were granted federal status. They had to settle for a vague promise that "the matter would be given full consideration after independence," a promise that was quickly forgotten.[3]

The transition to independence was also marred by violence, notably the mutiny of southern soldiers at Torit in Equatoria in August 1955, when the soldiers refused to obey orders to march north. Some of the mutineers fled into the bush, where they formed the core of later guerrilla forces.

After independence, political life in Khartoum was dominated by northern parties and political forces. Within a year, demands were made to promulgate a constitution based on Islam as the official religion of the country and Islamic law as a basic source of legislation. This trend caused anxiety and instability in the south. The Southern Federal party won 40 of the 48 southern seats in Parliament in 1958 on a platform that demanded a federal system, equal status for English with Arabic and for Christianity with Islam, and a separate military force in the south.

The situation was exacerbated when General Ibrahim Abboud seized power in November 1958. He tried to stamp out unrest in the south by force and sought to impose Islam and Arabic there. He viewed Christianity as an alien religion and expressed contempt for traditional African beliefs and languages. As a result, unrest escalated in the south. The Anya Nya guerrilla forces, which included soldiers who had deserted alongside local tribesmen, ambushed military convoys and raided garrisons, causing major social dislocations. The Anya Nya demanded secession of the south and establishment of an independent state there. Some Nuba politicians, whose territory adjoined the south, supported this demand and joined the rebellion.[4]

The Abboud regime fell in 1964, in part because of its policies in the south, and was replaced by a broad-based civilian government. This regime convened a Round Table Conference in Khartoum in 1965 to negotiate an end to the strife in the south. All the northern and southern parties were represented, but the participants were far too divided to reach agreement. Most northern parties rejected federation, whereas that was the minimum demanded by the south. Moreover, soon after the conference the Islamic-oriented parties gained power in the Parliament, and the civilian politicians reverted to General Abboud's pattern of using force to restore order in the south.

The Sudan experienced another coup d'état in May 1969, led by young officers who were impatient with the divisions in the ranks of the political forces and their failure to solve the problems in the south. The new head of state, Colonel Ja'far Muhammad Numairi, articulated a concept of Sudanese citizenship that rejected the assimilative approach of Abboud and the northern politicians. He asserted that unity must be based on the "objective realities [of] the historic and cultural differences between the north and south." Specifically, he recognized "the right of the southern people to Regional Autonomy within a United Sudan."[5]

Over the next two years, Numairi appointed an increasing number of southerners to the regional administration in the south and crushed the Islamic parties, which removed them temporarily from the political scene. Meanwhile, control over the Anya Nya was consolidated in the hands of Colonel Joseph Lagu in 1970. Finally, a peace conference convened in 1972 in Ethiopia and rapidly reached agreement on the lines of a political settlement.

This Addis Ababa Agreement was operationalized through the Regional Self-Government Act for the Southern Provinces, which was incorporated into the constitution that Numairi promulgated in 1973. The main provision was that the three southern provinces would amalgamate into one large region with its own regional assembly. The assembly would elect a High Executive Council (HEC) that would be responsible for public order and local administration in social, economic, and cultural fields. The regional government would have an independent budget, drawn in part from local taxes. The southern region would be represented in the national assembly in proportion to its population. Finally, most of the Anya Nya forces would be absorbed into the army and would serve in the south.

The constitution of 1973 was noteworthy because it stressed the heterogeneous nature of the Sudan. It legitimized customary law and non-Muslim personal status law alongside Islamic law. It also recognized that English could be a principal language in the south, although Arabic would be the official language of the country as a whole. And it allowed indigenous tribal languages to be taught in southern schools. Finally, the constitution expressed respect for Christianity and "noble spiritual beliefs" as well as Islam, and specified that there must be no discrimination among citizens on the basis of religion, race, language, or sex.[6] The concept of a homogeneous country was clearly rejected in favor of the idea of unity in diversity.

Following the Addis Ababa Accord, Joseph Lagu became a major general in the army, and Abel Alier, a southerner who had headed the government delegation to the negotiations, was appointed interim president of the HEC in the south. Elections were held for the regional assembly in November 1973. Despite the autonomous status of the south, Numairi intervened frequently. He proposed candidates for the southern presidency, and in 1980 he even dissolved the HEC and regional assembly, although he lacked the constitutional authority for this step. Moreover, Numairi promoted the rivalry between Alier and Lagu, emphasizing the tribal dimension since Alier came from the dominant Dinka and Lagu belonged to a small Equatorian tribe.

Lagu, in fact, began to argue that Equatoria should be separated from the other two provinces, a move that would weaken the south as a bloc vis-à-vis the north but would give the Equatorian tribes greater control of local affairs. Such a major change would require approval of the regional assembly, two-thirds support in a referendum in the south, and then three-quarters support in the national assembly in Khartoum. Nevertheless, Numairi short-circuited these processes when he abruptly decreed on June 5, 1983, that the south would be redivided into three separate provinces, as it had been before the Addis Ababa Accord. This high-handed act was evidence of Numairi's increasingly arbitrary and autocratic style of rule. It also heated up the rebellion that was already being renewed in the south, although some political groups in Equatoria embraced the redivision.

The political promise of Addis Ababa remained unrealized. Similarly, southerners were keenly disappointed with the economic results. The south lacked internal financial resources to undertake development projects or even rehabilitate the infrastructure and social services that had been destroyed during the civil war. But the central government failed to provide funds that would enable the HEC to launch development efforts. The south continued to lag behind the north in every economic and social indicator.

Two particular projects generated the most controversy.[7] One was the multimillion-dollar construction of the Jonglei Canal through the Sudd marshes in order to channel the White Nile and increase water availability for development efforts in the south, north, and Egypt, which was footing half the bill. Southerners were highly suspicious of the project: Some feared that Egyptian peasants would be moved to the canal area, others felt that it would harm the environment and disrupt the life-styles of the neighboring tribes, and still others argued that the money could have been spent better on local economic projects. As the rebels accelerated their operations in 1983, the guerrilla Sudanese Peoples Liberation Army (SPLA) forced the French construction firm to stop digging the canal. The canal remains two-thirds complete, an empty ditch, hostage to the political crisis.

The second controversy surrounded the oil discovered by Chevron Oil Company in Upper Nile Province in 1979. Southerners hoped that oil revenues could benefit their region and that large numbers of local residents could be employed in the rigs and refinery. Numairi, however, stated that anticipated revenue would benefit the country as a whole, not a particular region. Moreover, he decided to place the oil refinery not in the south but at Kosti, a major rail and river junction in the north. The site had been selected by Chevron on technical grounds, but it infuriated southerners. The SPLA viewed the oilfields as a prime target and believed that closing down the Chevron operations would contribute to undermining Numairi. It harassed the oil workers to the point that Chevron closed down its well digging and survey operations in February 1984. These remain on hold, pending resolution of the civil strife.

A final issue that shocked the south was Numairi's imposition of an Islamic penal code in September 1983 as a prelude to transforming the entire country into an Islamic state. His measures were denounced by many northern politicians, including al-Sadiq al-Mahdi, head of the moderate Muslim-oriented Umma party. Al-Mahdi argued that Numairi was misapplying Islamic legal concepts. Secular politicians criticized the turn away from a nondenominational political system. Christian leaders were particularly outspoken, objecting to the laws as destroying the spirit of reconciliation and respect for religious and cultural differences on which the Addis Ababa Accord had been based. They argued that non-Muslim Sudanese would become second-class citizens.

RECENT DEVELOPMENTS

Numairi's redivision of the south, the perceived discrimination in development programs, and the imposition of Islamic law led to massive disaffection among and alienation of southern citizens. Mutinies spread among southern soldiers, culminating in a lengthy mutiny at Bor in Upper Nile in early 1983.

One of the most prominent defectors was Colonel John Garang de Mabior, an agricultural economist who headed the army research center in Khartoum. In the summer of 1983, Garang created the SPLA and its political wing, the Sudanese People's Liberation Movement (SPLM). Unlike the Anya Nya, which had sought secession of the south, the SPLM made its main demands the overthrow of Numairi and the establishment of a united socialist country. Power should be shared by the non-Arab tribes from the east and west as well as from the south.

Within a year, Garang consolidated his control over the scattered rebel groups in the south and established contact with disaffected northerners in Khartoum and the west. The ability of the SPLA to close down the construction of the Jonglei Canal and the oil rigs demonstrated its political sophistication. The SPLA also attacked river and road communications, compelling the military forces to remain confined in their barracks and hampering civilian transport. Its operations were initially spread across Upper Nile and Bahr al-Ghazal, but it moved into Equatoria by 1985. There it faced political obstacles, since the Equatorian tribes resented the influence of the Dinka. Some of their politicians charged that Garang (a Dinka) let his tribe dominate the SPLA. Despite some armed conflict between Equatorian tribes and the SPLA, the SPLA gained allies in the eastern part of the province and managed to move within thirty miles of Juba, the capital city.

As the political situation deteriorated throughout the Sudan, Numairi imposed emergency rule in April 1984 and announced in June that an Islamic state would be formed in which he would be the permanent, unchallengeable ruler. The southern members of the national assembly protested, along with most northern politicians and all the church leaders. Lagu and Alier presented a joint protest to Numairi in which they emphasized that the unity of the Sudan could only be based on recognizing the cultural differences between north and south and respecting the religious beliefs of all the Sudanese people. Numairi was compelled to backtrack. In September 1984, he withdrew the proposal to amend the constitution and ended the state of emergency. But he kept the division of the south into three provinces, even though Equatorian politicians were the only southerners who supported the move. In March 1985, Numairi even called for a cease-fire with the SPLA and negotiations to end the civil war. These measures were too little, too late. Numairi was toppled from power the next month. A Transitional Military Council (TMC) and a civilian Council of Ministers ruled jointly for one year, until May 1986.

Southerners and northerners alike had high hopes for the transitional government and felt a great sense of relief at the ouster of Numairi after nearly fifteen years of increasingly autocratic rule. However, the transitional government proved too weak and too hesitant to undertake a serious reform of the system.[8] It instituted an interim constitution that reestablished democratic practices, and it carried out elections in a free atmosphere. But it failed to cancel the Islamic penal code of September 1983, even though the courts did not enforce its provisions. Moreover, elections could not be held in thirty-seven of the sixty-eight southern districts because of the war, and so the constituent assembly contained only a handful of southern delegates.[9] Most of those MPs came from Equatoria, which skewed the results toward those groups that opposed the SPLA and that objected to reunifying the southern provinces.

Most importantly, the TMC and cabinet never negotiated with the SPLM to end the war. Only the alliance of trade and professional unions, which had launched the uprising against Numairi, attempted negotiations. The alliance sent emissaries to Addis Ababa to meet with Garang and other SPLM leaders. This effort resulted in a conference in Ethiopia in March 1985, attended by SPLM leaders and a mix of union and political party activists from Khartoum. The Koka Dam Declaration issued at this meeting stated that both sides agreed to repeal the September Islamic laws. This was the key condition placed by the SPLM on holding further talks. The Declaration also outlined an agenda for a constitutional conference that would resolve the basic issues of power-sharing in the central government and the form of rule in the regions. From the perspective of the SPLM, this meant ensuring that the Arabs in Khartoum and the central Nile Valley could no longer dominate national political life but would share authority with ethnic groups from other regions. Moreover, a federal system would be established which would devolve major decision-making powers onto the regions and would reunify the south. The SPLM was willing to argue and resolve these matters at the constitutional conference. Its only unalterable precondition was abrogation of the September penal laws.

The Koka Dam Declaration came too late to affect the deliberations of the transitional government. By then the fighting in the south was more serious and widespread than it had been under Numairi. The chairman of the TMC had argued in favor of retaining Islamic laws, although he was willing to modify the 1983 decrees in order to eliminate incorrect and excessive punishments. Moreover, he was suspicious of negotiating with the SPLM and stated at times that a constitutional conference could be held even without the SPLM's presence. These pronouncements, which seemed to represent the majority view in the TMC and cabinet, fueled the suspicions of southerners. Garang noted bluntly: "certainly the SPLA cannot be expected to enter a national dialogue to negotiate the best possible outcome of second class citizenship. Religious, racial, tribal or any other form of sectarian dictatorship in the Sudan is a recipe for disaster."[10]

During the transitional year, the government's military position became increasingly precarious. The SPLA dominated the countryside and raided key towns in Upper Nile and Bahr al-Ghazal. The only serious opposition there came from such tribes as the Nuer which backed the Anya Nya II, a guerrilla movement based on the original Anya Nya but now funded and armed by the government. The SPLA also entered north and east Equatoria, and blocked the main roads to Kenya and Uganda. SPLA forces even moved north into Central Province, on the Blue Nile, and southern Kordofan. They clashed with Baqqara Arab tribesmen in Kordofan; contacted Abyei, a Dinka stronghold outside the south; and seemed to be trying to link up with Nuba territory further west, where some elements backed the SPLA. As a result of these multipronged advances, the Defense Minister conceded that the SPLA often had "the upperhand in the battlefield" and warned that it could develop into a conventional army, as it already fielded twelve battalions totaling 12,000 men. He concluded that negotiations were essential: "We are engaged in a war in which there can be no victor and no vanquished."[11]

The elections held in April 1986 did not result in a majority for any political party. Al-Mahdi's Umma party gained 39 percent of the seats, which forced him to make political concessions to the (DUP) in order to form a coalition government. The DUP, which controlled 24 percent of the seats, sought an Islamic constitution and criticized the idea of negotiating with the SPLM. Moreover, the militant Islamic National Front, with 20 percent of the seats, comprised a tough and outspoken opposition bloc that would try to prevent any modification of Islamic law and any concessions to the south. Southern parties gained only 12 percent of the seats in Parliament, far less than their demographic weight, and were relegated to marginal service ministries by the Umma-DUP coalition forces. Although all the southern politicians rejected Islamic law, their views were disregarded by that dominant bloc. As a result, the southern MPs formed a bloc of African parliamentarians, together with the Nuba-based Sudan National party. Traditional party lines and racial divisions have clearly been reasserted inside the assembly.

The war in the south and the related issue of Islamic law are the thorniest political problems facing the new government. Al-Mahdi articulated a three-pronged approach for ending the war. He would first work to convene a constitutional conference to tackle the fundamental legal and political issues. Second, he would strengthen the armed forces so that they could maintain the country's security and enable the government to negotiate with the SPLA from a strong position. Third, he would seek an agreement with Ethiopia to stop aiding the SPLA and to persuade it to negotiate.

This approach has not borne fruit. Although al-Mahdi and Garang met in Addis Ababa on July 31, 1986, they differed on the key issue of Islamic law. Garang insisted that cancellation of the September decrees meant returning to the secular constitution of 1956. Al-Mahdi argued that canceling them meant that new Islamic laws might be legislated that would take the rights of non-Muslims into account. Although they agreed to conduct followup meetings and al-Mahdi himself believed that the talks had been productive, a profound gap was evident. Garang appears to have left the meeting believing that no political accommodation was possible.

The military side of the conflict increased over the summer. The SPLA besieged several towns and shot down a civilian airliner in August, in order to close all the airspace to the government. Al-Mahdi responded to SPLA pressures by ordering the armed forces to adopt a more assertive posture, improving security at airports in the south, shaking up the military high command, and labeling the SPLA a terrorist organization. Whether the new high command can formulate a more effective military posture remains doubtful, given the low morale among the troops, the limited funds available, and the difficulties that face a regular army in combat with guerrilla forces in the swamps and forests of the south. In addition, discontent is high among the Nuba and southern soldiers in the regular forces.

Moreover, al-Mahdi's categorization of the SPLM as terrorist heightens the tension. Al-Mahdi argues that he will only negotiate if the SPLM takes the initiative by requesting talks and by implementing a cease-fire prior to the negotiations.[12] Neither prospect seems likely. Al-Mahdi also places much of the blame for the military escalation and diplomatic stalemate on the Ethiopian government, which he believes wants to keep the new democratic regime in Khartoum off balance and weak by bolstering the rebellion in the south. Thus, north-south talks appear more distant than they did when the elected government came to power in May 1986. The government seems determined to pursue the military route, even though thirty years of strife have shown that negotiations and political accommodation are the only way to resolve the conflict without tearing the country apart. Such accommodation will require that the government in Khartoum share power with the south and that it institute fundamental laws that do not discriminate among citizens of different religious faiths. Given the composition of the coalition government, the philosophical background of al-Mahdi, and the strong pressures from the Islamic fundamentalist movement in the north, it is doubtful that any such power-sharing and nondiscriminatory laws can be crafted, much less implemented.

PUBLIC POLICIES AND LAWS

The major laws affecting ethnic relations and the north-south divide have already been described. Their basic outlines will be reviewed here.

According to the provisional constitution that came into force upon independence in 1956, the legal system in the Sudan was to be secular, with the code based on English common law. Customary law could be applied in rural areas, where it would vary by tribal traditions. Personal status law—marriage, divorce, and inheritance—was particular to each religious community. Different codes applied to Muslims, Christians, and adherents of traditional beliefs. The constitution provided for a unitary system of rule, with power centralized in Khartoum and the provinces having limited authority.

Islamic-oriented political parties, such as the Umma, People's Democratic party (subsequently the DUP), and the Islamic National Front, pressed for the promulgation of a permanent constitution that would incorporate Islamic law and make Islam the official religion. Draft constitutions along those lines were debated in Parliament in 1957–58 and 1966–69. Those trends were resisted by secular political groups in the north, including the Communist party, and by the southern politicians. In both 1958 and 1969, promulgation of Islamic constititions was aborted only by military coups d'états.

Numairi, who came to power in 1969, instituted a permanent constitution in 1973. As mentioned above, for the first time this provided regional autonomy for the south, which was extended to the northern provinces in 1980. It also guaranteed racial and religious equality. The Addis Ababa Accord, on whose basis the long civil war had ended, was incorporated into that constitution.

While the constitution remained the legal basis for Numairi's regime, he altered it fundamentally through presidential decrees. In June 1983, Numairi decreed the division of the south into three provinces, an important violation of the Addis Ababa Accord. In September 1983, he revised the penal code to conform to his interpretation of Islamic law.

In June 1984, he proposed amendments to the constitution that would make him president for life and "leader of the faithful," strip the legislative assembly of even the right to question the government, make Islamic law the sole source of legislation, and delete from the constitution references to nondiscrimination on the grounds of religion. These drastic amendments were resisted by the normally docile assembly, and Numairi had to withdraw them.

The constitution for the transitional period, which came into force in October 1985, established the provisional constitution of 1956, as amended in 1964, as the basis for the transitional period. It also included unification and self-rule of the south, as instituted in 1972–73, and regionalization of the north. Despite the secular underpinnings of the 1956 constitution, the Islamic decrees of 1983 were not revoked. The TMC decided that only the constituent assembly, which would be elected in April 1986, would have the political and moral authority to decide whether to eliminate those laws, retain them, or modify them. In fact, the interim constitution stated that both Islamic law and customary law were the bases of the legal system, in an attempt to balance the contradictory trends within the country.

The constituent assembly elected in 1986 is charged with drafting and passing a permanent constitution. Until then, the transitional constitution remains in force, as modified to meet the new political circumstances. Prime Minister al-Sadiq al-Mahdi has stated that he would prefer to see the constitution amended rather than draft a new text. However, some other parties want to start from scratch, so that they can draft a constitution based on either Islamic principles or entirely secular codes.

A complicating factor is the proposal, agreed on in the Koka Dam Declaration, that a national constitutional conference be convened to draft a new constitution. The SPLM and alliance of unions maintain that this conference will make the final decision on the constitution, and the constituent assembly can only ratify it. Some other political parties argue that the assembly can amend the draft constitution. This might mean that if, for example, the national constitutional conference agreed to a secular constitution, the assembly (in which the SPLM is not represented) could alter that basis and introduce Islamic legal provisions.

A further complicating factor is the issue of Numairi's laws of September 1983. Al-Mahdi has stated that these laws must be annulled, and the Koka Dam Declaration made that the basic condition. But the political groups differ profoundly as to what should replace those laws. The SPLM insists on a secular criminal code, as do the southern parties in Khartoum, the Nuba Sudan National party, and the communist and socialist groups. In contrast, Umma and DUP assert that new laws need to be instituted that would correct the September code but retain their Islamic essence. Al-Mahdi suggests that different laws could apply to

Muslims and non-Muslims, although in practice this would mean that secular codes would be enforced in the south and Islamic codes in the north. In practice, al-Mahdi's view does not differ substantively from the hardline Islamic National Front, which is willing to exempt non-Muslims from Islamic laws in areas where they form the majority.[13]

SUMMARY AND CONCLUSIONS

The Sudan is a country composed of myriad tribes, widely varying ethnic groups, and profound religious differences. Pressures toward fragmentation are strong, as ethnic variations tend to be rooted in particular regions. Of the many cleavages, the one with greatest political salience is the north-south divide between the predominantly Muslim and Arab north and the African peoples of the south. Political alliances occasionally cut across that divide, as demonstrated by Nuba support for southern demands and periodic tactical coalitions between southern groups and northern parties. But the fundamental issues that separate the two parts of the country remain unresolved. The issues of power-sharing and regional decentralization can be agreed on, potentially, since they would benefit several northern groups such as the Nuba and Fur in the west and the Beja in the east, as well as the southerners. But all central governments have hesitated to implement fully a regional or federal system, for fear of reducing their own power and for fear of the pressures toward fragmentation that could be released. Some even imagine that the country could break into several pieces.

The key issue of the identity of the Sudan, however, is the most difficult to resolve. Political forces that seek a homogeneous polity, based on the Arab and Muslim aspect of the country, press for an Islamic constitution, complete Arabization and, ultimately, conversion of the non-Muslim peoples to Islam. Political forces that seek a heterogeneous polity, based on the equal status of all the ethnic and religious groups, press for a secular constitution in which individuals will be free to practice their religious faith but the legal system will make no distinction among the citizens. Some argue that if this heterogeneity is not recognized, the non-Muslim areas should secede: this is now the minority view, but it could gain support if an acceptable compromise is not reached. The tension and instability in the system resulting from these conflicting trends are likely to continue to bedevil the Sudan, weaken prospects for institutionalizing democracy, and foster further violence in the south.

NOTES

1. The following sections are largely based on John O. Voll and Sarah P. Voll, *The Sudan: Unity and Diversity in a Multicultural State* (Boulder, Colo.: West-

view Press, 1985), pp. 6–23. Also Ann Mosely Lesch, "The Fall of Numeiri," *Report* No. 9, Universities Field Staff International (UFSI), 1985, p. 3.

2. Abel Alier, "The Southern Sudan Question," in Dunstan M. Wai, ed., *The Southern Sudan* (London: Frank Cass, 1979), p. 13. For general background see A. M. Lesch, "Rebellion in the Southern Sudan," *Report* No. 8, UFSI, 1985.

3. Bona Malwal, *People and Power in Sudan* (London: Ithaca Press, 1981), p. 47.

4. Interview with Philip Ghabboush, May 27, 1986; see also A. M. Lesch, "Party Politics in the Sudan," *Report* No. 9, UFSI, 1986, p. 2.

5. The declaration was issued on June 9, 1969; quoted in Alier, "Southern Sudan Question," pp. 25–26.

6. For Key provisions of the constitution, see Lesch, "Rebellion in the Southern Sudan," p. 7.

7. For details on these issues, see pp. 8–10.

8. The transitional period is critiqued in A. M. Lesch, "Transition in the Sudan," *Report* No. 20, UFSI, 1985, pp. 1–4.

9. Details on the elections are provided in A. M. Lesch, "Party Politics in the Sudan," pp. 6–9.

10. Garang's statement was made over the SPLA radio on October 19, 1985; quoted in A. M. Lesch, "Confrontation in the Southern Sudan," *Middle East Journal* 40, No. 3 (1986): p. 412.

11. Interview in *al-Sharq al-Awsat,* October 9, 1985, quoted in ibid.

12. Interview with al-Mahdi, September 21, 1986.

13. Interview with Dr. Hasan al-Turabi, head of the Islamic National Front, on May 19, 1986.

BIBLIOGRAPHY

Abd al-Rahim, Muddathir. *Imperialism and Nationalism in the Sudan, 1899–1956.* Oxford: Clarendon Press, 1969.

Abu Hasabu, Afaf. *Factional Conflict in the Sudanese National Movement, 1918–1948.* Khartoum: Graduate College Monograph, University of Khartoum, 1985.

Badal, Raphael Koba. "Oil and Regional Sentiment in Southern Sudan." *Discussion Paper* No. 80, Department of Geography, Syracuse University, 1983.

Bechtold, Peter K. *Politics in the Sudan.* New York: Praeger Publishers, 1976.

Beshir, Mohammed Omer. *Revolution and Nationalism in the Sudan.* London: Rex Collings, 1974.

———. *The Southern Sudan: Background to Conflict.* London: Hurst, 1968.

———, ed. *Southern Sudan: Regionalism and Religion.* Khartoum: Graduate College Monograph No. 10, University of Khartoum, 1984.

Cudsi, Alexander S. "Islam and Politics in the Sudan." In *Islam in the Political Process,* edited by James P. Piscatori. London: Cambridge University Press, 1983.

Deng, Francis Mading. *The Dinka of the Sudan.* New York: Holt, Rinehart & Winston, 1972.

Hamid, Muhammad Beshir. "Confrontation and Reconciliation Within an African Context: The Case of Sudan." *Third World Quarterly* 5, No. 3 (1983): 320–29.

———. "Devolution and the Problems of National Integration." In *Essays in Sudan Politics,* edited by Peter Woodward. London: 1986.

———. "The Martial Arts of Survival." *Africa Contemporary Record* 14 (1981–82): B90-B106.

———. "The Politics of National Reconciliation in the Sudan." Occasional Paper, Center for Contemporary Arab Studies, Georgetown University, Washington, D.C., 1983.

Holt, P. M. *The Mahdist State in the Sudan, 1881–1898.* Oxford: Clarendon Press, 1970.

———, and M. W. Daly. *The History of the Sudan.* Boulder, Colo.: Westview Press, 1979.

Khalid, Mansour. *Nimeiri and the Revolution of Dis-May.* London: Routledge & Kegan Paul, 1985.

Lesch, Ann Mosely. "Confrontation in the Southern Sudan." *Middle East Journal,* 40, No. 3 (1986): 410–28.

———. "The Fall of Numeiri." *Report* No. 9, Universities Field Staff International (UFSI), Indianapolis, Ind., 1985.

———. "Party Politics in the Sudan." *Report* No. 9, UFSI, 1986.

———. "Rebellion in the Southern Sudan." *Report* No. 8, UFSI, 1985.

———. "Transition in the Sudan: Aspirations and Constraints." *Report* No. 20, UFSI, 1985.

Malwal, Bona. *People and Power in Sudan—The Struggle for National Stability.* London: Ithaca Press, 1981.

———. *The Sudan: A Second Challenge to Nationhood.* New York: Thornton Books, 1985.

Mawut, Lazarus Leek. *Dinka Resistance to Condominium Rule 1902–1932.* Khartoum: Graduate College Monograph No. 3, University of Khartoum, 1983.

O'Fahey, R. S. *State and Society in Dar Fur.* New York: St. Martin's Press, 1980.

Sammani, Mohammed Osman. *Jonglei Canal: Dynamics of Planned Change in the Twic Area.* Khartoum: Graduate College Monograph No. 8, University of Khartoum, 1984.

Voll, John Obert. "A History of the Khatmivvah Tariqah in the Sudan." Ph.D. diss., Harvard University, 1969.

———, and Sarah P. Voll. *The Sudan: Unity and Diversity in a Multicultural State.* Boulder, Colo.: Westview Press, 1985.

Wai, Dunstan M., ed. *The Southern Sudan: The Problem of National Integration.* London: Frank Cass, 1973.

Warburg, Gabriel. *Islam, Nationalism and Communism in a Traditional Society: The Case of Sudan.* London: Frank Cass, 1978.

Waterbury, John. *Hydropolitics of the Nile Valley.* Syracuse, N.Y.: Syracuse University Press, 1979.

Woodward, Peter. *Condominium Rule and Sudanese Nationalism.* Totowa, N.J.: Barnes & Noble, 1979.

SWITZERLAND

Carol Schmid

The migration of foreign labor since the end of World War II has been critical in sustaining the economy of Switzerland. The number of foreign workers, or "guest workers" as they are euphemistically termed, increased markedly from 250,000 in 1950 to almost 1.1 million by the end of the 1970s. The migration of large contingents of foreign workers from Southern Europe and the European periphery to Switzerland has created a number of socioeconomic and political problems generally associated with the presence of minority groups. These problems include discrimination with respect to work and education, higher unemployment rates, segregation in housing, and exclusion from political participation and representation. The problems have been exacerbated since Switzerland does not think of itself as a country of immigration in the sense one applies this concept to the United States, Canada, or Australia.

This chapter seeks to elucidate the status of foreign workers in Switzerland by discussing a number of areas: hostility toward immigrants and its relationship to class and a racist ideology; the social and economic background of the foreign worker problem; laws and social policies governing guest workers; and recent developments influencing the assimilation and social stratification of migrants in Switzerland. An important underlying theme will be the similarities and differences between foreign workers in Switzerland and those of racial and ethnic minorities more generally.

A RACIAL CONTEXT

Those employing a racist ideology use physical and cultural characteristics as the criteria for assigning people to superior and subordinate positions. Where the minority group is not physically distinguishable, the superior group uses social and cultural characteristics, including names, language, religion, or other prominent and readily visible cultural traits to justify its position. These criteria, which may be either real or imaginary, serve to distinguish the group from the native population and to justify its subordination. Stephen Castles and Godula Kosack observe that the Swiss "racialist" says that foreigners' physical and mental characteristics which are based on heredity cannot be assimilated. However, the immigrants referred to are not colored people, but Southern Europeans, primarily from Italy.[1] This attitude is similar to the widespread view concerning colored people in Britain.

Even though foreign workers are drawn from a variety of countries from Southern Europe and the European periphery (see Table 25), because "typical evaluations of ethnic categories depend upon the relative position of groups in a system of stratification,"[2] there is a tendency, on a cognitive level, for many Swiss to group all foreign workers (and some refugees), together. The over-foreignization initiatives in Switzerland, for example, did not make any distinction between the nationality of foreign workers.

According to William Peterson:

Many Swiss see in the large blocs of foreigners a danger to society, partly because many come from areas quite distinct from Swiss culture (southern Italy, Spain, and other Mediterranean countries), partly because the legal impediments to naturalization are so great that they are unassimilable almost by definition.... In this thoroughly middle class society, where the embourgeoisement of workers and of Socialists in particular has been all but total, the foreign laborers have introduced a new type of proletariat.[3]

While prejudice toward foreign workers is widespread, there is also differentiation among national groups based on factors such as cultural and geographical distance from the receiving nation, distinguishability of the immigrant group, size of the group, recentness of arrival, and social status and economic position. Switzerland had few colored people, and there is little evidence of color discrimination against Africans and Asians, most of whom work for international organizations or large corporations and have high status and well-paid occupations. The more numerous Italians and Spaniards, on the other hand, face more prejudice.[4] The size of the group alone is not the deciding factor. Turks, even though they make up a very small portion of the foreign population, appear to face even more hostility than foreign workers from Southern Europe. This is at least in part attributable to their more recent migration, their higher concentration in unskilled jobs, and their distinctiveness in terms of religion and culture.

The visibility of foreigners in Switzerland has recently been exacer-

Table 25
Foreign Nationals in Switzerland, 1860–1983, Selected Years

Year	Germany	France	Italy	Austria	Other Europeans	Other Non-Europeans	Foreign Pop. (thousands)	Percent of total pop.
1860	41.0	40.2	12.0	3.4	2.6	0.9	117	4.6
1880	44.8	25.5	19.8	6.1	2.8	0.9	212	7.4
1900	43.9	15.4	30.5	6.3	2.9	1.0	383	11.6
1920	37.2	14.1	33.5	5.5	8.7	1.0	403	10.4
1941	35.1	10.8	43.2	-	7.7	3.1	222	5.2
1960	15.9	5.3	59.3	6.5	7.4	5.7	584	10.8
1970	11.8	5.2	53.6	4.4	13.6	11.3	983	15.9
1980	9.6	5.2	47.1	3.6	15.7	18.8	893	14.2
1983	9.0	5.1	43.7	3.3	19.7	19.2	926	14.5

Source: Statistisches Jahrbuch der Schweiz (various years).

bated by a sudden influx of refugees. Currently, there are more than 22,000 requests for political asylum. The low status of Turks, who comprise the largest single national group, has been aggravated by 7,000 asylum seekers. While Turks argue that they are legitimate refugees, government authorities do not appear to share this opinion. In 1985 only 171, or 10 percent, were granted refugee status. The second largest group of asylum seekers is composed of Tamils from Sri Lanka, who are even further removed from Swiss culture than are the Turks. They occupy a position close to the bottom of the ethnic stratification ladder. Significantly, only twenty-three Tamils, or 3 percent of those seeking refugee status since 1984, have been allowed to stay permanently in Switzerland.[5]

Intraethnic relations within the same group, as well as interethnic relations between various immigrant groups, also characterize ties between foreign workers and the host populations. Hans-Joachim Hoffmann-Nowotny, in one of the few studies dealing with this aspect of ethnic relations, found that contact between Swiss and Italians was positively correlated with knowledge of German, living in the same neighborhood with Swiss, duration of stay, education, income, and nationality of colleagues in the workplace.[6]

"Race relations" is ordinarily thought to involve the interaction of individuals who are physically different from one another. Furthermore, it is commonly assumed that physical characteristics, especially differences based on skin pigmentation, are the best indicators of prejudice and discrimination between peoples. This assumption is not borne out in the Swiss context. Instead, there is a complex interaction of cultural and class factors. Where white immigrant workers have the same position as racial minorities, the same type of prejudice is used to maintain their subordinate position. In order to more fully understand the complex factors influencing the position of foreign workers in Switzerland, it is necessary to trace the genesis and development of the problem.

HISTORICAL BACKGROUND

Switzerland was the source of massive outmigration in the eighteenth and nineteenth centuries. In the eighteenth century, between 300,000 and 350,000 mercenaries emigrated from Switzerland.[7] A reminder of this period may be observed in the Papal guard, which still includes uniformed Swiss. By 1900, however, this trend had reversed itself, and there was an influx of Italian emigrant workers to Switzerland. The Swiss term *Überfremdung* (which may be translated as over-foreignization and connotes fear of loss of identity owing to the presence of a large number of foreigners) came into usage prior to World War I.[8]

In contrast with the situation today, proposals for controlling foreign penetration in the first decade of the twentieth century concentrated almost exclusively on the promotion of naturalization. One concern during this early period of immigration was that annual naturalizations would lag far behind annual increases in the foreign population. A second issue of concern was the higher birth rate of foreigners than that of Swiss. In order to remedy this situation, after 1900 compulsory naturalization of children of foreigners was demanded. Work on a bill to be introduced to the Federal Council was interrupted by the outbreak of the war.[9]

From 1850 to 1917, control of immigration was the prerogative of each canton and was generally loosely administered. In order to enter Switzerland, foreigners were required only to have a passport, to bear no criminal record, and to assure authorities that they would not become a charge on public welfare. Conditions changed in 1917 when the government created the Federal Aliens' Police, an agency that corresponds to the U.S. Immigration and Naturalization Service. Direction of immigration was then delegated to the federal government, and the admission of foreigners was subordinated to the country's ability to absorb them. In 1925, the voters approved a new article to the Constitution which explicitly gave the Swiss Confederation the right to legislate in matters of immigration.[10]

The first wave of immigration was composed primarily of citizens from the neighboring countries of Germany, France, Italy, and Austria. In 1914, foreigners made up 15.4 percent of the resident population in Switzerland, only slightly less than in 1974, when they reached a new peak at 16.5 percent of the population.[11] The first wave of immigration, however, in contrast to the second wave of foreigners which arrived after World War II, had a higher proportion of German, French, and Austrians and a lower percentage of Italians and Europeans from nonbordering countries. In the interwar years, marked by the Great Depression, the percentage of foreigners declined to approximately 5 percent, similar to the level in 1860.

Massive postwar dependence among Western European countries on a foreign workforce occurred first in Switzerland. Relative to its neighbors, Switzerland emerged unscathed from World War II. Therefore, in comparison to the French and German, the Swiss economy experienced an early demand for manufactured goods, which led to a long period of economic expansion. This in turn led to a massive personnel shortage, especially in manual labor, and a demand by employers for foreign labor. One of the first bilateral labor treaties was signed with Italy in 1948. Since this time, it has been assumed in Switzerland that foreign workers will comprise a complementary workforce to fill essential economic gaps in the labor market, rather than as immigrant population.[12]

As migration continued after World War II, the proportion of Italians increased steadily, reaching a peak in 1960 (see Table 25). Over the next two decades there was a significant shift in the composition of the foreign labor force toward more foreigners from the European periphery, so that by 1880, in descending order, 47.1 percent came from Italy, 10.9 percent from Spain, 9.6 percent from Germany, 5.2 percent from France, 4.9 percent from Yugoslavia, and 4.3 percent from Turkey. Despite a reduction in the number of foreigners between 1970 and 1980, Yugoslavs and Turks have increased in both absolute numbers and as a share of the foreign population.[13]

The 1970s witnessed a change from temporary migration to settlement. By 1970, Switzerland had clamped down on the number of foreigners. Although there was a total outflow of 105,000 immigrants between 1969 and 1976, the foreign population did not drop.[14] The reason was that existing legislation gave more and more of the workers the right to have their dependents join them. In terms of numbers, the departing workers were replaced by the wives and children of the workers who remained. By 1983, the foreign population had stabilized at approximately 926,000 in Switzerland, over half of whom were employed.

Despite the large contingent of foreigners in Switzerland, the concept of "immigration" or "immigrant" is missing from all official documents and the headings of official statistics. Instead, one finds the expressions "resident alien population," "aliens subject to control," "employed aliens," and "alien labor force."[15] Even though there is no formal immigration policy as such in Switzerland, a distinct set of *ad hoc* rules toward foreign workers has evolved. Coupled with demographic and structural factors, they influence the assimilation and integration of the migrants and, in particular, their children into the larger socioeconomic and political order. The next section, focuses on the demographic and structural factors shaping public policy and the law as they pertain to foreign workers and refugees.

IMMIGRATION AND IMMIGRANT POLICIES

With minor alterations, the Federal Law of Abode and Settlement of Foreigners (ANAG), which was enacted in 1931, is still valid today. The law provides for three main categories of foreigners: those with an annual permit (*Jahresaufenthalter*), those with a permit of permanent residence (*Niedergelassene*), and those with a seasonal permit (*Saisonarbeiter*). The annual permit serves as both a work and a residence permit.

All foreign workers are initially subject to residence and work requirements. To work in Switzerland, a foreigner must obtain a permit. Seasonal permits are issued for a maximum of nine months to foreigners with seasonal jobs in an occupation that has an expressly seasonal character, such as work in the tourist industry and construction. It does not allow the foreign worker to be accompanied by his or her family. Another category is the frontier worker who is wholly nonresident and commutes daily into Switzerland.

The annual permit is the primary instrument of Swiss immigration regulation. This permit is usually valid for a year when granted for the first time. Annual permits must be renewed regularly each year during the first five years of residence and afterward once every two years. After fifteen months these workers can be joined by their families, who can also receive annual permits allowing them to work. Since foreigners have no right to renewal, the authorities may refuse an application and force the holder to leave the country. This is likely to happen if the foreigner is unemployed and unable to find a new job very soon.[16]

The permit of permanent residence is granted at the discretion of the pertinent authorities, after at least ten years of residence. This permit entitles foreigners to rights in the job market equal to those of citizens (with the exception of certain occupations that are reserved for Swiss citizens or that demand a special Swiss examination). Although a permanent residence permit has to be renewed every three years, this is merely a formality, and can be revoked only if the holder commits a serious offense. A permanent permit does not, however, entitle one to political rights, including the right to vote.

A permanent residence permit is also issued to immigrants who request asylum and are subsequently allowed refugee status. By the end of 1983, there were 33,166 acknowledged refugees in Switzerland. Between 1978 and 1985, the number of requests for political asylum increased fifteenfold, from under 1,400 to over 22,000. Although Hungarians in 1956 and Czechs in 1968 were allowed to enter the country freely, this is no longer the case today. The last large wave of political refugees who were allowed to enter Switzerland were Vietnamese.[17]

Thus, there has been a significant change in the composition of the refugee applicant pool, from Eastern European to Third World countries. According to a recent *Wall Street Journal* editorial, "Since 1981 new and more liberal legislation has encouraged thousands throughout the world to seek asylum in Switzerland for no other reason than to share in its economic blessings. A family granted asylum may receive as much as $1,800 a month in subsidies."[18] This has generated an intense debate, similar to that in the United States about the fate of Latin Americans from countries such as Haiti and Nicaragua, concerning the distinction between economic and political refugees. Switzerland has also spawned its own sanctuary movement, with many priests and ministers active in the issue. The increase of individuals seeking asylum is almost certain to lead to a revision of the law, making it more restrictive. This has been confirmed in the percentage of asylum seekers granted refugee status: it decreased from 75 percent in 1982, to 36 percent in 1983, to 24 percent in 1984, to just 14 percent in 1985.[19]

In spite of the fact that many children and adults have spent a considerable amount of time as permanent residents, Switzerland has taken a stand against widespread naturalization. Technically, a permanent resident in Switzerland can apply for naturalization after twelve years, but because of the complexity of other considerations involved, the probability that naturalization will occur under current conditions is not very great. Cantons and communes may impose their own regulations concerning minimum length of residence, and since time spent in one commune may not be transferred to another, residence requirements may take considerably longer than twelve years. Many communes also impose high fees for naturalization. In addition, before citizenship is granted, the applicants must prove that they are "sufficiently assimilated." Naturalization is not considered a means of solving the foreigner problem. The proportion of foreigners being naturalized has rarely exceeded 1 percent in any given year. Between 1973 and 1983, approximately 109,000 foreigners were permitted to become naturalized Swiss citizens. Unlike the United States, where children born to legal immigrants on American soil are automatically entitled to American citizenship, children born to foreign parents do not gain the right to Swiss citizenship.[20]

Switzerland made some concessions to the thousands of foreign workers and their dependents in the country after severely restricting further in-migration of workers in 1970. Historically, Switzerland has been more restrictive than West Germany in regard to foreign worker policy. Since Switzerland is not a member of the European Economic Community, all foreign workers (including the large Italian contingent) are initially subject to residence and work requirements. For instance, the Italians (who represented 90 percent of the new entrants in the early 1950s and still comprise almost half of the foreign resident population) as well as all other foreign workers were initially restricted to one canton and bound to an employer or an occupation, or both, for at least five years. Family migration was not foreseen. Preference was given to individuals unaccompanied by family members. In the early 1950s, when the economic boom was viewed as a passing phenomenon soon to be followed by a depression, foreigners were not encouraged to settle. Although the desires of the migrant workers who did not plan to expatriate themselves initially coincided with the attitudes and intentions of the receiving country, this situation became increasingly illusionary.

Annual permit holders could apply for family unification only after ten years' residence. Seasonal permit holders had no such rights at all.[21] During the 1960s and 1970s, less stringent regulations were introduced with respect to family migration and movement within the job market.

Currently, seasonal workers who have accumulated thirty-six months of employment during four consecutive seasons may have their status changed to that of an annual permit without restrictions regarding choice of canton, employer, or occupation. When granted an annual work permit, they can also request permission for family reunification. Prior to the liberalization of foreign worker policy and the stabilization of the immigrant population, there was a public outcry against *Überfremdung*.

In Switzerland, immigration became one of the most debated political issues in the postwar period. Pressure from groups campaigning against "foreign domination" helped to restrict the entry of new foreign workers in 1964 and subsequent years. The campaign against foreigners reached a climax in June 1970 when all male Swiss citizens (women were not enfranchised on the federal level until 1971) were asked to vote in a referendum as to whether to limit the proportion of foreigners to 10 percent of the population in both the country as a whole and in each canton (with the exception of Geneva). Acceptance of this referendum would have meant the expulsion of a large number of immigrants from Switzerland. The move was sponsored by a newly formed right-wing party, the National Action Against Over-Foreignization of People and Country. It was opposed by the Federal Council (the executive branch of the Swiss government composed of seven members from the four major parties), the Parliament, the trade unions, and all major parties. Even so, it was defeated by only a modest majority (54 percent).

In late 1972, the right-wing National Action began to collect signatures for an even more drastic proposal. Under its terms there would have been a sharp reduction in the number of foreigners—two out of every five would have been expelled by 1978. The referendum was defeated in 1974 by a margin of about two to one. The two most recent initiatives, which attempted to liberalize the status of foreign workers, were also turned down (in April 1981 and June 1982). The 1981 initiative would have abolished the category of seasonal workers. By maintaining this category, the Swiss have been able to keep tighter control over the foreign population. The 1982 initiative, which was narrowly defeated, turned down a proposed new Aliens Law which would have reduced the time needed to secure a permanent permit and to unite families.

The 1981 and 1982 Swiss votes seem consistent with current foreign worker policy: on the one hand, measures designed to stabilize and control the number of new immigrants, and on the other, economic integration of those already in Switzerland. With an unemployment rate of only 1 percent, one of the lowest in the world, the tension caused by foreign workers, and more recently refugees, does not seem to be rooted exclusively in the fear of losing jobs to lower priced labor as is arguably the case in France and England. Rather, it seems to be based in the threat to the Swiss way of life and "Swissness" that a large foreign population poses for the delicately balanced Swiss society. A closer examination of the 1970 referendum reveals a strong relationship between the size of the community in which people grew up and the way they voted, with the percentage opposed to immigration decreasing from farm to village to large city. "The immigrant workers apparently symbolized to these conservative Swiss a trend towards economic and social modernization, a trend they feared and hoped to reverse by halting immigration."[22] The rise of a large-scale nativist reaction to the presence of foreign workers in Switzerland occurred in the 1970s during an economic recession. As economic conditions improved, the over-foreignization issue seemed to have lost some of its importance until the refugee problem again stirred public sentiment.

In spite of the indirect relationship between the unemployment rate in Switzerland and the over-foreignization movement, there can be little doubt that the high rate of growth of real wages and the low level of inflation in Switzerland are partly attributable to the influx of a large pool of low-cost unskilled and semiskilled workers.[23] Denis Maillat observes that, "From 1950 on immigrants have been directed into the less well paid branches of the secondary sector, which entailed a certain stagnation of the wage growth of these branches. During the following years the ranges of wages widened, i.e. the difference between the high wage and low wage sector increased," with Swiss moving disproportionately into the better paid jobs, while foreign workers remained in the low-wage industries.[24]

RECENT DEVELOPMENTS

Immigration since World War II has been seen primarily in economic terms. Since the economic boom was expected to last only temporarily, immigration policy aimed at rotation as a means of preventing immigrants from staying permanently. After vigorous protest from the electorate, a ceiling for annual permits was established in 1970, at about 10,000 permits per year (excluding family members). In 1972, a total of 244,000 seasonal permits had been issued. By 1976, this was cut back to only 91,000. At the same time, the issuance of permits for new frontier workers was reduced from 40,000 in 1974 to 14,000 in 1976.[25]

Many foreigners were forced to leave Switzerland during the recession, either voluntarily or involuntarily when their permits were not renewed. However, attempts to strictly manipulate the number of foreigners have gradually lost some of their effectiveness, as the percentage of foreigners with permanent residence permits has risen: from 23.5 percent in 1960, to 37.2 percent in 1970, to currently more than three-fourths of the foreign population (see Table 26).

The increase in the number of foreigners with residence permits slowed

Table 26
Foreign Residents in Switzerland in 1983 (in thousands)

Nationality	Total	Permanent Permits	Annual Permits	% Permanent Permits
Italian	404.8	368.4	36.4	91.0
Spanish	104.2	82.7	21.5	79.3
German	83.5	64.8	18.7	77.6
Yugoslavian	58.9	30.2	28.7	51.2
Turkish	48.5	31.3	17.2	64.5
French	46.8	38.1	8.6	81.5
Austrian	30.1	26.5	3.6	88.0
Portuguese	19.7	6.1	13.6	31.0
Others	129.1	68.2	60.9	52.8
Total	925.6	716.3	209.2	77.4

Source: *La Vie Economique*, June 1984.

down after 1975, but because annual permits continued to be reduced, an increasing proportion of the foreign population has permanent status. The reduction in the number of annual permits granted and the relative stabilization in the numbers of permanent permit holders has brought the resident foreigners down from 16.5 percent of the population of Switzerland in 1974 to 14.5 percent in early 1984. Currently, very few new annual permits are distributed, with those issued going disproportionately to dependents.[26]

The transformation from temporary migration to permanent settlement has profound implications for Swiss society. The nature of this transformation can best be seen by focusing on a number of demographic and structural factors. First, one can see a visible aging of the foreign worker population. Because permanent status takes ten years to achieve, the resident population has a distinctly older age structure than was the case in the early 1970s. Forty to forty-four years is now the model age group for males with permanent permits. Very few immigrants have reached retirement age, so they continue to subsidize the pensions of the old indigenous population. As husbands were joined by their wives and children, the percentage of foreigners actively employed dropped from 79 percent in 1960 to 66 percent in 1980. Nevertheless, they continue to have a higher labor force participation rate than the native population.[27]

A second demographic factor related to the age of the migrant population is the fertility rate. The overall contribution of foreigners to Swiss fertility dropped from 31.4 percent of all births in 1974 to around 20 percent in 1982. Part of the steep drop after 1977 was related to the introduction of a new law that allowed children of a Swiss mother and foreign father to receive Swiss citizenship (previously they were only entitled to their father's nationality).

In 1982, about 17 percent of children in compulsory schooling were non-Swiss. In some urban neighborhoods, as many as half the children were foreigners. These children continue to be disadvantaged in comparison to Swiss nationals—proportionately more attend special classes for children with learning disabilities, and fewer complete the upper grades of compulsory school. In addition, foreign children are less apt to obtain vocational training and more likely to work in semiskilled or unskilled occupations. Although the percentage of children completing compulsory schooling has improved in recent years, foreign children remain disadvantaged because of their concentration in the lower social strata.[28]

Foreign workers in Switzerland are concentrated among skilled and unskilled workers. Although the proportion of those engaged in such low-paying occupations as hotel and restaurant work, domestic work, and agriculture has declined since 1956, the majority of foreign immigrants is still found in jobs requiring physical labor. The extreme labor shortage in Switzerland in the late 1960s helped to reduce the wages between different branches of the secondary sector of the economy. "Low wage branches were forced to improve their salaries because, on the one hand, they wanted to keep some part of their indigenous work force, and on the other hand, remain sufficiently attractive to immigrants for whom they had a great need."[29] This trend has aided Swiss foreign workers to achieve a higher standard of living than their German counterparts.

In a recent study of immigrants in Frankfurt and Lippstadt, Germany, and in Zurich and Frauenfeld, Switzerland, Ulrike Schöneberg found that, on a number of dimensions relating to aspects of employment, foreigners in Germany registered less positive attitudes than foreigners in Switzerland. Even if our examination is narrowed to Italians in Germany (where they comprise a group on the top of the foreign stratification system, since they are members of the European Economic Community and may freely migrate to and from Germany, and where the Turks comprise a third of the immigrant population) and in Switzerland, we find that significant differences still remain. Concerning job discrimination, 19 percent of Italian foreign workers in Switzerland as compared to 33 percent of those living in Germany, said they were disadvantaged in securing work in comparison to citizens. With regard to their chances in the future, the Italians in Switzerland also have a more positive perspective than those in the Federal Republic of Germany: in Switzerland, 52 percent judged their chances in the future to be "rather good" as compared to only 26 percent who had this opinion in Germany.[30] Thus, although Italian immigrants are decidedly less well off in Switzerland than the native population, unique demographic and structural factors have been instrumental in shaping more positive attitudes and economic integration for Italian foreign workers in Switzerland than for their counterparts in West Germany. This is also true in regard to segregation within the host society and the quality of housing.[31] Foreign workers are more concentrated in segregated and low-cost housing in Germany than in Switzerland, although, migrants in both countries tend to occupy the least desirable accommodations.[32]

The spatial distribution of the foreign worker population makes them more visible to the Swiss population. The foreign community is concentrated in the urban cantons. In 1983, foreigners accounted for 29 percent of the population in Geneva, 20 percent in Vaud, 18 percent in Basel-Stadt, and 17 percent in Zurich. With the exception of Ticino (an Italian-speaking canton bordering on Italy), immigrants were underrepresented in rural areas (although seasonal workers are often found in the tourist industry in the rural areas). This urbanism contrasts with current trends among the Swiss. The 1980 census and migration data for 1981 and 1982 indicate a trend toward the suburbs, with all major cities losing population.[33]

Different foreign groups show different distributions within the various language areas of Switzerland. Spaniards and Portuguese are concentrated in French-speaking Switzerland, while Turks and Yugoslavs are almost exclusively employed in the German-speaking cantons. Concentration of a particular nationality group alone, however, seems to be a poor indicator of ethnic hostility or racism.

Recent election returns point to a complex equation that includes the percentage of foreigners, individual perceptions of economic disadvantage, and visibility of the foreigners. Recently, the National Action and the Vigilance parties, two right-wing parties dedicated to the reduction of foreigners, have made their greatest inroads in the cantons of Geneva, Vaud, and Bern. Geneva, in addition to having the highest percentage of foreigners, also has about 2,600 people awaiting decisions on asylum applications. On October 13, 1985, the Vigilance party emerged as one of the two strongest parties in Geneva's cantonal Parliament. It won nineteen seats, a gain of twelve, thus almost matching the number of seats held by the Liberals (twenty seats), in the hundred-seat Parliament. The main message of the Vigilance party was that an influx of migrants and "false refugees" has been aggravating a housing shortage and threatening jobs.[34] In the city of Lausanne in the canton of Vaud, a similar situation prevailed.

Although Bern contains a lower percentage of foreigners than either Geneva or Vaud, the foreigners are more visible. By the end of 1986, the canton of Bern will be responsible for "taking care" of 1,000 refugees. In a secret ballot on September 9, 1985, 85 percent of the voters in the small town of Sonceboz decided against accommodating six Tamils from Sri Lanka.[35] The vote appears to be more than just a xenophobic response. At least part of the problem stems from a feeling that the Tamils will not "fit in" and that they may take away economic resources from the community.

The negative view of foreign workers and refugees can be traced to two sets of factors: factors unique to Switzerland and factors characteristic of right-wing movements in general. Switzerland is a culturally and socially diverse country, consisting of twenty-six highly autonomous cantons. It contains four linguistic groups and two major religions, as well as large differences between rural and urban cantons. Despite its heterogeneity, Switzerland has managed to mitigate the problems of its citizen minorities through a complex system of compromises and a conscious effort to promote a common identity and attachment to the Swiss nation.[36] This ability to absorb native linguistic groups has not carried over to the assimilation of foreign workers and refugees. In fact, a number of Swiss observers have suggested that a small multicultural, multilingual society with a fragile identity can easily feel endangered by immigration.[37] The term *Überfremdung*, which was coined in Switzerland, conveys this feeling. Currently, Switzerland contains the highest percentage of foreigners of any of the major Western European countries.

The problems of foreign workers have been amplified by the nature of direct democracy in Switzerland. Through the referendum, at the demand of 100,000 citizens, federal legislation must be submitted to the electorate for acceptance or rejection. Through this process one of the small parties, such as the National Action, may successfully launch a referendum against a law passed by a large majority of the federal Parliament. This has happened on several occasions. Furthermore, the multiparty system and proportional representation also allow smaller parties to play a part in city, communal, cantonal, and federal bodies.

There are significant similarities between those voting for right-wing parties in Switzerland and other countries. As Rudolf Heberle puts it, "such movements are supported by those who for some reason or other had failed to make a success in their business or occupation, and those who had lost in their social status or were in danger of losing it."[38]

Although there are few quantitative studies of recent voting patterns, qualitative evidence suggests that anti-foreign worker and anti-refugee sentiment comes disproportionately from middle-aged individuals who believe they have been left behind and failed to achieve a higher standard of living which they deserve.[39] The foreign workers and refugees have become scapegoats for their displaced hostility.

SUMMARY AND CONCLUSIONS

It has not been possible for Switzerland to exploit the short-term economic advantages of foreign workers without social, cultural and political repercussions. Many problems experienced by recent immigrants to Switzerland and their impact on society are similar to those of colored immigrants in Britain and blacks in the United States. Even though the majority of foreign workers are not physically distinguishable from the native population, right-wing parties, such as the National Action, portray immigrants as possessing physical and mental characteristics, based on heredity, which cannot be assimilated. In addition, they link foreigners to real grievances in the society, such as a shortage of apartments. The campaign against over-foreignization also has an element of romantic anti-industrialization, looking back to an idealized self-sufficient agrarian nation.

The movement of thousands of foreigners into the Swiss labor market has increased the mobility rates of Swiss workers into the ranks of skilled working-class and white-collar occupations, while foreign immigrants are disproportionately concentrated in less skilled jobs. Willem Albeda distinguishes four phases in the development of labor stratification in Western Europe, from the beginning of large-scale immigration after World War II through the recession in 1972. In the first phase, guest laborers were used to temporarily relieve certain bottlenecks in the labor market. Next, there was a movement to fulfill functions that the indigenous labor force saw as unpleasant, inferior, or too insecure. The third phase saw foreign migrants occupy, in principle, all unskilled positions. The final phase witnessed a slight diversification of jobs, with foreign immigrants doing the physical labor in a developed economy. By 1972, Albeda points out, Switzerland was already in the fourth phase, while Germany and France were in the third stage and the Netherlands was entering the second.[40]

Since this time, Switzerland has entered into a new phase characterized by ethnic stratification among foreign workers and some degree of mobility from unskilled and semiskilled to skilled jobs. Preliminary evidence suggests that early migrants to Switzerland have obtained a limited degree of mobility and social and economic integration within Swiss society. According to the study conducted by Schöneberg, 11.5 percent of the

Italian sample had Swiss wives, 18.3 had perfect knowledge of German, and 41.9 percent said they had experienced some mobility from their first job in Switzerland.[41]

The relative calm and progress of the last few years are currently being strained by a stream of asylum seekers, primarily from poor countries. The refugee question has drawn attention to the large contingent of foreign migrants, the vast majority of whom by now have resided in Switzerland for over ten years. With more and more Third World groups seeking political asylum (including a substantial number of Turks, Tamils, and Africans), the potential for invidious distinctions between ethnic and racial minorities now exists. Whether or not this will occur remains to be seen.

NOTES

1. Stephen Castles and Godula Kosack, *Immigrant Workers and Class Structure in Western Europe* (London: Oxford University Press, 1985), pp. 455–57. In this chapter the terms "foreign workers," "immigrants," "migrants," "guest workers," and "aliens" are used interchangeably, even though they have slightly different connotations.

2. Tamotsu Shibutani and Kian M. Kwan, *Ethnic Stratification* (New York: Macmillan, 1965), p. 115.

3. William Petersen, "On the Subnations of Europe," in Nathan Glazer and Danial P. Moynihan, eds., *Ethnicity, Theory and Practice* (Cambridge, Mass.: Harvard University Press, 1975), pp. 195–96.

4. Castles and Kosack, *Immigrant Workers,* p. 446. The situation for Africans may change if a substantial number of less skilled individuals seek refugee status in Switzerland.

5. "Härtere Gangart in der Zulassungspraxis," *Tages-Anzeiger* (foreign edition), February 4, 1985, p. 2. "Swiss Dilemma: Who's a Political Refugee?" *Wall Street Journal,* November 20, 1986, p. 31.

6. Hans-Joachim Hoffman-Nowotny, *Soziologie des Fremdarbeiter-Problems* (Stuttgart: Enke, 1973).

7. W. Bickel, *Bevölkerungsgeschichte der Schweiz seit dem Ausgang des Mittelalters* (Zurich: Büchergilde Gutenberg, 1947), p. 91.

8. Mark J. Miller and Phillip L. Martin, *Administering Foreign Worker Programs* (Lexington, Mass.: Lexington Books, 1982), p. 7.

9. Hans-Joachim Hoffmann-Nowotny, "Switzerland," in Tomas Hammer, ed., *European Immigration Policy* (Cambridge: Cambridge University Press, 1985), pp. 207–8.

10. M. Gardner Clark, "The Swiss Experience with Foreign Workers: Lessons for the United States," *Industrial and Labor Relations Review* 36 (July 1983): 607.

11. Carol L. Schmid, *Conflict and Consensus in Switzerland* (Berkeley: University of California Press, 1981), p. 137.

12. Miller and Martin, *Administering Foreign-Worker Programs,* pp. 7–8.

13. Hoffmann-Nowotny, "Switzerland," pp. 209–10.

14. W. P. Böhning, *Guest Worker Employment with Special Reference to the Federal Republic of Germany, France and Switzerland-Lessons for the United States?* Working Paper NB–5 (College Park: University of Maryland Center for Philosophy and Public Policy, 1980), p. 26.

15. Hans-Joachim Hoffmann-Nowotny and N. Killias, "Switzerland," in R. Krane, *International Labor in Europe* (New York: Praeger Publishers, 1979), pp. 46–47.

16. Hoffmann-Nowotny, "Switzerland," p. 218.

17 Ibid., pp. 220, 210; *Tages-Anzeiger*, February 4, 1968, p. 2. According to this article, Eastern Europeans, as a group, are still the most likely to be awarded refugee status, even though the percentage granted refugee status as a whole has declined. *Wall Street Journal*, November 20, 1985, p. 31.

18. *Wall Street Journal*, November 20, 1985, p. 31.

19. *Tages-Anzeiger*, February 4, 1986, p. 2.

20. Hoffmann-Nowotny, "Switzerland," p. 222, and Carol Schmid, "Gastarbeiter in West Germany and Switzerland: An assessment of Host-Society—Immigrant Relations," *Population Research and Policy Review* 2(1983): 233–52.

21. W. P. Böhning, *Studies in International Labour Immigration* (New York: St. Martin's Press, 1984), p. 130.

22. Seymour Martin Lipset, "The Revolt Against Modernity," in P. Torsvik, ed., *Mobilization Center—Periphery Structures and Nation-Building* (Bergen: Universitetsforlaget, 1981), p. 477, and C. P. Kindleberger, *Europe's Postwar Growth* (Cambridge, Mass.: Harvard University Press, 1976), p. 46.

23. Böhning, *Studies in International Labour Migration*, pp. 61–106.

24. Ibid., p. 102.

25. Paul White, "Switzerland: From Migrant Rotation to Migrant Communities," *Geography* 70 (April 1985) 169.

26. Ibid., p. 170.

27. Ibid., and Schmid, "Gastarbeiter in West Germany and Switzerland," p. 235.

28. Hans-Joachim Hoffmann-Nowotny, "The Second Generation of Immigrants: A Sociological Analysis with Special Emphasis on Switzerland," in Rosemarie Rodgers, ed., *Guests Come to Stay* (Boulder, Colo.: Westview Press, 1985), pp. 110–33.

29. Schmid, *Conflict and Consensus in Switzerland*, p. 142, and Böhning, *Studies in International Labour Migration*, p. 102.

30. Ulrike Schöneberg, "Bestimmungsgründe der Integration und Assimilation ausländischer Arbeitnehmer in der Bundesrepublik Deutschland und der Schweiz," in Joachim Hoffmann-Nowotny and Karl-Otto Hondreich, eds., *Ausländer in der Bundesrepublik und in der Schweiz*, (Frankfurt: Campus Verlag, 1982), pp. 477–88. In the German sample, 47 percent of the workers were unskilled and 24 percent were skilled. In contrast, in Switzerland 26 percent of the sample were unskilled and 40 percent of the workers were employed. These differences, in addition to the higher compensation of Swiss workers, are reflected in average family income in 1981—approximately $963 per month for Italian aliens in Germany and $1,454 per month for those in Switzerland.

31. The more limited resources of Italian families in Germany than in Switzerland, as well as the larger size of German cities, appear to limit opportunities

for contact with the host populations and the ability to learn the German language. (A total of 51 percent of Italian foreign workers in Switzerland have contact with the host population and three-fourths speak some German, as compared to 24 percent and 45 percent, respectively.) Schöneberg, "Bestimmungsgründe," pp. 482–84.

32. Even when a distinction is made between Italian workers in highly concentrated accommodation (over 30 percent foreigners) versus less concentrated quarters, 86 percent of the Italian immigrants in Zurich have a bath, toilet, and central heating in their apartment, compared to only 46 percent in Frankfurt. For those in more highly concentrated living situations, the comparable rates are 61 percent in Zurich and 30 percent in Frankfurt. Doris Bühler, "Individuelle Determination der residentiellen Verteilung von Ausländern im städtischen Raum," in Hans-Joachim Hoffmann-Nowotny and Karl-Otto Hondreich, eds., *Ausländer in der Bundesrepublik Deutschland und in der Schweiz* (Frankfurt: Campus Verlag, 1982), pp. 384–85.

33. White, "Switzerland," pp. 170–71.

34. Right-Wing Party Gains in Geneva Election," *New York Times,* October 16, 1985, and "Genf: Sieg für die Vigilants," *Tages-Anzeiger* (foreign edition), October 15, 1985.

35. *Wall Street Journal,* November 20, 1985, p. 31.

36. Schmid, *Conflict and Consensus in Switzerland,* p. 6.

37. Hoffmann-Nowotny, "Switzerland," pp. 211–12, and Leonhard Neidhart, "Die Nationale Aktion lebt von den Zukurzgekommenen," *Tages-Anzeiger* (foreign edition), January 14, 1986, p. 10.

38. Rudolf Heberle, *From Democracy to Nazism* (Baton Rouge: Louisiana State University, 1945), p. 10.

39. *Tages-Anzeiger,* January 14, 1986, p. 10.

40. Hans Van Amersfoort, *Immigration and the Formation of Minority Groups: The Dutch Experience 1945–1975* (Cambridge: Cambridge University Press, 1982), pp. 187–188.

41. Schöneberg, "Bestimmungsgründe," pp. 479–82.

SELECT BIBLIOGRAPHY

Böhning, W. R. *Studies in International Labour Migration.* New York: St. Martin's Press, 1984.

Castles, Stephen, and Godula, Kosack. *Immigrant Workers and Class Structure in Western Europe.* London: Oxford University Press, 1985.

Hoffmann-Nowotny, Hans-Joachim. "The Second Generation of Immigrants: A Sociological Analysis with Special Emphasis on Switzerland." In *Guests Come to Stay: The Effect of European Migration on Sending and Recruiting Countries,* edited by Rosemarie Rodgers. Boulder, Colo.: Westview Press, 1985.

———. "Switzerland." In *European Immigration Policy,* edited by Tomas Hammar. Cambridge: Cambridge University Press, 1985.

———, and Karl-Otto Hondreich, eds. *Ausländer in der Bundesrepublik Deutschland und in der Schweiz.* Frankfurt: Campus Verlag, 1982.

Miller, Mark J., and Philip L. Martin. *Administering Foreign Worker Programs.*
    Lexington, Mass.: Lexington Press, 1982.
Schmid, Carol L. *Conflict and Consensus in Switzerland.* Berkeley: University of
    California Press, 1981.
————. "Gastarbeiter in West Germany and Switzerland: An Assessment of Host
    Society-Immigrant Relations." *Population Research and Policy Review* 2 (1983):
    233–52.

THAILAND

Suchitra Punyaratabandhu-Bhakdi
and Juree Vichit-Vadakdan

A RACIAL CONTEXT

We take as our point of departure the notion that racial distinctions[1] are inherently subjective, that they are to be defined, as Duane Lockard suggests, by "cultural norms with greater or lesser degrees of genetic differentiation serving as the basis for categories."[2] It follows, then, that the grounds on which racial distinctions are made are almost entirely culture- and context-dependent. Moreover, we observe that the greater the degree of genetic differentiation within a given society, the more likely it is that genetic differences provide the key defining properties of the social concept race. In societies characterized by relative genetic homogeneity, however, racial distinctions derive from other criteria. For the curious feature about the concept of race is that, regardless of the degree of genetic differentiation within any given society, discrimination based on racial distinctions exists. The question is not whether race is an issue but, rather, what form does it take and to what extent?

Thailand, with a population of some 55 million, enjoys a relatively high degree of ethnic, linguistic, religious, and cultural homogeneity.[3] Ethnic minorities account for no more than 15 percent of the total population. Central Thai, the official language, is almost universally understood, with the exception perhaps of the hill tribes in the north and the Muslim villages in the southern border provinces. Buddhism is the state religion. About 95.3 percent of Thais profess Buddhism, 3.8 percent Islam, and 0.6 percent Christianity.

Against this background of relative cultural and ethnic homogeneity, let us consider the criteria that form the basis for racial categorizations in the Thai context. The common approach which this handbook explores is the extent to which physical factors associated with groups/

minorities have resulted in social categorizations of a racial or quasi-racial character. The emphasis is on racial perception based on skin color, facial features, hair characteristics, body type, and so forth. In the Thai context, however, we take explicit note from the outset that racial distinctions are based overwhelmingly, on national origins and ethnic differences, and, to a lesser extent, on religion, rather than on physical features. Nevertheless, it is true that categorizations based on national and ethnoreligious factors have given rise to racial sterotypes that comprehend not only behavioral and sociopsychological traits, but also physical attributes. Thus, the Chinese are stereotypically distinguished by their paler complexions and "single-fold" (no crease in the) eyelid, Thai Muslims by their dark skins and Malay features, and Indians by their height, build, complexion, facial characteristics, and hair. It is common to hear people described as "looking Chinese," or "looking Indian," or "looking like a southern Thai," or "looking like a northeasterner." A pejorative connotation sometimes attaches to such descriptions.

Physical characteristics associated with, for example, "looking Chinese," or "having a Chinese face" become the basis on which social categorizations are made. Thus, a person with a "Chinese face" may be looked down on, considered physically unattractive, or given less than courteous treatment by sales and service personnel; or may be treated with indifference by petty bureaucrats and government officials. Unless offset by other characteristics such as a strong and impressive personality, an aura of dominance and importance, a family name of distinction, or a socially recognized title or rank (Ph.D. or M.D., General or Colonel), a person with a "Chinese face" will be stigmatized because of his or her looks and will be treated, however subtly, as a second-class citizen. It is not uncommon to hear remarks such as, "To think that such a famous name would have such a Chinese face!" or "He's certainly smart—what a pity he looks so Chinese."

Although racial prejudice extends beyond differentiation based on physical characteristics, such prejudice is deepened by visible physical distinctions. The Indian minority, for example, is easily distinguished from the average Thai or Sino-Thai by the following physical attributes: height and a heavier build; larger eyes and aquiline noses; and an abundance of body and facial hair. In terms of the racial sterotype, Indians are considered to possess a strong and repulsive body odor. Indian food and Indian dwellings are thought to exude a distinctive "Indian smell," which is considered unpleasant. In must be noted here that Thais tend to assign Hindus, Muslims, as well as Sikhs, to the same category—*khaek*, a generic term denoting all foreigners who are not Caucasian or of Mongolian extraction. Generally, the term *khaek* refers to persons of a darker complexion. Persons of Negroid racial stock are considered a subcategory of *khaek*. However, Arabs are also considered a subcategory of *khaek*.

Stereotypically, *khaek* are considered to be dirty, stingy, untrustworthy, and treacherous. Nevertheless, in actual interpersonal transactions, prejudices based on the stereotype may be temporarily put aside. Other evaluative criteria are used instead to assess relationships. These criteria may very well extend to considerations of economic status, professional and/or educational attainment, social position, and so on. Hence, regardless of how Thais verbalize their prejudices against *khaek,* wealthy *khaek* are quite readily accepted as neighbors, business associates, customers, and tenants.

Social prejudice against the Chinese can be summarized as follows. Chinese are dirty, crude, and crass, as well as uncouth in their manner and behavior. Although Chinese have business acumen, they are far too money- and profit-oriented. They lack the spontaneity to form meaningful, genuine friendships and relations with others. The calculating Chinese is the butt of many ethnic jokes. Thus, when a Chinese shows sincerity to a non-Chinese, it is the occasion for surprise. Selfish motives are imputed to most behaviors, even the most philanthropic.

Ethnic Chinese possess their own sterotypic prejudice against ethnic Thai. These prejudices are passed on from generation to generation, however inadvertently, through jokes, casual comments, and even serious moralizing on the virtues of being Chinese as opposed to being Thai. Ethnic Thais are thought to be lazy, irresponsible, lacking in endurance and physical stamina, too fun-loving, too present-oriented, wasteful, undisciplined, incompetent, and gullible in business matters. The Chinese frown on the Thais' spending patterns—typically, the feast to famine syndrome.

The preceding discussion notwithstanding, it is important to bear in mind that physical characteristics do not serve as the basis on which racial distinctions are made. They are important only because they constitute "clues" to racial categorizations. But they are often unreliable clues. Someone who "looks Chinese" may not be racially categorized (perceived) as Chinese whereas another person who in no way resembles the physical stereotype may in fact be assigned to the racial category Chinese. The reason is simple. Social categorizations of a racial character are based primarily on nationality and ethnoreligious considerations. Although there is some correspondence between these factors and physical features, the correlation is by no means strong—primarily because the melting pot of intermarriage has resulted in the present-day situation whereby most Thai, in particular those living in urban areas, must admit to mixed ancestry. Looks alone are highly deceptive.

For any discussion of race and race relations in Thailand to be mean-

ingful, adherence should be made to the criteria-in-use in social categorizations of race. How, then, is the social concept of race defined in
the Thai context? In Thailand, we find that race is virtually indistin-
guishable from the concept of "minority peoples," who are defined as
social groups whose ethnic background, language, culture, customs and
traditions, or religion set them apart from the mainstream Thai-Buddhist culture. The term "minority peoples" carries the additional connotation of existence of, or potential for, political conflict between the
subordinate group and the dominant culture. There are probably at
least twelve or thirteen identifiable minorities in Thailand. In view of
space limitations here, however, we will examine only those that have
figured more prominently in race relations or that are numerically
important.

For purposes of the present discussion, we distinguish between (1)
government-initiated public policies toward minorities, and (2) social
(private) acts of discrimination of a racial character. We note, moreover,
that the grounds for these two types of actions are quite different nor
are they in any way related. Public policies derive primarily from national
security and economic considerations, whereas social discrimination is
based on a perceived refusal on the part of minority races to assimilate
with or conform to the prevailing social and cultural norms of the dominant Thai-Buddhist bureaucratic culture. If, in the discussion that follows, we have paid less attention to private acts of discrimination, it is
simply because in Thailand, such discrimination has on the whole been
relatively unobtrusive and of minor proportions. Neither has it led to
protest on the part of the group that has been discriminated against,
nor has it occasioned political action on behalf of the racial group. The
explanation is rather straightforward. Such racial minorities as remain
out-groups in society by and large do so voluntarily. Even as the Thai
culture places value on assimilation and conformity, so has it also provided easy access for entry and assimilation. Throughout the centuries,
Thailand has remained an open society, unconcerned with new arrivals,
provided they become assimilated to the mainstream culture.

HISTORICAL BACKGROUND

The presence of minorities in Thailand can be explained by at least
four separate historical developments. The first concerns those minorities who, indigenous to the region, were supplanted by the dominant
Thai-Buddhist polity in the nineteenth and twentieth centuries. The
second relates to the seminomadic hill tribe minorities located along
Thailand's northern borders, who happen to fall under Thai jurisdiction
chiefly because of the way geopolitical boundaries were drawn at the
turn of the century, but who themselves may neither fully understand

nor necessarily subscribe to the concept of national identity and loyalty to a nation-state. Third, there are minorities inhabiting the southern provinces whose language, religion, and customs are identical to those of their Muslim Malay neighbors across the border and whose incorporation with Thailand is largely an accident of historical circumstance, or, to be more accurate, the result of an accord reached with the colonizing British in the late nineteenth century. The fourth development concerns minority groups who have sought haven in Thailand either for economic reasons (viz., the nineteenth- and early twentieth-century Chinese and Indian settlers) or for political reasons (notably, the Vietnamese, Kampuchean, and Laotian refugees in the post-World War II period).

Dictated primarily by national security considerations, the Thai government's response to minorities can broadly be classified into two types of policies: assimilation and integration with respect to certain groups; and denial of Thai citizenship and/or repatriation or expulsion for other groups. Since the treatment accorded to each racial group has varied widely, we will discuss each group separately.

Indigenous Khmer, Suey, and Yeuh Minority Races

These minorities are the original inhabitants of that part of northeastern Thailand that now comprises the provinces of Surin, Buriram, and Si Sa Ket. In fact, the Khmer, Suey, and Yeuh account for 2.5 million of a total of 3.5 million inhabitants. For the most part, these subsistence-level peasant farmers suffer from economic poverty and low literacy levels. Possibly because they have posed no security or political threat, however, the Thai government has not instituted any special programs to alleviate their condition, other than carrying out routine development activities directed at eliminating rural poverty, in accordance with the objectives specified in the Five-Year National Economic and Social Development Plans.

The Hill Tribes

About twenty different hill tribes inhabit the mountainous northern borders of Thailand. Together, their numbers total some 500,000. Virtually ignored by the Thai government, until 1960 the hill tribes led a largely self-sufficient existence, employing slash-and-burn cultivation methods and growing opium as their main cash crop. Now, however, approximately half are under the supervision of the Public Welfare Department. Of these, 127,683 are identified as Thai nationals in official household registration records, and 52,931 have been granted ID cards.

Southern Thai-Muslims

Islam was introduced to southeast Asia in the twelfth century A.D., chiefly through Arab and Indian traders. It spread from Sumatra to the Malay Peninsula to what is now southern Thailand. At the present time there are about 2.5 million Muslims in Thailand, most of whom are located in the southern border provinces of Pattani, Yala, Narathiwat, and Satun, where 75 percent of the population are Muslims. The Muslim provinces of southern Thailand have had a long history of political violence, but the roots of the problem have not been racial. Both historically and culturally, the border provinces, have been associated more closely with their Malay neighbors than with the dominant Thai-Buddhist polity. Most southern Thai-Muslims speak Malay and follow Malay customs. A social gulf separates them from the Thai-Chinese and Thai-Buddhists. Separatist and irredentist movements underlie the political unrest. The roots of political conflict can be traced back to 1902, when the state of Pattani was formally incorporated with Thailand. Since that time, there have been a series of organized movements, both within and outside the country, whose aims have been to disrupt the workings of the government through violent means.

The Indians in Thailand

Indians (persons of Indian subcontinental origin or of Indian descent) are by far the smallest of all the minorities. It is rather hard to obtain a precise estimate of their numbers. According to the Indian Embassy, in 1981 there were approximately 20,000 Indian nationals resident in Thailand. A census figure released earlier by the Ministry of Interior gave the number of Sikhs and Hindus as 59,948. This figure does not, of course, include the number of Indian Muslims. By any estimate, however, the total number of Indians in Thailand should not exceed 70,000, or roughly 0.13 percent of the total population. The great majority tend to live in urban areas, especially Bangkok, and, as Zakir Hussain notes, their occupations tend to be ethnically typed. Sikhs are mostly in the textile trade, Tamils in precious stones and export-import businesses, whereas North Indians from Uttar Pradesh and other provinces tend to be lower down on the economic ladder and are engaged mainly as night watchmen, hawkers, and milkmen.

A common observation is that the Indians have tended to live as a "silent minority" within Thai society. Resisting efforts to be assimilated, the various Indian enclaves have nevertheless become integrated into the economic system. Recent research shows that isolationist tendencies are perhaps beginning to break down in third- and fourth-generation

Indians, especially with respect to intermarriage with non-Indians and occupational choices.

Unlike other minorities, Indians in Thailand have never presented a political problem or a threat to national security. But they are, perhaps, the least esteemed ethnic group in Thailand. The Indian stereotype is one of low economic, and particularly low social status, unassimilable, and miserly. A Thai saying goes, "On your way, if you come across a snake or an Indian, kill the Indian first."

The Chinese

Of all the ethnic minorities, the Chinese are decidedly the most important, in terms both of the size of their population and the role they have occupied in the economic system. It is difficult to attach a precise figure to the number of Chinese because of the different methods used to identify who "counts" as Chinese and who does not. The general rule-of-thumb is to say that approximately one-tenth of the population is Chinese, which yields an estimate of roughly 5.5 million. These are mainly resident in Bangkok and other urban areas of Thailand.

Chinese traders appeared on the scene as far back as the Sukhothai period, 700 years ago. The Thai ruling elite long enjoyed a mutually beneficial relationship with the Chinese merchants and traders. Chinese seamen sailed trading vessels for the Thai monarchs. Chinese performed the function of tax and revenue collectors for the Crown. Other concessionary rights were granted to the Chinese in return for guaranteed income for the ruling elite. In the early Bangkok period, the Thai rulers brought in Chinese as immigrant laborers, serving as a cheap and dependable source of labor for national reconstruction and development. Over time, many of the original laborers branched out into the small retail trades or became hawkers and middlemen. By the early twentieth century, commerce and industry had come under the control and operation of the Chinese.

Until the late 1930s, the Chinese in Thailand enjoyed freedom and privileges unknown to Chinese immigrants in other countries. Throughout the course of Thai history, upwardly mobile Chinese were ennobled and co-opted by the ruling elite, a process that secured their loyalty to the elite, as well as ensuring a smooth assimilation into Thai society.

The early twentieth century, however, witnessed changes in the Chinese community. As increasing numbers of Chinese women immigrated to Thailand, Chinese society and culture in its stricter form was reinstated. In addition, the Chinese in Thailand were stimulated and attracted by the strong tide of nationalistic sentiment that was sweeping China at about the same time. Chinese schools and Chinese papers proliferated and thrived. This also contributed to the strengthening of Chinese identity and culture in Thailand.

The Thai government took retaliatory steps immediately prior to World War II. A series of economic policies were initiated that were intended to restrict Chinese activities. Included in the economic nationalism policies was the stipulation that certain occupations be held exclusively for Thais. Industrial and manufacturing concerns were required to employ at least 75 percent Thai nationals on their workforce. State control was extended over certain industries such as tobacco, salt, and liquid fuel. Moreover, during the war years, six areas of the country were banned to aliens, which effectively forced Chinese living in these areas to abandon their livelihood, businesses, and property.

Government measures against the Chinese during the war years included close supervision of Chinese schools and newspapers. Many were forced to close down in this period. Recalcitrant Chinese leaders and teachers were arrested and deported.

The Yuen

Yuen is a term used for people whose ethnic origin is Vietnam. We can distinguish four waves of immigrants. The first group sought political refuge in Thailand about 200 years ago. The descendants of this group can still be found in certain districts of Bangkok. The second group consists mainly of Roman Catholics who fled religious persecution in the early twentieth century and settled in the easternmost province of Chantaburi. The third wave of Yuen arrived at the end of World War II.

None of the above groups presented a problem. The children of the Yuen who were born in Thailand were granted Thai citizenship, and became socially and culturally assimilated. There was no discrimination against them. The problem arises with the fourth wave of Yuen after World War II. This problem is taken up in the next section.

Prior to World War II, with the exception of the Chinese it cannot be said that the Thai government had any specific policies with regard to minority races. Minorities were not perceived as problematic, either with respect to the economy or with respect to politics, including national security. As long as they did not constitute a problem, they were largely ignored by governments whose primary orientation lay in the direction of maintaining law and order.

POST-WORLD WAR II DEVELOPMENTS

Prior to World War II, the Thai government, as noted above, paid scant attention to minorities, with the exception of its policies toward the Chinese. It was not until the 1960s and 1970s that considerations of national security and a related desire to foster national integration prompted the government to introduce a series of measures designed to address these problems.

The Hill Tribes

By 1960, the hill tribes had become a problem on three different counts: (1) with the passing of the 1960 Narcotics Act, the sale of opium was banned and cultivation of the opium poppy became illegal; (2) the hill tribes' traditional slash-and-burn cultivation had severely damaged the forests and watersheds, resulting in soil erosion and flash floods; and (3) the risk of subversion and infiltration by communist agitators posed a serious security risk, the more so because the hill tribes did not possess a sense of Thai national identity or loyalty to the Thai nation. The government's solution was to establish a National Hill Tribe Committee in 1965 with sole responsibility for hill tribe affairs. Headed by the Minister of Interior, the committee is comprised of representatives from twenty-nine military, police, and civilian government agencies. The secretariat and coordinating body is the Division of Hill Tribe Welfare, under the Department of Public Welfare. A second body, the Committee on the Administration of Hill Tribe Affairs, was assigned responsibility for the coordination, planning, operation, and evaluation of development and welfare activities. The thirteen-member committee is chaired by the Permanent Secretary of Interior, with the Director of the Hill Tribe Division acting as Secretary and ex officio member. At the provincial level, Provincial Tribal Committees headed by provincial governors were set up for purposes of coordination and cooperation with the central government committees. In 1982, the government appointed yet another body, the Executive Committee on Security Problems Related to Hill Tribes and Opium Cultivation, chaired by a Deputy Prime Minister, to propose policies on the hill tribes and prevention of opium production.

In terms of actual policies, prior to 1969 the government had established only broad policy guidelines with respect to development activities. In 1969, however, a hill tribe program was formally set up with two basic goals: to instill a sense of Thai national identity and loyalty to the Thai nation; and to introduce new cash crops and agricultural methods, as substitutes for poppy growing and the traditional slash-and-burn cultivation. The program consisted of five major projects: (1) establishment of tribal welfare settlements as a means of creating permanent agricultural communities for the seminomadic and widely scattered hill tribes; (2) creation of coordinating centers for development and welfare operations, with mobile teams working in major tribal villages in the areas of occupational promotion, education, and health services; (3) set up of a Tribal Research Center on the campus of Chiengmai University to conduct socioeconomic and anthropological studies on the main tribal groups in the northern provinces, to assemble a data base on population and land use, and to conduct evaluative research on government-sponsored development programs; (4) institution of a Hill Tribes Relations Program for the purpose of generating a sense of belonging and national identification of the part of the hill tribes; and (5) establishment of an occupational training program for the hill tribes.

Southern Thai-Muslims

Muslims in the southern border provinces have presented a long-term political problem. Economic and social problems in this region have exacerbated the political dimension, and have reinforced secessionist and irredentist tendencies. Violence has been endemic, reaching a peak in 1975. At the present time, three separate movements are prominent in the south. The oldest is the Barisan Nasional Pembasan Patani (BNPP), which was formed toward the end of World War II and which directs its activities primarily against the Thai-Buddhist settlements in Yala, Pattani, and Narathiwat. Unlike the monarchist-oriented BNPP, the Barisan Revolusion Nasional is firmly committed to Islamic Socialism and conducts its activities mainly in the form of urban guerrilla warfare. The most recent organization is the Patani United Liberation Organization (PULO). Created in 1968, PULO is by far the most organized and effective of the three organizations, with a far-flung net of activities. In 1975, PULO was able to mobilize over 70,000 Muslims in a month-long protest against the killing of a Thai-Malay by marines.

Since the 1960s, separatist movements in the south have allied themselves with elements of the Communist party of Malaya to undermine and disrupt development programs instituted by the Thai government. Their guerrilla activities have had an adverse effect on the economy. Lack of public safety in rural areas has resulted in productivity levels far below what they normally should be.

Religious factors not only provide the underpinning for irredentism, but they also directly account for an educational system that places southern Thai-Muslims at a disadvantage in the competition for jobs and careers, both in government and in the private sector. For religious reasons, Thai-Muslims have traditionally preferred to send their children to *pondoks*, or schools that emphasize the teaching of Islam and Islamic culture. In 1961, *pondoks* were allowed to voluntarily register themselves with the Ministry of Education, in return for which they were formally granted the status of private schools and were rendered eligible for certain categories of government funding. Seven years later, the government decreed that all registered *pondoks* cease Malay language instruction. The same decree put an end to the establishment of new *pondoks*. In 1971, registration with the Ministry of Education was made compulsory for all remaining *pondoks*. In this manner were the religious schools brought under the control of the Thai government and forced to comply with the Ministry of Education's curriculum requirements. Not surprisingly, the Ministry's set texts tended predominantly to emphasize Thai-Buddhist values, customs, and culture. The additional requirement that instruction be conducted entirely in the Thai language, to the exclusion of Malay, was consistent with the government's policies on assimilation and integration, but it naturally generated a great deal of hostility as well as resistance.

Many *pondoks* found the situation unacceptable. In 1971, the Ministry of Education reported that 109 of 464 *pondoks* had closed down because they could not tolerate what they viewed as encroachment on their freedom to give religious instruction. Since 1971, the government has followed a policy of granting budgetary allocations only to that part of the curriculum that does not involve religious instruction. The teaching of religion has been left alone, except that the government, for reasons of national security, has insisted on having a say in the selection of religious instructors. One controversy that was ongoing at the time of this writing stemmed from the government's decision to place Buddha images in all schools. This has generated vociferous protest on the part of southern Muslim leaders.

All in all, however, the political situation in the south is better now than it was in the 1970s. Government policies designed to ameliorate social and economic conditions and to strengthen integrative mechanisms seem to be taking some effect. Since 1978, the government has actively promoted Islam and Islamic activities through: Koran reading competitions; annual meetings of Provincial Islamic Committees; support for Thai-Muslims making the pilgrimage to Mecca; and provision of places of worship and preparation of food in accordance with Muslim dietary laws in state hospitals in the south. With respect to education, since the early 1970s the government has given a special quota to Thai-Muslims, which allows them direct entry to government training schools, to state colleges and universities, and to the Police Academy, without having to compete with non-Muslims in entrance examinations. Special state scholarships have been made available to Thai-Muslims. A Center for the Study of Islam has also been set up on the Pattani campus of the Prince of Songkhla University.

The Fourth and Fifth National Economic and Social Development Plans (1977–81 and 1982–86) have paid special attention to the development of the southern border provinces. Several large-scale infrastructure projects have been launched, including highway construction, rural electrification, construction of a multipurpose dam in Yala province, and construction of ports in Pattani and Songkla. As regards the agricultural sector, the government has instituted several measures designed to boost rubber production and has set up a marketing center for agricultural products in Songkla. In addition to those government agencies that are directly involved in program implementation, the government has created two special planning units: the Center for Development of the Southern Region, which is responsible for research, analysis, and plan specification within the framework of the National Development Plan; and the Committee for the Accelerated Development of the Southern Border Provinces, which is charged with short- and long-term planning for the southern border provinces.

With respect to administration, the government has followed a policy since 1977 of assigning Thai-Muslim officials, or officials who speak the local Malay dialect, to the southern border provinces. All officials posted to the southern border provinces must attend an orientation course conducted by the Center for Administrative Coordination of the Southern Border Provinces. In addition, the government has created two kinds of advisory committees to assist with the administration of the south. They are (1) the National Islamic Central Committee and Islamic Provincial Committees, which advise the Ministry of Interior and provincial administrations on matters relating to Islam; and (2) the Advisory Committee to the Executive Committee of the Center for Administrative Coordination of the Southern Border Provinces. The twenty-eight member Advisory Committee consists of prominent local citizens from the four border provinces. It gives advice, makes recommendations, and brings local problems to the government's attention.

The Chinese

The economic policies initiated in the prewar period against the Chinese ostensibly invoked nationality as a basis for differentiation. The Thai authorities were careful not to cite race as a factor. Thus, naturalized Chinese nationals were purportedly granted equal rights with ethnic Thais under the law. This made naturalization an attractive option to many Chinese, the more so because the communist victory in China had not led to the anticipated euphoria or satisfaction with the new state of affairs. Chinese, therefore, earnestly sought to become Thai citizens.

The process of assimilation was further hastened by two separate developments. First, Chinese entrepreneurs, realizing their own political vulnerability, sought alliance with military and political figures. Power and economic wealth entered into a new liaison—a mutually enhancing and beneficial relationship which set the pattern for military and business interlocking directorates, and which, indeed, remains the pattern to the present time. The second major development had to do with a growing awareness on the part of the Chinese that it was an unrealistic option for them to remain a separate entity apart from the larger Thai society. Assimilation would afford them greater advantages and opportunities in the ongoing process of change and development that was taking place in Thailand. Moreover, the instability and drastic social and political changes in China were disquieting to many overseas Chinese, who experienced a loss of positive identification with the events of change.

Nevertheless, the question of Chinese assimilation is complex and ought not to be generalized. On the one hand, assimilation appears to have taken place successfully. Younger Chinese are Thai citizens, bearing Thai names and speaking Thai, if not entirely accent-free. Politically, Chinese allegiance and loyalty to the Thai polity is stronger today than it has ever been. On the other hand, within the Bangkok metropolis, enclaves, sections, and quarters of ethnic Chinese are evident. The ubiquitous shophouses owned and operated by resident Chinese is a resilient feature of the Chinese way of life. Among Chinese business circles, Chinese language, practices, customs, and values are maintained, attesting to the lack of social and cultural assimilation of Chinese into Thai society.

At the present, the questions of who is Chinese and how Chinese ought to be treated are not issues, either political or social. This is not to say that ethnic stereotyping or social prejudice do not exist. They do, but they are neither conscious nor malicious in intent. Although one source of rural poverty has sometimes been attributed to Chinese middlemen and moneylenders, no racial tension has occurred as a result.

The Yuen

In the period immediately after World War II, during the time of intensive struggle between the French and the Viet Minh, a large number of Yuen sought, and were granted, political asylum in Thailand. From the beginning, these Yuen were classified as political refugees whose presence on Thai soil was to be treated as temporary. With repatriation as the ultimate goal, the Thai government has firmly upheld its policies toward the Yuen refugees. There are two basic policies. First, the refugees may not move out of their designated areas of residence in the northeast of Thailand without permission of the Thai authorities. Second, the refugees, including offspring born in Thailand, may not change their status to legalized alien or naturalized citizens.

Political events thwarted the Thais government's original intention to provide temporary shelter to the Yuen. Initially, Thailand, was able to negotiate the return of only a few thousand refugees, who elected to return to North Vietnam. With the entry of the United States into the Vietnam War, however, further repatriation became impossible.

The total number of Yuen refugees is not known for certain. Estimates vary from 40,000 to 60,000, not counting children born in Thailand in the last thirty-five years. With high fertility rates, there is reason to believe that the Yuen in this latter group total between 70,000 to 100,000.

Residence restrictions have presented no difficulties to the energetic, persevering, frugal, hard-working, and enterprising Yuen. In fact, such restrictions may have reinforced group cohesiveness. The Yuen have turned inward in their cooperation, and their mutual dependence and assistance have borne fruit, as evidenced by their phenomenal economic success.

As a cohesive and highly visible group, the Yuen have become targets for scrutiny and attack. Their initial political sympathy for the Viet Minh and their allegiance to Ho Chi Minh have made them a continual source of apprehension and discomfort to the Thai authorities, particularly after Thailand sided with the United States against North Vietnam. Their wealth and enormous economic success have also made them objects of envy, blackmail, and extortion by unscrupulous individuals, corrupt officials in many instances.

Anti-Yuen sentiments have periodically occurred in the form of race riots, involving vandalism and looting of Yuen property and assets. Thus, the Yuen refugees remain a problem primarily because they have not been allowed to assimilate. Vietnam is reluctant to take them back and many Yuen, particularly the younger ones, have no desire to return. Continuing problems between Vietnam and Thailand over the Vietnamese occupation of Kampuchea and the expansion of Vietnamese influence in Southeast Asia have made the Thai authorities, as well as the Thai people, distrustful and hostile toward the Yuen in the northeast—an issue that remains to be resolved.

Vietnamese, Kampuchean, and Laotian Refugees

A post-World War II phenomenon, the Indochinese refugees, constitutes a special problem for Thailand. Although the influx of these refugees both by land and by sea ought not be seen as a permanent problem in terms of race relations in Thailand, the Thai authorities are especially worried about problems of national security associated with these refugees. Large refugee camps near the Thai-Kampuchea border invite Vietnamese aggression and incursion into Thai territory. In addition, the Thai authorities are concerned about escapees as well as espionage activities and subversive infiltration by undesirable elements from the refugee camps.

The Thai government maintains the following position on the Indochinese refugees: (1) Thailand will not and cannot bear the cost of keeping refugees; (2) Thailand will not absorb the Indochinese refugees; (3)

Thailand will continue to allow refugee camps to operate under the financing and supervision of external organizations;[4] (4) the United States and other countries should shoulder the burden of permanently settling the refugees because they are in a better position economically and because the United States was largely responsible for the conflict in Indochina, which resulted in the present-day refugee situation.[5]

PUBLIC POLICIES AND LAWS

We have already indicated that public policies in regard to race have arisen largely in response to perceived national security and economic threat. In no instance that we can think of has a public policy been instituted to solve problems of social prejudice and discrimination. We have discussed the public policies that have been applied to the different minorities. It remains to examine specific laws and statutes that have been enacted to facilitate implementation of those policies.

In light of the specific policies mentioned earlier, it should come as no surprise that parliamentary acts, government decrees, and other legislation fall into three broad categories: (1) laws concerning citizenship status, which in turn affect voting rights, ownership of land, and the right to employment; (2) laws and ministerial orders concerning curricula and instruction in schools; and (3) special rights for Muslims.

According to Article 7 of the Nationality Act of 1965, a person acquires Thai nationality at birth if any of the following conditions are met:

1. The person was born of a Thai father, in or outside the Kingdom of Thailand.
2. The person was born of a Thai mother outside the Kingdom of Thailand, but of an unknown father or one with no nationality.
3. The person was born in Thailand.

Article 10 of the same act stipulates that an alien who possesses all of the following qualifications may apply for Thai nationality:

1. Has come of age according to Thai law and the laws of the country of which s/he is a national.
2. Is of upright behavior.
3. Has a recognized profession.
4. Has been resident in the Kingdom of Thailand for no less than five years up until the time of application.
5. Has knowledge of the Thai language as stipulated in ministerial regulations.

Final determination is the prerogative of the Minister of Interior, subject to approval by His Majesty the King. It should be noted that the 1965

Nationality Act differs from the 1952 act in one important respect: alien women who marry Thai men no longer acquire Thai nationality automatically.

In 1972, security considerations led to a further tightening of the restrictions on acquisition of Thai nationality at birth. Revolutionary Decree No. 337 states that, "in the interest of national security,"

Thai nationality be rescinded for persons born in the Kingdom of Thailand of alien fathers, or of alien mothers and with no legal father; and whose father or mother at the time of birth

1. was resident in the Kingdom of Thailand by special permission;
2. was a temporary resident of the Kingdom of Thailand; or
3. had entered the Kingdom of Thailand in contravention of immigration laws.

This decree has direct application to the refugee population, for, in effect, children of refugees are automatically denied Thai nationality.

Thai nationals of alien fathers are not entitled to vote or to stand for election, unless they satisfy certain requirements. Article 18 of the Electoral Act of 1979 states that Thai nationals of alien fathers may vote only if they possess one of the following qualifications:

1. Possess at least a *mathayom 6* (Grade 10) or equivalent level of education, in accordance with Ministry of Education curriculum requirements.
2. Are in the military or have served in the military.
3. Are civil servants or local government employees, or were once civil servants or local government employees holding a tenured position or receiving a regular salary for a period of no less than five years.
4. Are, or have been, members of the national legislature, or provincial or local government councils, or village headmen.
5. Are paying or have paid personal income tax, household and land taxes, and local taxes for a consecutive period of no less than five years.

Article 19 of the same act stipulates that Thai nationals of alien fathers may stand for election only if they have certain educational attainments, which in this case means possession of at least a *mathayom 6* (Grade 10) certificate in accordance with Ministry of Education regulations.

Land tenure may become problematic for non-Thai nationals. The Land Act of 1954 states that aliens "may acquire land for residential, commercial, industrial, agricultural, burial, public charity, or religious purposes, in accordance with ministerial rules and regulations, and as authorized by the Minister of Interior" (Article 86), but it sets severe restrictions on the amount of land that may be held. For example, each family is allowed no more than 1 *rai* (0.40 acres) of land for residential purposes, and no more than 10 *rai* (4 acres) of land for agricultural or industrial purposes.

The most onerous restriction on aliens is no doubt the restriction on gainful employment. The Restriction on the Employment of Aliens Act of 1979 states categorically that the aliens may not engage in the following occupations: labor work; agriculture, animal husbandry, or forestry, unless of a specialized nature; carpentry; construction; bricklaying; driver of motorized and nonmotorized vehicles, except international pilots; sales; auditing and accounting; gem stone cutting; hairdressing or beautician; cloth-weaving; local handicrafts; goldsmithing and silversmithing; shoemaking; umbrella-making; handmade silk products; mattresses and quilted goods; agents or representatives, except for international business agents and representatives; engineering work, except for work requiring specialized skills; architectural work; pottery; dressmaking and tailoring; printing; tour guides; hawkers; secretarial work; or provision of legal services.

The list is comprehensive. It is possible to obtain dispensations, but these are generally reserved for work of a specialized nature. The real impact of restriction on employment for aliens is felt at the lower end of the economic scale. Not only are refugees, for example, denied citizenship, but they are also denied the right to work.

Moreover, aliens may not become government officials at either national, provincial, or local levels. Since the Thai bureaucracy is vast, encompassing many spheres of activity normally allotted to the private sector in more developed countries (universities and state enterprises are but two examples), prohibition of entry into the civil service represents a significant loss of opportunity. Entry into the armed forces or the police is even more restricted. A prospective applicant must not only be born a Thai citizen, but also his or her parents must both be Thai nationals.

The second major type of enactments has to do with education policies. These have primarily taken the form of ministerial orders and have been directed at preventing the use of non-Thai languages as the medium of instruction, and the hiring of non-Thai teachers. For example, no more than two hours of instruction a day may be given in a foreign language in any school, private or public. All teaching staff must satisfy Thai language requirements and must have obtained at least a Grade 6 certificate from the Thai Ministry of Education.

The third major category of laws and legislation concerns the Thai-Muslims. The most important of these is the 1946 Act on the Application of Islamic Laws in the Four Southern Border Provinces. The act provides Muslims in these provinces with the right to opt for the application of Islamic law concerning inheritance and family affairs, in place of Sections

Five and Six of the Civil and Commercial Code. The Act also provides for the appointment of two Islamic judges, known as *Dato Yuthitham,* to provincial courts. Their judgment on a case is final.

SUMMARY AND CONCLUSIONS

Race relations in Thailand are inextricably linked to national origins and ethnoreligious factors. In social terms, the history of race relations can be generally characterized as one of acceptance, accommodation, and cooperation. Traditionally, there have been few social barriers to assimilation. The barriers that exist are political and represent a deliberate intervention by government to prevent certain minorities who entered the country in the post-World War II period from becoming legal resident aliens or naturalized citizens. The reasons for this have been based primarily on economic and national security grounds. There is little indication that the Thai government is about to change its stance, and on the whole, it has had the public's support in this matter.

NOTES

1. The authors wish to make explicit that the term "race" as it is used in this chapter denotes the social concept of race, as distinct from biological race.

2. Duane Lockard, "Race Policy," in F. I. Greenstein and N. W. Polsby, eds., *Handbook of Political Science, Volume 6: Policies and Policymaking* (Reading, Mass.: Addison-Wesley, 1975), p. 245.

3. Some Thai scholars disagree with this characterization, claiming that to depict Thailand as basically a homogeneous society is to project the "official image." These scholars argue that Thailand is a rather heterogeneous society where different ethnic groups live together. See, for example, William G. Skinner, *Chinese Society in Thailand* (Ithaca, N. Y.: Cornell University Press, 1957); Boonsanong Punyodyana, *Chinese-Thai Differential Assimilation in Bangkok: An Exploratory Study* (Ithaca, N. Y.: Cornell University Press, 1977); Peter A. Poole, *The Vietnamese in Thailand: A Historical Perspective* (Ithaca, N. Y.: Cornell University Press, 1970). We agree that there is something to be said for this perspective, that cultural heterogeneity can be discerned. Nevertheless, Thailand does not have political division based on race, unlike, for example, the situation in neighboring Burma or Malaysia.

4. The Thai authorities, in particular the military, are directly responsible for determining the location of these camps, for maintaining peace and order in the camps, and for overseeing that the camps constitute no threat or problem to Thai national security. The assistance and care provided for refugees have aroused resentment and envy in local Thai villagers, who perceive their living standards to be inferior to those of the refugees.

5. There is yet another minority we have not mentioned. These are the illegal migrant laborers from Burma who work in the northern and western border provinces, particularly in the mines, who provide a welcome source of cheap

and industrious labor. The outcry from the press, however, has centered on job competition and job scarcity facing Thai nationals. In spite of anti-alien public sentiment, there is not enough political will to keep out alien laborers. This issue will remain unsolved as long as official policy on alien laborers remains unclear and unacceptable to officials working in the border areas.

BIBLIOGRAPHY

English Language Publications

Hussain, Zakir. "The Silent Minority: Indians in Thailand." Bangkok: Social Research Institute, Chulalongkorn University, 1982.

Poole, Peter, A. "Thailand's Vietnamese Minority." *Asian Survey* 7, No. 12 (December 1967): 886–95.

Royal Thai Government, Department of Public Welfare, Ministry of Interior. *Hill Tribes and Welfare in Thailand.* Bangkok: 1971.

Skinner, G. William. *Chinese Society in Thailand: An Analytical History.* Ithaca, N.Y.: Cornell University Press, 1957.

———. *Leadership and Power in the Chinese Community in Thailand.* Ithaca, N. Y.: Cornell University Press, 1958.

Thomas, M. Ladd. *Political Violence in the Muslim Provinces of Southern Thailand.* University of Singapore: Institute of Southeast Asian Studies, Occasional Paper No. 28, 1975.

———. "Some Observations on Interaction of Local Authority and Development Programs in the Four Muslim Provinces of Thailand." Northern Illinois University: Center for Southeast Asian Studies, 1971.

Thai Language Publications

Buruspat, Kajadpai, ed. *The Chinese in Thailand.* Bangkok: Phrae Pitaya Press, 1974.

———. "The Problem of Minority Groups and National Security." *National Education Journal* 18, No. 6 (August-September 1983): 3–20.

Dhiravekin, Likit, ed. *Minorities in Thailand.* Bangkok: Prae Pitaya Press, 1978.

Pitsuwan, Surin. "Political Conditions Leading to Violation of Human Rights in the Southern Border Provinces." *Thammasat University Journal* 12, No. 3 (September 1983): 108–28.

Prasertsri, Supot. "Education and Culture of Southern I-San." *National Education Journal* 18, No. 6 (August-September 1983): 51–63.

Royal Thai Government, Ministry of Foreign Affairs. *Thai Muslims.* Bangkok: 1978.

———, National Economic and Social Development Board, Office of the Prime Minister. *Fifth National Economic and Social Development Plan, 1982–1986.*

———. *Royal Gazette* 69, Section 10 (February 12, 1952), "The Citizenship Act of 1952," 106.

———. *Royal Gazette* 71, Section 78, Special Issue (November 30, 1954), "The Land Act of 1954," 50–57.

————. *Royal Gazette* 82, Section 62, Special Issue (August 4, 1965), "The Citizenship Act of 1965," 2–6.

————. *Royal Gazette* 89, Section 190, Special Issue (December 13, 1972), "Revolutionary Decree No. 337," 206–8.

————. *Royal Gazette* 96, Section 12, Special Issue (February 3, 1979), "The Electoral Law of 1979," 7–8.

————. *Royal Gazette* 98, Section 150, Special Issue (September 14, 1981), "Ministry of Education Regulations Regarding Minimum Standards for Private Schools in Southern Thailand," 35–39.

Suthasan, Arong. "Analysis of Concepts Relating to Minority Groups." *National Education Journal* 18, No. 6 (August-September 1983): 21–31.

TRINIDAD

Stephen D. Glazier

One can stand on any street corner in Port of Spain (Trinidad's capital city) and literally watch the world go by. Trinidad is among the most cosmopolitan of Caribbean nation-states, with peoples of all continents represented and almost every possible racial admixture present. It has been called a microcosm of the world's races.

Trinidad society is based on the complex interaction of thirteen ethnic groups, of which two predominate: blacks—descendants of African slaves as well as some recent migrants from Africa and the United States—and Indians—descendants of indentured laborers imported from India between 1845 and 1917. People of Indian descent are called East Indians in order to distinguish them from West Indians.

There are many separate groups of whites. The largest of these groups consists of foreign-born whites (mostly Europeans). In 1976, only 2,000 U.S. citizens were resident on the islands; the number of Americans has remained stable. The bulk of European whites are of British origin (with Germans, Swiss, and Italians also present). In addition, there are local whites, sometimes known as French Creoles (who live predominantly in the north of the island), and Portuguese (who number between 4,000 and 5,000 and are comparatively wealthy as a group), Jews, and Middle Easterners who are lumped together and called "Syrians." Spanish-speaking Venezuelans are included in the white group, along with a small number of Cubans and Dominicanos.

Trinidadians distinguish between three additional groups: (1) people of mixed blood called "Coloureds," or disparagingly, "Douglas" (from the Hindi word meaning bastard), the word "Douglas" usually reserved for mixed East Indian and black children; (2) a sizable group of Chinese who have remained ethnically separate; and (3) about 200 Amerindians (Trinidadians classify all Amerindians—whether of Arawak or Carib descent—as "Caribs"). The Amerindian population of Trinidad is racially mixed. Amerindian features are not readily discernible; for many, one would not know that they were Indian unless they were to reveal it themselves. Amerindians are concentrated in the central region around Arima.

In 1960, blacks constituted about 42 percent of the population and East Indians about 40 percent. In recent years, the East Indian birthrate has exceeded that of the blacks, and it is estimated that in the 1990 census East Indians will be the majority group. Ramesh Deosaran states that in 1970 the Indian population exceeded the African population in Trinidad (excluding Tobago) by 11,000.[1] Between 1959 and 1970, the percentage of the black population actually decreased. According to the 1970 census, whites constitute slightly less than 2 percent of the population; Coloureds (peoples of mixed blood) about 15 percent; and Chinese less than 1 percent. It is estimated that the next census will indicate a higher "Coloured" or mixed population.

Of these groups, Creoles are at the pinnacle of the social structure, with only the Chinese (of the various non-Creole groups) enjoying a comparable status. The Chinese, who occupy a very special position, are mainly urban and, for the most part, wealthy.

THE ISLANDS

The nation-state of Trinidad and Tobago is composed of two main islands some sixteen miles apart. They are the southernmost islands of the Lesser Antilles chain in the Caribbean, separated from mainland Venezuela by only seven miles and the Gulf of Paria. Of the two islands, Trinidad is the largest (1,864 square miles) as well as the most ethnically diverse. The bulk of the population of Tobago is black, although there has been considerable movement of various nonblack ethnic groups from Trinidad to Tobago in recent years (notably East Indians and Chinese).

The population of Trinidad and Tobago was estimated at 1,154,000 in 1980. The last official census was taken in 1970 when the total population was found to be 940,716. The next official census will be in 1990. Emigration is a big factor in estimating Trinidad's population. Trinidadians who leave the island do not tend to return. For example, it is estimated that 30 percent to 40 percent of Trinidadians who engage in studies abroad do not ever return to the islands.

The population is not evenly distributed over the land area. It is concentrated almost exclusively in a continuous urban belt extending eastward of Port of Spain to Tunapuna, westward to Chaguaramas, and northward into the Northern Range. About one-third of the population lives within ten miles of Port of Spain. About 56 percent of the population lives in the two cities of Port of Spain and San Fernando. The overall density of population is 510 per square mile, the sixteenth highest in the world.

A RACIAL CONTEXT

As anthropologist Franz Boas pointed out in *Race, Language and Culture*, race, ethnicity, culture, and language are often confused, but they are not the same.[2] More recently, anthropologists, especially Fredrik Barth, have emphasized that ethnic groups are not to be considered as natural entities—as "races" or anything of the sort—but as sociocultural creations: group identities established and maintained in particular social arenas by people with definable political and economic needs.[3]

In his study of politics and race in Guyana, E. Greene emphasizes the "social conception of race" in the Caribbean.[4] Racial categories include (but also go beyond) strict biological criteria. In Trinidad, for example, the official census has "allowed" respondents to categorize themselves into "White, East Indian, Mixed, Syrian, Lebanese, or Chinese" for racial classification. However, it has been noted that the peoples of Trinidad classify themselves much differently than would a physical anthropologist. In his research, Greene was most concerned with what people think the word "race" means when they encounter it in their daily lives and suggests that it may be best to think of "race" in terms of "a group of people who are felt to be similar in their essential nature," not a group of people who look similar. This sociopsychological measure of race has been used successfully by other researchers in the region: most notably, the late Vera Rubin[5] and David Lowenthal[6] in his discussions on the different ways in which "race" and "ethnicity" are used by West Indians.

Jan Knippers Black contends that party slogans, national mottoes, and middle and upper class ideology to the contrary, Trinidadians are neither racially nor culturally a unified people.[7] In general, he notes, interethnic relations have been characterized by want of knowledge and lack of communication. My own studies, however, reveal considerable communication between various island groups.[8]

According to Black, the greatest distinction in Trinidadian society is between and among Creoles and non-Creoles. The social system works to the advantage of light-skinned Creoles and to the disadvantage of darker-skinned Creoles and East Indians through education, job opportunities, wealth distribution, values, and patterns of interaction. Creoles, regardless of their relative whiteness, feel superior to non-Creoles. Chinese, East Indians, Portuguese, Middle Easterners (Syrians), Jews, and Spanish-speaking Latin Americans are classified as non-Creoles, although some Portuguese may be considered Creoles if they are married to Creoles or possess other Creole traits. People of mixed blood may be classified as Creole or non-Creole depending on their family or reference group.

Relationships between race, color, class, and social and economic mobility in Trinidad have been much studied.[9] In a study of racial discrimination in the private sector, Acton Camejo found substantial relationships between race, color, and elite status within private business organizations and concluded that "the evidence clearly suggests that the 'whiter' the person the less formal qualifications were demanded of him being hired into top or middle management positions in private business organizations."[10]

There have been few studies of income distribution among the major racial grouips. Francis Henry took a random sample of 2,744 households and found that 43 percent of Indians, 32 percent of Africans, and only 8 percent of whites were living below the poverty line.[11] Jack Harewood's study, based on 1960 census figures, demonstrates a strong correspondence between median household monthly income and race: white = over $500; mixed = $112; African = $104; and Indian = $77.[12] In all these studies, it is apparent that wages were lower in rural than urban areas. East Indians were primarily rural dwellers.[13] As more East Indians have moved into urban and suburban areas, however, their incomes have gone up in relation to those of blacks. The economic status of whites vis-à-vis the rest of the population has remained much the same.

Physical factors associated with the various ethnic groups on Trinidad have resulted in social categorizations of a racial or quasi-racial character; especially with regard to skin color, facial features, hair characteristics, and, to a lesser extent, body type. The importance of these factors varies according to social class. For the upper classes, especially Creoles, they are of extreme importance. Light skin and staight hair are the ideal. They are less so for the lower classes. As in the United States, color is the most significant criterion for Creoles, probably followed by hair type and then facial features. Body type is not seen as particularly relevant.

Class, especially wealth, can alter one's racial category. A popular saying among Trinidadians is "If you rich you white, if you poor you black." Lloyd Braithwaite, in his classic study, discusses the difference between being white and being "Trinidad white" (that is, "passing" for white in Trinidad).[14]

Color is not as much a problem for French Creoles who take their whiteness for granted. For many Creoles, color is not as important as ancestry, and many shun contact with white Europeans and Americans because they may not be of "pure" ancestry. Both Creoles and Coloureds shun association with those whom they feel are darker than they.

There is a notion among some Creoles and Coloureds that certain values and personality traits such as laziness, poverty, promiscuity, and low IQ are directly related to skin color.

Language

The official language of Trinidad and Tobago is English. There are various dialects, often related to the social class of the speaker. Linguists have noted the persistence of French patois and Spanish patois, as well as a standard Spanish dialect.[15] Both French and Spanish patois have been greatly influenced by Trinidadian English with respect to vocabulary, intonation, and tempo of speech. Older East Indians speak numerous Indian languages, particularly Hindustani (also called *Desi Bhasa*). Some East Indians attempt to maintain their language in the home but are not always successful. Some scholars have suggested that Indian lanugages may die out in Trinidad.[16] The Chinese, to the contrary, have succeeded in maintaining their own language in the home, and many Chinese children are bilingual. Language is a political issue in Trinidad and Tobago, and many East Indians see attempts to establish literacy standards for voting as prejudicial.

Religion

Christianity is the majority religion of Trinidad and Tobago. Sixty-three percent of the population identify themselves as Christians. Of these, the majority are Roman Catholic (33 percent) or Anglican (18 percent). There are some problems with these figures, however, inasmuch as Trinidadians are religious pluralists.[17] They attend a variety of religious services, while officially reporting themselves as adherents to Catholicism or Anglicanism. Very few identify themselves as members of African-derived sects such as Shango or Rada, but Shango and Rada ceremonies are well attended. Of the two, Shango has a much larger following. Also of note is the growth of Pentecostalism and the persistence of obeah. The Trinidad Constitution guarantees freedom of religion, and there are sixteen recognized (government-sanctioned) religious groups on the island. Of Trinidadians who do not identify themselves as Christian, 25 percent identify themselves as Hindu, 6 percent as Muslim, and 6 percent as Other.

Researchers have emphasized the dominance of Christianity, if not in content, at least in form. Of special note are various syncretisms of Christianity and African tribal religions such as the Spiritual Baptists.[18]

In many respects, Hinduism and Islam have come to resemble Christianity on Trinidad. Nevertheless, Hinduism is still important to East Indians, even among those East Indians who profess to be Christians. Apart from social identification, religious affiliation in Trinidad is widely recognized as playing a significant role in intergroup and intragroup relations.[19]

BACKGROUNDS OF MAJOR ETHNIC GROUPS

Blacks

The first black slaves in Trinidad were brought from the Dutch in the early seventeenth century. Records indicate that 400 slaves were purchased sometime before 1610.

Carlos III of Spain was greatly interested in populating Trinidad, which had been subject to prior neglect. In 1783, he issued a royal proclamation (or *Cedula*) for the colonization of the island. By its terms, a home and grants of land were offered to "all foreigners, the subjects of powers and nations in alliance with me," as long as they were Roman Catholics. Attracted by large areas of uncultivated land in Trinidad, many from Grenada, Guadeloupe, Martinique, and St. Lucia flocked to the island. This included whites (who were to be allocated thirty-two acres of land and sixteen acres for each slave) and free men of color (who were to be given sixteen acres for themselves and sixteen acres for each slave).

To give some idea of the volume of the slave traffic, when the *Cedula* was proclaimed in 1783, the population of Trinidad was 2,763, of which 126 were whites, 295 free people of color, 2,032 Amerindians, and 310 African slaves. Fourteen years later, the census indicates a population of 17,718, made up of 2,151 whites, 4,476 free people of color, 1,082 Amerindians, and 10,009 African slaves. Between 1783 and 1831, over 155,000 black slaves were brought to Trinidad to work on the plantations.

East Indians

A total of about 143,000 indentured laborers were brought from India between 1845 and 1917, mainly from northern India. Because they embarked from Calcutta, they were known as "Kalkatiyas" to distinguish them from those who migrated from the port of Madras in the south and were referred to as "Madrasis." One out of every six immigrants was a Muslim, the remainder being Hindu. In Trinidad, the ratio of Hindus to Muslims has decreased. Today, about one in four is a Muslim.

The ship *Fatel Rozack* brought the first 225 indentured Indian migrants to Port of Spain harbor on May 3, 1845. They came under contract and were allocated, usually in small groups, to the estates or plantations where they were required to work for a stipulated number of years after which they were given the choice of "free" return passage to India, reindenture, or, as time went on, small parcels of land to farm. In Trinidad, complicated rules and ordinances stipulated conditions of service. For example, some of the regulations dealt with the needs of plantation laborers, including food, shelter, wages and hours of work, and medical care. As

Donald Wood has pointed out, a majority of these regulations served the interest of the planters and not East Indian laborers.[20]

Joseph Nevadomsky notes that between 1845 and 1917 (when the indenture system was abolished), East Indians necessarily had to accommodate their previous values and behaviors to the requirements of the plantation system. Sugar dictated the social structure. Because Indian laborers were treated as an undifferentiated group and held the same position in relation to the means of production, equalitarian norms replaced caste norms. In addition, during the first twenty-five years of indenture, the lopsided three to one ratio of men to women resulted in some family instability. Immigrants entered into common law unions, intercaste marriage and cohabitation were unavoidable, and the authority of the East Indian male was undermined.

The majority of Indians who finished their indenture reestablished themselves in villages adjacent to the estates to which they had been indentured, on land leased to them by the estate or by the government. They engaged in wet rice production, sugarcane production, vegetable farming, and petty trading. Over several generations, many East Indians moved into urban areas and established themselves in the professions.

In the period just after World War I, the vast majority of East Indians in Trinidad were isolated from much of what was going on in the rest of the society. However, rural villages were not static, closed entities.[21] Linkages existed between villages and government agencies. There were also opportunities in shopkeeping and trade as well as teaching (usually within the Presbyterian Church system). A number of sociologists and historians have argued that during the postindenture period, the traditional Indian joint family system was reinstituted. Barton Schwartz, on the other hand, has argued that this would have been impossible owing to inadequate generational time, the presence of dicordant cultural factors, and the lack of economic cohesiveness brought on by increasing social mobility.[22] As Nevadomsky contends, the evidence is inconclusive. The information is simply not available to do more than hazard some rough approximations of what Indian social organization and culture were like during this period.

Generally, ethnographic studies of rural East Indians have focused on their alleged cultural and structural conservatism. Morton Klass, Morris Freilich, Robert J. Smith, and Yogendra K. Malik are examples of this focus.[23] For example, Klass claims that the community of "Amity" is a faithful reproduction of a generalized North Indian culture. He concludes that structurally and culturally "Amity" is an "Indian" rather than a "West Indian" village.[24] Malik's study of East Indian politics and elites postulates that the failures of East Indian politicians to develop a strong, cohesive political organization are linked directly to Indian retentions. Among dissenting voices are those of Daniel J. Crowley, Arthur and Juanita Niehoff, and Barton Schwartz.[25] The Niehoffs and Schwartz present considerable data indicating that the caste system was virtually wiped out in the process of accommodation to Trinidad society.

After World War II, universal suffrage and the demise of the colonial era thrust East Indians into the political arena, and, as Selwyn Ryan notes, signaled Indian political integration to the wider society on a massive scale.[26] Through formal education and occupational change, rural East Indians are clearly gaining in social and economic mobility.

Creole

White, native-born, Trinidad elites refer to one another as Creoles. Sometimes they are called "white Creoles," and at other times, French Creoles (although many cannot claim French ancestry). As Bridget Brereton points out, Creole is a word of many meanings. In the late nineteenth century,

a French Creole was a person of European descent, could be French, but also Spanish, Irish, English or Corsican, and even German, who was born on the island and who considered himself, and was considered by others, to be a member of the French Creole group. He might have ancestors of African descent, but in order to be accepted as a member of this group, he would have to be regarded as "pure white" descent.[27]

Sometimes people not actually born on Trinidad but possessing other necessary criteria were "adopted" as French Creoles. This pretty much describes the meaning of the term today, but in recent years it has become much more difficult to be "adopted" into Creole society.

Trinidad elites think in terms of extended families. This is so much the case that there is a question as to whether or not Creoles consider individual identity outside the family group. Many Creole families have been on Trinidad since the late 1700s. In 1783, the Spanish governor of Trinidad opened the island to settlers from other Catholic islands. Planters from Martinique, Guadeloupe, and Haiti took advantage of this opportunity and were granted considerable landholdings—much of which remains intact. Landholdings are important economically because Trinidadian Creoles do not work for wages, but derive most of their incomes from rents, royalties, and capital ventures. Four families continue to operate family plantations—although they are very much removed from day-to-day activities and decision making. All maintain their ancestral homes, although most do not actually live there. One prominent family has considered opening up its ancestral home as a museum.

Communication patterns follow what linguist Basil Bernstein would label a "restricted code."[28] Conversations—even among equals—are highly formalized. Most conversations consist entirely of a long series of perfunctory questions to which only a limited number of responses could be deemed appropriate. Most of these questions are the equivalent of "How are you?" in American culture. But in contrast to American culture, there are more standard questions and more standard responses. It can take up to ten minutes to get to the business at hand—if one ever does get down to business. In my observations, over half of all conversations terminate before anything of substance is ever said.

As Maurice Bloch has pointed out, ritual—whether in language, song, or movement—represents an increasing restriction of communication, an elimination or narrowing of choice. He contends that "formalized language rules out the possibility of contradiction."[29] For Trinidadian Creoles, who are already at the pinnacle of power, it is seen as advantageous to avoid contradiction and possible controversy.

All Creoles dress conservatively. There is little variation especially for the men whom the "Creole uniform" is a long-sleeved, white, loosely cut shirt, dark pants, and black dress shoes. A coat and tie may be worn on formal occasions, and a tuxedo on very formal occasions.

Male Creole dress contrasts with that of the middle classes who tend to wear "shirt-jacks" with long tails left outside over the trousers. Most government officials—customs officers and so on—wear matching shirt jack and shorts in khaki or brown. These, it should be added, are a relatively neat adaptation to the tropics, while a long-sleeved cotton shirt is not. It makes little difference to Creoles, however, since Creoles turn their air conditioners to the highest setting.

Female dress is also conservative, plain, and a bit dowdy. Once or twice a year, Creole females purchase fancy dress gowns to attend various charity balls and coming out parties. These are usually originals from Paris, New York, or London. Many husbands allow their wives to travel to the United States to buy a gown. Once worn, these formal dresses are never worn again—at least not on Trinidad. Like Creole males, Creole women's clothes differentiate them from the rest of the population. For must of the year, they do not dress as stylishly as the rest of the female population, but once or twice each year they are visibly better dressed.

Creole elites see themselves as surrounded by lesser beings. They also believe, as does the rest of the Trinidadian population, that "you are who you are seen with"; therefore, the possibility of pollution exists everywhere. Elites carefully regulate their environment and avoid situations (such as shopping) when one could come into contact with inferiors. For this reason, they spend a great deal of time indoors.

Finally, Trinidadian Creoles have very clear genealogies and maintain that other Trinidadians have very "fuzzy" genealogies. It is not so much that non-Creoles might have African or Indian blood in their backgrounds—because this is true for some Creole families also—but that

Creoles have their genealogies all worked out and non-Creoles do not. Like most people, elites fudge their genealogies, but unlike nonelites, Trinidadian Creoles try to make their lines of descent consistent. Children are encouraged to memorize genealogies, and most children can recite their family trees.

Chinese

The Chinese occupy an anomalous position in the Trinidadian social structure.[30] In some contexts, they are considered honorary whites. In other contexts, they are considered East Indians. The ambiguous position of Chinese has given rise to complex interaction rituals. For example, shopping in a Chinese grocery store is an uncomfortable experience for most Trinidadians, but it is also something that most Trinidadians must do several times a week. Certain rules are followed in order to make this experience more predictable, and therefore more comfortable, for all concerned: (1) one never addresses a Chinese grocer unless the grocer is standing behind the checkout counter; (2) one always addresses a Chinese grocer who is standing behind the checkout counter— even if nothing is to be purchased; and (3) when a grocer is not behind the counter, one should never approach him directly but should stand silently next to the counter until the grocer comes to help. These rules do not apply in black-owned or East Indian-owned stores, but must be observed in all Chinese establishments.

The Chinese are mostly urban; more than one-third reside in Port of Spain. They are not localized as a group. There is no Chinatown in either of the two major cities, partly because Chinese shops are so located that they are not in competition with other Chinese shops. Most Chinese live above or adjacent to their businesses. They are major distributors for dry goods, manufactured items, and food, are among the best educated members of the society, and share many Creole values. Before the 1949 revolution in China, children were sent to their homeland for higher education. Now, their children are sent to North America or Europe. Marriages are ideally endogamous, but some parents permit marriage with educated, white European expatriates and Americans.

RELEVANT PUBLIC POLICY AND THE LAW

In the 1970s, the government appointed a Commission of Enquiry into Racial and Colour Discrimination in the Private Sector. The commission found that the lighter an applicant's skin, the better his or her chances of getting employment in a bank in Trinidad. It was found that there was not as much discrimination in the Central (government) Bank, but that East Indians were underrepresented. The commission recommended legislation "to make discrimination in employment on the grounds of race or color an offense" and suggested that a Race Relations Board be established. To date, neither recommendation has been implemented by the government.

Leonard Glick contends that compared to nations such as Nigeria, Malaysia, India, and Pakistan, the nations of the Caribbean have experienced relatively little in the way of serious and sustained ethnic conflict.[31] He cites the Black Power revolt of 1970 in Trinidad as the only case in which ethnic differences have played a central role in political events.

SUMMARY AND CONCLUSIONS

As noted, the Trinidadian social structure is based on the complex interaction of thirteen separate ethnic groups (depending on how one wishes to classify "ethnic group"). Because Trinidad is a relatively small place, these groups have had extensive contact with one another and are much more interdependent than ethnic groups in North America, Europe, and Asia. Therefore, it is impossible for scholars to deal with ethnic groups in Trinidad as they have been dealt with in other places. In the nation-states of the Caribbean, ethnic and/or racial groups are not—and have never been—totally isolated from one another.

Race and politics in Trinidad have always been very much intertwined. For example, during the visit of the British-appointed commission under Major E.F.L. Wood in 1921, one can see much evidence of many issues faced in contemporary Trinidadian politics. Africans and French Creoles told members of the Wood Commission that they favored a directly representative government. The East Indian community, on the other hand, was very much divided. East Indians wanted proportional representation, although they differed as to how such representation was to be achieved. There have been a number of excellent studies of race and politics in Trinidad, notably, those of Selwyn D. Ryan, James Millette, and Yogendra K. Malik.[32] Unfortunately, there have been fewer recent studies of comparable quality. As noted previously, proposals for an English language test for screening voters have met with heavy resistance from East Indians.

Differences separating East Indians and blacks in Trinidad run deep; they have to do not only with cultural practices, but also with personality traits and fundamental attitudes and values. Paradoxically, they are rooted in common historical experiences. Since the beginning of the indenture system, blacks have perceived East Indians as a people who deserved scorn because they were willing to play the role of landless laborers, little better than slaves in the eyes of most blacks. After emancipation, blacks rejected estate labor. To blacks, East Indians seemed to willingly accept the most abject social status in the Caribbean. East Indians, on the other hand, do not see things that way. They do not seek approval from blacks or whites, but see themselves as proud heirs to one of the world's oldest and most complex civilizations.

There are two long-standing debates in the study of Trinidadian social structure: (1) the debate as to whether or not race and color are truly an issue on the island, and (2) the debate as to whether Trinidadian social structure is essentially consensualist or pluralist.

As a group, social scientists seem to have come to a negative conclusion regarding Caribbean race relations. Coleman Romalis notes that most sociological literature stresses the fragmented nature of Caribbean nation-states: racial and ethnic divisions that are deeply entrenched in the central economic and political institutions in the region.[33] According to Romalis, Guyana, Trinidad, and Jamaica are riven by ethnic divisions, and in national and regional terms such fissures act as actual barriers to political coherence and social solidarity.

Caribbean peoples themselves do not agree, and many believe their own promotional and tourist literature which touts the islands as a paradise where a mixture of races lives in perfect harmony. Many Trinidadians insist that race relations are better in Trinidad than in the United States. Although many have visited the United States and found less "racialism" there than expected, they still assert that race is less of an issue in Trinidad.

With regard to consensualists and pluralists, consensualists (most notably Lloyd Braithwaite) emphasize class distinctions in Trinidadian society and deemphasize the significance of race and ethnicity. Pluralists (notably M. G. Smith) believe that race and ethnicity continue to play an important part in Trinidadian social structure. Don Robotham and other Caribbean scholars have suggested that Smith's plural society theory is nothing more than a scientific abstraction derived from the ideological consciousness of the Jamaican anti-colonial middle class of the period.[34] Stephen D. Glazier indicates that Smith's theory is valuable, but the higher one's position in the social system, the more uniform one's behavior.[35]

All Trinidadian elites and would-be elites conform to patterns of behavior identified by Peter J. Wilson.[36] According to Wilson, Caribbean social structure is built on two antithetical but diametrically related value systems that he calls "reputation"and "respectability." Reputation is indigenous, philosophically egalitarian, and embodied primarily by males, whereas respectability is metropolitan, class conscious, and embodied primarily by females, but partially internalized by men with age.

Individuals in Trinidad find that, in order to be considered respectable, they must conform to rigidly defined behavioral patterns. They must be extremely careful about whom they are seen with, where they go, how they act, how they dress, and so on. The assumption is sometimes made that Trinidadian society allows all its members tremendous flexibility and freedom. Such is not always the case.

The quest for "respectability" serves many functions in Trinidad. It is a symbolic system that unites upwardly mobile blacks, East Indians, Chinese, and Creole elites, and may play no small part in promoting island harmony. Common bonds of respectability, for example, sometimes take precedence over ethnic differences. Still, as a carryover of the British colonial mentality, respectability does have its darker side. It sometimes makes for organizational inefficiency, and many men suffer because the system is so rigid—for example, white Creole males who are largely confined to their homes.

Trinidad's late prime minister, Dr. Eric Williams, concluded his *History of the People of Trinidad and Tobago* by noting that for his people there can be no "Mother Africa"; there can be no "Mother India": "The only Mother we recognize is Mother Trinidad and Tobago."[37] While there is much truth in Williams' words, he also should have mentioned "Mother England" because British-derived notions of respectability are among the greatest barriers to racial and ethnic harmony on these islands.

NOTES

1. Ramesh Deosaran, "Some Issues in Multiculturalism: The Case of Trinidad and Tobago in the Post-Colonial Era," *Ethnic Groups* 3 (1981): 204.

2. Franz Boas, *Race, Language and Culture* (New York: Macmillan, 1960).

3. Fredrik Barth, "Introduction," in Fredrik Barth, ed., *Ethnic Groups and Boundaries* (Boston: Little, Brown, 1969), pp. 9–38.

4. E. Greene, *Race vs. Politics in Guyana* (Mona, Jamaica: Institute of Social and Economic Research, University of the West Indies, 1974).

5. Vera Rubin, "Culture, Politics and Race Relations," *Social and Economic Studies* 2 (1962); see also Vera Rubin and M. Zavalloni, *We Wish to Be Looked Upon* (New York: Columbia University Press, 1969).

6. David Lowenthal, *West Indian Societies* (London: Oxford University Press, 1972).

7. Jan Knippers Black, *Area Handbook for Trinidad and Tobago* (Washington, D.C.: U.S. Government Printing Office), p. 77.

8. Stephen D. Glazier, "Caribbean Ethnicity Revisited; Editor's Introduction," *Ethnic Groups* 6 (1985): 85–97.

9. E. Ahiram, "Distribution of Income in Trinidad-Tobago and Comparison with Distribution of Income in Jamaica," *Social and Economic Studies* 15 (June 1966): 103–20; Allen Schwartzbaum and Malcolm Cross, "Secondary School Environment and Development; The Case of Trinidad and Tobago," *Social and Economic Studies* 19 (September 1970): 368–88; Winston Dookeran, "East Indians in the Economy of Trinidad and Tobago," in John G. LaGuerre, ed., *Calcutta to Caroni* (Port of Spain: Longmans Caribbean Limited, 1974), pp. 69–83; Jack Harewood, "Racial Discrimination in Employment in Trinidad and Tobago Based on Data from the 1960 Census," *Social and Economic Studies* 20 (September 1971):

267–93; Michael Lieber, *Street Scenes: Afro-American Culture in Urban Trinidad* (Cambridge, Mass.: Schenkman, 1981).

10. Acton Camejo, "Racial Discrimination in Employment in the Private Sector in Trinidad and Tobago: A Study of the Business Elite and the Social Structure," *Social and Economic Studies* 20 (September 1971): 305.

11. Frances Henry and Saberwal Satish, *Stress and Strategy in Three Field Situations* (New York: Holt, Rinehart & Winston, 1975).

12. Jack Harewood, "Racial Discrimination in Employment," p. 29.

13. E. Ahiram, "Distribution of Income in Trinidad-Tobago," p. 118.

14. Lloyd Braithwaite, "Social Stratification in Trinidad," *Social and Economic Studies* 2 (October 1953): 5. See also H. Hoetink, "Race and Color in the Caribbean," Sidney W. Mintz and Sally Price, eds., in *Caribbean Contours* (Baltimore: Johns Hopkins University Press, 1985).

15. Douglas Taylor, *Languages of the West Indies* (Baltimore: Johns Hopkins University Press, 1977); Dell Hymes, ed., *Pidginization and Creolization of Languages* (New York: Cambridge University Press, 1971).

16. M. A. Durbin, "Formal Changes in Trinidad Hindi as a Result of Language Adaptation," *American Anthropologist* 75 (1973): 1670–81; Mervyn Alleyne, "A Linguistic Perspective on the Caribbean," in Sidney W. Mintz and Sally Price, eds., *Caribbean Contours* (Baltimore: Johns Hopkins University Press, 1985), pp. 155–77.

17. Stephen D. Glazier, *Marchin' the Pilgrims Home: Leadership and Decision-Making in an Afro-Caribbean Faith* (Westport, Conn.: Greenwood Press, 1983), p. 19.

18. Stephen D. Glazier, "Syncretism and Separation: Ritual Change in an Afro-Caribbean Faith," *Journal of American Folklore* 98 (January 1985): 49–62. See also George Eaton Simpson, *Black Religion in the New World* (New York: Columbia University Press, 1978), pp. 111–21.

19. Yogendra K. Malik, *East Indians in Trinidad: A Study in Minority Politics* (London: Oxford University Press, 1971); J. C. Jha, "Indian Heritage in Trinidad (West Indies)," *Eastern Anthropologist* 27 (September 1974): 211–34; Deosaran, "Some Issues in Multiculturalism," p. 203.

20. Donald Wood, *Trinidad in Transition: The Years After Slavery* (London: Oxford University Press, 1968), p. 120.

21. Joseph Nevadomsky, "Social Change and the East Indians of Rural Trinidad: A Critique of Methodologies," *Social and Economic Studies* 31 (January 1982): 92–93.

22. Barton M. Schwartz, "Patterns of East Indian Family Organization in Trinidad," *Caribbean Studies* 5 (April 1965). See also Joseph Nevadomsky, "Marital Discord and Dissolution Among the Hindu East Indians in Rural Trinidad," *Anthropos* 79 (1984): 113–28.

23. Morton Klass, *East Indians in Trinidad: A Study of Cultural Persistence* (New York: Columbia University Press, 1961); Morris Freilich, "Cultural Diversity Among Trinidadian Peasants," Ph.D. diss., Columbia University, 1960; Robert J. Smith, "Muslim East Indians in Trinidad: Retention of Identity Under Acculturative Conditions," Ph.D. diss., Cornell University, 1963; Malik, *East Indians in Trinidad*, p. 7.

24. Klass, *East Indians in Trinidad*, p. 239.

25. Daniel J. Crowley, "Plural and Differential Acculturation in Trinidad,"

American Anthropologist 59 (1957): 817–24; Arthur Niehoff and Juanita Niehoff, *East Indians in the West Indies* (Milwaukee: Milwaukee Public Museum Publications in Anthropology, 1960).

26. Selwyn D. Ryan, *Race and Nationalism in Trinidad and Tobago: A Study of Decolonization in a Multiracial Society* (Toronto: University of Toronto Press, 1972), p. 31.

27. Bridget Brereton, *Race Relations in Colonial Trinidad, 1870–1900* (New York: Cambridge University Press, 1979), p. 3.

28. Basil Bernstein, "A Socio-Linguistic Approach to Socialization," in John Gumperz and D. Hymes, eds, *Directions in Sociolinguistics* (New York: Holt, Rinehart & Winston, 1970); Fathi S. Yousef, "Communication Patterns: Some Aspects of Nonverbal Behavior in Intercultural Communication," in E. Lamar Ross, ed., *Interethnic Communication* (Athens: University of Georgia Press, 1978), pp. 49–62.

29. Maurice Bloch, "Symbols, Song, Dance, and Features of Articulation: Is Religion an Extreme Form of Traditional Authority?" *European Journal of Sociology* 15 (1974): 55–81.

30. Gerald Bentley and Frances Henry, "Some Preliminary Observations on the Chinese in Trinidad," *McGill Studies in Caribbean Anthropology*, Occasional Paper No. 5, Frances Henry, ed. (Montreal: Center for Developing Area Studies, McGill University, 1969), pp. 19–33; Glazier, "Caribbean Ethnicity Revisited," pp. 91–93.

31. Leonard Glick, "Epilogue: "The Meaning of Ethnicity in the Caribbean," *Ethnic Groups* 6 (1985): 234. See also Ivar Oxxal, *Race and Revolutionary Consciousness* (Cambridge, Mass.: Schenkman, 1971).

32. Ryan, *Race and Nationalism;* James Millette, *The Genesis of Crown Colony Government: Trinidad, 1783–1810* (Port of Spain: Moko Enterprises, 1970); Yogendra K. Malik, *East Indians in Trinidad.*

33. Coleman Romalis, "Some Comments on Race and Ethnicity in the Caribbean," in Frances Henry, ed., *Ethnicity in the Americas* (The Hague: Mouton, 1976), pp. 417–28.

34. Don Robotham, "Pluralism as Ideolgy," *Social and Economic Studies* 29 (March 1980): 68–89.

35. Stephen D. Glazier, "Cultural Pluralism and Respectability in Trinidad," *Ethnic and Racial Studies* 6 (July 1983): 351–55. See also M. G. Smith, *The Plural Society in the British West Indies* (Berkeley: University of California Press, 1965); Farley S. Braithwaite, "Race and Class Differentials in Career (Value) Orientation," *Plural Societies* 7 (Spring 1976): 17–31.

36. Peter J. Wilson, *Crab Antics* (New Haven, Conn.: Yale University Press, 1973); Peter J. Wilson, "Respectability and Reputation: Two Suggestions for Caribbean Ethnology," *Man* 4 (1969): 70–84.

37. Eric E. Williams, *History of the People of Trinidad and Tobago* (Port of Spain, PNM, 1962), p. 281.

BIBLIOGRAPHY

Ahiram, E. "Distribution of Income in Trinidad-Tobago and Comparison with Distribution of Income in Jamaica." *Social and Economic Studies* 15 (1966): 103–12.

Alleyne, Mervyn. "A Linguistic Perspective on the Caribbean." In *Caribbean Contours*, edited by Sidney W. Mintz and Sally Price. Baltimore: Johns Hopkins University Press, 1985.

Bentley, Gerald, and Frances Henry. "Some Preliminary Observations on the Chinese in Trinidad." In *McGill Studies in Caribbean Anthropology*, Occasional Paper No. 5, edited by Frances Henry. Montreal: Center for Developing Area Studies, McGill University, 1969.

Black, Jan Knippers. *Area Handbook for Trinidad and Tobago.* Washington, D.C.: U.S. Government Printing Office, 1976.

Braithwaite, Farley S. "Race and Class Differentials in Career (Value) Orientation" *Plural Societies* 7 (1976): 17–31.

Braithwaite, Lloyd. "Social Stratification in Trinidad." *Social and Economic Studies* 2 (1953): 1–168.

Brereton, Bridget. *Race Relations in Colonial Trinidad, 1870–1900.* New York: Cambridge University Press 1979.

———. *A History of Modern Trinidad, 1783–1962.* Port of Spain: Heinemann, 1981.

Camejo, Acton. "Racial Discrimination in Employment in the Private Sector in Trinidad and Tobago: A Study of the Business Elite and the Social Structure." *Social and Economic Studies* 20 (1971): 31–40.

Crowley, Daniel J. "Plural and Differential Acculturation in Trinidad." *American Anthropologist* 59 (1957): 817–24.

Deosaran, Ramesh. "Some Issues in Multiculturalism: The Case of Trinidad and Tobago in the Post-Colonial Era." *Ethnic Groups* 3 (1981): 199–225.

Dookeran, Winston. "East Indians in the Economy of Trinidad and Tobago." In *Calcutta to Caroni*, edited by John G. LaGuerre. Port of Spain: Longmans, 1974.

Freilich, Morris. "Cultural Diversity Among Trinidadian Peasants." Ph.D. diss., Columbia University, 1960.

Glazier, Stephen D. "An Annotated Ethnographic Bibliography of Trinidad." *Behavior Science Research* 17 (1982): 31–58.

———. "Cultural Pluralism and Respectability in Trinidad." *Ethnic and Racial Studies* 6 (1983): 351–55.

———. *Marchin' the Pilgrims Home: Leadership and Decision-Making in an Afro-Caribbean Faith.* Westport, Conn.: Greenwood Press, 1983.

———. "Caribbean Ethnicity Revisited; Editor's Introduction." Special Issue, *Ethnic Groups* 6 (1985): 85–97.

———. "Syncretism and Separation: Ritual Change in an Afro-Caribbean Faith." *Journal of American Folklore* 98 (1985): 49–62.

Glick, Leonard. "Epilogue: The Meaning of Ethnicity in The Caribbean." *Ethnic Groups* 6 (1985): 149–64.

Harewood, Jack. "Racial Discrimination in Employment in Trinidad and Tobago Based on Data from the 1960 Census." *Social and Economic Studies* 20 (1971): 267–93.

Hoetink, H. "Race and Color in the Caribbean." *Caribbean Contours*, edited by Sidney W. Mintz and Sally Price. Baltimore: Johns Hopkins University Press, 1985.

Jha, J. C. "Indian Heritage in Trinidad (West Indies)." *Eastern Anthropologist* 27 (1974): 211–34.

Klass, Morton. *East Indians in Trinidad: A Study of Cultural Persistence*. New York: Columbia University Press, 1961.

Lieber, Michael. *Street Scenes: Afro-American Culture in Urban Trinidad*. Cambridge, Mass.: Schenkman, 1981.

Malik, Yogendra K. *East Indians in Trinidad: A Study in Minority Politics*. London: Oxford University Press, 1971.

Nevadomsky, Joseph. "Marital Discord and Dissolution Among the Hindu East Indians in Rural Trinidad." *Anthropos* 79 (1984): 113–28.

———. "Social Change and the East Indians of Rural Trinidad: A Critique of Methodologies." *Social and Economic Studies* 31 (January 1982).

Niehoff, Arthur, and Juanita Niehoff. *East Indians in the West Indies*. Milwaukee: Milwaukee Public Museum Publications in Anthropology, 1960.

Oxxal, Ivar. *Race and Revolutionary Consciousness*. Cambridge, Mass.: Schenkman, 1971.

Rubin, Vera, and M. Zavalloni. *We Wish to Be Looked Upon*. New York: Columbia University Press, 1969.

Ryan, Selwyn D. *Race and Nationalism in Trinidad and Tobago: A Study of Decolonization in a Multiracial Society*. Toronto: University of Toronto Press, 1972.

Schwartz, Barton M. "Patterns of East Indian Family Organization in Trinidad." *Caribbean Studies* 5 (April 1965).

Smith, Robert J. "Muslim East Indians in Trinidad: Retention of Identity Under Acculturative Conditions." Ph.D. diss., Cornell University, 1963.

Williams, Eric E. *History of the People of Trinidad and Tobago*. Port of Spain, PNM, 1962.

Wilson, Peter J. *Crab Antics*. New Haven, Conn.: Yale University Press, 1973.

Wood, Donald. *Trinidad in Transition: The Years After Slavery*. London: Oxford University Press, 1968.

UNION OF SOVIET SOCIALIST REPUBLICS

Samuel P. Oliner

A RACIAL AND ETHNIC CONTENT

The USSR comprises one-sixth of the global land mass and consists of over one hundred nationalities and ethnic groups, twenty-two of whom have over 1 million people. Most racial groups are represented on Soviet soil with the exception of the Negroid stock (other than visiting African students and diplomats). The dominant ethnic groups are the Russians and their "younger brother Slavs"—the Ukrainians and Belorrussians. It should be understood that Ukranians and Belorussians are not on the same footing as the 140 million Russians (sometimes also known as Great Russians). Although there are fifteen Soviet Socialist Republics comprising some 281 million people, for administrative purposes the Soviet Union is divided into fifty-three administrative regions.

The non-Russian ethnic groups of the USSR can be divided into two large groups. First are the Europeans who subscribe to Christianity and comprise Armenians, Georgians, the three Baltic republics (Latvia, Estonia, and Lithuania), Ukrainians, Poles, Bessarabians; and smaller groups. These ethnic groups have historically had cultural ties with the West and feel friendly toward Western visitors. The second group are Muslim people who have kin and co-ethnic groups in the Middle East and Asia in general. These areas are known as the Crimea, Central Asia, Siberia, and North Caucasus.

In this largest multinational country, there are conflicting claims about the status of the ethnic groups and their relationship to the dominant ethnic group, the Russians. The Soviet government and Soviet scholars

This chapter was written with the assistance of Jackie M. Fleury, a psychology graduate student.

assert that interethnic conflict or problems have virtually been eliminated. To be sure, while there was such strife and oppression under the Tsars, under the Soviets these polarizations disappeared with the advent of Marxism/Leninism. Some Soviet scholars make unusually optimistic claims about national harmony. For example, B. G. Gafurov makes the following claim: "The greatest achievement in the solution of the national question was that national discord and enmity were replaced by fraternal friendship and cooperation of all nations and nationalities of the Soviet Union."

I. P. Tsamerian and S. L. Ronin introduce their publication with the following comment: "The purpose of this publication is to acquaint the public with one of the major social triumphs of our day: namely the way in which the problems of nationalities have been solved in the Soviet Union."

David Kowalewski states that in 1972, on the occasion of the fiftieth anniversary of the Union of the Soviet Socialist Republics, Leonid Brezhnev said:

By now ... solving the nationalities problem, overcoming the backwardness of previously oppressed nationals, is ... habitual for the Soviet people. We must remember the scope and complexity of the accomplishments, in order to appreciate the wisdom ... of the party, which took upon itself such a task and accomplished it.[1]

Finally, V. I. Kozlov, section head of the USSR Academy of Science, Institute of Ethnography, in discussing ethnic amalgamations, says: "Mixed marriages are a powerful factor in ethnic assimilations. The children of those marriages usually adopt the nationality of one of their parents, thereby severing the ethnic lines of the other parents."[2]

Western scholars are skeptical of these optimistic claims of assimilation and racial and ethnic amalgamation, known respectfully as *sblizhenie* and *sliyanie*, or the drawing and merging together of ethnic groups under the Russian banner. Many in fact see an increase in ethnic conflict, inequality, ethnic nationalism, and underground publications. Among these scholars are Clem, 1982; Beloff, 1980; Bennigsen, 1979; Harap, 1979; Dima, 1980; Lapidus, 1983, Oliner, 1983; Rakowska-Harmstone, 1977; Anderson and Silver, 1983; Perakh, 1978; and Wixman, 1982.[3]

If Soviet claims of interethnic harmony were indeed correct, it would behoove the Western world to acknowledge them. The preoccupation of American sociologists with the subject of internal minority relations testifies to the enormity of the perceived problem and the lack of adequate solutions. It might be expected that the Soviets would welcome the advent of new concepts and strategies, particularly those that appear so hopeful. But such interest has not been forthcoming for a number of reasons, including the secretive nature of Soviet society. The impossibility for Western scholars to study ethnic and nationality problems in the USSR simply renders information largely inaccessible.[4]

Regardless of reasons, until very recently Western social scientists have shown deplorable lack of interest in the status of Soviet minorities and Soviet society in general. This disinterest is regrettable for several reasons. First, it tends to reinforce the notion that minority problems are exclusively a by-product of Western imperialism. Colleges and universities promote this point of view by failing to provide courses that would broaden the student's perspective. Second, the elimination of this large spectrum of humanity cannot fail but support a distorted vision of human behavior. Human patterns of behavior are frequently remarkably similar, despite cultural and geographical peculiarities. Discerning the pattern is the basic quest of social science theorizing; inherent in its discovery is the potential promise of applied solutions.

This chapter seeks (1) to understand the major disjunctive social processes that help account for interethnic strife. These are: (a) internal colonization, (b) russianization, russification, and sovietization, and (c) ethnic inequality that contributes to current ethnonationalism and conflict in the Soviet Union; and (2) to sketch some specific examples of ethnic and political conflict among the major Soviet nationalities and ethnic groups today.

Of course, a number of different explanations account for ethnic and racial polarization and antipathy. Before we address the above-mentioned disjunctive social processes, we want to briefly focus on the role of color and racism in the USSR. Unlike the United States, South Africa, and some Western European nations, the role of color as a symbol of inferiority and racism does not play nearly as important a role in explaining intergroup polarization. In the United States and most certainly in South Africa, people of color have been segregated or separated from whites and have been relegated to inferior social, economic, and political status. They have never been invited to assimilate, integrate, or amalgamate.

What appears to prevail in the Soviet Union is discrimination against nationalities and ethnic groups based largely on the charges by the dominant groups that many minorities do not want to assimilate (Russify) and modernize and join the advanced and superior Russian culture and its Soviet political system. The nationalities are accused of backwardness and of reverting to narrow bourgeois nationalism and tribalism. Some Soviet nationality leaders respond with a countercharge of great Russian chauvinism and gross disregard and disrespect of their ancient culture and life-styles. For our purposes, however, it appears more fruitful to explain disharmonious intergroup relations by focusing on three disjunctive social processes: internal colonization, Russification, and ethnic inequality.

"Internal colonization" is a recent concept introduced into sociology by Robert Blauner and others, although classic colonization has been studied by Marx and Engels, J. A. Hobson, V. I. Lenin, and others. Blauner, more than anyone else, has brought the construct of internal colonization into race relation theory.

Colonization is social, political, and economic domination over a region or ethnic group, inhabited by people of a different race, religion, and culture in an area that is subordinate to the mother country.[5] The attributes of both classical and internal colonization are as follows: (1) the entry of the colonizer is by conquest; (2) the colonizers constrain, transform, or destroy indigenous values and life-styles; (3) the colonizer has and holds legal power and governmental control over the lives of the colonized; (4) there is social domination based on racism against indigenous people who need to be Christianized, modernized, and civilized; (5) there is a definite separation between the colonizer and colonized. When one looks at the history of Tsarist and Soviet expansion, it is clear that a number of regions, especially the Muslim Central Asian republics, are internal colonies, be it of a less oppressive nature. Rocky L. Rockett in his *Ethnic Nationalities in the Soviet Union* convinces us that

both the internal colonial and the classical colonial approaches are most applicable in cases where racial and cultural differences are extreme. In the case of the Soviet Union, the Slavic/Muslim cultural contrast is sufficient to warrant an analysis of the relationship between these two groups of people from a colonial perspective. Also, the fact that most of the seventeen major nationalities have at one time existed as autonomous nations suggests the possibility that these nations may today exist as colonies to be the dominant Russian nation.[6]

Nicholas Dima assures us that the Soviet Union is dominated by the Russians who are among the most mobile Soviet nationality, migrating from rural to urban areas and from city to city all over the USSR. In contrast, non-Russians, who are less educated people in the Soviet Union, are most often confined to rural areas. Concentrating on Russian predominance, John A. Armstrong tells us that Slavic predominance is expressed in the less obvious ways. It manifests itself in overrepresentation of East Slavs in better jobs and all-union offices, especially in the military and diplomatic service. This overrepresentation annoys the Asians and other smaller groups.[7]

We will next look at the processes of Russianization, Russification, and Sovietization and their consequences for Soviet intergroup relations.

HISTORICAL BACKGROUND: RUSSIANIZATION, RUSSIFICATION, AND SOVIETIZATION

Russianization began in approximately 1552 when Ivan the Terrible freed the Russian people from Mongol vassalage and the European Russians emerged as the dominant Russian group. Through conquest and imperialistic expansion, their sovereignty extended to the Pacific Ocean by 1654. However, they discovered an indigenous people, who frequently proved easier to conquer than to rule. The policies of these early Russian imperialists regarding minority peoples were similar to those of the Soviet ruling powers today; their objective was simply to assure the supremacy of the European Russian political, economic, and cultural institutions of the time.

Three basic policies have emerged during the last four centuries designed to control minority and ethnic nationalities: (1) Russianization, (2) Russification, and (3) Sovietization.

"Russianization," the process whereby minority groups are persuaded or coerced into learning the Russian language, is directed primarily at non-Russian elites. Persuasion frequently takes the form of seduction via promise of upward mobility in the Russian-speaking upper professional and social classes. Coercion is usually expressed through the compulsory study of the Russian language in the education system.[8]

Early in their history, the Russians recognized that effective ruling required the "co-opting" of the elites of non-Russian nationality groups. One policy was to enlist their loyalty via promises of high positions and prestige in Moscow. This had two advantages. Numerically overwhelmed by Russians and qualitatively seduced by what was believed to be their obvious cultural superiority, the Russian government hoped that these elites would become advocates among their own indigenous populations. Even if such aspirations did not succeed, the policy nonetheless had the undisputed advantage of leaving native homelands without legitimized leaders who might become successful organizers of rebellion.

Efforts to linguistically Russify or Russianize elites of nationality groups began early in Russian history. Eventually, the policy was extended to include all educational institutions. Sometimes the exclusive language of instruction was Russian, as was the policy of Catherine in the Ukraine and of Nicholas I in Poland. During various regimes, greater latitude and bilingual instructional patterns were maintained. Generally, greater latitude was characteristic in Central Asia where compulsory Russianization was not attempted—probably based on a pragmatic attempt to avoid confrontation with the Muslim hierarchy.[9] This was sometimes accompanied by efforts to suppress indigenous culture, as was again the case of Poland under Nicholas I.

"Russification" includes Russianization but goes beyond it. It is aimed not only at minority elites, but also at all individuals within minority groups. Moreover, it involves the imposition of the Russian language, as well as of Russian cultural, political, and economic values in such a manner that minority peoples will internalize them as their own. Its objective is no less than the transformation of non-Russians into Russians.

Under the Tsars, Russification meant the imposition of the values of a socioeconomically stratified society headed by a highly centralized political institution at whose head was the "father" of all, in the form of the Tsar; the values of Russian culture as exemplified in its historical and cultural heroes; and the values of the Russian Orthodox Church which was imposed with different intensity under different regimes. In contemporary Soviet society, this means the imposition of the values of Soviet-Marxist-Leninist norms, as interpreted by its Great Russian architects and bureaucrats via the Great Russian culture.

The political system ensured the dominance of Russian economic interests. The policy of conquest began under Ivan the Terrible had its strategic component, but its major attraction was economic exploitation. The promise of sables, furs, and other resources offered by the vast lands to the east and west proved an irresistible lure to the advancing Russians who took full advantage of them. The Russian nobility lived lavishly and elegantly. Even the Russian peasant, once freed from serfdom, was able in some cases to acquire land from those he displaced among other ethnic groups. As noted above, even when they constituted a minority among ethnic groups, Russians acquired ownership of much of the land and other resources. True enough, some non-Russian elites gained entry to this select circle, but many more remained outside it.

The policies of Russification varied among the conquered peoples, to some extent depending on the size of the conquered groups. Thus, flexibility cannot be regarded as a response to the recognition of the legitimacy of nationalistic diversity, but a pragmatic adjustment. Many historians view Tsarist policy right from the beginning as designed to integrate all peoples into the mainstream as designed by the European Russians who defined their roles as "elder brothers." Many groups, such as the Cherkes tribes, too small to matter, were exterminated. Howewer, as Marc Raeff sees it, their view was not so much predicated on the suppression of nationalities, as their unconsciousness of it.

The goal of social, economic, and political conformity remained constant in the policy of the imperial government with respect to non-Russian lands and people through the 1917 period. At no point was it conscious of or aware of the dynamic force of nationalism and nationality. Yet the Russian government did not aim at eradicating nations and nationalities. It simply felt that their way of life should change in the process of natural evolution which their membership in the empire could speed up and help along.[10]

It was a myopic view, for the problems of minority groups did not cease to plague the Empire throughout the Tsarist rule.

The policy of "Sovietization" includes both Russianization and Russification, but adds other elements particularly suited to this new age. It includes both modernization and industrialization. Hence, Sovietization may be regarded as an essentially modern variation of Russification. The early Bolsheviks conceived their ultimate aim to be Sovietization, but looked toward Russianization and Russification as the mediating vehicles. The three processes are inextricably intertwined and mutually reinforcing, and are frequently used interchangeably.

It is helpful to regard these processes as a continuum of intensity encompassing lesser to greater amounts of modification in the life-styles of minority groups. Russianization, with its limited emphasis on language and culture directed primarily at non-Russian elites, would be on the low end of the continuum. Sovietization, which requires not only the adoption of Russian economic, political, and cultural values, but also the acceptance of modernization and industrialization, portends the most dramatic overhaul of nationality groups, some of whom continue to live essentially in nonmodern and nonindustrialized life-styles.

The problems of the nationalities continued to plague the new Bolsheviks. Convinced that their dissatisfaction was caused primarily by the oppressive tactics of Tsarism, Lenin encouraged nationality groups to break away. Equally convinced of the inherent attractiveness of the new communist ideology, Lenin advocated the principle of "free determination." "Free determination" meant that those nationalities who wished to secede from the Russian orbit could do so. Lenin's hope, of course, was that they would not. Indeed, he was convinced that once given the right to determine their own destiny, these nationality groups would voluntarily link their fortunes with those of the new regime. In short, what Tsarism had failed to accomplish through coercive means, Lenin hoped to achieve voluntarily.

Recognizing his error, Lenin sent out the Red Army, which together with local communists, "recaptured" these territories and established communist regimes in the Ukraine, Azerbaidjan, Armenia, Georgia, and Belorussia as well as in Muslim areas in Central Asia. The new relationship was formalized in treaties that gave Russia control over military and economic matters. So ended this excursion in "self-determination."

The repression of minorities begun under Lenin in his later years reached its full expression under Stalin, who assumed the mantle of power upon Lenin's death in 1924. While paying due homage to the principle of "self-determination," Stalin made it immediately clear that to take this principle seriously would be an act of sabotage:

Of course the border regions of Russia, the nations and tribes which inhabit these regions...possess the inalienable right to secede from Russia...but the demand for secession . . . at this present stage of revolution . . . is a profoundly counterrevolutionary one.[11]

Although Stalin's excesses were abandoned, the ideology of *sblizhenie* and *sliyanie*—the drawing and merging together of nationalities under the Russian banner—was reaffirmed by the liberalizating Nikita Khrushchev at the CPSU Congress of 1961:

Communists do not wish to preserve and perpetuate national distinctions. We depend on the natural process of an ever closer fusion of nations and nationalities. . . . It is essential that we insist on the education of the masses in the spirit of proletarian internationalism and Soviet patriotism.[12]

Official Soviet ideology is based on the articulated desire to transform all Russian peoples into a unified monotype—the new "Soviet Man" who alone can build Utopia. While there may not be a tradition of racism in Russia based on color as in the United States and South Africa, there is discrimination based on the failure of individuals and groups to accept the Russian invitation to join and accept the superior Russian culture and patriotism, as well as its Marxist-Leninist-Soviet ideology. Recently, we see more literature on the pervasive chauvinism of the dominant ethnic group, the Russians. Probably the best work on ethnic Great Russian domination has been recently compiled by Professor Edward Allworth in a work titled *Ethnic Russia: The Dilemma of Dominance* [New York: Columbia University Press, 1971]. Although the Soviet government doesn't want to see Russia return to "Social-Christian ideology," it wants to attain a unified, assimilated Soviet people. And yet, that kind of act implies the deculturization of various nationalities and ethnic groups. The ethnic Russian nationalists want to establish the dominance of Russian culture. This view is espoused by Roman Szporluk:

In fact, ideas close to those of the union [Christian union that is ultra-nationalistic] have been presented in *Samizdat*, *Veche*, *Zemlia*, and *Moskovski Sbornik* publications. They are not uncompromisingly hostile to the government, but they base their conception of Russian ethnic unity on cultural [religious, spiritual] features, and they judge political problems through an ideological culturalist prism.[13]

A primary tool for fashioning the new Soviet person is via the imposition of the Russian language. Although Russian was customarily taught in non-Russian schools throughout the early years of the new communist regime, the number of hours devoted to its study increased sharply after 1938.[14] Compulsory study of the Russian language was abrogated in the 1959 Education Reform Act, but many of the republics, recognizing that entrance to the universities and upward social mobility was impossible without it, made both their native languages and Russian compulsory.

The *lingua franca* of the Soviet Federation is, of course, Russian. It is the language of trade and commerce, the post office, telephone directories, the armed forces, official speeches, inscriptions on medals, and international communications. According to I. F. Desheriev and I. D. Protchenko, transactions of correspondence and business in state institutions and organizations within autonomous republics and provinces are now conducted primarily in Russian.[15]

Accompanying the institutionalization of Russian linguistic supremacy is the attempted establishment of Russian cultural supremacy in general. This takes essentially three forms. The first is the positive projection of Russian heroes, poets, writers, artists, and so on, and the second, is deemphasis, derision, and, in some cases, legal bans on non-Russian historical and cultural communications. "Nonassimilationist," "bourgeois nationalism," and "counterrevolutionary" are the commonly voiced epithets that suppress local cultural manifestations. Although all groups have suffered this in various ways, some have suffered more than others. Muslim Russians have been accused of being chained by the constraints of their Islamic teaching and oppressive practices toward women. Jewish culture has been virtually eradicated, and as part of the third form, large numbers of Slavs have been colonized in non-Slavic areas such as the Baltic States, Central Asia, and parts of Siberia.

The policy of "resettlement" and internal colonization, which began under the Tsars, continues unabated. Hundred of thousands of Russians have settled in the three Baltic states and the six predominantly Muslim Constitutional Republics of Central Asia, and they have also penetrated into the smaller groups of the vast Siberian region. Millions of Russians have settled in non-Russian republics and provinces, frequently establishing cities. They make little effort to learn local languages or customs, and, consistent with Soviet ideology, they expect locals to emulate them. They serve many functions: providing security, ensuring loyalty, and generally accelerating the processes of fusion, amalgamation, and modernization. Although more successful in urban areas, the more remote villages have also been strongly affected. As Brian Silver concludes:

Both urbanization and exposure to Russians have been shown to have a substantial impact on the Russification of the Soviet minority nationalities. Exposure to Russians affects urban natives, revealing that Russification is a function not only of the relative proportions of Russians in the area, but of the weakening of traditional village ties and the exposure of modern technology, mass communication and the urban life-style.[16]

Permeating all social and cultural processes is Marxist-Leninist ideology, which is interpreted and implemented by the ubiquitous Communist party of the Soviet Union. Centrally controlled and dominated largely by the Great Russians, the party extends throughout all of the Soviet Union. Its primary function is no less than the "sovietization" of all society. "Party-mindedness" is the purifying ideological commitment which is a minimum for upward mobility and acceptance by the Soviet political apparatus. Economic policies determined by the Kremlin are based on increased modernization and urbanization. It is primarily Russian and Russified technologists and specialists who are spreading and interpreting the process.

ETHNIC INEQUALITY

Despite the Soviets' claims to the contrary, a number of scholars have addressed the issue of social stratification and ethnic inequality: Jones and Grupp, 1984; Lapidus, 1984; Cole, 1984; Karklins, 1984; Clem, 1982; Zaslavsky, 1982; Kowaleski, 1980, 1981, 1982; Dima, 1980, 1982; Rockett, 1981; Gitelman, 1980; Lipset and Dobson, 1973; Pankhurst and Sacks, 1980; Carrere d'Encausse, 1978; Yanowitch, 1963; and Rakowska-Harmstone, 1974.[17]

Rocky L. Rockett identifies internal migration, Soviet linguistic and educational policies, differential modernization and urbanization, and political oppression as the more significant determinants of ethnic inequality in the Soviet Union. Rockett states:

The contention is that the Soviet regimes' inter-republic exchange of cadres policy, linguistic and educational policies; and remnants of Stalin's nationalities' policy all combine to work in the opposite direction of the stated goal of realizing socioeconomic equality . . . differential urbanization and modernization—is highly influential in the maintenance of socioeconomic differences between the nationalities but is not directly attributed to nationalities policy.[18]

Since the Tsarist days, there has been much internal migration—especially the ethnic Russian migration into the territories of other non-Slavic groups. This is illustrated in an article by Ralph S. Clem who points out that socioeconomic differences, particularly in the rural areas of their own ethnic territory, led to the outmigration of Russians, including the non-Russian lands.[19] There the Russians in many cases took the better jobs, which decreased the local inhabitants' opportunities for upward mobility.

Jerry Pankhurst and Michael P. Sacks observe that social differentiation exists in the Soviet Union as in other industrial countries. Some Soviet citizens have better access to the comforts of life than other citizens.[20] Because the Russian group has greater skills, which are necessary for a complex industrial society, they have the greater advantages in the

Soviet Union. Their predominance is seen in the area of higher ranking managers, in diplomatic and all-union offices, and in the military.[21] In the area of higher education the Russians are also overrepresented. Although that may not be true in all of the republics and regions, it does appear to hold true in the Ukraine, Georgia, Belorussia, Moldavia, Lithuania, and Latvia, where the Russians are overrepresented compared to the natives.[22]

Although the Soviets' ultimate goal may be ethnic equalization and modernization in the USSR, the more the communist cause is identified with Russian nationalism, the less appeal it has to the non-Russian minorities. Although some Soviet scholars look at ethnically differentiated access to higher education as a nonissue, a careful look at the practice shows otherwise. Not only do the minorities resent the institutional bias in education and employment, but they also feel the pressure to emulate Russian values and culture in order to climb up the social and economic ladder. There is also, as in the capitalist world, competition over the allocation of limited resources among different republics and ethnic groups. The displacement or noninclusion of ethnic managers and leaders in their own native lands frequently leads to ethnic tension.[23] Furthermore, ethnic dissatisfaction is also generated by unequal budgetary allocations directed by Moscow, although the significance of these budgetary factors affects members of various social classes differently.[24]

In sum, what appears to exist in the USSR today is not just a stratified society, but also ethnic inequality based on unequal access to education, which in turn, is based partly on social class and social origins of groups. The minorities in the USSR have an extra burden because they are not Russian and the Russian language is not their native tongue. To be sure, the minority elites do have a better life, but they can't protect the social-cultural interest of their homeland because they have been coopted by the privileged social class which enjoys the good life.

We will look at some major Soviet non-Russian peoples and attempt to highlight some aspects of ethnic nationalism, interaction, and attitudes toward the Russians.

THE CURRENT STATE OF ETHNONATIONALISM IN THE USSR

We would be remiss if we failed to note at the outset that the economic and social well-being of many minority groups has greatly improved under the Soviets. Measured in terms of access to goods, medical services, pensions, holidays, and general economic advances, many have seen great improvements. Although there is some doubt that these have been allocated equitably, the Soviet government has provided many services.[25] One can only speculate regarding what each might do given a real rather than an illusory choice of political autonomy today. Nonetheless, current evidence strongly suggests that nationality feelings continue to reamin high—indeed, in some ways perhaps more acute than at the beginning of the Soviet regime.

Teresa Rakowska-Harmstone notes:

The new nationalism results from a dual process involving (1) a change in content as a result of superimposition of new conflicts on top of old ethnic differences, and (2) a shift in the main locus of nationalistic impulses to the new national elites. Old ethnic antagonisms have been reinforced by powerful new conflicts between the demands of the center and the aspirations of the various national groups.[26]

Nationalistic aspirations in the political, economic, and cultural domain appear to be growing.

Rakowska-Harmstone goes on to say that the ethnic nationalists are pressuring the central leadership in these areas. Each republic is trying to maximize political autonomy. Examples of how they are attempting to do so are (1) by the local elites trying to obtain control of the power structure and decision making and achievement of fair representation at the all-union level, (2) by sabotaging and failing to comply with all-union policies, (3) by forming local "backscratching" groups and "family circles," and (4) by cultivating factional "pull" in Moscow. Other research indicates that the local elites' efforts to increase ethnic cadres in the republic, state, and party institutions have greatly disturbed the central leadership becuse it not only poses a challenge to the central political control, but it also seems to generate opposition and anxiety among the nontitular nationalities that fear being usurped from their dominant positions.[27] Economically, central leadership is being pressured by the local elites to approve local projects and to grant to their republics larger shares of resources that are allocated by the central planning authorities or to minimize their republics' contributions. Culturally, the local elites are pressuring the central leadership for greater freedom to promote their local national cultures. Rakowska-Harmstone claims that the new ethnic elites perceive themselves as second-class citizens because they do not have equal access to power and the comforts of life. This fosters antagonism toward those in central leadership.[28]

Given the restrictions on research within the Soviet Union, data that support the notion of nationalistic strivings are neither systematic nor complete. Recent emigrés, journalists, a few Western scholars, underground publications that have managed to reach this country, and official census data are the primary sources from which conclusions are drawn. We will call on all of these resources in presenting the summary picture of the state of minority nationalism as it exists in the Soviet Union today.

The concept of nationalism has many definitions and is discussed by a number of writers: Lapidus, 1984; Rakowska-Harmstone, 1974; Kuzio, 1981; Weeks, 1979; Wixman, 1982; and Wozniuk, 1977.[29] For our purposes here, the one developed by Brian Silver seems most appropriate. Silver sees the terms "national identity" and "ethnic identity" as meaning essentially the same thing. Both imply "an individual emotional attachment to certain core symbols of his ethnic group." While an ethnic group might need to retain traditional practices and language in order to maintain its cohesiveness, an individual may be committed to only a few of these in order to express attachment to the group. In short, "an individual may retain his ethnic identity even while forsaking such practices," for the essence of one's ethnicity lies in one's personal and subjective attachment to these symbols, rather than in one's overt practice of them.[30] As Silver further points out, it is this aspect of ethnicity that appears to be most durable and sustained even when groups ostensibly acculturate.

The emotional attachments of the group of individuals we will be speaking about are exressed in several ways. (1) They indicate awareness of belonging to an ethnic or nationality group by designating themselves as members of the group. (2) They identify the native language of the group as their own native language. (3) They express a desire to maintain and develop the cultural aspects of the group—its language, history, art, and literature. This ethnic desire is sometimes so intense that a few court imprisonment and even death in order to maintain it. (4) In cases where they are not living in the group's recognized homeland, they express the desire to return to it. Here, too, some may be willing to court severe penalties in order to realize the desire.

In the following pages we will focus only on the status of Ukrainians, the Baltic States, the Caucasian area (Armenia, Georgia, and Azerbaidjan), Central Asia, Crimean Tatars, and the Jews.

The Ukrainians

The Ukrainians, a Slavic group comprising some 50 million people at the beginning of the 1980s, are frequently regarded as the chief rivals to the Russians. Although part of the Russian Empire for over 300 years, the 1959 census showed that only 6.5 percent claimed Russian as their native language. Although their protests of Russian sovereignty and dominance have taken many forms throughout history, its contemporary form is primarily in the cultural domain.

The chief articulate spokesmen for Ukrainian nationalism are the cultural elite—the scholars, educators, poets, artists, and professionals. Much of their protest has been directed against linguistic Russification. They are concerned that more Ukrainian should be taught at both lower and higher levels of education and that Ukrainian should be cleansed of non-Ukrainian and especially Russian elements. They have also sought the spread of Ukrainian literature in the native tongue rather than in translation.

This expression of Ukrainian identity has been both restrained and intense. Humor and sarcasm, such as the sardonic letter cited below, is one form it has taken. The letter, printed in the Komsomol paper of the Ukraine in the 1960s, commented: "It is, of course, very nice that our pupils are being acquainted with these works [the writings of Oles' Honchar and O. Dovzhenko] in Russian, but they would be just as good in the original."[31] In February 1963, a large conference of scholars, educators, and communication specialists requested the establishment of public education in Ukrainian outside the Republic. In 1964, the Writers Union of the Ukraine, concerned about the inadequate supply of Ukrainian books, undertook the sponsorship of 544 libraries in boarding schools and donated part of their own earnings and books. Generally, there are many requests for more Ukrainian films, records, and songs.

The above suggests the presence of ethnic identification, but does not necessarily reflect the intensity of the feeling. A measure of intensity is the degree to which individuals are ready to risk public censure, loss of jobs, arrest, and even death itself on behalf of such feelings. Evidence for such intensity exists, now with more frequency. Many intellectuals, including non-Ukrainians such as Andrei Sakharov, do not acknowledge Russia's right to forcibly keep the so-called National Republics within its Empire. They accuse the Soviets of forced amalgamation of peoples. They regard the Ukraine, Baltic States, the Urals, Siberia, the Far East, Central Asia, Kamchatka, Crimea, Caucasus, Transcaucasia, and Bessarabia as colonies.

The Ukraine is economically strong and resents the transfer of its resources to these other regions.[32] Between 1965 and 1966, some twenty Ukrainian intellectuals were arrested and sentenced for allegedly spreading and copying censored literary and historical works regarding the Ukrainian language and culture. As reported in the *Chronicle* (an underground newspaper), 139 Ukrainian intellectuals again risked imprisonment when they wrote a letter of protest to L. I. Brezhnev, A. N. Kosygin, and N. V. Podgorny while he was still President of the Supreme Soviet protesting the legality of the trials. Some were subsequently dismissed from the Ukrainian Academy of Sciences, others lost their jobs, still others were expelled from party membership and some imprisoned.[33] In March 1968, a leaflet was distributed in Kiev University calling for resistance to the Russification of Ukrainian culture. Oles Honchar's novel, *The Cathedral*, a work expressing a strong nationalist Ukrainian theme, has enjoyed wide circulation in Ukrainian *Samizdat* (underground publication). Those accused of either copying or circulating the work have suffered severe reprisals.[34]

Because of these main arrests, Vladimir Wozniuk indicates that

Ukrainian dissenters have subordinated themselves to a more orthodox program within the federated system.[35] This research further reveals that 72.3 percent of the 1960 Ukrainian taxes went dirctly to the all-union budget. The Ukrainians, in turn, were not granted any part of the resources that were allocated by the central planning authorities.

The Baltic States

Evidence of strong nationalistic feeling is also available for the Baltic States of Estonia, Latvia, and Lithuania. Linguistic Russification among all these groups is insignificant—less than 1 percent on the average.

In addition to *Samizdat* ventures in nationalist literature and sentiments, protest among these groups has taken an interesting form. David Kowalewski indicates that Estonians and Lithuanians have been increasingly concerned over environmental issues. They have openly criticized the side-effects of "breakneck industrialization" and disregard for their nations' natural beauty such as destruction of forests and pollution of the air.[36] Adoption of Western modes of dress, architecture, and popular culture is strongly evident. *My Fair Lady* and *West Side Story* had long popular runs in Estonia. Commenting on the twenty-fifth anniversary celebration of the Soviet Socialist Republics celebrated in 1965 in these states, Jaan Pennar observes:

The constant theme of the celebrations, which included native dancing and singing, speeches about past glories under the Soviets, promises for the Communist future, and keynote addresses by Suslov, Kosygin, and Mikoyan in Wilnus, Riga, and Tallinn—the capitals of the three republics, was nationalism.[37]

Although the Russians have generally been quite tolerant of this expression in these particular states, they are paying a high price for this tolerance. The Baltic States have the highest per capita income and are the most economically advanced area, even though they frown on greater investment allocation from the central planning authorities because they fear that it would bring in more Russians.[38]

Victor Zaslavsky feels that the Baltic States' advanced economics along with their high percentage of specialists have created the major preconditions for a nationalist movement. Zaslavsky goes on to say that the Soviet regime neutralizes the nationalist threat by means of the centrally planned economy, federalism, and the passport system.[39]

Anti-Soviet incidents occur more regularly in the Baltic States than in any other part of the Soviet Union, where national groups such as Armenians and Georgians have asserted their claim to maintain their religious, linguistic, and other ethnic traditions. Youths at pop-music concerts recently ended up running through the city of Liepaja, a Latvian coastal town, shouting, "freedom, give us freedom."

Lithuania is one of the most nationalistic of the three Baltic States. At a 1978 Vilna soccer match against the Soviets, anti-Russian slogans were shouted, and Soviet propaganda banners were torn down. The Baltic States regard themselves as "Western States" and should not be under the Great Russian domination. Indeed, one can see Western-style culture in Riga, the capital of Latvia. The historic link with Germany can be seen in Tallinn, capital of ancient Estonia. In Estonia, people can buy a TV attachment for $50 that enables them to watch TV programs from Finland. The Baltic people have an ironic half-mocking attitude toward the Russians. Officially, the Moscow connection is justified on the basis of great economic improvement. Privately, feelings and attitudes are quite different. One *Samizdat* states this attitude in the following words: "Love and friendship between Lithuanians and Russians? It is the friendship and love between a lamb and a wolf." In Lithuania, the Kremlin tries hard to reduce the power of the Roman Catholic Church. Despite this effort, about 40 percent of the population in Lithuania are still regular church-goers. In this region, as in the Ukraine, the Soviets expend great effort to make sure the Russian language is spoken. Yet the Baltic people try to avoid speaking Russian whenever possible. Although the prosperity is largely due to Russian investment, acceptance of Russian people is rather unimpressive. The Baltic people are still nationalistic; a few even want independence. The Kremlin is trying hard to reduce anti-Soviet sentiments and acts.[40]

The Caucasian Area: Armenia, Georgia, and Azerbaidzhan

Linguistic Russification has been insignificant in the Caucasian area— averaging approximately 1 percent for all the many groups living there. The range among groups has also been small, the highest being 2 percent for the North Ossetians of the North Caucasus and the low 0.3 percent of the Chechens. Even among the Georgians, who are considered a varied group, the percentage was no larger than 0.4 percent. The Georgians and Armenians are very protective of their language and have fought to maintain their language as the official language of their republics.

Armenian flourishes as the official language for everyday business. The Armenian Church still functions and is apparently well attended, although much of its financial support comes from diaspora funds. Customary betrothal and other rituals are still maintained, particularly among peasant groups. A large number of Armenian university graduates (a proportionately larger percentage than that which characterizes many other nationality groups) appear to be devoting their energies to the study of Armenian problems.

Nationalist expressions are strongest among that group which Mary Matossian calls "the fellow-traveling Armenian nationalist." This group has come into frequent conflict with communist authorities, and some have been expelled from the party.

On the whole, Moscow has been quite tolerant of nationalist expressions here. Hence, there were no reprisals at nationalist celebrations held in Erevan in April 1965, commemorating the fiftieth anniversary of the 1915 Massacre of the Armenians in the Ottoman Empire. The Soviet Armenian poet Kevorak Emim was warmly received as he uttered these sentiments: "Our people were, are, and will be."

A number of indicators point to Armenian nationalism. Recent Armenian emigrés and emigré organizations in the United States tell of unrest, occasional riots, and a Soviet crackdown. Soviet leaders in Georgia have been targets of assassinations. Georgians claim that there have been at least two assassination attempts aimed at the leader of the Georgian Republic. In one, the bomb failed to go off. In the second, gunmen attacked his car and shot the Chairman's chauffeur in the shoulder but missed the party secretary. General anti-Soviet feelings resulted in the dynamiting of a statue commemorating the "liberation"of Georgia by the Russians in 1921. The Georgians, an ancient proud people, have a 3,000-year-old history and culture. They adhere to a way of life in which chivalry, honor, and ancient traditions are held in high esteem. Some regard the Great Russian materialistic culture as inferior.

Azerbaidzhan is the third Transcaucasian republic. Soviet Azerbaidzhan is bordered on the north by mountainous Daghestan ASSR, on the northwest by Georgia, on the southwest by Armenia and a small area of Turkey, on the south by Iran, and on the east by the Caspian Sea. Azerbaidzhan consists of two cultural worlds: one urban, in which Islam and its traditional customs, literature, and art have largely disappeared, and the other rural and isolated, in which women still wear black shawls and Muslim values are retained to some extent. The Azerbaidzianese, who are Muslim, have a large amount of co-ethnics in Iran and have ties to the Near East. Historically, the country has not been unified. Its culture comes from Persia but its language and ethnic background are Turkish. Twentieth-century influence has been overwhelmingly Russian. Ronald Wixman says that one of the clearest indicators of why ethnic nationalism is very pronounced in this area is the distribution and migration patterns. He believes that, in spite of overpopulation and labor surplus, Caucasians have shown a great reluctance to migrate outside their traditional homeland.[41]

Central Asia

In summing up the attitudes of the Central Asian peoples, who are largely Islamic, Alexandre Bennigsen states:

Islam itself is not merely a religion. It encompasses not only a corpus of directly religious beliefs and rites, but also a complex aggregate of cultural, psycological and social traditions, attitudes and customs governing the whole way of life of the Muslim community. Its "rooting" in every level of society is certainly deeper than that of any other religion of the world, and many of the traditions, attitudes and customs of Islam are not contingent on the strict observance of the faith.[42]

Teresa Rakowska-Harmstone concludes:

In retrospect, the role played by the Russians in Central Asia was not an agreeable one and did not endear them to the local population. It would be naive to suppose that they are liked there. In spite of all the natives, the Russians have become identified with hardship and oppression at every stage of development since the revolution, and for all the emphasis on druzhba narodov and socialist brotherhood, they still represent an alien rule and privileged minority.[43]

The Tadzhiks continue to adhere to their customs, dress, language, and religious practices, despite hostility from the party. Parents who sent their children to Russian schools were criticized publicly at debates held in Kazakhstan and the Tatar Republic. Representatives of the Kazakh intelligentsia demanded that only persons who knew the Kazakh language should hold responsible posts in Kazakhstan. Cultural life in the native languages flourishes among all the Turkish peoples of Central Asia; even Shakespeare has been translated into native languages. Native language publications have increased, and there has been instensified interest and research in national heritage, resulting in the reissuance of banned, suppressed, and well-nigh forgotten materials, as well as textbooks in native poetry, literature, and history. Caution, however, is exercised when these impinge on official Russian interpretations. It is not surprising, therefore, that linguistic Russification has been very small.

Geoffrey Wheeler indicates that the elites in Central Asia feel they are culturally and morally Russia's superiors. They regard themselves in education and technical know-how as equals and resent being treated as "second-class citizens."[44] An important point is made in a recent article by Gail Warshofsky Lapidus. She feels that the increase of culturally and scientific elites is not only a way of rewarding and coopting elites, but also of channeling them away from political and administrative areas.[45] Bennigsen writes that, although there is no evidence of open protest among the local elites, there is a noticeable increase in the tension between them. Bennigsen maintains that the Central Asian elite will demand access to the Muslims outside Soviet borders; further rehabilitation of the political past; and greater ethnic representation of the party and state apparatus.[46]

Other research points out that the Central Asians feel they are exploited economically by the Russians who have invested huge capital in their region. They feel the Russians have done so for their own profit and do not deserve either their loyalty or respect.[47] The Central Asians are demanding greater allocations of capital investment funds, so that they can diversify their economies.[48]

The Soviet regime, then, pays much attention to this region for the following reasons: (1) Some of these regions, such as Tajikstan and Kazakstan, have co-ethnics in China and Afghanistan; therefore, the Soviets have to be ever vigilant about the images they project in their treatment of the Central Asian peoples. (2) The Central Asian Muslims have a much larger population increase; hence, for geopolitical reasons, it is not very comforting to the Slavic Russians. (3) The Central Asians continue to resist Russification and persist in holding on to a sense of strong Muslim self-identity and separateness. There is, of course, criticism of the Muslim people and their clergy by writers who espouse the regime's ideology.

One prolific writer on modernization and the Muslim nationalist movement in Central Asia is Nugman Ashirov, who says that Muslim religious organizations, though propounding modernity, do nevertheless adhere to the backward notion that God creates and predetermines everything.[49]

The Crimean Tatars

Peter Reddaway tells us that while the adult men were at the front during World War II and able-bodied older men and younger men were in labor camps, the entire Crimean Tatar population was deported to Siberia and Central Asia. The KGB forced 200,000 defenseless women, children, and the infirm into trains for resettlement. This move resulted in the death of 50 percent of the population, which was slanderously accused of being disloyal to the Soviet motherland, and destroyed their culture and autonomy.[50]

An appeal by Representatives of the Crimean Tatar People to the World Public Opinion was published in the *Samizdat* of June 21, 1968. The million or so Crimean Tatars now living outside their homeland territory are demanding the right to return.

According to Reddaway, more than 500 pages from *Samizdat* available in the West have been devoted to this issue, and the number is growing steadily.[51] The documents include cases of individual and group protest in the form of public lectures, protest letters, and demonstrations. Research of protest demonstrations in the Soviet Union indicates that from 1965 to 1978 the Crimean Tatars have been the second most active, accounting for 14.5 percent of all events—second only to Soviet Jews with 35.0 percent.[52] Their protests have been followed by mass arrests, expulsion from the party, job loss, and imprisonment. At least one protest letter contained the names of 16,000 Crimean Tatars. It was addressed to Professor M. Vakhabov who had written a critique of the Tatars accusing them of bourgeois nationalism in *A Chronicle of Human Rights in the USSR*, Nos. 5–6, November–December 1973. Other members of the Soviet intelligentsia have taken up the cause, including General Pyotor Grigorevich Grigorenko, a Ukrainian, who was eventually imprisoned for his support.

Toward the end of 1969, a Tatar-initiated referendum purporting to record the feelings of Tatars now living outside their homeland reported that the overwhelming majority wished to do so.[53] Several thousand have indeed attempted to so do but, according to *Samizdat*, have been subjugated to police brutality and harassment. Victor Zaslavsky claims that economic and political reasons are involved in the obstinate refusal of the central leadership to recognize the Tatars' rights. One example that he gave was that of weighing the protest of the Tatars versus the potential dissatisfaction of the Ukrainians if the Tatars were to return; the leadership, as previously shown, decided in favor of the Ukrainians.[54] Hélène Carrère d'Encaussé states that, although certain cultural rights were restored by a 1967 decree, they were not given back their collective rights. This decree failed to mention a restoration of their republic and omitted the term "Tatar nation," substituting "Tatars having resided in Crimea." It is felt that this eliminated the permanent bond between ethnic identity and soil, which is one of the four criteria determining a nation's existence. D'Encaussé also observes that recently the Tatar movement has followed three lines of action: (1) harassing the Soviet authorities with mass petitions, (2) linking Tatar demands with those of the democratic movement in the Soviet Union, and (3) going to the Crimea in spite of the ban.[55]

The Jews: Latent Racism

Perhaps the most striking evidence of the latent nature of ethnicity is the behavior of Soviet Jews during the last several years. Among all non-Russian groups, the Jews show the largest degreee of linguistic Russification. The 1959 census indicated that only somewhat more than 20 percent still claimed Yiddish as their mother tongue, and, by 1970, the figure was reduced to approximately 17 percent. Evidence of any Jewish cultural life is rare. Yiddish is taught nowhere in any school in the Soviet Union; there is no Jewish press to speak of, Yiddish cultural productions are exceedingly rare, and the handful of synagogues scattered throughout the Soviet Union are attended primarily by a smattering of old men. By all classic indices of ethnic identity, it seems fair to say that until the late 1960s the Jews were the most successfully Russified of all minority groups. Beginning in 1968, however, events occurred which totally reversed this judgment.

On October 30, 1968, a letter signed by twenty-six Lithuanian Jews appeared in the *New York Times* and *The Washington Post*. It was in protest against anti-Jewish discrimination and growing anti-Semitism in the Soviet Union. Shortly thereafter, hundreds of letters written by Jews began to be reported in the Western press. Some emerged via *Samizdat*, others were sent directly to Israeli or U.N. officials, and a very small percentage were sent to Russian officials. William Korey estimates that between February 1968 and October 1970, some 220 letters of appeal made their apperance. The themes of the letters varied: protests against officially sponsored anti-Semitism, the publication of over a dozen books and articles that are blatantly anti-Semitic, protest against the absence of Jewish cultural institutions, letters expressing simple ethnic pride and even some expressing religious interest.

D'Encaussé points out that increasing action is being taken to restore the Jews' cultural heritage. To accomplish this objective, she says that the Jews play with the interpretation of the laws. For example, a network was set up to teach Hebrew, which is considered to be illegal.[56] Most impressive in the letters, however, is a theme that had dominated many of them since: an expression of strong love for Israel and an accompanying desire to emigrate there.

While assessment of the pervasiveness of this newfound ethnicity (or perhaps heretofore suppressed ethnicity) must be speculative, several factors are evident. First, the letters and protests emerged from several areas of the Soviet Union, suggesting that it was not a localized phenomenon. Some of those familiar with the scene have claimed that from several hundred thousand to as many as one-half million Jews would emigrate to Israel given the opportunity. Currently, many are awaiting Soviet permission to leave the USSR.

Some researchers, however, including Thomas E. Sawyer, believe that central authorities are using Jewish emigration to rid themselves of harmful activists. As more Jews emigrate, Sawyer suggests, those who remain in the Soviet Union will be subject to increasing discrimination. The Soviets consider the Jews who immigrated traitors, which leaves them with a feeling of distrust of the Jews who remain. Sawyer and others indicate that the sociopolitical position of the Jews who have remained has deteriorated. Even though they are allowed to join the Communist party, they are barred from party/state leadership roles. So Jewish activist leaders are not only focusing on emigration rights, but also on religious and political rights for the Jews who have remained in the Soviet Union.[57]

The Jewish ethnic impulse has indeed become so strong that some observers believe it to be the most militant protest movement today. Despite the horrendous consequences that may have endured, the Jews have undertaken ventures judged enormously daring by Soviet standards. Examples are numerous. A "sit-in" in front of the Presidium of the Supreme Soviet occurred on February 18, 1971. Thousands appeared at the synagogue during Simchat Torah (a Jewish festival) as a form of ethnic assertiveness and defiance. Jewish dissidents hold scholarly seminars in their private apartments under the watchful eyes of the KGB. Despite the ban on contacts with other Western Jews, visitors report being widely sought after, albeit surreptitiously. Several thousand have indeed managed to obtain emigration visas, the most famous recent cases being those of Valery and Galina Panov, and Alexander Ginzburg, who is part Jewish.[58]

Officially encouraged, anti-Semitism is prevalent throughout the USSR. In 1977, it was reported that not a single Jew had been admitted to Moscow University. The media are very anti-Semitic and put on campaigns against the Jews. Harris O. Schoenberg says:

The new Soviet racism is not restricted to denying Jews educational and employment opportunities. It manifests itself as well in a massive multimedia campaign, directed ostensibly against Zionism. That would be harm enough since, as Zaslavsky points out, "*Zionist* is not a neutral, intellectual concept in the contemporary USSR, but a symbol that agitates strong anti-Semitic emotions." To make sure that the average Soviet citizen does not miss the point, Soviet propagandists incorporate all the basic anti-Semitic stereotypes. For example, in *The Creeping Counter-Revolution*, a book published by the Soviet authorities in 1974, Vladimir Begun traces "zionist gangsterism" to the teachings of the Torah (the first five books of the Bible) and the Talmud. The Torah is characterized as "an unsurpassed textbook of blood-thirstiness, hypocrisy, treason, perfidy, and moral degeneracy—all the lowest human qualities." The Jewish religious ethic, according to Begun, teaches "shamelessness and cynicism" and plays "an exceptionally harmful role." The synagogue he describes as a base "for subversive activity," and overt anti-Semitic outbreaks he justifies as part of the class struggle.[59]

Social movement theory holds that when one individual or group is persecuted, the individual or the group will join any social movement or political party that will help alleviate the individual's or group's oppressed state.

Dissident physicist Aleksandr Voronel, who now resides in Israel, has said:

When intellectuals who have built their lives on professional achievement perceive barriers to their advancement, they find themselves in a crisis that is tantamount to the loss of the meaning of life. And they begin to search for a new source of meaning. Having been rejected as Russians, they revive their old cultural reference group and become again Jews and Zionists. For the latter, Israel offers a positive option which restores their feelings of self-pride.[60]

Russian leaders have been showing a film to some audiences, including the Red Army, entitled *Secret and Open Things* which opens with a crack of a pistol shot and the narrator points out that a Jewish woman tried to kill Lenin. During a sequence that shows Hitler invading Russia, the narrator says: "Jewish capital helped Hitler to power." Soviet propagandists such as Trofim Kichko, Yurii Ivanov, Vladimir Begun, Vladimir Bolshakov, Yevgenii Yevseev, Valery Yemelyanov, Lev Korneyev, among a number of others, have written such vicious books and articles that surpass the infamous "Protocols of the Elders of Zion." The persistent theme in this writing is that Jews are fifth columnists inspired by their religion and the religious teaching and that the ultimate aim of the Jews is to seek "mastery of all mankind." Tass, the famous communist news agency, has strongly endorsed this image of Jews and has made sure that the Soviet public gets to know about it.[61]

SUMMARY AND CONCLUSIONS

Despite the claim that issues of ethnic relations and national grievances within the Soviet Union have been given scant attention, Marxist polemics disguise both the extent and range of the problem. Having willed the existence of the new international Soviet man, Soviet sociologists tend to treat him as a reality. If indeed some ethnic feeling forces itself on their vision, official responses indicate that it is merely a temporary aberration—a lapse into bourgeois nationalism and temporary "negative attitudes" that will inevitaly be altered in the internationalization process. Furthermore, minority voices are instigated by the imperialist West and the chauvinist Han Chinese.

Reluctance to deal with the issue may stem from fear of what such exposure may reveal. First, the actual policies implemented toward minority groups under the new communist regime show more of a historical continuity with the hated Tsarism than it does with any new ideology. Sovietization is but modernized Russification—more powerful because of its greater efficiency and technological resources. Second, as minority groups in this country have long recognized and American sociologists belatedly so, the treatment of minority groups is part of a broader "class" struggle wherein dominant groups attempt to maintain their power. Official Russian ideology recognizes no classes in Soviet Union—and Soviet sociologists would be hard pressed to ignore this aspect in any realistic discussion of the problem. Third, Soviet sociologists, like American sociologists some years ago, may simply have tended to underestimate the power of ethnicity and cultural nationalism. The world currently faces two polarizing trends. On one hand, the march toward internationalism and global cooperation seems inevitable, given an increased recognition of the interdependence of the planet. On the other is the equally strong move toward "tribalism" or ethnicity. A glance at a world map will tell us that oppressed minorities and nationalities are everywhere registering grievances and national rights. Models and strategies for reconciling these apparently contradictory drives are sadly lacking.

By all current indications, inequality, ethnicity, and nationalism remain strong forces in the Soviet Union, and we would agree with Professor Szporluk, among a number of other scholars, that Soviet leaders can't afford to ignore these forces. Russian policy has wavered between coercive repression and limited concesisons. The present era is characterized by the latter. But again, as experience from other sources indicates, minor concessions rarely appease—more frequently they lead to "rising expectations." The burgeoning growth of ethnic nationalism in the Soviet Union may be just such a phenomenon. It is our judgment that it will not disappear—we suspect that it will continue to grow. What the Soviet Union will do, however, remains to be seen. Certainly, one could venture a guess that geopolitical considerations such as the threat from China, the status and effectiveness of the detente, the political strength of Mikhail Gorbachov, the Middle East situation, and the Afghanistan conflict could affect the status of minorities in the USSR. We do not, however, foresee, as some do, that the minorities/nationalities and dissidents are going to bring about the dissolution of the Union of the Soviet Socialist Republics. As a superpower, the dominant nationality, the Russians, cannot and will not permit that.

NOTES

1. B. G. Gafurov, member of the Central Committee of the Communist party and chief editor of its periodical, *Sovremennity vostok*, delivered a lecture to the Diplomatic Corps in Moscow on October 12, 1961. I. P. Tsamerian and S. L. Ronin, *Equality of Rights Between Races and Nationalities in the USSR* (UNESCO, 1962), p. 9. See other footnotes here on Gafurov and Brezhnev. David Kowalewski, "Protest for National Rights in the USSR: Characteristics and Consequences," *Nationalities Papers* 8, No. 2 (Fall 1980): 179–95.

2. V. I. Kozlov, "The Dynamics of the National Composition of the USSR's Population and Problems of Demographic Policy," *Current Digest of Soviet Press* 35, No. 43 (1968): 12.

3. Ralph S. Clem, "Ethnicity and Its Implications," *Bulletin of the Atomic Scientists* 38, No. 6 (June/July 1982): 53–58; N. Beloff, "Russia and the Hundred-Headed Hydra," *Virginia Quarterly Review* 56, No. 3 (Summer 1980): 385–95; Alexandre Bennigsen, "Several Nations or One People? Ethnic Consciousness Among Soviet Muslims," *Survey* 24, No. 3 (Summer 1979): 51–64; Louis Harap, "Socialism, Anti-Semitism, and Jewish Ethnicity," *Journal of Ethnic Studies* 6, No. 4 (Winter 1979): 65–84; Nicholas Dima, "A Hypothetical Model of Migration in the Soviet Union," *Nationalities Papers* 8, No. 1 (Spring 1980): 87–94; Gail W. Lapidus, "Ethnonationalism and Political Stability—The Soviet Case,"*World Pol-*

itics, No. 36 (July 1984): 555–80; "The Nationality Question and the Soviet System," *The Soviet Union in the 1980s* 35, No. 3 (1984): 98–112; Samuel P. Oliner, "Soviet Nationalities and Dissidents: A Persistent Problem," *Humboldt Journal of Social Relations* 10, No. 1 (1982/83): 19–49; Robert V. Daniels, *Russia: Roots of Confrontation* (Cambridge, Mass.: Harvard University Press, 1985).

4. Teresa Rakowska-Harmstone, "Ethnicity in the Soviet Union," *Annals of the American Academy of Political and Social Science* 433 (September 1977): 73–87; B. Anderson and B. Silver, "Estimating Russification of Ethnic Identity Among Non-Russians in the U.S.S.R.," *Demography* 20, No. 4 (November 1983): 461–85; M. Perakh, "Contemporary Dissent in Russia: Rise, Development, Trends," *Partisan Review* 45, No. 2 (1978): 248–64; Ronald Wixman, "Ethnic Nationalism in the Caucasus," *Nationalities Papers* 10, No. 2 (Fall 1982); 137–56.

5. Robert Blauner, *Racial Oppression in America* (New York: Harper & Row, 1972).

6. Rocky L. Rockett, *Ethnic Nationalities in the Soviet Union* (New York: Praeger Publishers, 1981), p. 23.

7. Dima, "Hypothetical Model," p. 87; Y. Bilinsky, "Expanding the Use of Russian or Russification," *Russian Review* 40, No. 3 (1981): 320; John A. Armstrong, "Federalism in the U.S.S.R.: Ethnic and Territorial Aspects," *Publius, the Journal of Federalism* 7, No. 4 (1977): 104.

8. I am indebted to the following scholars who have used the concepts of Russification, Russianization, and Sovietization: Ivan Dzyuba, *Internationalism or Russification?* (London: Weidenfeld and Nicolson, 1968); Paul G. Rubel, "Ethnic Identity Among Soviet Nationalities," in E. Allworth, ed., *Soviet Nationality Problems*, (New York: Columbia University Press, 1970), pp. 211–30; V. V. Asparturian, "The Non-Russian Nationalities," in A. Kassof, ed., *Prospects for Soviet Society* (New York: Praeger Publishers, 1968), pp. 143–98; F. C. Barghoorn, *Soviet Russian Nationalism* (New York: Oxford University Press, 1956).

9. G. Wheeler, "Russian Conquest and Colonization of Central Asia," in T. Hunczak, ed., *Russian Imperialism from Ivan the Great to the Revolution* (New Brunswick, N.J.: Rutgers University Press, 1974), p. 284. For a discussion of Russian expansion and conquest of nation-states and ethnic groups, see: W. Kolarz, *Russia and Her Colonies* (Hamden, Conn.: Anchor, 1967); Kolarz, *The People of the Soviet Far East* (Hamden, Conn.: Anchor, 1969); R. Charques, *The Twilight of Imperial Russia* (Englewood Cliffs, N.J.: Essential Books, 1959); S. A. Zenkowshy, *Pan-Turkism and Islam in Russia* (Cambridge: Harvard University Press, 1960); T. Rakowska-Harmstone, *Russia and Nationalism in Central Asia* (Baltimore: Johns Hopkins Press, 1970); Marc Raeff, "Patterns of Russian Imperialism," in Allworth, ed., *Soviet Nationality Problems* (New York: Columbia University Press, 1971), pp. 22–42.

10. Raeff, "Patterns of Russian Imperialism," p. 37.

11. Samuel Bloembergen, "The Union Republics: How Much Autonomy?" *Problems of Communism* (September/October 1967): p. 34. Also see Robert Conquest, *Soviet Nationality Policy in Practice* (New York: Praeger Publishers, 1967). For additional discussion of autonomy and self-determination, see Peter G. Stercho's "Soviet Concept of National Self-Determination: Theory and Reality from Lenin to Brezhnev," *Ukrainian Quarterly* 29, Nos. 1–2 (Spring and Summer 1973, respectively).

12. Cited in William Forwood, "Nationalities in the Soviet Union," in George Schopflin, ed., *The Soviet Union and Eastern Europe: A Handbook* (New York: Praeger Publishers, 1970), p. 202. For contemporary status of nationalities, see Hélène Carrère d'Encaussé's "Party and Federation in the USSR: The Problem of Nationalities and Power in the USSR," *Government and Opposition* 13 (September 1978): 133–50.

13. Roman Szporluk, "History and Russian Ethnocentrism," in Edward Allworth, ed., *Ethnic Russians in the USSR: The Dilemma of Social Dominance* (New York: Pergamon Press, 1980), p. 47.

14. Barghoorn, *Soviet Russian Nationalism*, p. 10; for further discussion of linguistic Russification, see Pedro Ramet, "Linguistic Assimilation in Ukraine," *Ukrainian Quarterly* 35, No. 3 (Autumn 1979): 237–53; George Gibian, "Reviving Russian Nationalism," *The New Leader* 62 (November 19, 1979): 13–14.

15. Brian Silver, "The Status of National Minority Languages in Soviet Education: An Assessment of Recent Changes," *Soviet Studies* 26, No. 1 (January 1974): 39. Also see Tonu Parming, "Population Processes and the Nationality Issue in the Soviet Baltic," *Soviet Studies* 32, No. 3 (July 1980): 398–414.

16. Brian Silver, "Social Mobilization and the Russification of Soviet Nationalities," *American Political Science Review* 68, No. 1 (March 1964): 65.

17. E. Jones and F. Grupp, "Modernization and Ethnic Equalization in the USSR," *Soviet Studies* 36, No. 2 (1984): 159–84; Lapidus "Ethnonationalism," pp. 555–80; "The Nationality Question and the Soviet System," *The Soviet Union in the 1980s* 35, No. 3 (1984): 98–112; J. P. Cole, *Population and Peoples in Geography of the Soviet Union* (London: Butterworths, 1984); R. Karklins, "Ethnic Politics and Access to Higher Education: The Soviet Case," *Comparative Politics* 16, No. 3 (April 1984): 277–94; Clem, "Ethnicity," pp. 53–58; V. Zaslavsky, *The Neo-Stalinist State* (New York: M. E. Sharpe, 1982); D. Kowalewski, "The Crimean Tatars: Ten Years of Rehabilitation in Ethnic Groups," *International Periodical of Ethnic Studies* 2, No. 4 (1980): 343–58; D. Kowalewski, "National Rights Protest in the Brezhnev Era: Some Determinants of Success," *Ethnic and Racial Studies* (Great Britain) 4, No. 2 (1981): 175–88; D. Kowalewski, "The Religious-National Interlock: Faith and Ethnicity in the Soviet Union," *Canadian Review of Studies in Nationalism* 9 (Spring 1982): 97–111; Dima, "Hypothetical Model," pp. 87–94; Dima, "Contemporary Soviet Modernization and Its Ethnic Implications: 1959–1979," *Journal of Social, Political and Economic Studies* 7 (Winter 1982): 337–48; Rockett, *Ethnic Nationalities*, pp. 1–153; Z. Gitelman, "Moscow and the Hundred-Headed Hydra," *Virginia Quarterly Review* 56, No. 3 (Summer 1980): 385–95; S. Lipset and R. Dobson, "Social Stratification and Sociology in the Soviet Union," *Survey* 19, No. 3 (Summer 1973): 114–85; Jerry Pankhurst and Michael P. Sacks, eds., *Contemporary Soviet Society—Sociological Perspectives* (New York: Praeger Publishers, 1980); H. Carrère d'Encaussé, "Party and Federation in the USSR," *Government and Opposition* (Great Britain) 13, No. 2 (Spring 1978): 133–50; Murray Yanowitch, "The Soviet Income Revolution," *Slavic Review* 22, No. 4 (December 1963): 683–97; T. Rakowska-Harmstone, "The Dialectics of Nationalism in the USSR," *Problems of Communism* 23 (May–June 1974): 1–22.

18. Rockett, *Ethnic Nationalities*, p. 140.

19. Clem, "Ethnicity," p. 57.

20. Pankhurst and Sacks, *Contemporary Soviet Society*, p. 111.

21. Armstrong, "Federalism in the U.S.S.R.," p. 104.

22. Karklins, "Ethnic Politics," p. 291.

23. Lapidus, "Ethnonationalism," p. 568.

24. Zaslavsky, *Neo-Stalinist State*, p. 109.

25. V. Holubnychy, "Some Economic Aspects of Relations Among the Soviet Republics," in E. Goldhagen, ed., *Ethnic Minorities in the Soviet Union* (New York: Praeger Publishers, 1968), pp. 50–120. For additional discussion of minorities, see Robert Conquest's writings in *The Nation Killers* (New York: Macmillan, 1970). See also R. Conquest, "The Deported Nationalities—An Unsavory Story," *Problems of Communism* (September/October 1967); Paul Hollander, *American and Soviet Societies* (Englewood Cliffs, N.J.: Prentice-Hall, 1969), pp. 316–20; Walter Kolarz, *Russia and Her Colonies* (Hamden, Conn.: Anchor Books, 1967), pp. 67–87; William J. Parente, "The Nationalities Revival in the Soviet Union," *Midstream* (August–September 1971): 59–65.

26. Rakowska-Harmstone, "The Dialectics of Nationalism," pp. 12–15.

27. Lapidus, "The Nationality Question and the Soviet System," pp. 98–112.

28. Rakowska-Harmstone, "Ethnicity in the Soviet Union," p. 79.

29. Lapidus, "'Nationality Question," pp. 98–112; Rakowska-Harmstone, "The Dialectics of Nationalism in the USSR," pp. 1–22; T. Kuzio, "The Russian Idea— Fact and Fiction," *Ukrainian Review* (Great Britain) 34, No. 1 (1981): 3–38; A. Weeks, "Russia—The Chosen Nation," *Freedom at Issue*, No. 50 (March/April 1979): 23–29; Wixman, "Ethnic Nationalism," pp. 137–56; V. Wozniuk, "Nationalism and Dissidence in the Soviet Union: The Ukrainian Case," *Potomac Review* 8, No. 3 (Spring 1977): 1–12.

30. Brian Silver, "Social Mobilization and the Russification of Soviet Nationalities," *American Political Science Review* 68, No. 1 (March 1974): 46. For excellent discussions of ethnic nationalism as well as other forms of nationalism, see L. Wirth, "Types of Nationalism," *American Journal of Sociology* 61 (May 1936); H. Kohn, *Nationalism, Its Meaning and History* (New York: Van Nostrand, 1965); I. Lightbody, "Nationalism as a Function of Ethnic Demand," *Canadian Journal of Political Science* 11, No. 3 (September 1969): 118–35.

31. Y. Bilinsky, "Assimilation and Ethnic Assertiveness Among the Ukrainians of the Soviet Union," in *Erich Goldhagen, ed., Ethnic Minorities in the Soviet Union* (New York: Praeger Publishers, 1968), p. 166. For more discussion of the Ukrainian problem, see Michael Pap in W. Gurian, ed., *Soviet Imperialism* (South Bend: University of Notre Dame Press, 1953), pp. 43–73. See also Ivan Dzyuba, *Internationalism or Russification?* (London: Weidenfeld and Nicolson, 1968).

32. Rakowska-Harmstone, "Ethnicity in the Soviet Union," pp. 73–87.

33. Peter Reddaway, ed., *Uncensored Russia* (New York: American Heritage Press, 1972), p. 78. For further manifestations of nationalism in the Ukraine, see Roman Szporluk's "The Ukraine and the Ukrainians," in Zev Katz et al, eds., *Handbook of Major Soviet Nationalities* (New York: Free Press, 1975). Also see Mark Perakh's "From Sakharov to Samolvin: Contemporary Russian 'Free Thinking' on Nationality Question," *Ukrainian Quarterly 34*, No. 3 (Autumn 1978): 201–17.

34. For further discussion of the problems of Russification and problems of Ukrainian language, see Walter Dushnyck, "The Assault Against the Ukrainian Language," *Ukrainian Quarterly* 35, No. 3 (Autumn 1979): 229–36.

35. Wozniuk, "Nationalism and Dissidence," pp. 4–9.

36. Kowalewski, "National Rights in the Brezhnev Era: Some Determinants of Success," p. 177.

37. Jaan Pennar, "Nationalism in the Soviet Baltics," in Erich Goldhagan, ed., *Ethnic Minorities in the Soviet Union* (New York: Praeger Publishers, 1968), p. 198.

38. Rakowska-Harmstone, "The Dialectics of Nationalism in the USSR," p. 14.

39. Zaslavsky, *Neo-Stalinist State*, p. 117.

40. For more details, see Robin Knight's "How Baltic States Torment Russia," *U.S. News & World Report* (September 25, 1978), 43–44; Parming, "Population Processes," pp. 398–414. Also I. Vuorjoki's "The Baltic Question in Today's World," *Baltic Review* 38 (August 1971); Adelaida Lemberg, "Russification in the Baltic States," *Baltic Review* 33 (January 1967).

41. Wixman, "Ethnic Nationalism," p. 146.

42. Bennigsen, "Several Nations," p. 53.

43. Teresa Rakowska-Harmstone, *Russia and Nationalism in Central Asia* (Baltimore: Johns Hopkins University Press, 1970), p. 93.

44. Geoffrey Wheeler, "Islam and the Soviet Union," *Asian Affairs* 10, No. 3 (1979): 250.

45. Lapidus, "Ethnonationalism," pp. 555–580.

46. Bennigsen, "Several Nations," p. 63.

47. Beloff, "Russia and the Hundred-Headed Hydra," p. 393.

48. Rakowska-Harmstone, "The Dialectics of Nationalism in the U.S.S.R.," p. 14.

49. Wheeler, "Islam," pp 40–49.

50. Reddaway, *Uncensored Russia*, p. 249. Also see Adrei Sakharov's "Letter to the Soviet Academy of Science," *Russia*, No. 1 (1981): 25.

51. Reddaway, *Uncensored Russia*, p. 252. For a further discussion of this minority, see Robert Conquest's writings in *The Nation Killers* (New York: Macmillan, 1970). See also Conquest, "The Deported Nationalities—An Unsavory Story"; Hollander, *American and Soviet Societies*; Kolarz, *Russia and Her Colonies*.

52. Kowalewski, "The Crimean Tatars: Ten Years of Rehabilitation," p. 346.

53. Reddaway, *Uncensored Russia*, pp. 263–69.

54. Zaslavsky, *Neo-Stalinist State*, p. 122.

55. Hélène Carère d'Encaussé, *Decline of an Empire* (New York: Newsweek Books, 1980), p. 196.

56. Ibid., p. 205.

57. Thomas E. Sawyer, *The Jewish Minority in the Soviet Union* (Boulder, Colo.: Westview Press, 1979), pp. 120, 217–18.

58. Benjamin Pinkus, *The Soviet Government and the Jews 1948–1967* (Cambridge: Cambridge University Press, 1984), pp. 341–63.

59. Harris O. Schoenberg, "The Solution Is Escape," *Society* 16 (May 1979), p. 12.

60. Ibid., p. 12.

61. For additional information on anti-Semitism in the Soviet Union, see Erwin H. Epstein, "Ideological Factors in Soviet Educational Policy Towards Jews," *Education and Urban Society* 10 (Fall 1978): 223–54; William Korey, "Kremlin's War Against the Jews," *Reform Judaism* (December 1978); William Korey, "Soviet Jewry: Plight and Prospect," *Midstream* 23, No. 4 (April 1977): 18–27;

William Korey, "Updating 'The Protocols of the Elders of Zion,' " *Midstream* (May1976): 5–17; S. L. Shneiderman, " 'High' Anti-Semitism Revived," *Midstream* 22, No. 7 (August/September 1976): 76–80; Mikhail Agursky, "Russian Neo-Nazism—A Growing Threat," *Midstream* 22, No. 2 (1976): 35–42.

BIBLIOGRAPHY

Allworth, Edward. *Ethnic Russians in the USSR: The Dilemma of Social Dominance*. New York: Pergamon Press, 1980.

———. *Soviet Nationality Problems*, New York: Columbia University Press, 1971.

Anderson, B., and B. Silver. "Estimating Russification of Ethnic Identity Among Non-Russians in the USSR." *Demography* 20, No. 4 (November 1983): 461–85.

Armstrong, J. "Federalism in the USSR: Ethnic and Territorial Aspects." *Journal of Federalism*, No. 4 (1977): 104.

Asparturian, V. V. "The Non-Russian Nationalities." In *Prospects for Soviet Society*, edited by A. Kassof. New York: Praeger Publishers, 1968.

Cole, J. P. *Population and Peoples in Geograpahy of the Soviet Union*. London: Butterworths, 1984.

Conquest, R. *Soviet Nationality Policy in Practice*, New York: Praeger Publishers, 1967.

Daniels, Robert V. *Russia: Roots of Confrontation*. Cambridge, Mass.: Harvard University Press, 1985.

Forwood, William. "Nationalities in the Soviet Union." In *The Soviet Union and Eastern Europe: A Handbook*, edited by George Schopflin. New York: Praeger Publishers, 1970, p. 202.

Goldhagen, Erich. *Ethnic Minorities in the Soviet Union*. New York: Praeger Publishers, 1968.

Jones, E., and F. Grupp. "Modernization and Ethnic Equalization in the USSR." *Soviet Studies* 36, No. 2 (1984): 159–84.

Katz, Zev. *Handbook of Major Soviet Nationalities*. New York: Free Press, 1975.

Kozlov, V. I. "The Dynamics of the National Composition of the USSR's Populations and Problems of Demographic Policy." *Current Digest of Soviet Press* 35, No. 43 (1968): 12.

Lapidus, Gail W. "Ethnonationalism and Political Stability—The Soviet Case." *World Politics* (No. 36 (July 1984): 555–80.

Oliner, Samuel P. "Soviet Nationalities and Dissidents: A Persistent Problem." *Humboldt Journal of Social Relations* 10, No. 1 (1982/83): 19–49.

Pinkus, Benjamin. *The Soviet Government and the Jews 1948–1967*. Cambridge: Cambridge University Press, 1984.

Rakowska-Harmstone, Teresa, *Russia and Nationalism in Central Asia*. Baltimore: Johns Hopkins University Press, 1970.

Rockett, Rocky L. *Ethnic Nationalities in the Soviet Union*. New York: Praeger Publishers, 1981.

Sawyer, Thomas E. *The Jewish Minority in the Soviet Union*. Boulder, Colo.: Westview Press, 1979.

Tsamerian, I. P. and S. L. Ronin. *Equality of Rights Between Races and Nationalities in the USSR*. New York: UNESCO, 1969.

Wixman, Ronald. "Ethnic Nationalism in the Caucasus." *Nationalities Papers* 10, No. 2 (Fall 1982): 137–56.

Wozniuk, V. "Nationalism and Dissidence in the Soviet Union: The Ukrainian Case." *Potomac Review* 8, No. 3 (Spring 1977): 1–12.

UNITED KINGDOM

Barrie Axford

Much current theorising about the appearance and treatment of race in Britain is flawed. Whether conceptualized as part of a sociology of race relations or one of several versions of more or less vulgar Marxism, the tendency has been to offer theoretical accounts that are either excessively reductionist or conspiratorial in construction; or to designate "race relations" as a discrete area of sociological analysis. In this chapter an attempt is made to explain the thematization of race in contemporary Britain, by giving attention both to the historically conditioned discourse through which the meaning of racial categories is established, and to the conjunctural factors that mobilize them into the current politics of race. The account is sensitive to the needs of production, to the origins of what is widely and somewhat confusingly conceptualized as a "race relations problem," in the labor market requirements of the postwar British economy. At the same time the essential character of the current thematization of race requires that due attention be paid to the way in which legitimation needs are met in societies like Britain and how such needs articulate with the needs of production. The emphasis in this article is on majority attitudes and behavior and on responses to the presence of Afro-Caribbean (black) and Asian peoples in the United Kingdom, while acknowledging that the processes of social incorporation and exclusion have not reduced such groups to the status of mere objects.

A RACIAL CONTEXT

Race, or rather, as Robert Miles says, the fact that people of all classes continue to believe and act as if there are "races," is a matter of some social significance in Britain.[1] It is, of course, necessary to point out that the use of phenotypical variation between peoples as a means of ascribing worth, effecting social closure, or making sense of the world is a social construction not tied to any real scientific basis for categorizing human populations. This is in no way to diminish the salience of racial categorization for ordering the social world, since an enormous amount of evidence corroborates the famous dictum, that if people believe something to be real, then it is real in its consequences. The significance of ideas about race, and even racist ideologies as components of the dominant culture, centers on the extent to which identities are secured by reference to racial categories and the ways in which these are mobilized in particular conjunctures to realize new forms of politics. As Miles and Paul Rich have pointed out, the social construction of race has been a dynamic process in which there have been a variety of formative influences.[2] Consequently, not only the origins of ideas on race are important, but also the ways in which they have been refurbished or even superseded over time.

The social construction of race and the meaning of racial categories in Britain may be examined via the perceptions and behavior of individual subjects and groups, and via the manner in which the concepts of race and nation have been connected in popular discourse and more formal political ideologies. Until recently, the term "ethnic" was not widely used in Britain, although it is reasonably clear that opposition to the presence of Asians and other "immigrants" was often expressed in terms of an antipathy to their cultural practices and the inferred threat to British culture and traditions, rather than simply to their physical appearance or genotype. Even today, however, when official discourse and informed opinion make fairly free use of concepts like "ethnicity" (partly to inform shifts in public policy), popular perceptions remain largely innocent of the major religious, linguistic, and cultural differences between those ethnic groups who are either casually or resentfully called "Pakis," or "coloureds," or known by the generic "immigrants." This term, synonymous since the mid–1950s with "New Commonwealth" or "coloured" migration expresses the generally negative image of non-whites in popular consciousness. As Michael Banton suggests, what white Britons disliked (and apparently continue to dislike in quite substantial numbers) was the very idea of a black or brown Briton. From this inauspicious starting point the issues of immigration, or rather its control, and national identity, became connected.[3]

The implied significance of racial perceptions in ordering world-views or patterning behavior should not be left unqualified, either in respect to the formation of exclusive identities, or in relation to the position of migrants in the labor market. There is a good deal of evidence (admittedly much of it anecdotal) to suggest that racial perceptions do not always create whole identities of a regressive kind. On the contrary, ambiguities about the use of racial categories as boundary markers on social interaction, or the legitimacy of ethnic identities, are legion. Whites in general remain hostile to black and Asian immigration, even to that of dependents. Their views on living in a multiracial Britain, however, show much more variation and ambivalence. Relatively few believe that whites and nonwhites should be kept apart, though a larger proportion (some 39 percent) see problems arising when the two live in the same area. Moreover, white people are divided on the legitimacy of blacks and Asians preserving their own culture and way of life. On recent survey evidence, some 50 percent are in favor of a multicultural society where ethnic identities are not lost, while 40 percent are against.[4]

At one level, these data may be interpreted as an endorsement of the sort of pluralism sanctioned in the United States, especially since the blossoming of "ethnic consciousness" during the 1960s, but the putative significanace of the sentiments lies in the fact that they suggest an apparent willingness to disaggregate the concepts of "race," "ethnic," and "nation." Previously, these cateogries have been interchangeable, or at least overlapping, and the tendency, most powerfully evoked in some brands of racist/nationalist ideology, has been to subsume race to nation in terms of some inchoate identity called "Britishness," characterized by a perceived racial homogeneity and, tenuously, by cultural affinity. In practice, this notion has been tolerable only by the recognition of peripheral and subordinate national identities within the United Kingdom, which subsists as a multinational state. This recognition has yet to be realized in terms of substantial political devolution, but the existence of particular national/ethnic identities in, for example, Scotland and Wales, has made it difficult to manipulate a form of overarching "Britishness" in which citizenship could be made to correspond to a single, uniform national identity.

It is not clear that this reasoning extends to the ethnic identities of "immigrants," where the people concerned are held to be racially distinct and their cultures a further affirmation of their "un-Britishness." The data reported above do suggest, however, that it might be. Even if the notional salience of ethnic identities is discounted, it is apparent that the assimilationist perspective on group relations, in the recent past upheld by many whites, allowed for racial factors to be discounted where "immigrants" were prepared to become "more like us." The stereotypes of Afro-Caribbeans and Asians seem in part constructed on the basis of their degree of adaptation to British "culture," the Afro-Caribbeans being seen as more British than the Asians, and on this measure at least, evaluated more favorably.

All this points to considerable ambiguity and confusion with regard to the use and appropriateness of racial categories, not least when they are combined with the concept of "nation." Although racist ideologies or nationalist dogmas that make use of racial concepts, have always found fertile soil among white Britons, including the working class, their reception has not, for the most part, resulted in the formation of racial identities that are exclusive and easily capable of mobilization into an unequivocally racist politics. In part, this may be understood in terms of the common gap between attitudes and behavior, but more crucial is the extent to which racial identities have been mediated by other identities and traditions, the whole being subject to the vicissitudes of conjunctoral forces. For the working class, this would appear to involve some kind of tradeoff betwen the universality of class identity and the particularity of national or racial identity, although the scale of "working-class racism" suggests that the operation of trade union consciousness has not been a major factor in the war against racism. Furthermore, it is not the case that nationalist ideologies and sentiments need always make use of racial imagery. In Scotland, as Miles says, nationalism does not seem to have been expressed in terms of the idea of race, while in England the concepts of race and nation have frequently been linked in racist and nationalist ideologies.[5] In some respects, this may reflect the lack of an "authentic" English ethnic or national identity as much as it suggests different historical experiences. Although much can be made of the fact that the English have never bothered to define their national identity, and so may be more susceptible to racist initiatives than the Scots, in the absence of an appreciable body of research on the question of English identity, it is unwise to speculate too far.[6]

HISTORICAL BACKGROUND

The idea that racial attitudes and racism in the Britain of the 1980s can be explained as the current manifestation of attitudes and ideologies fostered since the heyday of Britain's imperial past ignores the contribution of even earlier traditions associated with national identity. Such traditions, which with the Empire bequeathed a legacy of racial antipathy, are in fact much more introspective. They articulate a defensive nationalism that is quite out of keeping with the wider racial identity bruited by supporters of a pan "Anglo-Saxonism" during the Imperium, and certainly at odds with the professed Commonwealth ideal of multiracialism which struggled to surface and survive in the wake of Empire.[7] Although, as Hannah Arendt says, racism provided the element of continuity between imperialism and nationalism, the manifestations of racism in Britain since the late 1960s, the so called new racism, all employ a narrow, instinctive concept of national identity. These manifestations are indicative of the attempt to forge a new ideological definition of itself during the uneasy and demoralizing transition from imperial back to national status.[8] Compared to earlier exegeses, the disciples of the new racism rarely evoke any concepts of white racial superiority, or of "pure" races. Instead, they appeal to the historic roots of "community" and national identity, with the emphasis on threats to "national cohesion" and the importance of "allegiance."[9]

To some extent, these are circumlocutions, means of avoiding making direct observations about race, where such remarks, at least by respectable politicians, are proscribed. This has not always been the case, and much of the more robust and racist examples of popular discourse on race derive from imperial and pre-imperial times. The period when Britain was involved with slavery saw blacks described in brutal, dehumanizing terms. The racial stereotypes established then survived the abolition of slavery in the eighteenth century. During the time of British imperial expansion in the nineteenth century, although most of the cruder ideologies justifying subjugation had been abjured, arguments in favor of imperialism were often couched in terms of a deterministic relationship between biological characteristics and cultural attributes. African "races"were cast as savage and childlike, and hence incapable of self-government. At the same time, Liberal justifications of empire stressed the export of the civilizing virtues of parliamentarism and the Whig tradition.

Although a great deal has been written about the impact of the Empire on the racial perceptions of succeeding generations of Britons, a good deal of it is based on limited evidence. No doubt the "imperial legacy" has influenced the way in which white Britons perceive and evaluate the membership of racial categories, just as it has influenced the amorphous concept of citizenship that is at the heart of the postwar debates on immigration. However, it may be thought somewhat unlikely that the politics of race in contemporary Britain has been entirely anticipated in belief systems nurtured during a quite different past. This is not to argue that there has been no continuity in beliefs; rather, it is to suggest that in some ways the migration of "New Commonwealth" populations to Britain must be understood as de novo, because it constitutes the first direct experience of different racial groups by the bulk of the British people. Consequently, it is a mistake to see the politics of race in Britain as arising out of racial conditions already existing in society. In contrast, the tendency in some recent, historical treatments of the "black presence" in Britain has been to suggest a continuity of racism and the centrality of racial cleavages in British society during the past.[10]

The migration in question also constituted part of the movement of free labor from periphery to core in the world system. In the first instance, migrants (who, of course, were formerly colonized people) were allocated to places in the labor process, on the basis not of their race, but of particular gaps in the labor market. The subsequent use of racial images to lock migrant workers into semiskilled and unskilled jobs suggests, as Miles says, an apparent correlation between phenotypical variation and position in the labor market.[11] However, these images serve largely as a convenient means of exclusion, which appear "natural," precisely because they permit appeals to history and tradition. Elsewhere in Europe the allocation of migrant labor to "appropriate" places in the labor process has also been subject to the imperatives of market need. In the case of continental migrant labor, however, the imagery of alien and inferior cultures has been employed, where phenotypical differences between indigenous and migrant labor forces are absent.

In Britain, the thematization of race cannot be understood either as the reproduction of racial beliefs and ideologies transmitted from earlier periods, or even as a means of meeting the abstract "needs" of British capital. Instead, the present conjuncture represents a confrontation between the demands of particular national and racial identities, received from the past and refurbished via contemporary ideologies, and the realities of a qualified market society, which labor migration has rendered multicultural.

THE POLITICS OF RACE: PUBLIC POLICIES AND LAWS

The preceding discussion provides some clues for understanding the contemporary political and social management of race. In particular, the historical legacy is somewhat ambivalent in respect to racial categories and with regard to "national origins" as the basis of citizenship rights. British society was race conscious before the postwar migration from the new Commonwealth, no doubt because of the amorphous "colonial mentality," as well as the influence of more specific ideologies of racial and cultural difference. At the same time, it is difficult to specify the precise nature of the relationships between such traditions and their possible manifestations in current thought and practice.

Moreover, while British experience in this area displays certain idiosyncracies that might make it appear unique, it also exhibits important aspects of a general problematic common to other advanced states, namely, the tensions that arise between the statuses of citizenship and nationality in a period of large-scale labor migration. To ascribe much of the inheritance of British racial attitudes to the imperial legacy underestimates the diverse sources of cultural tradition, and their significance in explaining the meaning of racial categories in Britain. In addition, any undue emphasis on historical and cultural factors may well obscure the material basis for current attitudes and the politics to which they give rise, in the labor market requirements of the British economy. In this respect, migration to Britain should be seen as part of the internationalization of labor supply which occurred during the long wave of capitalist expansion from 1945 to the early 1970s.

Migration to Britain does appeal unusual, however, in two main respects. First, a majority of the migrants have not been sojourners, even if their original intention was not to settle permanently. Elsewhere in Europe an annual turnover of about 50 percent has not been unusual.[12] A second distinguishing feature of British immigration is its background in an originally imperial concept of subjection to the British Crown. This was initially expressed in an undifferentiated category of citizenship, which established the rights of inhabitants of British colonies and Commonwealth countries to enter and settle in Britain. The legal framework within which the bulk of migration from the Caribbean and the Indian subcontinent took place was the 1948 British Nationality Act, which created separate but overlapping categories of citizenship of the United Kingdom and colonies and of the Commonwealth. The Commonwealth included citizens of ex-colonies who had subsequently become members of the Commonwealth, within the status of British Subject. They were given unrestricted rights of entry to and settlement in Britain, equal rights with U.K. citizens, and the possibility of acquiring U.K. citizenship after a qualifying period of residence.

The British case is sometimes held up as unusual because of this "imperial legacy." Even in the absence of a colonial heritage, it may be argued that recent labor migration leading, however tenuously, to a multicultural society would have raised questions of rights and citizenship, in the sense that this status implies notions of equal social worth and equal natural rights, regardless of national origins. At all events, whatever the original position, Britain is no longer anomalous when compared to other European countries. Since 1962 there has been a marked shift away from the universalisms of the 1948 Act, while in countries like West Germany, which has long been dependent on "guest workers" rather than colonial labor, there has been a grudging move toward longer term security of residence and freedom of entry for dependents.[13]

The erosion of citizenship rights, seen as too generously extended in the colonial period, has been a major feature of immigration law and policy. Curiously, the British Nationality Act of 1981, which makes explicit use of concepts and criteria originally formulated in immigration law as the basis of new categories of citizenship, remains ambiguous in its commitment to a racially exclusive national identity in the form of British nationality. Moreover, even the enduring popular concern with immigration control is ambiguous. The racial character of opposition often seems less obvious than fears about immigration as a threat to British culture and traditions.

Any account of the politics and policy of race should thus be sensitive to the demands of national tradition, including imperial tradition, which stresses the particularity of people, or their origins, as in the case of black or Asian British. At the same time, what might be regarded as subject only to the peculiarities of British tradition is in fact influenced by the more general question of the rights of citizens, when the migration in question is voluntary and economically based. Consequently, although parallels have not infrequently been drawn between the "xenophobic" reactions to Jewish immigrants to Britain in the early years of this century and reactions to "New Commonwealth" migrants in the 1960s, it is as well to be cautious in distinguishing between the purposes of migration in each case.

In Britain, racial imagery and stereotypes may appear to result from differences of color and culture which are natural to human society, and thus permit appeals to tradition which can be represented as dissociated from, or anterior to, the claims of liberalism and individualism. Although this dissociation is highly questionable for the ethnic minorities present in contemporary Britain, the feeling that race is a natural rather than a systematic characteristic, with its roots in ancient and authentic traditions, considerably helps maintain or reinforce a sense of exclusive identity. An unambiguous understanding of race (racial categories, racism) as natural in origin, on the other hand, encounters the essentially universalistic norms of rights and citizenship which are the political realizations of individualism. Of course, it is possible to overestimate the significance of citizenship rights in the British context, where compared to other countries, notably the United States, there has been an absence of a generally accepted body of legal doctrine and a reluctance to admit universal principles in law, especially where these expressed concern for the "rights of men" per se.[14]

The British "sense of fair play" notwithstanding, the argument here is that an inchoate liberalism, with limited embodiment in statute law, still less enshrined as constitutional dogma, has had and will continue to have a poor defensive record against both institutionalized and popular racism. However, the point is not to present liberalism as an immutable constraint on diverse expressions of racism, but rather to suggest that too obvious a violation of its norms, with their implicit appeal to generalizable interests, regardless of race or color, offends against the predominant mode of legitimation in British society. Requirements of legitimation are met in part by a system of formal or procedural democracy. This system elicits mass loyalty without, for the most part, involving active participation. The universalistic concept of citizenship, intimately connected with the development of the modern, capitalist state, nonetheless constitutes an essential means of securing requisite inputs of mass loyalty.[15] In Britain, as elsewhere, this implies that state policies as well as the attitudes and behavior of individuals and groups are constrained by the existence of a universalistic value system, even though this may be attenuated by the impact of more particularistic belief systems and/or conjunctural forces.

This complex of traditions means that what may be termed "formal racism" in Britain is compelled to function through self-denial.[16] Although it is sustained by and through socialization into a culture imbued with racial imagery and stereotypes, it promotes ambivalence rather than coherence of identity. On an attitudinal level, this process can be observed in the apparent self-contradictions and inconsistencies that have been found in empirical studies of racial prejudice, or the psychodynamics of race, as well as in the limited work done in Britain on "black identity."[17] On a practical level, it seems best exemplified by ambiguities of policy which are otherwise liable to be understood as simply involving contradictions in intentions, or bad faith on the part of policymakers.

For much of the postwar period, race has widely been considered to be an issue of great potential conflict, sufficient to disrupt the cautious mainstream of British politics. Yet, it has rarely intruded with anything like the dramatic effect its reputation deserves. There may be many reasons for this seeming paradox, including the difficulties of mobilizing and sustaining a politics peripheral to the main concerns of part organizations and other opinion leaders. In addition, it is possible that the independent effect of racial tensions may be submerged in public concern over less emotive but more pressing matters like inflation or unemployment. The handling of race may perhaps constitute a paradigm for growing disillusion with the conduct of public affairs.

There is general agreement, however, on the significance of an elite consensus concerning the substance of the proper relationships between race and politics. This includes an all-part consensus, which, at least from the mid–1960s to the late 1970s, removed race from the agenda of interparty rivalry. In operational terms, party leaders identified a problem of immigration control, while at the same time emphasizing the need for anti-discriminatory and assimilationist policies. The effect of the consensus was to immunize race as a conflict area, without defusing racial tensions.

This paradoxical state of affairs continues to characterize the politics of race in Britain, although some commentators suggest that the consensus was broken around the time of the election of the Conservative government in 1979.[18] Indeed, the outward signs of a breakdown are manifest in the increased volume of partisan discord over the application of the immigration rules, in disagreements over nationality legislation, and, of course, in renewed conflict over race during the election campaign in 1979. But those who interpret these as indicators of the demise of the consensus mistake its fundamental character. The consensus is not just an exercise in bipartisanship, proving illusory or pragmatic in the face of pressures from within the ranks of party supporters and from the wider political environment. It is, as indicated above, an expression of the constraints operating on state action, which has to be carried out under the limiting condition of formal democracy and in accord with dominant, universalistic, value systems. In Britain, such constraints often appear contradictory, but in the main they have worked to proscribe radical solutions to what is widely identified as a problem. Of course, the difficulty lies in being able to specify the tolerances within which the constraints are effective, and hence their limits. Evidence for the breakdown of the consensus, however, would not consist merely in recording an increase in the intensity of "adversary politics" over race, but would require a demonstration of a resolution to the ambiguities of policy, attitudes, and behavior noted earlier.

One important consequence of the overt, bipartisan aspect of the consensus has been the immunization of race as a conflict area, most obviously at elections. Nonetheless, the politics of race does not constitute a pristine model of elite autonomy, nor indeed have elites been consistently more liberal or more sensitive than nonelites, in the familiar politics of democratic elitism. On the contrary, race, especially the question of black and Asian immigration, has been placed on the political agenda, albeit sporadically. These interventions have been most often made by "outsider" groups and politicians, and only occasionally by leaders from the major parties of government. A measure of the success of these interventions from outside the elite consensus is that government policy often seems to be purely reactive—responding to but seldom creating demand. Even Margaret Thatcher's populist appeal in 1978, when she gave voice to the "legitimate fears" of the British people that their culture was being "swamped" by immigrants, were prompted, in part, by fear of the limited electoral success of the neo-fascist National Front and its brand of lumpen nationalism. The urban disorders of 1981 and 1985 were further occasions when the government was pressured into immediate, "fire brigade" action, characteristically dealing with the symptoms of unrest rather than its causes.

The empirical mold of public policy is not its only feature. Successive governments have experienced pressure from what Donley Studlar calls "outside initiators," or they have been confronted by the need to take some action on immigration or race, however precipitate or symbolic.[19] The point is that, for the most part, they have successfully managed these pressures, through a combination of "centre statecraft" and particular policy outputs that institutionalize a fundamental ambivalence about race. "Statecraft" has involved the shifting of responsibility for the management of race relations away from the central government into the hands of what Jim Bulpitt refers to as "peripheral" agencies. Such agencies include local government, the police forces, and a succession of more or less corporatist bodies (at present the Commission for Racial Equality), which are charged with promoting racial harmony.[20] Although the particulars differ in respect to race, this method of agenda management is a modal phenomenon in British government, a reflection of

a preferred policy style. The preference for indirect forms of incorporation, or "buffers," may be seen as a further increment in the depoli-
ticization of race. It represents an attempt to generate consensus through
conciliation procedures, rather than to institutionalize and legitimate
conflicting demands through party politics, or the representational forms
of an ethnic pluralism. Interestingly, the buffering institutions have always enjoyed low public and official esteem and are being superseded
as mechanisms of social and political incorporation.

The policies administered by these and other bodies should be seen
as a whole, even if their most obvious quality over the years has consisted
of an attempt to separate or particularize what are really inseparable
phenomena: the question of immigration control and the matter of relations between existing immigrant and host populations. In the manner
outlined above, both of these problems raise questions of citizenship
rights, but the functional separation of "race relations" and "immigration" in official discourse has obscured this fact. Only a pragmatic connection is allowed between the two, reiterated once again at the 1985
Annual Conference of the Conservative party, namely, that "firm immigration control is a necessary precursor of good race relations." The
political charge attached to the concept of citizenship is thus defused.
Immigration control is treated simply as a managerial solution to the
problem of "numbers," and racial categories as convenient, though in
law they are seldom explicit means of effecting this control. From the
late 1960s onward, racially discriminatory immigration controls have
substantially reduced immigration from the New Commonwealth. Indeed, primary migration is virtually at an end, in a country that generally
experiences much higher emigration than immigration. People who are
accepted for settlement now fall into two main categories: (1) those who
are accepted on arrival in the United Kingdom, of whom the great
majority in recent years has comprised dependents of those already
settled, and (2) a much smaller number accepted for settlement on completion of four years in approved employment, under the 1971 Immigration Act.

A number of legislative and administrative markers chart the shift
away from the principle of the right of free entry for Commonwealth
citizens. The Commonwealth Immigrants Act of 1962 introduced a
voucher system operated by the then Ministry of Labour and related to
specific employment, or to the skills of the applicant, to apply to citizens
whose passports were not issued in the United Kingdom. In 1968, a new
Commonwealth Immigration Act withdrew the remaining right of entry
and settlement from passport-holders lacking "close connection" with
the United Kingdom. This was defined by birth or descent from a British-
born parent or grandparent, or by naturalization or adoption. The act
was hurriedly passed to control the entry of East African Asian passport-

holders, while preserving the unrestricted right of entry to white settlers in East Africa holding the same class of passport. During 1971, an increase in the number of entry vouchers available under this act was the means of responding specifically to the political plight of Ugandan Asians threatened with expulsion by President Amin. The criteria of "close connection" with the United Kingdom anticipated the granting of "right of abode" in Britain to "patrials" in the 1971 Immigration Act. "Right of abode," primarily by nationality, has finally become part of the definition of British citizenship in the terms of the 1981 British Nationality Act. In this "common-sense" and incremental fashion, the concepts of nationality, citizenship, and immigration have become interrelated. There is a strong mutual dependence of categories of citizenship and those derived from immigration control.

In domestic matters, the questions of race and race-related "problems" resonate throughout policy responses in areas like urban policy, education, employment policy, and, most emotively of all, public order and policing. However, governments have often been "race blind" in the application of ameliorative policies to what are identified as more general social problems or pathologies. Paradoxically, they have been obsessed by the idea that blacks (especially) and Asians are a source of special problems, which if left untreated will constitute a threat to social stability. Among such perceived threats are the alleged rootlessness and criminality of black youth, and the fear that black youth unemployment might underlie riotous behavior. Under the general rubric of promoting racial harmony, a number of policy responses are extant. Anti-discrimination legislation in the form of the various Race Relations Acts provides a core of race-specific policy. In the main, however, public policy consists either of race-shy initiatives in a number of key sectors, informed by an ideology of equal opportunity, or of measures aimed essentially at preserving social stability and order.

In many ways, the Scarman Report on the Brixton disorders is a paradigm for these contradictory imperatives, and a measure, too, of the tensions within the liberal democratic ethos.[21] Apart from being a notable example of the crisis management techniques employed by British governments, the Scarman Inquiry, and more particularly the report, seemed to augur a more direct and explicit attack on racial disadvantage. In fact, Lord Scarman's findings and recommendations, quintessentially liberal, perfectly express what John Solomos calls the contradictory linkage between social justice ideolgy and a concern with social stability.[22] The report, though primarily concerned with policing, is also vigorous in its attack on the causes of racial disadvantage. On policing and public order, Scarman made eighteen formal recommendations and a further twenty detailed suggestions. The Home Office and the police have enacted, or at least tried to enact, every one. These include the demand for more sensitive "community policing" and the establishment of local police-community liaison committees, a form of representation that models the indirect structures already extant in community relations. On the social and economic backgroud to the riots, the report makes two formal recommendations and twenty specific sugestions in employment, housing, education, and race relations. The Conservative government has not formally implemented any one of these recommendations, and in the aftermath of the disorders in 1985 the official response has been to treat only the public order dimensions of the occurrences. No similar, wide-ranging judicial inquiry has been set up.

Scarman nicely captures the character of public policy, which at least since the early 1960s has demonstrated a fundamental ambiguity over race. This ambiguity was initially expressed in the apparent contradiction between increasingly tough and discriminatory immigration laws, and an insistence, in domestic matters, on a racial equality of opportunity. Of late, the emphasis on immigration has shifted to a concern with the problems of the black British, that is, with the Afro-Caribbean and Asian communities settled in British cities. Official discourse now stresses the virtues of multiculturalism rather than assimilation, but the images of violence (mugging, rioting) associated with the second generation of black British require them to be treated as a potential threat to social and political order. In both phases, the gap between official tolerance and discrimination experienced by the black and Asian communities is stark. In part, this must reflect the tendency for policymakers to eschew a more direct and radical approach to racial disadvantage, in favor of general and largely ameliorative measures. The treatment of race and racism in policy terms (though this is also apparent in popular discourse) has been consistently to present it as something else, to sublimate it in a wider politics of poverty, the "inner cities," or law and order.

To restate the argument directly; public policy over race often seems ambivalent or even contradictory. It is "of a piece," however, and needs to be understood as the outcome of tensions within prevailing traditions associated with citizenship, nationality, and identity. The elite consensus is, in a sense, a formal expression of the ambivalence in the liberal-democratic ethos. The continued ambivalence over race is thus crucial to this formulation. Any shift in the management of race issues, or in popular attitudes and behavior which indicates a resolution of ambivalence in whatever fashion, is damaging to the argument. Many commentators have noted the existence of a consensus over the handling of race. In general, however, they have treated it either as a pragmatic response to the conflict potential of the issue or as some aspect of a developing institutionalized racism, for which functional equivalents (in the form of "pseudo biological culturalism," or an exclusivist version of national identity) can easily be found.[23]

The idea of the consensus as a product of the legitimation needs of British society is foreign to most such interpretations. In seeking a materialist understanding of racism, these interpretations slip too easily into economic reductionism or ingenious structuralism without regard for the complex dialectics of the relations between production and legitimation. Even Solomos, et al., whose analysis is sensitive to the legitimation needs of a society undergoing a period of crisis, depict the treatment of race since the mid–1970s as part of a fundamental reworking of state policies and popular attitudes, leading to a form of "authoritarian populism."[24] In brief, if the treatment of race ever demonstrated a degree of ambivalence, the deepening crisis of British capitalism has forced a resolution, and in a regressive fashion. The question is, therefore, how far do recent events suggest a resolution to the fundamental ambivalence over race, a change in the maner of its thematization, and thus a possible shift in the legitimation needs of British society?

CONTEMPORARY EVENTS

Much of the recent discussion of an implacable racialization of British politics centers on changes in Conservative party ideology and government practice since the late 1970s. These changes are seen primarily as part of a reconstruction of culture in line with the needs of British capitalism, which is in the throes of a crucial transition to a higher level of technology. During this period, class conflict which had been latent throughout the years of collectivist consensus (1950s and 1960s), has resurfaced; structural unemployment has become rife, and other social pathologies associated with industrial decline (like violence and threats to public order) have been more apparent. In response, the "politics of Thatcherism" consists of an appeal to the organic unity of the nation, at once exclusivist and defensive, and recourse to the seeming paradox of a free-market economy sustained by a strong state.[25] Thatcherism (like Powellism before it) represents a break with the postwar consensus that had previously dominated British politics. It also displays an apparent willingness to embrace some of the mores of the "New Right," complete with theories of racial nationalism. A. Sivanandan has summarized the consequences of this putative ideological break for immigrant communities, already cast as (at least) symptomatic of Britain's decline:

The nature and function of racism (began) to change . . . the rationale . . . was no longer exploitation but repatriation, not oppression but repression—forged on the ideological level through the media . . . and the schools and effected on the political level . . . through the police and courts principally.[26]

The reality may be more irresolute or contradictory than might be inferred from such accounts. A strong state unencumbered by any liberal-democratic scruples or the patrician qualities of the *ancien régime* has not so far been established, and the radicalization of culture, including the stress on the naturalness and superiority of national traditions, has not been unequivocally realized.

Margaret Thatcher's appeal to nativist sentiments in 1978 inaugurated a tougher stance on immigration and race by the Conservative party.[27] The initiative was no doubt a piece of political opportunism, designed both to distance the party from the prevailing consensus and, at the next general election, to pick up the votes of those disaffected enough to consider supporting parties of the extreme right. Even within the party the initiative did not go uncontested. By April 1978, the message, though formalized, was couched more obviously in the mold of bipartisan dualism, being concerned to "improve race relations and take full account of present anxieties."[28] However, the party did enter the 1979 election with a commitment to introduce a new Nationality Act to define entitlement to British citizenship, to tighten immigration controls, and to take firm action against illegal immigrants and overstayers. Once in office the more radical proposals (e.g., for a register of those Commonwealth wives and children entitled to entry and settlement under the 1971 Immigration Act, and a quota system, covering all non-European Economic Community [EEC] nations, to control entry for resettlement) were effectively dropped. Despite some pressure from far-right elements in the party, there is no evidence that these measures are likely to be revived. The more vigorous policy toward illegal entrants and overstayers resulted in a number of well-publicized actions by police and immigration officials, particularly during 1980, without producing a dramatic rise in the number of illegal immigrants being detected and removed from the United Kingdom.

The experience of the Conservative government in respect to the Immigration Rules, which given substance to the statutory provisions, reveals evidence of conflict and confusion, but no dramatic break with past practice. Instead, as in the highly emotive and symbolic issue of the right of women settled in the United Kingdom to bring husbands or fiances into the country, policy has consisted of a series of contradictory attempts either to liberalize and extend the "concessions" introduced by the Labour government in 1974, as a consequence of the 1981 Nationality Act, or to limit them on the pretext that "arranged marriages" by the Asian community facilitate the evasion of immigration control. In the apparent denouement to this issue, in a case before the European Court of Human Rights, in May 1985, the government was found guilty of sex (though not racial) discrimination.

The Nationality Act of 1981 was itself based on a Green Paper published by the Labour government in 1977 and constitutes the first attempt to codify a concept of British citizenship, though Nationality itself remains significantly undefined in the act. This lack of clarification does not facilitate Britain's acceptance of the obligations under the European Convention of Human Rights, Protocol 4, which inter alia, recognizes the right of a person not to be deprived of the right to enter the country of which he or she is a national. The definition that has been attempted employs a combination of patriality and a right of abode in the country, and those principles relate an individual to a category of citizenship. Since the same principles apply to the definition of British Citizen, and to British Overseas Citizenship, acccording to close connection with a given territory, the residual category of British Subject in the meaning of the act is necessary to accommodate the potentially stateless. Thus, although the act might appear to represent a shift away from a tradition of citizenship based on residence (*ius soli*) toward one based on descent (*ius sanguinis*), aspects of both are retained.

For all their dislike of the apparatus of Keynesian corporatism, the Conservatives have not dismantled the machinery of race management, either legislative (the Race Relations Act) or implementive (the Commission for Racial Equality—CRE). The position of the established machinery of conciliation and mediation remains marginal, not least in its ability to influence policy, but this, too, is not new. The most recent report of the CRE, which was highly critical of immigration control procedures, has been dismissed by the Home Office as "fundamentally flawed."[30] Broader social issues with a race component also continue to be handled as problems for short-term amelioration. None of this seems markedly at odds with earlier practice, nor is it wildly out of step with the way the Labour party conducted itself when in government. Even today, when that party has, to quote one observer, "polished up its radical credentials" on race, no Front Bench spokesperson for Labour would seriously question the need for firm immigration control.[31] In opposition since 1979, the party has denounced the Immigration Rules as racist and sexist, and since 1983 has been committed to repeal both the 1971 Immigration Act and the 1981 Nationality Act, with the object of replacing legislation that discriminates on racial grounds. This having been said, the politics of race in Britain is not conspicuous for dramatic reversals in policy. Ironically, too, it is the Labour party, determined to strengthen the Race Relations Act of 1976 and to promote a wide range of affirmative action measures, which also finds itself divided on the legitimacy of setting up "black sections" with in the party.[32]

Unquestionably, the area in which the Conservatives are held to deviate most sharply from the consensus is that of law and order. At least an augury of authoritarian statism is seen to lie in the emphasis placed on public order and the government's apparent willingness to indemnify "state violence" by police forces whose conduct in the policing of largely black and Asian areas has been a major source of tension for many years. In this respect, recent attention has focused on policing as a contributory factor in the urban disorders of 1981 and 1985. Yet a history of "routine repression" can be found in the implementation of the notorious "sus" law, as well as catalogued in the folklore of immmigrant communities since the 1960s.[33] The official response to the disorders has been to treat them as *sui generis*, and, quintessentially, as manifestations of criminal or otherwise socially malign behavior, requiring improvements in police tactics and equipment. Other contributory factors may be allowed but solutions to the material problems of inner cities in general and migrant communities in particular have in practice been submerged in the broader warp of monetarist policy, or, as in the case of programs of affirmative action, have been ruled inadmissible on ideological grounds.

There is an obvious danger in culling a range of empirical evidence, sometimes of an anectodal nature, to support a more abstract formulation. Nonetheless, it does appear that the imputed shift in the management of race by the Conservatives has been more equivocal and certainly more contested than is sometimes claimed. Forces within the party, often labeled the "new right," have pressed strongly, if not always consistently, for an interpretation of "Britishness" which employs a more specific racial root. The Conservative leadership, while not entirely resistant to their blandishments, has in fact retained the essentials of the much vilified consensus, treading uneasily between the extremes of liberalism and populism within its own party ranks.[34] The provisions of the Nationality Act, the continued sublimation of race in the wider social issues of employment, urban deprivation, and public order all point to continued ambivalence over race. Of course, many Conservatives (many white British per se) also feel ambivalent about the idea of a multiracial Britain. But to suggest that this ambivalence has been resolved in favor of a racially specific policy of repatriation based on domestic repression is not supported by the available evidence. On the contrary, the use of the slogan "Labour say he's black, Tories say he's British" at the 1983 general election, reveals further ambiguities in both the discourse and strategies of the politics of race. The appeal to a common British citizenship implied here is certainly at odds with the exclusive definitions of national identity trafficked by the "new right." This remains true even in the face of the assumption that the slogan was an opportunist bid to attract the vote of middle-class Asians. The direction of public policy has been neither to systematically politicize race nor, fundamentally, to racialize (formal) politics.

At the same time, evidence for racializing British politics, or for resolving ambivalence in a regressive manner, should be canvassed beyond the confines of policy or the statements of leading politicians. The nature of popular attitudes and behavior may provide an insight into the claim that "Thatcherism" has established a bridgehead in the popular culture and has dispensed with the need for a fundamental ambivalence over race. In this respect, one might expect the success in refurbishing a sense of national cohesion and a connection between race and national identity, as well as the effect of economic crisis on attitudes and behavior toward immigrants, to be revealed in more pronounced and widespread expressions of racial antipathy and a greater willingness to ascribe praise or blame on the basis of membership of a notional racial group.

Predictably, the evidence is confused and relatively unenlightening despite Stuart Hall's claim that "the social core of racism has been enjoying a steady unremitting rise in popularity"[35] In the late 1970s, Christopher Husbands opined that, although the National Front was bankrupt as an electoral force, its racist platform was quite simply a mirror-image of the feelings of the white electorate.[36] It is entirely in keeping with the idea of an ambivalent popular consciousness about race that people should reject the crude racism of the neo-fascist right and, significantly, its violent, bully-boy image and yet cleave to what Husbands calls "consensus" racism, altogether more genteel. As suggested earlier, this has been effectively managed in the electoral realm, and to date the party system has been able to accommodate racism, albeit uneasily. It is perhaps less easily contained in the wider social environment.

Sections of the Asian population have become the victims of more virulent abuse and organized violence. The fact that it is the cultural practices of such groups, rather than skin color per se, which have often made them the objects of derision and animosity does nothing to alleviate the harshness and tenuousness of their existence in certain localities. Surveys conducted by the Policy Studies Institute also indicate a high and enduring level of discrimination against people of Asian and Afro-Caribbean origins in the housing and labor markets.[37] It is difficult to know whether to attribute these phenomena to some more or less independent racist dynamic, or as in some treatments of "working-class racism," to see such attitudes mediated by material factors, like competition for jobs in depressed areas, and sharpened by the interventions of radical politicians. The tendency has been to relate the crasser examples of racial antipathy, like the simian chanting of "sambo, sambo" at black football players, even by sections of their own supporters, to a general decay of standards in Britain. This in turn is associated with the collapse of organized religion, the decay of family life, and the increasing dispossession of sections of the working class from work.

From these sorts of indicators, it is only a short step to the plausible hypothesis that the complex of traditions that sustained ambivalence over race no longer operates. Instead, for the bulk of the population, an inherent conservatism and a defensive nationalism are reinforced by a decline in the scope of tolerance and the expanded scope for purely instrumental attitudes, indifference, or cynicism, especially on the part of the marginal, white populations of the inner cities. Apart from the difficulty of establishing the extent of the "decay" in British moral standards, it is also not clear that there is a necessary connection between moral decay and antipathy toward blacks and Asians. In the wake of the 1985 riots, although public support for the government and its stress on law and order rose sharply, there is nothing to suggest that this attitude is tied in any specific way to increased fears of particular ethnic groups, even though there is a generalized concern about the level of violence in society.

Among the population at large, ambivalence over race-related questions is widespread. Among all subgroups in the population, including those who see themselves as unprejudiced, black and Asian immigration continues to be very unpopular. Nevertheless, there appears to be considerably more support for legislation against racial discrimination in the depressed mid–1980s than in the affluent late 1960s. A majority of whites perceive both widespread prejudice against blacks and Asians, and discrimination in respect of job opportunities.[38] Unfortunately, there is little evidence as to how these cognitions are evaluated, and what relation, if any, they have to the support expressed for anti-discrimination measures. The meaning attached to racial categories and the extent to which identities, national or otherwise, are being refurbished via racial imagery in the Britain of the 1980s thus remains unclear. Although a degree of ambivalence continues to mark public responses to the presence of black and Asian people in Britain, this quality may indeed be under threat, not only from the peripheries of politics and society (football hooligans, street gangs, etc.), but also in the wash of cynical pessimism that is attending Britain's decline.

But perhaps more direct evidence is available in the extent to which race is undergoing a regressive thematization, a racialization, in fact. For example, the "race riots" of 1980, 1981, and 1985 are sometimes presented as occasions of intercommunal violence, or, in the style of much current and romantic rhetoric, part of the "fight back" of black youth— their proto-rebellion. While the disorders clearly underline the extent of anti-police sentiments, and in a direct fashion remind us that migrants are the agents as much as the objects of political activity, it is less clear that either of these descriptions fits. The disorders occurred in localities that are not racially or ethnically exclusive; they were not instances of ghetto violence. Intercommunal tensions, insofar as they were expressed, included conflicts between blacks and Asians as well as between blacks and whites. The involvement of youths from different ethnic groups in collective violence displays a strong element of ritual rather than the continuation of politics by other means. Furthermore, even if street politics of this kind may be interpreted as the only political resource of the powerless, in particular of second-generation blacks, it is open to question as to how far this view is shared by large sections of black and Asian youth, who do not all experience British society as unremittingly racist.

That the disorders also express the rage and frustration of sections of the black and Asian population is, however, undeniable. Whether they are an intimation of new forms of political response is much more difficult to predict. It is hard to say if the disorders will serve to deepen ambivalence, or in some cathartic fashion hasten its demise. As a means of placing racial disadvantage more firmly on the political agenda, their contribution is likely to be minimal.[39] In terms of policy, their most significant effect lies in hastening changes to policing techniques and legislation on public order.[40]

There are other dimensions to the current thematization of race in Britain, which in the past has been notable for the manner in which political elites have managed its conflict potential. In this endeavor, they have been assisted by the homogenizing character of British political culture and the reluctance to admit the legitimacy of specifically ethnic demands via conventional representative and brokerage structures, like political parties. The preferred mode of incorporation, at least in the recent past, was by way of the established machinery of conciliation, which offended the sensibilities of black and white alike. Much of this scenario remains true in 1987, but there are signs of change. At one remove, the (probably overestimated) significance of the "ethnic vote" has pushed the major political parties into greater awareness of ethnic constituencies. Previously, the Labour party took the allegiance of blacks and Asians for granted, while the Conservatives scarcely contested the field. Today, partly as a result of the class-dealignment of British politics, when both parties see their traditional support being eroded and public disillusion with the party system rife, they see some salvation in wooing the ethnic vote. But their interest still seems largely in blacks and Asians as voters rather than as activists or candidates. For nonwhites, electoral politics does not offer an important vehicle for expressing demands; they are simply too few in number and too dispersed to make an impact at the national level.[41]

The possibility of black and Asian activists acting as ethnic brokers from within conventional party structures also seems remote. In some ways, the debate within the Labour party on the appropriateness of "black sections" emphasizes this point. Although a concern with ethnicity and multiculturalism pervades official thinking in the Labour party and is often expressed powerfully in the policies of Local Education Authorities and the like, it is also clear than an insistence on mulitculturalism and respect for the legitimacy of ethnic identities does not extend to the realm of politics, to representative structures. The possibility of a full-blown pluralism of the American variety is proscribed on the grounds of its incompatibility with dominant strains in the political culture. Nonetheless, British politics exhibits the same tendency to fragment and succumb to centrifugal forces: single-issue politics and partisan dealignment, also observed in the American polity. Similarly, the prospects for the kind of bureaucratic-bargaining politics of topocracy familiar in the United States is inhibited in the context of the much more centralized British state, and the demographic and political difficulties of establishing black power bases in particular localities. The militant multiculturalism pursued by Councils in Labour-controlled authorities may thus either be regarded as a palliative for the failure to mount a more substantive attack on disparities in economic and political power, or another illustration of the fundamental ambivalence in white British attitudes, wherein an insistence on a generalized equality for all races is contradicted by the failure to require a comparable equality in specific areas like housing or politics.

SUMMARY AND CONCLUSIONS

The treatment of race in British politics and society is ambivalent. This ambivalance can be observed in popular and official discourses and in public policy, as well as on the wider terrain of politics. In one respect, the ambivalence is functional for the management of what is generally described as an issue area with high conflict potential, since it has served for the most part to keep tensions within manageable limits. In a more profound sense, it expresses a contradiction that is immanent in societies where universalistic value systems compete with more particularistic traditions, and both are subject to the vagaries of conjunctural forces, especially of the economic variety. This contradiction is sometimes characterized as that between system integration and social integration, but the critical point is that neither is reduced to the imperatives of the other as in many other accounts of race in Britain. Thus, the peculiarities of British tradition in securing national and racial identities are acknowledged. It is also emphasized, however, that the universalistic concept of citizenship still constitutes an essential means of securing legitimacy in a late-capitalist order like Britain, where the phenomenon of postwar labor migration has served to highlight the tensions between the two. As a result, both public policy and popular attitudes about race are ambivalent, and racial and national identities are inconsistent and fragmented rather than whole and exclusive or whole and inclusive.

Of course, it may be suggested that all this perversely ignores the extent of racism in Britain, which is reflected more accurately in the spate of racial attacks and arson. The racism has been institutionalized in the state's peevish attempts to inhibit the movement of dependents into the United Kingdom, or has been witnessed more forcefully in the "law and order" responses to the urban disorders. On this account, the radicalization of culture in a regressive manner and the racialization of society have proceeded, more or less unchecked in recent years, and the politics of Thatcherism has as its racist denouement the forcible repatriation of black and Asian people. The purpose of the argument here is not to offer a sanguine alternative to these dire prognoses, in the pious language of the assimilated or "multi-ethnic society." Rather, it is to suggest that, while the deepening of the "British crisis" may well result in a regressive resolution to the systematic ambivalence over race, it has yet to do so. As a theoretical position, the argument recognizes the possibility of legitimation needs being met in such a way that amibvalence over race is no longer required. The theoretical possibilities at least, which are then available, include both regression to some form of fascist, authoritarian state, or the emancipation of those members of the working class previously divided by the social constructs of race and nation. On the available evidence, a number of prognoses are possible. In the meantime, the meaning of race in social life and its treatment in public policy remain ambivalent. Whether this phenomenon is a uniquely British one, or, as intimated above, is common to many advanced states requires much more research. To reiterate: the likelihood is that labor migration leading to the creation or enlargement of multicultural societies will present challenges both at the level of the justification of rights and citizenship, and to the prevailing traditions associating citizenship with nationality. The tensions between these aspects, considered in the context of the legitimation of the social order as a whole, will in some considerable measure constitute the politics of race in those societies.

NOTES

1. Robert Miles, "Racism and Nationalism in Britain," in Charles Husbands ed; *Race in Britain: Continuity and Change* (London: Hutchinson, 1982) pp. 329–49.

2. Ibid., pp. 1–84, and Paul Rich, "Conservative Ideology and Race in Modern British Politics," unpublished manuscript, 1984.

3. Michael Banton, *Racial and Ethnic Competition* (Cambridge: Cambridge University Press, 1983), pp. 64–65.

4. Colin Brown, *Black and White in Britain: The Third PSI Survey* (London: Heinemann Educational Books/Policy Studies Institute, 1984), pp. 270–72.

5. Ibid., pp. 287–97.

6. There is no lack of journalistic comment on this matter and, of course, there is a considerable literature on nationalism in the wake of its "revival" during the 1960s. Work that combines on historical approach to the question of identity with material on contemporary attitudes is rare, but see Douglas Schoen, *Enoch*

Powell and the Powellites (London: Macmillan, 1977), and, though not an empirical study, Tom Nairn, *The Break-Up of Britain* (London: New Left Books, 1977).

7. For a useful examination of these themes, see Paul Rich, "Liberal Racialism, Empire and the Quest for Commonwealth," unpublished manuscript, 1984.

8. Hannah Arendt, *The Origins of Totalitarianism*, 2d ed. (London: Allen & Unwin, 1958).

9. John Casey, "One Nation: The Politics of Race," *The Salisbury Review* 1 (Autumn 1982): 25. See also Rich, "Liberal Racialism."

10. Peter Fryer, *Staying Power: The History of Black People in Britain* (London: Pluto Press, 1984).

11. Miles, "Racism and Nationalism in Britain," p. 286.

12. John Salt, *Migration in Post-War Europe*, J. Salt and H. Clout, eds. (Oxford: Oxford University Press, 1976), pp. 80–83.

13. See the comparative discussion in Stephen Castles, Heather Booth, and Tina Wallace, *Here for Good* (London: Pluto Press, 1984), pp. 11–39. At the same time, the recent growth in the intensity of anti-immigrant sentiments in, for example, France, should also be noted.

14. For example, Disraeli expressed a preference for the "rights of Englishmen" as against the "Rights of Men."

15. The theoretical basis for this discussion is to be found in Jurgen Habermas' conception of a "legitimation crisis" in advanced capitalism. With Alan Brier, I have elaborated on this theme in relation to race in a number of papers. See, for example, "The Idea of a Politics of Immigration in Britain," unpublished manuscript, 1982.

16. Barrie Axford and Alan Brier, "Race and Formal Politics in Britain," unpublished manuscript, 1980.

17. See Rae Sherwood, *The Psychodynamics of Race* (Brighton: Harvester Press, 1980). On the contradictions found in the attitudinal makeup of self-confessed racists, see Michael Billig, *Fascists: A Social Psychological View of the National Front* (London: Harcourt Brace Jovanovich, 1978).

18. For an account of race and party politics, see Zig Layton-Henry, *The Politics of Race in Britain* (London: Allen & Unwin, 1984). See also A. M. Messina, "Race, Party Competition and Policy Formation in the Post-Concensus Period," *Parliamentary Affairs* 38, No. 4 (Autumn 1985): pp. 423–36.

19. Donley Studlar, "Nonwhite Policy Preferences, Political Participation, and the political Agenda in Britain," unpublished manuscript, 1984.

20. Jim Bulpitt, "Continuity, Autonomy, and Peripheralisation: The Anatomy of the Centre's Race Statecraft in England," *Government and Policy* 2 (1985): 129–47.

21. Lord Scarman, *The Brixton Disorders April 10–12 1981: Report of an Inquiry*, Cmnd 8427 (HMSO), 1981.

22. John Solomos, "Problems, But Whose Problems?: The Social Construction of Black Youth Unemployment and State Policies," unpublished manusript, 1984.

23. The expression is taken from Martin Barker, *The New Racism* (London: Junction Books, 1981), p. 43.

24. John Solomos et al., *The Empire Strikes Back*, CCCS, ed. (London: Hutchinson, 1982), pp. 9–47.

25. On this matter, see Paul Rich, "Conservative Ideology and the Politics of Race," and Andrew Gamble, "Smashing the State, Thatcher's Radical Crusade," *Marxism Today* 29, No. 6 (June 1983): 21–29.

26. A. Sivanandan, "Challenging Racism: Strategies for the 1980's," *Race and Class* 25, No. 2 (Autumn 1983): 6.

27. These remarks were made on the Granada Television program, "World in Action," January 30, 1978.

28. William Whitelaw, in a speech to the Central Council of the Conservation Party in Leicester, April 7, 1978.

29. "Apparent" since the decision of the Court raises questions as to how the government can deal with all who marry non-EEC nationals, without offending liberal opinion on one side and anti-immigrant feeling on the other.

30. Commission for Racial Equality, *Immigration Control Procedures*, 1985.

31. Layton-Henry, *Politics of Race*, p. 156.

32. Some black and Asian members of the Labour party have demanded the right to form special "black sections" of local constituency parties. The National Executive Committee of the party has ruled against the legitimacy of such bodies, and Labour candidates selected by General Management Committees containing "black section" representations are in an anomolous constitutional position.

33. The "sus" law, which made it an offense for a "suspected person or reputed thief" to frequent or loiter in a public place with intent to commit a crime, was part of the Vagrancy Act of 1824. This offense was replaced in 1981 by the Criminal Attempts Act.

34. Robert Behrens and John Edmunds, "Kippers, Kittens and Kipper Boxes: Conservative Populists and Race Relations," *Political Quarterly* 52 (1981): 342–47.

35. Stuart Hall, "Cold Comfort Farm," *New Socialist*, No. 32 (November 1985): 12.

36. Christopher Husbands and Jude England, "The Hidden Support for the National Front," *New Statesman* 46 (May 12, 1979).

37. Brown, *Racial and Ethnic Competition*, p. 296.

38. Colin Airey, in R. Jowell and C. Airey, eds., *British Social Attitudes: The 1984 Report* (Aldershot: Gower, 1984), pp. 122–30.

39. See Studlar, "Nonwhite Policy Preference." See also John Benyon, "Turmoil in the Cities," *Social Studies Review* 1, No. 3 (January 1980): 3–9.

40. In which respect they must be considered along with the heightening of class conflict revealed in the Miners strike of 1984–85. During the current session of Parliament, the goverment has laid a new Public Order Bill before the House of Commons, which extends the incitement to racial hatred provisions of existing legislation to cover people who possess racist material with a view to publication or distribution. At the same time, the bill creates new offenses concerned with control of demonstrations, marches, and the like.

41. Among a burgeoning literature, see Marian Fitzgerald, *Political Parties and Black People* (Runnymeade: Runnymeade Trust, 1984).

BIBLIOGRAPHY

Anwar, Muhammed. *Race and Politics*. London: Tavistock, 1985.

Banton, Michael. *Promoting Racial Harmony*. Cambridge: Cambridge University Press, 1985.

Benyon, John, ed. *Scarman and After*. Oxford: Pergamon Press, 1984.

Cashmore, Ernest, and Barry Troyna. *Black Youth in Crisis*. London: George Allen & Unwin, 1982.

Glazer, Nathan, and Ken Young, eds. *Ethnic Pluralism and Public Policy*. London: Heinemann, 1983.

Hall, Stuart, et al. *Policing the Crisis: Mugging, the State and Law and Order*. London: Macmillan, 1978.

Joshua, Harris, Tina Wallace, and Heather Booth. *To Ride the Storm*. London: Heinemann, 1983.

Katzenelson, Ira. *Black Men, White Cities*. London: Oxford University Press, 1973.

Miles, Robert, and Annie Phizacklea. *White Man's Country: Racism in British Politics*. London: Pluto Press, 1984.

Rex, John, and Sally Tomlinson. *Colonial Immigrants in a British City*. London: Routledge & Kegan Paul, 1979.

Sivanandan, A. *A Different Hunger*. London: Pluto Press, 1982.

Taylor, Stan. *The National Front in English Politics*. London: Macmillan, 1982.

UNITED STATES

Jay A. Sigler

A RACIAL CONTEXT

The United States of America is a nation of immigrants. The English, Dutch, Swedes, and French struggled for control of its coastal areas until, by the middle of the seventeenth century, English mastery was virtually assured in the land stretching from Massachusetts to Virginia. By the middle of the eighteenth century, the French and Spanish competitors were pushed to the far north and the far south. But none of these groups competing with the English was seen as a "race," except in a very loose use of the word. Indians and blacks were usually regarded as some sort of separate "race," and race categories were reserved for those who were fundamentally "different" from the white Anglo-Saxon dominant majority. Even though white Anglo-Saxons no longer form a majority in the United States, due to the immigration of other Europeans, race categories are fairly clear-cut in America and are not easily confused with ethnic or religious distinctions. Race is a well-understood fact of American life.

Census information is collected in a way that describes American racial groups, not ethnic groups. Statistics of the resident population "by race and Spanish origin" are to be found in the 1980 population census, issued in December 1983. The census also collected data on "selected ancestry groups," including Dutch, English, French, German, Greek, Hungarian, Irish, Italian, Norwegian, Polish, Portuguese, and Russian statistics. So it seems that official distinctions between race and ethnicity have been made in the collection of data used by the U.S. Census Bureau. These categories do not necessarily correspond with popular usage, but they are pertinent.

For most purposes, the census only distinguishes race by the terms "white" and "black," but the official view of race used by the Census Bureau was based on "self-classification by people according to the race with which they identify" with "householders and families . . . classified by the race of the householder."[1] Census officials regarded "white" as an appropriate category, but if a response different from the specific race categories listed on the questionnaire was elicited (such as Canadian, German, Italian, Lebanese, or Polish), it was counted as "white." The officially designated race categories are: "white, black, American Indian, Eskimo, Aleut, Japanese, Chinese, Filipino, Korean, Asian Indian, Vietnamese, Hawaiian, Guamanian, Samoan." Persons of Spanish/Hispanic origin were treated in a separate category, which may or may not be interpreted as racial. Obviously, since origin, nationality group, and ancestry were called for, more than mere language distinctions were involved. Census officials cautioned that "persons of Spanish origin may be of any race."[2] Nonetheless, attempts were made to separate Puerto Ricans from Mexican-Americans, Cubans, and "other Spanish," a reflection of the recognition that these Hispanics were treated differently from other American ethnics. For our purposes, as for those of the census, Spanish-origin Americans can be regarded as belonging to a racelike category.

Census officials have honestly confronted the existence of race and racial categories in American life. Sociologists and anthropologists may dispute the exact boundary lines between ethnic, linguistic, religious, and racial groups, but in spite of academic wrangling the lines are clear enough for practical purposes. Most Americans know what the boundaries are. When called on to identify themselves by race, most Americans are able to respond. Spanish speakers may be confused on the subject, but they, too, know the current rules of the game.

Whether Jews or gypsies are a race is not an important question in America. Our racial categories are rooted in a different and specific historical past. To understand the past is the best guide to the race relations situation of the present. Americans are a pragmatic people, and it is the practical consequences of the physical appearance and the language and cultural signals used by individuals which provide the best quick indicators of racial status. Those physical/linguistic/cultural factors have been established by a special historical experience. Italian-Americans are not now perceived as a "race" in America. Puerto Ricans seem to be seen in racial terms. The bases for these distinctions are not logical, but they are deeply felt.

It is difficult and unfair to fit people into precise racial categories, but such groupings are made in America and elsewhere, "the racial label being determined in large part by the dictates of society."[3] In our society, Irish-Americans, Jewish-Americans, Polish-Americans, Armenian-Americans, and other hyphenates are usually seen as ethnic groups or as assimilated "Americans." Members of so-called racial groups find assimilation much harder and, in many cases, virtually impossible. Race and ethnicity are distinguishable in America.[4]

RACE RELATIONS IN AMERICA BEFORE 1950

Officially speaking, the United States admits to having problems of race or race relations.[5] This nation is especially heterogeneous in terms of religion, nationality, ethnicity, class language, and, of course, race. But prevailing American values emphasize the values of equality of opportunity, fair play, and individualism. In spite of such groups as the Ku Klux Klan, the American Nazi party, and the John Birch Society which have been actively racist, the popular view held by most Americans is that race and race prejudice is less of a social problem today than ever before in the nation's history. While there is some evidence to justify current attitudes, in fact there is better evidence to suggest that race relations in America are still a major source of stress and social tension.

Europeans who came to America for settlement encountered various groups whom they designated as "Indians." These groups were of diverse cultures, languages, and levels of civilization and organization. Yet they were lumped together as "Indians," essentially a racial classification based on the skin color and other physical attributes of the indigenous population. Thus, the nation was founded on a European invasion of a continent that was sparsely settled by inhabitants who appeared to be physically "different."

European policies toward the indigenous populations of America were mixed. In a few places, accommodation was achieved. For the most part, conflict emerged after tribes were drawn into struggles among competing European powers. The principal conflicts between Indians and Europeans arose over a struggle to gain control over Indian lands. Gradually, the attitudes toward Indians shifted to racial hostility as the prejudice grew that the Indians did not deserve their own land.[6]

The relationships of the Spanish and the French with the Indians were more amicable than those of the English colonists. English clergy made numerous efforts to convert the Indians to Christianity, with some success. But as the English population rose, friction increased and outright warfare often emerged. As early as 1644, after numerous bloody battles between English settlers and Indians in Virginia, a treaty was signed between the colonists and the Powhatan Indians, initiating the reservation system for Indian lands. This treaty assigned certain lands to Indians as a sanctuary against white incursions, a virtual recognition "that assimilation of the two peoples was unlikely."[7]

In practice, white incursions on Indian lands occurred frequently, often in spite of treaty guarantees or land reservations. Indians were perceived by early Americans as fundamentally different, and their rights were often ignored. Official policy, as in the 1787 Northwest Ordinance of the newly independent United States, was frequently benign, but land thefts and violence toward Indians were common events.[8]

Finally, by 1830, an overt policy of taking away Indian lands emerged. This policy was actively sponsored by President Andrew Jackson. The passage of the Indian Removal Act of 1830 gave an official stamp to a policy of forced racial movement. Indian groups were compelled to leave their lands and to migrate westward to "reservations" in Oklahoma and other Great Plains states. In one vivid example, 4,000 Cherokees died in the course of a march made at gunpoint.[9]

Native Oklahoma Indians resisted the movement into the Plains. War between Americans and Plains Indians broke out in the 1830s, with atrocities on both sides. Overt Indian resistance to white policies continued until 1890 when, in a massacre of Indians at Wounded Knee, South Dakota, 300 defenseless Indian men, women, and children were gunned down by American troops. Several massacres had occurred before, committed by both sides, but the brutality of the incidents is still shocking today.[10] In the end, the Indians were defeated, humiliated, disarmed, and made dependents of the U.S. government. This was the first chapter of race relations in the United States of America. Some have described the policy as essentially genocidal in character.[11] However, for those Indians who are left in America today, the issues of tribal rights and the rights of Indian individuals on and off the reservations remain uncertain.

Blacks in America became the nation's second source of race relations problems. As Thomas F. Gossett so eloquently explained the situation, the English colonists already had a race problem with Indians when they imported another, with the arrival in 1619 of the first boatload of Negro slaves.[12] The first African blacks in America were twenty indentured servants sold to Virginia settlers just one year before the *Mayflower* arrived. Black slavery gradually emerged as a legal institution. While white indentured servants had the prospect of gradual freedom, lifetime servitude for blacks and their children became the rule in Virginia, Maryland, and other Southern states. The view of a black person's social status became one of permanent social inferiority as slaves formed a large part of the labor force of the South. Black women and children, together with black men, became an essential feature of the plantation economy.[13]

The importation of slaves increased as planters came to realize that low-cost labor could increase profits. Slaves became treated as property, to be used by owners as they saw fit. Slave women were often used for breeding purposes. Slaves did not enjoy a legal family life, nor could they marry, nor make contracts. Slave families could be separated at any time. Parents of slave children had no legal authority or control of them.

Although some historians have argued that black slavery was not especially brutal,[14] most would agree that slaves were regarded as subhuman and were devoid of the rights available to other Americans, and even to aliens in this country.

Actually, there were free blacks in early America, too. However—and this shows the imprint of racism—even unenslaved blacks were not treated as well as whites. Voting was difficult and often impossible. Property rights were limited by law. There was always the risk of being brought into slavery, and the final means of social control was intimidation. Burnings, lynchings, and brutalization of blacks by whites remained a threat even for so-called free blacks.[15]

The American Civil War was fought partly over the issue of slavery. By 1860 many Americans in the North thought of slavery as a moral evil. But there were also Northerners who were opposed to the abolition of slavery, especially Irish immigrants who were in direct competition with freed blacks for jobs.[16] In the armies of the North, black enlistees were, at first, rejected, but by the end of the Civil War about 186,000 black troops had been enrolled. Even then, however, blacks served in segregated units under white officers.[17]

The famous Emancipation Proclamation was signed by President Abraham Lincoln on January 1, 1863, while the war was still in progress. Lincoln's decision was primarily tactical, intended to advance the cause of the Union. The Proclamation only freed the slaves who lived in areas under Confederate control. The president's feelings did not run so deeply that he was willing to declare all slaves free throughout the nation.

After the Civil War, slavery was legally terminated by the ratification on December 18, 1865, of the Thirteenth Amendment to the Constitution. There had been little advance planning for the needs of the newly freed slaves, and in order to assist them, Congress immediately established the Freedmen's Bureau. Statutes were passed providing direct federal aid, including food, clothing, supplies, job placement, educational facilities, and homestead land to former slaves. Despite President Andrew Johnson's 1866 veto of the Freedmen's Bureau Bill (which proposed to extend its life), the Bureau served the needs of blacks very well until its ultimate abolition in 1872.[18]

In 1868, the nation adopted the Fourteenth Amendment to the Constitution, which established, in a legal sense only, full citizenship of former slaves in the state where they resided and in the United States. This amendment later became the cornerstone of minority rights policies in America, through the interpretation of the "equal protection of the laws" clause found at the end of its first section.

The formal process of terminating slavery in America was completed in 1870 when the Fifteenth Amendment to the Constitution was ratified. This amendment states that the right of the citizens to vote "shall not be denied or abridged by the United States or any state on account of race, color or previous condition of servitude." The amendment also gives Congress the power to enforce its provisions by "appropriate legislation." Unfortunately, the struggle for the passage of "appropriate legislation" is still continuing today, as Congress receives evidence of interferences with the voting rights of blacks and other minorities.

It took nearly one hundred years after independence to achieve a free American society. Thomas Jefferson attempted to attack the institution of slavery in his original draft of the Declaration of Independence, but the section was stricken from the Declaration at the insistence of Southern representatives in the Continental Congress. Jefferson was an advocate of the gradual deportation of slaves from America on the grounds of his own view of racial policy. Jefferson warned Americans that "the two races, equally free, cannot live in the same government."[19]

Modern American race policy stems from the three great post-Civil War amendments, which express the fundamental views of race. However, the word "race" occurs only once in the Constitution—in the Fifteenth Amendment. There is no official constitutional statement of racial policy except as it impacts on voting. This silence regarding race is a source of confusion and constraint when approaching racial issues, since there is a tendency to avoid direct recognition of these sensitive matters. However, American legislation sometimes explicitly mentions race. Still, no Supreme Court could deny what Justice Roger Taney once brazenly admitted—that blacks had been "regarded as beings of an inferior order ...altogether unfit to associate with the white race, either in social or political relations; and so far inferior, that they had no rights which the white man was bound to respect."[20] Taney's portrayal of pre-Civil War policy toward enslaved blacks is accurate. Fortunately, that policy was expressly changed by the ratification of the Thirteenth, Fourteenth, and Fifteenth amendments. The import of those changes for race policy will be explored.

Congress passed seven civil rights acts from 1866 until 1875. One act was passed over a presidential veto, and three were struck down by the Supreme Court as unconstitutional. Congress did not enact any other significant civil rights legislation until 1957. These seven acts represent the sum and substance of official American race policy prior to the civil rights movement of the 1950s and 1960s.

The most far-reaching of the post-Civil War statutes was the so-called Ku Klux Klan Act.[21] This act imposed penalties on those who deprived "any person or any class of persons of the equal protection of the laws or of equal privileges or immunities under the laws." It was intended to reach private acts of discrimination, especially violent ones. This statute was intended to protect black voters from intimidation and blacks in general from the terrorism and violence which so often was a first resort of whites who wanted "to keep blacks in their place." In 1883 and 1887, the Supreme Court delivered a devastating blow to black civil rights when it declared Section 2 of the act unconstitutional.[22]

An even more damaging blow to the better treatment of blacks was delivered by the Supreme Court in 1896 in its decision in the infamous case of *Plessy v. Ferguson*.[23] This case created the "separate but equal" doctrine of constitutional law, providing a basis for a renewed series of state "Jim Crow" legislation which became the greatest burdens blacks had to bear until modern times. These laws were similar to South African "petty apartheid" in that they attempted to segregate every aspect of life—schooling, religion, housing, recreation, transportation, employment, and so on. When a victim of a Jim Crow law claimed that he had been deprived of his rights pursuant to the Thirteenth and Fourteenth amendments to the Constitution, Justice Henry Brown replied for the Court majority that the Constitution did not "abolish distinctions based upon color...or a commingling of the two races upon terms unsatisfactory to either."[24] Brown denied that equal rights would come from "an enforced commingling of the two races."[25]

American blacks suffered indignities and injustices for decades afterward. Worse still, violence directed against blacks accelerated. Even as late as the 1940s, Swedish social scientist Gunnar Myrdal observed:

in the South the Negro's person and property are practically subject to the whim of any white person who wishes to take advantage of him or to punish him for any real or fancied wrong or insult! A white man can steal from or maltreat a Negro in almost any way without fear of reprisal, because a Negro cannot claim the protection of the police or courts ... Violence may occur at any time, and it is the fear of it as much as violence itself which creates the injustice and insecurity.[26]

Over 3,000 blacks were lynched in the South between 1882 and 1936.[27] This, then, was the situation for American blacks living in the South prior to 1950. Life was somewhat better for the one-third of the black population living outside the South.

Mexican-Americans are another group that has tended to be regarded as a "race" in America. Official census publications lump persons of Spanish origin together, but Mexican-Americans are reported separately. There are about 5.5 million such persons living in America.

Some Mexican-Americans were indigenous to the Southwestern regions of the United States when they were overpowered by white settlers during territorial struggles. Many Mexican-Americans came across the border as temporary workers (*Braceros*), while still others entered illegally as undocumented aliens. Although the legal number of Mexican-Americans living in the United States is known, no one is certain of the number of "illegals."

Hispanic communities have existed in the Southwest since the seventeenth century. Some became American by virtue of the 1853 Gadsden Purchase which enabled the United States to acquire Texas, New Mexico, and parts of Colorado and Arizona. Utah and Nevada were acquired from Mexico in 1948. California was acquired in 1847 when Mexico surrendered it to John C. Fremont. Outnumbered by the whites, they were generally regarded as social inferiors. Only in New Mexico was political power retained to any degree.

The basic conflict was over land. Like the indigenous Indians, the Mexican residents lost most of their lands. Unlike the Indians, the Mexicans were not herded into reservations, but were included in the Southwestern economy.[28] At least the Mexicans were experienced at farming, ranching, and mining—which the Indians were not—and they formed a cheap and tractable labor pool for the dominant "Anglos."

Extensive migration from Mexico took place in the 1900s as political and economic instability caused many to flee Mexico. Meanwhile, economic development in the American Southwest was rapidly taking place, providing much-needed jobs, especially for farm laborers and railroad workers.[29] Unionization among Mexican workers was severely discouraged. Most of the jobs were rural and migratory, preventing much opportunity for social or economic advancement. Active repression and discrimination were employed to keep Mexicans and Mexican-Americans at the lower rungs of the social ladder.[30] Only with the outbreak of World War II did conditions begin to improve, as the wartime labor shortages and the need for more urban labor began to break down the old patterns. Opportunities came with the war, but many doors remained shut.

Discrimination against Mexican-Americans became more acute, in a way, once they sought entry into the mainstream of American life. It was common in the Southwest for Mexican-Americans to be excluded from public and private places, denied access to real estate, or even to be forbidden to render jury service.[31]

In 1943, the so-called Zoot-Suit Riots broke out in Los Angeles. These involved mostly Mexican youths and some blacks who adopted exaggerated clothing and organized themselves into flamboyant bands. Clashes between white servicemen and zoot-suiters broke out after months of friction. City police tended to blame the Mexicans and rounded up many of them, sometimes with considerable brutality. This episode has been interpreted in various ways, but it shows, at least, that antagonisms between Mexicans and "Anglos" could lead to large-scale urban riots.[32]

After the war, new patterns of immigration emerged, and an increasing political awareness also developed. In a few areas, Mexican-Americans began to improve their social status.

ASIAN IMMIGRANTS

Chinese immigration to the United States began in the 1840s, forming the first Asian wave of immigration. At first, they were well received on the West Coast, where they supplied much needed cheap labor. Hostility to the Chinese did not break out until some of them sought jobs in California mining camps. Yet, by the 1860s, there were over 50,000 Chinese in California, which was about 10 percent of the population.

An active anti-Chinese movement developed in the San Francisco area, where competition for jobs was fiercest. In response to mass meetings, state and local governments passed anti-Chinese laws intended to drive the Chinese out. Special taxes were placed on Chinese laundries, special "bonds" were required of new immigrants, and a tax was imposed on "pigtails" by a "queue" ordinance. These openly discriminatory acts were mostly unconstitutional, but few state courts were prepared to support Chinese rights.[33]

The demand for an end to Chinese immigration became a national issue in the 1880s. Finally, in 1882 Congress passed a Chinese Exclusion Act, prohibiting further Chinese immigration for ten years. This act was renewed in 1892 and "made permanent" in 1902. The goal of the anti-Chinese movement had been attained, but these goals were popular nationally, especially among workingmen. Chinese exclusion was both racist and economic in origins, leading one scholar to conclude that discriminatory legislation was often broadly supported, even by forces that were liberal in other social matters.[34]

During World War II, the Chinese became our allies against the Axis powers, including the Japanese. It was possible to regard Chinese as "friends" and Japanese as "enemies." But the "sly, tricky Jap" of World War II became our ally within a few years after the end of the war. The Chinese revolution under Mao-Tse-Tung became a "bad" or communist revolution. As a result of these shifts in foreign policy, the popular views of Chinese and Japanese became reversed after World War II.

Japanese immigration to the United States began later than that of the Chinese. Most Japanese immigration took place between 1870 and 1924. After that date, as a result of anti-Asian immigration laws, Japanese migration virtually ended. No quota for Japanese migration was established after 1924.

The first generation of Japanese to America was drawn from the middle and lower classes who lived their lives in self-segregated fashion far from the American mainstream. Many of the "Issei," as they called themselves, returned to Japan after earning some money. Those who stayed lived in a sharply different life-style from the Americans around them.[35]

The children of the Issei suffered considerable difficulty in entering American life. Although legally citizens, the "Nisei" had limited access to jobs, schools, and housing, and were often openly denied opportunities because of their race. Evidence of race discrimination against the Nisei was clear enough. However, the outbreak of World War II caused an anti-Japanese hysteria on the West Coast which led directly to serious denials of basic civil liberties.

The wartime evacuation and internment of Japanese-American citizens during World War II is one of the most painful episodes in American history. Some authors have referred to the internment as virtual American "concentration camps" like those of Nazi Germany.[36] Although many Japanese-Americans were unjustly deprived of their property, their businesses, and even their livelihood, brutality and genocide were not in evidence at these so-called relocation centers.[37] But lives were seriously disrupted from January 29, 1942, until January 2, 1945, when, in spite of Supreme Court inaction, the Japanese-Americans were no longer held in detention. Executive Order 9066, signed by President Franklin D. Roosevelt, had authorized the building of "relocation camps" scattered over seven states. More than 110,000 Japanese, most of them American citizens, lost their homes and possessions to live behind barbed wire, for no other offense than having as little as one-eighth Japanese blood.

THE REVOLUTION IN AMERICAN RACE RELATIONS

The current state of American race relations is the product of far-reaching changes in attitudes and policies since the 1950s. These changes were largely provoked by a much more militant position by black Americans which paved the way for a general reconstruction of race relations, called by some a "civil rights revolution" and by others a "black revolt." There is no doubt that the desperation and dissatisfaction of blacks had reached a boiling point by the 1950s. A direct challenge to dominant American racial attitudes was created because earlier moderate policies had failed to gain the attention of dominant whites.[38]

Black Americans had raised their expectations during the post-World War II era. The war itself had opened many job opportunities which had been unavailable to them earlier. The experiences of black soldiers had also expanded their horizons. Although President Harry S Truman ended segregation in the armed forces by issuing an Executive Order in 1948, black soldiers came to understand the depth of race attitudes in America.[39] Most important was the vast migration of blacks from the South to cities in the North and West. This mass migration is one of the major events of modern American history, as large numbers of blacks sought a new and better life in other regions of the country.

The chief black interest group of the twentieth century is the National Association for the Advancement of Colored People (NAACP). The name alone suggests that race relations has been a major American problem, since "colored" was the name applied by whites to blacks. The NAACP has pursued a policy of using the courts as a means of combatting discrimination. Since 1931, the NAACP has followed a strategy of undermining racial segregation by expanding the promise of the equal protection of the laws clause of the Fourteenth Amendment to the Constitution. In particular, the group aimed to destroy the effects of the vicious *Plessy v. Ferguson* decision of 1896, which propped up the system of Jim Crow segregationist legislation which had spread through the entire nation. Finally, in 1954, the NAACP gained its legal victory, destroying the foundations of segregation and scoring the most important blow for equality in race relations in the history of the nation. The Supreme Court, under Chief Justice Earl Warren, was prepared to correct historic wrongs against blacks by giving new life to the equal protection of the laws clause first given to the nation after the Civil War.[40]

Unfortunately, Chief Justice Warren's reasoning in the *Brown* case did not rest entirely on the Fourteenth Amendment, but also on some questionable social science data. The full import of the decision is somewhat in question and deserves close attention because it is the cornerstone of modern American race relations policy. Warren found that the separation of black from white children in public education "solely because of their race generates a feeling of inferiority as to their status in the community that may affect their hearts and minds in a way unlikely ever to be undone." He also ruled that segregation by means of separate educational facilities is inherently unequal. This segregation was held to deprive the black plaintiffs of the equal protection of the laws. While this decision clearly dealt with state-enforced segregation on the basis of race, the questions of other forms of racial separation in the community were not considered. The *Plessy* case was effectively dead, but the new lines of American race relations policy were not drawn with any precision.

Racial segregation in public facilities beyond schools was forbidden in 1954 and 1955.[41] Racial segregation in public transportation was ended in 1956.[42] Privately endowed public recreational facilities were ordered desegregated in 1966.[43] In 1968, sixteen state laws that had prevented interracial marriages were held to be unconstitutional.[44] Yet in spite of these judicial victories on behalf of the principle that segregation was improper, Louis M. Steel, NAACP Associate Counsel, declared in 1968 that the Supreme Court had "never committed itself to a society based upon principles of complete equality," but had instead hit at the most overt and obnoxious racial barriers.[45] For his bluntness, Steel lost his job with the NAACP, but he was essentially correct because the Court has never held social equality to be a constitutional objective.

As we will see later, there is some ground for regarding the constitutional basis for the reform of American race relations as inadequate. Yet, these important Supreme Court rulings did lay the basis for a fresh start in a nation that had long been haunted by the specter of race. This fresh start has provided a benchmark for race relations in America and elsewhere, while also heightening the awareness of race problems in other nations that have seen the American example as significant.

One of the most interesting constitutional doctrines that evolved in America is the development of "suspect classifications" of legislation. The Supreme Court has held that race is a "suspect category," meaning that legislation based on racial categories would be treated to much more judicial scrutiny than normal legislation. Unlike most legislation, race-based legislation would be presumed to be invalid. Only a "compelling government interest" could uphold such statutes.[46] The Court has consistently held that racial considerations may not be used by legislatures to burden members of minority races, but it has not definitely decided whether racial distinctions intended to confer a benefit are also offensive to the Constitution. That is the central problem of affirmative action policy in America, which raises the question of whether sound public policy stops at requiring public neutrality toward the races or whether stronger, more positive steps toward aiding disadvantaged racial groups should or could be taken.

National legislation to aid blacks and other races began to flow only after the Supreme Court broke the logjam on American race policy. On September 9, 1957, the first national civil rights bill enacted since 1875 was able to slip through Congress, thanks mostly to the efforts of Senate Majority Leader Lyndon B. Johnson. The 1957 act established a Civil Rights Commission empowered to investigate and gather evidence on voting and race discrimination.[47] Certain other rights were protected, such as the right to sit on grand and petit juries. The Civil Rights Commission has been a major source of information about the dimensions of American race policies.

In 1960, because of the inadequacies of the voting rights protections of the 1957 statute, a stronger act was passed to protect voters and those who were assisting blacks to register. This act also made traveling in interstate commerce and "willfully attempting to or damaging by fire or explosive any building" a federal criminal offense.[48] This was intended to discourage acts of violence aimed at civil rights activists. Both federal protection of black voting rights and the powers of the Civil Rights Commission were expanded.

In June 1963, President John F. Kennedy proposed an act intended to eliminate racial discrimination in private facilities open to the public.

President Kennedy was slain later that year, but his work was carried to fulfillment by President Lyndon Johnson. In 1964, the most sweepng civil rights act in American history was passed.[49] Public accommodations, voting, education, public facilities, and employment were all reached by some provisions of the statute. This means that hotels, motels, restaurants, lunchrooms, theatres, and other public places cannot discriminate or segregate "on the ground of race, color, religion, or national origin." The black rights movement now embraced all races and religions in America. Petty apartheid was legally dead in the nation.

The act also makes various types of employment discrimination unlawful. An Equal Employment Opportunities Commission was created to oversee the enforcement of the law concernng job discrimination. The Commission was in the vanguard of race policymaking until the Reagan years and began developing rules that laid the basis for the affirmative action controversy.

Two more major pieces of race policy legislation have been passed by Congress. In 1965, the Voting Rights Act finally put the federal government in the business of intervening on behalf of blacks and others seeking to register to vote.[50] In 1968, an omnibus civil rights act was passed which was aimed at housing discrimination and the protection of Indians and others who sought to exercise rights not to be discriminated against.[51] The 1968 Civil Rights Act made unlawful the refusal of a private individual to sell or rent housing to another because of his race, color, religion, or national origins. Because it reached private acts of discrimination, this was an important attempt to change private behavior toward an individual victim of race discrimination. But this was also the last major national civil rights act. The mood of the nation has shifted rightward ever since, away from further positive legislation to promote greater racial equality.

The mobilization of blacks also aided the rights of other race groups. Groups such as American Indians, which had suffered more than a century of neglect, became the objects of congressional concern. Indians had been regarded as virtual "wards of the state," but an effort toward Indian self-government started in the 1960s. Congress, the Bureau of Indian Affairs, and the Indian groups began to make new arrangements for Indian rights. Title II of the Civil Rights Act of 1968 gave Indians their first benefits from the civil rights movement. Prior to the passage of that act, Indians had no federally protected rights while living on reservations. Title II was intended to preserve tribal government, as well as extend to individual Indians most of the protections available to other Americans under the Constitution.

Most, but not all, of the federal Bill of Rights, has been extended to the Indians on reservations. The right to counsel is limited, since Indians must bear the expenses. There is no right to a grand jury. Freedom of religion exists, except that establishment of religion is not prohibited, a concession to Indian religious practices. Habeas corpus and bill of attainder restrictions apply to limit the power of Indian tribal councils. Tribal courts were restricted in their powers over criminal offenses to those involving minor offenses only. In spite of official efforts to push for Indian self-government, the major concern of Indians has been to obtain better treatment on reservations and fairer disposition of Indian lands, many of which were claimed under old treaties with whites.[52] Major Indian issues are still unresolved, as the composition of the Bureau of Indian Affairs and the policies of the Interior Department touch the lives of Indians most intimately.[53]

One of the most interesting features of American Indian policy has been a statutory version of an affirmative action scheme. Since 1934, the Bureau of Indian Affairs has been required by law to give preference in hiring to Indians.[54] This policy is limited to Indian reservations, but it is an important recognition of the inferior and dependent social status of those Indians. The Supreme Court, too, has long recognized that Indians are "intrinsically dependent."[55]

Mexican-Americans were identified by the Supreme Court in 1954, which recognized "the ethnological and statistical identifiability of the Mexican-American classification."[56] Until that date, Mexican-Americans were not treated as a group by national authorities. In the past, Mexican-Americans had been subjected to many of the exclusionary practices used against blacks in the South, including literacy test, exclusion from juries and grand juries, intimidation, and murder.[57]

One of the major by-products of the civil rights movements was the removal of language barriers to the political participation of Spanish speakers. In the Voting Rights Act of 1965, Congress made it easier for those whose primary language was Spanish to have access to the ballot. In 1970, Congress suspended the language requirements and the literacy tests altogether.[58] Furthermore, many states made their elections bilingual, sometimes voluntarily and sometimes as a result of the enforcement of the voting laws. However, a command of English is still necessary for virtually all public employment.

An English-only policy of teaching in American public schools came under attack in the late 1960s. In 1979, the U.S. Department of Health, Education and Welfare required school districts to "take affirmative steps to rectify . . . language deficiencies" when national-origin minority group children in a school system were unable to speak and understand the English language.[59] In 1968, Congress had passed a Bilingual Education Act. While there is no constitutional right to bilingual or bicultural education, many states and the federal government were moving in that direction until the 1980 election of President Ronald Reagan whose administration has discouraged further development.

AFFIRMATIVE ACTION: THE FRONTIERS OF RACE POLICY

As indicated above, American Indians have been given special hiring preferences since 1934. Similarly, and for other than racial reasons, veterans, retired people, disabled persons, and other politically popular groups have in various ways been given economic and social opportunities denied to the general population. Special treatment and preferences for groups is not new in America, but affirmative action on behalf of racial minorities was not attempted on any large scale until the 1970s. It has met with widespread opposition, which has grown until the Civil Rights Commission itself was packed by President Reagan with opponents of affirmative action, as was the Reagan Justice Department.

Preferential treatment for blacks and other racial groups is, by definition, unequal treatment. Providing special opportunities for racial minorities in education and employment may be a useful technique to rapidly advance the social and economic opportunities of those groups, but it also comes at considerable cost. For one, such policies cannot be "color blind," but are based on racial categories which the Supreme Court has held to be suspect when used for the purposes of discrimination. Positive or "benign discrimination" may be geared to assist, rather than hamper, racial groups, but it is nonetheless a challenge to the principle of equal protection of the laws when examined in the light of congressional intentions. In the clearest statement on this sensitive issue, a leading scholarly article has aptly concluded:

Viewed in this light the prohibition against discriminatory legislation is a demand for purity of motive. It erects a constitutional barrier against legislative motives of hate, prejudice, vengeance, hostility, or, alternatively, of favoritism, and partiality. The imposition of special burdens, the granting of special benefits, must always be justified. They can only be justified as being directed at the elimination of some social evil, the achievement of some public good.[60]

In fact, affirmative action began in 1967 with President Lyndon Johnson's Executive Order requiring that federal contractors take affirmative action to insure equal employment opportunity without regard to race and sex.[61] This step launched a series of actions and activities by other federal agencies, followed by state and local actions, aimed at placing larger numbers of American racial groups in good jobs and good schools. However, policy leadership in affirmative action was assumed by the Equal Employment Opportunity Commission (EEOC) which attempted to expand opportunities beyond federal contractors to reach state and local employers. The EEOC has achieved some successes, but it has come under direct political attack since 1980 and is no longer vigorously pressing forward on affirmative action plans.[62]

The federal effort to pursue affirmative action remedies reached its height under President Jimmy Carter who urged his staff to obtain more "unrepresented minorities" in the federal civil service. He also directed his office of Federal Contract Compliance Programs to pressure private employers to hire more women and minorities. The U.S. Department of Education also placed stringent guidelines on public education to obtain more women and minorities on their staffs. Ronald Reagan reached the White House in 1980 standing on a platform that opposed "quotas, ratios, and numerical requirements." He took steps to dismantle the bureaucratic machinery that supports affirmative action. Pressure on government agencies and private contractors was relaxed. In 1985, he threatened to rescind the Executive Order of 1967 which had been tacitly upheld by every President since Lyndon Johnson. Although Reagan retreated from this act, he continued to use his Justice Department as a leader in anti-affirmative action activities.[63]

The fight over the future of affirmative action policies has been taken out of the executive branch. The Congress has refused to act on the matter, for fear of irritating voters one way or another. Only the courts are still active in pursuing affirmative action remedies, and then only under constraints developed by the interpretations of the Supreme Court. The question of the effectiveness of such programs is no longer being debated.

The most well-known action of the Supreme Court is the 1978 *Bakke* case.[64] The decision involved a state medical school which had reserved a specific number of places in each entering class for minority applicants. Bakke, a white applicant, insisted that if some places had not been reserved for minorities he would have been admitted, since some minorities were admitted with much lower test scores and college grades. The Justices were badly split, although the majority did agree that Bakke should be admitted. Apparently, the state had gone too far in setting a specific fixed quota for minority admissions. But affirmative action plans that made race a factor were not held to be impermissible. Race could be taken into account as a remedy for past disadvantages.

The reasoning became clearer in the *Weber* case, decided in 1979, a year after *Bakke*. Weber was a blue-collar worker who ran afoul of a voluntary affirmative action agreement made between the Kaiser Aluminum Company and the United Steelworkers. This agreement required the company to set up two lists of applicants for a special training program (one white, one black). The Supreme Court upheld the voluntary program, in spite of Weber's claim that he had fallen victim to preferential treatment.[65]

In 1984, the U.S. Supreme Court ruled six to three that a federal district court may not prevent a city from following its seniority system in choosing employees for layoffs because of budget difficulties, even though strict compliance with the seniority system would force layoffs of blacks who had been hired pursuant to affirmative action goals established by a consent decree under Title VII of the Civil Rights Act of 1964.[66] The Court majority said that affirmative action plans would give way to seniority rights (1) the seniority system was adopted with discriminatory intent, or (2) there was a proven victim of discrimination who was entitled to an award. The Justice Department hailed this decision as support for its broader opposition to all quotas, regardless of a seniority system. As of this writing, neither the Supreme Court nor the lower federal courts support the Justice Department's interpretation. They will allow the use of affirmative action in consent decrees under Title VII, without requiring that the relief be limited to actual victims of discrimination.[67] Both the Reagan administration and the courts agree that proven victims of race discrimination are entitled to an affirmative action-type remedy, but since "discriminatory intent" must be shown, such cases will be rare indeed. It remains to be seen whether lower courts and the Supreme Court will complete the retreat from affirmative action policies. Plainly, in public education, courts may still apply such remedies to correct a pattern of discrimination within a school district, but race-conscious employment opportunities and affirmative action programs are under severe attack. Apparently, "voluntary affirmative action plans contracted between the parties are easier to defend in the courts than those mandated *ab initio* by federal trial courts."[68]

Black scholars do not agree on the extent of black gains in American race relations since the pivotal *Brown* decision of 1954. Some progress has been made in improving the social and economic status of blacks, but is it enough? The Congress has ceased legislating on behalf of blacks and other racial minorities. Affirmative action is under attack. Judgment must be made. Has American race relations dramatically improved, especially for the largest minority, the blacks?

Thomas Sowell, a prominent black economist takes a conservative line. He believes that race prejudice has been a powerful force in American history, but he contends that today it is not, since "various non-white groups equal and exceed the economic level of various white groups," when using family income as a measure of comparison.[69] However, according to Sowell's own table, only Japanese and Chinese families were above the national averages in 1977, while blacks, Cubans, Mexicans, Puerto Ricans, and Indians were far below the averages. Thus, by confusing race and ethnicity, Sowell blames the blacks and Hispanics for their own lack of industry. In fact, recent evidence shows that Asian-Americans do not enjoy great success in America. The data on which Sowell relied are not sound.[70] Sowell has opposed aggressive public policies on behalf of racial minorities in America because of his belief in the power of the private marketplace and his distrust of the power of black rights leaders. He has contended for years, as the Reagan administration now holds, that affirmative action policies are both unnecessary and pernicious.[71] From Sowell's point of view, official race policy is now adequate, but the groups themselves should rely more on their own initiative to advance themselves.

Another black perspective argues that race in America has become less salient than class. This transition in American history signifies that "race relations in America have undergone fundamental changes in recent years, so much so that now the life chances of individual blacks have more to do with their economic class position than with their day-to-day encounters with whites."[72] This assessment, if true, would suggest that black-white relations are much better than they have ever been before in America. In September 1978, the Association of Black Sociologists passed a resolution condemning the thesis just stated, saying that there was abundant evidence "that documents the significance of race as a critical variable in the denial of opportunity for whites." The resolution contended instead that "the life chances of blacks (e.g., employment, housing, health care, education, etc.) are shocking and that discrimination in some areas is so pervasive that the income and employment gaps between blacks and whites have widened."[73] There is a split in the interpretation of data which threatens to divide the forces for social progress.

Some other analysts have argued that class, not race, now steers the course of race relations in America.[74] Although there is no longer a monolithic white majority that resists the advances of minority races, it is probable that race continues to play a significant role in the lives of most minority group members. For those few who have managed to enter the mainstream of employment, housing, and education in America, there probably is greater acceptance than ever before, but year after year the general employment and housing statistics imply that vast numbers of minority race members are still at or near the bottom of the social heap.[75] Race prejudice in America has decreased, but opportunities for racial minorities do not appear to have dramatically improved in the areas of income and housing, as revealed by statistics gathered by the Bureau of the Census.

Mindful of these considerations, some black scholars contend that black progress in America is a myth or illusion. Alphonso Pinkney believes that racism is still a persistent problem. He admits that there is a black middle class, but he contends "they are still considered black first and middle class second."[76] Even wealthy blacks, he says, are victims of racial discrimination in housing. Private clubs still have white-only policies, even in cities with black mayors. Furthermore, black entry into the middle class has often been accomplished through affirmative action programs, giving these newcomers a precarious hold on their newly acquired status. While most urban blacks live in slums as a virtual underclass, even those who have escaped poverty because of recent public policies have not escaped exposure to race discrimination.[77] It is probably true that progress in American race relations has been significant, but Pinkney alerts his reader to the limited gains of blacks thirty years after the *Brown* decision. Other racial groups could make a similar showing.

There are also signs that the gains of blacks and other racial minorities on the legal front are much less meaningful than early liberal commentators had assumed. The reinterpretation of the Thirteenth, Fourteenth, and Fifteenth amendments to the U.S. Constitution made by U.S. courts in the 1950s and 1960s appears to have been much less sweeping in effect than was first assumed. True, segregation by public agencies is now unlawful, but desegregation of society has proven to be much more difficult to attain. Official desegregation efforts have been largely limited to public education, and even there progress has been extremely slow in urban school districts.[78]

Public opinion polls show an increasing acceptance among whites of the process of racial integration.[79] There has also been an increase in the number of black elected officials at the federal, state, and local levels.[80] Many of these changes have taken place in the South, a former bastion of anti-black attitudes. Nonetheless, implementation of the civil rights laws has gone extremely slowly, and there may have been slippage in black employment in the past few years while whites have been better off.[81]

American Indians are still among the poorest Americans. Half of the nation's 1.5 million Indians live on 300 reservations where few job opportunities can be found, literacy is low, and infant mortality is high. In 1985, Ross O. Swimmer, the principal chief of the Cherokee Nation of Oklahoma, was made head of the Bureau of Indian Affairs, the chief federal agency dealing with Indian problems. It remains to be seen whether this unusual appointment will substantially improve the lot of American Indians.

In America, race seems to have a strong correlation with poverty. Census Bureau figures show that in urban areas blacks are three and a half times more likely than whites to be below the poverty line. "Spanish-origin" people are a bit less than three times as poor as urban whites. Even what the Census Bureau calls "Asian and Pacific Islanders" are 40 percent more likely to be poor than are whites.[82] These figures may change in the future, but today it is highly likely that race is a major factor in the life opportunities of Americans.

CONCLUSION

The limits of socially acceptable policies may have been reached in American race relations. At least, no major improvement in official policies seems likely in the current policies of the American Supreme Court, which once seemed to be pressing most actively for improvements in race relations. It may be too early to say whether there will also be no further enhancement of the social and economic positions of racial minorities, but this seems very likely for most groups.

The Supreme Court itself has begun to recognize that *Brown v. Board of Education* has not resolved the problems of racial separation in the housing patterns that prevail in American communities. The 1974 decision in *Milliken v. Bradley* shows that the limits of judicial intervention on behalf of segregation have been determined.[83] The decision held that a court cannot include white suburbs in a busing order to remedy a city's de jure segregation unless the suburbs also knowingly and deliberately perpetrate de jure segregation. This means that white suburbanites who wish to avoid the perils of racially mixed schools may safely escape them by moving to the suburbs. Unless the school boards and other public authorities have designed a haven for "white flight," the courts will not question the social circumstances which, all too often, result in center city public schools with huge minority enrollments surrounded by suburbs with minimal minority enrollments in public schools. The Court has gone as far as it is willing to go in desegregating American schools.

The equal protection of the laws clause of the Fourteenth Amendment does not seem to guarantee or promise full racial equality. Even if blacks or other racial minorities are being treated differently because of their race, courts have held that they have not been victims of wrongful discrimination unless the discrimination is shown to have been "intentional."[84] Private acts of discrimination that do not implicate a governmental unit are regarded as beyond the reach of the Fourteenth Amendment to the Constitution. In 1883, the Supreme Court held that "individual invasion of individual rights is not the subject matter of the Amendment."[85] This view signifies that essentially governmental functions must meet the standards of the amendment, so that elections, public facilities, and public functions generally cannot rest on a segregated or discriminatory basis. However, truly private associations may practice discrimination, even if such groups enjoy a public license, such as a liquor license.[86] Clearly, such an interpretation of the equal protection of the laws requirement allows race discrimination to stand whenever there is no significant state involvement.[87]

Recent Supreme Court decisions in the affirmative action area also show a reluctance to press forward the boundaries of equal protection. On the contrary, the Court has shown itself willing to intrude into both public and private schemes for preferred treatment of racial groups, fearing that the establishment of racial quotas might somehow detrimentally affect private parties. While the limits on public programs of affirmative action have not yet been established, there is little doubt that the Court, the current administration, and conservative politicians look askance at race and minority preferences.

The Reagan administration has maintained an active campaign to roll back minority preferences. The White House aimed to reverse a twenty-year-old Executive Order which had allowed government contractors to set numerical hiring and promotion goals. The administration asserted that the Constitution must be "color blind," meaning that even the elimination of racial prejudice and oppression was an insufficient justification for racial preferences. This view was not shared by most blacks but was favored by whites.[88]

In 1983, the Census Bureau reported the highest black poverty rate since 1968, with 9.9 million or 35.7 percent of black Americans categorized as poor. Black unemployment has persistently been more than twice that of whites.

Critics of American race policies have begun to emerge. One of the strongest, Alan David Freeman, concludes that "as surely as the law has outlawed racial discrimination, it has affirmed that Black Americans can be without jobs, have their children in all-black, poorly funded schools, have no opportunities for decent housing, and have very little political power without any violation of antidiscrimination law."[89] Freeman points out that the color-blind theory of racial discrimination suggests that racial discrimination is essentially cured and should not be reintroduced by utilizing quotas for racial minorities. But he insists that from the point of view of the victim the failure to press onward to improve the conditions of life of racial minorities assumes, contrary to fact, that the victims of discrimination are now threatening to oppress the perpetrators.

A more sweeping interpretation of events is provided by Derrick Bell, who contends that the 1954 desegregation decision arose out of a brief period when the interests of blacks and whites happened to coincide, making the *Brown* decision inevitable. *Brown* was a decision valuable for whites as well as for blacks, because there were evident social and economic advantages to the abandonment of segregation, as well as foreign policy and Cold War gains. Poorer whites may not have wanted desegregation, but more affluent whites felt comfortable with it at first. This convergence of interest between blacks and well-off whites now seems to be nearly over.[90] This interpretation seems much more plausible than James A. Kushner's harsh and polemical judgment on American "apartheid."[91]

Major sociologists have tended to regard race relations as a subcategory of ethnic relations. From that perspective, American policy appears more positive. The ability of American society to absorb and assimilate newcomers has been remarkable.[92] This positive view is probably true for most ethnics, but it seems to be partly false for racial minorities. A leading American sociologist, Nathan Glazer, has campaigned actively against affirmative action, bilingualism, and group rights in general. He contends that gradually the victims of race discrimination will advance economically as they have in the past (meaning ethnic groups) without active state intervention.[93] Glazer is an optimist about the future of American race relations, relying, as he does, on the history of earlier ethnic groups. However, Indians and blacks have long been at the bottom of the heap in America, and the evidence suggests that they and some other racial groups (including Hispanics) will not be easily "assimilated."[94] As it is, Glazer and some other white American sociologists have advocated gradualism and have opposed activism in race matters.

The recent migration of Kampucheans and Vietnamese to the United States is a fair test of American race policy. Does the United States have a serious problem of race prejudice and bigotry directed at these newest immigrants? Numerous reports of violent incidents directed against them have appeared in the newspapers. The Civil Rights Commission claims it doesn't know whether this is a serious national problem.[95] On the basis of the past history of American race relations, there is a strong probability that these Asians will confront protracted periods of hostility, and their "assimilation" into the United States will be extremely difficult.

NOTES

1. Appendix B, U.S. Department of Commerce, Bureau of the Census, *1980 Census of Population, General Social and Economic Characteristics, Part I, United States Summary*, p. B–3.

2. Ibid., p. B–5.

3. Peter I. Rose, *They and We: Racial and Ethnic Relations in the United States* (New York: Random House, 1968), p. 9.

This issue greatly troubles American scholars, who have not yet established clear definitions of what is meant by race relations. Some mean only "black-white" relations, and others only minority relationships with a "majority." Still others concentrate on ethnic relations, combining race and ethnicity as one general category. However, more than scholarly disputation is involved. Catholics, Jews, and Southern Europeans were once victims of severe prejudice, but their assimilation has proceeded rapidly, while certain racial groups remain outside of mainstream American life. Race cuts deeper than ethnicity in America. The confusion that occurs when race and ethnicity are mingled analytically is vividly displayed in Stanley Lieberson, *A Piece of the Pie: Blacks and White Immigrants Since 1880* (Berkeley: University of California Press, 1980). A distinguished black scholar has made the same error, producing a flawed book: Thomas Sowell, *The Economics and Politics of Race* (New York: William Morrow, 1983).

5. Anti-discrimination and affirmative action policies have emerged in response to past troubles, but no definite statement on race relations exists to guide policymakers.

6. Joseph Hraba, *American Ethnicity* (Itasca, Ill.: F. E. Peacock, 1979), p. 210.

7. Gary B. Nash, *Red, White, and Black* (Englewood Cliffs, N.J.: Prentice-Hall, 1974), p. 65.

8. Joe Feagin, *Racial and Ethnic Relations* (Englewood Cliffs, N.J.: Prentice-Hall, 1978), p. 195.

9. Virgil Vogel, *This Country Was Ours* (New York: Harper & Row, 1972) tells the story of the "Trail of Tears."

10. Ralph Andrist, *The Long Death* (London: Collier/Macmillan, 1964), p. 32, describes one of the most brutal of all white atrocities committed in 1864 by a minister, Colonel John Chivington, and some Colorado volunteers against 200 unarmed Indians at Sand Creek, Colorado.

11. See Feagin, *Racial and Ethnic Relations*, p. 196.

12. Thomas F. Gossett, *Race, the History of an Idea in America* (New York: Schocken Books, 1965), p. 3.

13. E. Franklin Frazier, *The Negro in the United States*, rev. ed. (New York: Macmillan, 1957), pp. 29–30.

14. See Robert Fogel and Stanley Engerman, *Time on the Cross* (Boston: Little Brown, 1974). This view of black slavery holds that the system was essentially benign, if only for economic reasons, since slaves were valuable as property. Actually, there is much historical evidence that confutes this thesis. High death rates, frequent illness, and poor housing of slaves have been documented.

15. See Winthrop D. Jordan, *White over Black* (Baltimore: Penguin, 1968).

16. Anti-draft riots in Northern cities during the Civil War sometimes turned into attacks against blacks.

17. Alphonso Pinkney, *Black Americans* (Englewood Cliffs, N.J.: Prentice-Hall, 1975), pp. 19–20.

18. Many critics contended that the benevolence of Radical Republican leaders of the time was tainted by political opportunism. Yet, many of the Republicans sincerely had honorable motives.

19. Philip S. Forer, ed., *Basic Writings of Thomas Jefferson* (New York: John Wiley & Sons, 1944), pp. 439–40. Jefferson privately believed that blacks were an inferior race, and he was opposed to the sexual "mixture" of blacks and whites. He was himself a slaveowner, although he referred to slaves as "servants."

20. *Dred Scott v. Sanford*, 19 How. 393, at 407 (1857). This case was essentially overruled by the ratification of the Fourteenth Amendment.

21. 17 Stat. 13 (1871).

22. *United States v. Harris*, 106 U.S. 629 (1883) and *Baldwin v. Franks*, 120 U.S. 678 (1887).

23. 163 U.S. 537 (1896).

24. Ibid., p. 540.

25. Ibid., p. 544.

26. Gunnar Myrdal, *An American Dilemma* (New York: McGraw-Hill, 1964; first published in 1944), p. 530.

27. Probably 3,275, according to G. Franklin Frazier, *The Negro in the United States* (New York: Macmillan, 1957), p. 160.

28. Hraba, *American Ethnicity*, p. 237.

29. Carey McWilliams, *North from Mexico* (New York: Greenwood Press, 1968).

30. Matt Meier and Feliciano Rivera, *The Chicano: A History of Mexican Americans* (New York: Hill & Wang, 1972), p. 184.

31. Ibid., pp. 247–48.

32. Roger Daniels and Harry H. L. Kitano, *American Racism* (Englewood Cliffs, N.J.: Prentice-Hall, 1970), pp. 76–77.

33. Harry H. L. Kitano, *Race Relations*, 2d ed. (Englewood Cliffs, N.J.: Prentice-Hall, 1980), pp. 236–37.

34. Ibid., p. 239.

35. See John Connor, *Tradition and Change in Three Generations of Japanese Americans* (Chicago: Nelson-Hall, 1977).

36. Allan P. Bosworth, *America's Concentration Camps* (New York: W. W. Norton, 1967), and Roger Daniels, *Concentration Camps U.S.A.* (New York: Holt, Rinehart & Winston, 1971). The classic work remains Morton Grodzins, *Americans Betrayed* (Chicago: University of Chicago Press, 1949).

37. There have been numerous accounts written by camp victims which describe the pain, isolation, and harshness of their conditions, but deliberate brutality was not evident.

38. For a description of these moderate policies, see Herbert Garfinkel, *The Negro in the United States* (New York: Macmillan, 1957).

39. Truman's Executive Order 9981.

40. *Brown v. Board of Education of Topeka,.* 347 U.S. 483 (1954).

41. *Muir v. Theatrical Park Association*, 347 U.S. 397 Baltimore, 250 F. 2d 386 (4th Cir., 1955).

42. *Brauder v. Gayle*, 142 F. Supp. 707 (M.D. Ala. 1956); affirmed, 352 U.S. 903 (1956).

43. *Evans v. Newton*, 382 U.S. 296 (1966).

44. *Loving v. Virginia*, 388 U.S. 1 (1967).

45. Lewis M. Steel, "Nine Men in Black Who Think White," *New York Times Magazine*, October 13, 1968, pp. 15–16, 112, 115, 117, 118, 120, 122.

46. *McLaughlin v. Florida*, 379 U.S. 184 (1964); see also *Loving v. Virginia*, 388 U.S. 1 (1967). Sex has not been held to be a suspect category, so that sex distinctions in statutes are supposedly less suspicious than race distinctions. A standard below that for race has been established, a standard of "heightened scrutiny" (*Personnel Administrator of Massachusetts v. Feeney*, 422 U.S. 256 [1979]). So the Supreme Court perceives race relations to be on a higher plane of protection than other forms of discriminatory policies.

47. 71 Stat. 634 (1957).

48. 74 Stat. 86 (1960).

49. 78 Stat. 241 (1964).

50. 79 Stat. 437 (1965).

51. 82 Stat. 81 (1968). Congress had written an even broader statute in the Civil Rights Act of 1866. Indeed, the scope of the Ku Klux Klan Act of 1871 was also broader in reaching private acts of discrimination.

52. Legally, terminated Indians are non-Indians. They are regarded, in law, as part of American society and enjoy the protections available to other Americans. However, terminated (off-reservation) Indians do not receive special federal aid. The Bureau of Indian Affairs and the Indian Health Service provide education, housing, and health care for reservation Indians only.

53. See Stephen Cornell, "Crisis and Response in Indian-White Relations:

1960–1984," *Social Problems* 32 (October 1984): 44–59 for a careful review of political events in Indian affairs.

54. 25 U.S.C. Sec. 472. See Mescalero, *Apache Tribe v. Hickel,* 432 F. 2d 956 (10th Cir. 1970).

55. *Board of Commissioners of Creek County v. Seber,* 318 U.S. 705, 715 (1943).

56. *Hernandez v. Texas,* 347 U.S. 475 (1954).

57. According to the California State Advisory Commission to the U.S. Commission on Civil Rights, *Political Participation of Mexican Americans in California* (1971).

58. 84 Stat. 315 (1970), made permanent by 89 Stat. 400 (1975).

59. *Federal Register* 35, No. 139 (July 18, 1979), pp. 11594–95.

60. Joseph Tussman and Jacobus ten Broek, "The Equal Protection of the Laws," *California Law Review* 37 (September 1949): 343.

61. Executive Order 11367 which amended Order 11246. See also Federal Contract Compliance Manual, 1978.

62. For one attempt at measuring its own success, see Equal Employment Opportunity Commission, *Minorities and Women in State and Local Government–1975* (1977).

63. William Bradford Reynolds, Assistant Attorney General, Civil Rights Division, has led the assault. For a reasoned justification for his position, see Reynolds, "Individualism vs. Group Rights: The Legacy of Brown," *Yale Law Journal* 93 (1984): 995–1005. Reynolds opposes all "race-conscious decision making," including court-ordered busing as well as affirmative action programs.

64. *University of California Board of Regents v. Baake,* 438 U.S. 265 (1978).

65. *Steelworkers v. Weber,* 443 U.S. 193 (1979).

66. 52. U.S.L.W. 4767 (June 12, 1984).

67. See *NAACP v. Detroit Police Officer's Association,* 591 F. Supp. 1194 (E.D. Mich. 1984).

68. *Wygant v. Jackson Board of Education,* 746 F. 2d 1152 (6th Cir. 1984) at 1159.

69. Thomas Sowell, *The Economics of Politics and Race* (New York: William Morrow, 1983), p. 187.

70. U.S. Commission on Civil Rights, *Success of Asian Americans: Fact or Fiction?* Clearinghouse Publication 64 (September 1980).

71. Thomas Sowell, "Are Quotas Good for Blacks?" *Commentary* (June 1978): 39–43.

72. William Wilson, *The Declining Significance of Race: Blacks and Changing American Institutions* (Chicago: University of Chicago Press, 1978). In later writings, Wilson has been concerned with the special problems of female-headed households among blacks.

73. Quoted in Alphonso Pinkney, *The Myth of Black Progress* (Cambridge: Cambridge University Press, 1984), p. 15.

74. See H. Edward Ransford, *Race and Class in American Society* (Cambridge: Schenkman Publishing, 1977).

75. The best and clearest evidence for continued racial inequality is U.S. Commission on Civil Rights, *Social Indicators of Equality for Minorities and Women* (August 1978). Little has changed to dispute these indicators. The latest census figures are still in accordance with these findings.

76. Pinkney, *Myth of Black Progress*, p. 107.

77. Douglas Glasgow, *The Black Underclass: Poverty, Unemployment, and Entrapment of Ghetto Youth* (San Francisco: Jossey-Bass, 1980).

78. See U.S. Commission on Civil Rights, *With All Deliberate Speed: 1954–19??* (1981). While the percentage of black students attending white majority schools increased from 23 percent in 1968 to 38 percent in 1978, in the 1978–79 school year over 60 percent of all minority students attended schools that were composed of at least 80 percent minorities. This fact is probably explained by housing segregation patterns, by the whites' desertion of public schools, and only partly by failures of school administrators.

79. D. Garth Taylor, Paul B. Sheatsley, and Andrew M. Greeley, "Attitudes Toward Racial Integration," *Scientific American* 238 (June 1978): 43.

80. *Statistical Abstract of the United States*, 1984, p. 261.

81. Melville J. Ulmer, "The Mismeasure of Unemployment," *New Perspectives* 17 (Spring 1985): 19–23, argues against the statistical evidence gathered by several federal agencies. But most observers do not agree with Professor Ulmer.

82. U.S. Department of Commerce, Bureau of the Census, *Poverty Areas in Large Cities* (February 1985), pp. 12–13.

83. 418 U.S. 717 (1974).

84. *Village of Arlington Heights v. Metropolitan Housing Development Corp.*, 429 U.S. 252, 265–68 (1977).

85. Civil Rights Cases, 109 U.S. 3 (1883).

86. *Moose Lodge No. 107 v. Irvis*, 407 U.S. 163 (1972).

87. Just what constitutes significant state involvement is subject to judicial interpretation. See *Reitman v. Mulkey*, 387 U.S. 367 (1967) and *Norwood v. Harrison*, 413 U.S. 455 (1973).

88. CBS/New York Times poll, Spring 1985, cited in *New York Times*, October 7, 1985, p. A20.

89. Alan David Freeman, "Legitimatizing Racial Discrimination Through Antidiscrimination Law: A Critical Review of Supreme Court Doctrine," *Minnesota Law Review* 62 (1978): 1049–1119, 1050.

90. Derrick A. Bell,"*Brown v. Board of Education* and the Interest-Convergence Dilemma," *Harvard Law Review* 93 (1980): 518–33.

91. James A. Kushner, "Apartheid in America," *Harvard Law Journal* 22 (1979): 547–685.

92. See Stanley Lieberson, *Ethnic Patterns in American Cities* (New York: Free Press, 1962) and his later book, *A Piece of the Pie*.

93. Nathan Glazer, *Ethnic Dilemmas* (Cambridge, Mass.: Harvard University Press, 1983).

94. The 1986 unemployment rate among reservation Indians was 49 percent, according to the Bureau of Indian Affairs.

95. Dr. John H. Bunzel, Commissioner, quoted in *New York Times*, August 31, 1985, p. 8.

BIBLIOGRAPHY

Bianchi, Suzanne M. *Household Composition and Racial Inequality*. New Brunswick, N.J.: Rutgers University Press, 1981.

Daymont, Thomas A. "Racial Equity or Racial Equality." *Demography* 17 (1980): 379–93.

Franklin, John Hope. *From Slavery to Freedom.* New York: Alfred A. Knopf, 1967.

Frazier, E. Franklin. *Black Bourgeoisie: The Rise of a New Middle Classs in the United States.* New York: Free Press, 1957.

Hermalin, Albert I., and Farley Reynolds. "The Potential for Residential Integration in Cities and Suburbs: Implications for the Busing Controversy." *American Sociological Review* 38, No. 5 (October 1973): 595–610.

Lake, Robert M. *The New Suburbanites: Race and Housing in the Suburbs.* Washington, D.C.: Center for Urban Policy Research, 1981.

Lieberson, Stanley. *Ethnic Patterns in American Cities.* New York: Free Press, 1962.

————. *A Piece of the Pie: Blacks and White Immigrants Since 1880.* Berkeley: University of California Press, 1980.

————, and Glenn V. Fuguitt. "Negro-White Occupational Differences in the Absence of Discrimination." *American Journal of Sociology* 73 (1967): 188–200.

Myrdal, Gunnar. *An American Dilemma: The Negro Problem and Modern Democracy.* New York: McGraw-Hill, 1944.

O'Hare, William P. *Poverty in America: Trends and New Patterns.* Washington, D.C.: Population Reference Bureau, 1987.

Parrillo, Vincent. *Strangers in These Shores.* 2d ed. New York: John Wiley, 1985.

Pettigrew, Thomas F. *The Sociology of Race Relations.* New York: Free Press, 1980.

Simkus, Albert. "Residential Segregation by Occupation and Race in Ten Urbanized Areas, 1950–1970." *American Sociological Review* 43 (1978): 81–93.

U.S. Commission on Civil Rights. *Affirmative Action in the 1980s: Dismantling the Process of Discrimination.* Clearing House Publication 70, 1981.

U.S. Commission on Civil Rights. *The Economic Progress of Black Men in America.* Clearing House Publication 91, 1986.

Wilson, William Julius. *The Declining Significance of Race.* 2d ed. Chicago: University of Chicago Press, 1980.

WEST GERMANY

Lutz Holzner

DEFINITION OF STUDY AREA

West Germany is the more popular unofficial name of a sovereign country officially constituted on May 5, 1955, as the Federal Republic of Germany (Bundesrepublik Deutschland or BRD). The BRD is one of the three successor states to emerge from the Greater German Empire (Grossdeutsches Reich), commonly referred to as Nazi Germany, after its defeat and unconditional surrender and dismemberment through the Potsdam Conference Declaration of August 2, 1945. The other two successor states are the German Democratic Republic (Deutsche Demokratische Republik or DDR), more commonly known as East Germany, and the Republic of Austria (Republik Osterreich). Theoretically, all three states share the historical and moral burden of guilt for the holocaust, the systematic genocide of Jews, Gypsies, and other racial minorities during the Nazi era. Only the BRD, however, has officially accepted this dubious heirloom of its predecessor state. West Germans, more than East Germans or Austrians, have as a result developed particularly sensitive and guilt-ridden attitudes toward race and race relations which are probably unlike any other in the world.

The BRD has not been chosen for inclusion in this publication for this reason alone, but also because it has the most acute current minority problem of the three German-speaking countries. A relatively large proportion of the otherwise homogeneous population in the BRD is of foreign origin. Most controversial is the permanent presence of Turks whom many Germans perceive as a greater threat than any other foreign minority group present. The discussion and handling of this problem, including the reaction of the German public and the legal status of the Turks in the BRD, are of widespread interest given the notoriety of

German racism and atrocities of the past. Included in this discussion are the German political organizations and parties, government, the media both in the BRD and abroad, and the scientific community.

A RACIAL CONTEXT

The BRD is racially and ethnically as homogeneous as most other nation-states in Western, Central, and Eastern Europe. As of 1985, 57 million people, or 92.7 percent of the 61.5 million total resident population including West Berlin, were of Germanic (German) stock. Almost 4.5 million, or only 7.3 percent, were non-German, excluding allied troops and their dependents. Traditional tribal differences and some friction among the German people themselves still exist in the BRD and are expressed through historical regionalism, folklore, architecture, and distinct dialects. Some of the dialects are so different that all states of the Federal Republic together with the other German-speaking countries including the DDR (East Germany), Austria, and Switzerland have High German taught in all schools and used by the media. Overall, however, most Germans in the BRD share a sense of national cohesion based on a common national history through more than one hundred years (since 1871), the all-pervasive German cultural heritage, and modern mobility which tends to weaken regionalism.

The cohesive ethnic-cultural and political-societal bonds among the German tribes of the BRD were also fostered through the commonly shared experience of total defeat and unconditional surrender in 1945, the stunning economic recovery since approximately 1955, and the concomitant successful integration of over 12 million German refugees from the Eastern provinces of the German Empire within the boundaries of December 12, 1937, including Southern East Prussia, Pomerania, and Silesia (now incorporated into the state of Poland); Northern East Prussia (now part of the Soviet Union); and from the so-called Sudeten land in Bohemia (Czechoslovakia); as well as many descendants of expatriate Germans who had lived for centuries in Yugoslavia, Hungary, Rumania, and Russia (later Soviet Union). In addition, approximately 3.5 million refugees from the German Democratic Republic (East Germany) were also fully integrated, until the construction of the Berlin Wall and the Death Strip along the East German-West German border on August 13, 1961, stopped most of this migration.

Before 1940, the most significant racial minority in Germany including the territory of the present BRD was the German-Jewish population which numbered approximately 550,000 persons before 1933. Another approximately 450,000 German-speaking Jews lived in Austria. Through both emigration (until 1939) and mass extermination during the holocaust, the Jewish minority of Germany entirely disappeared by 1945 and has been replaced by only a few thousand individuals in the BRD and West Berlin since then.

After 1945, a new racial component developed in the BRD through the offspring of black American occupation personnel and German mothers. These approximately 600,000 persons of mixed parentage (mulatto) have never been subject to group discrimination or racial prejudice, as in all cases their mother and/or their families raised them as Germans without any further contact with their U.S. American fathers. The main concern of current race relations in the BRD including West Berlin lies in the foreign labor population and their families, particularly the Turkish minority. The 1984–85 non-German component of the resident population of the BRD and West Berlin consists of the following nationalities: Turkish 1,552 million; Yugoslavian 613,000; Italian 565,000; Greek 292,000; Austrian 172,000; Spanish 166,000; Dutch 109,000; Portuguese 99,500; and others 867,000.[1] Most of these foreigners had originally been recruited as "guest" laborers (*Gastarbeiter*) during the West German reconstruction and economic growth period starting in approximately 1955 and ending in November 1973 when the West German Parliament (*Bundestag*) declared an end to the recruitment efforts and closed all recruitment offices abroad. Until this point, it was believed that foreign workers returned routinely to their respective home countries to be replaced by an equal number of new recruits. The end of recruitment was conceived to have ended the influx, thus reducing the number of guest workers in the country. This did not happen. Many foreigners obviously decided to remain permanently in the BRD and bring their families. This in fact constituted immigration.

Different groups of immigrants showed different integrative behavior. Those citizens of Italy, Spain, Yugoslavia, and Greece who chose to stay permanently in the BRD made great and in most cases successful efforts to integrate with the German people and their way of life. The Turks, on the other hand, added a component of foreign attributes that these other groups had not displayed: they were obviously distinct in appearance (height, facial features), culture, and religion (Muslim, food habits, a glaringly inferior status of women), dress (particularly the women), and speech (which does not belong to the Indo-European language family as do the languages of all the other above-mentioned minorities). They displayed no apparent willingness to integrate into mainstream German culture, partly because of their strictly temporary status as migratory laborers which citizens of European Economic Community member countries do not share.

Ethnocentrism and/or xenophobia toward foreigners in general exists in practically all ethnically and culturally homogeneous European societies including France, Great Britain, Switzerland, and the Netherlands. As a rule, however, prejudice and discrimination occur only in conjunction and confrontation with clearly discernible ethnic or racial minorities which consist of a considerable number of individuals, as, for example, the German-speaking South Tyrolians in Italy, the German-speaking Alsatians in France, or the Basques in Spain.

The popular definition of minority expressed through numerical means alone, however, is insufficient inasmuch as practically any criterion chosen could make an individual a member of a minority (if fewer than half of the total population of a country makes a minority).[2] Hans Jochim Hoffman-Nowotny defines a minority as a category of any number of persons who (1) suffer social prejudice which is (2) coupled with fixed characteristics, most commonly acquired through birth, such as race, sex, ethnic background, and religion, which in turn (3) exert a negative and stereotyped emotion on the part of the majority.[3] This definition fits the Turks in the BRD. The native German population identifies and perceives them as a discernible group of strangers. They are a "social race" (*Gesellschaftsrasse*)[4] and as such are confronted with isolation, stereotyped prejudice, condescension, and, less frequently, hostility as shown, for example, through occasional racist graffiti or rude behavior in public directed against Turks. But in the context of the West German's hypersensitive awareness of embarrassment through guilt and worldwide scrutiny (holocaust), responsible strata of society and government at all levels make every effort to avoid what the world public might construe as neo-racism in Germany.

At the same time, however, the interests of the German "state" as perceived and postulated by the Basic Law (*Grundgesetz*), a temporary constitution of the BRD, are being protected in the name of the German people through the federal and the respective state and local governments (communities). This includes job protection for Germans and citizens of other EEC countries in times of recession; maintenance of the quality and subjects of instruction in the public schools; prevention of residential concentrations (ghettoes) of Turks in cities; and concern about high birthrates among Turks and low birthrates among Germans, suggesting a possible eventual "foreignization" (*Uberfremdung*) of Germany by people who refuse to integrate. These two goals, avoiding racist discrimination but protecting German interests, are not entirely synchronized, which creates the dilemma of the current push and pull of the so-called guest-worker question (*Gastarbeiterfrage*), or, more to the point "the Turkish problem" (*die Turkenfrage*).

HISTORICAL BACKGROUND OF FOREIGN WORKERS IN GERMANY AND THE BRD

According to the West German Basic Law (*Grundgesetz*), the Federal Republic of Germany is not an immigration country. It does not seek to increase its national population through nationalization of foreigners. This policy is a long-standing principle in Germany and predates the inauguration of the BRD. In fact, prior to the creation of the first German nation-state in 1871, almost all German-speaking states were classical emigration countries. During the nineteenth century, German-speaking Europe changed gradually from a predominantly agrarian to an industrial society. Landless farmhands, impoverished craftshop workers, home-weavers, handimen, and so forth, became more and more superfluous and sought a better life abroad, above all in the United States. Except for religious or political refugees, most German emigrés belonged to the lower strata of society. The ruling classes long perceived that this exodus of the poor and destitute helped prevent dangerous social unrest, perhaps revolution.[5] But by 1871 Germany found itself short of personnel for its booming industries in the exploding cities.

A basic precondition for industrialization in nineteenth-century Europe was the existence of labor reserves, almost always in rural areas. Evicted peasants and destitute artisans, who had lost their livelihood through competition from the new capitalistic method of production, flooded into the new industrial towns and became part of the proletariat. Once local labour reserves were used up, labour migrants were induced to come from farther afield. Often they crossed national frontiers in their search for employment. The social history of industrialization is that of mass movements from country to town; international migration is a special case within this general pattern.[6]

In Germany, too, foreign laborers became the necessary answer to the ensuing personnel shortage. They numbered 207,000 in 1871 already, yet increased their ranks to 1.250 million by 1910. In addition, another 1 million seasonal migrants worked annually on the large farm estates in the East. They came predominantly from "Congress Poland" and Galicia (Southern Poland, part of the Austro-Hungarian Empire). To ensure their temporary status, the seasonal workers were forced to return home during winter months (*Karenzzeit*), so as not to meet the requirements necessary for a permanent residency permit. Most industrial workers were permitted to remain year round, but obtained only temporary resident permits and could be forced to return.

Some strata of society repeatedly expressed fear of concentrations of foreigners in Germany. Workers dreaded the competition on the labor market. The authorities perceived larger concentrations of foreign workers as a potential political and/or national threat. Economic recessions led repeatedly to mass expulsions of foreigners, mainly Poles, as, for example, in 1907. Yet in realilty, the demands of the economy made absolute restrictions on further recruitment not feasible. Migrant workers, then as now, were needed in the growing industrial economy.[7]

As a result of the Great Depression and mass unemployment after

World War I, fewer foreigners found work in Germany. This changed after the Nazis assumed control of the government in 1933. State contracts (*Staatsverträge*) were signed with Italy, Hungary, the Netherlands, Poland, and Czechoslovakia to allow approximately 500,000 persons annually to work in Germany.[8] "During the war there was a tremendous increase in the number of foreign workers as they were used to replace the eleven million German men withdrawn from the labor force for military service between May 1939 and September 1944. By 1944, 7.5 million foreign workers were employed in the Reich."[9] Some of these workers were recruited through agreements made with friendly countries, but more were pressed into service in the occupied areas and 1.8 million persons were prisoners of war.

The BRD recovered quickly and miraculously from the devastation of World War II. In spite of the enormous influx of over 15 million German refugees, soon labor shortages began to emerge again. Contrary to popular belief, seasonal or temporary workers do not take jobs away from indigenous unemployed. They perform tasks which native workers, including unemployed, will not undertake. Already in 1952, seven years after the end of the war, the agricultural and construction sectors of the economy were short of labor, while at the same time 9.5 percent of the German labor force was unemployed. In 1955, the first labor-recruiting agreement was signed with Italy while 1.07 million Germans were still unemployed. In the following years, similar agreements were signed with Spain, Portugal, Yugoslavia, Greece, and Turkey. Thus, the foreign worker migration into the BRD can be described initially as a succession from different countries, not unlike the immigration waves of different ethnic groups into the United States during the nineteenth and twentieth centuries, although, of course, on a much smaller scale. There was no attempt or intention to integrate these persons, nor did most of them seek integration, as they came to work, save money, and return home as quickly as they could. Until approximately 1973, most foreign workers in the BRD were predominantly young male adults, not eager at all to remain in the foreign land. They were indeeed "guest workers."

With the gradual development of one South European country after another, workers returned home to open businesses or to find jobs in their native economies, only to be replaced in the BRD by eager workers from another country. The temporary nature of the guest workers in the BRD, which was not challenged by most of the involved persons themselves, is best illustrated by the rapid decline of their numbers from 1.3 million to 900,000 during the one recession year of 1966–67 alone.

While citizens of EEC countries (Italy, much later Greece, and as of 1985 Spain and Portugal) possess the right of free choice of residence and job search within the community, citizens of nonmember countries have to rely on temporary labor contracts (Yugoslavia, Turkey). The federal government of the BRD through its labor-recruiting offices in the foreign labor departments then provided applicants who were examined by German physicians and, providing they had a clean police record, received a contract, as a rule for one year.

The oil crisis of 1973 and later structural changes in the economy precipatated an unemployment problem in the BRD which became increasingly severe, reaching the highest level since World War II in July 1985. When in November 1973 the labor-recruiting offices abroad were closed, it was hoped that, as in the past, the foreign workers present would routinely return home; without new recruits coming in, the overall numbers of foreign workers would rapidly decline. This did not occur. The economics of the sending countries did not provide enough jobs for all their workers to return from the BRD. Many decided to stay in Germany and bring their families. For about every worker leaving the BRD after 1973, a dependent family member of one who stayed moved in. Today, 1.2 million of the almost 4.5 million foreigners in the BRD are children of school age or younger; 1.3 million are other nonworking dependents; only 1.9 million are actually working.[10] "Unlike earlier migrants, whose return followed the German policy of 'rotation' of workers, 43 percent of foreigners now living in Germany (BRD) have been there for 10 years or more."[11] The policies of government and the expectation of the West German public that, as in the past, foreign labor could be recruited temporarily to meet short-term employment needs and dismissed at will are no longer operable. The "guest worker" has become an immigrant, and the BRD has become an immigration country.

A major debate in the BRD has subsequently commenced:

Apart from extremist views that foreigners must be repatriated at any cost, most views can be classified into two camps. The "liberal" view holds that foreigners must be allowed free choice, that is, to "Germanize" if they wish or to maintain their separate identity.... The "conservative" views ... give the immigrants a stark choice, either "Germanize" or leave.[12]

Apparently, the majority of the German public has come to prefer the latter idea. The Turks comprise only 33 percent of the foreign population in the BRD. But with their fixed socioracial characteristics acquired through birth, particularly appearance (race), religion (Muslim), and language, they represent not only the most alien group in the BRD, but also the most stubborn resisters to integration. To a society bent on avoiding embarrassing "racist" attitudes and behavior, yet inclined to protect its own interest at the same time, the answer can only lie in subtle force to integrate as many as possible and earnestly encourage the others to leave.

RECENT DEVELOPMENTS

During the 1950s and 1960s, the expanding economy of the BRD necessitated the recruiting of foreign workers. Between 1955 and 1973, approximately 8 million foreign laborers came to work temporarily in the BRD. The overwhelming majority (about 75 percent) returned home, both on a routine "rotation" and in particular great numbers during the recessive periods 1966–67, 1973, and after 1980. Most of the remaining 1.9 million workers and their 2.6 million dependents, however, are permanent immigrants: by the end of 1984, over 80 percent of all foreigners had lived four or more years in the BRD; 62 percent eight or more years; 48 percent ten or more years.[13] It is obvious that the majority of foreigners in the BRD today tends toward permanent or long-term stay rather than the earlier "rotation." Most of the presently employed foreign workers are indispensable for the West German economy, despite an annual overall national unemployment rate between 8 and 9 percent. Studies have shown that, as in the state of Hessen, regions and communities with a high percentage of foreign worker populations are not identical with regions and communities with high unemployment.[14] The unemployment rate among foreigners in the BRD exactly coincides with the national average.

The majority of foreign workers fill jobs that Germans are reluctant or unwilling to undertake: well-paying but often health-hazardous, dangerous, or noxious work in manufacturing industries (smelters, chemicals, plastic, rubber, glass, asbestos, gravel pits); in construction (tarring, handiwork at construction sites); in underground mining; in the automobile industry (repetitive assembly line work); in low-status service work (cleaning in hospitals and office buildings, garbage collection, street sweeping); and in transportation (train track work, subway maintenance, porters in stations). It has been estimated that at least 1.4 million foreigners are essential to fill such jobs in the BRD at all times, regardless of the current or future unemployment level.

Foreigners, most recently Turks, willingly undertake such undesirable jobs abroad because of desperate financial need to support their families at home. In addition, many come from rural regions (Anatolia) and have no skills of any kind. In fact, some have never had any previous contact with modern technology (electricity), motor vehicles, telephones, industrial machines, and so on. Such persons need some training to perform even a nonskilled job; they would hardly be able to obtain such jobs in the less developed and job-short economies of cities in their home countries. Most workers have little or no formal education, have never lived or worked in urban environments, do not know how to read or write, and have no vocational qualifications.[15]

Once they obtain the necessary skills and a well-paying job in the BRD, the workers quickly realize that they could never hope to maintain a similarly high standard of living for themselves and their families if they returned to their home country. Nor would they enjoy a similarly secure social protection under the law. The West German social protection laws (unemployment compensation, unemployment aid after one year out of work, welfare, cash bonuses to children [*Kindergeld*], compulsory social health care, compulsory retirement pension) are among the best in Europe and apply equally to guest workers. The more work years accumulated, the higher benefit reaped.

After a decade of sometimes angry and emotional debate, in which some voices from the left (labor unions), and the right demanded that "foreigners go home" (*Ausländer raus*), it appears that the West German public has reached a consensus. They have reluctantly consented to integrate those foreigners, including Turks and their dependents who are inclined to stay permanently, but continue to encourage persons to leave through severance payments or other financial incentives. This consensus has been the result of a variety of arguments and counterarguments, including, most embarrassingly, those from former Nazi racists who have joined in the chorus of anti-foreign sentiments, as, for example, Professor Heinrich Schade (emeritus Dusseldorf, 1974). Schade had been assistant to the notorious Nazi anthropologist and "race hygienist," Professor Otmar Freiherr von Verschuer (emeritus Munster, 1965) and had been the colleague of another of Verschuer's assistants, Dr. Josef Mengele. In the 1970s, Schade published books and articles on the ethnic and cultural death of the German people through "foreignization."[16] He also co-signed the infamous Heidelberg Manifesto of June 17, 1981, which called for the total expulsion of all foreigners from the BRD under the slogan "Germany for the Germans."[17]

No responsible politician, intellectual, or even common citizen of the BRD would, of course, want to publicly support such views. In fact, most West Germans who object to foreigners do so not because of race and ethnic survival, but because of the imagined competition on a tight job market or their ability, with their numerous children, "to get the benefits of our system for nothing." And it is above all the intolerance of the small things that are different in the everyday appearance of the foreigners—their life-style and even their way of thinking. After all, a community does not only possess a "somatic norm image: i.e., an idea of how the members of community ought to look and behave externally, but it also possesses an internal-mental norm-image."[18]

Such prejudice in largely homogeneous societies that contain minorities is based on judgments that rest on aspects of "ethocentrism." Ethnocentrism is defined as a pattern of criteria of judgments of what the in-group, the "we," think about that out-group, "the others." Ethnocentrism is the basis for a feeling of natural superiority because one's own cultural values are measures of evaluating others.[19] European nations are notoriously ethnocentric. In West Germany as elsewhere, such cultural value measurements are often quite trivial. For example, the Turks have no curtains in their windows; they don't send their fourteen-year-old daughters to school but make them carry the books of their eight-year-old brothers; the women wear boorish head scarfs and long pants under their skirts; the Turks don't drink alcohol; they don't wash their windows every week; they drive old and dirty cars. In contrast, racism in the United States is based on the skin color of blacks alone. In other words, in West Germany it is the intolerance of the homogeneous culture over the "other," the simply being different or having different wants or needs, that creates most of the strained relations toward the Turkish minority in the BRD.

RELEVANT PUBLIC POLICIES AND LAWS

Post-World War II legislation pertaining to foreigners in the BRD clearly reflected the intent to permit guest workers to have only temporary status. The earlier unamended Alien Act (*Ausländergesetz*) explicitly controlled the influx of foreign nationals into the country by extending only temporary work and residence permission and prescribed civil liberties of citizens of countries outside the EEC and Austria, Switzerland, and Lichtenstein, and persons seeking political asylum.[20] The Alien Act was "much more severe and restrictive than its predecessor, the Aliens Police Decree of the Third Reich (APVO), dated August 22, 1938, and found in the *Reichsgesetzblatt* I, 1053."[21]

Since Turkey is not a full member of the EEC, most Turkish nationals in the BRD were faced with the temporary and insecure position of migratory laborers. Resident permits were granted for one-year periods only and were dependent on a person being employed. Employment was legal only through an employment permit issued at the time of recruitment and renewend on an annual basis. Unlimited residence permits and unlimited work permits were difficult to obtain and were largely left to the discretion and whim of local clerks. The Right of Residence (*Aufenthaltsberechtigung*), similar to the resident alien status in the United States, was almost impossible to get. Nationalization in the BRD is granted only after extensive years of residence (as a rule ten years or more), proof that the applicant is fully integrated into the "economic and social life of society." The applicant must also demonstrate oral and written fluency in German unless he or she is a spouse of a German citizen. While all other above-listed regulations were recently liberalized, the fluency law was upheld on May 23, 1985, through the Federal Court *Koblenz* (File: AZ: gk 97/84) which denied a Syrian national and his dependents, legally residing and working in the BRD since 1968, German citizenship on the grounds that he could not communicate effectively in German.

Until recently when resident and work permit regulations were improved, foreign workers from non-EEC countries, initially employed on labor contracts of a fixed duration, were not permitted to change jobs during this period (usually one year), a violation of contract. Whether or not foreign workers were employed on fixed contract, they did not possess the right to change jobs or occupations without special permission of the local Labor Department authorities (*Arbeitsamt*). (As a rule, foreign workers from non-EEC countries are not permitted to engage in self-employed occupations, including opening stores or other businesses unless authorities grant exceptions. Exceptions are made primarily in cases of specially needed services and local demands such as ethnic restaurants or stores dealing in ethnic-religious foods or Turkish travel agencies.) After five years of legal residence and work in the BRD, labor permits could be granted for three instead of the usual one year and changes in job and occupation became easier. Still, this was not a right or entitlement but had to be granted on an individual basis by the authorities. Similarly, the Right of Residence (*Aufenthaltsberechtigung*, a residence entitlement) which provided considerable improvements in the worker's position, was "given only after a careful examination of the foreigner's personal life and political behavior."[22]

In recent years, the strict and often discriminatory laws have been improved concomitant with the general acceptance of foreigners as permanent immigrants. Although the state of Hessen is somewhat more liberal than some others in the BRD, its new package of "Rights of Foreign Workers and Their Families" may illustrate the improved legal status of foreigners in the BRD.[23] Foreign workers who have resided legally and without interruption in the BRD for five years are given an unlimited residence permit. The period of residence is considered legal and without interruption if the person has had a valid residence permit at all times during the past five years. During the first five years, the residence permit is renewable annually or, in some cases, biannually. Short absences, such as a vacation in the worker's home country, are not counted as an interruption of residence. If one's stay in the BRD is interrupted by military service in one's own country, the waiting period of five years is extended by the length of military service.

In order to obtain an unlimited residence permit, the worker must first have a special work permit. The Labor Department (*Arbeitsamt*) of the place of residence will issue a special work permit if the person has been employed (but not self-employed) without interruption in the BRD for the past five years. Temporary unemployment under entitled unemployment benefits is not considered interruption of employment. A special work permit is valid for five years. An unlimited work permit is

granted if a person has resided in the BRD legally and without interruption for at least eight years.

These improvements in residence and work permit status are now
entitlements and must be granted by the authorities upon application,
provided the following additional requirements are met: the applicant
must be capable of making himself or herself understood "in a simple
way" in the German language. The applicants receive a brochure in
which they are advised in their own language that when they are

talking to an official at the Registration Office for foreigners you must be able
to understand and answer simple questions about your personal living conditions. You do not have to know how to write, and you are not required to have
taken a German language course. Even if you have some difficulties in communication, don't worry: in the interest of equal treatment for everyone, the
officials must assume that this requirement is fulfilled.[24]

In addition, the applicant for unlimited residence and work permits is
required to have a flat in which each person has at least nine square
meters of living space. Another requirement is that the person have no
criminal record. Minor crimes and misdemeanours, which are not serious
enough to lead to expulsion from the country or to denial of a residence
permit, will be ignored. If the applicant has children who live in the
BRD, they must go to school as long as they are of school age (fourteen).
The schools are required to provide certificates confirming the children's
enrollment and regular attendance.

Unemployment is no longer a reason to deny an unlimited residence
permit, not even if the workers are no longer entitled to unemployment
benefits or unemployment aid. They must be able to show, however,
that they can support themselves and their families. Special regulations
apply to social welfare recipients. Applicants will be given unlimited
residence permits if their home countries have a welfare treaty with the
BRD; among these countries are Austria, Belgium, Denmark, France,
Greece, Great Britain, North Ireland, Iceland, Italy, Luxemburg, Malta,
the Netherlands, Norway, Portugal, Spain, Sweden, Switzerland, and
Turkey. An applicant on welfare from Yugoslavia, Morocco, or Tunisia
can be denied a permanent residence permit only if this does not result
in "undue hardship." The authorities must take personal living conditions into account and must consider what effects it would have on the
family if a person's residence in the BRD were to end. Every applicant
has the right to appeal. Once a foreigner has obtained an unlimited
residence permit, the authorities are not allowed to put a time limit on
welfare.

The Right of Residence, which is equivalent to the U.S. resident alien
status, will be granted to any foreigner who has resided legally and

without interruption in the BRD for eight years. The Right of Residence guarantees workers and their families a secure stay in the BRD. They can no longer be expelled from the country except in especially grave cases (serious crimes or endangering the security of the BRD). The Right of Residence does not make these persons German citizens. They do not give up their citizenship, and they can return to their home country at any time. German citizenship is not granted automatically upon application after a specified number of years under the Right of Residence.

The requirements for the Right of Residence include those for an unlimited residence permit and proof that the person is integrated in the economic and social life of the BRD. This means above all that the applicants must be capable of providing for themselves and their families. "This is always the case if you have a job and are in possession of a special work permit."[25] As a rule, the husband or wife must also be granted the Right of Residence whether or not he/she has a work permit. Children under the age of sixteen do not need a residence permit, but when they reach that age they can immediately apply for the Right of Residence, provided they have resided legally and without interruption in the BRD for at least eight years. If the applicant and the other members of the family speak German well, they may obtain the Right of Residence after only five years. In this case, they must present diplomas or certificates showing that they have successfully completed a German language course. German school completion diplomas are, of course, also accepted.

The intent of all this new legislation is clearly to integrate the foreign workers and their families who intend to remain permanently in the BRD. This includes improved regulations for family reunions. The applicants may bring their families (or a new wife or husband) after having lived in the BRD legally for only one year, but they must be financially able to provide for their families and may not at the time of application be welfare recipients. They must have a health insurance policy for themselves and their families, and must show proof that they have rented a flat. As a rule, only a spouse and children under the age of eighteen will be allowed to join as well as one parent or in-law, in case husband and wife work and have small children.

The integrative concern has also caused the legislature to liberalize the rules for expelling young foreigners for breaking the law:

Young foreigners who live in the BRD with their parents often have hardly any ties to their home countries. They feel at home in the BRD. If any of these young people get into trouble with the law they should not be expelled from the country except in cases of extremely serious criminality. These young people should have the opportunity to be rehabilitated here.[26]

As a matter of principle, youths and young adults whose lives are centered in the BRD may not be expelled from the country even if they have committed a crime. A youth is a person who, at the time of the crime, was at least fourteen but not eighteen years of age. A young adult is someone who was at least eighteen years but not yet twenty-one years old at the time of the crime. If they grew up in the BRD, it is always assumed that their lives are centered there.

Their lives are also considered to be centered here if their parents reside here legally, if the youths or young adults are working, studying or receiving vocational training here, if their social ties (for instance their circle of friends) are stronger here than in their home country.[27]

INTEGRATION

In recent years, West Germans have accepted the idea that the era of "rotation" is over and that most foreigners including Turks are there to stay. The urgent goal is no longer whether or how foreigners may be induced to leave but how best to integrate them into German society. This goal appears to be particularly important in relations with foreign children of school age who were born in or were brought to the BRD and have little if any contact with their parents' homeland, but are often under direct or indirect pressure from their parents not to assimilate. Such an attitude is common among Turks (Muslims), particularly concerning their daughters. Unless integrated, these children will become strangers in two worlds, unable to compete successfully with their German cohorts on the job market or otherwise.

The lot of adolescent Turks is even more precarious. Many were brought to Germany past the compulsory school age with little if any formal schooling in Turkey. They therefore, have little chance of securing jobs in a job-tight economy where they compete with German trade school and high school graduates for apprentice positions. It has been estimated that the BRD needs between 700,000 and 800,000 new jobs each year just to employ German youth. Even the unemployment rate among Germans with college degrees is rising. If the number of foreign workers' children who come of age are added, the number of new jobs needed each year reaches 1 million.

Turkish children and adolescents are in the very midst of the integrative tug of war between German society and the Turkish communities in the BRD. While there is no specific definition of what "integration into German society" really means, it minimally requires that the children at least learn the language of the host society, complete a school education, and learn a trade or be otherwise prepared for some kind of job.[28] The German legislature on both the federal and state level has made many efforts to enable Turkish children to achieve meaningful school integration in German public schools, including the hiring of Turkish teachers or, whenever available, bilingual teachers; preparatory schooling in Turkish with German as a foreign language for preschoolers and older children who do not speak German; reduction of the teaching load of teachers who teach foreign children; and increased pay for such teachers: sabbaticals with full pay for teachers who take special training at universities for the purpose of teaching foreign children.[29]

Problems connected with the schooling of Turkish children, aside from the expected language difficulties and consequent generally poor performance in most subjects include the reluctance of Turkish parents and organizations to allow the integration of Turkish Muslim children into the ordinary German school routine. Approximately 80 percent of all Turkish children in the BRD attend the religious Koran Schools in the afternoons. These schools are protected and sponsored by the Turkish Idealists Organization, the right-wing National Savior party, or the ultrarightist underground group of the Gray Wolves which leans toward the right-wing Party of National Movement under *Alparslan Türkesch* and does not hesitate to use force, including murder, to keep Turks living abroad from leaving the path of true belief and behavior. Even the Turkish teachers themselves complain time and again that Koran instructors tell children to forget what they were taught in the German schools in the morning. Girls who work and play along with German boys and girls in school are told in the afternoon that they must always walk one pace behind boys, not to swim, dance, do sports, or befriend Christian children.[30] It is well nigh impossible for children to make their way in a Western democratic society having been repeatedly told that union members and social democrats are of the devil (*Seytan*). The religion and ideology of Turks in the BRD prevent integration of any substantive kind: "Their 'religious ghetto mentality' is usually unpenetrable from the beginning."[31]

Generally, integration can be achieved in three ways.[32] *Monistic* integration is achieved through a minority's submission and total acculturation within the majority. This is often the declared goal of totalitarian societies and would undoubtedly suit many members of majorities even in nontotalitarian societies. A more ideal form is *interactionist* integration which achieves mutual assimilation of both majority and minority, whereby each accepts the process of permanently interdependent relationships which lead to a new *modus vivendi* of both partners in a new community. This is usually a long-term process and often occurs when majority societies have been invaded by powerful minorities. *Pluralistic* integration, on the other hand, is achieved through dissimilation whereby both partners retain their differences but tolerate each other and coexist. The U.S. black ghetto is an example of such dissimilated pluralistic integration.

Dissimilated ghetto integration is almost unanimously opposed in West Germany for varying reasons.[33] The ensuing developments of ethnic concentrations particularly in older, less desirable residential wards of cities are perceived as a threat to the cherished order of things.[34] Urban wards with noticeable foreign resident populations remind many of the American ghettoes and the problems they entail. Concern has often been voiced over the possible effects of presumed unacceptable hygienic practices (such as raising and slaughtering goats and sheep in the urban environment), a possible rise in the crime rate, and the overall physical deterioration of buildings and facilities. More liberal democratic voices are concerned about the political embarrassment that the mere appearance of ethnic or racial discrimination through residential isolation might create for post-World War II West Germany. But no matter what the concern, all sources advocate the breakup of Turkish quarters or, what many in exaggeration call "Turkish ghettoes," both to avoid such embarrassment, and to provide Turks with better housing, more equal treatment, and general acceptance into the mainstream of German society.[35]

Housing segregation is one of the most visible and widely-discussed elements of the immigrant question. A nearly unanimous view, held by the government, academics and journalists, holds that ghetto development must be prevented because such separation of Germans and foreigners would hinder any possible future integration of permanent settlers.[36]

The BRD has made a concerted effort to disperse perceived ethnic ghettoes: notably, influx control ordinances on an intracommunity (urban ward) level and forced resettlement of Turks through massive urban renewal and housing rehabilitation schemes. Rent levels have been raised, thereby attracting German and foreign residents with higher incomes while forcing out many of the lower income residents, both foreign and German, and those individuals and families unwilling to spend more money on housing because they consider their stay only a temporary one.[37] Actually, these "ghettoes" are no more than concentrations of Turkish families in single apartment buildings scattered loosely about a given ward. Recent research has shown that no city in the BRD possesses a Turkish (or any other) ghetto even remotely comparable in segregation index levels to black or ethnic ghettoes in U.S. cities.[38] In addition, even "the fear, constantly expressed by politicians, editorial writers and letters to newspapers, of Turks piling up in the poorest inner city neighborhoods is given the lie" once detailed research probes into intraurban migration patterns.

Like Germans and other foreigners, Turks (in German cities) originate predominantly in middle status wards and stay (in their intra-city migratory behavior) within that range of housing quality. If the stereotype were accurate, they should live predominantly in the poorest wards. Neither element is seen in these movement data.[39]

As a matter of fact,

although the primary residences of foreigners are more concentrated than their secondary residences . . . (once the workers bring their families and need larger apartments) . . . and although foreigners seem to move within a more restricted set of locations than Germans, the differences are not substantial and do not lead to ghetto formation in the short or intermediate term.[40]

SUMMARY AND CONCLUSIONS

The Federal Republic of Germany is an immigration country but only to a limited degree. Immigrants to classical immigration countries such as Australia, Canada, or the United States usually knew that they were making a major move, that they had to burn their bridges, and that they confronted the difficult task of adjusting to a different society. In contrast, foreign workers in West Germany do not leave everything behind; above all, they always know that their home country is nearby and not inferior. The ties therefore remain direct and strong. Immigrants to America who didn't make it returned to their home countries and they knew they had failed in what they had set out to accomplish. Between 1907 and 1924, for example, 38 percent of all European immigrants to the United States returned to their home countries.[41] Their failure as immigrants was not always or even predominantly one of economics. In most cases it was their realization that they didn't like the new world and that they "could not adjust." They did not expect, however, that the host society would permanently tolerate them unless they adjusted or accept them warmly and equally unless they eventually spoke and behaved and felt like Americans. The Turks in West Germany are in a difficult situation. They are de facto immigrants, but few wish to accept this fact. The German host society, sensitive to its racist past, tries hard to "integrate" the Turks and feels rejected when they don't go along. Only time will tell whether the Turkish immigrants in the BRD will become an entirely integrated part of society, which is particularly difficult in a homogeneous nation-state.

There is already a new group of underdogs in Germany even more alien than the Turks, who are now the foremost target of German xenophobia and prejudice: the so-called "asylants" (*Asylanten*) from Afghanistan, Pakistan, Bangladesh, India, Syria, and so on. They are not very numerous, but they are coming. During the 1970s, about 5,000 persons annually asked for asylum in the BRD. By 1978, the annual number was already over 30,000 and, by 1980, over 100,000. Only approximately 20 percent prove to be real political refugees for whom the West German right of asylum applies (Article 16 of the Basic Law). Eighty percent are "economic refugees" and are eventually repatriated, but not before a thorough examination of their asylum application, which, as a rule, takes between two and three years. During this time, all "asylants" and their dependents are fed, clothed, and housed, often in hotels, and their children attend school. West German taxpayers have therefore found another target for their scorn and prejudice. The reasoning is that if the Turks have proven so difficult to assimilate, how can anyone expect Afghani or Tamils to settle comfortably within German society and culture? Yet without integration they remain alien and isolated.

Homogeneous nation-states such as the BRD face a difficult task in the present age of worldwide migration and uprooting and mixing of people of greatly different backgrounds. It is imperative that such countries maintain their laws for both protecting the rights of their minorities and easing their integration, while protecting the values and integrity of their own indigenous culture. West Germany seems to be trying to do just that.

NOTES

1. Ausländerzentralregister (Bonn: 1984); Stat. Jahrbuch der BRD 1984; Bundesforschungsanstalt für Landeskunde und Raumordnung, Heft 17, Laufende Raumbeobachtung (Bonn: 1984).

2. Michael Banton, *Racial Minorities* (London: 1972).

3. Hans-Jochim Hoffman-Nowotny, "Rassische, ethnische und soziale Minderheiten als Zukunftsproblem internationaler Integrationsbestrebungen," in *Minderheiten*, ed. R. Kurzrock (Berlin: Colloquium Verlag, 1974), p. 174.

4. Peter I. Rose, "Zur Sozialpsychologischen Analyse von Minderheitenkonflikten in der Gegenwartsgesellschaft," in R. Kurzrock, ed., *Minderheiten* (Berlin: Colloquium Verlag, 1974), p. 19.

5. Peter Marschalck, *Bevölkerungsgeschihte Deutschlands im 19. und 20. Jahrhundert* (Frankfurt: Suhrkamp, 1984).

6. Stephen Castles and Godula Kosack, *Immigrant Workers and Class Structure in Western Europe* (London: Oxford University Press, 1973), p. 15.

7. Ray C. Rist, *Guestworkers in Germany: The Prospects for Pluralism* (New York: Praeger Publishers, 1978), p. 58.

8. Klaus J. Bade, *Vom Auswanderungsland zum Einwanderungsland? Deutschland 1880/1980* (Berlin: Colloquium Verlag, 1983).

9. Rist, *Guestworkers in Germany*, p. 59.

10. Gerhard Spörl, "Nirgends zu Hause—Vom Auswanderungsland zum Einwanderungsland," *Die Zeit.* November 2, 1984, pp. 1, 4–5.

11. John O'Loughlin and Gunther Glebe, "Migration of Germans and Foreigners in German Cities," unpublished paper presented at Urban Geography Specialty Group Special Session on International Perspectives and Processes of

Urbanization, Association of American Geographers, Annual Meeting (Denver, Colo.: April 28, 1983), p. 1.

12. Ibid., p. 1.

13. Hessischer Minister des Innern, Referat Pressearbeit, "Ausländer-Politische Grundsätze der Hessischen Landesregierung," in *Ausländer in Hessen* (Wiesbaden: 1984), p. 36.

14. Ibid., p. 37.

15. Castles and Kosack, *Immigrant Workers*, p. 97; see also Ursula Mehrländer, "Minderheiten in der BRD: Soziale Probleme ausländischer Arbeitnehmer," in R. Kurzrock, ed., *Minderheiten*, pp. 165–82.

16. Heinrich Schade, *Völkerflut und Völkerschwund. Bevölkerungswissenschaftliche Erkenntnisse und Mahnungen* (Neckargemund: Vowinckel, 1979).

17. Klaus-Dieter Thoman, "Rassenhygiene und Anthropologie: Die zwei Karrieren des Professor Verschuer," *Frankfurter Rundschau, Dokumentation* en (Frankfurt: May 20, 1985), p. 20.

18. Gert Raeithel, *"Go West"—Ein psychohistorischer Versuch über die Amerikaner* (Frankfurt: Syndikat, 1981), p. 11; see also Friedrich Heckmann, *Die Bundesrepublik: ein Einwanderungsland? Zur Soziologie der Gastarbeiterbevölkerung als Einwandererminorität* (Stuttgart: Klett-Cotta, 1981).

19. Rose, "Zur Sozialpsychologischen Analyse," pp. 21–22.

20. Lutz Holzner, "The Myth of Turkish Ghettos: A Geographic Case Study of West German Responses Towards a Foreign Minority," *Journal of Ethnic Studies* 9, no. 4 (1982): 65–85, particularly 67–68.

21. Fritz Franz, "The Legal Status of Foreign Workers in the Federal Republic of West Germany," R. E. Krane, ed., *Manpower Mobility Across Cultural Boundaries: Social, Economic, and Legal Aspects. The Case of Turkey and West Germany* (Leiden: E. J. Brill, 1975), pp. 46–60, 52; S. Paine, *Exporting Workers: The Turkish Case* (London: Cambridge University Press, 1974), pp. 69–70; D. Rojahn, "Die Rechtsstellung des Gastarbeiters in der BRD," in H. Reimann and H. Reimann, eds., *Gastarbeiters* (München: Goldmann, 1976), pp. 85–99; W. Kanein, *Ausländergesetz (Aliens Act)*, annotated 2d ed. (München: 1974); *Ausländergesetz (Aliens Act), Bundesgesetzblatt* I, 353 (Bonn: April 18, 1965).

22. Castles and Kosack, *Immigrant Workers*, p. 101.

23. Hessian Ministry of the Interior, Department of Public Information, *The Rights of Foreign Workers and Their Families in Hessen* (in English) (Wiesbaden: December 1984).

24. Ibid., pp. 2–3.

25. Ibid., p. 5.

26. Ibid., p. 10.

27. Ibid.

28. Olaf Schumann, "Die Fremden als Herausforderung; Der asoziale Geist des westlichen Denkens," in Rolf Italiaander, ed., *Fremde raus? Fremdenangst und Ausländerfeindlichkeit Gefahren für jede Gemeinschaft* (Frankfurt: Fischer Taschenbuch Verlag, 1983), pp. 52–53; see also K. Bingemeyer and E. Meistermann-Seeger, "Probleme der Integration," in E. Neubert, ed., *Leben als Gastarbeiter. Geglückte und missglückte Integration* (Opladen: 1972), pp. 17–24; ed. Wilfried Röhrich *Vom Gastarbeiter zum Bürger*, Beiträge zur Sozialforschung, Vol. 2 (Berlin: Dunker und Humbolt, 1982), p. 94.

29. Hessischer Kultusminister, *Zur Lage der ausländischen Kinder und Jugendlichen in Hessen*, Bildungspolitische Information No. 2/81 (Wiesbaden: September 1, 1981); Hessischer Minister für Wirtschaft und Technik, *Kleine Anfrage der Abgeordneten Lütgert u.a. (SPD) betreffend MBSE in Hessen—LD 9/3736* (Darmstadt: November 20, 1980); Bayerisches Staatsministerium für Arbeit und Sozialordnung und der Landeshauptstadt München, *Ausländische Jugendliche in Bayerischen Grosstädten* (München: July 1980); Sener Sorrgut, "Zur Sozialisation der Kinder türkischer Emigranten in Schule und Familie," in H. Müller, ed., *Ausländerkinder in deutschen Schulen. Ein Handbuch* (Stuttgart: 1974), pp. 28–41.

30. Shawn Christoph and Henning Christoph, "Die deutschen Türken," *Geo* (1972): 32.

31. Johan Bouman, "Der gläubige Moslem zwischen Kulturschock und Akkulturation—Zur religiösen Krise der Gastarbeiter," in Rolf Italiaander, ed., *Fremde Raus?*, p. 63; see also Sener Sorgut "Zur Sozialisation der Kinder Türkischer," pp. 39–41; A. Th. Khoury et al., *Muslimische Kinder in der Deutschen Schule* (München: Verlag für Christlich-Islamisches Schrifttum, 1981).

32. Bingemeyer and Meistermann-Seeger, "Probleme der Integration," pp. 19–20.

33. Holzner, "The Myth of Turkish Ghettos," pp. 65–66.

34. H. Reimann and H. Reimann, "Federal Republic of Germany," in R. E. Krane, ed., *Manpower Mobility*, pp. 63–87; Ernst Giese, "Reumliche Diffusion auslandischer Arbeitnehmer in der BRD 1960–1976," *Die Erde* 109 (1978): 92–110; Ernst Giese and Josef Nipper, "Zeitliche und Räumliche Persistenzeffekte bei Räumlichen Ausbreitungsprozessen, analaysiert am Beipiel der Ausbreitung ausländischer Arbeitnemher in der Bundes republik Deutschland," *Karlsruher Manuskripte zur Mathematischen und Theoretischen Wirschafts—und Sozialgeographie*, Vol. 34 (Karalsruhe: April 1979); W. G. S. Thomas, "Gastarbeiter in Western Germany," *Geography* 59 (1974): 348–50.

35. Hans-Joachim Hoffman-Novotny and Karl-Otto Hondrich, eds., *Ausländer in der BRD und in der Schweiz* (Institutional Determinants for Spatial Concentration and Social Segregation of Foreign Workers in Urban Areas of West European Immigration Countries), (Frankfurt-New York: Campus Verlag, 1981); Der Spiegel, "Die Türken kommen-rette sich wer kann," *Der Spiegel* 27, no. 31 (July 30, 1973): 24–34; U. Herlyn, "Soziale Segregation," in W. Pehnt, ed., *Die Stadt in der BRD. Lebensbedingungen, Aufgaben, Planung* (Stuttgart: 1974), pp. 89–106; W. F. Killisch and K. J. Moch, "Bevölkerungs-Sozialgeographische Untersuchung als Grundlage der Sanierungs—und Sozialplanung," *Erdkunde* 30 (1976): 253–65; ed. E. Klee, *Gastarbeiter: Analysen und Berichte* (Frankfurt: Suhrkamp, 1977); "Misstrauen belastet das Verhältnis von Einheimischen Und Gastarbeitern," *Die Zeit*, No. 2 (January 11, 1980); U. Mehrländer, "Soziale Aspekte der Ausländerbeschäftigung," *Schriftenreihe des Forschungsinstituts der Friedrich Ebert Stiftung*, Vol. 103 (Bonn-Bad Godesberg: Verlag Neue Gesellschaft, 1974); P. Rothammer et al., *Die Integration ausländischer Arbeitnehmer und ihrer Familien in ausgewählten Städten—Probleme, Massnahmen, Steuerinstrumente* (Berlin: Deutsches Institut für Urbanistik, 1974).

36. O'Loughlin and Glebe, *Migration of Germans*, pp. 1–2.

37. Holzner, "Myth of Turkish Ghettos," p. 66; see also Jürgen Hoffmeyer-

Zlotnik, *Gastarbeiter im Sanierungsgebiet: Das Beispiel Berlin-Kreuzberg* (Hamburg: Hans Christian Verlag, 1977).

38. Paul Gans, "Bevölkerungsgeographische Veränderungen in der westlichen Unterstadt Mennheims zwischen 1970 und 1976," *Mennheimer Geographische Arbeiten* 2 (1978): 41–84; Holzner, *Myth of Turkish Ghettos*, pp. 65–85; John O'Loughlin,, "The Distribution and Migration of Foreigners in German Cities," *Geographical Review* 70 (1980): 253–75; J. R. Clark, "Residential Patterns and Social Integration of Turks in Cologne," in R. E. Krane, ed., *Manpower Mobility*, pp. 61–76; J. R. Clark, *Turkish Cologne: The Mental Maps of Migrant Workers in a German City*, Publications in Geography, No. 19 (Ann Arbor, Mich.: 1977); Helga Reimann, "Die Wohnsituation der Gastarbeiter," H. Reimann and H. Reimann, eds., *Gastarbeiter*, pp. 131–48.

39. O'Loughlin and Glebe, *Migration of Germans*, p. 24.

40. Ibid., p. 31.

41. Raeithel, "Go West," p. 37.

BIBLIOGRAPHY

Adams, John S. "Directional Bias in Intra-urban Migration," *Economic Geography* 45 (1969): 302–23.

——, and Kathleen A. Gilder. "Household Characteristics and Intra-urban Migration." *In Social Areas in Cities*, Vol. 1, edited by D. T. Herbert and R. J. Johnston. London: John Wiley & Sons, 1976, pp. 41–79.

——, et al. "Intraurban Migration," *Annals*, A.A.G., #63 (1973): 152–55.

Bade, Klaus J. *Vom Auswanderungsland zum Einwanderungsland? Deutschland 1880/1980*. Berlin: Colloquium Verlag, 1983.

Banton, Michael. *Racial Minorities*. London: 1972.

Bartels, D. "Türkische Gastarbeiter aus der Region Izmir. Zur raumzeitlichen Differenzierung der Bestimmungsgründe ihrerr Aufbruchsentschlüsse." *Erdkunde* 22 (1968): 313–24.

Bayerisches Staatsministerium für Arbeit und Sozialordnung und der Landeshauptstadt München. *Äuslandische Jugendliche in Bayerishen Grosstadten*. München, July 1980.

Bingemeyer, Karl, et al., Eds. *Leben als Gastarbeiter. Geglückte und missglückte Integration*. Opladen: Westdeutscher Verlag, 1972.

Borris, Maria. *Ausländische Arbeitnehmer in einer Grosstadt: eine empirische Untersuchung am Beispiel*. Frankfurt: Europaische Verlagsanstalt, 1973.

Bouman, Johan. "Der gläubige Moslem zwischen Kulturschock und Akkulturation—Zur religiösen Krise der Gastarbeiter." In *Fremde Raus? Fremdenangst und Ausländerfeindlichkeit Gefahren für jede Gemeinschaft*, edited by Rolf Italiaander. Frankfurt: Fischer Taschenbuch Verlag, 1983.

Castles, Stephan, and Godula Kosack. *Immigrant Workers and Class Structure in Western Europe*. London: Oxford University Press, 1973.

Christoph, Shawn, and Henning Christoph. "Die deutschen Türken," *Geo* (1972): 8–34.

Clark, John R. "Residential Patterns and Social Integration of Turks in Cologne." In *Manpower Mobility Across Cultural Boundaries: Social, Economic, and Legal*

Aspects. The Case of Turkey and West Germany, edited by R. E. Krane. Leiden: E. J. Brill, 1975, pp. 61–76.

———. *Turkish Cologne: The Mental Maps of Migrant Workers in a German City*. Geographical Publications, No. 19. Ann Arbor, Mich.: 1977.

Esser, Hartmut. "Aufenthaltsdauer und die Eingliederung von Wanderern: zur theoretischen Interpretation soziologischer Variablen." *Zeitschrift für Soziologie* 10 (1981): 76–97.

Franz, Fritz. "The Legal Status of Foreign Workers in the Federal Republic of West Germany." *Manpower Mobility Across Cultural Boundaries*, edited by R. E. Krane. Leiden: E. J. Brill, 1975, pp. 46–60.

Franzen, Jürgen. *Gastarbeiter: Raumrelevante Verhaltensweisen*, Hannover: Jahrbuch der Geographischen Gesellschaft zu Hannover, 1978.

Gans, Paul. "Bevölkerungsgeographische Veränderungen in der westlichen Unterstadt Mannheims zwischen 1970 und 1976," *Mannheimer Geographische Arbeiten* 2 (1978): 41–84.

———. "Bevölkerungsentwicklung und Wanderungsverflechtungen Ludwigshafens seit 1970," *Mannheimer Geographische Arbeiten* 10 (1981): 105–15.

Giese, Ernst. "Räumliche Diffusion auslandischer Arbeitnehmer in der Bundesrepublik Deutschland 1960–1976," *Die Erde* 109 (1978): 92–110.

———, and Josef Nipper. "Zeitliche und Räumliche Persistenzeffekte bei Räumlichen Ausbreitungsprozessen-analysiert am Beipiel der Ausbreitung ausländischer Arbeitnemher in der Bundesrepupblik Deutschland." *Karlsruher Manuskripte zur Mathematischen und Theoretischen Wirtschafts—und Sozialgeographie*, Vol. 34 (Karlsruhe: April 1979).

Heckman, Friedrich. *Die Bundesrepublik: ein Einwanderungsland? Zur Soziologie der Gastarbeiterbevölkerung als Einwandererminorität*. Stuttgart: Klett-Cotta, 1981.

Heller, W. "Komponenten räumlichen Verhaltens in Gastarbeitern in der Bundersrepublik Deutschland." *Berichte zur Deutschen Landeskunde* 53 (1979): 5–34.

Herlyn, U. "Soziale Segregation." *Die Stadt in der Bundesrepublik Deutschland. Lebensbedingungen, Aufgaben, Planung*, edited by W. Pehnt. Stuttgart: 1974, pp. 89–106.

Hessian Ministry of the Interior, Department of Public Information. *The Rights of Foreign Workers and Their Families in Hessen* (in English). Wiesbaden: December 1984.

Hessischer Kultuminister. *Zur Lage der ausländischen Kinder und Jegendlichern in Hessen*. Bildungspolitische Information 2/81. Wiesbaden: September 1, 1981.

Hessischer Minister des Innern, Referat Pressarbeit. "Ausländer-Politische Grundsätze der Hessischen Landesregierung." *Ausländer in Hessen*. Wiesbaden: 1984.

Hessischer Minister für Wirtschaft und Technik. *Kleine Anfrage der Abgeordneten Lütgert u.a.—LD 9/3736*. Darmstadt: November 20, 1980.

Hoffman-Nowotny, Hans-Joachim. *Minoritätensoziologie*. Frankfurt: 1974.

———. "Rassische, ethnische und soziale Minderheiten als Zukunftsproblem internationaler Integrationsbestrebungen." *Minderheiten*, edited by R. Kurzrock. Berlin: Colloquium Verlag, 1974, pp. 173–82.

————, and Karl-Otto Hondrich, eds. *Ausländer in der Bundesrepublik Deutschland und in der Schweiz*. Frankfurt, New York: Campus Verlag, 1981.

Hoffmeyer-Zlotnik, Jürgen. *Gastarbeiter im Sanierungsgebiet: Das Beispiel Berlin-Kreuzberg*. Hamburg: Hans Christian Verlag, 1977.

Holzner, Lutz. "The Myth of Turkish Ghettos: A Geographic Case Study of West German Responses Toward a Foreign Minority." *Journal of Ethnic Studies* 9, n. 4 (1982): 65–85.

Hottes, Karl-Heinz, and P. Michael Potke. *Ausländische Arbeitnehmer im Ruhrgebiet und im Bergisch-Markischen Land*. Paderborn: Ferdinand Schoningh, 1977.

Ipsen, Detlev. "Wohnsituation und Wohninteresse ausländischer Arbeiter in der Bundesrepublik Deutschland." *Leviathan* 6 (1978): 558–73.

————. "Segregation, Mobilitat und die Chancen auf dem Wohnungsmarkt: eine empirische Untersuchung in Mannheim." *Zeitschrift für Soziologie* 10 (1981): 256–72.

Italiaander, Rolf, ed. *Fremde raus? Fremdenangst und Ausländerfeindlichkeit Gefahren fur jede Gemeinschaft*. Frankfurt: Fischer Taschenbuch Verlag, 1983.

Johnston, Ronald J. *Urban Residential Patterns*. London: G. Bell, 1971.

Khoury, A. Th., et al. *Muslimische Kinder in der Deutschen Schule*. München: Verlag für Christlich-Islamisches Schrifttum, 1981.

Killisch, W. F., and K. J. Moch. "Bevölkerungs—Sozialgeographische Untersuchung als Grundlage der Sanierungs—und Sozialplanung." *Erdkunde* 30 (1976): 253–65.

Klee, E., ed. *Gastarbeiter: Analysen und Berihte*. Frankfurt: Suhrkamp, 1977.

Krane, R. E., ed. *Manpower Mobility Across Cultural Boundaries: Social, Economic, and Legal Aspects. The Case of Turkey and West Germany*. Leiden: E. J. Brill, 1975.

Kurzrock, Ruprecht, ed. *Minderheiten*. Berlin: Colloquium Verlag, 1974.

Lichtenberger, Elisabeth. "Gastarbeiter—Leben in zwei Gesellschaften." *Mittelungen der Osterreichischen Geographischen Gesellschaft* 124 (1982): 28–65.

Marschalck, Peter. *Bevölkerungsgeschichte Deutschlands im 19. und 20. Jahrhundert*. Frankfurt, Suhrkamp, 1984.

Maarshall, Adriana. *The Import of Labor*. Rotterdam: Rotterdam University Press, 1973.

Mehrländer, Ursula. "Minderheiten in der Bundesrepublik Deutschland: Soziale Probleme ausländischer Arbeitnehmer." In *Minderheiten*, edited by R. Kurzrock. Berlin: Colloquium Verlag, 1974, pp. 165–82.

————. *Soziale Aspekte der Auslanderbeschäftigung*. Bonn-Bad Godesberg: Verlag Neue Gesellschaft, 1974.

Mehrländer, Ursula. "Soziale Aspekte der Ausländerbeschäftigung." *Schriftenreihe des Forschungsinstituts der Friedrich Ebert Stiftung*. Vol. 103. Bonn-Bad Godesberg: Verlag Neue Gesellschaft, 1974.

Meier-Braun, Karl-Heinz. "Die neue Völkerwanderung: werden aus Gastarbeitern Burger?" *Bild der Wissenschaft* 9 (1982): 104–19.

O'Loughlin, John. "The Distribution and Migration of Foreigners in German Cities." *Geographical Review* 70 (1980): 253–75.

————, and Gunther Glebe. *Migration of Germans and Foreigners in German Cities*. Unpublished paper presented at Urban Geography Speciality Group Special Session on International Perspectives and Processes of Urbanization,

Association of American Geographers, Annual Meeting, Denver, Col., April 28, 1983.

Paine, S. *Exporting Workers: The Turkish Case.* London: Cambridge University Press, 1974.

Peach, Ceri. "Conflicting Interpretations of Segregation." In *Social Interaction and Ethnic Segregation,* edited by P. Jackson and S. J. Smith. London: Academic Press, 1981, pp. 19–33.

Popp, H. "The Residential Location Process: Some Theoretical and Empirical Considerations." *Tijdschrift voor Economische en Sociale Geografie* 67 (1976): 300–5.

Raeithel, Gert. *"Go West"-Ein Psychohistorischer Versuch über Amerikaner.* Frankfurt: Syndikat, 1981.

Reimann, Helga. "Die Wohnsituation der Gastarbeiter." in *Gastarbeiter,* edited by H. Reimann and H. Reimann. Munchen: Goldmann, 1976, p. 131–48.

Reimann, Horst, and Helga Reimann. "Federal Republic of Germany." In *Manpower Mobility Across Cultural Boundaries,* edited by R. E. Krane. Leiden: E. J. Brill, 1975, pp. 63–87.

———, eds. *Gastarbeiter.* München: Goldmann, 1976.

Reisser, Craig. "Italian Foreign Workers in the Cultural Landscape of German Cities—The Case of Nurnberg." Ph.D. diss., University of Wisconsin, Milwaukee, 1985.

Rex, John. "A Working Paradigm for Race Relations Research." *Ethnic and Racial Studies* 4 (1981): 1–25.

———, and R. Moore. *Race, Community and Conflict.* London: Oxford University Press, 1967.

Rist, Ray C. *Guestworkers in Germany: The Prospects for Pluralism,* New York: Praeger, 1978.

de Riz, Peter. *Mobilität und Integrationsverhalten ausländischer Arbeitnehmer.* Frankfurt: Waldemar Kramer Verlag, 1979.

Rohrich, Wilfried, ed. *Vom Gastarbeiter zum Bürger* Beiträge zur Sozialforschung, Vol. 2. Berlin: Duncker & Humbolt, 1982.

Rojahn, D. "Die Rechtsstellung des Gastarbeiters in der Bundesrepublik Deutschland." In *Gastarbeiter,* edited by H. Reimann and H. Reimann. München: Goldmann, 1976, pp. 85–99.

Rose, Peter I. "Zur Sozialpsychologischen Analyse von Minderheitenkonflikten in der Gegenwartsgesellschaft." In *Minderheiten,* edited by R. Kurzrock. Berlin: Colloquium Verlag, 1974, pp. 17–27.

Rothammer, P., et al. *Die Integration ausländischer Arbeitnehmer und ihrer Famialien ausgewählten Städten—Probleme, Massnahmen, Steverinstrumente.* Berlin: Deutsches Institut für Urbanistik, 1974.

Schade, Heinrich. *Völkerflut und Völkerschwund. Bevölkerungswissenschaftliche Erkenntnisse und Mahnungen.* Neckargemünd: Vowinckel, 1979.

Schumann, Olaf. "Die Fremden als Herausforderung; Der asoziale Geist des westlichen Denkens." In *Fremde raus?,* edited by Rolf Italiaander. Frankfurt: Fischer Taschenbuch Verlag, 1983, pp. 48–56.

Sick, Wolf-Dieter. "Die innerstädtische Mobilität in Freiburg/Breisgau." *Festschrift für Wolfgang Meckelein.* Vol. 93. Stuttgart: Geographisches Institut der Unversität Stuttgart: 1979, pp. 257–66.

Sorrgut, Sener. "Zur Sozialisation der Kinder türkischer Emigranten in Schule und Familie." In *Ausländerkinder in deutschen Schuleno Ein Handbuch*, edited by H. Müller. Stuttgart: 1974, pp. 28–41.

Sowell, Thomas. *The Economics and Politics of Race. An International Perspective.* New York: William Morrow, 1983.

Spörl, Gerhard. "Nirgends zu Hause—Vom Auswanderungsland zum Einwanderungsland." *Die Zeit*, November 2, 1984: 1, 4–7.

Taeuber, Karl E. "Residential Segregation." *Scientific American: Cities, Their Origin, Growth and Human Impact.* San Francisco: W. H. Freeman & Co., August 1965, pp. 267–74.

Thoman, Klaus-Dieter. "Rassenhygiene und Anthropologie: Die zwei Karrieren des Professor Verschuer." *Frankfurter Rundschau: Dokumentationen.* Frankfurt: May 20, 1985, p. 20.

Thomas, W.G.S. " 'Gastarbeiter' in Western Germany." *Geography* 59 (1974): 348–50.

Yamamoto, Kenji. "Regional Distribution of Foreign Employees in the Federal Republic of Germany." *Geographical Review of Japan* 55 (1982): 85–112 (in Japanese; English summary).

BIBLIOGRAPHICAL NOTE

The literature on comparative race relations has been surprisingly slight. Until the past decade, most writing about race relations has concentrated on the United States, although race relations in Britain has become a topic of concern more recently. South Africa has always gained the attention of scholars because of its peculiar institutions. However, it is hard to disagree with Graham C. Kinloch's assessment that this literature has been generally parochial in character, lacking in theoretical and methodological sophistication, as well as sound empirical—as differentiated from historical—detail. Kinloch's own book, *The Dynamics of Race Relations* (New York: 1974), was one of the first truly comparative works in race relations. In this work, as in his other writings, Kinloch attempts to locate the societal and economic factors that produce different patterns of race relations. This emphasis on causative factors in a quest for an explanation of the current situation in race relations has been the dominant characteristic of most sociological research.

Some have discovered that certain societies have racial elites that impose their alien cultural values on indigenous populations. This view is best expressed by Philip Mason in *Patterns of Dominance* (Oxford: 1970). Pierre L. van den Berghe argues, in *Race and Ethnicity* (New York: 1970), that migration, forced and voluntary, has been a major cause of racial subordination. Orlando Patterson's *Slavery and Social Death* (Cambridge: 1984) finds in a comparative view of slavery a source of racial and economic exploitation for the benefit of colonialist elites. Roger Sawyer's *Slavery in the Twentieth Century* (London: 1986) defines slavery to encompass apartheid, debt bondage, and child labor.

Class differentiation, according to John Rex's neo-Marxist interpretation, is the true source of race relations. This interpretation, presented in *Race Relations in Sociological Theory* (London: 1970), has been popular in England. Robert Miles, *Racism and Migrant Labour* (London: 1982), holds this view, as does Annie Phizacklea and Robert Miles, *Labour and Racism* (London: 1980). In the United States, the classic work of Oliver Cox helped launch the study of race relations. His book, *Caste, Class, and Race* (New York: 1959), rests on a Marxian interpretation. An updated version of Cox's thesis can be found in Robert Blauner's *Racial Oppression in America* (New York: 1972). Another American work, Mario Barrera, *Race and Class in the Southwest* (Bloomington, Ind.: 1979), provides a similar view of Hispanic-Anglo relationships. R. E. Simon, *Class and Colour in South Africa* (London: 1969) provides a neo-Marxist framework for analyzing that society. More recently, Pierre-Michel Fontaine, *Race, Class and Power in Brazil* (Berkeley, Calif.: 1986) has taken a similar approach to explore the less than harmonious situation of race relations in Brazil, a nation previously held out as a model of stable race relations.

Pierre L. van den Berghe's *Race and Racism* (New York: 1978) is regarded, by most scholars, as the most influential work in comparative race relations. In this book, van den Berghe compares Mexico, Brazil, the United States, and South Africa. He concludes that racial patterns in these nations stem from historically different conditions, but that all four were part of the colonial expansion of European powers. Unfree labor conditions for subordinate groups prevailed in all four nations, and the indigenous population was severely curtailed. The four societies derived paternalistic systems, with a servile labor force, and all four experienced an erosion of paternalism in the direction of a "competitive" system of race relations as a result of industrialization and urbanization.

Graham Kinloch, *The Sociology of Minority Group Relations* (New York: 1979), accepts this view, but adds the argument that there are historic cycles in the evolution of race relations, as a plantation stage under colonialism disintegrates after the abolition of slavery, with indigenization flowing from independence, following minority rejection of the old order. He also describes two types of colonial situations and two types of noncolonial situations that result in differing minority group relationships. Paul B. Rich, *Race and Empire in British Politics* (Cambridge: 1986), shows that this approach does help explain the rise of racism and the nature of race relations under the British system. Donald Baker, *Race, Ethnicity and Power: A Comparative Study* (London: 1983), also fits squarely into the colonialist explanation of race relations. These authors agree that noncolonial developed societies are likely to have less racial differentiation than colonial or postcolonial societies. All these books are indebted to an early sociological study, John S. Furnivall's *Colonial Policy and Practice: A Comparative Study of Burma and Netherlands India* (Cambridge: 1948).

Migration and economic development may have introduced racial problems into noncolonial settings, so that race relations problems have arisen in nations that have previously been considered racially homogeneous. This view, by Michael Banton, explains the rise of race relations problems in modern Britain. Banton's *Race Relations* (New York: 1967) shows some sense of the situation. A clearer comparative statement of the situation appears in his *Race and Ethnic Competition* (Cambridge: 1983) which puts Britain into a larger perspective, among other nations undergoing change after substantial immigration of foreign groups. J. M. van Amersfoort, *Immigration and Minority Group Formation, the Dutch Experience, 1945–75* (Cambridge: 1982), provides a detailed explanation of the impact of new immigrants on a quite homogeneous society. There is very little material available on the issue of whether race relations are improving as the result of the termination of colonial rule by Western nations. However, there is a tendency to explain racial tensions as a new type of "internal colonialism," a term that seems to be in vogue among left-leaning social scientists. Many of the essays in William Beer, *Ethnic Autonomy—Comparative Dynamics: The Americas, Europe and the Developing World* (Oxford: 1979) rest on this interpretation.

Much of the writing in the field seems to derive from liberal sentimentality, aimed at improving the condition of disadvantaged racial minorities through "integration" into the larger society by ending or limiting race discrimination. This view of American life is expounded in Oscar Handlin, *Race and Nationality in American Life* (New York: 1957), Milton M. Gordon, *Assimilation in American Life, The Role of Race, Religion and National Origins* (Oxford: 1964), and in the well-received *Beyond the Melting-Pot* (Cambridge: 1963), written by Nathan Glazer and Daniel P. Moynihan. Most race relations textbooks in the United States are in this genre. A typical example is James W. Vander Zanden's *American Minority Ethnic Relations* (New York: 1963). Benjamin Ringer's *"We the People" and Others* (London: 1985) attempts to prove that racism and separatism are imbedded in American institutions. Gilberto Freyre's *New World in the Tropics* (New York: 1959) provides a comfortable assimilationist view of Brazil, but this book is much in dispute among experts in the field.

Michael Omi and Howard Winant, *Racial Formation in the United States* (London: 1986) challenges the assimilationist model, but holds that race is an important category of sociological analysis. Doubtless, there will be a continuing debate within the field of sociology about whether race is a legitimate category of analysis. John Stone, *Racial Conflict in Contemporary Society* (Cambridge: 1985) is a fine comparative study that accepts the saliency of race as a category. A useful collection of essays on this debate in America is provided in Richard Alba, *Ethnicity and Race in America: Towards the Twenty-First Century* (London: 1975). Race and ethnicity are deliberately confused with economics in Thomas Sowell, *The Economic and Politics of Race: A Comparative Survey* (New York: 1983), which is an attempt at a comparative survey.

As far as can be determined, the term "race" was first introduced by Count George Louis Buffon in the early eighteenth century. Buffon did not provide any precise meaning but employed "race" to designate the broad sections of humankind, using common observation of physical differences and similarities. For Buffon there were three "great races": Europeans, Negroes, and Asiatics. Subdivisions of the great races could be made, such as the division of Europeans into Nordic, Alpine, and Mediterranean types. Buffon did not link race with intelligence or other mental traits. This task was performed by the famous biologist Linnaeus (Carl von Linne) in 1738. Linnaean classification was part of his grand scheme for including humans in the order of nature, so that all animate parts of the creation were described in a single comprehensive model. The system of nature classified by Linnaeus was frequently revised. By 1758, he was able to distinguish several different types within the category of *Homo sapiens*: Wild man (four-footed, mute, hairy); American (red, choleric, erect); European (white, sanguine, brawny, blue-eyed, flowing hair); Asiatic (yellow, melancholy, rigid); African (black, phlegmatic, relaxed); monstrous (various freaks of nature).

The lengthy story of the development of modern anthropology need not be entered into here. Suffice it to note that the idea of race is in dispute among contemporary anthropologists, few of whom would agree with the twentieth-century figure, Carlton S. Coons, who, in his book *The Origin of the Races* (New York: 1962), identified five highly distinct subspecies of *Homo sapiens*: the Australoid, Caucasoid, Mongoloid, Congoid (African Negroes and Pygmies), and Capoid (Bushmen and Hottentots), each of which has a separate developmental history from a more primitive ancestral type. The controversy among anthropologists began to become a social issue in 1940, with the publication of Ruth Benedict, *Race and Racism* (London: 1940). The use of anthropology by advocates of race prejudice alarmed liberal scientists, mindful of Adolf Hitler's perversions of the idea of race to justify a German "master race." Several books were written in an attempt to discredit all such attempts to base race prejudice on science. The best of these is Theodore Dobzhansky, *Heredity, Race and Society* (New York: 1959). The United Nations itself enlisted the services of leading sociologists, biologists, and anthropologists to explode race doctrines based on pseudoscience, producing UNESCO's *Race and Science* (New York: 1951). Sociologist Michael Banton has produced the most useful writing on the concept of "race." His book, *The Idea of Race* (London: 1977), clarifies much of the confusion surrounding the word. Banton's later book, *Promoting Racial Harmony* (Cambridge: 1985), attempts to interpret recent data on race relations in a fresh manner.

One unfortunate effect of this body of literature intended to refute the various "myths" surrounding the word "race" is that many social scientists have avoided this kind of research altogether, for fear, perhaps, of being perceived as racists themselves. Yet "racism" or "racialism," the conversion of the idea of race in order to discriminate and dominate, is quite a separate matter. Ruth Benedict, *Race and Racism* (London: 1940), did distinguish racism from the study of race, something that many standard books on race relations still fail to do. Indeed, in its current usage, racism is at present both a concept and an epithet. The history of racism as an idea has been traced many times. Two of the best books are Louis L. Snyder, *The Idea of Racialism* (London: 1970), and Thomas F. Gossett, *Race: The History of an Idea in America* (Dallas: 1963). Finally, it has been argued that racism is best understood as a kind of psychological fantasy, a means of explaining the deeply felt irrational hatred that motivates many bigots, but even infects well-meaning whites. This view is expounded in Joel Kovel, *White Racism* (New York: 1970), and in the controversial *Black Skin, White Masks* (New York: 1967). There is no doubt that the apartheid system as practiced in South Africa is based on blatant racism. Many books prove the point. One of the best is R. M. Price and C. G. Roseberg, *The Apartheid Regime* (Berkeley, Calif.: 1980).

What is unsettled is whether race is a concept *sui generis* or whether it is a special case of more general sociological concepts, such as class or other aspects of social stratification. Against the thesis that no special categories pertaining to race are necessary, a view has arisen to describe societies that have more or less permanent social divisions: the plural society school of thought. According to this interpretation, plural societies are riven by cleavages of caste, race, ethnicity, language, or religion into quasi-independent subsystems. Seen from this vantage point presented in this volume, racial divisions can be regarded as a special instance of structural or social pluralism as distinguished from ethnic divisions, which are a case of cultural pluralism. Van den Berghe's *Race and Racism: A Comparative Perspective* (New York: 1970) accepts both structural pluralism and the independent validity of race as a category. The best representative book on cultural pluralism, which emphasizes ethnicity, is Crawford Young, *The Politics of Cultural Pluralism* (Madison, Wis.: 1976). Racial relations, then, is an element of the general ethnic relationships among groups in the setting of a plural society. There is a strong body of opinion that places ethnicity at the center of the study of plural societies. Richard Schermerhorn, *Comparative Ethnic Relations* (New York: 1970), rests on this view. David Nicholl, *Three Varieties of Pluralism* (New York: 1974), makes the point that First and Third World varieties of pluralism differ widely.

Genocide, the deliberate slaughter of human beings because of their group identity, seems a clear case of racist policies. Leo Kuper's *Genocide*

(London: 1981) is the leading book on the subject. A few social scientists would contend that racial tensions are a major source of international instability. Chris Mulland, *Race, Power and Resistance* (London: 1985), makes this point, as does Hugh Tinker, *Race, Conflict and the International Order* (New York: 1977).

APPENDIX:
RACIAL/ETHNIC DIVISIONS

AUSTRALIA

Background Notes (August 1986)

Population (1986): 15.3 million

Groups	Percent
Europeans	96
Aboriginal	1.1
Asian	2

World Factbook (1986)

Population (July 1986): 15,793,000

Divisions	Percent
Caucasian	99
Asian and Aborigine	1

BRAZIL

Background Notes (September 1985)

Population (1985): 122 million

Groups	Percent
Portuguese, Italian, German, Japanese, African, American Indian	
White	55
Mixed	38
Black	6
Indian	1

<u>World Factbook</u> (1986)

Population (July 1986): 143,277,000

<u>Divisions</u>	<u>Percent</u>
Portuguese, Italian, German, Japanese, African, Amerindian	
White	55
Mixed	38
Black	6
Other	1

CANADA

<u>Background Notes</u> (March 1985)

Population (1985): 25.2 million

<u>Groups</u>	<u>Percent</u>
British	45
French	29
Other European	23
Indigenous Indian and Eskimo	1.5

<u>World Factbook</u> (1986)

Population (July 1986): 25,644,000

<u>Divisions</u>	<u>Percent</u>
British Isles origin	45
French origin	29
Other European	23
Indigenous Indian and Eskimo	1.5

FIJI

Background Notes (November 1985)

Population (1985): 686,000

Groups	Percent
Indian	50
Fijian	45
Europeans, other Pacific Islanders, overseas Chinese	5

World Factbook (1986)

Population (July 1986): 715,000

Divisions	Percent
Indian	50
Fijian	45
Europeans, other Pacific Islanders, overseas Chinese	5

FRANCE

Background Notes (July, 1986)

Population (1985 est.): 55,041,000

Groups

Celtic and Latin with Teutonic, Slavic, North African, Indochinese, and Basque minorities

World Factbook (1986)

Population (July 1986): 55,239,000

Divisions

Celtic and Latin with Teutonic, Slavic, North African, Indochinese, and Basque minorities

INDIA

Background Notes (May 1985)

Population (1983, est.): 746,000,000

Ethnic Groups	Percent
Indo-Aryan	72
Dravidian	25
Mongoloid	2
Other	1

World Factbook 1986

Population (July 1986): 783,940,000

Ethnic Divisions	Percent
Indo-Aryan	72
Dravidian	25
Mongoloid or other	3

JAPAN

Background Notes (June 1985)

Population (1985, est.): 120,301,000

Groups	Percent
Japanese	99.4
Korean	0.6

World Factbook (1986)

Population (July 1986): 121,402,000

Divisions	Percent
Japanese	99.4
Other, mostly Korean	0.6

MALAYSIA

Background Notes (February 1986)

Population (1985 est.): 15.7 million

Groups	Percent
Malay and other indigenous	59
Chinese	32
Indian	9

World Factbook (1986)

Population (July 1986): 15,820,000

Peninsular: 12,854,000

Sabah: 1,293,000

Sarawak: 1,525,000

Divisions	Percent
Malay	50
Chinese	36
Indian	10
Other	4

NETHERLANDS

Background Notes (November 1984)

Population (1983): 14.3 million

Groups

Predominantly Dutch with some Indonesian and Surinamese

World Factbook (1986)

Population (July 1986): 14,536,000

Divisions	Percent
Dutch	99
Indonesian and other	1

NEW ZEALAND

Background Notes (October 1984)

Population (1983): 3.25 million

Groups	Percent
Europeans	85.7
Maori	8.9
Other Polynesian	2.7

World Factbook (1986)

Population (July 1986): 3,305,000

Divisions	Percent
European	87
Maori	9
Pacific Islander	2
Other	2

SINGAPORE

Background Notes (August 1984)

Population (mid-1983): 2.5 million

Groups	Percent
Chinese	77
Malays	15
Indians	6
Other	2

World Factbook (1986)

Population (July 1986): 2,584,000

Divisions	Percent
Chinese	76.4
Malay	14.9
Indian	6.4
Other	2.3

SOUTH AFRICA

Background Notes (May 1985)

Population (1983 est.): 31.1 million

Groups

White (English and Afrikaner)

Black (Colored, Asian, African)

World Factbook (1986)

Population (July 1986): 31,241,000

Bophuthatswana: 1,688,000

Ciskei: 781,000

Kwazulu: 4,554,000

Lebowa: 2,310,000

Transkei: 3,063,000

Venda: 423,000

Divisions	Percent
African	69.9
White	17.8
Colored	9.4
Indian	2.9

SUDAN

Background Notes (August 1985)

Population (1984, est.): 21.1 million

Groups

Arab-African, black African

World Factbook (1986)

Population (July 1986): 22,932,000

Divisions	Percent
Black	52
Arab	39
Beja	6
Foreigners	2
Other	1

SWITZERLAND

Background Notes (January 1985)

Population (1984, est.): 6.5 million

Groups

Mixed European stock

World Factbook (1986)

Population (July 1986): 6,466,000

Divisions	Percent
Total population:	
German	65
French	18
Italian	10
Romansch	1
Other	5
Swiss nationals only:	
German	74
French	20
Italian	4
Romansch	1
Other	1

THAILAND

Background Notes (July 1985)

Population (1984): 51 million

Groups	Percent
Thai	75
Chinese	14
Other	11

World Factbook (1986)

Population (July 1986): 52,438,000

Divisions	Percent
Thai	75
Chinese	14
Other	11

TRINIDAD and TOBAGO

Background Notes (September 1984)

Population (1980): 1,079,000

Groups (1980)	Percent
African	40.8
East Indian	49.7
Mixed	16.3
White	1.7
Chinese	0.5

World Factbook (1986)

Population (July 1986): 1,204,000

Divisions	Percent
Black	43
East Indian	40
Mixed	14
White	1
Chinese	1
Other	1

UNION OF SOVIET SOCIALIST REPUBLICS

Background Notes (October 1985)

Population (1984): 273.8 million

Groups (1979)	Percent
Russian	52
Ukrainian	16
Uzbek	5
Belorussian	4

World Factbook (1986)

Population (July 1986): 279,904,000

Divisions (1979)	Percent
Russian	52
Ukranian	16
Other ethnic groups (over 100)	32

UNITED KINGDOM

Background Notes (January 1984)

Population (1980, est.): 55.9 million

Groups

British, West Indian, Indian, Pakistani

World Factbook (1986)

Population (July 1986): 56,458,000

Divisions	Percent
English	81.5
Scottish	9.6
Irish	2.4
West Indian, Indian, Pakistani	2.0
Welsh	1.9
Ulster	1.8
Other	0.8

UNITED STATES

World Factbook (1986)

Population (July 1986): 240,856,000

Divisions (1980)	Percent
White	80
Black	11
Spanish Origin	6.2
Asian and Pacific Islander	1.6
American Indian, Eskimo and Aleut	0.7

WEST GERMANY

Backround Notes (February, 1985)

Population (1984, est.): 59,000,000

World Factbook (1986)

Population (July 1986): 60,734,000

Divisions

Primarily German, Danish minority

Sources

Background Notes on the Countries of the World. U.S. State Department.

World Factbook, 1986. U.S. Central Intelligence Agency.

Compiled by B.J. Swartz

INDEX

Abboud, Ibrahim, 269–70
Abraham, C.E.R., 163 n.4, 164 n.7
Adam, Heribert, 259 n.34
Adams, P., 210 n.15
Affirmative Action: Australia, 7–9; Japan, 149; Netherlands, 179–80; United States, 406–7, 409–14
African National Congress, 240, 246–53
Agricultural Landlord and Tenants Ordinance (Fiji), 89
Ahiram, E., 333 n.9, 334 n.13
Airey, Colin, 392 n.38
Albeda, Willem, 295–96
Algeria, 102
Ali, Ahmed, 97 nn.7, 12; 98 nn.22, 99 nn.55, 57
Alier, Abel, 270, 279 n.2
Alleyne, Mervyn, 334 n.16
Allworth, Edward, 346, 363 n.8
Amin, Samir, 43, 49–51
Andrist, Ralph, 417 n.10
Apartheid, 238–58
Arendt, Hannah, 372, 391 n.8
Armstrong, John A., 342, 363 n.7, 365 n.21
Assimilation policy, 219, 343–48, 385–90, 432–40
Association of Southeast Asian Nations, 9

Atawere, D., 210 n.12
Atmore, Anthony, 258 n.1
Australia: Aborigines, 1–6, 8–19; Asians, 1–3, 9–19; citizenship, 4–9; convicts, 3–5; Human Rights Commission, 5, 15; Immigration Reform Group, 13; Indochinese, 2, 8–9, 18–19; Japanese, 17–18; Kanakas, 3; League of Rights, 15; Racial Discrimination Act of 1975, 5–6; Vietnamese, 12–13, 18; violence, 15–16
Awatere, Donna, 195
Axford, Barrie, 391 n.16

Baake, Alan, 410–11
Bade, Klaus J., 440 n.8
Bagley, Christopher, 169, 188 n.6
Ballinger, William, 241
Banton, Michael, 150 n.10, 168–69, 186, 187 nn.1, 2; 188 n.19, 370, 390 n.3, 440 n.2
Barghoorn, F. C., 363 n.8, 364 n.14
Barker, Martin, 391 n.23
Barnes, Leonard, 241
Bartels, Dennis, 59 n.4
Barth, Frederick, 323, 333 n.3
Basham, A. L., 125 n.4–7
Bauer, Peter, 59

Bedggood, D., 196, 210 nn.14, 18, 20
Behrens, Robert, 392 n.34
Bell, Derrick, 415, 420 n.90
Beloff, N., 362 n.3
Benjamin, Geoffrey, 229 n.9
Bennigsen, Alexandre, 355–56, 362 n.3, 366 nn.42, 46
Bentley, Gerald, 335 n.30
Bernstein, Basil, 328, 335 n.28
Berreman, G. D., 123, 126, n.26
Beteille, Andre, 126 nn. 15, 22
Bhaktivedanta, A. C., 125 n.9
Biko, Steve, 255
Bilinsky, Y., 363 n.7, 365 n.31
Billig, Michael, 391 n.17
Black, Jan Knippers, 323, 333 n.7
Blainey, Geoffrey, 16–19, 20 n.11
Blake, D. J., 164 n.6
Blauner, Robert, 342, 363 n.5
Bloch, Maurice, 329, 335 n.29
Bloembergen, Samuel, 363 n.11
Blumer, Herbert, 254, 260 n.57
Boas, Franz, 323, 333 n.2
Böhning, W. P., 297 nn. 14, 21, 23, 24
Booth, Heather, 391 n.13
Bosworth, Allen P., 418 n.36
Botha, Louis, 238
Bouman, Johan, 442 n.31
Bovenkerk, Frank, 168, 182, 185, 187 n.3, 188 n.15, 189 nn.33, 49
Braithwaite, Farley, 335 n.35
Braithwaite, Lloyd, 332, 334 n.14
Brazil: blackness, definition of, 28–31; Indians, 24–25; mullatoism, 29–33; slavery, 29–31; United States comparison, 35–36
Brereton, Bridget, 328, 335 n.27
Brewer, John D., 260 n.69
Brezhnev, Leonid, 340, 352
Brier, Alan, 391 nn.15, 16
Brooks, Edgar, 255, 258 n.12, 260 n.62
Brown, Colin, 390 n.4
Bryce, James, 239, 258 n.12, 259 n.18

Bulpitt, Jim, 378, 391 n.20
Bundy, Colin, 258 n.4
Butadroka, Sakiasi, 68, 84–86
Buthalezi, Gatsha, 257–58
Buxton, Earl, 240

Camejo, Acton, 324, 333 n.10
Campfens, Hubert, 188 n.30
Canada: Anglo-Canadians, 48–55; Chinese, 54; Constitution, 44; Doukhobors, 50; Eurocanadians, 44; Innuits, 53; Kwakiutls, 55; Metis, 44–45, 50, 53–55; Quebec, 45–48; Riel rebellion, 45–47
Carter, Jimmy, 410
Casey, John, 391 n.9
Caste, 117–25, 219–20
Castles, Stephen, 282, 296 nn.1, 4; 391 n.13, 440 n.6, 441 nn.15, 22
Cell, John, 238, 258 n.11, 259 nn.16, 35
Charques, R., 363 n.9
Chen, Peter S. J., 229 n.3
Chirac, Jacques, 107, 111
Chon, Chun, 150 n.8
Christoph, Shawn, 442 n.30
Churchill, Winston, 244, 248
Civil Rights Act of 1964 (U.S.A.), 411–13
Civil Rights Act of 1968 (U.S.A.), 407–8
Civil Rights Commission (U.S.A.), 406–7, 416
Clammer, John, 230 nn.10, 11, 12, 14
Clark, J. R., 443 n.38
Clark, M. Gardner, 296 n.10
Clem, Ralph, 348, 362 n.3, 364 nn.17, 19
Cohen, Robin, 258 n.6
Collares, Alceu, 28
Colonialism, 29–31, 118–25, 155–63, 213–18, 234–37, 326
Comber, Leon, 229 n.1
Commission of Enquiry into Racial and Colour Discrimination (Trinidad), 330

Commission for Racial Equality (U.K.), 378–79, 384
Common Market (European Economic Community), 103, 433
Communal representation, 78–82
"Communal roll," 78
Conde, David, 150 n.7
Connor, John, 418 n.35
Conquest, Robert, 365 n.25, 366 n.51
Conrad, Robert, 26, 36 n.2
"Consocialism," 95
Convention Relating to the Status of Refugees, 136, 142, 146
Cornell, Stephen, 418 n.53
Costa-Lascoux, Jacqueline, 107, 112 n.1
Cottaar, Annamarie, 188 n.20
Cox, Oliver C., 123, 125 n.1, 126 n.25
Creswell, Frederic, 241
Cross, Malcolm, 333 n.9
Crowley, Daniel J., 327, 334 n.25
Cruson, Cees, 188 n.10
Curson, P. H., 194, 209 n.3

D'Encausé, Hélène, 359, 364 n.12, 366 n.55
D'Estaing, Valéry Giscard, 103–4, 110–11
Da Valle Silva, Nelson, 36 n.1
Daniels, Robert, 363 n.3
Daniels, Roger, 418 nn.32, 36
Davis, Kingsley, 122–23, 125 n.2
De Holand, Sergio Barque, 27, 36 n.10
De Jong, Lou, 188 n.16
De Mello Franco, Afonso Arinos, 33–34
De Oliveira, Eduardo, 28
De Vos, George, 150 n.4, 12; 151 n.23, 152 n.66
Dean, Warren, 38 n.22
Degler, Carl, 28, 36 n.8
Deoaran, Ramesh, 333 n.1
Derrick, R. A., 98 n.16
Desai, Ashok, 99 n.49
Desai, I. P., 126 n.32

Desheriev, I. F., 347
Dima, Nicholas, 342, 362 n.3, 363 n.7, 364 n.17
Do Nascimento, Abdias, 27–28, 33, 38 nn.13, 15
Dookeran, Winston, 333 n.9
Dovzhenko, O., 352
Dreyfus Affair, 110
Dumont, Louis, 123
Durbin, M. A., 334 n.16
Durkheim, Emile, 140
Dushnyck, Walter, 365 n.34
Dutt, N. K., 120, 126 n.12
Dzyuba, Ivan, 365 n.31

East, Herschel, 246
Edmunds, John, 392 n.34
Eiselen, W. M., 253
Elich, Joed, 189 nn.39, 41, 47
Emancipation Proclamation (U.S.A.), 399
Emerson, Rupert, 164 n.12
Engerman, Stanley, 417 n.14
England, Jude, 392 n.36
Enloe, Cynthia, 164 n.14
Entzinger, Hans, 188 n.8
Epstein, Erwin H., 366 n.61
Equal Employment Opportunity Commission (U.S.A.), 409
Equal protection of the laws, 414–16
Essed, Philomena, 188 n.9
Ethnicity, 29–31, 118–25, 155–63, 168–73, 183–87, 195–96, 219–21, 264–67, 295, 301–3, 323, 326–31, 339–52, 370–76, 413–16
European Convention of Human Rights, 384
European Court of Human Rights, 383
Evans, Gareth, 20 n.3

Feagin, Joe, 417 nn.8, 11
Fernandes, Florestan, 26–28, 34, 36 n.5, 38 nn.17, 29
Fifteenth Amendment (U.S.A.), 399–400
Fiji: Chinese, 71–72, 79–82; civil

service, 90–94; Communal repre-
sentation, 77–82; Europeans, 72,
83, 87, 90; Fijians, 70–82, 90–94;
Indians, 70–82, 90–94; land own-
ership, 86–90; *mataqali*, 73; "out-
bidders," 68; racial balancing, 76–
77, 83–88; Rotumans, 72
First, Ruth, 254, 260 n.60
Fisk, E. K., 97 n.11
Fitzgerald, Marian, 392 n.41
Fogel, Robert, 417 n.14
Foner, Philip, 417 n.19
Fong, Pang Eng, 229 n.7
Foon, Chew Sock, 229 n.5
Forwood, William, 364 n.12
Fourteenth Amendment (U.S.A.),
399, 414–16
France: Algerians, 103–9; *bidonvilles*,
107; black Africans, 109–10; immi-
gration, 102–8, 111–13; Mauri-
tians, 104; Moroccans, 103–6;
racist parties, 111–12; Spanish,
103–5
Franz, Fritz, 441 n.21
Frazier, E. Franklin, 417 nn.13,
27
Freedmen's Bureau (U.S.A.), 399
Freeman, Alan David, 415, 420
n.89
Freilich, Morris, 327, 334 n.23
Freyre, Gilberto, 23–24, 36 n.11
Fryer, Peter, 391 n.10
Furnivall, J. S., 68, 97 n.2, 164
n.11

Gabboush, Philip, 265, 279 n.4
Gafurov, B. G., 340, 362 n.1
Gamble, Andrew, 392 n.25
Gandhi, M. K., 120–25, 243
Gans, Paul, 443 n.38
Genocide, 397–98
Ghurye, G. H., 118, 120, 125 nn.3,
10
Gibson, K. D., 210 n.24
Giese, Ernst, 442 n.34
Giliomee, Hermann, 259 n.34
Glasgow, Douglas, 420 n.77
Glazer, Nathan, 415–16, 420 n.93

Glazier, Stephen D., 332, 333 n.8,
334 nn.17, 18; 335 nn.30, 35
Glebe, Gunther, 440 n.11
Glick, Leonard, 331, 335 n.31
Gorbachov, Mikhail, 362
Gordon, Milton M., 163 n.2, 164
n.6
Gordon, Sir Arthur, 69–70
Gosling, L. A. Peter, 230 n.10
Gossett, Thomas F., 398, 417
n.12
Goudsblom, Johan, 188 n.13
Graves, T. D., 209 n.2
Greene, E., 333 n.4
Greenland, H., 210 n.17
Greenstein, F. I., 318 n.2
Grocott, P. H., 98 n.31
Grodzins, Morton, 418 n.36
Guestworkers. *See* Switzerland; West
Germany
Guha, B. S., 120, 126 n.16
Guinzberg, Alexander, 360
Gumede, J. T., 247
Guy, Jeff, 258 n.2

Habermas, Jurgen, 391 n.15
Hall, Stuart, 386, 392 n.35
Harap, Louis, 362 n.3
Harewood, Jack, 324, 333 n.9
Harris, Marvin, 60 n.6
Hasenbalg, Carlos, 26, 31, 36 n.6, 38
n.23
Hassan, Rita, 229 n.9
Heberle, Rudolph, 294–95, 298
n.38
Heckmann, Friedrich, 441 n.18
Henderson, James, 246
Henry, Francis, 324, 334 n.11, 335
n.33
Hertzog, J.M.B., 238, 241–45, 250
Hobson, J. A., 342
Hoernle, R.F.A., 243
Hoetink, H., 156, 164 n.5, 334
n.14
Hoffman, Stanley, 35–36, 39 n.30
Hoffman-Nowotny, Hans-Joachim,
296 nn.9, 13; 297 nn.15, 16, 17,

20, 28; 298 n.37, 426 n.3, 442, n.35

Hoffmeyer-Zlotnick, Jürgen, 442 n.37

Hofmeyer, Jan H., 249–50, 260 n.48

Hollander, Paul, 365 n.25

Holubnychy, N., 365 n.25

Holzner, Lutz, 441 n.20, 442 nn.33, 37; 443 n.38

Honchar, Ole, 352

Hondrich, Karl-Otto, 442 n.35

Hraba, Joseph, 416 n.6, 417 n.28

Human Rights Act (New Zealand), 207

Husbands, Christopher, 386, 392 n.36

Hymes, Dell, 334 n.15, 335 n.28

Imperialism, 48–55, 118–25, 154–63, 341–45, 372–74

India: Aryans, 118–20; Brahmins, 119, 121; caste, 117–25; Constitution, 124; Shudras, 119–22; Sikhs, 125; untouchables, 120–25

Institute of Race Relations (South Africa), 240–43

Intermarriage, 120–21, 220–21, 251–54, 323

Internal colonialism, 342

International Convention on the Elimination of All Forms of Racial Discrimination, 5

International Covenant on Civil and Political Rights, 136, 146, 183

International Covenant on Economic, Social, and Cultural Rights, 136, 147

Irish Republican Army, 10

Jabavu, D.D.T., 248

Jackson, Andrew, 398

Japan: Ainu, 148; Alien Registration Law, 141; Chinese, 131, 140–41; exclusion policy, 132–33; Koreans, 129–50; Koreans, assimilation of, 142–46; Koreans, education of, 135–40, 145–46; Koreans, social

insurance, 146–48; Koreans, unemployment, 137–41; Nationality Law, 135; Okinawans, 129–30, 148; racism, 133–35, 149

Jefferson, Thomas, 400

Jenkins, David, 229 n.6

Jews, 170, 173–74, 185, 215, 351, 358–60, 424–25

Jha, J. C., 334 n.19

Jo, Yung-Hwan, 151 n.22

Johnson, Andrew, 399

Johnson, Lyndon, 406–9

Jones, J. D. Rheinallt, 243

Jordon, Winthrop D., 417 n.15

Kadalie, Clements, 241

Kagan, Richard, 151 n.3

Kahn, Herman, 133, 150 n.15

Karis, Thomas G., 260 n.68

Keegstra, James, 59

Kennedy, John F., 406–7

Khrushchev, Nikita, 346

Kim, Kyongduk, 147

Kim, Yong Mok, 150 n.3

Kim, Yongdal, 151 n.47

King-Boyes, M.J.E., 20 n.1

Kirk, J., 258 n.7

Kitano, Harry H. L., 418 nn.32, 33

Klass, Morton, 327, 334 nn.23, 24

Klee, E., 442 n.35

Köbben, André, 169, 187, 188 n.7, 189 n.50

Kolarz, Walter, 363 n.9, 365 n.25

Kong, Chiew Seen, 229 n.3, 230 n.13

Koohn, Chan Chee, 229 n.8

Koot, Willem, 188 n.25

Koreans. See Japan

Korey, William, 359, 366 n.61, 367 n.61

Kosack, Godula, 282, 296 n.1, 440 n.6, 441 nn.15, 22

Koslov, V. I., 340, 362 n.2

Kosygin, A. N., 352

Kowalewski, David, 340, 353–54, 362
    n.1, 364 n.17, 366 nn.36, 52
Koya, Siddiq, 80, 84
Krane, R. E., 441 n.21, 442 n.34, 443
    n.38
Ku Klux Klan, 397–98, 400–401
Kulkarni, V. G., 229 n.6
Kuper, Leo, 97 n.3
Kushner, James, 415, 420 n.91
Kwan, Kian M., 296 n.2
Kyong-Hae, Kim, 152 n.56

Lagu, Joseph, 270–73
LaGuerre, John G., 333 n.9
Lal, Brig, 98 nn.32, 42, 43
Land ownership, 86–90
Langdon, Godfrey, 240
Language, 122–24, 215–22, 263–68,
    301–3, 311, 317, 325, 329–30,
    342–50, 425–27
Lapidus, Gail W., 356, 362 n.3, 365
    nn.23, 27, 29; 366 n.45
Layton-Henry, Zig, 391 n.18, 392
    n.31
Lee, Changsoo, 133
Lee, Kwang Kyu, 150 n.18, 151
    nn.42, 49; 152 nn.51, 58, 63
Lee, Wangse, 152 n.57
Legassick, Martin, 258 nn.1, 10
Lembede, Anton, 248
Lenin, V. I., 342, 344–46
Lerner, Natan, 189 n.38
Lesch, Ann, 279 nn.1, 6, 7, 8,
    10
Levine, S., 210 n.10
Lewis, I. M., 29, 38 n.21
Leys, Norman, 241
Lieber, Michael, 334 n.9
Lieberson, Stanley, 416 n.3, 420
    n.92
Lijphart, A., 99 n.44, 189 n.42
Lim, Linda Y. C., 230 n.10
Lincoln, Abraham, 399
Lipset, Seymour Martin, 297 n.22
Lloyd, D. T., 99 n.45
Lockard, Duane, 150 n.1, 301, 318
    n.2
Lodge, Tom, 260 n.51

Loram, Charles T., 240, 242
Lowenthal, David, 323, 333 n.6
Lucassen, Jan, 188 n.12
Luthuli, Albert, 252, 255, 260
    n.55

Macmillan, W. M., 241, 246
McQueen, Humphrey, 20 n.2
Macrae, J., 200, 210 n.26
McWilliams, Carey, 417 n.29
Madoc, Kenneth, 20 n.7
Magna Carta, 77
Maillat, Denis, 290
Malan, D. F., 245, 249–50
Malaysia: Chinese, 156–63; class
    structure, 155–63; imperialism,
    155–63; Indians, 162; Malays, 155–
    63; tin industry, 158–60
Malik, Yogendra, 327, 331, 334 n.19,
    335 n.32
Malwal, Bona, 279 n.3
Mamak, Alexander, 75, 98 nn.21, 37;
    99 n.52
Manasse, Ernst Moritz, 163 nn.1,
    3
Mandela, Nelson, 248–49, 253–54,
    257
Manne, Robert, 20 n.8
Maoris, 194–209
Mara, Sir Kamasese, 80, 84–86, 95–
    96
Marks, Shula, 258 nn.1, 2
Marschlack, Peter, 440 n.5
Martin, Philip L., 296 nn.8, 12
Marx, Karl, 185–86, 342–46,
    369–70
Maso, Benjo, 189 nn.39, 41, 47
Mason, Philip, 164 n.9
Mathews, Joe, 255
Mbeki, Govan, 253
Means, Russell, 58
Mehrländer, Ursula, 441 n.15, 442
    n.35
Meier, Matt, 417 n.30
Meller, Norman, 98 n.24–28
Merton, Robert K., 140, 151
    n.33
Messina, A. M., 391 n.18

Miles, Robert, 168, 185–86, 187 nn.4, 5; 191, 209 n.1, 210 n.29, 211 n.38, 369–71, 390 nn.1, 2,; 391 n.11
Miller, Mark J., 296 n.8
Millette, James, 331
Mills, Lenox, 164 n.12
Milne, R. S., 92, 98 n.36, 99 n.51
Mintz, Sidney, 334 nn.14, 15
Mitterrand, François, 111
Mohammad, Mahathir bin, 229 n.8
Moog, Vianna, 26, 36 n.4
Mota, Carlos Guilherme, 27–28, 36 n.12, 38 n.16
Moura, Clovis, 27–28
Muss, Flip, 188 n.29
Mussert, Anton, 173
Myrdal, Gunnar, 123, 126 nn.27, 28; 242, 255, 259 n.23, 401, 417 n.26

Narayan, Jay, 99 n.6
Nash, Gary B., 417 n.7
National Aboriginal Conference, 8
Native Land Trust Board (Fiji), 88–90
Nazism, 173–74, 244–45, 249–50, 361, 378, 404, 431
Neame, L. E., 260 n.47
Nesfield, John C., 120, 126 n.13
Netherlands: Chinese, 172; Constitution, 183; ethnicity, 167–73, 180–87; Huguenots, 170–72, 175; immigration, 167–69, 179–81; Indonesia, 1, 67–69, 173–80; Jews, 170, 173–74, 185; migrant workers, 167–70; Antilles, 177–81; racism, 171–76, 180–86; South Mollucans, 178–79; Surinam, 167–69, 177–80; Tamils, 179; Turks, 167–69, 176, 179–81
Nevandomsky, Joseph, 327, 334 n.21
Neville, R.J.W., 229 n.4
New Zealand: Chinese, 197–98, 202–3; Maoris, 192–209; Maoris, representation, 205–7; "overstayers," 202–3; Pakehas (Europeans), 192–97, 203–5; Polynesians, 192–95, 199–200, 209; racism, 195–98, 209; Tongans, 202; Treaty of Waitangi, 195–97, 206–8; Western Samoans, 202
Ngubane, J., 260 n.42
Niehoff, Arthur, 327–8, 335 n.25
Nipper, Josef, 442 n.34
Nooij, Ad, 188 n.21
Norton, Robert, 98 nn.33, 34, 35
Numairi, Muhammad, 269–77

O'Loughlin, John, 440 n.11, 442 n.36, 443 n.38
Oliner, Samuel P., 363 n.3
Olivier, N.J.J., 260 n.52
Oxxal, Ivar, 335 n.31

Pachai, Bridglal, 259 n.28
Paine, S., 441 n.21
Pak, Chong Sun, 147
Palestine Liberation Organization, 109
Pandharinath, H. Prabhu, 125 n.8
Pankhurst, Jerry, 348, 364 nn.17, 20
Panov, Valery, 360
Parente, William J., 365 n.25
Parks, Rosa, 147
Patel, A. D., 80
Pennar, Jan, 353, 366 n.37
Pennix, Rinius, 188 n.22, 189 n.48
Perakh, Mark, 365 n.33
Perkins, Charles, 20 n.16
Peterson, William, 282, 296 n.3
Pevner, Herman, 151 n.37
Phenotypes, 69–73, 156–58, 180–82, 187, 191, 225–26, 283–84, 324, 429
Phizacklea, Annie, 185–86, 187 nn.4, 5; 189 n.43
Ping, Lee Loh, 229 n.2

Pinkney, Alphonso, 412–13, 417 n.17, 419 n.73, 420 n.76
Pinkus, Benjamin, 366 n.58
Plaatje, Sol, 247
Plural society analysis, 23–38, 68, 157–59, 179–81, 213–18, 332–33, 379–80, 437–38
Podgorny, N. V., 352
Poliakov, Leon, 168
Polsby, Nelson, 318 n.2
Poole, Peter A., 318 n.3
Premdas, Ralph, 97 n.5, 98 nn.19, 39; 99 n.58
Price, Sally, 334 nn.14, 15
Protchenko, I. D., 347
Punyodyana, Boonsanong, 318 n.3

Rabuka, Sitveni, 97
Rabushka, Alvin, 97 n.4
Race Relations Act (New Zealand), 207–9
Race Relations Acts (U.K.), 380–84
Racial Discrimination Act of 1975 (Australia), 5–6
Racial stereotyping, Australia, 9
Raeff, Marc, 344, 363 nn.9, 10
Raeithal, Gert, 441 n.18, 443 n.41
Raffles, Sir Stamford, 214–15
Rakowska-Harmstone, Teresa, 350, 356, 363 nn.4, 9; 364 n.17, 365 nn.26, 28, 32
Ransford, H. Edward, 419 n.74
Rath, Jan, 189 n.45
Reagan, Ronald, 408–10, 413–15
Reddaway, Peter, 365 n.33, 366 nn.50, 51, 53
Reddy, Jairam, 86, 95–96
Reeves, W. P., 197–98, 210 nn.19, 21
Reimann, H., 442 n.34, 443 n.38
Reischauer, Edwin, 133–34, 150 n.11
Reubsaet. T. J., 188 n.24
Rex, John, 27–28, 38 n.14
Reynolds, William Bradford, 419 n.63
Rhodes, Cecil, 239
Rhoodie, E., 260 n.65

Rich, Paul, 258 n.8, 259 nn.14, 19, 22, 25, 29; 370, 390 n.2, 392 n.25
Riel, Louis, 59 n.3, 63 n.9
Right of residence (West Germany), 432–36
Ringeling, Anco, 188 n.25
Risely, Herbert, 126 n.11
Rist, Ray, 440 nn.7, 9
Rivera, Feliciano, 417 n.30
Robotham, Don, 332, 335 n.34
Rockett, Rocky L., 342, 348, 363 n.6, 364 nn.17, 18
Rodriguez, José Honório, 25
Romalis, Coleman, 332, 335 n.33
Ronin, S. L., 340, 362 n.1
Roosevelt, Franklin D., 404
Rose, Peter I., 416 n.3, 440 n.4, 441 n.19
Rose-Innes, Richard, 239, 259 n.15
Ross, E. Lamar, 335 n.28
Rothammer, P., 442 n.35
Rubin, Vera, 323, 333 n.5
Ruland, Loes, 189 n.36
Ryan, Selwyn, 328, 331, 335 nn.26, 32

Sacks, Michael P., 348
Sakuna, Sir Lala, 88
Salt, John, 391 n.12
Satish, Saberwal, 334 n.11
Sawyer, Thomas E., 359, 366 n.57
Scarman Report (U.K.), 380–81
Schade, Heinrich, 431, 441 n.16
Schermerhorn, R. A., 124, 126 n.30–31
Schmid, Alex, 178, 188 n.26
Schmid, Carol L., 296 n.11, 297 n.29, 298 n.36
Schoen, Douglas, 390 n.6
Schoenberg, Harris O., 360, 366 n.59
Schöffer, I., 188 n.11
Schönberg, Ulrike, 292, 295–96, 297 n.30, 298 n.41
Schriener, Olive, 239, 258 n.13
Schumann, Olaf, 441 n.28

Schwartz, Barton, 327–28, 334
  n.22
Schwartzbaum, Allen, 333 n.9
Sectional representation, 78
Segregation, 235–50, 401–6
Seme, Pixley, 247
Sheatlsey, Paul B., 420 n.79
Shepsle, Kenneth, 97 n.4
Shepstone, Sir Theophilus, 235
Sherwood, Rae, 391 n.17
Shniederman, S. L., 367 n.61
Shobei, Shiota, 150 n.5
Silcock, T. H., 164 n.13
Silver, Brian, 347, 351, 364 nn.15,
  16
Simpson, George Eaton, 334 n.18
Singapore: Chinese, 213–26; cultural
  policy, 222–23; education, 222–25;
  employment, 221–23; Eurasians,
  213–14; Indians, 215, 221–22,
  227–29; Jews, 215; language pol-
  icy, 223–25; Malays, 213–29; plu-
  ralism (multiracialism), 213–18,
  224–29
Sisulu, Walter, 252
Sivanandan, A., 382, 392 n.26
Skidmore, Thomas, 27, 36 n.7
Skin color, 28–33, 69–73, 156–58,
  179–82, 187, 197–98, 234–38, 301–
  3, 323–24, 326, 386–89, 432
Skinner, William G., 318 n.3
Slavery, 28–33, 235, 326–27, 398–
  401
Smith, M. G., 97 n.3, 332, 335
  n.35
Smith, Robert J., 327, 334 n.23
Smuts, Jan, 238, 243–46, 250
Sneider, Daniel, 147, 152 nn.64,
  67
Sobuke, Robert, 253
Social class, 28–35, 155–63, 184–87,
  226–29, 256–59, 328–30, 332–33,
  412–15
Solaun, Mauricio, 38 n.19
Solomos, John, 380, 382, 391 n.22,
  392 n.24
South Africa: apartheid, 238–58; Af-
  rican National Congress, 240, 246–

256; Afrikaaners (Boers), 233–38,
  245–58; Bantustans (Homelands),
  253–58; "coloureds," 234, 246–58;
  education, 235, 255–58; franchise,
  235, 242—46, 257–58; Glen Gray
  Act, 239–40; Indians, 243–44,
  257–58; Native Lands Act, 237–39;
  Pass laws, 251–52; Rand revolt,
  238; Sharpesville riots, 254;
  Suppression of Communism Act,
  252–53; Tomlinson Report, 251–
  52; Transvaal, 235, 237; Zulus,
  234–35, 251–55, 257–58
Sowell, Thomas, 411–12, 416 n.3,
  417 nn.69, 71
Spoonley, Paul, 209 nn.1, 6; 210
  nn.10, 13, 25, 29; 211 n.38
Spörl, Gerhard, 440 n.10
Srinivas, M. N., 122, 126 n.21
Stalin, J. V., 345–46
Steele, Louis M., 405–6
Steinmetz, S., 173, 188 n.17
Strijdom, Johannes, 251–52
Studlar, Donley, 378, 391 n.19, 392
  n.39
Subraces, 217–18
Sudan: Addis Ababa Accord, 270–71;
  Anya Nya, 269–74; Bejas, 264,
  278; Constitution of 1973, 270;
  Dinkas, 265–67, 272–74; Islam,
  263–72, 276–78; Nubas, 264, 275,
  278; Nubians, 264–65; Nuer, 265–
  66, 274; Muhammad Numairi,
  269–77; Sudanese People's Libera-
  tion Army, 271–73
Suzman, Helen, 254
Sweezy, Paul, 45
Switzerland: Italians, 282, 288, 293,
  296; migratory labor, 281–88, 293–
  96; residency laws, 286–91; Spanish, 282, 286, 293; Tamils, 284,
  294, 296; Turks, 282–86, 292, 296;
  unemployment, 290–91; Vigilance
  Party, 292–94; Yugoslavs, 286
Szporluk, Roman, 264, 354 n.13,
  362

Tambo, Oliver, 248
Taney, Roger B., 400–401

Taylor, D. Garth, 420 n.79
Taylor, Douglas, 334 n.15
Ten Broek, Jacobus, 419 n.60
Thailand: Chinese, 302, 307–8, 312–
13; Indian, 306; *khaek*, 302–4; lan-
guage, 301, 311, 317; "minority
peoples," 303–9; Nationality Act of
1965, 315–16; refugees, 305, 314–
17; separatist movements, 310–11;
Yuen, 308, 313–14
Thatcher, Margaret, 378, 382–83,
388–90
Thirteenth Amendment (U.S.A.),
399–401
Thoman, Klaus-Dieter, 441 n.17
Thompson, Leonard, 245, 259
n.32
Thompson, Virginia, 164 n.12
Thomson, Lloyd D., 20 n.5
Tiek, Goh Cheng, 229 n.1
Tiwari, K. N., 210 n.23
Trapido, Stanley, 258 n.3
Trinidad: blacks, 326, 331–32; Car-
ibs, 321; Chinese, 321–23, 330,
333; "coloureds," 321–23; creoles,
322, 328–30, 333; East Indians,
326–27, 331–32, 333; racialism,
323–33
Trlin, A. D., 198, 207, 209 n.4, 210
n.22, 211 n.37
Trocki, Carl A., 229 n.2
Truman, Harry S, 404
Tsamerin, I. P., 340, 362 n.1
Tsunoda, Tadanobu, 150 n.13
Tsutomi, Ikegami, 134
Turnbull, C. M., 229 n.2
Tussman, Joseph, 419 n.60

Uichiro, Sakamoto, 150 n.14
Ulmer, Melville J., 420 n.81
Union of Soviet Socialist Republics:
Armenians, 351–52, 354–55; Belo-
russians, 339, 345–47; Central
Asians, 355–57; Crimean Tatars,
357–58; Estonians, 339, 353–54;
Georgians, 339, 345–49, 351; Jews,
351, 358–61; Latvians, 339, 347–
49, 353–54; Lithuanians, 339, 347,

349, 353–54; Muslim peoples, 339,
342–43, 347, 355–58; Poles, 339;
racism, 358–60; Russification, 341–
47, 351–58; Ukrainians, 339, 343–
45, 349, 351–53
United Kingdom: Afro-Caribbeans,
369–78, 385–90; Asians, 369–71,
377–79, 386–90; British Nationality
Act of 1981, 375, 383–86; Jews,
376; migration, 370, 374–84, 386–
90; Race Relations Acts, 380–85;
racism, 371–90; violence, 380–81,
385–89
United Nations Economic and Social
Council, 107
United States of America: affirmative
action, 406–14; Asians, 396, 403–4,
413; blacks, 396, 398–401, 404–14;
Civil Rights Act of 1964, 411; Civil
Rights Act of 1968, 407–8; Civil
War, 399–401; Emancipation Proclamation, 399; Fourteenth
Amendment, 399–400, 413–15;
Hispanics, 396, 401–2, 408–9, 411,
416; Jews, 396; Indians, 396–98,
407–9, 413; NAACP, 405–6; violence, 397–404; voting, 399–401,
406–8
Urban, Greg, 36 n.2

Vakhabov, M., 358
Van Amersfoort, Hans, 174, 188
n.18, 298 n.40
Van Den Berghe, Pierre, 164
n.10
Van Dijk, Teun, 189 n.34
Van Donselaar, Jaap, 189 n.32
Van Eck, H. J., 244, 259 n.30
Van Heek, F., 172, 188 n.14
Vasili, Raj, 92, 98 n.29, 99 n.56
Verwoerd, H. F., 250–52
Vilakazi, Absalom, 255, 260
n.61
Visibility theory, 44, 50–51, 61
n.6
Viviani, Nancy, 20 n.14
Vogel, Virgil, 417 n.9

Voll, John O., 278 n.1
Voronel, Aleksandr, 360

Wagatsuma, Hiroshi, 150 n.19
Walker, R. J., 210 nn.11, 16
Wallace, Tina, 391 n.13
Walsh, A. C., 98 nn.14, 20
Walshe, Peter, 259 n.40, 260 n.44
Ward, A., 211 n.36
Warren, Earl, 405–6
Watters, R. F., 97 n.10
Weber, Max, 155, 171
Webster, A., 209 n.5, 210 n.8
Welsh, David, 258 n.5
West Germany: Alien Act, 432; "asylants," 439–40; Basic Law, 426; blacks, 425; Greeks, 425, 428, 434; guestworkers, 425–40; integration policy, 435–40; Jews, 424; racism, 424, 426, 429–432; right of residence, 432–36; Turks, 423–26, 428–40; Yugolavs, 425, 428, 434
Wheeler, Geoffrey, 356, 366 nn.44, 49
White, Paul, 297 n.25, 298 n.33

White Australia policy, 2
Willems, Wim, 188 n.20
Williams, Eric, 333, 335 n.37
Wilson, Peter J., 332, 335 n.36
Wilson, William, 419 n.72
Wixman, Ronald, 355, 366 n.41
Wojak, W. G., 20 n.4
Wolf, Eric, 43
Wolpe, Harold, 245, 258 n.9, 259 n.33
Wood, Donald, 327
World Council of Indigenous Peoples, 10
Wozniuk, Vladimir, 352

Xume, A. P., 247, 249

Yakamura, Masaaki, 151 n.25
Yanowitch, Murray, 364 n.17
Yoneyama, T., 151 n.19

Zaslavsky, Victor, 353, 358, 364 n.17, 365 n.24
Zavelloni, M., 333 n.5
Zenkowshy, S. A., 363 n.9
Zubaida, S., 189 n.46
Zundel, Ernst, 59

ABOUT THE CONTRIBUTORS

C. E. R. ABRAHAM earned his doctorate at Oxford University. Abraham is Associate Professor at the School of Social Sciences, Science University, Penang, Malaysia. He has written significant articles dealing with race relations, as well as with housing issues. His doctoral dissertation analyzed race relations in West Malaysia. He was designated Selangor State Government Scholar and won the Goldthorpe Memorial Award of the Victoria Institution, Kuala Lumpur.

HENRY ALBINSKI is Professor of Political Science and Director of the Australian Studies Center, Pennsylvania State University. The author of several leading books and articles on Australia, Albinski also served as Visiting Professor of Political Science, University of Melbourne during 1985–86.

ALAN B. ANDERSON is Associate Professor of Sociology at the University of Saskatchewan. He is co-author of a general overview of the development of sociology in Canada in the *Handbook of Contemporary Developments in World Sociology* (1975). As a specialist in race and ethnic relations, he is co-author of *Ethnicity in Canada: Theoretical Perspectives* (1981). He is also the author of a wide variety of articles about race and ethnic relations in Europe and the Caribbean.

BARRIE AXFORD is Senior Lecturer in Politics at Oxford Polytechnic. He also lectured at Stanford University from 1971 to 1973. Axford's publications include contributions to books on the political sociology of race and on political leadership, as well as articles in these areas. He has a forthcoming book on the politics of the world system and an introductory text on comparative government.

JOHN CLAMMER is Reader in the Department of Sociology at the National University of Singapore. He has written extensively about ethnicity, race, and national integration in Singapore. Clammer is author of *Straits Chinese Society* (1980), *The Ambiguity of Identity* (1979), *Ethnographic Survey of Singapore* (1977), and *Singapore: Ideology, Society and Culture* (1985).

DOUG DANIELS is Professor of Sociology, University of Regina. His Ph.D. thesis research concerned West Saskatchewan native politics and modernization. He has been a consultant with the Bene nation Indians in the Northwest Territories. The author of many articles on race relations, Daniels has studied, among other places, in Peking and Mongolia. He recently returned from a sabbatical trip to South Africa and Australia.

ANANI DZIDZIENYO is Associate Professor in the Center for Portuguese and Brazilian Studies, and Afro-American Studies Program, Brown University. A Ghanian, Dzidzienyo was educated in Ghana, the United States, and the United Kingdom. He is author of *The Position of Blacks in Brazilian Society* (1971) and several major papers on African links with Latin America, including a contribution to Pierre-Michel Fontaine's, *Race, Class and Power in Brazil* (1985). Dzidzienyo has two forthcoming books dealing with Afro-Brazilian subjects.

JOED H. ELICH studied sociology at the University of Tilburg (Netherlands), Oslo, and the University of Northern Illinois. He is currently a researcher at the Center for the Study of Social Conflict at the State University of Leiden. He has been working in the field of migration and ethnic and race relations since 1980, and has written about migrants in the Netherlands and Dutch migrants overseas. His Ph.D. thesis, completed in 1986, deals with Dutch migrants in Australia.

RAJ S. GANDHI earned his doctorate at the University of Minnesota. He is a Professor of Sociology at the University of Calgary, Canada. Prior to joining the faculty at Calgary in 1977, he was Assistant Professor of Sociology at the University of Saskatchewan (1967–68) and also at San Diego State University (1966–67). Gandhi has taught in India at the Maharaja Sayajirao University. He has published over forty articles in professional journals and is the author of *Locals and Cosmopolitans of Little India* (1974). Social stratification in India is one of Gandhi's main interests.

STEPHEN D. GLAZIER studied anthropology at Princeton University and also at the University of Connecticut, where he earned his Ph.D. He has conducted research in Trinidad since 1976 and has published extensively on Caribbean topics. Glazier's most recent books are *Marchin' the Pilgrims Home: Leadership and Decision-Making in an Afro-Caribbean Faith* (1983) and *Caribbean Ethnicity Revisited* (1985). Currently, he is Associate Professor of Social Science at Westmont College.

LUTZ HOLZNER is Professor and Chairman of the Department of Geography at the University of Wisconsin in Milwaukee. He served as Visiting Professor at the Johan-Wolfgang-Goethe University in Germany in 1985 and has lectured at numerous other European universities. Holzner has conducted research in Western Europe and South Africa. He is the author of numerous professional journal articles, especially about problems of urban geography and about the special situations of South Africa and foreign minorities in West Germany.

YUNG-HWAN JO is Professor of Political Science at Arizona State University, in affiliation with its Center for Asian Studies. He taught three years at Keio University, Tokyo, and for a year at Academia Sinica, Taiwan. His recent book, *Russia vs. China, What Next?* (1980), was translated into Korean. His earlier works include *U.S. Foreign Policy in Asia* (1978), *Korea's Response to the West* (1970), and an edited book, *Political Participation of Asian-Americans* (1980). Professor Jo publishes in Japanese, Chinese, and Korean journals, as well as in English language publications. His current research has been concerned with the treatment of Koreans in Japan, China, and the United States.

ANN LESCH earned her Ph.D. in Political Science from Columbia University, conducting research in comparative politics and Middle East studies under a fellowship from the Middle East Institute at Columbia University. Lesch was the Middle East Program Officer with the Ford Foundation from 1977 to 1984 and currently resides in Cairo. She served as Associate Middle East Representative for the American Friends Service Committee in Jerusalem from 1974 to 1977 and before that worked for the Foreign Policy Research Institute in Philadelphia. Lesch frequently travels to the Sudan. In addition to numerous journal articles, she is the author of *Arab Politics in Palestine, 1917–1939* (1983) and *Political Perceptions of the Palestinians on the West Bank and the Gaza Strip* (1985).

SAMUEL P. OLINER is Professor of Sociology, Humboldt State University, California. He is founder and editor-in-chief of the *Humboldt Journal of Social Relations*. Oliner is the author of *Restless Memories: Recollections of the Holocaust Years* (1980) and is currently the senior author of a forthcoming book dealing with the international study of the rescue behavior in Nazi-occupied Europe. Oliner is founder and research director of the Altruistic Personality Project and the Institute for Righteous Acts, involing research that takes him all over the world.

RALPH PREMDAS is Visiting Professor of Political Science, McGill University, Canada. He has written extensively on ethnic and race relations in the Pacific and the Caribbean. Premdas is author of *Communal Politics in Fiji* (1978).

SUCHITRA PUNYARATABANDHU-BHAKDI earned her Ph.D. at the University of California, Berkeley. She is now Assistant Professor, Graduate School of Public Administration of the National Institute of Development Administration in Thailand. Her Ph.D. dissertation was a case study of the organizational effectiveness of the Ministry of Agriculture.

PAUL RICH is currently Visiting Lecturer, Department of Politics, University of Bristol, England, but is also Lecturer at the University of Warwick. His previous work includes a study of South African liberalism and industrialization, *White Power and the Liberal Conscience* (1984) and a study of British racial thought, *Race and Empire in British Politics* (1986). He has also written extensively on both South African and British literature and politics and is currently working on a study of U.S. and British policy toward South Africa since World War II.

CAROL SCHMID received her Ph.D. in sociology from McMaster University, Canada. She has been a Visiting Professor at the University of Trier, West Germany. Currently, Schmid is teaching at Guilford Technical College in North Carolina. Her main publications include works on political sociology and aspects of race and ethnic relations in the United States, Canada, West Germany, and Switzerland. She has received numerous awards, including a Fulbright Fellowship, a German Study Visit Grant, an award from the National Endowment for the Humanities, and the American Sociological Association Problems of the Discipline grant.

JAY A. SIGLER is Professor of Political Science and Public Policy at Rutgers University. He is Director of the Graduate Program in Public Policy. The author of many articles and over a dozen books, Sigler has written *Minority Rights* (1985), *Understanding Criminal Law* (1983), and *The Legal Sources of Public Policy* (1980) in recent years. He is co-author of *Human Rights Documents* (1987). Sigler received many awards, including the Lindback Award for Distinguished Teaching and Research.

PAUL SPOONLEY is a Senior Lecturer in the Department of Sociology, Massey University, New Zealand. He teaches courses in race and ethnic relations and structural inequality. He was chief editor and contributor to *New Zealand: Sociological Perspectives* (1982) and *Tauiwi: Racism and Ethnicity in New Zealand* (1984). In 1985, he was Visiting Professor at the University of California, Irvine, and later completed a comparative study of neo-fascism and anti-Semitism, while based in Britain.

ANDREW D. TRLIN is a Reader in the Department of Sociology, Massey University, New Zealand. He is best known for his studies of immigrants in New Zealand and his recently published work on anti-discrimination legislation in New Zealand and Australia. He was editor of *Social Welfare and New Zealand Society* (1977), author of *Now Respected, Once Despised: Yugoslavs in New Zealand* (1979), and author of several other works on minorities in New Zealand.

JUREE VICHIT-VADAKDAN is a Professor at the National Institute of Development Administration in Thailand. An anthropologist by training, she received her Ph.D. from the University of California, Berkeley. Her dissertation on the urban middle-class Chinese in Thailand was a valuable source of her further work in the area of race realtions.